The Psychology of Language

Timothy B. Jay

Upper Saddle River, New Jersey 07458

Library of Congress Cataloging-in-Publication Data

Jay, Timothy.
    The psychology of language / Timothy B. Jay.
       p. cm.
    Includes bibliographical references and index.
    ISBN 0-13-026609-4
      1. Psycholinguistics
  P37 .J39 2002
  401'.9–dc21   2002074949

Editor in Chief: Leah Jewell
Senior Acquisitions Editor: Jayme Heffler
Editorial Assistant: Kevin Doughten
Senior Managing Editor: Joanne Riker
Production Liaison: Fran Russello
Project Manager: Ellen Sklar/P. M. Gordon Associates, Inc.
Prepress and Manufacturing Buyer: Tricia Kenny
Art Director: Jane Conte
Cover Art: *Words Coming out of Mouth*. Scott Swales/Stock Illustration Source, Inc.
Permission Specialist: The Permissions Group, Inc.
Director, Image Resource Center: Melinda Lee Reo
Executive Marketing Manager: Sheryl Adams
Marketing Assistant: Ronald Fox
This book was set in 10/12 Sabon by TSI Graphics, Inc.
and was printed and bound by RR Donnelley and Sons.
The cover was printed by Phoenix Color Printer.

 © 2003, by Pearson Education
Upper Saddle River, New Jersey 07458

Printed in the United States of America
10 9 8 7 6 5 4 3 2 1

ISBN 0-13-026609-4

PEARSON EDUCATION LTD., *London*
PEARSON EDUCATION AUSTRALIA PTY, LIMITED, *Sydney*
PEARSON EDUCATION SINGAPORE, PTE. LTD
PEARSON EDUCATION NORTH ASIA LTD, *Hong Kong*
PEARSON EDUCATION CANADA, LTD., *Toronto*
PEARSON EDUCACIÓN DE MEXICO, S.A. DE C.V.
PEARSON EDUCATION—JAPAN, *Tokyo*
PEARSON EDUCATION MALAYSIA, PTE. LTD
PEARSON EDUCATION, *Upper Saddle River, New Jersey*

Preface

It took me two years to write this book. The first year I spent writing the book *I wanted to write*, and the second year I spent writing the book *my reviewers* wanted to adopt. As anyone who has authored a text knows, writing is an arduous task, painful at times. A textbook cannot be written without some compromises, making decisions about what to include and what to omit. In this text I aimed to cover the classic paradigms and standard issues, but I also wanted to include more than these. I wanted to broaden the scope of psycholinguistics to include more research on the emotional and cultural aspects of language. I wanted to pay closer attention to the idiosyncratic nature of our personal linguistic practices. I wanted to recognize each of us situated in our unique speech communities with our own emotional attachments to words and their meanings. I wanted to pay homage to the foundational studies in psycholinguistics but at the same time invigorate a new generation of students of language with exciting and cutting-edge research. After the second round of revisions, I think I can offer you this text. I breathed a sigh of relief when it became clear from the final round of reviews that students would not find this book boring; in fact, they would probably engage many of the topics very enthusiastically.

By the time I started working on *The Psychology of Language,* I had spent twenty-five years studying emotional language, offensive language, taboo language, and cultural influences on speech. I have become quite familiar with the process of asking questions about little-studied areas of human communication. As I started outlining this textbook, it was clear that most of the emotional aspects of speech I studied had remained outside of the mainstream of psycholinguistic research. It always bothered me to open new textbooks on language acquisition and see no mention of the fact that children readily acquire and use taboo speech. All of us who have raised children know how disturbing, humorous, frustrating, and problematic this aspect of language development can be. It also bothers me to look in the index of important books like Gernsbacher's *Handbook of Psycholinguistics* (1994) or Elman et al.'s *Rethinking Innateness* (1996) and not find an entry for "emotion." Can this be right? Can we really construct a theory of language, develop a way of studying language, without addressing topics like emotion and culture? Can we really understand language acquisition by ignoring its cultural and emotional contexts? I don't think so, and that is one of the reasons why I wrote this book—to include emotion and culture in the outline of traditional language phenomena. In the end, the book aims to offer something familiar to language scholars and something new to both scholars and students.

Part One is designed to parallel other texts in psycholinguistics with respect to scope and outline. The material is similar to that covered in other books, but much of it is unique. Chapter 1 uses traditional material to set the stage for the rest of the text: What is language? Do animals have language? What is the history of psycholinguistics? And so on. Chapter 2 examines the neurological basis for language. It is positioned early in the text to establish the importance of neuroscience in language studies and to introduce the role of emotion in language into the neuroscience literature. Some instructors may not be comfortable with this early emphasis on neuroscience at first glance; however, neuroscience is becoming more prominent in psychology textbooks, and our students must be properly prepared. Chapter 3 takes a fairly traditional journey through the speech perception literature, with one exception: It covers theories of speech perception that are currently motivating research questions rather than outlining all of the models that have emerged historically. Chapter 4 is a long chapter on words and word recognition. The first part covers traditional material on the nature of reference, semantic meaning, and the organization of the mental lexicon. The second part concentrates on recent research on the topic of lexical access. I have included the connectionist theory (Seidenberg & McClelland, 1989), which has been gaining increasing attention in recent years. Since this is a long chapter, some instructors may wish to cover the material in Chapter 4 as two separate topics. Chapter 5 is dedicated to the topic of sentence processing. It is filled with many examples of parsing problems and the sentence processing models that have been developed to account for parsing research phenomena. I have also addressed the issues of individual differences in processing, emotional involvement, and working memory constraints. Chapter 6 covers speech production and uses errors in the production process to suggest the stages of production. This approach is fairly traditional. I have included research on Freudian slips, which has often been avoided, I suggest, because there is no adequate theory to explain them. Another unique feature of this chapter is the inclusion of speech production models that incorporate gestures. Chapter 7 is dedicated to writing and reading processes. I have developed material on the process of writing and the stages of writing that are not generally detailed in psycholinguistics textbooks as they are here. I am convinced that basic and applied research on the writing process will become more important in the future. Writing research needs more thorough attention from students of language and classroom instruction to make progress in this area. The reading section covers research on deaf reading, reading tongue twisters, and Chinese reading processes. I included a connectionist model of reading with traditional models. These first seven chapters are meant to cover the traditional material and lay the foundation for the rest of the text.

Part Two extends beyond traditional topics to include important research on the emotional and social aspects of language use. Chapter 8 addresses the topic of discourse in conversations and narratives. I have drawn on a lot of material from Gernsbacher's influential *Handbook* (1994) and the work of H. Clark (1996) on conversation. What will be new for many readers here is the material on storytelling, joking, and humor. Chapter 9 provides extensive and up-to-date coverage of figurative speech, including metaphors, irony, idioms, and name-calling. Chapter 10 is the first of two chapters on language development. It concentrates on phonological, lexical, and grammatical development. Chapter 11 is probably the most controversial chapter, covering the topics of emergence, emotion, and embodiment. I look back at the literature demonstrating how a word's affective components are classically conditioned. I look forward to cutting-edge research on less well known concepts such as emergence and embodiment of language because they are helpful in understanding the emotional and cultural aspects of language acquisition. Chapter 12 examines the nature of language and thought, linguistic relativity, bilingualism, and categorical language. Readers will find the material on slang, sex talk, taboo words, and language standards both informative and provocative. Chapter 13 covers what I call applied psycholinguistics—the application of psycholinguistic research to everyday problems and settings. These contexts include classroom instruction, law, forensic linguistics, doctor-patient dialogues, mass communication, and human factors (ergonomics).

The pedagogical features of each chapter are similar to those employed in other textbooks. Each chapter opens with a set of critical thinking questions. These are meant to stimulate inquiry into what lies ahead and to expose the content and structure of the chapter. Students probably will not use these questions unless the instructor develops their pedagogical or functional utility. For example, I use these kinds of questions in review sessions prior to examinations. The content of each chapter is meant to expose *central issues* on the topic and the *experimental methods* designed to address those issues. Each chapter contains exercises designed to stimulate interest in the topic at hand. There are also throughout each chapter a number of boxed features in the form of discussion questions, special topics, and review questions. These boxed materials are designed as points of departure that push the reader to integrate the material in the box with text material. Like the critical thinking questions, instructors have to make the material in boxed sections prominent in classroom discussion to persuade students to use and think about them. Each chapter ends with a list of recommended Web sites.

Acknowledgments

First I have to thank the people at Prentice Hall who encouraged me to write this text and supported me throughout the many phases of its production. Before I started this project, I had several conversations about language with my sales representative, Ed Weisman. Ed was the one who originally asked me to submit a prospectus. From there, editor Jennifer Gilliland helped me outline and flesh out the initial draft of the text. When Jennifer moved on, Jayme Heffler took over and helped me redesign the nature and scope of this book. I have many thanks to offer to Jayme. It was her faith and encouragement that kept me working to improve the quality of the book. I will forever be grateful for her guidance and support. I also thank Prentice Hall assistants April Dawn Klemm and Lauralee Lubrano for helping me with the day-to-day chores involved in publishing a textbook.

As for those from my institution, Massachusetts College of Liberal Arts, who were very helpful, I thank my Psychology Department chair, Professor James May, MCLA college president Thomas Aceto, former academic dean John Hess, and the current academic dean, Randall Hansis, for allowing me to work with a reduced teaching load, which provided the time I needed to complete this book on schedule. I thank the students in my human communication and perception courses who read earlier versions of the manuscript and made helpful comments and suggestions in class. It was very instructive to me to observe what was working and not working in a classroom environment, and the book has been greatly improved by my students' input. Their feedback helped me make sure I was reaching them with something interesting, informative, and beneficial to their educational goals. They were candid enough to tell me what they did not like, which was very helpful. Thanks to my teaching and research assistants, Tim Duncan and Krista King, whose able assistance convinced me that one could write a textbook, teach, and collect data at the same time. Thank you to Linda Kaufmann for her library help and to Darlene Truskowski and her assistants, who helped me assemble the final draft of the manuscript.

I am deeply indebted to my reviewers for their critical and insightful comments. It is abundantly clear to me that I could never have written the final draft of this book without my reviewers' input. They helped me make this book what it needed to be. I hope that each reviewer will see that I have incorporated his or her suggestions in this book, sometimes to the letter. I hope they all realize how important their comments were to me.

Christina Kakava	Mary Washington College
Jonathan Walters	Norwich University
Michael J. Cortese	Washington University
Ann Eisenberg	University of Texas at San Antonio
Michael Spivey	Cornell University
Richard L. Lewis	Ohio State University
Wendelyn Shore	Pacific Lutheran University
Danny R. Moates	Ohio University
Matthew J. Traxler	University of South Carolina

Table of Contents

Part 2: Applied Psycholinguistics 267

Chapter 8 Discourse: Text and Conversation 269

Chapter 12   Language and Thought in a Social Context   431

Chapter 13   Applied Psycholinguistics   482

PART 1
Introduction to the Psychology of Language

Chapter 1
An Introduction to the Psychology of Language

Critical Thinking Questions

These questions are intended to guide your reading and note taking. They preview the chapter content and important issues.

1. What is the scope of psycholinguistic research?
2. What kinds of methods do psycholinguists use to conduct research on language?
3. What are the broad issues in psycholinguistics?
4. What are the historical roots of psycholinguistics?
5. What disciplines are comprised in psycholinguistics?
6. What is language?
7. What are the structural components of language?
8. Is the faculty of language unique to humans?

Exercise 1.1. **Language**
This exercise is intended to get you thinking about language. Before you continue reading, take out your notebook and write down answers to these questions. What is your definition of language? Do you know of any evidence that indicates that nonhuman animals have language? What advantages for everyday existence does language afford humans? Review your answers when you have finished the chapter.

This chapter introduces you to the field of psycholinguistics and sets the stage for the remainder of the book. It will probably not make you all "tingly and excited" about psycholinguistics (Can any introductory chapter do that?), but it will provide a broad outline that is intended to

- Define language and its components
- Reveal the scope of the discipline
- Describe some major questions and controversies
- Sample research methods used to study language
- Place psycholinguistics in a historical context

This chapter is divided into two main sections: the nature of language and its components and the nature and scope of psycholinguistics. We begin with language and its components.

What Is Human Language?

Human language is a structured system for combining words that makes it possible for us to communicate to others, to think about our immediate environment, or to imagine. Language is not just speaking; language and speech are *not* the same thing. **Speech** is the oral production of language. **Language** is more abstract and multimodal; it can be manifested through signs, symbols, finger spelling, written words, and Braille. We can further define language by looking at its properties (R. Brown, 1965; Clark & Clark, 1977; Hockett, 1960). There seems to be some agreement among language scholars that language has the following six properties:

1. *Language is communicative.* It allows us to communicate with others who share the same language.

2. *Language is arbitrary.* The relationship between a referent, object, idea, process, or description and its symbol (word) is not fixed but arbitrary.

3. *Language is structured.* Language has a pattern to it that is based on rules. Only certain patterns of words or sounds that follow these rules are permitted in a language.

4. *Language is multilayered.* It can be analyzed as speech sounds, as units of meaning, as words, as phrases, or as sentences.

5. *Language is productive.* It has the potential to use a small set of rules to generate a limitless number of novel sentences.

6. *Language is evolutionary.* Languages change over time; some aspects become obsolete.

LANGUAGE IS COMMUNICATIVE

Communication is behavior directed at another member of the same species that affects the recipient's behavior and the initiator's subsequent behavior. I mention this first because acts of communication do not necessarily involve language. When one cat hisses at another causing the second cat to run, that is not language, but it is communication. Cat hissing fails to incorporate the other five properties of language (hissing is not arbitrary, structured, and so on).

Communicativity refers to the *function* of language. We can write, speak, or use sign language to express how we are feeling, and others can read, listen or watch, and understand what we are thinking and feeling. Language is used to communicate ideas from one person to another and to make others do things. A goal is formulated in the mind of a speaker (e.g., I need to borrow some money) and put into sentence form (e.g., "Can you loan me a dollar?"). When the listener hears that sentence, it affects his or her subsequent thought and behavior (e.g., "Sure. Pay me back later."). Human language functions to affect other humans, similar to forms of animal communication.

LANGUAGE IS ARBITRARY

Language is based on arbitrary symbolic references to things, ideas, processes, and relationships. There is no a priori relationship between words and their referents. Arbitrariness means that there is no causal link between objects in the environment or ideas and the names we give them. You can call those objects on your feet anything you want; they do not have to be called *shoes*. Call them *cows* if you want. Words are arbitrary symbols that represent, refer to, suggest, or stand for something else. Without **arbitrary reference,** the symbol might have to resemble its referent. A cowlike symbol would be used to represent a cow. This symbolic language system affords abstraction, which allows us to talk about things that are not in the immediate context or that do not exist at all.

LANGUAGE IS STRUCTURED

We will address language structure in more detail in a minute. For now, remember that language is composed of rule-governed or acceptable patterns of sounds, letters, and meaningful words. Random orderings of letters, sounds, and words usually do not have meaning. An acceptable pattern of letters or sounds form words, and an acceptable pattern of words form sentences. An acceptable pattern of sentences form paragraphs, stories, and discourse. Randomizing the sentences in a story would make less sense to us than having the sentences in the acceptably structured order.

LANGUAGE IS MULTILAYERED

A meaningful sentence can be analyzed at more than one level. Each level has varying degrees of meaningfulness. A sentence can be viewed as a system of sounds produced concurrently with a system of words and phrases. We can analyze an utterance at the level of sounds, like *b* or *t;* at the level of words, like *bat, tab, but,* or *tub;* or at the level of sentences, like *Tab put the bat in the tub but could not make it float.* Sentences can be analyzed within paragraphs, like this one explaining that language is multilayered. We can also talk about language at the level of chapter-sized units, for example, to answer a question like "What is the topic of Chapter 1?"

Does Language Have an Emotional Layer?

Every spoken sentence contains emotional information, which would lead one to believe that there are emotional layers in speech. One layer involves the way the sentence is produced in terms of loudness and stress on the words in the sentence. This aspect of emotion in speaking may be present in all languages (Haiman, 1998), including primate communication (Cheney & Seyfarth, 1990). Speech is also accompanied by nonverbal cues about emotion in facial expression, gesture, and body posture. Another layer of emotion is encoded in word choice. For example, the amount of perceived anger in a sentence like "I'm disappointed in you" is less than in "I'm pissed off at you." The emotional layers of word meaning are culturally determined and acquired through experience. Knowing that *pissed off* is more emotional than *disappointed* comes from the experience of hearing and speaking these expressions in social contexts.

LANGUAGE IS PRODUCTIVE

Language has an unbounded capability to generate creative and novel utterances. Using the *rules* for ordering words in sentences and a set of arbitrary symbols, we can produce an infinite number of unique and meaningful sentences and phrases. At another level of analysis, we can use the limited set of *sounds* in a language to create an unlimited set of meaningful words and sentences. The **productivity** of language permits us to create unique expressions that have never been said or heard before. This property makes languages inherently creative and flexible enough to express new utterances used to describe or think about everyday life. All human languages have the capability to express ideas and thoughts in other languages, although the specificity or clarity of expression might vary greatly across languages. This creative aspect of language leads to the next property.

LANGUAGE IS EVOLUTIONARY

Languages are organic, growing new words and expressions and killing off expressions that are no longer useful (obsolete). Languages grow words that are functional for everyday life. Trends in popular culture, mass communication, advertising, medicine, technology, and science are important sources of new words and phrases. Languages also undergo change through contact with other languages. Globally speaking, when cultures interact, words that are useful in one language are borrowed into another. Modern English has evolved from Middle English, which evolved from Old English. English in America is filled with words borrowed from other languages in contact with English (Flexner, 1976). Like living species, languages also become endangered and undergo extinction.

These are the properties of languages. Although languages differ in many respects, they share these six common attributes.

Do Animals Have Language?

Since Darwin's time, scholars have been studying the relationships between human behavior and that of other species. Many scholars in the past century have addressed the question of whether nonhuman animals have language (see Cheney & Seyfarth, 1990; Premack, 1986). While it is accepted that members of the same species communicate with each other, whether this communication constitutes "language" is debatable.

All normal humans acquire a language with little difficulty. Do animals have similar language capabilities? Studies of animal communication have used as subjects chimpanzees, orangutans, whales, dolphins, and bees (Premack, 1986). For example, we know that when a honeybee returns from a foraging mission, he signals information about his trip to the bees in the hive by doing a "dance." The survival of the hive depends on accurate information in the dance. The components of the honeybee dance tell coworkers what direction to fly in, how far to fly, and the quality of the source (Von Frisch, 1962). Stingless bees communicate in a similar manner (Nieh, 1999). This is clearly bee communication; however, it lacks the productive properties of human language. There is no room for creativity or abstraction in this system; it is bound to the stimuli in the context. Bees do not tell jokes about pollen, nor do they lie about where it is located.

The answer to whether animals have language rests on how we define language. We can find a more compelling argument for animal language with nonhuman primates. It is clear from the studies that primates in the wild communicate with each other, vocalizing information essential to survival (Cheney & Seyfarth, 1990; Premack, 1986; Van Larwick–Goodall, 1971).

NONHUMAN PRIMATE COMMUNICATION

Primate communication studies include both laboratory and field studies of nonhuman primate capabilities and habits. Researchers have tried to teach language to primates, with mixed results. Attempts to teach vocal speech to chimpanzees have not been successful (Hayes & Hayes, 1952; Kellogg & Kellogg, 1933). Successful training programs were those that capitalized on the chimps' skill at symbolic gesturing and their ability to communicate via computer. Gardner and Gardner (1969; Gardner, Gardner, & Van Cantfort, 1989) initiated a long-term project to teach American Sign Language (ASL) to a young female chimp named **Washoe.** The sign language program produced impressive results and has been the basis for teaching ASL to gorillas and an orangutan.

The Gardners tried to raise Washoe under conditions similar to those in which humans learn language. Caretakers used ASL around the chimp but did not make a special effort to teach it to her. Twenty-two months into the project, Washoe had acquired a vocabulary of thirty signs, which she used appropriately and also used spontaneously in novel situations. She was also a creative signer. When Washoe saw a swan, an animal for which she had no sign, she invented the sign, *water + bird* from two signs she had learned before. Washoe, similar to a 2-year-old human, appeared to have mastered the basics of sign language, simple word ordering, and applying signs in new contexts.

The Gardners' research gained the attention of psycholinguists but not uncritically. Terrace, Petitto, Sanders, and Bever (1979) examined the tapes of Washoe and another chimp named Nim with their trainers. They found that many of the signs (39 percent) were not spontaneous but were imitations of the trainers' signing. O'Sullivan and Yeager (1989) countered that the chimps' signing skills depended on how they were taught and what kind of situation they were in, that is, a training versus "conversational" context. They observed spontaneous signing only 14 percent of the time in the training condition but 60 percent of the time in the conversational setting.

David Premack (1971) employed a different line of primate research. He used a token system (somewhat like refrigerator magnets with symbols on them) to demonstrate that his chimp, Sarah, had rudimentary symbolic thought. Premack was not so much interested in communication as he was in Sarah's conceptual capacity to answer questions that involved reasoning, such as "name of," "not name of," and "if-then" types of questions. For example, in the "name of" condition, Sarah would be shown an apple to see if she would respond with the token for apple, which she usually did. Premack's system is more artificial than ASL, and Sarah did not use the symbols spontaneously outside of the testing situation. In contrast, the signing chimps did converse outside of testing situations.

Another approach to teaching primates language was adopted by Rumbaugh (1977), who used a computer keyboard system to teach chimpanzee, Lana, to construct and respond to computer messages. Sue Savage-Rumbaugh, using this technology, has published impressive language learning results with pygmy chimpanzees (bonobos) (Savage-Rumbaugh & Lewin, 1994). Bonobos are thought to be more intelligent and more likely to gesture and vocalize in their natural environment than chimpanzees. Unlike chimpanzees, bonobos readily learn language and do not need language training to make associations between objects and symbols (Brakke &

Savage-Rumbaugh, 1996; Savage-Rumbaugh, McDonald, Sevik, Hopkins, & Rubert, 1986). Savage-Rumbaugh, Shanker, and Taylor (1998) described their work with Kanzi, a laboratory-raised bonobo who exhibited linguistic and cognitive skills similar to a 2½-year-old human.

One final noteworthy project on natural animal communication is the research of Dorothy Cheney and Robert Seyfarth with vervet monkeys and baboons (Cheney & Seyfarth, 1990, 1999). They pioneered the study of vervet monkeys' predator alarm calls in East Africa. Vervet monkeys signal to their kin about the presence of predators in their habitat, which are eagles, snakes, and leopards. When monkeys voice these alarm signals, the other monkeys run in fear, but how they respond depends on which predator is referenced. Leopard alarms send the monkeys into trees, but eagle alarms send them under bushes. Cheney and Seyfarth's studies of baboons demonstrated similar socioemotional uses of vocalizations and warnings. Female baboons are able to recognize and differentiate the threat grunts and screams of their close relatives and those of nonkin. Cheney and Seyfarth's research reveals the social, emotional, and familial purposes of primate communication in natural settings, which has qualities similar to human speech.

As animal communication researchers become more aware of how primates communicate in their natural environments, better comparisons can be made between primate communication and human language. One aspect of human cognition that might separate us from animals who communicate well is the facility of metalinguistic awareness, the awareness of language as a system.

METALINGUISTIC AWARENESS

Metalinguistic awareness is our conscious awareness of how language works. It is our ability to think of language as an object. It takes time to develop a high level of awareness, but every normal adult has metalinguistic awareness; it includes our feeling about the "correctness" of language that comes from listening and speaking it. Whereas adults are able to tell when a verb is missing from a sentence, a young child might just say that it "sounds funny." A high level of linguistic awareness is probably not available to nonhuman animals. Metalinguistic awareness tells us, for example, that word order makes a difference in English: *a Venetian blind* and *a blind Venetian* are two different things. When we speak, the words and thoughts seem to come to us with ease much of the time. The underlying "rules" we use to construct sentences seem implicit and out of awareness. We may not notice the rules until something goes wrong. When someone says, "Have a dice nay," instead of, "Have a nice day," our metalinguistic awareness tells us that the first sentence does not make sense but the second one does. Linguists analyze languages in order to find their rules. All languages are *rule-governed* from this point of view, but the rules differ from language to language. French speakers place adjectives after nouns, not before them, as in English: Americans drink *red wine* and French drink *vin rouge*. Rules of language exist at different levels of awareness.

A language has an abstract *ideal* form represented by its accepted (implicit) rules. A language also has a *real* form that sounds like what speakers say on the street. Speech on the street contains errors, but the ideal form does not. The Swiss linguist Ferdinand de Saussure (1916/1966), whose work had a great impact on the field of linguistics, first drew the ideal-real distinction. Saussure called the ideal form of language *la langue*, and he called what we hear on the street *la parole*.

WHY STUDY LANGUAGE?

One question that might come to mind at this point is the value of studying language as a communication system. There are plenty of academic and personal reasons to study language. On the academic level, the study of language can provide a deeper understanding of the social sciences and humanities. Knowledge about language is important to understand social studies on topics such as education, intelligence, personality, memory, group interaction, and cognition. Language plays an important role in studies of logic, composition, literature, history, international relations, religion, and philosophy. Psycholinguistic research also has applications to emerging trends in electronic communication, artificial intelligence, speech therapy, medicine, law, mass communication, and sociopolitical thought. These will become clearer as we advance through the text.

On a personal level, we grow up in a language-rich environment that provides a basis for our psychological development and cultural awareness. Language is our tool for self-awareness, identity development, social interaction, problem solving, and intellectual and psychological growth. Language may be most important to us because we can do things with it. By speaking, we can do things with people such as elicit help, provide directions, make people laugh, ask questions, insult enemies, display intelligence, conduct business, and earn a living. We revisit the past, imagine the future, and solve our everyday problems with language. Through our personal conversations, dialogues, narratives, and stories, we create and remember our existence (that should seem important!). Another way to consider the importance of language is to imagine your life after brain damage that left you without some of your language skills. How would you live if you could not communicate to others or understand what others are writing, saying, or gesturing?

We will leave the depressing thought of a life without language to look at the components of language. Understanding the nature of linguistic rules is crucial to psycholinguistics because the rules determine what combination of language components (e.g., sounds, words, word prefixes and suffixes, phrases, and sentences) are acceptable in a language. We look at these components next.

Components of Language

Like a chemist would examine a compound to discover its molecules, linguists analyze language by breaking it down into its smaller components. To discuss language research in later chapters, it is necessary to have an understanding of the component parts of language (unfortunately, it is more necessary than it is exciting). The discussion proceeds from the smallest components of language (*phonemes*) to the largest units of language (*discourse*).

PHONEMES

The smallest unit of sound is a *phone*, which is a single vocal sound. We produce different speech sounds by changing the way air goes through our vocal tract. Not all vocal sounds we can make are part of the language we speak. For example, you can make a "click" sound with your tongue, but it is not a phone in English. The smallest vocal sound that can make a difference in meaning in a language is called a **phoneme.** Phonemes are discrete speech categories. English has about forty phonemes consisting mainly of consonants and vowels, as shown in Table 3.1 p. 66 Some languages have more phonemes (e.g., African dialects), and some have less (e.g., Hawaiian). The sound corresponding to the first letter in *toy* is the phoneme symbolized by /t/. If we replaced the /t/ in *toy* with another phoneme, for example /b/, it would change its meaning, in this example to *boy*. Note that although phonemes can correspond to letters, they are speech sounds, not letters.

We are good at discriminating different phonemes from each other in our language. We are not so good at discriminating the different phones that correspond to the same phoneme. For example, it is difficult for us to distinguish the /p/ sound in *pin* from the /p/ sound in *spin*. If you hold your hand in front of your mouth and say these words, you notice that the /p/ in *pin* has a puff of air that is missing in *spin*. So our discrimination is good *across* phoneme categories but poor *within* categories. Each language has a different set of phonemes. In English there is a difference between phonemes /r/ and /l/, but in Japanese these are perceived as the same phoneme, much as English speakers perceive the two /p/ sounds in my example.

Phonemes are combined according to *phonotactic rules*. For example, /b/ cannot be followed by /t/ in English. There are no words in English that begin with *bt-*. Further, all acceptable combinations of phonemes are not meaningful. *Wuf* is an acceptable combination of phonemes in English but it has no meaning. So the sound system contains the meaningful set of phonemes in the language and a set of rules that specify how they can be combined sequentially (phonotactic rules).

MORPHEMES

The next component in the hierarchy of language is the **morpheme,** which is the smallest unit of language that carries linguistic meaning. They include root words (e.g., *bake*), suffixes (e.g., -*ed*), and prefixes (e.g., *un-*). The word *unbaked* has three morphemes. The words that convey the bulk of the meaning are referred to as *content morphemes*. These are contrasted with *function morphemes*, which add details to the meaning of the content morpheme or help adapt it to the context of the sentence in which it occurs. The suffix -*ism,* the prefix *anti-*, the conjunction *and,* and the article *the* are function morphemes.

Function morphemes include a subset of suffixes referred to as *inflections*, which are added to words to fit a sentence context. Inflections in English include verb tense (e.g., *-ed* and *-ing*, as in *played* and *playing*), verb and noun number (e.g., *we pass, he passes*) plurals (e.g., *cats, horses, nouns*), noun possession (e.g., *John's hat*), and adjective comparison (e.g., *dumber, dumbest*). *Morphological rules* indicate how to combine morphemes to stems and words in the acceptable order.

Phonemes and morphemes are the building blocks of words. Some linguists refer to our knowledge of morphemes as the **lexicon.** The average adult English speaker has a lexicon of over 80,000 morphemes and a *vocabulary* or repertoire of words (over 100,000) assembled from combinations of morphemes. *Semantics* is the study of the meaning of morphemes, words, and sentences. Semantics also refers to relationships between words in the lexicon. What words "mean" is a very complex topic that we address in Chapter 4.

SYNTAX

Syntax refers to the way a language permits users to assemble words to form phrases and sentences. A sentence is comprised of at least two parts, a *noun phrase* (NP) and a *verb phrase* (VP). The NP contains at least one noun, which is often the subject of the sentence, along with the words used to describe the noun. The VP contains at least one verb and what the verb acts on, if that is stated. In the sentence *Lazy scholars ignore their texts, Lazy scholars* is the NP and *ignore their texts* is the VP. We use these kinds of **grammatical rules** in our language to assemble words and phrases in the proper order.

Look at the following two sentences:

1. *Bob coffee the spilled.

2. Bob spilled the coffee.

English does not allow sentences like 1. Although you might not be able to describe grammatical rules of English, you can make a metalinguistic judgment reflecting an implicit knowledge of grammaticality. Word strings 1 and 2 differ in grammatical acceptability. You are aware that something is wrong with 1. (Note that it is conventional in psycholinguistics to use an asterisk to indicate that a string of words is ungrammatical.) String 2 obeys the rules but violates the acceptable word order for noun and verb phrases.

Psycholinguists use the word *grammar* in a particular way. You might recall having to write sentences in school according to a standard that your teacher called "correct grammar." By the teacher's definition, good sentences start with a capital letter, are punctuated correctly, and do not end with a preposition. The teacher's definition of a grammar is a **prescriptive grammar;** it prescribes standards for a "right" way to speak or write. This is *not* what psycholinguists mean when they speak of grammars. When psycholinguists write about a grammar, it is *descriptive.* A

descriptive grammar contains the rules that are needed to produce sentences in the language. English grammar uses a *subject-verb-object* (SVO) order. Sentences in English in the active voice use SVO ordering. An example of a simple SVO sentence is sentence 2. But not all languages use the SVO rule. Japanese, for example, is *a subject-object-verb* (SOV) language.

A descriptive grammar also accounts for the relationships between sentences; for example, it shows how active sentences are related to passive sentences.

3. The coffee was spilled by Bob.

Our metalinguistic awareness tells us that sentence 3 means the same thing as sentence 2. A descriptive grammar accounts for how active sentences are related to their passive forms. You might want to think of a grammar as computer software that can produce sentences but no ungrammatical sentences.

DISCOURSE

The highest level of language analysis is **discourse,** the multisentence language used in conversations, dialogues, and narratives. Figure 1.1 outlines the components

DISCOURSE
(conversation, story, narrative, paragraph)

SENTENCE UNITS
(acceptable syntactic structure)

PHRASES
Noun phrases (noun + descriptor)
Verb phrases (verb + what it acts on)

WORDS
(from the vocabulary)

MORPHEMES
(from the lexicon)

PHONEMES
(from the set of acceptable phones in the language)

Figure 1.1. Levels and Components of Language Think of speech production processes as running from the top to the bottom of the figure and speech comprehension processes as ordered roughly from the bottom to the top of the figure.

of language and suggests strategies for comprehension and production that are covered in later chapters. We move on to discuss the field of psycholinguistics.

The Scope of Psycholinguistic Research

Psycholinguistics is an interdisciplinary field that draws on psychology and related disciplines to study language processes. It focuses on processes used to acquire, produce, or understand language. Psycholinguists initiate research first by asking questions about language and then devising a research plan to answer them. Psycholinguists usually specialize in one facet of language (e.g., speech perception), just as physicians may specialize in one kind of medicine (e.g., proctology). One way to describe the work of psycholinguistics is by describing its fields of expertise (see Gernsbacher, 1994), which is how I planned the chapters in this book, summarizing areas of specialization in each chapter. I describe what we know about human language by reviewing the research conducted on different aspects of language.

You will soon discover that language is a complex *neurological, psychological,* and *sociocultural* phenomenon (see Jay, 2000). Speaking and understanding language draws on neurological structures in the brain, psychological processes (e.g., memory, inference), and sociocultural knowledge (e.g., social status, politeness, gender orientation). Most psychological research is carried out in the context of a single language; however, cross-linguistic and bilingual comparisons are also essential but studied less. The scope of psycholinguistics is usually limited to one of four general topics: language acquisition, language comprehension, language production, or pragmatics. We look at these four topics next.

LANGUAGE ACQUISITION

Language acquisition refers to how and when children learn to speak and understand their native language (or in bilingual communities, two languages). Developmentalists are interested in the factors that shape acquisition, such as learning, brain maturation, social interaction, and cognitive development. The acquisition period spans prenatal development through adolescence. The goal of language acquisition research is to describe how a child becomes competent to produce and understand language, select the proper processing strategies, and achieve language "milestones" (e.g., first spoken word).

Developmental research produces data charting the "normal" course of language comprehension and production. This would include when children first begin to use negatives (e.g., *no* or *not*) in speech. Developmental norms are useful to compare typical children to language-delayed children, who may suffer from severe neglect or brain dysfunction. Childhood language disorders (e.g., autism) are also understood through comparison to typical development. Generally speaking, a child's linguistic performance is a function of age (with wide variations) and the language being acquired. Children learn simple grammatical forms before they learn complex forms. For example, they understand and produce the active voice (sentence 4) in English before the more complex passive voice (sentence 5).

4. Farmer Brown chased the rabbit.

5. Wasn't the rabbit chased by Farmer Brown?

Sentence 5 is structurally more complex than 4, and it has more words in it than 4. Adding words to sentences also places a burden on the young child's limited memory span. Developmentalists are interested in why children use sentences like 4 before they use sentences like 5.

Other issues in language acquisition include these:

- Does bilingualism add to or subtract from language acquisition?

- How do children learn irregular verb forms (e.g., *go–went*)?

- How does the mother's prenatal speech affect learning?

We address language acquisition questions in Chapters 10 and 11.

LANGUAGE COMPREHENSION

Comprehension refers to how we understand written, spoken, or signed language. Comprehension involves a complex string of processes that begin with phoneme perception and end with a derived meaning. Comprehension includes making inferences and constructing a mental model of what is being discussed, as well as using information about the topic of discussion, the setting in which the speech occurs, and the speaker's gestures and emotional state. Psycholinguists are interested in discovering the comprehension strategies we employ to derive meaning from speech and text and describing how comprehension occurs in real time. Does comprehension occur all at once, or does it unfold in stages fashion? If it unfolds in stages, what are the stages?

One question of interest in comprehension research is how we resolve lexical **ambiguity.** How do we find the "right" meaning when a word has more than one meaning—for example, *seal, lead, bank,* or *fine?* Context helps (e.g., *river bank*), but how do we derive meaning if a word is out of context? Ambiguity also operates on the sentence level. How do we determine the meaning of an ambiguous sentence like *Bob shot the robber in his underwear?* Part of the solution depends on how we parse the sentence, that is, assign a structure to it. Does the phrase *in his underwear* go with Bob or with the robber? Who is wearing the underwear? It is difficult to disambiguate the sentence without more linguistic or contextual information. Ambiguity is one of many problems to be resolved in written and spoken language. The following are some other issues of interest in comprehension studies:

- Are metaphors (e.g., "time is money") understood directly, or are their literal meanings computed first?

- Do listening and reading use the same areas of the brain?

- How does word imagery affect comprehension?

- What strategies do we use to parse sentences?

As you can see from these questions, the research on comprehension is complex and wide-ranging. We encounter more questions about comprehension in Chapters 4 and 5.

LANGUAGE PRODUCTION

Language production refers to how a person creates speech, sign language, or text, beginning with an initial idea or message and ending in the spoken, signed, or written form. The production process on the surface seems simple, but cognitively it is a complex process. Speech production unfolds in a fraction of a second from an unconscious idea into the final spoken sentence. Sometimes we find ourselves hesitating and searching to find the right words to express a thought. We sense the complexity of speech production when it is labored, when we make mistakes, and when the words we say do not capture our complete thoughts.

Some analysts have proposed that speech production unfolds through a series of stages that begin with an overall message, followed by word selection and then assembling the words into a sentence prior to assigning speech sounds to be articulated (Levelt, 1989). Psycholinguists have used speech errors, hesitations, and pausing phenomena as a window into the production process. Where and how errors and pauses occur provides some insight into the overall process. Some of the issues in language production being explored include these:

- How do we select the right words and create a sentence framework for them?

- How are gestures integrated into spoken messages?

- Can a language-delayed child catch up later?

- How are our emotional states encoded in speech?

Speech production is covered in Chapter 6. Other issues on this list are discussed throughout the text.

PRAGMATICS AND DISCOURSE

Studies of **pragmatics** focus on how social situations affect language processes. Pragmatic analyses demonstrate how speech depends on *who* is listening (e.g., one's age, gender, and socioeconomic status), *where* a conversation is taking place (e.g., a dorm room, a retail store, a doctor's office), the *topic* of discussion (e.g., politics, sexual desire, balancing chemical equations), and the speaker's and listener's *goals* (e.g., seduction, placing a bet, buying a car). Whereas speech production and comprehension studies commonly employ the word or sentence as a unit of analysis, studies of pragmatics involve strings of sentences in discourse. *Discourse* is multisentence speech such as conversation, dialogue, written text, stories, jokes, and narrative.

Understanding discourse relies in part on knowledge of schemas. **Schemas** are cognitive frameworks for organizing interrelated concepts. For example, our "storytelling schema" contains concepts about the plot, the setting, the main characters, and the theme of the story. We use our knowledge of story schemas when we listen to stories and when we tell stories. We have schemas for many situations—for example, teacher-student classroom dialogue, doctor-patient interviews, dining out, and doing the laundry. Other examples of pragmatics research include topics such as conversational turn taking, psychotherapy, police interrogation, learning to tell a story, giving courtroom testimony, and the role of politeness in business transactions.

Some of the issues in discourse analysis include the following:

- What gender differences appear in conversations? What do they mean?

- Why are metaphors used in psychotherapy?

- Is one dialect of a language better than another?

- What kinds of speech constitute sexual harassment?

Analysis of pragmatics and discourse is relatively new to the field, but it is providing some of the most exciting and diverse (maybe even tingly) research in psycholinguistics. Many of these everyday issues are addressed Part Two.

A Sample of Research Methods in Psycholinguistics

One way to understand the field of psycholinguistics is to examine the questions it generates and the methods it uses to answer questions about acquisition, comprehension, production, and pragmatics. Psycholinguistic research is based on controlled experimental studies conducted in the laboratory, naturalistic observations in the field, case studies, cross-linguistic comparisons, and psychobiological measures.

Research is generally not a "one-shot deal" but a programmatic one, asking a series of questions that converge on an answer to a particular problem. The results of a single experiment generally suggest follow-up questions to be answered in subsequent research. In each chapter, we examine a series of experiments that address major questions and converge on answers to them.

The Experiment Schema

Psychology laboratory experiments generally consist of *independent variables* (IVs) that interest the experimenter (e.g., age, gender, location of brain damage, sentence complexity, ambiguity) and *dependent variables* (DVs) that measure subjects' reactions to, or are a function of, the independent variables (e.g., reaction time, brain wave activity, subjective ratings). The experimental method allows the researcher to control the variables involved and to determine the causal relationships between the IVs and the DVs in the experiment (e.g., increasing sentence complexity causes increases in reading times).

Some research methods are unique to psycholinguistics and are rarely employed in other sciences. For example, the *lexical decision task* is an experimental task that asks subjects to decide if a string of letters (e.g., *jete* or *neat*) is a word or not. The task can be used to determine what factors affect word recognition and reading processes. Other methods are more general than this, for example, the *word association task*. In a word association task, the experimenter presents a subject with a target word (e.g., *money*), and the subject responds with the first word that comes to mind (e.g., *owe*). Word association provides a window into the subject's associations, and it has been used in the fields of counseling, child development, personality, abnormal psychology, speech pathology, and social psychology. Let's look at a sample of research methods for the areas of psycholinguistic research.

Question: When Do Children Learn to Use Negations?

If we wanted to observe how children use negation (*no, not,* etc.) between the ages of 2 and 4 years, we would get a sample of 2-year-olds and 4-year-olds and record the differences between the two groups. Another way to approach this question would be to use a longitudinal study, which samples the development of individual children at periodic intervals. For example, a child's use of negation would be recorded monthly from age 2 through age 4 and compared to other children during this period (R. Brown, 1973). The longitudinal method is time- and labor-intensive, but it provides more reliable data than the cross-sectional method. Other developmental methods could include experimental studies using imitation, fill-in-the-blank, interview, and standardized testing methodologies.

Question: How Do We Comprehend Metaphorical Language?

Comprehension studies aim to elucidate the processes or strategies that we use to derive meaning. A standard method is to record simple reading times for sentences that vary in linguistic complexity. A topic currently being debated is the comprehension of metaphors (e.g., "time is money"). One issue is whether people compute literal *and* metaphorical meanings simultaneously or one after the other. For some kinds of judgments, activating literal and metaphorical meanings will slow down the processing time. For example, participants in one experiment were presented with sentences like *My job is a jail* and asked if they are literally true. The time it took to make the decision was recorded. This sentence is literally false but it is metaphorically true. Sentences like these took *longer* to judge than sentences that did not have metaphorical interpretation (e.g., *My job is purple*). The metaphorical meaning was available during the literalness judgment and slowed reaction time, indicating that the metaphorical meaning was immediately available.

Question: What Do "Slips of the Tongue" Reveal about Speech Production?

Speech production processes are difficult to study in a laboratory setting. There are fewer studies on production processes than on comprehension processes. One traditional analysis of speech production is based on spontaneous speech errors. Errors in speech production are used as evidence of a stagelike production process. A **slip of the tongue** occurs when one segment of speech (e.g., a sound, syllable, or word) is exchanged involuntarily for another segment in the same sentence. "Have a dice nay" is a slip involving speech sounds. In this example, notice that the sentence structure is intact and has the right words. Only the initial speech sounds of two words were exchanged: /n/ is switched with /d/. This error tells us that speech sounds were selected after the words and sentence frame were put together in the speech production process.

Question: How Do Speakers Take Turns in Conversations?

Research methods on discourse processes use observations of colloquial speech in everyday settings. A trend in discourse production research is to analyze strategies used in conversations, dialogues, question asking, and interviews. For example, in a study of turn taking in conversations, observers recorded the techniques the speaker used to signal the end of his or her turn. Speakers signaled that they were finishing by pausing, ceasing gesticulations, relaxing their body posture, looking at the next speaker, and letting their speech volume trail off. These cues signaled the next speaker to jump in when the current speaker ended.

Question: How Does Brain Damage Affect Speech Processing?

Language comprehension and production studies include extensive use of psychobiological measurements like brain imaging techniques, brain wave activity, and cerebral blood flow. These studies (see Chapter 2) show what areas of the brain are active during particular tasks. For example, reading a printed word aloud and naming an object activate different areas of the cerebral cortex. Language research also employs case studies of *brain-damaged* patients and those with language disorders in order to determine what language processes are lost when an area of the cortex is dysfunctional. Damage in a patient's occipital lobes is more likely to affect visual or reading processes than auditory or listening processes.

Question: How Does the Language One Is Learning Affect How It Is Learned?

Cross-linguistic studies compare observations of people using different languages. One issue is to determine what language-specific characteristics affect language processing. Cross-linguistic comparisons are used to determine universal aspects of language acquisition as well as the unique aspects of a particular language. One outcome of cross-linguistic research is the notion that aspects of language that are repeatedly stressed will be acquired before those that are not stressed. Children learning Hebrew, for example, acquire the concept of gender before children learning to speak French because gender is stressed more frequently in Hebrew than it is in French. Developmentalists employ extensive cross-linguistic sampling of children's spontaneous speech. With the advent of computers and Internet access, these data are collected and archived in searchable language databases (MacWhinney & Snow, 1985).

Discussion Question
Select one psycholinguistic component (acquisition, comprehension, production, or pragmatics), and design an experiment that would examine a question about it. How would you conduct this experiment (indicate who, what, where, and when), and what kind of results would you anticipate?

Theoretical Issues

Language and thought have been explored since the time of Plato, who examined in *Cratylus* the relationship between words and the objects to which they refer. So psycholinguistics is part of a long tradition of seeking answers to questions about language and thought. Research in this textbook touches on some long-argued broader theoretical issues about language.

NATURE VERSUS NURTURE

Is language the product of learning (nurture), or is it innate (nature)? This is the *nature versus nurture* question. There is no simple answer; some aspects are more built-in than others are. Language is the product of both learning and biological predispositions. One approach for psycholinguists is to determine what is innate and what has to be learned. The human infant is capable of being sensitized to the sounds in any language, but the child's brain becomes most sensitized to sounds in its native language by the end of the first year. So infants come prewired to learn any language, but the language environment they live in directly affects what is important. Similarly, children who are severely neglected for long periods of time will exhibit language delay. Learning plays an important role in social and cultural aspects of language. Emotion is one area of research that is gaining attention in neuroscience, and it may revive an interest in Pavlovian conditioned meaning.

PSYCHOLOGICAL VERSUS BIOLOGICAL MODELS OF LANGUAGE

Is language best characterized as a set of psychological strategies and processes or as patterns of brain activity? This is a question about what type of analysis is appropriate to describe language and how it works. With the growing influence of research in neuroscience, psycholinguistics is leaning more toward brain-inspired models of language, which link language processes to neural patterns. Like the nature-nurture issue, the resolution lies in determining what about language is psychological and what is neurological. On the one hand, I am convinced that discourse processes such as those involved in writing text or telling a story rely heavily on mental models or schemas of how to complete those activities. On the other hand, 140 years of research on brain-damaged patients, including recent research on brain imaging, clearly support a biological analysis of language processes. One model is not necessarily better than the other; they just provide different kinds of information about a particular question.

AUTONOMOUS VERSUS INTERDEPENDENT PROCESSES

Are language processes mediated by a set of autonomous processes or by an interdependent network of information? The autonomy argument concerns the relationship between processes used to produce and comprehend language. It assumes that language processing can be described as a set of separate "modules" that operate like different parts of the cerebral cortex (Fodor, 1983), each dedicated to performing a specific task independently of other modules (e.g., word recognition). Each module contributes to a different stage of the comprehension or production process. For example, reading aloud uses one module to decode visual input at the beginning of the task and a separate module to perform the articulatory operations at the end of the task.

The interdependent view is that language processes operate as one large network of interconnected operations that feed off each other (e.g., visual processing, semantic processing, articulatory performance). This network of *parallel distributed processes* (Rumelhart, McClelland, & the PDP Research Group, 1986) activates the parts of the network that are required to complete a given task. Different parts of the network (e.g., visual processing and word recognition) interact to permit reading and articulation.

For example, text perception uses incoming visual stimuli to activate word meanings. At the same time, expected word meanings activate articulatory codes. These processes are not separate from each other; they are interconnected by bidirectional links that feed forward and backward into each system. When you read *Apples grow on . . . ,* the higher levels of the network begin to activate *trees* before you set eyes on the word.

LANGUAGE RULES VERSUS STATISTICAL REGULARITIES

Do children acquire an abstract set of rules about language, or do they store the statistical probabilities about language in memory? The rules argument proposes that children compute rules from language input (Pinker, 1999). For example, children learn that most verbs in the past tense end with *-ed.* The past tense rule gets overextended by the child to irregular verbs (e.g., *goed*) until the irregular forms are discovered as exceptions to the rule.

An alternative interpretation is that children compute the regularities of language, the transitional probabilities between words and word endings (Rumelhart et al., 1986). The regularities are stored in the network of letter patterns, sounds, and meanings. The child is highly likely to hear *-ed* when someone is talking about a past action, so *-ed* becomes associated with every past action. However, some verbs like *go* never occur with *-ed.* Initially, the child produces the most likely word, *goed,* because it is the most probable form. With more practice, the *-ed* ending linked to *go* is deactivated in the network and replaced by the more probable *went.*

The nature of these broader theoretical issues will make more sense when we read about particular issues like verb endings later on. The next section places psycholinguistic research in a historical context so that you history buffs will have something to be excited about.

Antecedents of Psycholinguistics

The point of examining the history of psycholinguistics is to understand the origins of contemporary research. I have outlined research issues that emerged in the past and remain with us today. I also point to the chapters in the text where these issues are discussed as a way of foreshadowing what lies ahead.

Psycholinguistics has evolved through five eras: structuralism (late nineteenth century) and functionalism (early twentieth century), behaviorism (early to mid-twentieth century), linguistics (postbehaviorism through Chomsky), cognitive (late 1960s to early 1980s), and cognitive science (Kess, 1992). Psycholinguistics came to fruition after a debate about language between linguists, behaviorists, and cognitive psychologists in the 1950s and 1960s. Questions about language encompass research from linguistics, neuroscience, artificial intelligence, computer science, anthropology, philosophy, and psychology.

STRUCTURALIST AND FUNCTIONALIST VIEWS OF LANGUAGE

In the second half the nineteenth century, interest in language research intensified. Modern-day neuroscience was being born in the field of medicine in France, Germany, and England. Shortly thereafter, in Europe and America, psychologists who came to be known as structuralists attempted to describe the structure of the human mind and of sensations, images, and feelings. **Wilhelm Wundt** is credited with establishing the first experimental psycholinguistic laboratory in Leipzig, Germany, in 1879. Wundt used language as a means of studying the mind. He wrote extensively about language acquisition, comprehension, production, sign language, and reading, all of which remain topics of interest today. Wundt developed a theory of speech production using the sentence as the unit of analysis. He regarded production as a sequential process that begins with a complete or whole thought that becomes sequentially organized and articulated. The comprehension process, he reasoned, was essentially the same as production, but in reverse, proceeding from sound segments to the complete thought. Wundt's conceptualization of production and comprehension set the stage for the theories we discuss in Chapters 5 and 6.

Shortly after Wundt's work in structuralism began, prominent American psychologist William James (1890) developed the functionalist view of thought. Functionalists like James were interested in what people do with language and thoughts, rather than the structure of the mind. Functionalists were pragmatic reasoners; they believed that the value of knowledge depended on its usefulness. This question of language function has carried over into research on discourse (see Chapters 7, 8, and 9). The subject of emotion was of keen interest to Wundt and James, and it is addressed throughout this text, especially in Chapter 11.

Functionalism was important because it could be applied to practical problems like those children face when learning to read. From a functionalist perspective, Edmund Burke Huey (1908/1968) developed what might be considered by today's standards a "modern" theory of reading. He refined the use of an important laboratory device known as the *tachistoscope*, which was designed to present text materials very rapidly to human subjects in order to record *reaction time* (RT). The processes underlying reading can be elucidated by assuming that longer RTs reflect the difficulty or complexity of the reading material. Huey developed the idea of *eye-voice span* in reading by observing how the voice lags behind the eye when we read aloud. Huey's research is a precursor to word recognition and reading research (see Chapters 4 and 7).

BEHAVIORISM

Structuralist and functionalist points of view were supplanted in America by a growing trend to make psychology a more rigorous science. In the early 1900s, behaviorists tried to establish psychology as an empirical science with all the requisite tools of the scientific method but devoid of mental constructs like *mind*, *thought*, and *imagery*. Behaviorists like John Watson and B. F. Skinner wanted a psychology based on observable behavior (e.g., rats pressing levers), not mental constructs. **Behaviorism** became firmly established in

America through the work of Watson and in Russia by Ivan Pavlov, who worked out the rudiments of classical conditioning (Hilgard, 1987). Pavlov demonstrated how an originally neutral stimulus (bell), when frequently paired with a reflex (salivating to meat powder), would elicit the reflexive response. In the 1950s, the classical conditioning paradigm was used to account for how words acquired emotional meaning (see Chapter 11). At the end of the 1950s, the notion of language changed, as we see next.

LINGUISTICS: THE SKINNER-CHOMSKY DEBATE

The pivotal juncture in the history of psycholinguistics involved a nature-versus-nurture-type debate. Is language a product of operant conditioning, or is the potential for language innate? B. F. Skinner, in his book *Verbal Behavior* (1957), argued for the behaviorist position. Skinner's book was predicated on the principles of operant conditioning, developed two decades earlier during the behaviorist domination of American experimental psychology. Skinner's view was that speech was a product of operant learning processes such as reinforcement, extinction, and generalization.

A linguist from MIT, Noam Chomsky, critically reviewed Skinner's book in 1959 and successfully challenged its assumptions. Chomsky's rationalist argument was that the potential for language was an inborn or innate mental capacity. Chomsky argued that children's patterns of language acquisition were too systematic to be the product of parents' operant conditioning. Chomsky's perspective changed how scholars defined language: the potential for language was universal and innate, not the product of operant conditioning. Infants were predisposed to acquire language with a built-in *language acquisition device* (LAD), according to Chomsky. Comparing these two accounts of language acquisition is referred to as the Skinner-Chomsky debate.

Chomsky alone did not sway psychologists. The shift away from behaviorism was assisted by prominent psychologists like George Miller of Harvard University, who encouraged cognitive psychologists to examine Chomsky's theory of language structure as a model for speech processing. Miller proposed that linguists' questions about language could be translated into fruitful psychology experiments. Psychologists looked to linguistic theory to guide laboratory research, and psycholinguists spent the next decade trying to verify aspects of Chomsky's argument. Chomsky's view of language and language acquisition are addressed in Chapters 5 and 10, and his theory of sociopolitical thought is covered in Chapter 13.

History

A good example of Miller's work is *The Psychology of Communication* (1967). Books published in this era documented the commingling of psychology and linguistics. Informative explanations of Chomsky's theories of grammar include Lyons (1970) and Greene (1972). Readers interested in a historical account of psycholinguistics from the time of Wundt to Chomsky can consult Blumenthal (1970).

COGNITIVE PSYCHOLOGY

The work of Chomsky and Miller signaled an oncoming revolution in psychology. The transition from behaviorism to the cognitive perspective has been referred to as the **cognitive revolution** (see Gardner, 1985). The cognitive revolution was crucial to the birth of psycholinguistics, and it turned attention away from behaviorism toward language and mental processes. Cognitive psychology became the study of how people perceive, organize, remember, and use information. Cognitive psychology and psycholinguistics converged to study how people produce and comprehend language, as discussed in Chapters 3, 5, and 6.

COGNITIVE SCIENCE

Psycholinguistics since the mid-1980s has turned toward a cognitive science point of view. **Cognitive science** is a multidisciplinary effort that integrates research linguistics, psychobiology, artificial intelligence, cognitive psychology, and cognitive neuroscience perspectives in order to understand more clearly how humans think and communicate (see the box "Psycholinguistics and Related Disciplines"). Cognitive neuroscience is a field of research that links the brain and nervous system to cognitive processing. Psycholinguists are currently incorporating research on language from, and contributing research to, cognitive psychology, cognitive science, and cognitive neuroscience (Gazzaniga, Ivry, & Mangun, 1998). The cognitive and neuroscience frameworks for language have set the agenda for research in the twenty-first century, as is made clear in Chapters 2 and 14. A timeline of psycholinguistic research (covered throughout this text) appears in Figure 1.2, to which you can refer while reading as you learn who these scholars are. It would be interesting for you to ask your instructor where he or she fits on this timeline.

Psycholinguistics and Related Disciplines

Historically, the ideas of the various disciplines interested in language have overlapped and cross-pollinated, so it would be misleading to not mention these ties. Each discipline has its own methods of inquiry and its own opinions about what constitutes an important problem. Psycholinguistics is influenced by research in linguistics, sociolinguistics, philosophy, anthropology and ethology, neuroscience, computer science and speech technology, speech pathology, and communication studies.

LINGUISTICS

It should be clear by now that contemporary linguists and psycholinguists are interested in similar issues (e.g., How do we parse sentences?), and these will be noted throughout this text. **Sociolinguistics,** a subfield, focuses on the social and contextual

Circa 386 B.C.	Plato—Cratylus
1755 A.D.	Samuel Johnson writes dictionary of English
1797	Itard—The Wild Boy of Aveyron

Structuralist-Functionalist Era

1828	Noah Webster publishes dictionary of American English
1838	Morse code is introduced
1861	Paul Broca—Localization of speech area
1874	Hughlings Jackson—Language and brain
	Carl Wernicke describes sensory aphasia
1876	Bell invents the telephone
1879	Wundt—Experimental Laboratory Leipzig, Germany
	Francis Galton published first study of word associations
	Wundt standardizes studies of the word association experiment
1885	Ebbinghaus—Memory & Nonsense Syllables
	Cattell shows that letters are easier to read when they create a word
1890	James—Principles of Psychology
1904	Jung & Ricklin—Word Association
1905	Binet & Simon incorporate vocabulary questions in intelligence test
1908	Huey—Reading Processes
1910	Kent & Rosanoff establish word association norms

Behaviorist Era

1913	Pavlov—Classical Conditioning
1916	Freud—Lectures on Psychoanalysis
1921	Sapir publishes anthropological view of linguistics
1923	Ogden & Richards—The meaning of meaning
1926	Piaget—Language and Thought of the Child
1932	Bartlett—Remembering
1935	Stroop—Semantic interference
	Zipf shows the relationship between word frequency and length
1945	tape recorder is available to record speech
1947	speech spectrograms are introduced
1948	Wiener—Cybernetics
	Shannon—Information Theory
1949	Wada—Cerebral dominance
1950	Lashley—Problem of Serial Order
1951	Miller, Heise, & Lichten demonstrate how expectation affects word perception
1954	Osgood & Sebeok's book Psycholinguistics names the new field
1955	Austin lectures on "how to do things with words"
1956	Whorf—Language, Thought & Reality
1957	Skinner—Verbal Behavior
	Osgood, Suci & Tannenbaum—Semantic Differential
	Chomsky—Syntactic Structures

Linguistic Era

1959	Penfield & Roberts—Speech and Brain
	Chomsky—Review of Skinner's Book
1961	Kimura—Cerebral Dominance
1962	Miller—Psychology and linguistics
	Vygotsky—Thought and Speech
1963	Katz & Fodor develop semantic theory

Figure 1.2. Psycholinguistics Timeline

1965	Brown—"psycholinguistics" further defined
	Chomsky—Aspects of a Theory of Syntax

Cognitive Psychology Era

1967	Neisser—Cognitive Psychology
	Geschwind—Model of Aphasia
	Quillian develops idea of semantic network
	Miller—The Psychology of Communication
	Lenneberg—Biological Foundations of Language
	Gazzaniga & Sperry demonstrate cerebral lateralization of lexicon
1968	Gardner & Gardner—Chimpanzee sign language
	Atkinson & Shiffrin—Model of memory
1969	Paivio—Mental Imagery
	Searle—Speech Acts Theory
	Sperry, Gazzaniga & Bogen—Split Brain Studies
	Collins & Quillian test semantic network proposal
1970	Rubenstein introduces the lexical decision task
1971	Meyer & Schvaneveldt demonstrate priming in lexical decision by related words
	Fillenbaum & Rapoport use scaling method to study lexical memory structure
1972	Ervin-Tripp—On Sociolinguistic Rules
1973	Brown—A First Language
1975	Grice—Logic and Conversation
	Thorne & Henley—Language and Sex
	Lakoff—Language and a Woman's Place
	Gibson & Levin—The Psychology of Reading
1976	Rosch provides evidence of basic level concepts
1977	Curtiss—Genie
	Clark & Clark—The Psychology of Language
1978	Shapiro & Shapiro—Tourette Syndrome
1980	Kutas & Hillyard—brain potentials, the N400 response
1982	Gilligan—In a Different Voice
1983	Fodor—Modularity of Mind
	Anderson—Act* Theory

Cognitive Science Era

1986	Rumelhart & McClelland—Parallel Distributed Processes
1987	Van Lancker—Nonpropositional Speech
	Just & Carpenter—reading and language comprehension
1988	Kintsch—discourse comprehension
	PET used to localize lexical processes in the brain
1989	Seidenberg & McClelland—Model of Word Recognition
	Rayner & Pollatsek—The Psychology of Reading
	Levelt—Spoken Language
1990	Cheney & Seyfarth—How Monkeys See the World
1991	Corballis—The Lopsided Ape
1994	Posner & Raichle—Images of Mind
	Gernsbacher—Handbook of Psycholinguistics
	Pinker—The Language Instinct
	Bialystok & Hakuta—second-language acquisition
1996	Clark—Using Language
	Elman et al.—connectionist perspective on development
1997	Jusczyk—infant speech perception
1998	Gazzaniga—Cognitive Neuroscience
	Miller—WordNet
1999	Pinker—Words and Rules

aspects of speech. Questions about how speech production is affected by class, race, gender, education, social status, social setting, or occupation are some examples. Sociolinguistics provides insight into group dynamics and settings that are not always part of the psychologist's experimental design. Fieldwork, discourse analysis, and case studies have provided valuable information about social aspects of speech, and they remind us that one important function of language is the facilitation of social interaction.

PHILOSOPHY

Interest in the philosophy of language and meaning predates experimental psychology by centuries. Questions about the nature of meaning and reference, rational thinking, semantics, learning, hermeneutics (the interpretation of literature), association of ideas, existence, awareness, logic, reasoning, and sociopolitical thought all come from philosophical inquiry.

ANTHROPOLOGY AND ETHOLOGY

Anthropology has a long history of contributing information about the structural components of languages, especially in native cultures. Anthropologists show how a culture constructs its unique view of the world through language. Ethologists (and anthropologists) study nonhuman animals, especially primates, in natural settings and make comparisons of the communicative capacities of humans and nonhumans.

NEUROSCIENCE

Neuroscience is a multidisciplinary science of the nervous system. It includes medicine, psychology, psychiatry, biology, and brain imaging. Done mainly from a biological or medical point of view, researchers interested in neurological aspects of language study anatomy, physiology, prenatal development, genetics, synaptic transmission, brain and nervous system disease, and brain imaging technology.

COMPUTER SCIENCE AND SPEECH TECHNOLOGIES

In this category are several disciplines that use computers, computer technology, and computer software to discover what language is and does. The analogy between mind and computer is not new. In *Cybernetics* (1948), Wiener showed that the concept of a learning machine (computer) was applicable to living machines (animals) because the performance of both as systems was conceptually similar. Another important link to electronic communication studies was Shannon (1948), who described how coded information is transmitted over electronic channels. This early view is now known as *information processing*. Psychologists adopted many concepts from information theory. The idea that humans have limited channel capacity for speech, the effects of noise on comprehension, and the distinction between serial and parallel processing all come from information theory.

Interest in *artificial intelligence* (AI) has grown tremendously within the computer sciences. Although computer programs can rival human performance at the game of chess, they are not capable of understanding and comprehending speech at the level of human adult functioning. Speech synthesis and speech analysis programs are currently advancing toward this goal. A good example of state-of-the-art technology can be found at Web sites for Bell Labs' Lucent Technologies or Dragon Speech Recognition systems.

Recent interest in the language technology field has turned to *natural language processors* (NLPs). NLPs are computer programs that attempt to understand everyday language. A related interest has been the development of computer lexicons or electronic dictionaries that simulate how linguistic information about words is organized in human memory. Miller and his colleagues at Princeton are pioneering research under the project name of *WordNet* (Fellbaum, 1998).

SPEECH AND HEARING DISORDERS

Speech and hearing specialists work with people who have atypical language development, deafness, and language disorders. Patients who manifest deficits or delays in comprehension or production are compared to normal language users. The patients' performance on standardized tests is used to explore questions about which aspects of language development are related to general cognitive development and which are uniquely linguistic.

COMMUNICATION STUDIES

Communication studies examine social and political implications of human language use. They look into how a therapist's credibility is undermined when he or she uses profanity, how a speaker's persuasiveness on an audience is affected by the use of humor, and the nature of sexual harassment. Political and social forces in a culture shape word meanings and conceptual reasoning about everyday problems (e.g., war or abortion). These studies provide insight into the pragmatic uses of language and the effects of culture and media on everyday speech.

Key Terms

ambiguity	cognitive revolution	comprehension
arbitrary reference	cognitive science	cross-linguistic studies
behaviorism	communication	descriptive grammar

discourse
grammatical rules
Edmond Burke Huey
language
language acquisition
language production
lexicon
metalinguistic
   awareness
morpheme

natural language
   processors
nature versus nurture
phoneme
pragmatics
prescriptive grammar
primate
   communication
productivity
schemas

Skinner-Chomsky
   debate
slip of the tongue
sociolinguistics
speech
syntax
Washoe
Wilhelm Wundt

What Lies Ahead?

Immediately ahead in Chapter 2 is a study of how the brain processes language. The brain is placed next in the sequence of chapters to reflect the increasing influence of neuroscience on psycholinguistic research. The book continues its sequential analysis of psycholinguistic processes by looking at speech perception in Chapter 3, words and word recognition in Chapter 4, and sentence processing in Chapter 5. The next three chapters change the sequencing from comprehension to production by examining speech production in Chapter 6, and writing and reading processes in Chapter 7. The second half of the book, which concentrates on social and emotional aspects of language, begins with the topic of discourse in Chapter 8. Chapter 9 follows up on the topic of discourse by looking at how we process figurative speech. The next two chapters concern the topic of language acquisition. Chapter 10 covers language development: phonology, lexicon, and grammar. Chapter 11 examines how language learning affects a person's emotional expression and behavior. The final three chapters of the text cover applications of psycholinguistic research to broader everyday situations and problems with language. Chapter 12 covers culture, dialect, education, and censorship; Chapter 13 includes a wide range of applied psycholinguistics in therapy, police interrogation, courtroom testimony, and doctor-patient dialogue. The format covers the "traditional" topics in Part One and attempts to cover some challenging new ground in Part Two.

Suggested Web Sites

Language links: http://psych.wisc.edu/courses/psy_lang/links.htm
Psycholinguistics Web Site: http://www.psyc.memphis.edu/POL/POL.htm

Chapter 2
Brain and Language

Critical Thinking Questions

1. What areas of the brain are important for comprehending and producing language?

2. How does aphasia (language loss or disorder) affect language production and comprehension?

3. What methods are used to study how the brain processes language?

4. What cognitive processes are lateralized in the left hemisphere and in the right hemisphere of the brain?

5. What role do subcortical structures play in language processing?

Exercise 2.1. **Language, Brain, and Emotion**
This exercise is designed to show you that brain damage can affect one's ability to perceive the emotional content of speech. Read each of the following sentences, and rate each on a 9-point scale of arousal (1 = not arousing at all, 9 = most arousing possible, 5 = moderately arousing). Do the same for fear (1 = completely unfearful, 9 = very fearful, 5 = moderately fearful).

1. **Jody giggled and laughed.**

   Arousal rating _____ Fear rating _____

2. **Tom's wife and children had all died in a car crash.**

   Arousal rating _____ Fear rating _____

(Exercise Continues)

(Exercise 2.1, Continued)

3. **As the car was speeding down the hill, Mike stepped down to find that he had no brakes.**

    Arousal rating _____   Fear rating _____

4. **Sally waved her hands in the air and yelled for help as the boat was sinking.**

    Arousal rating _____   Fear rating _____

Adolphs, Russell, and Tranel (1999) conducted experiments with a subject (SM), who had damage to the **amygdala,** a part of the brain that deals with emotion. The researchers wanted to study SM's recognition of unpleasant emotions expressed in the form of facial characteristics, words, and sentences and then compare her responses to those of normal subjects.

SM was read a list of sentences including those in this exercise and was asked to rate how arousing and fearful they were. SM was severely impaired at recognizing how arousing these negative sentences were. She rated sentences that represented fear and anger as "relaxing." When normal subjects were read a sentence such as *As the car was speeding down the hill, Mike stepped down to find that he had no brakes,* they rated it as high as possible, 9, on the fear scale. SM rated it 6. SM gave *Sally waved her hands in the air and yelled for help as the boat was sinking* a 3 on the fear scale. She rated the sentences depicting fear 5 standard deviations below the mean for the normal control subjects.

Are your reactions like the "normal" subjects in the experiment? What do SM's responses tell you about the amygdala's role in language comprehension? What kinds of language problems do you think SM would have "on the street"?

This chapter focuses on the neuropsychological aspects of language. It is intended to

- Describe the areas of the cortex that are involved in language processing, that is, the "localization" of language function

- Describe the language problems exhibited by patients with aphasia and brain dysfunction

- Introduce research methods used in neuroscience

- Provide evidence of the lateralization of cognitive processes

- Provide evidence of subcortical involvement in emotional aspects of language processing

This chapter describes the relationship between brain structures and language processes. Neuroscience research is becoming increasingly important to psycholinguists' conceptualization of how language functions, which is the reason for placing this chapter early in the text. Interest in how the brain produces and reacts to speech is centuries old. Throughout history, physicians have been interested in how the brain controls human behavior and thought. Reports of loss of language abilities due to brain damage have been around since the sixteenth century. Patients were identified with what we would now call **aphasia,** speech disturbances due to brain dysfunction. Psychologists have incorporated the work of brain surgeons into theories of language since the birth of psychology in the late 1800s.

One influential study that emerged during the early days of psycholinguistics was Lenneberg (1967), *Biological Foundations of Language.* Lenneberg asked questions about brain and language that are still being asked today. Has the human brain evolved specialized areas dedicated only to speech? How does language acquisition unfold in the course of physical maturation? Is there a "critical period" for language learning? What do language disorders reveal about normal brain functioning? How does language influence cognition? Psycholinguists working in neuroscience are pursuing answers to these kinds of questions.

Though we cannot cover all of Lenneberg's questions, we can use them to approach the central issues. For students to understand how the brain is involved in language processing, six factors must be addressed: (1) the anatomy of the human brain, (2) language localization, (3) models of how brain damage affects language processing (aphasiology), (4) neuroscientific methods used to examine language processes, (5) lateralization of cognitive processes, and (6) the role of emotion in language processing. As we address these six issues, you will see that different parts of the brain are associated with different language functions. The **cerebral cortex** has evolved specialized comprehension and production functions, but exactly what parts of the brain operate on language and when depends on whether it is written, spoken, or signed. Comprehension and production areas also interact with subcortical emotion areas, as demonstrated in Exercise 2.1. Together these brain areas are interdependently involved in the neurological, psychological, and sociocultural aspects of communication. We begin our study with an analysis of the language-related areas of the human brain.

The Human Brain

Learning how the brain functions is essential for a complete understanding of modern psycholinguistics. To understand the relationship between the brain and language, we need to explore the structural anatomy of the brain. To construct a model of "normal" language functions, psycholinguists capitalize on observations on and experiments with healthy individuals and on studies of people with language disorders as a result of brain injuries, tumors, and diseases.

Neuroscientists have debated the evolution of brain structures—which parts of the brain evolved earliest and how different parts are interconnected. The human brain has evolved over tens of thousands of years, expanding from the base of the brain near the spinal cord and brain stem to central areas and then onward and upward to frontal areas, somewhat in the way one builds a house from the basement to the roof. Figure 2.1 shows a side view of the four lobes of the cerebral cortex: the frontal, temporal, parietal, and occipital lobes, on the front, side, top, and back of the cortex, respectively. Each of these areas carries out a different language task. Visual processing is carried out in the occipital lobe, and auditory processing is carried out in the temporal lobe. Two different areas—**Broca's area** and **Wernicke's area**—are involved in speech articulation and auditory-semantic interpretations. Damage to Broca's area produces **nonfluent aphasia,** difficulty primarily with articulating fluent speech. Damage to Wernicke's area produces **fluent aphasia:** The person can speak easily, but the speech makes little sense. We cover these in detail in the section on aphasiology.

As mentioned, each lobe makes a different contribution to understanding and producing language, a division of labor is known as **localization** of function. The visual functions needed to process printed language (text) take place in the visual cortex in the occipital lobe (rear of the brain). Hearing spoken speech begins in the auditory cortex in the left hemisphere's temporal lobe. Interpretive functions take place in the temporal and parietal areas. We explore these localized functions in more detail throughout the chapter.

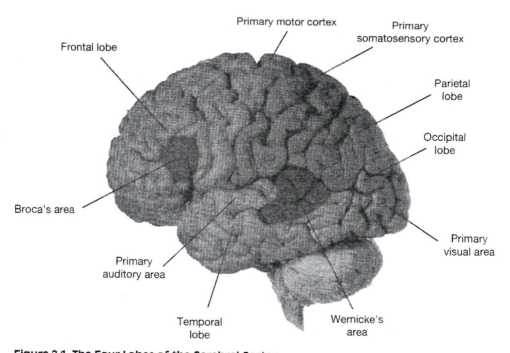

Figure 2.1. The Four Lobes of the Cerebral Cortex
Note. From *Biological Psychology* (fig. 1.5), by Klein, Stephen B., © 2000. Reprinted by permission of Pearson Education, Inc., Upper Saddle River, NJ.

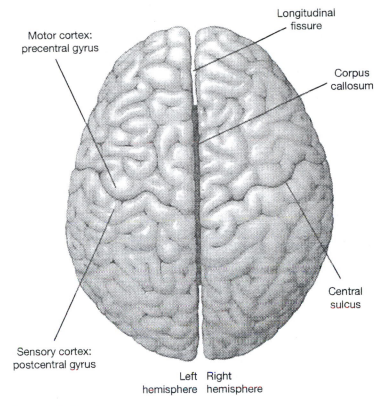

Longitudinal fissure

Motor cortex: precentral gyrus

Corpus callosum

Central sulcus

Sensory cortex: postcentral gyrus

Left   Right
hemisphere hemisphere

Figure 2.2. The Cerebral Cortex: View from Above
Note. From *Brain, Mind, and Behavior,* by Floyd E. Bloom and Arlyne Lazerson © 1985, 1988, 2001 by Educational Broadcasting Corporation. Used with the permission of Worth Publishers.

The two cerebral hemispheres are separated externally by a longitudinal fissure, which is a deep groove in the cortex. The hemispheres are connected internally by the **corpus callosum,** as is illustrated in Figure 2.2. The corpus callosum allows the two hemispheres to communicate with each other through millions of bands of nerve fibers. Neuroscientists (see Brodmann, 1909; Penfield & Roberts, 1959) discovered that the sensorimotor areas of the cortex have opposite-side or *contralateral organization.* For outgoing motor functions, this means that stimulation of the right motor cortex will make a body part on the left side of the body move. Stimulation of the left motor cortex makes the right side move.

Vision and hearing operate contralaterally too. Visual information from the left side of a scene travels to the right occipital area. Visual information from the right side of the scene travels to the left occipital area. This contralateral information is shared with the other hemisphere within milliseconds via connections in the corpus callosum. Hearing is organized with both contralateral processing and *ipsilateral processing* (processing on the same side of the body). The primary information from the right ear travels to the temporal area in the left hemisphere via contralateral pathways. The right-ear information travels to the left temporal area.

The contralateral auditory pathways dominate over same-side (ipsilateral) information, which travel to the auditory areas on the same side.

SUBCORTICAL INVOLVEMENT IN SPEECH

Speech areas in the cerebral cortex evolved over time on top of the **limbic system** and **basal ganglia.** Lamendella (1977) and others (Jay, 2000) urge us to broaden the concept of language to include processes associated with the limbic system and basal ganglia. Lamendella suggested that the interconnections of the limbic system with the speech areas in the cortex are the link to studying emotion and language phenomena.

The *limbic system* inhibits and instigates instinctive patterns, such as feeding, mating, fight-or-flight responses, anger, and aggression. The limbic system allows conscious control over motor actions necessary to satisfy emotional needs. The right hemisphere elaborates the input generated by the limbic system in a manner that retains its "rich affective value" (Lamendella, 1977, p. 199). The *amygdala* is a small, almond-shaped structure that plays a role in emotional recognition, especially negative emotions such as fear and anger. Adolphs et al. (1999) suggest that the amygdala plays a significant role in processing negative emotional arousal (e.g., fear), and a person with an impaired amygdala has difficulty processing dangerous and threatening speech (recall Exercise 2.1).

The *basal ganglia* with related structures are involved in motor movement. Dysfunction in the basal ganglia can result in movement disorders such as Parkinson's disease, Huntington's chorea, and Tourette syndrome (TS). TS is a tic disorder characterized by uncontrollable tics, motor movements, vocalizations, and cursing. The uncontrollable cursing in TS provides a nexus for neurological, psychological, and sociocultural aspects speech (Jay, 2000). We address subcortical involvement in emotional speech later in the chapter with the topic of right-hemisphere speech.

Review Question
What are the names of the four lobes of the cerebral cortex? What language functions are associated with each lobe as described in this section? What subcortical areas are associated with language processes?

Language Localization

Language localization refers to language functions being carried out by areas of the cerebral cortex. We have just read that speech production is handled by Broca's area. The argument that speech was localized in the frontal areas of the left hemisphere was formulated in Europe in the mid- to late 1800s. The localization of cognitive functions in specific brain areas has been a topic for research since Franz Joseph Gall's study of phrenology, or measuring the bumps on a person's head, which immediately preceded Broca's work.

Most textbooks in psychology and cognitive neuroscience trace classic research on language localization to the nineteenth-century physician and anthropologist Paul Broca. It was Broca's 1861 description of the brain of his patient, **Leborgne,** that provided the first clinical evidence that the facility for articulate speech was located in the left frontal lobe. Broca's research, along with that of Hughlings Jackson and Carl Wernicke, proved that brain damage to different areas of the cortex produce different patterns of language difficulties, laying the foundation for present-day aphasia research.

One important aspect of Broca's research that has generally been ignored is the details of Leborgne's *emotional speech* ability. Despite his aphasia, Leborgne retained the ability to curse when he was angered. Only Jackson (1874/1958) noted the common occurrence of profanity in aphasic speech. Leborgne's ability to curse when angered raises some questions about how emotional aspects of speech are integrated with core language processes.

BROCA AND LEBORGNE

Broca's description of Leborgne and his evidence for the localization of articulate speech in the frontal lobe were published in his 1861 report, *"Remarques sur le siège de la faculté du langage articulé, suivies d'une observation d'aphémie."* Complete English translations of this article are not easy to find, although secondary references to this work as the landmark of language localization are plentiful. Herrnstein and Boring (1965) published Mollie D. Boring's translation of the article in their book, *A Sourcebook in the History of Psychology.* Another accessible version of this translation appears in Benjamin's (1997) *History of Psychology* in a chapter titled, "The Physiological Roots of Psychology." These books contain Broca's description of Leborgne; a man brought to the hospital at age 51 with cellulitis of the right leg. He could comprehend what was said to him, but when Leborgne was asked about the origin of his disease, he replied "only with the monosyllable *tan*, repeated twice in succession and accompanied by a gesture of his left hand" (Herrnstein & Boring, 1965, p. 224). Leborgne remained in the hospital at Bicêtre for twenty-one years until his death. Broca described Leborgne as follows:

> Since his youth he had been subject to epileptic attacks, yet he was able to become a maker of lasts, a trade at which he worked until he was thirty years old. It was then that he lost his ability to speak and that is why he was admitted to the hospice at Bicêtre. It was not possible to discover whether some other symptom accompanied the onset of his affliction. When he arrived at Bicêtre he had already been unable to speak for two or three months. He was then quite healthy and intelligent and differed from a normal person only in his loss of articulate language. He came and went in the hospice,

where he was known by the name of "Tan." He understood all that was said to him. His hearing was actually very good, but whenever one questioned him he always answered, "Tan, tan," accompanying his utterance with varied gestures by which he succeeded in expressing most of his ideas. If one did not understand his gestures, he was apt to get irate and added to his vocabulary a gross oath "*Sacre nom de Dieu!*" ("Goddamn!") Tan was considered an egoist, vindictive and objectionable, and his associates, who detested him, even accused him of stealing. These defects could have been due largely to his cerebral lesion. (Herrnstein & Boring, 1965, p. 224)

Leborgne died on April 17, 1861, and Broca performed an autopsy as soon as possible and reported what was to become the key observation in the history of neuroscience. Broca had found the first clinical evidence that language was localized in the third convolution of the left frontal lobe (see Figure 2.1). This area of cortex became known as *Broca's area*. *Broca's aphasia* is a term for damage in Broca's area causing the loss of articulate speech and some comprehension skills. Today these two terms appear frequently in texts where language disorders are discussed.

Review Question
Where is Broca's area? Describe what happens when it is damaged.

Aphasiology

We shall now consider *aphasiology*, or what we have learned about language localization from studies of aphasic patients like Leborgne. Aphasias involve all language modalities. Patients can have trouble with signing, reading, or writing language, as well as with speaking. The importance of looking at forms of aphasia is that they inform us about normal language functions. Broca's era marked a time when postmortem autopsy was used to examine brain-language links. When a physician had a patient with speech-related symptoms who died, he would perform an autopsy to determine the location of the defect. Modern surgical techniques and brain imaging have reduced much of the guesswork.

THE GESCHWIND MODEL

The localization of language abilities is now widely accepted by many psycholinguists as the **Geschwind model** (see Howard, 1997). Norman Geschwind (1970) is the American neurologist who recently updated and elaborated the model, which originated in the work of Wernicke and Ludwig Lichtheim in the late 1800s. Geschwind described how different areas of the cortex interact to produce and comprehend speech.

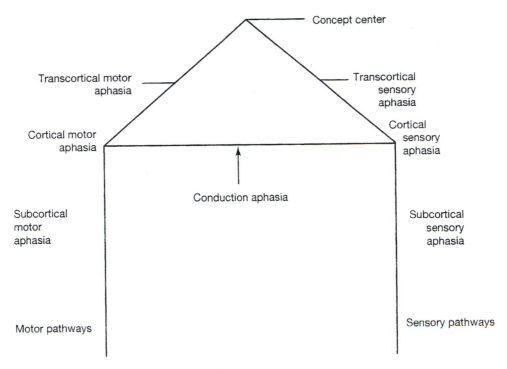

Figure 2.3. Geschwind's View of Aphasia

Figure 2.3 illustrates a "concept center" with motor and auditory pathways. Motor pathways work to produce speech, and auditory-sensory pathways work to comprehend it. Aphasia is represented as damage on a path or center in the house-shaped diagram in Figure 2.3. Damage or dysfunction along these pathways will disrupt the representation of speech at that point and produce a unique pattern of symptoms, some that result in comprehension difficulties and some that result in the inability to produce spoken or written language. The common types of aphasia are labeled on the diagram.

Damage to the motor area of the cortex will produce what is known as *pure word mutism*. Word mutism is caused by cortical damage; it is not a defect with the speech or vocal apparatus, such as the tongue or larynx. The patients cannot say words at all. The mouth and vocal apparatus work fine; the defect is in the cerebral cortex near the frontal area and motor strip. Damage to the auditory area will produce *pure word deafness*, the inability to process speech. It is the result of cortical damage in the temporal area and is not the result of damage to the ear or middle ear.

From the symptoms of aphasia, Geschwind constructed a model of normal language comprehension and production. The comprehension of a spoken word takes place in Wernicke's area, and the production of speech takes place in Broca's area. Geschwind's model suggests that once the meaning of a spoken utterance is understood, Wernicke's area constructs a representation of a verbal response. The representation could be an auditory neural image of the response, which is transferred to the *arcuate fasciculus,* a bundle of fibers connecting Wernicke's area with Broca's area.

Language can be communicated through visual and spoken modalities. Geschwind's model suggests that the secondary visual cortices in the occipital lobe and *angular gyrus* in the parietal lobe are the areas responsible for comprehending written words. A *gyrus* is a rounded, elevated convolution in the cortex. The angular gyrus borders the left occipital lobe and has connections to Wernicke's area.

Broca's Aphasia

Broca's aphasia is the result of damage in the third convolution of the frontal lobe, which is near the motor cortex. Patients with Broca's aphasia have difficulty producing speech. They can speak, but only very haltingly, leaving out many function morphemes and words, producing an abbreviated form of syntax. Here is an example of Broca's aphasia:

INTERVIEWER: Were you in the Coast Guard?

PATIENT: No, er, yes, yes . . . ship . . . Massachu . . . chusetts . . . Coast Guard . . .
   years. (*raises hands twice with fingers indicating "19"*)

INTERVIEWER: Oh, you were in the Coast Guard 19 years?

PATIENT: Oh . . . boy . . . right . . . right.

INTERVIEWER: Why are you in the hospital?

PATIENT: (*points to paralyzed arm*) Arm no good. (*points to mouth*) Speech . . . can't
   say . . . talk, you see.

INTERVIEWER: What happened to make you lose your speech?

PATIENT: Head, fall, Jesus Christ, me no good, str, str . . . oh Jesus . . . stroke.

INTERVIEWER: Could you tell me what you've been doing in the hospital?

PATIENT: Yes sure. Me go, er, uh, P. T. nine o'cot, speech . . . two times. . . . Read . . .
   wr . . . ripe, er, rike, er, write . . . practice. (Gardner, 1975, p. 61)

As noted earlier, there are two forms of aphasias: *fluent* and *nonfluent.* Fluent aphasia does not interrupt the flow of speech, whereas nonfluent does, as we see in the example just given. Broca's aphasia has been characterized as nonfluent aphasia or *expressive* aphasia. Broca's aphasics may exhibit *apraxia,* which is a difficulty in programming articulations, or *dysarthria,* which is a loss of control over articulatory muscles. These problems with language production are not limited to speech. Broca's aphasics also have difficulty with handwriting, *agraphia,* as can be seen in Figure 2.4. The handwriting resembles the patient's spoken language. This patient also has *anomia,* which is difficulty selecting the correct word for either written or spoken language.

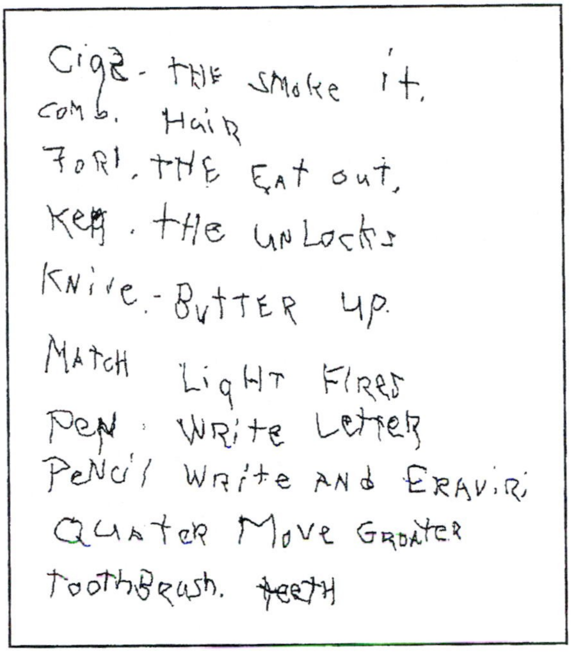

Figure 2.4. Sample of the Handwriting of a Patient with Broca's Aphasia

Note. From R. H. Brookshire (1997). *Introduction to Neurogenic Communication Disorders,* 5/e, Mosby, 1997, fig. "Writing Sample from Patient with Broca's Aphasia" Reprinted by permission of W. B. Saunders Company.

Wernicke's Aphasia

Wernicke's aphasia is the result of damage near the auditory area near the back of the temporal lobe (Wernicke's area). Wernicke's aphasia is characterized as fluent aphasia or *receptive* aphasia. The problem is not disfluency in speaking; in fact, Wernicke's aphasics are fluent speakers. The problem is a decreased ability to understand the language of others and decreased meaningfulness of their speech production. Wernicke's patients have comprehension problems in all modalities. Damage to the pathway between Wernicke's area and the angular gyrus is associated with an impaired ability to comprehend written words, known as **alexia.**

Fluent aphasia results in speech that is a sort of agrammatical "word salad" in which words, phrases, and nonsense words are jumbled together. Here is an example of speech from a patient with Wernicke's aphasia:

> Boy, I'm sweating. I'm awful nervous, you know, once in a while I get caught up. I can't mention the tarripoi, a month ago, quite a little. I've done a lot well. I impose a lot, while, on the other hand, you know what I mean. I have to run around, lookt it over, trebin and all that sort of stuff. (Gardner, 1975, p. 68)

Some of these words and expressions have meaning in isolation, but the way they are tossed together in strings makes little sense. A non-English speaker might perceive this as fluent normal speech because it "sounds" normal. English speakers would readily perceive the nonsense words and failures to express a complete thought in sentence form.

Other Forms of Aphasia

What would happen if a person suffered extensive brain damage that extended from Wernicke's area all the way through Broca's area? If you are thinking that there would be many problems with language, you are right. This type of damage is called **global aphasia,** and it results in a loss of all speech abilities. *Conduction aphasia* is characterized by good comprehension of spoken language but impairment in repeating what was heard. People with conduction aphasia cannot read aloud, but they can comprehend written material. They do have problems with writing, usually using incorrect letters or reversing letters in words. *Transcortical aphasia* can appear in motor or sensory form. *Transcortical motor aphasia* results in nonfluent speech and difficulty in naming (**anomia**), although the ability to echo another person's speech is retained. Comprehension is good, and repetition is too. The damage is in front of or behind Broca's area. *Transcortical sensory aphasia* is characterized by fluent speech and the ability to echo or repeat. Comprehension of spoken language is poor, as are reading and writing. Damage involves the zone between the temporal and parietal lobes. These forms of aphasia are outlined in Table 2.1.

Before leaving the topic of aphasiology, the question of age of occurrence must be addressed. Studies have shown that age of onset of brain damage is an important determinant of speech localization (Lenneberg, 1967). For left cerebral damage before the age of 5 years, there is a good chance that speech can shift to the right hemisphere. After the age of 5, however, it is more likely to be represented bilaterally or in the left hemisphere. The ability of language to relocate in areas of the cortex amid early brain damage is what Lashley (1950) called *equipotentiality.* As long as there is some cortical tissue that evades the damaged area, the functions in one part of the cortex (Broca's area in this case) can be taken over by a nearby region. In the case of language processes, this must occur before the age of 5 years. Now we turn to the question of adequacy regarding the classic model of aphasia.

Review Question
If you had speech samples from patients with brain damage, what would you look for in the samples to diagnose each patient's type of aphasia?

Table 2.1. Site of Lesion and Characteristics of Aphasias

Disorder	Site of Lesion	Spontaneous Speech	Speech Comprehension	Repetition	Naming
Broca's aphasia	Left frontal cortex rostral to base of motor cortex	Nonfluent	Relatively intact	Poor	Poor
Global aphasia	Anterior and posterior language areas	Nonfluent	Poor	Poor	Poor
Transcortical motor aphasia	Areas anterior and superior to Broca's areas	Nonfluent	Relatively intact	Intact	Poor
Wernicke's aphasia	Posterior part of the superior and middle left temporal gyrus and left temporoparietal cortex	Fluent	Poor	Poor	Poor
Conduction aphasia	Temporoparietal region, above and below posterior Sylvian fissure	Fluent	Relatively intact	Poor	Intact
Anomic aphasia	Posterior part of the superior and middle left temporal gyrus and left temporoparietal cortex	Fluent	Relatively intact	Intact	Poor
Transcortical sensory aphasia	Posterior to Wernicke's area around boundary of occipital lobe	Fluent	Poor	Intact	Poor

From *Biological Psychology* by Klein, Stephen B., © 2000. Reprinted by permission of Pearson Education, Inc., Upper Saddle River, NJ.

PROBLEMS WITH THE GESCHWIND MODEL

Not everyone agrees that the Geschwind model describes why aphasics have difficulty with language (Caplan, 1994). The Geschwind model posits that Broca's aphasia results in production deficits and that Wernicke's aphasia results in comprehension deficits, assuming that language processes evolved along the sensory and motor tracks in the cortex. One assumption is that Broca's patients have intact language representation but cannot put representation into sentence form. There may be other reasons why Broca's patients perform as they do; for example, problems with language may stem from processing difficulties (e.g., lexical access or mapping syntax to thematic roles) rather than representational failures (Zurif & Swinney, 1994).

One problem with the traditional interpretation of Broca's aphasia stems from the general and global nature of comprehension tests used to screen patients. These tests are too general to determine whether problems with syntax or semantics affect comprehension. Although Broca's aphasia is usually described as a production failure, comprehension problems also accompany damage in Broca's area. Following up on the idea that Broca's aphasics may have undiagnosed comprehension problems, Caramazza and Zurif (1976) tested the comprehension abilities of patients with Broca's, Wernicke's, and conduction aphasia. Subjects were presented auditorily with *reversible* and *nonreversible* sentences. A nonreversible sentence is one in which the nouns cannot be interchanged, for example, *The cookie the girl is eating is hot.* Only the girl can eat the cookie. A **reversible sentence** requires that the listener to pay careful attention to the syntactic structure to derive the intended meaning, for example, *The dog the cat is biting is black.* Either the cat or the dog could be biting. Subjects were asked to choose from two pictures the one that represented the sentence they heard.

It came as no surprise that the Wernicke's patients did poorly with both reversible and nonreversible sentences, in line with classic problems with comprehension processes. But for both the conduction patients and the Broca's patients, the type of sentence made a big difference. Both did very well with the nonreversible sentences but performed at the chance level with the reversible sentences. The results suggest that Broca's aphasia is not limited to production problems but that comprehension problems involving syntax appear when semantic cues are missing, as they are in reversible sentences.

AN ALTERNATIVE: PROCESSING IMPAIRMENT

When we look more closely at the tasks used to reveal syntactic, lexical, and semantic problems in aphasia, we see that an alternative interpretation of previous research is possible. At present, no single alternative model to Geschwind's has emerged but results from several studies have shown that aphasics' language processing difficulties proceed through different stages. The notion that aphasics' problems come from processing difficulties is referred to as the **processing impairment** view. One important variable in previous research is the amount of time allowed for the patient to complete the task at hand. From a processing impairment point of view, some experimental tasks may not provide enough lexical access time or enough time to integrate information at the end of a sentence with meanings from the beginning. The processing impairment approach describes aphasics' problems with language tasks in terms of processing times and processing strategies, as opposed to basing difficulties on representational failures, as in Geschwind's model.

Linebarger, Schwartz, and Saffran (1983) gave Broca's patients a list of sentences and asked them to indicate whether they were grammatical or not. Performance overall was high, and subjects were able to detect ungrammatical sentences that used wrong pronouns such as, *The little boy fell down, didn't it?* Notice that the pronoun at the end of the sentence has to be compared with the noun that comes earlier in the sentence. This study suggests that subjects performed poorly on the reversible sentence task used by Caramazza and Zurif (1976) because they did not have enough time to construct the appropriate syntactic representation of the reversible sentences. It may be also be the case that not having enough time to find word meanings causes the Broca's patient to adopt a simple subject-verb-object (SVO) comprehension strategy to understand sentences (Zurif, 1995). Using this strategy, the aphasic would map the first noun as the subject of the sentence and the second noun as its object. This SVO strategy would work for sentences like *It was the dog who chased the boy* but not for passive sentences like *It was the boy whom the dog chased*, which Broca's aphasics fail to comprehend. Related research by Zurif and colleagues confirms that Broca's patients are sometimes unable to activate word meanings quickly enough or that their activation times are slower than those of normal language users (Prather, Zurif, Stern, & Rosen, 1992; Zurif, Swinney, Prather, Solomon, & Bushell, 1993). Another interpretation is that problems with lexical access signal an impairment of the initial syntactic analysis *before* the thematic mapping (SVO) is conducted (see Zurif & Swinney, 1994).

The Geschwind model can be contrasted with a holistic network model of parallel distributed processes, or PDP (McClelland, Rumelhart, and the PDP Research Group, 1986; Seidenberg & McClelland, 1989). A holistic account of aphasics' language-related problems suggests that they can arise from lesions throughout the network rather than in one location (e.g., Wernicke's area). All the lesion would have to do to impair comprehension would be to disrupt a component of the comprehension process, such as lexical access. Patients' comprehension difficulties would then be the result of a disruption of a single factor, like lexical access, that affects performance on a variety of measures. Lesions in a variety of locations in the neural network could affect the lexical access process (see Caplan, 1994). To date, no mechanism for lesioning the simulated network can account for the pattern of symptoms that patients exhibit.

We shift our focus from the classic studies of aphasia to look at the modern study of language processes via brain imaging and electrophysical measures.

Review Question
Describe Geschwind's model of language and contrast it with the processing impairment view.

Brain Imaging and Electrophysiological Studies of Language

In the past, to determine the location of a brain anomaly, an autopsy had to be performed. Now neuroscientists use brain imaging to take pictures of the living brain. Images of the brain have been possible since the X-ray. Modern techniques are essentially new and improved X-rays. For example, *computerized axial tomography* (**CAT**), also called simply *computerized tomography* (CT), sends X-rays slices through a patient's skull, measuring the radiation that gets through. The setup is illustrated in Figure 2.5. Instead of the single picture provided by older X-rays, CAT uses the computer to assemble a two-dimensional picture of the brain.

Positron emission tomography (**PET**) uses a computer to monitor the amount of energy being expended by different areas of the brain. A radioactive tracer is injected into the blood, which mixes with glucose, the brain's energy source. PET gives a picture of the cerebral blood flow (CBF) in the brain when it is at rest or involved in language-related tasks. The task-related brain activity is compared with the resting state of activity. The most active neurons in the cortex will use the most glucose, appearing as a different color on the computer. PET can detect functional lesions, areas of low metabolism or hypometabolism (low glucose use) that are not detected by other imaging techniques.

Posner and Raichle (1994) used PET to show how a given speech task will activate a particular area of the cortex, depending on the nature of the task. The task-related CBF patterns are shown in Figure 2.6. As can be seen in the figure, passively viewing words activates areas in the occipital and parietal lobes. Listening to words activates the auditory cortex and Wernicke's area. Generating verbs activates Wernicke's and Broca's areas. Speaking words activates Broca's area.

Recently, the more powerful and less harmful *magnetic resonance imaging* (MRI) technology has evolved. In MRI, a patient is placed inside a circular tunnel, which is surrounded by a whirling magnet that generates a magnetic field. The patient's head is exposed to a radio-frequency pulse, and the signals emitted from the tissues are measured. As in CAT, a computer constructs a two-dimensional image that displays energy levels (see Figure 2.7). MRI provides a more precise and accurate picture than CAT. The newest version of MRI, known as *functional MRI* (**fMRI**),

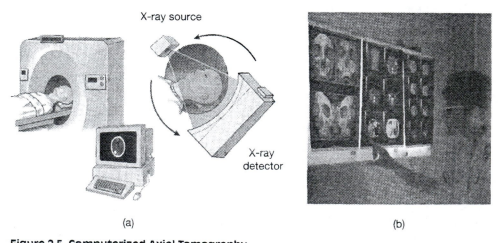

(a)   (b)

Figure 2.5. Computerized Axial Tomography

Note. From *Biological Psychology* by Klein, Stephen B., © 2000. Reprinted by permission of Pearson Education, Inc., Upper Saddle River, NJ.

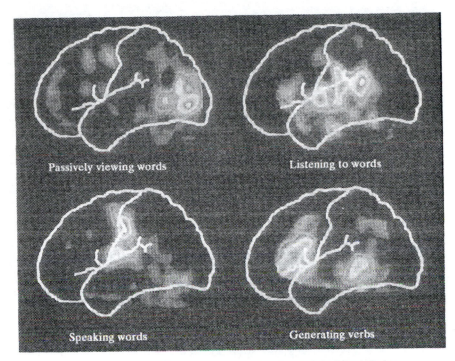

Figure 2.6. Cerebral Blood Flow Patterns during Speech-Related Tasks
Note. From *Images of mind* by Michael I. Posner and Marcus E. Raichle, New York: Scientific American Library, 1994.

measures increases in oxygen consumption to construct brain images. Subjects perform mental tasks while in the MRI device, and differences in the amount of oxygen consumed are analyzed and compared to resting states.

EVENT-RELATED POTENTIALS

The *event-related potential* (**ERP**) procedure uses microelectrodes placed on the scalp to measure the amount of electrical activity in the brain. ERP is not an image of the brain; it is an electrophysiological measure of brain wave activity in response to an "event" in the experimental task. The components of the brain waveform—for example, its amplitude, negative electrical peaks, and positive electrical peaks—change in response to sensory, motor, and cognitive event processing. Some components of the wave have been found to index syntactic and semantic processing. The **N400,** a negative deflection of the brainwave occurring 400 milliseconds (ms) after the onset of a word stimulus, is especially sensitive to the semantic aspects of words. Kutas and Hillyard (1980) discovered the N400 by comparing brainwave activation in response to the last word in three types of sentences: normal sentences (*It was his last day at work*), semantically anomalous sentences (*He spread the warm bread with socks*), and physically different sentences (*She*

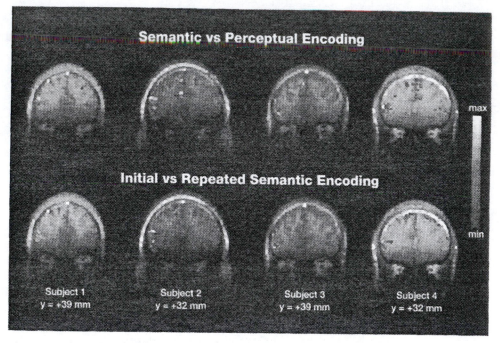

Figure 2.7. Functional Magnetic Resonance Images of Normal Individuals and Patients with Tumors

Note. From *Cognition*, by Ashcroft, © 2000. Reprinted by permission of Pearson Education, Inc., Upper Saddle River, NJ.

put on her high-heeled shoes). The N400 amplitudes increased in response to anomalous sentences when compared to normal sentences. Physically deviant sentences elicited a positive wave rather than the N400. The pattern of brain waves is illustrated in Figure 2.8.

The N400 reactions to semantic anomalies are modality-independent. They occur as a result of visual or auditory input and with American Sign Language (ASL). The N400 occurs during lexical integration when there is a semantic mismatch between words in a sentence context. The N400 can be used to study comprehension deficits in aphasics. Swaab, Brown, and Hagoort (1997) studied spoken-sentence comprehension in three groups of impaired patients: those with right-hemisphere damage (used as controls), with low comprehension ability (severe deficits), and with high comprehension ability (mild deficits). The researchers assumed that comprehension problems occur because aphasics have difficulty integrating word meanings in on-line comprehension tasks. Subjects were presented with sentences in which the last word matched the previous context and with sentences in which the last word was anomalous. Results supported the idea that aphasics have an impaired ability to integrate lexical information into a sentence context. High comprehenders showed N400 responses similar to unimpaired subjects. Low comprehenders with severe deficits had delayed and reduced N400 responses.

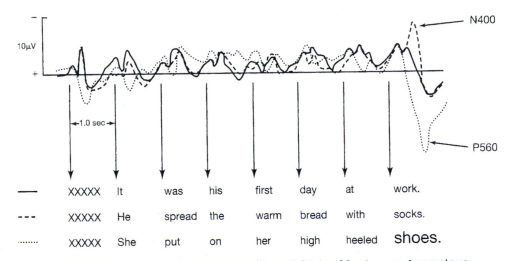

Figure 2.8. ERP Waveforms in Response to Different Sorts of Sentences Anomalous words at the end of a sentence elicit a large negative deflection in ERP (N400); words that make sense syntactically but appear differently on the page elicit a positive wave (P560) but not the N400. *Note.* Reprinted with permission from "Reading senseless sentences: Brain potentials reflect semantic incongruity" by M. Kutas & S. A. Hillyard, *Science, 207.* Copyright 1980 American Association for the Advancement of Science.

Modern brain imaging and recording techniques allow psycholinguists to locate language-related functions in the cerebral cortex and to monitor how brain activity shifts as a function of task demands. Further, these methods permit comparisons across subject populations and across language modalities. Having addressed the nature and location of language-specific areas of the cortex, the next task is to discuss the lateralization of cognitive and linguistic functions.

Lateralization

In addition to studying the localization of specific language functions, psycholinguists have also been interested in what cognitive processes are handled by the left hemisphere compared to those handled by the right hemisphere. The language lateralization argument is that articulate language is located in the frontal lobe of the left cerebral cortex for most, but not all, speakers. Because language is so important to cognition, the left hemisphere is known as the "dominant" or "major" hemisphere. Recall from the discussion of anatomy that the brain and body have a contralateral organization. Motor movement and sensation on the right side of the body are governed by the left sensorimotor cortex, and vice versa. As for the lateralization of cognitive and linguistic tasks, there is some consensus about their locations, which are summarized in Table 2.2, which shows that the left hemisphere handles general language functions and the right hemisphere handles emotional and pragmatic aspects of language. Note that the right hemisphere also specializes in general visual-spatial tasks.

SEX DIFFERENCES AND LANGUAGE LATERALIZATION

Evidence from a variety of cognitive tasks has shown that many language functions are lateralized in the left hemisphere, while visual-spatial functions are lateralized in the right hemisphere. It has also been observed that males and females do not perform the same on language and spatial tasks. Women tend to outscore men on language-related tasks, and men tend to outscore women on visual-spatial tasks (Kimura, 1992). At the anatomic level, it is known that women have more inter-hemispheric connections via the corpus callosum than men (Allen, Richey, Chai, & Gorski, 1991). What do these findings imply about language lateralization? Is language lateralized differently in female and male brains? Two lines of evidence, brain imaging studies and aphasia research, suggest that the answer is yes.

Research using fMRI to measure cerebral blood flow during language tasks supports differential language organization in male and female brains (Shaywitz et al., 1995). In this research, subjects had to decide if two nonsense strings (e.g., *jete, lete*) rhymed. Blood flow patterns measured during the rhyming task showed activation lateralized in the left hemisphere of male subjects, but in female subjects the activity was bilaterally represented. The Shaywitz and colleagues study was one of

Table 2.2. Lateralization of Function

Function	Left Hemisphere	Right Hemisphere
Visual system	Letters, words	Complex geometric patterns Faces
Auditory system	Language-related sounds	Nonlanguage environmental sounds Music
Somatosensory system		Tactile recognition of complex patterns Braille
Movement	Complex voluntary movement	Movements in spatial patterns
Memory	Verbal memory	Nonverbal memory
Language	Phonetic Semantic Syntactic Arithmetic	Emotional Intonation Pragmatic Prosody
Spatial processes		Geometry Sense of direction Mental rotation of shapes

Adapted from: *Fundamentals of Human Neuropsychology* by Bryan Kolb and Ian Q. Whishaw © 1980, 1985, 1990, 1996 by W.H. Freeman and Company. Used with permission.

the first to demonstrate sex differences in functional language processing. More recently Jaeger et al. (1998) used PET to measure cerebral blood flow during a reading task. Subjects read real and nonsense verbs and pronounced past tense forms. During the past tense task, males showed left-lateralized activation while females displayed bilateral activation.

The second line of evidence draws from aphasia research. If males have greater unilateral language representation, we would expect the consequences of left-hemisphere brain damage to be more severe for males than for females, who have bilateral representation. Studies show that males are more frequently the victims of aphasia after left-hemisphere damage than females. Females also have a better chance of recovery from left-hemisphere damage than males. These findings lead researchers to conclude that language is more unilaterally represented for men than for women (see Levy, 1972), although these interpretations are not without controversy (Caplan, 1994).

LATERALIZATION OF SIGN LANGUAGE AND BILINGUALISM

If the right hemisphere is superior to the left on tasks requiring spatial reasoning, we might wonder if sign language, which is produced through spatial references, is represented in the right hemisphere (RH). Poizner, Klima, and Bellugi (1987) found that signers with **left-hemisphere damage** exhibited language problems similar to aphasic speakers with Broca's or Wernicke's aphasia, suggesting that sign language relies on general language representations and processes in the left hemisphere (LH). However, the right hemisphere is critical for other cognitive and extralinguistic functions in sign language. For example, signers with **right-hemisphere damage** presented difficulty with nonlinguistic tasks (e.g., music), while their signing remained unaffected. Hickok, Say, Bellugi, and Klima (1996) tested the performance of two native signers, one with RH and one with LH damage. They found that the LH-damaged signer was impaired on tasks involving the use of space (e.g., where in space the sign was made) for encoding *syntactic* information but performed well on tasks where spatial information was encoded *iconically* (e.g., when the sign looks similar to its referent), not syntactically. The RH-damaged patient showed the reverse: poor use of spatial information encoded iconically but good performance using space for encoding syntactic information. These studies suggest that grammatical aspects of signing are represented in the left hemisphere with general language functions and that nonlinguistic iconic aspects of signing are represented in the right hemisphere with visual-spatial functions.

Recent research with brain imaging techniques have further clarified the lateralization of language in signing and bilingual populations. Bavelier et al. (1998) used fMRI to compare sentence processing in English and ASL. They found that classic left-hemisphere areas were used by both normal and signing subjects, suggesting a left-hemisphere role in natural language regardless of modality. In addition, deaf and hearing ASL users heavily used right-hemisphere activation. Some right-hemisphere activation represents spatial aspects of ASL, as we have seen previously. The right hemisphere also plays a role in extragrammatical discourse processing in deaf and hearing language users, for example, for role playing, topical coherence, and spatial discourse devices.

The extragrammatical narrative device of role playing in ASL relies on linguistic references and extrasyntactic devices such as signing style and facial caricature to differentiate roles in the narrative. While linguistic references use left-hemisphere resources, extrasyntactic devices require right-hemisphere activation. Lowe, Kegl, and Poizner (1997) studied the narrative abilities of an ASL-fluent, hearing signer with RH damage. During the narrative task, she could correctly reassign first-person references at the sentence level but could not employ pragmatically appropriate devices such as changing her gaze, using caricature, or shifting her body position. Hickok et al. (1999), who examined the extrasyntactic discourse functions in two deaf signers with RH damage, also studied hemispheric asymmetries in discourse processing. One subject showed difficulty maintaining topical coherence, while the other had difficulty using spatial discourse devices. Even though the two were equally impaired on nonlinguistic spatial tasks, they showed different patterns of extragrammatical impairment. As in a hearing population, discourse functions are dissociated from one another in ASL. Linguistic spatial devices are incorporated into general language processing rather than general spatial characteristics of signing.

Research by Neville et al. (1997) indicates that the nature and timing of language acquisition play a significant role in the development of brain language systems. When ASL is acquired early on, there is an increased role for the right hemisphere and the parietal cortex, which occurs in both hearing and deaf native signers. However, an increased role for posterior temporal and occipital areas occurs only in deaf native signers and may therefore be attributable to their lack of auditory stimulation. These results suggest that there are organizational constraints on brain systems that mediate language, including different specializations of cortical regions with a bias for the left hemisphere to mediate language functions. If cerebral organization is time-dependent for deaf signers, we might wonder what happens to cortical specialization in foreign-language learning or bilingual speakers or signers.

Several brain imaging studies are informative about bilingual representation of language (see Cabeza & Nyberg, 2000). Soderfeldt et al. (1997) found that sign language in bilinguals activates a network similar to that underlying spoken language. Perani et al. (1996) concluded that brain regions activated by native-language processing, compared to foreign-language processing, selectively activates several brain regions. They suggested that some brain areas are shaped by early maternal language, but learning a foreign language later in life does not activate these areas. A study by Kim, Relkin, Lee, and Hirsch (1997) supports this conclusion about age of acquisition of a second language. Kim and colleagues studied native-language and foreign-language activation as a function of when the second language was learned. They showed that in Broca's area, foreign languages acquired in adulthood were spatially separated from native languages. However, second languages acquired at an early age tend to activate overlapping areas within Broca's area. Interestingly, in Wernicke's area, there was no separation of languages based on age of acquisition.

These studies of sign language and second-language learning support the generalization that language is lateralized in the left cerebral hemisphere for most people and that second-language learning may overlap these areas, depending on the age of acquisition. The right hemisphere plays a role in extragrammatical and pragmatic aspects of language and in nonlinguistic aspects of sign language processing.

SPLIT-BRAIN STUDIES

Recall that the corpus callosum is a band of fibers that allows communication between the left and right hemispheres. A **split-brain patient** is one who has had these fibers severed by surgery (a *commissurotomy*) to relieve seizures due to epilepsy. The patient now has what amounts to a split brain instead of a pair of interconnected hemispheres.

Split-brain patients are used in experimental studies of language lateralization to assess what functions are lateralized in one hemisphere. Sperry, Gazzaniga, and Bogen (1969) pioneered studies with split-brain patients in the 1960s. An experimental situation is illustrated in Figure 2.9, which shows how different messages can be presented simultaneously to the subject. The content of the left side of the visual field is processed by the right hemisphere, and the content of the right side of the visual field is processed by the left hemisphere. The contralateral organization of the information in each hemisphere is illustrated in Figure 2.10. In the experimental setting, a subject views a screen with a left field and a right field. The subject stares at the middle of the screen as words and pictures are rapidly projected by a tachistiscope on one side of the screen. The brief exposure time (50 ms) prevents the subject from shifting the eyes to one side or the other during exposure. What happens to the message after exposure depends on the nature of the material and which hemisphere is activated.

Verbal Input

When a word like *art* is projected on the right side of the screen, the left hemisphere has no problem processing it because this is the general language side of the brain. The subject reports what was seen, "Art." The right hemisphere handles words differently. When the word *he* is projected on the left side of the screen, the subject cannot say what has been seen and reports, "Nothing." But the right hemisphere does exhibit some language representation. When *he* is projected to the right hemisphere, the subject can point to the item with the left hand. The left hand can also write the word, even though the word cannot be articulated (see Sperry, 1968).

In these early experiments with split-brain subjects, the right hemisphere adequately processed nouns (e.g., *boy* or *pen*) but had difficulties with verbs. When the right hemisphere was presented with simple commands like *smile* or *frown,* subjects

Figure 2.9. The Lack of Information Transfer between Hemispheres in Split-Brain Patients The word *HEART* is flashed on a screen such that *HE* goes to the right hemisphere, and *ART* goes to the left hemisphere. The split-brain patient can verbally report seeing only *ART*. However, if asked to point to the word *HE*, the patient can do so with the left hand. *Note.* From *Biological Psychology* by Klein, Stephen B., © 2000. Reprinted by permission of Pearson Education Inc., Upper Saddle River, NJ.

did not execute them. While the right hemisphere performs well with spatial tasks, its language functions are limited. In a procedure similar to those described previously, Gazzaniga and Hillyard (1971) presented split-brain patients with visual scenes and then asked them to chose between pairs of sentences presented auditorily, identifying which sentence described the scene. They found that the right hemisphere could distinguish between affirmative and negative sentences but did not distinguish between different syntactic orderings, for example, *The man kicked the horse* versus *The horse kicked the man*. The right hemisphere also performed poorly with future tenses and singular versus plural nouns.

Visual-Spatial Input

Considerable evidence has accumulated showing that the right hemisphere is better than the left at performing visual tasks, those that require spatial analysis. Subjects shown visual shapes (deconstructed triangles or squares) can readily find those shapes when hidden from view with the left hand. In comparison, the right hand performs only at a chance level at this spatial task. Split-brain patients asked to reproduce a simple line drawing show the predominance of visual-spatial pro-

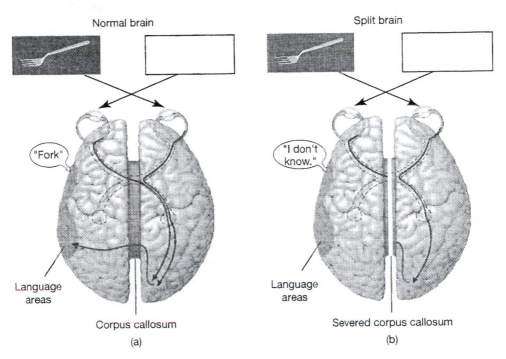

Figure 2.10. Verbal Identification of Objects by Normal and Split-Brain Individuals When a fork is presented to the left visual field, a normal person can identify it as a fork, but a split-brain patient cannot. *Note.* From *Biological Psychology* by Klein, Stephen B., © 2000. Reprinted by permission of Pearson Education, Inc., Upper Saddle River, NJ.

cessing in the right hemisphere. Figure 2.11 illustrates that the left hand is better at reproducing the simple line representation than the right hand.

In a series of studies, Gazzaniga and colleagues (e.g., Metcalfe, Funnell, & Gazzaniga, 1995) have examined the cognitive and linguistic abilities of JW, a split-brain patient who had a language-dominant left hemisphere and is slowly developing language perception and naming functions in his right hemisphere. Metcalfe et al. showed that when asked to make judgments of old versus new, his right hemisphere was better able than his left to reject new events (e.g., categorized lists of words, faces, line patterns) similar to the originally presented material. In this regard, the right hemisphere keeps a more veridical account of what it experiences than the left. The left hemisphere is more prone to generalization and inferencing; it is more capable of mental manipulation, inference, imagination, semantic association, and complex language production. Evidence related to the right-hemisphere superiority in judgments of old versus new comes from N400 ERP in split-brain patients (Kutas, Hillyard, & Gazzaniga, 1988). Recall that the N400 is a response to the semantic relatedness of words. The N400 occurs when words are semantically unrelated and is produced in a graded manner such that the more unrelated the words are, the greater the response. Kutas and colleagues found that the left

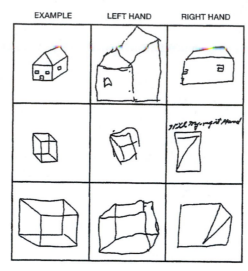

Figure 2.11. Reproduction of Drawings by Right-Handed Split-Brain Patients When asked to redraw the example, split-brain patients were unable to do so with any accuracy with their dominant right hand; the drawings made by the nondominant left hand are much more accurate.
Note. From *Biological Psychology* by Klein, Stephen B., © 2000. Reprinted by permission of Pearson Education, Inc., Upper Saddle River, NJ.

hemisphere but not the right produced the N400 response. The interpretation is that the left hemisphere is sensitive to semantic comparisons and semantic similarity but the right hemisphere is not so sensitive. The right hemisphere is more concerned with constructing a veridical record of verbal input, not generalizing or inferring from that input. In a way, the left and right hemispheres work in coordination, the right hemisphere providing a check on the left hemisphere's ability to generalize.

> **Review Question**
> According to split-brain research, what functions are carried out by the left hemisphere? What functions are carried out by the right hemisphere?

THE WADA TEST

The **Wada test** is named after Juhn Wada (1949), a Japanese surgeon who developed it to obtain information about language lateralization prior to brain surgery. The Wada test works as follows: Sodium amytal is injected into the carotid artery via a catheter in the femoral artery in the upper leg, deactivating the hemisphere on the side of the injection. The patient rests on the operating table with arms raised, counting backward. The arm on the contralateral (opposite) side of the injection will fall. The counting is temporarily halted and will take from one to three minutes to resume if the injection involves the dominant (usually left) hemisphere. Counting will resume within 20 sec if the nondominant side is injected.

The Wada test has been used with normal and brain-damaged patients to provide evidence of speech laterality. The results of a study by Rasmussen and Milner (1977) showed that 96 percent of normal right-handers have speech lateralized in the left hemisphere and 4 percent have speech lateralized in the right hemisphere. For normal left-handers and those with mixed handedness, 70 percent had left-hemisphere lateralization, 15 percent had right-hemisphere lateralization, and the remaining 15 percent had bilateral representation. Notice that most left-handers have speech lateralized in the left hemisphere such that laterality is not dependent on handedness, as was once thought.

We turn now to the topic of right-hemisphere speech and its links to subcortical structures in language processing.

RIGHT-HEMISPHERE SPEECH AND SUBCORTICAL INVOLVEMENT IN EMOTIONAL SPEECH

Research from aphasiology, brain imaging, split-brain studies, and the Wada studies support the central tendency for core language processes to lateralize in the left hemisphere. What, then, is the role of the right hemisphere in language processing, as these studies also point to noncore language processing in the right hemisphere?

As outlined in Table 2.2, the left hemisphere does not predominate on all auditory tasks. The right hemisphere is superior on tasks involving the detection of emotional affect, such as deciding if the voice represents a happy, sad, or angry reading. The right hemisphere is also better than the left hemisphere at tasks involving the identification of declarative or interrogative voicing in sentences. Emotional aspects of speech require right-hemisphere involvement. Studies of brain-damaged patients reveal that RH damage impairs the ability to produce or to comprehend emotional aspects of speech.

In the past two decades, research has clarified which language functions are distributed in the right hemisphere (see Beeman & Chiarello, 1998; Ross, Thompson, & Yenkosky, 1997; Van Lancker, 1987; Van Lancker & Cummings, 1999). An important attempt to describe right-hemisphere speech was made by Van Lancker (1972), who revived a distinction made by Hughlings Jackson (1874/1958) about articulate speech. Jackson described the ability to generate novel, grammatically sound sentences as **propositional speech.** Propositional speech is impaired by LH damage such as Broca's aphasia. He contrasted propositional speech with automatic or **nonpropositional speech** like that used in idioms, clichés, and expletives. Nonpropositional speech is not propositionally or grammatically novel, consisting as it does of well-learned and often repeated expressions. This does not mean that automatic speech has no meaning, as we will see in Chapter 9. Following Jackson's distinction, Van Lancker found that nonpropositional speech is common in the verbal output of patients with LH damage, as we shall see shortly.

A different picture emerges for patients with RH damage. The majority of RH-damaged patients do not emote normally. They do not swear at all; in fact, they have difficulty producing or understanding spoken emotional expressions and facial expressions of emotion. RH-damaged patients are emotionally blunted and indifferent to the emotional aspects of sentences like those used in Exercise 2.1. In contrast, one fact that seems clear about LH-damaged aphasics is that they are emotional people. Like Broca's patient Leborgne, about half of Broca's aphasics and Wernicke's aphasics retain the ability to curse when frustrated or excited. Broca's aphasics frequently produce clichés, automatic speech, nonsense words, and *recurrent real word utterances* (**RRWUs**). Nonpropositional recurrent speech remains when the ability to construct articulate speech is interrupted by brain damage. For example, Code (1987, 1989) recorded spontaneous right-hemisphere speech production despite RH damage. Here is an example of some of the RRWUs recorded from a Broca's aphasic (Code, 1987, p. 67):

Alright	away away away	Bill Bill
Bloody hell	bloody hell bugger	fuck fuck fuck
Fuck off	goody goody	Oh you bugger
I can't	yep	pardon for you
Sister sister	so so	paper and pencil

Notice that the sample of automatisms contains automatic phrases and emotional words not unlike Leborgne's profanity. The words *bugger* and *bloody hell* indicate that the patient learned English in the United Kingdom. The point of looking at this sample is to show that the RRWUs are not merely meaningless nonsense words. Some of these RRWUs have strong emotional content, an aspect of speech that is frequently expressed in emotionally reactive LH-damaged patients. The picture is quite different for RH-damaged patients.

Gardner and his associates (Brownell, Potter, Michelow, & Gardner, 1984; Winner & Gardner, 1977) provided evidence that RH-damaged patients have difficulty perceiving the emotional aspects of metaphors. They have difficulty matching pictures to their corresponding metaphorical statements. For example, *He has a heavy heart* is matched with a picture of a man carrying a large heart rather than a picture of a man with a sad face. RH-damaged patients show sensitivity to the literal aspects of words but not the connotative or emotional aspects of words. Unilateral brain damage interferes with the appreciation of the emotional aspects of speech.

Ross, Homan, and Buck (1994) reviewed evidence to support the idea that the right hemisphere not only contributes to emotional aspects of speech but also modulates aspects of gesture and affective **prosody,** which is the rhythmic and intonational quality of speech, including speech duration, pitch, loudness, tone, and intonation. The affective-prosodic quality of speech, along with gestures, is a component of speaking that occurs concurrently with the literal content of the speech. Emotional prosody projects onto an utterance that a speaker is happy, sad, anxious, fearful, or angry. The loss of prosodic features of speech, or **aprosodia,** produces a right-hemisphere counterpart to the aphasias of the left hemisphere. Wolfe and Ross (1987) reported the case of a woman with RH damage who had propositional speech. She could repeat propositional speech presented to her but could not repeat the affective and prosodic features of that speech. The patient also exhibited a form of *sensory aprosodia:* She could not identify sadness, happiness, boredom, anger, surprise, or neutral aspects of auditory presentations, and she could not identify facial emotions when pantomimed.

Ross, Homan, and Buck (1994) used the Wada test to study affective and propositional aspects of speech. With the right hemisphere "asleep," subjects were asked to recall an emotional life experience they had previously identified before the procedure. They dramatically altered their stories under the Wada procedure for the recall of the affective content. At the same time, the factual content remained. Many of the alterations of the previous experiences were minimalizations of the originally expressed emotions. Ross and colleagues suggested that the left hemisphere modulates positive social emotions and the right hemisphere handles the primary negative emotions.

Although we have spent the entire chapter outlining the relationship between language processing and brain mechanisms, let's not forget that language is the product of one's psychological development and cultural heritage. This point is made by Lamendella (1977) in a review of limbic involvement in human communication. Lamendella proposed that emotionally charged speech represented an intersection of the limbic system with general language systems. Emotion in speech comes from limbic functions that have found linguistic representation mainly for the purpose of the expression of affect. Speakers select words that are emotionally charged, having a special tie-in to the limbic system, perhaps via the right hemisphere. Insults give emotional release to speakers and cause an emotional reaction in the person addressed. Cultures differ in the extent to which they allow affective expressions during speech. The depth of emotional expression also differs widely from person to person. American Sign Language allows a great deal of freedom to express emotions and attitudes toward what is being said. In this sense, ASL may be more emotionally satisfying than vocal speech. Foreign-language learners may feel frustration at having failed to express affect in a foreign language, and bilinguals revert to their mother tongue to express strong emotions through the language that has the best tie-in to limbic expression. Lamendella's point was that limbic information processing is of interest not as an extragrammatical fringe to language but because it raises questions under discussion in psycholinguistics. Humans have developed neocortical modules for articulate communication, but we are also the beneficiaries of a limbic communication system for aggression, appetite, affect, and social interaction (see Jay, 2000; Lamendella, 1977). For many reasons, studies of right-hemisphere speech processing and limbic involvement have been treated as extragrammatical, noncore aspects of language (see Caplan, 1994). Perhaps when we understand core language processes better, psycholinguists will integrate what we know about subcortical and right-hemisphere language processing into a more comprehensive model of language that includes culture and emotion.

Review Question
How does language use satisfy emotional needs? For the bilingual, why would one language be more emotionally satisfying than another?

Key Terms

alexia	fluent aphasia	PET
amygdala	fMRI	processing impairment
anomia	Geschwind model	propositional speech
aphasia	global aphasia	prosody
aprosodia	localization	reversible sentence
basal ganglia	Leborgne	right-hemisphere
Broca's area	left-hemisphere damage	damage
CAT	limbic system	RRWUs
cerebral cortex	N400	split-brain patient
corpus callosum	nonfluent aphasia	Wada test
ERP	nonpropositional speech	Wernicke's area

What Lies Ahead

The next chapter looks at how we perceive speech. We outline the articulatory and acoustic properties of speech and examine what cues listeners use to segment continuous speech. We look at how infants learn to perceive sounds in their native language and how this affects their ability to hear the sounds in another language.

Suggested Web Sites

Human Brain Atlas: http://www.med.harvard.edu/AANLIB/home.html
Phineas Gage information: http://www.hbs.deakin.edu.au/gagepage/pgage.htm
History of aphasiology: http://www.medinfo.ufl.edu/other/histmed/roth/

Chapter 3
Speech Perception

Critical Thinking Questions

1. How do we segment everyday speech?

2. How does English phonology compare with that of other languages?

3. Can humans perceive phonemes that are not in their native language?

4. What are the important articulatory properties of speech?

5. What are the important acoustic cues in speech?

6. What acoustic information is used to perceive vowels? To perceive consonants?

7. How do we perceive continuous speech segments?

8. Is there a "module" for speech perception?

9. Is there one unified theory of speech perception?

Exercise 3.1. **Synthetic Speech**
Lucent Technologies of Bell Laboratories has a Web site (http://www.bell-labs.com/project/tts/voices.html) that demonstrates text-to-speech (TTS) synthesis. In the demonstration, visitors can type in a body of text to be synthesized and vary components such as pitch, volume, gender, and vocal tract. Go to the Web site and give it a try. Can you speculate about what acoustic qualities make TTS sound unnatural?

When you look at the words on this page, they fall into neat, segmented patterns. Each word is separated from every other word, and every letter in every word is discernable from the other letters in the word. Spoken speech is not like this. Fluent speech is a continuous flow of changing sounds, rhythms, intonations, odd nonspeech sounds, and pauses. We can listen to a political speech ("My fellow Americans . . .") and dissect paragraphs, sentences, and words within sentences. But once we start looking for the sounds within words, the analysis gets a bit tricky. Words sound as if they blend into each other (e.g., "Mahfellamuruhcans"), and we cannot tell exactly where one word ends and the other begins. This is a segmentation problem: How do we segment the continuous flow of speech? To make our analysis even more difficult, we also "fill in" some of the sounds that we miss within words or that are drowned out by noises. How we integrate linguistic knowledge and general knowledge in the speech perception process is a controversial topic. Besides problems with segmentation and integration, scholars studying speech perception have raised a number of issues, including these:

- Is speech perception a general auditory capacity or a language-specific process?

- Is there a special "module" for speech in the human brain?

- What is the "object" of speech perception? A phoneme? A syllable?

- How does a newborn learn the sounds of its native language?

This chapter is dedicated to addressing these questions and controversies. Answers to them can be drawn from a multitude of sources. Research on the problems of speech perception is quite active and diverse (see Kluender, 1994). The cognitive science view of speech perception has produced several ways to study the phenomenon: (1) to describe the domain of sounds across languages to convey phonetic distinctions, (2) to study the structure and function neural "hardware," (3) to develop computational models and simulations of the domain, (4) to develop mechanical speech recognition devices, and (5) to describe the general cognitive processes of learning and categorization that are used in speech perception. Since our goal is to explain matters of importance to psycholinguists, only a limited number of topics can be covered here. This chapter is therefore intended to

- Outline the components of spoken speech

- Describe the articulatory and acoustic properties of speech

- Outline how listeners process speech segments and continuous speech

- Discuss the biological development of speech perception

- Describe models of speech perception

The identification of speech segments is a multilayered process. *Sensation* is the first stage, when the human ear detects sounds from the environment. Sensation is the registration that something is heard, that a sound was audible. Determining what a sound means brings us to the second stage, *perception*. During perceptual analysis, an attempt is made to recognize or identify a sound by matching it up to a representation stored in memory. *Identification* is the process of attributing meaning and emotional significance to the message.

Components of Speech

Exactly *what* perceptual processes are involved and *how* they are carried out is a matter of debate. Perhaps a good place to start the study of speech perception is to identify the structure of speech.

PROSODY

Prosody is a suprasegmental property of speech; it refers to the sound properties "above" the speech segment. Prosodic features are variations in speaking involving intonation, stress (accent), pause, rate, and duration (length). Prosodic features of pausing and word stress are cues for the segmentation of continuous speech. Vocal *pitch* is determined by how frequently the speaker's vocal cords vibrate. The faster they vibrate, the higher the vocal pitch. **Intonation** refers to changes in pitch (frequency) over time. The intonation of an utterance signals whether a person is making a statement or asking a question. Asking a question will produce a rising intonation contour, as the speaker's pitch gets higher at the end of the sentence. Other statements end with a falling intonation pattern.

Prosodic information helps determine the meaning of a word, phrase, or utterance. **Stress** or *accent* refers to the length, loudness, or pitch of a syllable. A stressed syllable has relatively greater length, loudness, or pitch than its unstressed counterparts. For example, the word *record* can refer to an object or an action. The meaning we attribute to the string depends on how it is stressed. *Rec´ord*, with the stress on the first syllable, can only be a noun; *record´*, with the stress on the last syllable, can only be a verb. Note that *accent* does not mean "dialect," nor does it refer to foreign-language differences in pronunciation. *Accent* refers to syllable stress, to which syllable is *accented* or emphasized by the speaker.

With reference to speech, *rate* refers to the number of speech segments (phonemes or words) produced or perceived per second. As speech rate increases, enunciation becomes more difficult for speakers and comprehension becomes more difficult for listeners. Rapid speaking rates result in reduced information about speech sounds because **acoustic cues** are available for shorter periods for analysis. Speech rate influences speech rhythmicity. Martin (1972) argued that one cue to important information in fluent English speech is its *rhythm*. The important information in English tends to be delivered at stressed intervals, like rhythmic beats in music.

Prosody also provides critical cues to the *emotional* meaning of an utterance. Fast rates of speech may signal a speaker's anxiety, and slower speech may signal depression. Vocal pitch is also informative. High-pitched speech may signal positive affect, whereas low-pitched speech may be more indicative of sadness or depression. Some forms of computer-generated speech also lack these prosodic features, making it sound nonhuman and lacking coloration and emotion. Maybe it is the lack of natural prosodic cues that made the **synthetic speech** sample in Exercise 3.1 sound unnatural?

PHONEMES

Phonemes are the distinctive sounds of a language that permit contrasts. A **phoneme** is a contrastive phonological segment of speech whose phonological realization is predicted by a rule. Phonemes can be regarded as the phonological units of speech. If you change a phoneme in a word, you change the word's meaning. This is usually demonstrated by looking at word and sound contrasts in pairs of words called **minimal pairs.** The phonological difference between the two words in each pair is minimal because the words are identical except for one sound segment that occurs in the same place in the sound string. For example, *rat-hat, hat-mat, mat-gnat* all shift meaning when the initial phoneme is changed. When you change the phoneme in the first member of a minimal pair, you change the perception of the word.

Phonemes are abstract representations of phonological units of a language. They are not physical sounds. They form the basis for meaningful contrasts in a language. The phonetic segment or **phone** is a member of a category of sounds that are contrastive. A phoneme represents a class of sounds in a language that are all regarded as the same. Consider the phoneme /p/ in English; this is a set of sounds that are very similar but not exactly the same. Compare the /p/ in *spin* with that of *pin*. Hold your hand in front of your lips and say each of these aloud. Notice that there is a puff of air in *pin* that is missing in *spin*. That puff of air is *aspiration*; we could say that this /p/ is *aspirated*.

The different sounds, or phones, that are classified as one phoneme are called **allophones.** We just read that English speakers classify two different /p/ phones as one phoneme and that an aspirated /p/ and an unaspirated /p/ are different phones that are perceived as /p/. They are allophones of /p/. Phones are usually represented in brackets such that [ph] represents the aspirated allophone and [p] represents the unaspirated allophone of /p/. These phones do not "contrast" because substituting one for the other does not change the meaning of the segment as it would in a minimal pair. *Pipe* begins with the aspirated version and ends with the unaspirated version of /p/. Replacing [ph] with [p] does not change the meaning of the word.

The important point is that a phoneme is a perceptual category of sounds learned through experience with a native language. Phonemic categories construct similarities across allophones but differences from one phoneme to another. The phonemic representations of words, along with phonological rules of the language, determine how sound segments are pronounced.

PHONOLOGICAL RULES

Phonological rules state what speakers know about the phonological regularities or predictable aspects of speech sounds in their native language. Phonology includes a set of phonemes in a given language and a set of rules for combining strings of phonemes. Through experience with our native language, we learn what combination of sounds obey the rules. We construct a metalinguistic awareness for the phonological rules. We understand what "sounds right" in our native language without explicit knowledge of the phonological rules.

Phonological knowledge includes **phonotactic rules** for what combinations of phonemes are permissible. It will become obvious on inspection that some strings are not permitted in English (see Fromkin & Rodman, 1998). For example, although /str/ is a permissible initial string, English has no words that begin with sound combinations like /stl/ or /tl/. Word phonotactics are based on syllable phonotactics. Only clusters that can begin a syllable can be used to begin a word, and only clusters that can end a syllable can end a word. Multisyllabic words follow phonotactic rules such that we can have a two-syllable word like *construct* (*con* + *struct*) but not *constluct* because we cannot initialize the second syllable with /stl/. Phonotactic rules vary from language to language.

Not all permissible sound combinations form "real" words. Some permissible sound strings will not be recognized as words. For example, *shime* is a permissible string of sounds in English, but it is not a word. Whereas *shime* sounds like a word in English but is not, a string like *stluct* does not sound like a word at all in English, not even a nonsense word. *Shime* does not violate phonotactic rules in English, but *stluct* does.

The phonemic analysis of spoken language is not limited to phonology because it can also be extended to the segments of a signed language like American Sign Language (ASL). Features of signs include hand configuration, place or location of the sign in front of the signer, and the movement of the sign away from or toward the body. The sign units that correspond to phonetic elements in spoken language are called *primes*. As spoken languages have impermissible sequences of sounds, so do signed languages have impermissible combinations of signed primes. Again, rules are language-dependent; what is forbidden in ASL may be permissible in Chinese sign language, and vice versa.

CROSS-LINGUISTIC PHONETICS

Phonology is the sound system of a language, which includes an inventory of sounds (phonetic and phonemic units) and rules for how they can be combined. The phonological systems of a language use a limited number of phonemes to produce an infinite number of utterances. This means that a small set of phonemes can be combined and recombined to produce an endless set of words and sentences. English uses only forty-six different phonemes and a set of phonological rules to produce over 100,000 words.

Phonetics is the study of speech sounds that occur in the languages of the world. Each language has its own set of phonemes and phonological rules. What constitutes a meaningful sound in one language may be ignored in another. A speaker of English may have learned to ignore contrasts that are meaningful in a foreign language. English speakers hear the /k/ sounds in *key* and *cool* as allophones of the same consonant. In Arabic, each of these sounds is a different phoneme. Say each of these words to yourself, and you can feel and hear the slight differences in how these sounds are produced. Conversely, Japanese speakers have difficulty distinguishing between /r/ and /l/ in English. Spanish speakers may not hear the English contrast between /s/ and /z/. One important question here is why languages come to use the sounds that they do. When we examine cross-linguistic commonalties in phonologies, it is apparent that speech is constrained by limitations on the articulatory and auditory hardware. Out of the hundreds of sounds that can be produced, a few combinations are favored.

The UCLA Phonological Segment Inventory Database is a representative sample of the phonological inventories of the world's languages (see Maddieson, 1984). Sound systems used across these languages range from languages that use as few as eleven phonemes (Rotokas, Mura) to more complex sound systems that use a set as large as 141 (!Xu). One can use the database to answer questions about the most common properties of the world's languages. The database contains some 869 phonemes. On close inspection, most of these phonemes are relatively rare, and a handful of consonants and vowels are very common. For example, all languages use stop consonants like /t/ and /b/. Over 80 percent of languages make a distinction based on voicing. Over 90 percent of world languages include fricatives (e.g., /s/ as in *sale* or /š/ as in *shale*). We will discuss these distinctions shortly.

The structure of the vowel systems across languages is as orderly as the consonant pool, perhaps even more so. Five- to nine-vowel sound systems predominate, and the sets of vowels used in languages with the same number of vowels have a lot in common. The large numbers of languages that use a five-vowel system tend to use the same five vowels. Humans have evolved a diverse set of languages, but our languages do exhibit systematic phonetic commonalties. Let's look more closely at the articulatory and acoustic properties of English phonetics.

Articulatory Phonetics

Figure 3.1 shows a cross-sectional view of the organs involved in speech. Restricting airflow in different ways along the vocal tract produces speech sounds. In some cases, the airway is completely closed; for other sounds, one or more speech organs between the vocal cords and the lips obstruct the airflow. The airflow is also shaped by the position of the mouth, tongue, and nasal cavity. Varying the place of obstruction, the amount of air, and how the sound resonates or vibrates produces consonants and

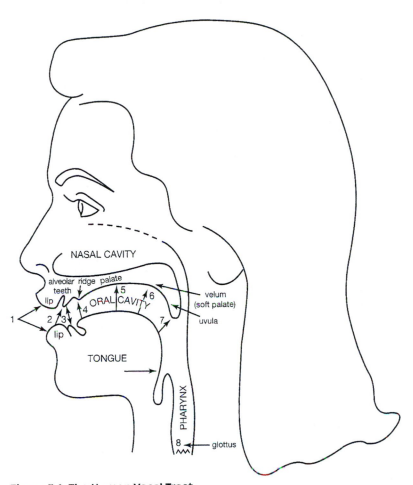

Figure 3.1. The Human Vocal Tract

Note. Places of articulation: 1, bilabial; 2, labiodental; 3, interdental; 4, alveolar; 5, palatal; 6, velar; 7, uvular; 8, glottal. From *An Introduction to Language, 6th edition,* by V. Fromkin © 1998. Reprinted with permission of Heinle & Heinle a division of Thomson Learning.

vowels. Figure 3.1 shows the locations for producing the eight types of **articulation:** *bilabial* (using both lips), *labiodental* (with lip against teeth), *interdental* (between the teeth), *alveolar* (against the ridge behind the upper teeth), *palatal* (against the hard palate), *velar* (against the soft palate), *uvular* (using the uvula), and *glottal* (in the throat).

    Consonant articulation differs from **vowel** articulation in that consonants always involve the closure or partial closure of the airway. Vowels are distinguished by the manner in which the long period of resonance is produced in the mouth or nasal passages. Consonants are produced very quickly and dynamically, while vowels are longer and steady.

CONSONANTS

A **phonetic alphabet** for English phonemes appears in Table 3.1. The symbols used are those adopted by the *International Phonetics Association* (IPA), along with some alternatives traditionally used by linguists in the United States. Using a phonetic alphabet, one can record a string of phonemes in an utterance, even if the source language is unknown. The symbol string can be pronounced by anyone who understands the phonetic alphabet. A classification of the articulatory features of consonants in English appears in Table 3.2. The *place* of articulation is plotted across the top of the figure, and the *manner* in which the air is obstructed is plotted down the left side. It would be helpful for the discussion if you would familiarize yourself with the terms and symbols in Tables 3.1 and 3.2.

Stop consonants are sounds that involve blocking the air stream briefly. The stops are /p, b, t, d, g, k/ as you might articulate in *pat, bat, till, dill, good,* and *could.* As you say these words aloud, notice that each is obstructed or stopped in a different manner. The /b, p/ stops, made with both lips, are bilabials. The ridge behind the teeth, the alveolar ridge, is used to produce /t, d/. The velum in the back of the mouth is used to produce the /k, g/ pair. As you say each member of a pair to yourself, notice that they differ in **voicing:** One member of each pair is *voiced,* and the other is *voiceless.* A *voiced* phoneme is one that employs the vocal cords in production. You can feel your vocal cords vibrating when you pronounce a voiced consonant. The *unvoiced* member of the pair is produced the same way but without activation of the vocal cords.

Table 3.1. Phonetic Symbols

The major consonants, vowels, and diphthongs of English and their phonetic symbols.

Consonants				Vowels		Diphthongs	
p	pill	θ	thigh	i	beet	ay	bite
b	bill	ð	thy	ɪ	bit	æw	about
m	mill	š	shallow	e	bait	ɔy	boy
t	till	ž	measure	ɛ	bet		
d	dill	č	chip	æ	bat		
n	nil	ǰ	gyp	u	boot		
k	kill	l	lip	ʊ	put		
g	gill	r	rip	ʌ	but		
ŋ	sing	y	yet	o	boat		
f	fill	w	wet	ɔ	bought		
v	vat	ʍ	whet	a	pot		
s	sip	h	hat	ə	sofa		
z	zip			ɨ	marry		

From *Psychology and Language: An Introduction to Psycholinguistics, 1st edition,* by H. Clark, E. V. Clark © 1977. Reprinted by permission of Brooks/Cole, an imprint of the Wadsworth Group, a division of Thomson Learning.

Table 3.2. English Consonants Classified by Manner and Place of Articulation

Manner of Articulation					Alveolar			Glottal
Stops	Voiceless	p (*p*at)			t (*t*ack)		k (*c*at)	
Stops	Voiced	b (*b*at)			d (*d*ig)		g (*g*et)	
Fricatives	Voiceless		f (*f*at)	θ (*th*in)	s (*s*at)	š (fi*sh*)		h (*h*at)
Fricatives	Voiced		v (*v*at)	ð (*th*en)	z (*z*ap)	ž (a*z*ure)		
Affricatives	Voiceless					č (*ch*urch)		
Affricatives	Voiced					ǰ (*j*udge)		
Nasals		m (*m*at)			n (*n*at)		ŋ (si*ng*)	
Liquids					l (*l*ate)	r (*r*ate)		
Glides		w (*w*in)				y (*y*et)		

From *Experimental Psycholinguistics: An Introduction*, by S. Glucksberg and J. H. Danks. Copyright © 1975 by Lawrence Erlbaum Associates, Inc. Reprinted with permission.

The *fricatives* use a partial obstruction of the airflow that produces a kind of rushing sound rather than a complete stop. Remember the /fr/ sound in *fricative* to help you recall what the term means. In English, the fricatives are /f, v, θ, ð, s, z, š, ž, h/ as you would hear in *fine, vine, thin, the, sip, zip, ship, azure,* and *hip.* As in the case of the stops, fricatives differ in voicing and place of articulation. The labiodentals /f, v/ are produced with lower lip and teeth. The dentals /θ, ð/ are produced with the tongue on the teeth. Alveolar fricatives /s, z/ use the tongue and alveolar ridge, while the palatal fricatives /š, ž/ use the back of the tongue against the palate. The /h/ is produced in the back of the mouth near the glottis without voicing.

A combination of fricative and stop articulation defines the *affricatives* /č, ǰ/, as in the words *churn* and *jury.* As you say these words, notice that the airflow is stopped at first and then followed by the fricative turbulence. One is voiced /ǰ/, and the other /č/ is voiceless.

Nasal consonants /m, n, ŋ/ are not produced in the oral cavity like the ones described so far. These consonants are produced by allowing air to escape through the nasal cavity while varying the position of the tongue, lips, and velum. Slowly produce these nasals, shifting from one to another, and notice how your tongue, lips, and velum are involved. Another four phonemes are closely related to vowel sounds. Two consonants /l, r/ are appropriately called *liquids* because they do not completely stop the airflow or produce a rushing sound. Examples of these two liquids would be the initial sounds in *lie* and *rye*. Cross-linguistically, /r/ can be produced in different manners. In English, it is done by cupping the tongue, but in French or Spanish, the tongue is trilled or flapped rapidly. The *glides* /ʍ, w, y/ are named for the manner in which they glide into position toward or away from the vowel, as /ʍ/ in *which,* /w/ in *witch,* and /y/ in *yule.* In words, glides must be either preceded by or followed by a vowel. Glides are transitional sounds sometimes referred to as *semivowels.*

VOWELS

As you consider the primary vowel sounds in English—*a, e, i, o, u*—and say them to yourself, notice that each vowel is voiced and that it is produced without obstruction. The articulation of vowels is determined by where they are produced in the vocal cavity—toward the *front, back, top,* or *bottom.* The vowels used in English are arranged according to the position of the tongue, as shown in Figure 3.2. Notice that letters *a, e, i, o,* and *u* are insufficient to describe the full set of vowels. There are at least twelve different vowel sounds represented by these phonetic symbols. Again, familiarizing yourself with this nomenclature now will make it easier to read

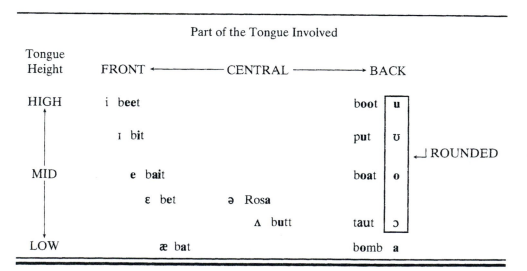

Figure 3.2. How American English Vowels Are Produced
From *Psychology and Language: An Introduction to Psycholinguistics, 1st edition,* by H. Clark and E. V. Clark
© 1977. Reprinted by permission of Brooks/Cole, an imprint of the Wadsworth Group, a division of Thomson Learning.

phonetic strings discussed elsewhere. It is instructive to pronounce the front vowels from high in the mouth /i/ to low /æ/. Also move from the front / I / to the back of the mouth /o/, examining what your vocal organs are doing throughout these transitions.

The vowels produced in the front of the mouth depend on the height of the tongue. From the high tongue height to low, the sequence is /i/ as in *beet*, / I / as in *bit*, /e/ as in *bait*, /ɛ/ as in *bet*, and /æ/ as in *bat*. Notice that most of the vowels from the back of the mouth /u, U, o, ɔ/ are produced by "rounding" the lips. The /a/ sound as in *bomb* is the exception. There are also two central vowels, /ə/ as in *Rosa* and [ʌ] as in *butt*. While all the vowels in English are oral vowels, other languages like French, use nasal vowels, letting some air go through the nose, as in *mon oncle*. In French, nasality is a feature of vowels that is important; in English, nasality is not a feature of vowel sounds; it affects only consonants.

The sounds we have studied up to this point are all single vowels or monophthongs. Vowels that are a combination of two phones are called diphthongs. Diphthongs are usually a vowel and a glide /w, y/ sound; the sound begins with a vowel and glides into the next sound. These pairings produce the diphthongs in English: /ay/ as in *bite*, /æw/ as in *bout*, /ɔy/ as in *boy*.

Note that a phonetic transcription can be read by anyone who understands these symbols, even if they do not understand what the sound string represents or the language from which it was derived. Phonetic transcription is a method of translating words into sound patterns, although the precise symbols used are not universal.

DISTINCTIVE FEATURES

Linguists have developed the notion of distinctive features of sound segments to contrast speech sounds. Distinctive features are hypothetical properties of sound waves or articulations that are used to differentiate one phoneme from another. For example, we described one unitary property of consonant pairs in terms of voicing (e.g., *fine* versus *vine*). One member of a minimal pair, *vine*, is voiced, and the other, *fine*, is unvoiced. The feature of voicing served to distinguish between the two (/f/ versus /v/), so voicing is a distinctive feature. Fricatives were defined as phonemes produced with turbulence or stridency. Nonfricatives are not strident; hence stridency can be a distinctive feature of languages. Other contrasts are possible (e.g., nasality). The goal of distinctive feature analysis is to find a set of features that will describe all of the phonemes in a language. Each phoneme would be represented as a package of these features, with some features (voicing) marked as present (+) and others marked as absent (–). Chomsky and Halle (1968) proposed that the forty-six phonemes in English could be described with a set of thirteen distinctive features. The utility of distinctive features is that a finite set of features can be used to convey all of the phoneme contrasts in the world's languages.

PHONEMIC CONFUSIONS

One interesting aspect of distinctive feature analysis is that it can be used to predict human performance in some speech situations. In particular, feature similarity across a set of sounds predicts their acoustic **confusability,** that is, perceiving one phoneme as another (Miller & Nicely, 1955). Words with similar features are mistakenly confused. We are likely to confuse sets of phonemes like /m-n/, /f-θ/, /v-ð/, /p-t-k/, /d-g/, /s-š/, and /z-ž/. Notice that most of these differ only in the place of articulation, although the last two differ in both place and manner of articulation. The overlap in manner and place of articulation can be used to predict phonemic confusions in speech settings that vary in noisiness. When speech loudness is low relative to background noise, people make many confusions. When voices are louder compared to background noise, they make fewer confusions. You probably notice these confusions in your everyday phone conversations (e.g., "Did you say 'mice' or 'nice'?").

Review Question
Can you spell your name using the International Phonetic Alphabet?

Acoustic Phonetics

Whereas articulatory properties of speech focus on the movement of the vocal organs, acoustic analyses focus on the nature of the sound waves as a packet of energy that can be sensed by the human ear. Here we rely on technology to give us an image of acoustics. Speech engineers are working on two phases of technology, one that will produce or synthesize humanlike speech and one that will segment and analyze speech in terms of meaningful units. Whether these technological projects will yield information about how humans actually perceive speech is not clear. One device that has been crucial in pursuing these technological goals is the *speech spectrograph*, developed in the 1950s.

THE SPEECH SPECTROGRAPH

A speech spectrograph analyzes speech sound waves and converts the acoustical energy in the sound waves into a picture. The image of the speech represents the acoustical properties of frequency, intensity, and duration of speech sounds. The resultant picture produced by the spectrograph is a **spectrogram.** Several speech spectrograms are displayed in Figure 3.3. Three isolated vowels are shown in the top row, diphthongs in the middle row, and words in the bottom row.

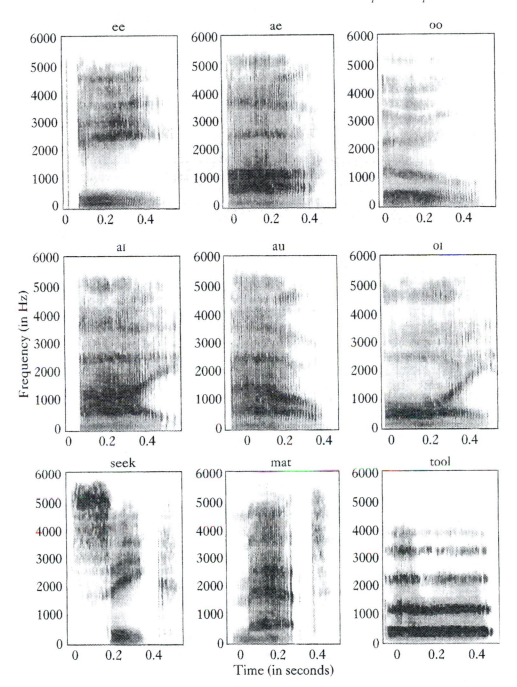

Figure 3.3. Typical Speech Spectrograms

Note. From *The Speech Chain: The Physics and Biology of Spoken Language,* by Peter B. Denes and Elliot N. Pinson © 1993 by W.H. Freeman and Company. Used with permission.

The sound's *frequency* spectrum is represented along the vertical axis. Frequencies of the component sounds are usually measured in cycles per second, or hertz (Hz). On the graph, the higher the sound frequency, the higher the image of it on the vertical axis. Most of the speech waveform is contained between frequencies of 100 and 6000 Hz. *Intensity* or loudness is represented by darkness, such that as intensity increases, darkness increases. Low-intensity sounds will appear very light or sketchy, but louder bands of sound are dark. Time or *duration* is the horizontal dimension, as we see speech unfolding from left to right. The longer the sound, the more space it covers on the horizontal plot. Silent periods will appear as gaps on the horizontal axis. The spectrogram will show transitions in frequency from high to low or vice versa. These **transitions** appear as dark curves tailing upward or downward. The transitions are apparent in the diphthong spectrograms in the middle row of Figure 3.3.

Looking at the figure, you will notice what appear to be dark layers or bands of sound energy. These spectral bands or packets of energy at different frequencies are called **formants.** The bottommost band is labeled F1. The spectrogram will reveal three to five formants. You can see the formants in the bottom right panel representing acoustics of *tool.* F1, the first formant, is below 1000 Hz; F2 is at 1000 Hz. Each speaker produces speech at a different pitch, depending on age, gender, and the characteristics of the vocal tract. The two formants correspond to the two predominant cavities in the vocal tract—the pharynx and the oral cavity. The shape of these structures will vary from person to person. The **fundamental frequency** (F0) is the rate at which the vocal cords vibrate, that is, the speaker's vocal pitch. F0 is roughly 125 Hz for males and 200 Hz for females. The fundamental frequency also produces a series of resonant *harmonics*, which are multiples of F0 that occur at regular intervals (128 Hz, 256 Hz, 384 Hz, etc.).

VOWELS

Vowels are distinguishable by the relative position of the first two formants, which are sufficient for identification in isolation. The vowel "ee" has a low F1 and a high F2, which can be seen in the upper left panel of Figure 3.3. This pattern is different from the one that identifies "oo," which has two low-frequency formants, as shown in the upper right panel of Figure 3.3. Since the spectrum of sound is affected by the size of the vocal tract, men, women, and children produce different values for the vowel formants. Therefore, it is not the absolute frequencies of the formants that are important but rather the pattern they produce in relation to each other that is the basis for recognition.

In the case of diphthongs, which are two vowels produced in a smooth glide, the formants move from one vowel pattern to the other pattern. The movement of the formants is a formant *transition*. The transitions are evident in the middle row of Figure 3.3. Notice that "aɪ" has a transition from lower to higher frequencies but "au" has a transition that ends on a lower frequency. Single vowels produced in isolation will not have transitions. Instead, they will produce relatively flat formant patterns referred to as *steady states*. When vowels are used in fluent conversations, they will be affected by the preceding and following consonants, which can be observed in the bottom panel of Figure 3.3 by looking at the vowels in the context of words. The formants of the "ee" in *seek* do not show the steady state pattern as in the top panel. Instead, they are affected by the preceding /s/ and following /k/.

CONSONANTS

Consonants produce a different spectrum of acoustic information on a spectrogram. Notice the fricative sound /s/ in *seek* in Figure 3.3. The turbulence associated with /s/ is visible as a thick column of high-frequency energy. The fricative /š/ has a similar pattern with a column of energy, and it includes low-frequency spectra due to the way it is produced. Because fricatives vary across place of articulation, the pattern of energy also varies.

With oral-stop consonants such as /t/ and /d/, there is sudden *burst* or release of air pressure immediately prior to the onset of the vowel sound. It will appear on a spectrogram as a thin line. The bursts are evident in Figure 3.4, which shows the spectrograms for the syllables /di/ and /ti/. The bursts of energy are difficult to see on the spectrographs because they are brief, low-intensity sounds. The transitions in the following formants may hold the clue to which particular stop consonants have been articulated, as well as the gap between the burst and the beginning of the voicing of the vowel sounds.

One benefit of spectrograph research is that it provided a basis for speculation about what acoustic features humans use to perceive speech. Speech processing seems to occur at three different levels (Studdert-Kennedy, 1976): (1) at an *auditory* level, consisting of frequency, intensity, and duration; (2) at a *phonetic* level, consisting of cues such as formant transitions that are used to identify phones; and (3) at a *phonological* level, where phonetic segments are converted into phonemes. These levels of perceptual analysis unfold sequentially. But how do these levels of analysis provide the cues humans use to perceive speech? Spectrograms aside, the psycholinguist wants to know the answers to some difficult questions. What cues are we using to categorize speech segments? What are the processes that underlie such categorization? First, let's look at some potential cues for speech perception.

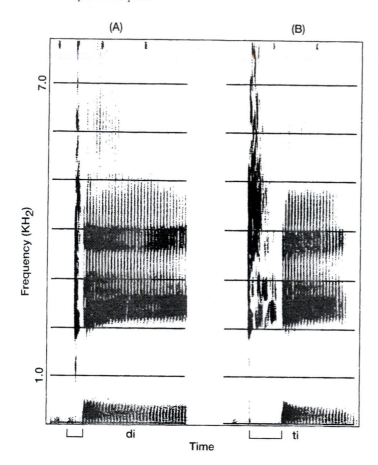

Figure 3.4. Spectrograms for the Syllables /di/ and /ti/ In each syllable, the initial burst is represented by the dark vertical line to the left. The onset of voicing is indicated by the start of the first formant (regular striations). *Note.* From G. H. Yeni-Komshian (1998) "Speech Perception" in J. B. Gleason & N. B. Ratner (eds), *Psycholinguistics, 2nd edition,* Figure 3.8, p. 130. Orlando, FL: Harcourt Brace. Reprinted by permission of Grace H. Yeni-Komshian.

Perception of Speech Segments

In this section, we consider the perception of isolated segments of speech. These tend to be studies using phonemes and syllables of natural or synthetic origin.

SPEECH SYNTHESIS

Speech synthesis works like a spectrographic analysis, but in reverse. Speech synthesis is accomplished by drawing a picture of speech similar to a spectrogram and feeding the picture into a synthesizer called the **Pattern-Playback** (see Denes & Pinson, 1993). The Pattern-Playback provided information about speech in the 1950s by converting the painted images of sounds into sound waves. Researchers would know they had captured the essence of a sound segment when the painted segment fed to the Pattern-Playback produced the desired sound patterns. A speech synthesis pattern looks like a schematic version of a spectrogram (see Figure 3.5). The top part of the figure is a spectrogram, and the bottom part is a painted pattern that can be "played." When the bottom part of the figure is fed into the Pattern-Playback synthesizer, it will produce a pattern of sounds like that recorded at the top of the figure. Readers can visit http://www.haskins.yale.edu/haskins/misc/sws/sentence/s6.html and see some of the Haskins Laboratory research.

VOWEL IDENTIFICATION

As noted earlier, the long steady-state segments on spectrograms tend to be vowel sounds. Most of the vowel sounds in the spectrograms in Figure 3.3 have three formants that provide the bulk of the information about the vowel. But we do not need all the information in all the formants to decide what we are hearing. We could filter out the formants F4 and F5 with little harm to identification. What seems to be important for vowel identification is the steady-state information in the first two formants and the types of transitions they produce (Delattre, Liberman, Cooper, & Gerstman, 1952). Even though the frequencies of the first two formants influence vowel perception of isolated speech segments in a laboratory setting, they may not be the objects of perception in syllables or continuous speech. In natural speech, vowels are produced in the context of consonants. This means that there will be transitions between vowels and the consonants they abut.

Some thirty years after Haskins Laboratory research was conducted, Jenkins, Strange, and Edman (1983) asked the next logical question about the perception of vowels in the context of consonants. They produced a set of consonant-vowel-consonant (CVC) stimuli that used nine different vowels and began and ended with [b] (*bib, babe, beeb, bob,* etc.). Jenkins et al. cut the syllables into three segments: (a) those containing the initial [b] + transitions to the vowel, (b) those containing only the central vowel steady state formants, and (c) those containing the transition to the final [b]. Subjects were asked to identify the vowels in different combinations of these three segments: (1) a + b + c, (2) a + silent gap + c, (3) b only, (4) b trimmed to the length of the shortest vowel, and (5) a + c.

Subjects were asked to identify the vowel segments in each stimulus. Subjects identified silent-center stimuli (2) as accurately as complete segments (1). More errors were made with steady-state information + temporal information segments (3) and abutted segments (5) than the complete segments (1). Performance was the worst for steady-state-only information segments (4). Recall that the original research had shown that information in (4) was sufficient for identification of *isolated* segments. Jenkins et al. interpreted the new contextualized results to mean that vowel duration and transitions were more important than short samples of steady-state information. Therefore, the identification of isolated vowels and the identification of vowels in continuous speech use different cues. Isolated segments can be identified by steady-state information, but these cues are less important than dynamic transition changes used to identify vowels in continuous speech.

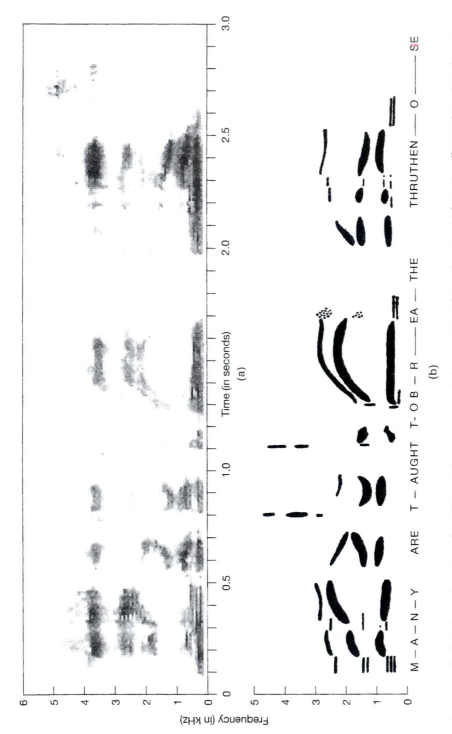

Figure 3.5. Typical Speech Synthesis Patterns The upper panel shows a sound spectrogram of a naturally produced sentence; the lower panel is a painted pattern that can be played on the Pattern-Playback to synthesize the same sentence. (Only the first three formats of the natural speech are represented in the painted pattern; they suffice to produce recognizable speech.)

Note: From *The Speech Chain: The Physics and Biology of Spoken Language,* by Peter B. Denes and Elliot N. Pinson © 1993 by W.H. Freeman and Company. Used with permission.

CONSONANT IDENTIFICATION

We have just read that listeners can identify vowels by their steady-state information when in isolation and by the transitions to abutting consonants in continuous segments. Relative to vowel cues, consonants are produced more briefly than vowels and with less acoustic energy than vowels. Consonants are marked by brief, broadband bursts of acoustic energy. Listeners could use the acoustical differences in duration and intensity to distinguish consonants from vowels. But how might they identify which particular consonant has been produced? If we remove the entire vowel portion of a syllable /ba/ and present the remaining consonant segment to a listener, what is heard sounds more like a "chirp" than the phone [b]. In natural speech, a stop consonant must contain sufficient information for it to be identified as [b]. Important consonant information must be encoded in the vowel information that was excised from the [b], resulting in the chirp perception. If this is the case, then the acoustic cues necessary to identify [b] are encoded in the vowel information that follows it. Stop consonants are more highly encoded than other consonants, but in natural speech, consonants are affected by the vowels they abut. That the information about a phone [b] is contained or encoded in the vowel that follows is referred to as **parallel transmission.**

PARALLEL TRANSMISSION: A SEGMENTATION PROBLEM

Parallel transmission presents a problem for the notion that speech can be segmented into discrete phonemes for perception. This problem arises from the nature of articulating syllables. In a syllable, consonant and vowel information is coarticulated. **Coarticulation** refers to the spreading of phonetic features either in anticipation of adjacent sounds or in perseveration of the articulatory process. Information about the first phoneme affects and overlaps the second phoneme. The articulation of the second phoneme is programmed into the articulation of the first phoneme. In other words, features of the first and second phonemes are transmitted in parallel, and the features overlap somewhat. Let's take one segment from the spectrogram in Figure 3.3 to illustrate this. First look at the "ee" pattern in the top row of the figure; then look at the pattern for *seek* at the bottom. Notice how the initial segment of the /s/ blends into the "ee." Where does the "ee" begin and the /s/ end? It is not clear. The /s/ has information about the nature of the following vowel encoded into it. Parallel transmission of acoustic information creates what is called the **segmentation problem;** we cannot tell where the phoneme segments are because the adjacent sounds affect each other through coarticulation.

Parallel transmission is problematic for a phoneme-based model of speech perception. Why? Because the phonemes blend together in speech segments. If phonemes are coarticulated, should we still think of them as individual phonemes with distinctive features, or should we abandon the idea of the phoneme as the object of perception? A great deal of evidence supports the phoneme as a unit of perception (Liberman, Harris, Hoffman, & Griffith, 1957). But there is also evidence that larger units (e.g., syllables) are used as perceptual units. Segui, Frauenfelder, and Mehler (1981) presented strong evidence for the syllable as the unit of perception. Subjects were asked to respond as quickly as possible when a segmental or syllabic target occurred in an utterance. Syllable targets (/ba/, /pi/, /dɛ/) were reported more quickly than phoneme targets (/b/, /p/, /d/). Evidence of this kind has been interpreted to mean that the syllable is directly available in a unitary form for auditory analysis, casting some doubt on the phoneme as the only unit of perceptual analysis.

CONTEXTUAL VARIATION: THE PROBLEM OF INVARIANCE

It is generally accepted that phonemes do not have invariant properties. For most phonemes, there are no cues that uniquely identify a phonetic category. **Invariance** is the term used to describe how a phoneme's acoustic properties change across contexts, that is, they are not invariant. We tend to perceive segments categorically across variations of speaker age and speaker gender, which produce changes in vocal pitch. The perception of phonemes depends on the linguistic-phonetic context in which they are produced. In other words, phoneme recognition varies from context to context.

Contextual variation refers to the finding that a given phoneme, such as /d/, will be produced differently, depending on its surrounding speech segments (Liberman, 1970). This can be illustrated by looking at the /d/ consonant in different vowel contexts. In Figure 3.6, the /d/ F1 frequency and transition cues are different, depending on the following vowel context. The transition "tails up" preceding /i/

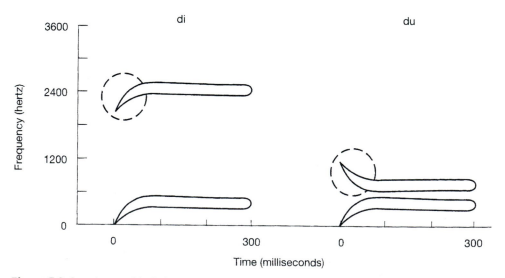

Figure 3.6. Spectographic Patterns Sufficient to Synthesize the Syllables /di/ and /du/
Figure "Simplified spectrographic patterns" from Glucksberg, S., & Danks, J.H. (1975). *Experimental psycholinguistics: An introduction*, Lawrence Erlbaum Associates. Reprinted by permission.

but "tails down" preceding /u/. F1 occurs around 2400 Hz in /di/ and at 600 Hz in /du/. The spectrogram clearly shows different transitional components of the /d/ in each context, yet these are both heard as /d/. What is heard as /d/ in one context is based on a different pattern of acoustic cues than the other. In other words, the acoustic pattern of the consonant is context dependent or determined by the vowel that follows it. **Context dependence** refers to the finding that consonant perception is a function of surrounding context.

VOICE ONSET TIME

Consider what happens when you hear a syllable like /*tip*/ that begins with an unvoiced consonant followed by a vowel (which is always voiced). There is a period of time between the end of the /t/ and before the /I/ where the voicing of the vowel has not yet begun. This lag before the voicing of the vowel is known as **voice onset time** (VOT). VOT is a feature of the spectrogram. It is a potential cue that could signal the difference between whether the syllable we heard was /*dip*/ with the voiced /d/ or /*tip*/ with an unvoiced /t/ consonant. The voicing of the vowel begins almost immediately with the voiced consonant, as in /*dip*/. But there is a delay of 40 to 60 milliseconds (ms) with the unvoiced consonant before the vowel, as in /*tip*/. You can see the small gap following /t/ in the word *tool* in Figure 3.3, and a more obvious gap in the spectrograms in Figure 3.4 and in the synthesized word *taught* in Figure 3.5.

Do listeners use the long VOT to identify the unvoiced consonant /t/ and the shorter VOT to identify /d/? Notice that VOT is not a distinctive feature of a phoneme. VOT relies on the relationship between consonant and vowel sounds in the speech segment. Because these consonant and vowel sounds occur simultaneously, the way one phoneme is articulated effects the articulation of its neighbors. Is VOT psychologically real? That is, do listeners use VOT to identify speech segments? The answer from several studies is yes. In one such study (Yeni-Komshian & Lafontaine, 1983), subjects were presented with synthetic stimuli that begin with a burst, followed by three formant transitions that lead to /i/, creating the perception of a CV syllable beginning with either /t/ or /d/. Since VOT is the cue of interest, the VOT between the burst and the formant transitions was varied from 0 ms (no delay) to 60 ms in increments of 10 ms, creating seven different stimuli. Subjects were give identification tasks (Is this /di/ or /ti/?) and discrimination tasks (Is this pair the same or different?) using the seven stimuli.

We can discuss the results in terms of which items were identified as one category versus the alternative, so let's look at what gets perceived as /di/. The results indicated that subjects identified all of the stimuli with a VOT of 20 ms or less as /di/ but none of the stimuli with VOT of greater than 30ms as /di/. The stimulus with a VOT of 30 ms proved to be a "crossover" stimulus, marking the border between /di/ and /ti/. VOTs on the other side of the border are perceived as a different syllable. As for discrimination, all stimuli under 30 ms VOT were categorized as "the same," /di/. The crossover stimulus was sometimes identified as /*ti*/ and sometimes /di/. This pattern of results for identification and discrimination of stimuli is referred to as *categorical perception*.

CATEGORICAL PERCEPTION

Categorical perception of speech refers to the finding that allophones such as [d] with VOTs between 0 and 30 ms in our previous example are perceived as the same phoneme, /d/. In other words, there is a class of sounds that all sound the same and between which a speaker cannot easily discriminate. However, there is a boundary to what is included in the /d/ category, and once we cross that boundary, another phoneme, /t/, will be perceived. This is the essence of categorical perception: poor discrimination *within* a category but excellent discrimination *across* phoneme boundaries. An idealized version is presented in Figure 3.7, showing the first four stimuli perceived as category A and the last four as category B. Discrimination is poor within each category but peaks at the border of each category between stimuli 4 and 5.

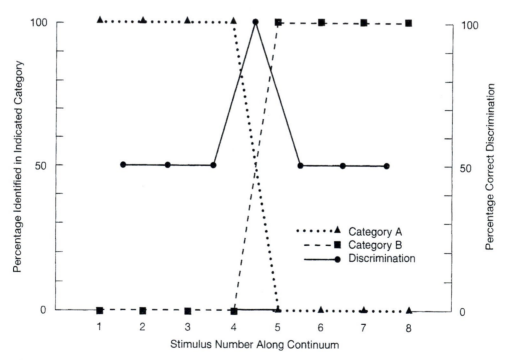

Figure 3.7. Categorical Perception: Identification Performance for Two Categories and Discrimination Performance between Categories
From "Motor Theory of Speech Perception: A Reply to Lane's Critical Review," by M. Studdert-Kennedy, et al., *Psychological Review, 77*, p. 235. Copyright © 1970 by the American Psychological Association. Reprinted with permission.

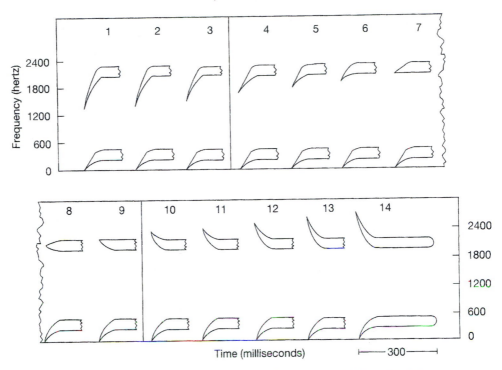

Figure 3.8. Schematic Spectrograms Demonstrating Categorical Perception
Note. After Liberman, Harris, Hoffman, & Griffith (1957).

Figure 3.8 illustrates how spectrograms can be used to demonstrate the phenomenon of categorical perception. Displayed are a series of sounds that have a second formant with a transition around 2000 Hz. The curve of the second formant transition varies across the series from a prominent upward-moving curve in segments 1 through 4 and a downward-moving transition in segments 10 through 14. When subjects hear these segments, they categorize the first three segments as /ba/, the next six as /da/, and the last five as /ga/, performing as if there are category boundaries between segments 3 and 4 and between segments 9 and 10. Notice that the different consonant variations (e.g., segments 4 through 9) are not discriminated but are perceived as members of one phoneme category. Subjects perform as if there are boundaries between one phoneme and another such that one phoneme is perceived on the left of the boundary and another phoneme on the right, as was hypothesized in Figure 3.7 (Liberman et al., 1957).

Over the past four decades, many experiments on the categorical perception of speech segments have been conducted, using discrimination and identification methodology similar to what has been described up to this point. These studies are too numerous to cover in detail, but we can summarize from them what acoustic cues are perceived categorically (see Yeni-Komshian, 1998).

Word initial voicing in oral stops /ti-di/	VOT
Word final voicing in oral stops /ab-ap/	Duration of preceding vowel
Place in nasal stops /ma-na/	Start and direction of second formant
Place in oral stops /ba-da-ga/	Start and direction of second formant
Voicing in final fricatives /as-az/	Duration of preceding vowel
Place in fricatives [sa-ša]	Frequency of turbulent noise
Liquids /la-ra/	Frequency of third formant

Discussion Question

Describe how categorical perception, parallel transmission, and context dependence might occur in American Sign Language.

PHONEME PROTOTYPES

It was mentioned earlier that a phoneme represented a category of acoustically different sounds that were perceived as the same phoneme. The example was that English speakers categorize [d] in /du/ and [d] in /di/ both as /d/, even though their F2 properties are very different. Why do we hear different sounds as the same phoneme? What is the basis for categorical perception? Kuhl (1991) suggested that vowel categories are structured around a **prototype** or best example of the category. There is plenty of research on prototypes in cognitive psychology. The research on categorization shows that the members of categories, be they dogs, birds, or cups, are not equally good members of the categories they occupy. A category has a *graded structure,* which is centered on an ideal or prototypical instance (Rosch, 1975, 1978). In this scheme, a phoneme represents a prototype or best example of the category of sounds. When we hear sounds, we compare them to the prototypes on a goodness-of-fit basis. Sounds that are near the prototype are perceived as the prototype, and those that deviate greatly from the prototype become perceptually different, depending on just how different they are from the prototype. Kuhl (1991) found that the tendency to generalize a background segment to another variant of the vowel category is greatest when the background stimulus is near the ideal or prototype. She referred to this tendency as a *perceptual magnet,* a phenomenon whereby variants of the vowel are perceptually assimilated to the prototype. Conversely, the greater the distance between the comparison stimuli, the greater the ability to discriminate between them.

Perception of Continuous Speech

Up to this point, we have been concerned mainly with the process of recognizing individual speech sounds. We have not addressed how people perceive speech sounds within the context of fluent speech. One controversy in speech perception is how conceptual knowledge is used to analyze the incoming acoustic cues. The debate is whether speech can be perceived on the basis of acoustic cues alone or whether general knowledge about speech interacts with the incoming data.

TOP-DOWN VERSUS BOTTOM-UP SPEECH PROCESSING

A perceptual analysis of a conversation or a visual scene is a good example of what cognitive psychologists call **bottom-up processing.** This process starts with the raw sensory data and works toward finding the concept or idea that the data represent to the perceiver. Consider an example in the visual system: Detecting the relative size, shape, and color of a bird provides enough information to tell you it is a kingfisher. Similarly, in speech perception, hearing the phonemes /l/ added to /pʊ/ tells you that the word is *pull* and not *push.* You analyze the available clues and come to a decision. You are working from the bottom (the data) up (to the concept).

Top-down processing works the other way, beginning with a concept and matching it to the incoming data. In the example, you know the kingfisher sits on the wire by the lake. When you see a bird on the line, you anticipate or expect that it is your kingfisher before you examine its color, size, and shape. Conceptual processing works this way in speech perception. When you hear a person saying, "Apples grow on . . . ," you have expectations about what the next word is going to be—a noun, probably *trees.* You have contextual and linguistic information about what the word is going to be before you hear it. Hearing the word *trees* will confirm your expectations. The role of top-down processing in the perception of fluent speech is a major point of controversy.

Does interactive (analytic and conceptual) processing of the speech signal occur, and if it does, where in the speech analysis does it take place? Plenty of research and ongoing debates about the nature of speech perception and word recognition are currently being conducted (see Gernsbacher, 1994, for some reviews). Several research methods are used to study spoken word recognition (e.g., perceptual identification, naming tasks, phoneme restoration). Lively, Pisoni, and Goldinger (1994) found that while these methods provided different ways to study access to the mental lexicon, no single task was sufficient to describe all the processes used in word recognition. The top-down versus bottom-up nature of speech recognition has not been completely resolved. Given space limitations, we consider just one of the experimental procedures used to study spoken word perception, the **phonemic restoration** paradigm. We address visual word recognition methodology in Chapter 4.

PHONEMIC RESTORATION: AUDITORY ILLUSION OR TOP-DOWN PROCESSING?

Warren devised one clever way to debate whether speech perception is an interactive process. Warren (1970) presented subjects with a tape-recorded sentence like this:

> The state governors met with their respective legi*latures convening in the capital city.

Where the asterisk appears, the /s/ was replaced with the sound of a cough. When the subjects were asked if any of the sounds were missing in the sentence, all but one said no, and the remaining subject guessed the wrong sound. The missing sound was processed as if it were there. The subjects "restored" the missing phoneme, hence the *phonemic restoration effect*. In a follow-up study, Warren and Warren (1970) demonstrated that listeners used both semantic and syntactic cues to fill in the missing sounds. They presented sentences like these:

> It was found that the *eel was on the shoe.
>
> It was found that the *eel was on the orange.
>
> It was found that the *eel was on the axle.
>
> It was found that the *eel was on the table.

All tape recordings used the same initial sentence frame with the last word spliced on at the end. The missing sound was replaced by a cough. Depending on the version heard, people claimed that they heard *heel, peel, wheel,* or *meal*. Notice that the restored phoneme depended on the semantics of the portion of the sentence that followed the missing segment. At this time, Warren and Warren's research was interpreted to mean that speech perception is an interactive top-down process and one that can travel back several words to fill in missing information. How can the context and speech signal come together to provide for speech perception? There have been a number of papers addressing phonemic restoration since Warren's original research. These papers address a central controversy in speech perception, whether speech is recognized from the bottom up through phonetic analysis or whether conceptual, top-down information plays a role in perception.

The controversy produces two general explanations for the role of context in phonemic restoration. Top-down context (word or sentence) interacts with bottom-up acoustic information to modify the acoustic representation. This produces a **sensitivity effect** whereby context modifies the listener's sensory system. The second explanation is that the context produces a **bias effect** by way of top-down context. The context provides additional sources of information that supplement the acoustic analysis, but context does *not* change how the sensory system operates. The question hinges on whether contextual information interacts during acoustic analysis or not. Does the context interact with acoustic analysis to change the listener's sensitivity, or does the acoustic analysis unfold in a bottom-up manner, its output biased by the context of the acoustic analysis? (Also see Green & Swets, 1966, on signal detection theory.)

This issue of top-down interaction with the perceptual process has not been fully resolved. Samuel (1981, 1986, 1996, 1997) revised the methodology used in Warren's phonemic restoration studies so that the target phonemes were either *replaced* by noise (as in Warren, 1970) or had noise *added* to them. Samuel's (1981) subjects were asked to judge whether the phoneme was replaced or had added noise. Samuel contrasted recognition of phonemes in words with the recognition of phonemes as isolated segments. He found a bias effect; subjects were more likely to respond that a phoneme was present in a word than in an isolated segment. In addition, subjects were better able to discriminate the presence of the phoneme or the noise in the isolated-segment context. However, according to Massaro (1994), this method confounds acoustic information with top-down information. Isolated segments have a bottom-up advantage over words because the abutting phonemes in the word context may degrade the acoustic segment when it is presented in the word context. The word could also produce coarticulation cues, which would not be present in the isolated-segment trials.

To overcome the confounding and coarticulation problems, Samuel contrasted the perception of pseudowords (e.g., *madorn*) with the perception of real words (e.g., *modern*). Samuel reasoned that like the isolated segments, the pseudowords would have a disadvantage relative to the words because subjects would not know what segments comprised the pseudowords. To overcome the advantage, each pseudoword was pronounced before it was presented in test trials. Results showed that subjects were more sensitive to changes in the pseudowords relative to changes in real words. But again, the method was not without confounds. Pseudowords averaged 10 percent longer in duration than real words, resulting in nonequivalent stimulus information. The longer duration might have produced the higher sensitivity scores.

In a final experiment, Samuel placed the test words in a sentence context, not unlike the Warren studies. The sentence context made the presence of the word either predictable or not predictable. This methodological change produced a shift in bias but not sensitivity, according to Massaro (1994). The predictable versus unpredictable sentence context here did not produce a confound in stimulus presentation. The general findings of these three experiments did not support a top-down role in the phonemic restoration procedure, according to Massaro and others (Mattingly & Liberman, 1988; Repp, 1992). They argue that a bottom-up analysis of words with missing segments provides sufficient cues to the identity of the excised phoneme. Top-down information is needed to cause the illusion. More recently, Samuel (1996, 1997) has provided more reliable evidence of top-down lexical influence on perception.

Samuel (1997) merged the phonemic restoration paradigm with a **selective adaptation** procedure to demonstrate that speech perception is mediated by phonemelike representations that are produced by top-down lexical activation. In the selective adaptation procedure, speakers identify members of speech continua (e.g., VOT variants of consonants /kɪ/ versus /gɪ/) before or after repeatedly hearing sounds (i.e., adaptation). The basic adaptation effect is a shift in contrast. If a repeated sound is voiced /gɪ/, after adaptation, fewer test items are identified as voiced relative to identification before adaptation takes place. After adaptation, stimulus sensitivity is reduced. The restoration procedure raises another question: What would happen if the repeated phoneme was not physically in the signal? Would restored phonemes produce the adaptation effect? If the answer is yes, then there must be a top-down lexical influence similar to acoustic stimulation that overrides lower-level codes. As Samuel put it, "If a lexically restored phoneme *sounds* like a phoneme and *acts* like a phoneme, it *is* a phoneme" (p. 98).

In the adaptation versus restoration paradigm, Samuel (1997) used real words, words with deleted phonemes, and words with phonemes replaced with noise. If the words with deleted phonemes produce adaptation but those with noise replacements do not, then the effect is a high-level lexical code and not top-down-driven activation of a phonemelike representation. Also, if phoneme restoration is driven by acoustic cues and not top-down activation, then the lexical status of a word is irrelevant to adaptation. If lexical status in not important, then adaptation to syllables /gɪ/ or /kɪ/ would occur equally often with phonemes /g/ and /k/ in words like *gift* and *kiss* and in nonwords *giss* and *kift*.

To answer these questions, Samuel (1997) used a set of real English words (e.g., *alphabet*), pseudowords with high lexical overlap (e.g., *orfabet*), and pseudowords with low lexical overlap (e.g., *exfabesh*). In the examples given, he tested for adaptation to /b/ and /d/ on the identification of syllables /bɪ/ and /dɪ/. Again, he was looking for lowered identification after repeated exposure to the adapters. The words and pseudowords were intact, had silent replacements, or had noise replacements of the target phonemes. In three experiments, Samuel demonstrated the adaptation effect with real words and with noise-replaced phonemes in real words and high-lexical-overlap words. The effect did not occur in low-lexical-overlap pseudowords like *exfabesh*. He found that silence-replaced words and pseudowords do not produce the adaptation effect, ruling out the possibility that phonemic restoration comes from high-level lexical activation. Phonemic restoration occurs because a top-down process has activated a phonemic code. Adaptation occurs at a sublexical level, mediated by a phonemelike representation produced through top-down lexical activation.

We return to the general question about phonemic restoration. When a listener reports that a word sounds intact in the phoneme restoration study, has a phonemic code been detected via true top-down activation, or has a lexical code provided the percept, meaning that the listener does not notice what is missing or added? Samuel's research suggests that the effect is mediated by lexical activation of a phonemic code. Alternatively, theorists who believe that speech perception is predicated on a bottom-up analysis and segregation of the auditory signal (e.g., Repp, 1992) argue that the process does not involve lexical interaction but occurs solely on the basis of speech cues segregated from other auditory sounds. For Repp (1992) and Mattingly and Liberman (1988), there are sufficient cues in the speech signal alone to identify the missing phoneme. These cues exist in the segments that abut the excised phoneme and can be segregated from the waveform as speech cues. We do not need to invoke top-down processing to explain the phenomenon.

We follow the problem of phoneme restoration with a look at a few models of speech perception that have been developed to account for the wide variety of empirical findings on the subject.

Theories of Speech Perception and Word Recognition

The nature of speech perception has been debated for well over a century. Technological and methodological innovations have aided these analyses. Since the work on spectrographic analysis of speech in the 1950s, several theories have been developed to define the nature of speech perception and word recognition. Speech perception models differ on what is the *object* of perception. Some researchers focus on the perception of speech segments such as phonemes and syllables; others extended the analysis to the perception and recognition of words. Recent accounts of word recognition attempt to conceptualize how the speech waveform is mapped into a memory representation. Most recognition models represent the mapping process as one of an *activation* of representations in memory and a *search* through the lexicon (Lively et al., 1994). This section outlines four theories that are part of the ongoing debate about speech perception. We begin by addressing whether speech is a general or specific form of perception, that is, the "modularity" question. Then we look at two speech perception theories that have contrasting views of the objects of perception: motor gestures versus auditory representations. We end with a look at two activation-search models.

MODULES AND MODULARITY

To what extent have we evolved mental or neural systems that are configured uniquely for a particular task such as face recognition or speech perception? This is the issue that is usually addressed as the question of *modularity*. The clearest and most extensive definition of modularity comes from Fodor (1983) in *The Modularity of Mind*. A *module* is a specialized, encapsulated mental organ that has evolved to handle specific information types of particular relevance to the species. The neuroscientist understands this in terms of layers or regions of the brain that operate under a division of labor, processing information in various ways. Few neuroscientists quibble with the use of the term. However, in cognitive science and psycholinguistics, the term embodies a different notion, one that goes beyond the claim about brain organization.

One of the lingering controversial issues for psycholinguists is to determine whether speech requires a special mode of perception, like the brain's resources dedicated to visual processing. The issue is whether speech is perceived through resources dedicated solely to speech or whether speech perception operates on *general* auditory resources. In other words, is there a speech module dedicated to the phonetic mode or not? To answer this question, we have to understand what Fodor meant by modularity.

Fodor (1983) specified the principal characteristics of modules, as follows:

- *Modules are domain-specific.* They operate exclusively with a single information type. Language and face recognition are used as examples.

- *Modules have mandatory commitment.* They are constrained to act whenever they can. Modules operate reflexively, providing predetermined outputs for predetermined inputs regardless of context.

- *Modules have limited access to underlying representations.* This means that perceptual forms are discarded during modular computation and are not available to other cognitive processes.

- *Modules have speed.* They work very fast.

- *Modules are encapsulated.* It is impossible to interfere with their inner workings. They are not influenced by knowledge or belief.

- *Modules have shallow outputs.* They provide limited output and have no intervening steps leading to that output.

- *Modules are unconscious.* It is impossible to think about or reflect on their operations.

Psycholinguists have interpreted modularization as an analogue to neural architectures dedicated to cognitive processes. Fodor suggested that modules should have a stereotyped pace and course of development and that they should exhibit a fixed neural architecture that would show consistent and characteristic breakdowns following insult to the system. In order to maintain that speech is a modular process, research has to support these constraints. Assumptions regarding the effects of the speech context and the role of the listener's knowledge in speech perception have provoked many debates. Opponents of modularity have used context and knowledge effects to argue against the theory. Whether there is a module for speech or whether modularity exists are issues of considerable controversy. Network models of speech perception (see Elman et al., 1996) pose an alternative view to modularity, as we shall see. Next we move on to look at theories of speech perception that have been influential.

MOTOR THEORY

Researchers at the Haskins Laboratory in the late 1950s (see Liberman, Cooper, Shankweiler, & Studdert-Kennedy, 1967) developed the theory of speech perception known as **motor theory** (MT). MT aims to explain on a one-to-one basis the perception of acoustic information in terms of the neuromotor programs that produced the articulation of those acoustics. The hypothetical *inverse problem*—that speech perception is the reverse translation of articulation—is solved by having the listener perceive speech by determining the causes of acoustic information he or she hears by modeling the articulation of that information. This is an efficient model because it uses the same mechanism for speech perception and speech production.

MT accounts for some perceptual phenomena, but it fails elsewhere. MT can account for the invariance problem, the fact that the initial phonemes in /di/ and /du/ are perceived as the same but are acoustically different. The solution lies in the invariant manner of producing both /d/ sounds, their articulatory histories. To account for humans' unique perception of speech sounds, Liberman and Mattingly (1985, 1989; Mattingly and Liberman, 1988) updated the model. Using a modular approach, these theorists proposed that humans have a speech-specific module that processes language differently than other speech sounds. The modular view can account for categorical perception by relegating phonetic processing to the unique speech module.

Whether speech is perceived through a special module or by general auditory processing remains a matter of debate (Remez, 1994). In another version of MT, C. A. Fowler (1984, 1986; Fowler & Rosenblum, 1991) favors phonetic *gestures* (coordinated vocal tract movements) as the objects of perception without resorting to a special speech module for an explanation. Fowler (1984) proposed that several overlapping phonetic segments (i.e., parallel transmission) influence the acoustic spectrum of speech. Fowler believed that the speaker extracts information from the acoustic spectrum into separate coincident articulations or underlying gestures. Perceptual judgments are made on the basis of the underlying gestures, not the sensory properties of the acoustic signal itself.

Several forms of research undermined the classic form of the model. First of all, the one-to-one relationship between perception and articulation was found to be false (MacNeilage, 1972). For any particular consonant, many articulatory programs will give rise to it; that is, there are no core properties or invariance in the signal that give rise to a consonant. Second, speech perception can be achieved without motor capacity, which would not be possible if the route to perception were through motor representation. Finally, research with infants and newborns has demonstrated that they have perceptual capabilities in the absence of articulatory or motor representations, providing strong evidence for perception without a motor component.

AUDITORY MODELS OF SPEECH PERCEPTION

An alternative view of speech perception focuses on an auditory mechanism for natural speech. Auditory models rely on linguistic-phonetic properties of sounds as objects of perception or more simply on auditory impressions of sounds as the objects of perception (Kluender, Diehl, & Wright, 1988). Ohala (1986) argued for the auditory model of speech perception through several lines of evidence. First, a vowel can be produced through several different forms of articulation that are categorized as the same. Second, a ventriloquist produces speech by fixing the jaw and lips. Third, mynah birds replicate speech sounds. Fourth, people with clinical articulation disorders approximate sounds of speech, not articulation. Additional evidence that proves even more problematic for a motor-gestural model of speech is the research by Kluender, Diehl and Killeen (1987), who trained a group of quail to distinguish and generalize natural segments of voiced stop consonants. These are quail that know nothing about articulation and have no linguistic experience, but they can distinguish between [b], [d], and [g] on the basis of avian auditory resources alone.

Kuhl (1991) offered a different defense of auditory perception that contrasted human adult and infant performance with adult macaques. Subjects were tested with synthetic five-formant tokens of [i]. Two groups of stimuli were designed around a "good" version of [i] and a "poorer" version of [i], as illustrated in Figure 3.9. The numerical scale for pitch uses units called "mels." For example, a pure tone of 500 mels is perceived as having half the pitch as a pure tone of 1000 mels. Kuhl measured how well subjects could notice differences between the central [i] in each group and other tokens from its group. Human adults and infants

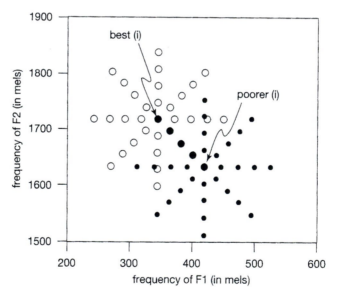

Figure 3.9. Kuhl's Experiment in Perceptual Goodness and Discrimination of Variants of the Vowel [i] When the discrimination standard was fixed the best [i], it assimilated its neighbors (open circles); when the set was fixed on poorer [i] (filled circles), performance of human adults and infants improved. Macaques discriminated well under both standards. From "Human and human infants show a 'perceptual magnet effect' for the prototypes of speech categories, monkeys do not" by Patricia K. Kuhl, *Perception & Psychophysics, 50,* (93–107). Redrawn with permission of Patricia K. Kuhl, 1991.

discriminated differences between [i] and its tokens in the poor group better than they discriminated the central vowel from tokens in the good group. The macaques performed equally well in both vowel groups. Kuhl proposed that human judgments were mediated by an auditory prototype representing the typical auditory effects of [i]. Variants of the prototype hindered discrimination when the standard was the good [i] but not when it was centered on the poor standard. The monkeys did not have differential discrimination, because they have not established phonetic perception on the basis of internalized auditory prototypes.

One theory that operates by matching speech sounds to prototypes through a series of stages is *phonetic refinement theory* (Pisoni, Nusbaum, Luce, & Slowiaczek, 1985). Analysis begins with auditory sensations and shifts to higher-level processes. Speech sounds are analyzed for patterns to be matched to a memory prototype. Words are identified by successively winnowing matches between each of the phonemes and memory representations of word candidates in memory. The word's initial sound, not the first phoneme alone, establishes the set of candidates. The problem for auditory models like phonetic refinement theory is to determine whether the psychoacoustic aspects of speech sounds underlie the perception of vowels and consonants. Research over the past decade has weighed heavily against the idea the listeners can identify auditory attributes of spoken speech segments. Variations in the duration, intensity, and frequency aspects of speech are not registered as such, but they do affect the linguistic aspects of speech. Listeners can rarely resolve the precise auditory characteristics that underlie phonetic attributes (Repp, 1982). Alternatively, if the auditory model is correct, listeners should not hear phonetic segments from nonspeech stimuli. People should hear vowels and consonants in a typical auditory signal but not in segments constructed with nonspeech signals.

Remez, Rubin, Pisoni, and Carrell (1981) demonstrated that speech perception could be achieved even when the natural acoustic cues were replaced with spectra that depart greatly from those made by the vocal tract. When listeners were asked to characterize sine wave replicas of sentences, they reported hearing electronic sounds, radio interference, electronic music, and the like. However, when another group of subjects were told to transcribe synthetic speech, they wrote down the sentence, indicating that the signal could simultaneously be perceived as phonetic and auditory information. This would suggest that phonetic and auditory perceptual analyses of sounds are independent, producing what has been described as *duplex perception*, the segregation of a speech analysis from an auditory analysis (Mann, Madden, Russell, & Liberman, 1981). Evidence like that of Remez et al. (1981) suggests a shift in emphasis away from psychoacoustic properties of individual speech elements to an emphasis on coherent patterns in the entire speech signal. The evidence suggests that the analysis of superficial acoustic cues should be abandoned in order to mount a study that takes into account particular speakers, their rate of speech and linguistic goals, and modulations in individual phonetic features. The Remez et al. study also proves problematic for a modular view of speech perception because the listeners' beliefs about the stimuli influenced their impressions of it. Beliefs would not influence the process if a speech module were encapsulated with mandatory commitment. The status of a modular speech mode is a topic of much current debate (see Norris, McQueen, & Cutler, 2000; Remez, 1994).

COHORT THEORY

Cohort theory is an activation-based model of word recognition developed by Marslen-Wilson and colleagues (Marslen-Wilson, 1987, 1990; Marslen-Wilson & Tyler, 1980; Marslen-Wilson & Welsh, 1978). In an activation-type model, the item to be perceived is recognized when its memory representation has reached its activation threshold and competing representations have been inhibited or deactivated. Marslen-Wilson (1987) viewed word recognition as a process of selecting the best candidate among possible alternative candidates. The set of alternative word candidates to be eliminated is the *cohort*. Marslen-Wilson (1985, 1987) found that listeners could recognize words within 200 ms of the beginning of the word on the basis of minimal acoustic-phonetic information.

Marslen-Wilson (1987, 1990) argued that listeners are sensitive to what he called the *recognition point* of a word, which is the point at which the word emerges from other candidates. In cohort theory, word recognition is a matter of discriminating and identifying what was spoken and what was not. The process of word recognition has three phases (Marslen-Wilson, 1987). First, the word recognition system makes contact with the acoustic-phonetic representation of the speech signal. This activates a set of candidates, the *word-initial cohort*, words with similar word-initial properties. Second, a selection process is used to choose one candidate from the cohort by a process of "winner takes all." Finally, the selected item is integrated into the ongoing discourse context. Figure 3.10 illustrates how the cohort theory recognizes the word *elephant*.

Cohort theory proposes that the lexicon or mental word dictionary is contacted on a bottom-up basis. Lexical representations are accessed by the acoustic-phonetic properties of the input. The word-initial cohort contains words that have phonetically similar initial phonemes (Marslen-Wilson, 1987), as illustrated in Figure 3.10. The selection mechanism is sensitive to the acoustic-phonetic properties of the input and to word frequency, semantics, and syntactic context. Candidates that are consistent with the incoming signal are activated, and those that are inconsistent drop out. Activation is a continuous process whereby candidates are judged against other members of the cohort (Marslen-Wilson, 1990).

Cohort theory as a model of speech perception has some positive and negative features. The theory acknowledges the rapid temporal nature of speech recognition. It also accounts for the importance of word-initial information and the left-to-right nature of the process. It is efficient, allowing a word to be recognized before all the phonemes are identified, if there are no competing candidates in the cohort. But this left-to-right strategy also produces a problem for the model in cases where listeners make word-initial cohort errors, as when the initial phoneme is missing, ambiguous, or inaccurate and thus instigates the wrong set of candidates. How would listeners recover from such a mistake and perceive the correct word? To correct the shortcoming, Marslen-Wilson (1987) suggested that the items could be

/ε/	/εl/	/εl ə/	/εl ə f/	/εl ə f ə/
aesthetic	elbow	elegiac	elephant	elephant
any	elder	elegy	elephantine	_____
•	eldest	element	_____	(1)
•	eleemosynary	elemental	(2)	
ebony	elegance	elementary		
ebullition	elegiac	elephant		
echelon	elegy	elephantine		
•	element	elevate		
•	elemental	elevation		
economic	elementary	elevator		
ecstacy	elephant	elocution		
•	elephantine	eloquent		
•	elevate	_____		
element	elevation	(12)		
elephant	•			
elevate	•			
•	_____			
•	(28)			
entropy				
entry				
•				
•				
extraneous				
•				

_____
(324)

Figure 3.10. How the Word *Elephant* is Recognized, according to Cohort Theory
Phonemes are recognized categorically and on-line from left to right as they are spoken. All words inconsistent with the phoneme string are eliminated from the cohort. The number below each column represents the number of words remaining in the cohort at that point in the process. Figure from "Psychological Aspects of Speech Perception" by D. W. Massaro, in *Handbook of Psycholinguistics,* edited by Morton A. Gernsbacher, copyright 1984, Elsevier Science (USA), reproduced by permission of the publisher.

represented by features rather than phonemically; however, this model did not specify how the acoustic signal is converted into phonetic features used for word recognition. Cohort theory has not generated as much interest in speech processing as comprehensive network models have, as we see next.

THE TRACE MODEL

TRACE is a *connectionist* model of speech perception and word recognition based on McClelland and Rumelhart's (1981) interactive activation model of visual word recognition. The connectionists' metaphor for memory representations or neural networks is that information is represented as a network of parallel distributed processes (PDP). The TRACE model (Elman & McClelland, 1986; McClelland, 1991; McClelland & Elman, 1986) consists of a connected network of processing units or *nodes* that are dedicated to perceiving acoustic features, phonemes, and words. The feature nodes are connected to the phoneme nodes, and the phoneme nodes are connected to the word nodes. Nodes that have interconnections at the same level accompany these between-level connections. Connections *between* levels are facilitatory, symmetric, and bidirectional. Connections *within* levels are inhibitory; that is, they compete for perceptual activation. Interactivity is achieved because higher-level lexical (word) information can influence activation levels of subordinate phonemes. The nodes facilitate or inhibit each other on the basis of their activation levels and interconnection strengths. The interactive network for visual perception is illustrated in Figure 3.11.

TRACE provides a description of the time course of speech perception through the concept of a *trace*. A trace represents the working memory model of the network, its connections, and the temporal distribution of the speech inputs. As

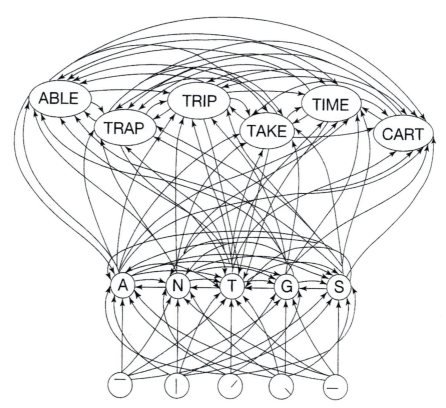

Figure 3.11. The Interactive-Activation Model of Letter Recognition Shows pattern of activation associated with T node in TRACE model.

From "An interactive-activation model of context effects in letter perception: Part 1. An account of the basic findings" by J. L. McClelland and D. Rumelhart, *Psychological Review,* 88, p. 380. Copyright © 1981 by the American Psychological Association. Reprinted with permission.

excitatory and inhibitory activation is passed through the network of nodes, the pattern of activation or trace is developed to represent the history of the spoken input prior to recognition.

TRACE is a dynamic model of the temporal process of speech recognition that has several positive features. It has bidirectional connections between different levels of analysis, accounting for bottom-up (data) and top-down (conceptual) processes involved in speech recognition. Inhibitory activation spreads within levels among inconsistent nodes, producing a winner-take-all activation. TRACE can account for problems unique to speech perception, such as phonemic restoration, ambiguous information, the segmentation problem, and categorical perception. TRACE can use high-level lexical information to resolve ambiguous phoneme segments in favor of segments that create words. The model has its weaknesses, too. First, TRACE provides for each phoneme the same amount of processing time, despite the temporal variability of speech (Klatt, 1989). Second, the model has a very small lexicon, consisting of monosyllabic words, and it is not clear how TRACE will perform with a sample of continuous more adultlike speech. TRACE continues to inspire research in speech perception and in visual word recognition studies.

Whether TRACE, cohort theory, an auditory-based model, or an updated version of MT will capture the field of speech perception is an open question at the moment.

FUTURE DIRECTIONS IN SPEECH PERCEPTION

Researchers continue to debate how speech is segmented and recognized. Norris, McQueen, and Cutler have been working on a new modular model for phonemic decision making during the recognition of spoken words. Their **Merge model** is predicated in part on the idea that feedback, an essential component of interactive models like TRACE, is *not* necessary to describe speech perception (see McQueen, Norris, & Cutler, 1999; Norris, McQueen, & Cutler, 2000). In this new bottom-up model, information flows from prelexical processing to the lexicon without top-down feedback. Phonemic decisions are based on the merging of lexical and prelexical information. The Merge model predicts lexical involvement in phonemic decisions about both words and nonwords through a process of competition between lexical hypotheses. It has extensions into research speech recognition, computational modeling, and reading.

Although the research reviewed in this chapter has focused on general characteristics of speech perception, there is evidence that information about an individual talker's voice plays a significant role in speech perception. Mullennix and Pisoni (1990) suggested that voice information is integrated with the phonetic form of a word and cannot be ignored when recognizing a spoken word. Goldinger, Pisoni, and Logan (1991) demonstrated that listeners encode the details of the speaker's voice into long-term memory and can use the information to facilitate recall. Palmeri, Goldinger, and Pisoni (1993) found that information about a speaker's voice is used in recognition judgments. These studies show that speaker-relevant information is not filtered out of lexical representations. A successful model of speech perception would have to account for the general properties of speech perception as well as these speaker-dependent effects.

One overarching problem for speech perception research is that speakers make categorical judgments on the basis of a variable set of acoustic cues. Research on speech variability has demonstrated that some sources of variability are more detrimental to speech recognition than others. Sommers, Nygaard, and Pisoni (1992) showed that words produced at multiple speaking rates were less intelligible than when the same words were produced at a single rate. Yet when words were presented at different amplitudes, they were identified as accurately as words presented at a single amplitude. These lines of research suggest that previous laboratory studies of speech perception have ignored the importance of variability in lexical representations and that this variability can be encoded in long-term memory and used to facilitate new speech patterns.

Contemporary research on speech perception is converging on several important themes (Lively et al., 1994): the activation of multiple candidates during the recognition process, determining a set of selection rules for the best candidates, the problem of translating the physical speech signal into a symbolic mental code in lexical memory, and aligning the word recognition process with the rest of cognition (e.g., learning, memory, categorization). The future of research in this area will require taking a broader perspective on the processes underlying speech perception than the previous views of speech perception.

Key Terms

acoustic cue	invariance	sensitivity effect
allophone	merge model	spectrogram
articulation	minimal pair	stress
bias effect	motor theory	synthetic speech
bottom-up processing	parallel transmission	top-down processing
categorical	Pattern-Playback	TRACE
perception	phone	transition
coarticulation	phoneme	voice onset time
cohort theory	phonemic restoration	voicing
confusability	phonetic alphabet	vowel
consonant	phonological rule	
context dependence	phonotactic rule	
distinctive features	prosody	
formant	prototype	
fundamental	segmentation	
frequency	problem	
intonation	selective adaptation	

What Lies Ahead

Chapter 4 takes up where we left off here. Here we discussed the role of acoustic and articulatory cues in speech perception, but we also noted that word knowledge affects the perceptual process. In the next chapter, we concentrate on words, word recognition, and the nature of the mental dictionary or lexicon.

Suggested Web Sites

X-ray Database for Speech Research: http://pavlov.psyc.queensu.ca/faculty/munhall/x-ray. Dynamic views of the vocal tract showing how the articulators operate in natural speech. You can actually see the places of articulation

Text-to-Speech Demonstration: http://www.bell-labs.com/project/tts/voices.html

Haskins Laboratory Site: http://www.haskins.yale.edu/Haskins/inside.html

Chapter 4
Words and Word Recognition

Critical Thinking Questions

1. What kinds of knowledge do we store in memory about words?

2. How are words related to things in the environment? To other words?

3. How are words stored in the "mental dictionary"?

4. What models have been developed to describe the mental dictionary?

5. What factors affect lexical access?

6. How do we recognize the meaning of ambiguous words?

7. What models have been developed to describe lexical access?

Exercise 4.1. Word Meaning
Before you begin reading this chapter, complete the following exercise. In your notebook, write a definition of the following terms without consulting a dictionary. What do these words mean?

contract	family	apple
ass	truth	catch

After you have written your definitions, reflect on which definitions were easy and which were difficult. How do you think ambiguity affects language processing?

Words

In this chapter, we examine our knowledge of words and how words are related to each other—that is, the structure of our mental dictionary or *lexicon*. In later chapters, we will go on to explore the many uses of words in conversations.

Psycholinguists want to know how knowledge of words is represented mentally. What is the nature of our internal lexicon? Is it set up like a dictionary? Psycholinguists also want to know how we find word meanings mentally, in the process known as lexical access. People seem to comprehend the meaning of many words without trouble but also occasionally grope for a word's meaning. In everyday tasks, lexical access is transparent and unconscious; we aren't even aware that we are doing it. Psycholinguists want to examine lexical access carefully to make it more visible.

What do words "mean"? Usually people think of a word's meaning in terms of its literal meaning or **denotation,** like what you might find in a dictionary. Words also have emotional overtones or **connotations.** *Ass* has a literal meaning in reference to an animal but also meanings in reference to a body part and a silly person. Each denotation has a different connotation. Exercise 4.1 was designed to help you reflect about the meanings of words. In the process, you may have noticed that the meaning attributed to *contract* depends on how you pronounced it or that a concrete word like *apple* was easier to define than an abstract word like *truth*. This chapter addresses the nature of words: word structure, word meaning, ambiguity, retrieval from memory, and word knowledge. First we will examine the structure of word knowledge and the relationships between words, and then we look at how we find words in the lexicon.

PHONOLOGY AND ORTHOGRAPHY

Spoken words have phonological structure and obey phonological rules, as we read in Chapter 3. Part of our knowledge of words is our awareness that they follow rules. "Real" words follow these rules, but not all strings of phonemes that follow the rules are real words (e.g., *shime*). All languages have rules for what constitute permissible strings of sounds in syllables and words, but the rules vary from language to language.

Written words also have rules that specify what constitutes a permissible letter string. **Orthography** is a method of mapping sounds onto written symbols. Orthographic rules govern spelling-to-sound correspondences. Languages differ in the regularity of the correspondence between spelling and sound. English is not as regular as Serbo-Croatian but is more regular than Hebrew. Our knowledge of words includes their phonological and orthographic patterns. We use phonology to recognize many written words.

What role does phonology play in word recognition? Readers seem to find word meaning in one of two ways, either indirectly by pronouncing the words they read or by accessing word meaning directly from print without phonology. The *indirect* route suggests that we translate spelling into sounds to find meaning. The *direct* route suggests that we map the orthographic string into a lexical representation, which can later be used to guide pronunciation but is not necessary for access. Word pronunciation can be performed by determining pronunciation via orthography (Venesky, 1970) or by directly accessing lexical representation via whole words.

One important factor underlying the efficacy of the indirect route is the degree to which the orthography of a language produces regular spelling-to-sound correspondences. Serbo-Croatian language has a straightforward orthography-to-phonology correspondence. A reader can rely on the indirect route because it reliably produces the correct response (Frost, Katz, & Bentin, 1987). English, however, has a far less obvious relationship between orthography and phonology. Hebrew is even less regular than English. In other words, languages vary in the degree to which spelling corresponds to sound. As correspondence between letters and sounds decreases, the effect on a speeded pronunciation task should increase. Regular languages should have faster pronunciation times than irregular languages. Frost et al. (1987) found larger frequency and lexicality effects in Hebrew than in English, and they found Serbo-Croatian to have the least amount of effect. Cross-linguistic comparisons support the notion that the dual routes are more probable in languages that have less predictable mappings between orthography and phonology.

We will address this issue of orthography in more detail in Chapter 7 when we explore reading processes. For now, it is important that we recognize that part of word knowledge is whether the word obeys regular spelling-to-sound rules or not. Another facet of word knowledge is a word's grammatical class.

GRAMMATICAL CLASS

A word's meaning contains information about its grammatical class, part of speech, or syntactic category. Words that come from the same syntactic category and are synonyms can be substituted for each other in sentences. Nouns, verbs, adjectives, adverbs, pronouns, prepositions, and conjunctions are traditional syntactic categories. Grammatical rules allow us to specify what are valid word strings in a language based on syntactic category. Syntactic categories can be grouped into two large classes of words: **open-class words** and **closed-class words.**

When you hear a sentence like *Jack and Jill went up the hill to fetch a pail of water,* you understand the basic content of the sentence through words like *Jack, went, hill, fetch,* and *water.* Content words form an open class of words consisting of nouns, adjectives, verbs, and adverbs. A language must have a large and expandable set of open-class words. Open-class words are constantly evolving due to sociocultural changes that demand the invention of new words and cause others to become obsolete. Open-class words are ordered within sentences around a smaller and closed set of function words. Closed-class words are oriented toward function, not content. They consist of articles, prepositions, and conjunctions. In our example, the function words are *and, up, the, a,* and *of.* Function words remain fairly stable over time. The grammatical classification of a word and the grammatical restrictions on its use are part of the knowledge we have about words.

MORPHOLOGY

What are the building blocks of word meaning? To answer that question, we need to establish a set of terms that can be used to describe words and word structure or *morphology.* **Morphology** is the study of the structure of words. *Morphological rules* are rules for the combination of *morphemes* to form stems and words. You will recall that a morpheme is the smallest unit of linguistic meaning or function. What you consider "root words" are called **free morphemes.** *Depend* is a free morpheme. Free morphemes are contrasted with **bound morphemes.** Bound morphemes are units of meaning that are attached to words. They have meaning but cannot stand alone. Bound morphemes must be attached to words as prefixes or suffixes. *Independence* has two bound morphemes: *in-,* meaning "not," and *-ence,* meaning "quality" or "condition." The bound morphemes are attached to the free morpheme.

Notice that the *in-* morpheme changes the meaning of the word *dependence* entirely. Bound morphemes that change the meaning of the root word are called **derivational morphemes.** Derivational morphemes are morphemes that are added to root morphemes to produce new words or stems. In contrast, **inflectional morphemes** are bound grammatical morphemes that are added to complete words according to rules of syntax. Inflectional morphemes do not change the basic meaning of a word, but they do change minor aspects of the meaning, such as tense (e.g., *-ed* added to verbs ending in unvoiced consonants to create the past tense), number (e.g., *-s* added to nouns to pluralize), or possession (e.g., *-'s* added to nouns to indicate ownership). So morphemes are the building blocks of word meaning that are combined according to morphological rules and grammatical or syntactic constraints.

This introduction covered some of the basic factors that make up our knowledge about words and their meaning. Another issue surrounding word meaning is the relationship between a word and what it points to in the world. We cover this issue next.

Words and Reference

Semantics is the study of the linguistic meaning of morphemes, words, phrases, and sentences. The field of semantics raises basic questions about words and their meanings. What do words mean? What is the relationship between a word and its meaning? One way to define word meaning is to look at what words refer to in the environment. Another way to define meaning is by comparing a word to related words.

At first glance, a word like *umbrella* would seem to have a one-to-one relationship with its meaning, but the reality is in fact more complex. *Umbrella* has more than one meaning; for example, it can refer to an object to repel rain or more abstractly to any protective force or influence. Thus even with a simple noun like *umbrella*, there is an imperfect relationship between the word and its meanings. **Reference** is the aspect of meaning that relates words to objects or events in the environment. When we consider words and their meanings in reference theory, the thing named is called the *referent*. The act of naming is *reference*. *Sense* is a related concept that refers to the relationship between words and other words, for example, between *umbrella* and *protective force*. Sense is the part of the meaning of a word that together with the context determines the referent. Knowing the sense of *president* (of the United States) allows one to determine that the referent in a conversation about "the president" is George W. Bush.

Some things in the environment have no words to describe them. There is no single word in English that refers to a dead tree, although there is one for a dead body, *corpse*. There is no word in English for the amount of toothpaste one puts on a toothbrush. We can call it a *squiggle, blob, chunk, swipe,* or *nurdle* of toothpaste, but there is no prescribed word for that amount. This is an instance of a referent without a label. Problems with reference occur when naming things in the environment and when translating from one language to another.

Some words cannot be translated into another language. What do we say when one language makes a distinction that does not occur in the second language? The lack of equivalent words poses a problem during translation. For example, Yiddish has a rich lexicon of words to describe ineptness, each with a slightly different sense, including *schlemiel, schlimazel, shlump, shmegegge, shmendrick, shmo,* and *shmuck* (Rosten, 1968). How do we translate these words into English, which does not make these distinctions? We can only give approximations of them in English.

What is the relationship between words and the things they refer to? Some references seem to have been made through *onomatopoeia*, in which the sound of the word bears some relationship to its referent. *Plop, swish, snap, crackle,* and *pop* are some examples. Most words are not onomatopoetic. Recall from Chapter 1 that the relationship between words and objects is arbitrary. We can decide that the name for a cow is *glerf* or *table* if we want. The relationship between a name and its referent is arbitrary and context-dependent: What we decide to call some object, event, or relationship depends on the context in which it occurs.

According to *reference theory*, a word means what it points to in the environment. On a simple level, word meaning must be understood by what is discussed locally. *Clock* means a particular clock that we are discussing in a situation. That particular clock might have a different reference if there are other clocks in the room or the building. We might have to refer to it as a *cuckoo clock* to distinguish it from others in the environment. The context provides the link between words and their referents. Labov (1973) demonstrated the influence of context on reference by presenting subjects with pictures of cups and bowls. Some of the referents appeared to be part cup and part bowl: They had a handle like a cup but a wide, low brim like a bowl. The subjects categorized the ambiguous object as a "cup" if it was said to hold tea but as a "bowl" if it was said to hold soup.

Another way to describe the meaning of a word is through *definition.* Definitions state the conventional ways to interpret a word. It is convenient to think of the meaning of words as stable, like definitions provided in a dictionary. For example, *plant* can mean a factory, a small leafy flower or bush, or a person deployed as part of a plot, among other things. The meaning of *plant* is all of these definitions; which one is understood depends on the context. In an industrial context, *plant* would be recognized to mean one thing, and in a horticultural context, it would mean something entirely different.

An alternative way to describe meaning in semantics is to define a concept as a bundle of **semantic features.** The semantic features of the concept "bird" are "has wings," "flies," "chirps," "has a beak," "lays eggs," and so on. Concepts that are similar have overlapping semantic features. The bundle of features for "bird" is similar to those used to define "insect" but very different from the bundle used to describe "games." Insects are similar to birds, but neither of these concepts has features like games. Definitions and lists of semantic features are conventional ways of describing a word's meaning; that is more or less how dictionaries are structured. But is the human lexicon structured like a dictionary or perhaps a thesaurus? The issue of interest to the psycholinguist is whether semantic features are psychologically real. Do they affect the way we process words or find their meanings? The answer to that question depends on how we conceptualize the structure of the internal lexicon, which we consider later in this chapter. But first we must address the notion that words have personal meaning and personal significance, as well as conventional meaning.

Subjective Aspects of Meaning

Contemporary psycholinguistics has focused on conventional meaning at the expense of personal or subjective aspects of word meaning. Other areas of psychology have a long history of studying how subjective uses of speech underlie personality, social, mental health, and psychodynamic processes. A comprehensive theory of word meaning must incorporate subjective and emotional aspects of words. Because words have personal emotional significance, words and reactions to them become tools for a therapist to examine how a person relates to his or her environment. The **word association** method was developed to find these links. Word associations are important because of what they reveal about word meaning.

WORD ASSOCIATION

Why would a psychoanalyst use a word association paradigm to try to understand a patient's unconscious inner life? In what way would a patient's response to a word reveal something about his or her personality? Carl Jung pioneered the use of word association as a technique to assess personality. Jung's elaborate experimental investigations led to widespread adoption of word association because associations brought emotional problems and other dimensions of personality to the fore. His work influenced Sigmund Freud in Vienna and American psychologists to use the association technique in psychoanalysis. Because reaction times and physiological measures can be studied, the word association technique pioneered and refined by Jung appealed to American experimental psychologists, as well as clinicians. Jung thought that the word associates would reveal how patients were blocking inner problems that he called *complex indicators*. A **complex** is a group of suppressed thoughts and feelings associated with guilt that produces a pattern of emotionally laden, delayed, or bizarre responses to words such as *mother* or *sex* (Jung, 1910, Jung & Riklin, 1904). Jung (1910) reported the case of a young wife who was jealous of her husband and had recurring fears about separation. This complex manifested itself on the word association test through unusual and delayed responses to the words *marry, contented, pray, happiness, fear,* and *false.*

Psychotherapy is predicated on the assumption that one's speech reveals one's inner conflicts. A person's emotional experience becomes attached to a word's meaning, and word associations reveal the nature of one's subjective associations. In **free association,** a subject is given a word and must respond with the first word that comes to mind. The free association method is assumed to be context-free. It taps how a person associates concepts in memory. These associations reveal information about both the structure of semantic relationships in the speaker's language and the speaker's subjective organization of words. Deese (1970) proposed that the free associations to a stimulus word represented everything the person thought of when presented with the word. I would add that associations go beyond semantic features and include emotional and physiological responses as well.

American clinicians Kent and Rossanoff (1910) adopted Jung's word association test as a part of clinical diagnosis. They created a set of word association tables based on the responses of one thousand normal subjects to a list of one hundred words. For example, the most frequent responses to the word *chair* were *table, seat, sit,* and *furniture* (see Table 4.1). These four responses accounted for half of the associations to the target word. The word also evoked idiosyncratic responses such as *beauty, idleness, teacher,* and *posture.* Bizarre word associations are characteristic of schizophrenic speech and may indicate psychogenic or neurological problems.

Miller (1995) noted that the Kent-Rossanoff data demonstrated that a single word activates a wide range of lexical knowledge. These data reveal associative relationships. The most frequent response to *chair* is *table*, a coordinate word, and both are hyponyms or subordinate terms, of *furniture. Rocker* is a hyponym of *chair. Furniture,* also a frequent associate, is a superordinate of *chair.* Some responses represented attributes of chairs, such as *wood, comfort, hard,* or *soft.* Some responses are parts of chairs, such as *seat, cushion, leg,* or *arm.* There are also responses that indicate

Table 4.1. Frequency of Word Associations for 1,000 Men and Women
Probe Word: CHAIR

191	table
127	seat
107	sit
83	furniture
56	sitting
49	wood
45	rest
38	stool
21	comfort
17	rocker
15	rocking
13	bench
12	cushion
11	legs
10	floor
9	desk, room
8	comfortable
7	ease, leg
6	easy, sofa, wooden
5	couch, hard, Morris, seated, soft
4	arm, article, brown, high
3	cane, convenience, house, large, lounge, low, mahogany, person, resting, rung, settee, useful
2	broken, hickory, home, necessity, oak, rounds, seating, use
1	back, beauty, bed, book, boy, bureau, caning, careful, carpet, cart, color, crooked, cushions, feet, foot, footstool, form, Govenor Winthrop, hair, idleness, implement, joiner, lunch, massive, mission, myself, object, occupy, office, people, place, placed, plant, platform, pleasant, pleasure, posture, reading, rubber, size, spooning, stand, stoop, study, support, tables, talk, teacher, timber, tool, upholstered, upholstery, white

what chairs do or what can be done with them, such as *sit, rest, comfort, ease,* or *seated.* Miller pointed out that aside from the idiosyncratic responses, adults tend to give four types of associative responses to noun probes: (1) superordinate, coordinate, and subordinate terms that arrange nouns as part of a taxonomic hierarchy, (2) attributive terms that modify values of attributes, (3) relationships that name a part of the whole or refer to the whole to which the part belongs, or (4) functional terms that describe what ends things serve or what is normally done with them.

In experiments with word association with children and adults, predictable patterns of responses have been observed (Jenkins, 1970; Palermo, 1963). Subjects are most likely to respond with a word that is similar in meaning (Ervin, 1957). Adults respond with a word that is in the same grammatical class as the stimulus word, but not all children do so. *Needle* will evoke words like *thread, pin,* or *sew. Doctor* will evoke *nurse, buy* evokes *sell, chair* evokes *table,* and so on. If the stimulus word is part of a word pair, subjects will respond with the mate; for example, *mother* evokes *father,* and *salt* evokes *pepper.* These and the other studies mentioned support the idea that meaning and grammatical class are the main dimensions of lexical organization and lexical access.

Exercise 4.2. **The Remote Associates Test**

The **Remote Associates Test (RAT)** was designed by Mednick (1962; Mednick & Mednick, 1967) to measure verbal creativity through word association. RAT is designed to measure individual differences in the ability considered fundamental to creative thinking. It is based strictly on "associative" interpretations, seeing the relationships between seemingly "remote" ideas. Subjects are presented with three words and are asked to find the term that connects them. For example, given *cookies, sixteen,* and *heart,* the remote associate is *sweet.* Try the following (answers appear at the end of the chapter):

stop, petty, sneak	elephant, lapse, vivid
lick, sprinkle, mines	shopping, washer, picture
stalk, trainer, king	sea, home, stomach
walker, main, sweeper	

Review Question

What is free association, and why is it used in psychotherapy?

THE SEMANTIC DIFFERENTIAL

To measure the affective or connotative meanings of words, Osgood, Suci, and Tannenbaum (1957) developed the **semantic differential** (SD). They conceived of meaning as a "mediated" response occurring between a stimulus and a response that was established through learning. One could tap this mediated affective response by asking subjects to rate how they felt about words on bipolar rating scales. Subjects are presented with a word such as *lazy* or *baby* and asked to rate the word on twenty 7-point bipolar scales (e.g., *weak-strong, happy-sad, tense-relaxed*). Our emotional feelings about *baby* would be indicated by how we rated the meaning of the word on the bipolar scales:

baby

weak - - - - - - - strong

active - - - - - - - passive

good - - - - - - - bad

A word like *baby* would tend to be rated weak, active, and good, while a word like *lazy* would come out closer to the weak, passive, and bad ends of the scales.

Using a data analysis technique known as factor analysis, it was found that the twenty adjective pairs were measuring three semantic groups: evaluation (*good-bad, happy-sad, beautiful-ugly*), potency (*strong-weak, brave-cowardly, hard-soft*), and activity (*active-passive, fast-slow, tense-relaxed*). Each group represents a different "factor" or aspect of emotional meaning. This means that a word was given very similar ratings on each of the adjective pairs *within* each of the three groups but different ratings on scales from the other two groups. These three dimensions represent connotative building blocks of word meaning. Words are most likely to differ on the evaluation dimension, reflecting our basic positive or negative reactions to objects and events. The SD has been conducted in a variety of languages and provides consistent results cross-linguistically. One of the problems with the technique is that it measures the affective reactions a word elicits but not its denotative meaning. It tells us how we feel about *mother* but not what *mother* denotes.

The psycholinguistic methods used to measure affective or connotative meaning are not as highly developed as those developed to measure the denotative aspects of words. However, several related affective measurement techniques are available. Emotional correlates can be assessed with physiological responses such as galvanic skin response, polygraph ("lie detector") measures, and pupillary response (Jay, 2000). These are more on-line (the response is recorded at the same time the word is presented rather than after the word has been accessed) measures of affect compared to the SD, which is an abstract and postemotional response measure of affect.

To this point, we have covered the nature of knowledge about words, how words are related to referents in the world, and how subjective experience influences associations between words. Now we move on to look at the structure of the internal lexicon.

Models of the Internal Lexicon

The words you know are in your mental lexicon. Two main questions about the lexicon occupy most of the remainder of the chapter. The question we address first is how words are associated with each other. After looking at models the lexicon, we address the second question, how we access words in the mental lexicon.

One might think of the lexicon as having a dictionary-type arrangement or as a thesaurus with synonyms and antonyms. Miller's (1995) word association research indicates that there are predictable relationships between a word and its associates. Most modern models of semantic memory are predicated on the idea that words are arranged in networks and that concepts are linked on a variety of levels (semantic, phonological, perceptual, and emotional). One notable exception to the network idea is the connectionist conceptualization of words. In Seidenberg and McClelland's (1989) **connectionist model,** there is no lexicon to be searched for word meaning. Instead, words are activated by input from connecting sublexical nodes, as discussed at the end of this chapter. The point is that not all models use a lexicon to explain semantic memory. A universally acceptable model of the mental lexicon—if there is one—has yet to emerge.

THE HIERARCHICAL NETWORK MODEL

Semantic memory is the part of memory that contains words, concepts, and facts about the world. The conceptual metaphor of semantic memory as a word network is not coincidental. Early models of semantic memory were formulated in the context of a computer-based metaphor for human memory, which linked words to each other and attempted to eliminate duplication of information due to limited storage. Collins and Quillian (1972) pioneered a model of knowledge analogous to computer storage that employed this principle of "cognitive economy" such that mental features of concepts were stored in only one place. For example, the knowledge that birds have wings is stored with the concept "bird," which eliminates storing "has wings" with every species of bird.

Using words from the animal kingdom, Collins and Quillian (1969, 1972) developed a hierarchical network model of semantic memory. A hierarchy is a classification system with superordinate and subordinate concepts. Figure 4.1 illustrates the hierarchical structure envisioned by Collins and Quillian. They assumed that memory was organized like a hierarchy of concepts with general terms at the top and

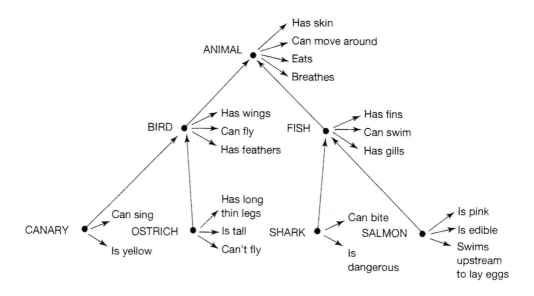

Figure 4.1. Collins and Quillian's Hierarchical Structure of Memory
Note. Figure from "Retrieval Time from Semantic Memory," by A. M. Collins & M. R. Quillian in *Journal of Verbal Learning and Verbal Behavior*, Volume 8, 240–247, copyright 1969, Elsevier Science (USA), reproduced by permission of the publisher.

subordinate, specific terms lower in the hierarchy. We might find branches of the hierarchy, such as *bird, fish, canary,* and *shark,* as we moved from top to bottom. Each *node* or juncture in the hierarchy represents a different concept. At the juncture of each node is stored the semantic features of the node. *Animal* stores the feature "has skin." *Salmon* stores "is pink." With each kind of animal are stored the semantic features specific to that instance (e.g., color, size, mating habits, song). More general semantic features ("breathes," "has skin") about animals were assumed to be attached to nodes at the top rather than with each instance, producing cognitive economy.

Collins and Quillian produced a set of **semantic verification** experiments to test their model. The semantic verification technique presents subjects with sentences in the form *An A is a B,* and the subject has to respond as quickly as possible if the sentence is true or false. *A canary is a bird* is an example of a true sentence, and *A chair is a bird* is an example of a false sentence. Subjects were presented with sentences containing information about animals that might be directly linked to them or that had to be accessed by traversing to another node in the hierarchy. It was assumed that the time it took to verify the sentences would indicate how far one was traveling mentally in the hierarchy. More immediate information would be accessed quickly relative to inferential information, which would take longer to find. *A bird can breathe* should take longer to verify than *An animal can breathe* because one has to traverse an extra link to get to the information in the first example. The predictions turned out to be true. A plot of the reaction times from the study appears in Figure 4.2. The data produced a *distance effect,* that is, the farther A is from B in the hierarchy, the longer it takes to verify *An A is a B* or *An A has a B.*

Although the initial findings were supportive, when other researchers attempted to verify the assumptions of the hierarchical model, support was not so clear. While the idea of cognitive economy is appealing for computers with limited memory storage, human memory is not necessarily subject to the same restriction. Humans have "cheap" and plentiful memory storage for word association but "expensive" attention-demanding cognitive processing functions. Alternative explanations for Collins and Quillian's data emerged. For example, Conrad (1972) argued that the "distance effects" in the hierarchical model were not based on mental distance but rather that reaction times were a function of the strength of association between the two terms in the sentence. *A canary can sing* is verified more quickly than *A canary has skin* because "has skin" is rarely associated with canaries while "singing" is. He argued against the notion of semantic distance in favor of the frequency of association between two terms, similar to word association effects. So while the animal taxonomy might provide a workable representation for discussing the relationships between one species and another in the biological sciences, the hierarchical model does not represent how the average person stores information about animals in memory, nor does it account for different arrangements of categorical information. No single organizational structure applies to all semantic domains. Fillenbaum and Rapoport (1971) demonstrated that while some categories are arranged hierarchically, others (e.g., odors) are not.

Another explanation for the verification task data was based on the notion of **typicality.** Typicality refers to the degree to which an instance of a taxonomic

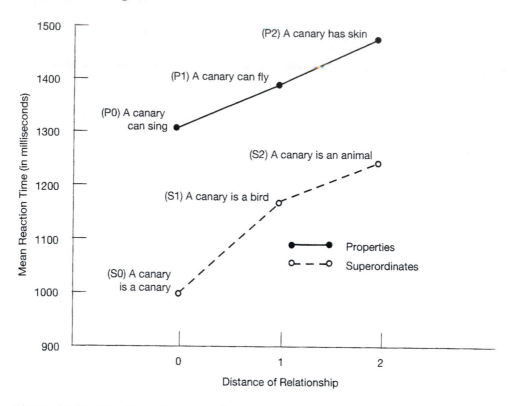

Figure. 4.2. Reaction Times for Answering Questions about Animals
Note. Figure from "Retrieval Time from Semantic Memory" by A. M. Collins & M. R. Quillian in *Journal of Verbal Learning and Verbal Behavior,* Volume 8, 240–247, copyright 1969, Elsevier Science (USA), reproduced by permission of the publisher.

category is a typical member of the category. Rosch (1973) and Rips, Shoben, and Smith (1973) argued that not all members of a semantic category are equally representative. Some members are more typical than others. For example, a robin is a very typical bird, but an ostrich is not. If you ask people to give an example of a bird, they usually say "robin" or "sparrow" but rarely "ostrich." They also respond more quickly to typical instances than to nontypical instances. Using sentence verification procedure, Rips et al. demonstrated that more typical members of a category are verified faster than atypical members. These results cast doubt on the hierarchical nature of the model because some members would have to be associated more closely to a subordinate node than others.

A third problem with the hierarchical model was the *category size effect*. In a taxonomy, the category *mammals* is a smaller category than *animals*. The animal category has more members and should produce longer verification times than decisions about mammals. Smith, Shoben, and Rips (1974) uncovered problematic results for the hierarchy model. They found that subjects verified *A dog is an animal* more quickly than *A dog is a mammal* even though *animal* is higher on the taxonomic scale than *mammal*. This runs counter to the category size effect and brings more doubt about the hierarchical model. One would have to employ some notion of associative strength or parallel search to account for this reverse category size effect. Although the original model had its flaws, it set the stage for more valid models of semantic memory.

THE SPREADING ACTIVATION MODEL

The **spreading activation model** (Collins & Loftus, 1975) is an improvement on the rigid hierarchical conceptualization of semantic information. The spreading activation model assumes that words are arranged in networks of nodes, but not hierarchically. All information is represented at the node level. Associated concepts, for example, "red" and "rose," are associated by links between nodes. The closer the relationship between concepts, the shorter the link. This appears in Figure 4.3 as a spider-web network rather than as a hierarchy. Properties of such concepts as "red" are treated as concepts and are represented as nodes in the network. The relationship between one node and another is determined by node length and by its place in the network. Related concepts are clustered together (e.g., "colors," "flowers," "vehicles") where semantic similarity is represented by distance. Physical closeness and number of interlinking nodes indicate semantic similarity.

Spreading activation refers to the idea that finding one concept in the network will activate concepts linked to it. When "truck" is activated, "car" and "vehicle" are activated, but to a lesser degree. The activation of one node spreads out to related concepts like a sound wave ripples outward from its source in all directions at once. The farther it travels, the weaker it becomes. The differential node lengths and clustering of concepts can account for the strength of association and typicality effects that were problematic for the Collins and Quillian model. Notice that the design of the spreading activation model is at the level of concepts. The underlying physical aspects of concepts (letters, acoustics) are not represented; neither are more general contextual or syntactic properties. The model fails to provide for the role of phonetic and feature information used to access words or how words are activated by the communication context. To overcome some of these difficulties, a more comprehensive spreading activation model has been proposed by Levelt and associates (Bock & Levelt, 1994; Levelt, 1989).

Bock and Levelt (1994) developed a lexical network model that represents word knowledge at three levels. A portion of the network is illustrated in Figure 4.4. The highest level is the *conceptual* level, which represents concepts such as "goat" and "sheep." Conceptual nodes are linked to other nodes through a variety of relationships similar to those in the Collins and Loftus model. The second level is the *lemma* level, which represents the syntactic aspects of words. In the Figure 4.4, *sheep* is represented as a noun and its gender in French is represented. The third level is the *lexeme* level, which represents the phonological properties of each word or lexeme. A lexeme is a word entry in the lexicon. For example, *sheep* is represented phonemically as /šip/. The three levels of representation allow the model to

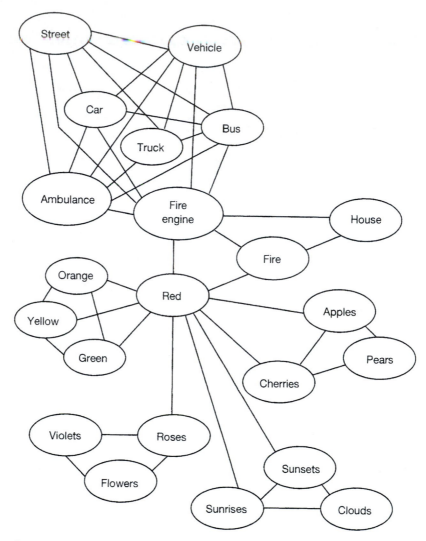

Figure 4.3. A Spreading Activation Model
Note. From "A Spreading Activation Theory of Semantic Processing" by A. M. Collins &
E. F. Loftus, 1975, *Psychological Review,* 82, p. 412. Copyright © 1975 by the American
Psychological Association. Reprinted with permission.

account for confusions that people make perceiving words or speaking words that
sound the same. It will account for cases where people have some sense of what a
word means and its syntactic category but cannot pronounce its lexeme (Brown &
McNeill, 1966).

Bock and Levelt's spreading activation model is more comprehensive than
Collins and Loftus's model because it accounts for phonological, syntactic, morphological, and conceptual information associated with word knowledge. Both activation models emphasize the sense of word meanings but put less emphasis on
their referential properties.

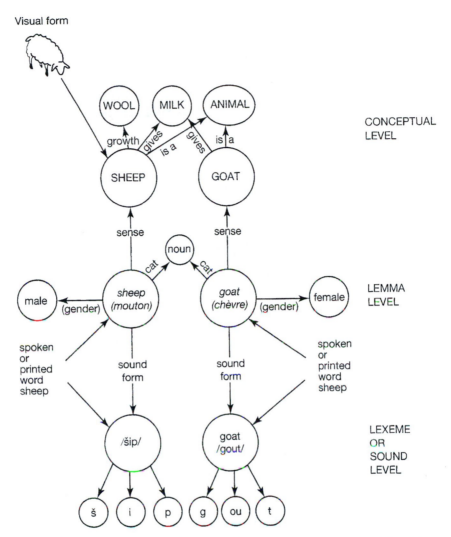

Figure 4.4. Part of the Lexical Network The arrows show connections within the network, not information flow.
Note. Figure from "Language production: Grammatical encoding" by Bock, K., & Levelt, W., in *Handbook of Psycholinguistics*, edited by Morton A. Gernsbacher, copyright 1994, Elsevier Science (USA), reproduced by permission of the publisher.

THE SEMANTIC FEATURE MODEL

Semantic feature models assume that concepts can be defined through a list of attributes or semantic features. In the wake of problems with the early hierarchical models, Smith et al. (1974) argued for a feature comparison model to explain the results of the sentence verification experiments. This model does not rely on a hierarchical taxonomy. Instead, the semantic feature model proposes that each concept is assumed to possess two levels of features: those that are necessary to *define* the concepts, as an instance of the category, and those that are *characteristics* associated with the concept but are not necessary to define it. For example, the defining features of *robin* include "has wings," "has feathers," and "has a beak." The characteristic features are more readily associated with robins such as "has a red breast," "eats worms," and "lays blue eggs."

Smith et al. (1974) believed that a two-stage feature comparison model could explain the results of the semantic verification experiments. The model is illustrated in Figure 4.5. If a participant is presented with a sentence such as *A robin is a bird,* the first stage compares the overall feature match-up of *bird* with *robin.* If many of the features overlap or if none of them do, either case would lead to a quick response. Since there is a great overlap of features between *bird* and *robin,* this results in a quick "true." A sentence like *A chair is a bird* produces almost no overlap and results in a quick "false." A second stage of comparisons is needed when there is a moderate degree of feature overlap in the first stage. Here only the defining features are compared. *An ostrich is a bird* will result in a defining feature count, resulting in a slow "true," and *A whale is a fish* will result in a slow "false" because there are many similarities between fish and whales, although the latter are mammals.

The feature comparison model will account for category size, distance, and typicality effects on the basis of feature overlap. One real problem with the model is whether features exist or not; It is possible that category judgments can be made without them. Another problem with the feature list idea is that it does not exhaust all we know about concepts. The semantic models to this point have considered the lexicon in isolation of other types of knowledge, for example, skills, sensory and perceptual information, and imagery. The next model of semantic memory attempts to place word knowledge within a larger context of knowledge and behavior.

THE ACT MODEL OF COMPLEX COGNITION

One of the most comprehensive models of semantic memory is John R. Anderson's **ACT model** (1983, 1993, 1996). ACT meant "adaptive control of thought" in the original model and "adaptive character of thought" in the updated 1996 version. Anderson intended ACT to cover the entire network of cognitions. It includes knowledge networks made up of propositional, imaging, spatial, and temporal information about actions, events, general semantics, and personal and autobiographical information. The network theory has three basic components: working memory, declarative memory, and production memory. The working memory component operates as a scratch pad, keeping track of information and outcomes. Declarative memory is a network that includes both semantic and episodic (autobiographical) information, each having different types of nodes. Semantic networks use type nodes to organize conceptual information, while episodic networks use token nodes to copy spatiotemporal information.

Anderson suggests that there are three types of knowledge codes in declarative memory. Abstract propositional representations are useful for verbal and sym-

Knowledge in Subject's Memory

Birds: flies, eats worms, is small, has feathers*, has wings*, builds nests, lives in trees

Robin: flies, eats worms, is small, has feathers*, has wings*, has red breast*, chirps, builds nests

Ostrich: can put head in the sand*, is tall, is clumsy, has wings*, has feathers*

*indicates defining feature

Feature Comparison Process

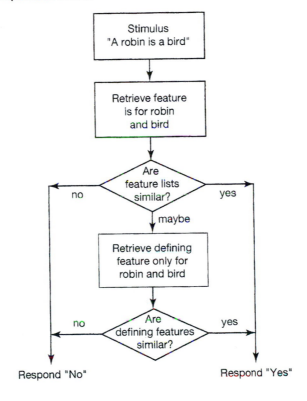

Figure 4.5. Feature Comparison Process
Note. From "Knowledge in Subject's Memory" from E. E. Smith et al., *Psychological Review,* 81, p. 222. Copyright © 1974 by the American Psychological Association. Adapted with permission.

bolic concepts and relationships. Temporal strings are used to code the order of a set of items. Spatial images are used to code spatial configurations of patterns or events. Working memory handles both new and old information. New information is stored in declarative memory through working memory. Stored information can be retrieved from declarative memory and copied into working memory. Semantic knowledge is represented in schemalike units called *chunks.* A potential chunk encoding of the letter *H* according to ACT (1996) is

Object

Isa H

Left vertical	bar 1
Right vertical	bar 2
Horizontal	bar 3

Lexical meaning is associated with a rich semantic and procedural network of concepts and skills (other networks, such as that of Collins and Loftus, operate primarily on the lexical level). The knowledge of procedures is stored in the production memory component of ACT. In this component, ACT holds the information used to carry out certain procedures, for example, tying one's shoelaces or computing mathematical sums. Procedural knowledge is knowledge that is displayed in our behavior without our being conscious of it. It is represented in units called *productions,* represented as rules or if-then statements (e.g., if the goal is to add two digits d_1 and d_2 in a column and $d_1 + d_2 = d_3$, then set as a subgoal to write d_3 in that column). Simple encodings of objects in the environment or transformations of production rules create individual units of knowledge. From a large knowledge database, the units appropriate to the environment are selected for activation. Figure 4.6 is a graphic display of a chunk encoding the fact that $3 + 4 = 7$.

One of the basic assumptions of ACT is that the recognition of a visual pattern from a set of features is identical to the process of *categorizing* the object, given the set of features. Employing a higher level of lexical processing, Anderson (1996) demonstrated how ACT could use history and context to learn the association between words that are used in the *New York Times* or in language databases (see Schooler, 1993). For example, during one time period, the word *AIDS* had a 1.8 percent probability of appearing in a *New York Times* headline, but if the word *virus* appeared in the headline, the probability of occurrence of *AIDS* rises to 75 percent. A similar pattern is found in the CHILDES database of children's speech with the words *play* and *game. Play* has less than a 1 percent probability of appearing in an utterance, but if the word *game* appears in the utterance, the probability of *play* climbs to 45 percent. ACT will learn the likelihood ratios of words and their associates and then activate chunk structures that are appropriate to the environment. The activation levels are sensitive to likelihood ratios similar to the word association data discussed previously.

The most attractive aspect of ACT is that it is a comprehensive network of information not only about words but also about living in the world. There is no reason to doubt that ACT could be expanded to include cultural and emotional information. If ACT can learn to tie shoelaces, it can store general information about the human body. It would be reasonable to include in ACT kinesthetic (body movement) information and emotional or physiological reactions.

Network Representation of an ACT Chunk

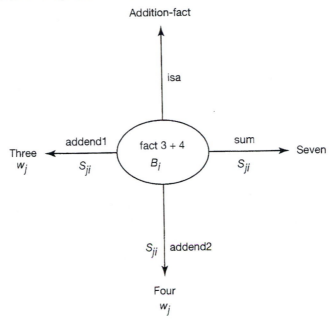

Figure 4.6. Network Representation of an ACT Chunk
Note. From "Network Representation of an ACT-R Chunk" from J. R. Anderson, *American Psychologist,* 51(4), p. 356. Copyright © 1996 by the American Psychological Association. Reprinted with permission.

The models of the mental lexicon have evolved substantially over the years, thanks to work in philosophy, linguistics, psychology, and computer simulation. Let us now look at a contemporary computer model of lexical information and word meaning.

WORDNET: AN ELECTRONIC LEXICAL DATABASE

The computer has revolutionized how cognitive science research is conducted. It has spurred new efforts to understand how the human mind works. Language databases are available to influence theories of the lexicon by providing evidence about ambiguity, frequency of occurrence, and selection preferences. The union of computational resources and linguistic theory has evolved into a number of natural-language-processing projects. Any theory of the lexicon must withstand the tests of computational treatments.

Cognitive psychologists and psycholinguists have formulated word meaning in terms of networks, diagrams with nodes to represent relations between meaning. **WordNet** is an exemplary model of a self-contained electronic lexical database that evolved from an electronic dictionary (Fellbaum, 1998). It lets readers explore words on the basis of semantic, not alphabetic, similarities. WordNet has a hierarchical structure that is motivated by theories of human knowledge organization and artificial intelligence. The basic unit of WordNet is the word, but it also contains collocations, idiomatic phrases, compounds, and phrasal verbs. WordNet does not decompose words into smaller units like a dictionary. Also unlike a dictionary, WordNet has entries such as *bad person* that cannot be reduced to a single word. WordNet separates words into syntactic categories, using scripts or frames (Schank & Abelson, 1977) to build the lexicon with verbs and nouns, and preserves structural and semantic relations among words in a particular context—for example, concepts used in economics are not treated as separate words. Instead, concepts like "buying" and "selling" are considered as part of a common "commercial transaction" frame.

WordNet can be used to analyze text and derive the meaning of the words by pruning complex words (removing inflections, suffixes, and affixes) until the lexeme is found. Although the database is built on words with similar meanings or synonyms, these "synsets" were not adequate to keep word meanings distinct. WordNet's design resembles a thesaurus in that a synset consists of all words that express a given concept. But unlike a thesaurus, the relationships between concepts and words are made explicit and labeled. The user selects the relationship of interest to move from one concept to the next. This hierarchical principle assumes that nouns are contained in a single hierarchy (Collins & Loftus, 1975). WordNet divides nouns into several categories, each with a different *unique beginner*. A unique beginner is a primitive semantic component in a compositional theory. Some unique beginners in the noun hierarchy are *animal, body, event, feeling, plant, shape,* and *time*. A representation of the relationships in the noun hierarchies based on unique beginners is illustrated in Figure 4.7.

WordNet is a work in progress that can be used for comparisons with psycholinguistic models of the lexicon. The project does have its lexical access problems. One has been dubbed the "tennis problem": Because WordNet focuses on the semantics of words and concepts rather than the semantics of discourse, no links reveal the shared role of words in a discourse topic. WordNet does not link *ball, net,* and *racket* in a way that shows that they are part of a concept like "court game." It would not show that *doctor, hospital,* and *HMO* are linked by a concept like "medical treatment."

CONCLUSIONS ABOUT THE MENTAL LEXICON

Psycholinguists and computational linguists have learned that word meaning cannot be understood through morphology alone. According to many scholars cited in this discussion, words and their meanings are better understood as parts of a network of associations between concepts with nodes and links that mark semantic relationships. Scholars try to understand a speaker's knowledge about language by

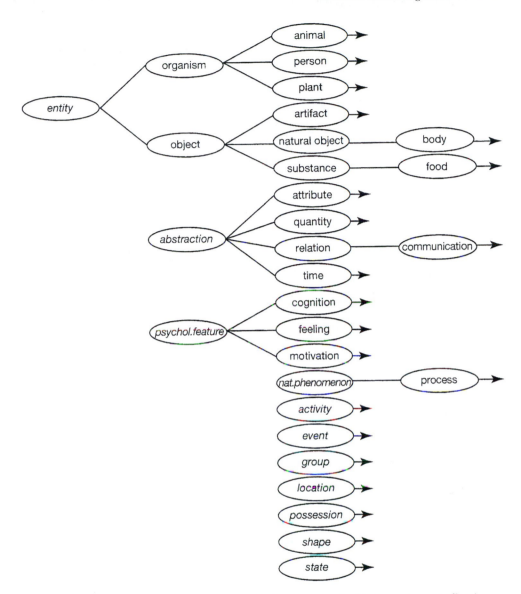

Figure 4.7. Diagrammatic Representation of Relations Reducing Noun Source Files to Unique Beginners Unique beginners appear in italics.
Note: From Fellbaum, Christiane (ed.), *WordNet: An Electronic Lexical Database.* Reprinted by permission of MIT Press.

breaking down word knowledge into its phonological, morphological, emotional, syntactic, and semantic aspects.

We now leave the topic of semantic memory to address the second question about words, how we access them in memory.

Review Question
Describe the models that have been developed to examine the mental lexicon.

Lexical Access

How we access a word's meaning is central to the comprehension of speech and writing. Lexical access has generated a great deal of research, and several theories have emerged to account for lexical processes. We shall address the factors that affect lexical access: frequency, semantic priming, morphological complexity, concreteness, emotional content, gesturing, and lexical ambiguity.

LEXICAL FREQUENCY

Most languages have a set of very common words that are used frequently, along with a relatively long list of words that are used infrequently. Zipf (1949) expressed this phenomenon as what has come to be known as **Zipf's law,** a straight-line relationship between probability of usage and frequency rank that is plotted in Figure 4.8. Zipf proposed that there was a "least effort" principle at work here. The more frequently a word is used, the easier it is to process. A great deal of psycholinguistic research has confirmed the influence of word frequency on language processing. Lexical frequency has been demonstrated to produce robust effects in *lexical decision tasks,* in which one has to decide if a string of letters is a word (Rubenstein, Garfield, & Millikan, 1970), and *word-naming tasks,* in which subjects have to pronounce the name of a visually or auditorily presented word (Forster & Chambers, 1973). The higher the frequency of the word, the faster it is identified as a word or named. These effects are obtained in both auditory and visual modalities (Howes, 1957; Savin, 1963). We look next at some ways word frequency influences task performance.

Foss (1969) used a **phoneme monitoring** task to study word frequency effects. In this version of the task, a subject had to listen to a string of continuous speech. At the same time, the subject had to press a button when a target phoneme /b/ was detected in the string words. The subject has to try to understand the speech while at the same time monitoring the presence of /b/ in the string. In this experiment, the target phoneme could appear following either a high-frequency or a low-frequency word. Foss found that phoneme monitoring times were slower following low-frequency words, presumably because low-frequency words are harder to process than high-frequency ones.

Frequency effects also depend on the syntactic class of the words in the stimulus set—for example, whether they are from open-class or closed-class categories. As noted earlier, open-class words are nouns, verbs, adjectives, and adverbs. Closed-class words are conjunctions, articles, and prepositions. Dramatic word frequency

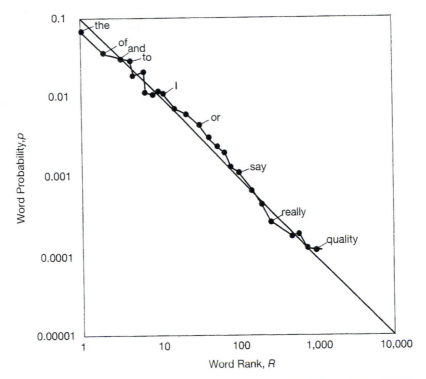

Figure 4.8. Zipf's Law: The Relationship between Probability of Usage and Word Frequency The probability of a word's occurring in a written text is plotted (on logarithmic scales) as a function of the word's frequency of occurrence. The result is a nearly straight line with a slope of −1.

Note: From *Language and Speech* by George A. Miller, 1981. Reprinted by permission.

effects in lexical decision tasks occur only with open-class words, not with closed-class words (Bradley, 1983; Bradley, Garrett, & Zurif, 1980).

The variable of word frequency plays a pivotal role in models of lexical access. But a note of caution is needed before we proceed. The degree to which lexical frequency affects lexical processing depends on the particular processing task—for example, lexical decision making, naming, or sentence verification. Balota and Chumbley (1984) found large frequency effects with lexical decision tasks, but naming tasks produced only moderate frequency effects. Semantic verification tasks produced small effects. Balota and Chumbley argued that these tasks involve decision processes that take place at different times, some of them after the lexical access has occurred. To make word-nonword decisions, participants may base their conclusions on the words' familiarity and meaningfulness (FM). Balota and Chumbley argued for a two-stage familiarity-based model in which low-frequency words may produce longer decision times because they are like nonwords on the familiarity dimension. If a stimulus is high on the FM dimension, participants make a quick yes response; items low on the FM dimension receive a quick no response. This model is illustrated in Figure 4.9.

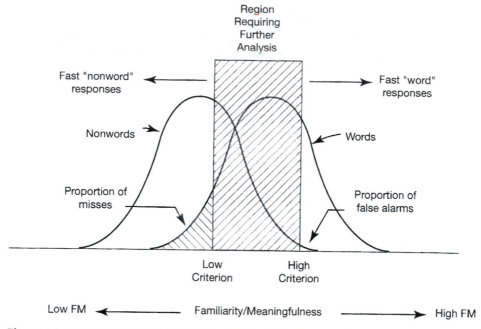

Figure 4.9. A Two-Stage Model of the Lexical Decision Task
Note. From "Are Lexical Decisions a Good Measure of Lexical Access? The Role of Word Frequency in the Neglected Decision Stage" by D. A. Balota & J. I. Chumbley, *Journal of Experimental Psychology: Human Perception and Performance,* 10, p. 352. Copyright © 1984 by the American Psychological Association. Reprinted with permission.

The items that are in the middle of the FM distributions prompt a more demanding and time-consuming analytic process, which increases reaction times. In the second stage, spelling and semantic checking may have to be used. The second stage may exaggerate the difference between low- and high-frequency words in lexical decision tasks. The high level of discrimination and decision making necessary to perform the lexical decision task may not be so essential to the naming task. The naming task can be performed for low-frequency words without the semantic checking process. Besides the effects of word frequency and lexicality, reaction times also depend on the specific items used. Both the nature of the low- (e.g., very low versus moderately low) and high-frequency words and how often they are repeated throughout the course of the experiment affect the distribution of reaction times (Balota & Spieler, 1999). One has to consider these factors when interpreting response times.

To be convincing that lexical frequency actually does affect lexical access, a task must directly link on-line lexical access process with word frequency. The task should monitor what occurs *during* lexical access rather than *after* access, as is the case in the phoneme monitoring task. One way to deal with postaccess criticism is to use **eye fixations** during reading as a measure of lexical access. As readers are scanning printed material, their eyes stop or fixate to take in information. Unusual, long, important, and low-frequency words are all good candidates for long fixation times.

Short words and high-frequency words need less gazing time. Rayner and Duffy (1986) measured how long readers visually fixated on words during a reading task. They found that word frequency clearly influenced the duration of eye fixations. Low-frequency words were fixated for 80 ms longer than words of higher frequency. Unlike the phoneme monitoring and lexical decision tasks, which are laboratory phenomena, eye fixations are a normal part of on-line reading. The eye fixation methodology during on-line reading is less susceptible to criticism of postlexical decision making than naming, phoneme monitoring, or lexical decision tasks.

Although frequency is a potent variable in lexical access experiments, it is difficult to use as an uncontaminated variable because frequency is correlated with several other variables, such as meaning, concreteness, and familiarity, that also affect lexical processes. One has to account for how accessing one word can affect associates.

SEMANTIC PRIMING EFFECTS

Recall from our discussion of word association that noun probe words reliably trigger words that are semantically related or grammatically related to the probe (*doctor-nurse*). Word association should affect lexical access. **Semantic priming** takes place when a word presented previously activates a semantically related associate.

In a semantic priming task, a subject is first shown a priming word, after which no response is required or measured. The priming word is not the locus of interest. In the next phase of the task, a second word is presented alone or in a sentence, and the subject is asked to name the word (naming task) or decide if the string of letters is a word or not (lexical decision task). The focus is on the semantic relatedness between the two words. The idea is that a related word will prime or speed up the recognition of the second. Meyer and Schvaneveldt (1971) used the lexical decision version of the semantic priming task and showed that a target word like *butter* was judged more quickly when it was primed by *bread* than it when it was primed with the unrelated word *nurse*. Lexical decision times to target words were faster when primes were semantically related to the target words.

Studies that have attempted to tease out the locus of semantic priming effects have found that they depend on the nature of the task. The results of studies that have used items that are from the same semantic category, such as *glove* and *hat*, but without strong associative relationships have demonstrated priming in lexical decision tasks but somewhat less powerful effects in naming tasks (e.g., Lupker, 1984; Schreuder, Flores d'Arcais, & Glazenborg, 1984; Seidenberg, Waters, Sanders, & Langer, 1984). Does this mean that there are "pure" semantic priming effects that do not implicate associative strength? Balota (1994) argued that there still might be lingering associative effects because pairs like *glove-hat* are more likely to co-occur than pairs like *glove-pen*. Priming could also be mediated within the word network, for example, *glove > clothes > hat*.

Priming research has produced a wealth of data for models of lexical access, but no single model of priming accounts for the diversity of data. It may be that multiple mechanisms account for the variety of results (Balota, 1994; Neely, 1991).

MORPHOLOGICAL COMPLEXITY

Psycholinguists are interested in how morphemes are organized in human memory, that is, whether words are stored as single root words stripped of their affixes or as root words plus morphemes. Does the lexicon consist of every root word (*depend*) and its affixed relatives (*independence, dependence, undependable, depending*, etc.), or is there a set of root words and a set of morphemes that can be affixed to them? If each word has a separate entry or lexeme in the mental dictionary, this would not be a very efficient strategy, using up places in memory for every variant of a root word when they share a common meaning. These issues raise questions about how morphology affects lexical access. Morphology is language-dependent, and so its effects will vary from one language to another. The discussion here is centered on English, although other comparisons are available (see "Mental Lexicon," 1999).

How are words accessed in the mental lexicon, as root words or as multiphonemic words? What is the basic form of a word that is stored? One idea is that each word (e.g., *judge*) and every variant of a word (*judged, judges, judgment, judicial*, etc.) has a separate entry or lexeme in the mental lexicon (Aitchison, 1987; Sandra, 1990). This means that when we produce or comprehend a word, we do so as a whole and not via root words and affixes. The more widely accepted hypothesis is that words are made of constituent morphemes that serve as the smallest units (MacKay, 1978; Taft, 1981; Taft & Forster, 1975, 1976). According to this view, when we listen to someone speaking, we break down or decompose words into morphemes. When we speak, we recombine morphemes to make multimorphemic words rather than accessing them whole. The **decomposition view** proposes that only the root word is stored in memory and that morphological affixes can be appended to it (Taft & Forster, 1975). To understand a word, the listener or reader strips the word of its affixes and comprehends the base word in relation to the stripped morphemes. The system fosters cognitive economy because every single word does not require a storage space; only the root words do. Affixes are added during comprehension or production. Speech production and comprehension research supports the decomposition view.

Taft (1981) used a lexical decision task to study morphological complexity and lexical access. Taft showed that unprefixed words (e.g., *chair*) are identified rapidly, as expected. However, *pseudoprefixed* words, those that appear to have more than one morpheme (e.g., *interest*), take longer to identify than prefixed words (e.g., *intermission*) or unprefixed words (e.g., *chair*). Taft reasoned that decision times were shorter for the prefixed words than for pseudoprefixed words because subjects strip away what seem to be prefixes only to find no valid root word.

More convincing evidence comes from research with long-term morphemic priming effects (Stanners, Neiser, & Painton, 1979; Stanners, Neiser, Hernon, & Hall, 1979). In these studies, subjects perform a number of lexical decision tasks. In a series of trials, subjects are presented with two forms of a word with the same root (e.g., *jump, jumped*). The question of interest is how the earlier presentation of one root form will affect the recognition of either form later in the experiment. Stanners, Neiser, Hernon, and Hall (1979) demonstrated that both *jump* and *jumped* equally primed *jump,* indicating that to produce the long-term priming from *jumped,* subjects had to access *jump* to recognize *jumped.* Further, Lima (1987) showed that this priming effect is not due to mere letter overlap. For example, *arson* does not prime *son,* but *dishonest* primes *honest.*

Additional evidence in support of the decomposition view comes from eye fixation research and speech production studies. Eye fixation studies indicate that pseudoprefixed words receive longer eye fixations during reading (Lima, 1987). The differences in fixation times occur even when words are matched for frequency, length, and syntactic category. Using a speech production paradigm, MacKay (1978) presented subjects with root word stimuli (e.g., *depend*). The subject's task was to respond with a variant of the root (e.g., *depending, undependable*). MacKay found that response time was a function of the number of morphemes added to the root word. Each morpheme added to the response time, although this study does not rule out postlexical access effects on reaction time because it is a production task.

Some caution is suggested regarding the decomposition view of lexical access as presented here. One qualification on complexity studies stems from the nature of the word sets used in the task (Balota, 1994). Decomposition may not be necessary, even though it is helpful in many cases. Rubin, Becker, and Freeman (1979) demonstrated that lexical decision time differences for prefixed and pseudoprefixed words occur only when the stimulus set contains 50 percent prefixed words. When the pool of prefixed words is reduced to the 10 percent level, the difference between prefixed words and pseudoprefixed words disappears. This suggests that frequency of occurrence may affect processing strategy. It may not be necessary to decompose a very frequent word into its morphological components. Frequently used words are generally easier to access than less frequent words, as noted earlier. Carroll (1999) argued that frequently used multimorphemic words like *impossible* are accessed as single words, while less common words like *imprecision* are decomposed into separate morphemes.

WORD CONCRETENESS AND IMAGERY

From word association and semantic differential studies we know that words evoke emotional responses. Words also evoke images, although they vary in the degree to which they activate **imagery.** The effect is sometimes discussed in terms of a word's abstractness versus concreteness. Concrete words like *knife, pumpkin, river, book,* and *doorknob* evoke concrete images. Abstract words like *truth, justice, democracy,* and *excuse* evoke less imagery. Concrete words such as *pumpkin* are more "imageable" than abstract words like *justice.* Word imagery has been found to be psychologically real; that is, words that are high in imagery are more easily recalled in memory tests than low-imagery words (Paivio, 1969).

The question of interest here is how concreteness affects lexical access. In lexical decision tasks, Bleasdale (1987) found that words primed each other when they were matched on concreteness or on abstractness. Concrete words primed concrete words, and abstract words primed abstract words. Concrete and abstract words did not prime each other. This would mean that concreteness does play a role in lexical access. One problem with word imagery studies is that word image-ability is correlated with lexical frequency, which is known to affect lexical access (Schwanenflugel, Harnishfeger, & Stowe, 1988). It could be that frequency is responsible for some of the imagery effects. High-imagery, high-frequency words like *student* are accessed and recalled better than low-frequency, low-imagery words like *excuse*. High-frequency, low imagery words like *justice* and low-frequency, high-imagery words like *elbow* fall in the middle range of access and recall scores (Paivio, 1969).

One consistent finding is that concrete words produce better lexical decision times primarily for low-frequency words but not high-frequency words (de Groot, 1989; Kroll & Merves, 1986). Kroll and Merves argued that this interaction might reflect postlexical decision processes rather than task-dependent word recognition processes. Bleasdale (1987) countered with better evidence to support an effect of concreteness on word recognition. In one experiment, either abstract or concrete words were preceded by the word *blank*. There was no reason to suspect that a neutral prime should affect word identification processes for abstract or concrete words differentially. After controlling for subjective familiarity, Bleasdale found consistent evidence of an advantage for concrete words over abstract words in naming performance on this version of the task. Problems with word frequency aside, this is the most convincing evidence that concreteness affects lexical access.

EMOTIONAL CONNOTATION AND LEXICAL ACCESS

The lexical decision task is useful to show how emotional features of words are used to recognize word meaning. Unlike many studies of emotion states, which involve postperceptual judgments, the lexical decision task permits an evaluation of on-line processing. The emotional properties of words have not been exploited in lexical access studies, as semantic features have. Emotional properties of a word may affect lexical access if these emotional properties (symbols) are important for survival.

From an evolutionary point of view, humans gather information for the purpose of survival. Information serves this function if it helps us *gain beneficial resources* for reproduction and *avoid danger* through fight or flight. Vakoch and Wurm (1997; Wurm & Vakoch, 1996) used the evolutionary account to explain the differential processing of words in the general and in the affective lexicons. In their view, the affective lexicon—the part of semantic memory in which emotion words are stored—is structured to avoid threats (Wurm & Vakoch, 1996). Words in the general lexicon are assembled by meaning, but their emotional properties are secondary. As noted in our discussion of the semantic differential, the emotional connotation of words can be described with a small set of semantic dimensions. Dimensions consistently found by researchers are evaluation (*pleasant-unpleasant*), activity (*lively-still*), and potency (*strong-weak*). Most models of lexical access are vague about which of these semantic properties are used in categorical perception or why. The Vakoch and Wurm approach makes it clear that evaluation, potency, and activity dimensions are used because they contribute to the survival of the organism. Along with lexical frequency, morphological complexity, and concreteness, the emotional quality of words affects how quickly they are accessed.

In their original study, Wurm and Vakoch (1996) examined the structure of the affective lexicon through lexical access. They demonstrated that the emotional properties of emotion words as measured by the SD influenced how quickly they are processed. From the evolutionary view, the rapid processing of words rated high on evaluation, potency, and activity makes sense. A sense of danger is activated when words connote strength, badness, and quickness (high activity). Subjects in this study were presented with words that varied on SD dimensions and were asked to make word-nonword judgments. The subjects in these experiments reacted very quickly to words rated high on strength, badness, and quickness dimensions. However for *powerful* words (high potency) that represent no clear danger if they are also *pleasant* (high evaluation), there is no need to attend quickly to these kinds of words. This is the pattern of response times that Wurm and Vakoch found. There was rapid processing of dangerous words but slower responses to words that were rated as powerful but pleasant. This pattern of lexical decision times showed that the affective lexicon exploits the connotative quality of words and is designed to avoid threats.

In the follow-up study, Vakoch and Wurm (1997) showed how the emotional connotation of words as measured by the SD influenced the speed of processing on the basis of gaining beneficial resources. They argued that the emotional information in the lexicon enables us to obtain valuable resources, the other survival motive. When the referent is beneficial (high evaluation) but difficult to obtain because it is fast (high activity) or strong (high potency), the word is processed very quickly. Words with referents that are less desirable or more difficult to obtain are processed more slowly. The general (not affective) lexicon appears to be structured for obtaining scarce and beneficial resources, according to this pattern of results. Otherwise, why would subjects respond differentially to the emotional qualities of words in the lexical decision task?

Vakoch and Wurm (1997) offer a methodological innovation over previous attempts to understand the structure of the lexicon. Many studies reviewed in this chapter have examined the lexicon through semantic priming. With that method, lexical access is facilitated by prior presentation of semantically related words. In Vakoch and Wurm's evolutionary view of words (1997; Wurm & Vakoch, 1996), the lexicon is studied via characteristics intrinsic to the words themselves (i.e., their dimension weights). Although Vakoch and Wurm focused solely on evaluation, potency, and activity aspects of meaning, they raised the issue of studying lexical access with nonsemantic dimensions of the lexicon.

An another potential factor in lexical access is the degree to which a word is associated with a gestural component.

GESTURES AND LEXICAL ACCESS

Anyone watching people engaged in conversation will notice that the dialogue is filled with hand gestures. What do **gestures** do for communication? There is accumulating evidence that besides communicating information to listeners, gestures help speakers formulate coherent speech during the lexical access stage (Krauss, 1998). Krauss proposed that lexical gestures are spatiodynamic features of concepts, which can facilitate lexical retrieval, depending on what is being said. Krauss has reported several lines of evidence that support a lexical access role for gesturing.

First, gestures are more common in spontaneous speech than in rehearsed speech. The proportion of time spent making gestures is significantly greater in spontaneous speeches compared to rehearsed speeches. Second, Krauss reasoned that if gestures play a role in lexical access, they must have a temporal relationship with the words they are presumed to facilitate. Gesture-speech asynchronies—onset of the gesture before or after the onset of the spoken word—were examined as subjects gave descriptions of pictures and photographs. All of the gestures were initiated prior to or simultaneous with the onset of the lexical item. The mean advance asynchrony was 990 ms, and there was a strong positive correlation between the length of the asynchrony and the duration of the gesture. Finally, because gestures reflect the spatiodynamic features of concepts, the facilitative effects of gestures depend on the conceptual content of what is being discussed. When subjects were asked to define twenty common English words, the amount of gesturing depended on the words' concreteness, activity, and spatiality. More than 40 percent of the time spent defining words like *adjacent, under, cube,* and *square* included gesturing, while less than 20 percent of the speaking time was devoted to gesturing for words like *thought* and *evil.* It seems clear that gestures facilitate speech production, but it is not clear exactly how gestures facilitate the lexical access process.

LEXICAL AMBIGUITY

One area of lexical access that has generated considerable research is the problem of **ambiguity.** The relationship between words and meanings is not one to one. Meaning can be shared by numerous words; for example, *pants, slacks,* and *trousers* are equivalent in meaning. Individual words are also ambiguous; most words have more than a single meaning. Each of the following words is ambiguous: *seal, drawers, wax, drive, run.* The first list of ambiguous words consisted of *homophones,* words that are pronounced the same but have different meanings. *Homographs* are words such as *bow* or *alum* that have the same spelling but different meanings and pronunciations. Readers and listeners commonly use the context to disambiguate ambiguous words. Does all this mean that ambiguous words are psychologically more complex than nonambiguous words? If ambiguous words are more complex, they should affect some aspect of processing time.

If ambiguous words are more complex than unambiguous words, they probably demand more attention. Ambiguity should affect a subject's ability to perceive a phoneme when attention is demanded elsewhere. Foss (1969, 1970) used the phoneme monitoring task to study ambiguous word processing. He had subjects listen to sentences and respond when they heard /b/. If the target phoneme occurs in a sentence *following* an ambiguous word, the detection response should take longer than if the previous word was not ambiguous. For example, it should take longer to detect the /b/ in *The men started to drill before* . . . than in *The men started to march before* . . . because *drill* is ambiguous here, whereas *march* is not. This is what Foss found; ambiguity increased the response time in the phoneme monitoring in these kinds of sentences. Ambiguity seemed to slow down the monitoring task by demanding more attention. Many researchers have since pursued the question of ambiguity.

EXHAUSTIVE ACCESS VERSUS SELECTIVE ACCESS OF MEANING

One of the central questions in ambiguity research is whether *all* the meanings of an ambiguous word are activated during sentence processing or whether semantic and syntactic cues in the sentence are sufficient to activate only one appropriate meaning. In our last example, the word *drill* presents the case (Simpson & Burgess, 1988). Does *drill* activate the "boring holes" meaning or the "performing military exercises" meaning or both? If the sentence were *The carpenter started to drill* . . , would only the "boring holes" meaning be activated, or would the "performing military exercises" meaning be activated too?

Most of the research on lexical ambiguity supports the **exhaustive access** view (Onifer & Swinney, 1981; Seidenberg, Tanenhaus, Leiman, & Bienkowski, 1982; Simpson & Burgess, 1988; Swinney, 1979; Tanenhaus, Leiman, & Seidenberg, 1979). In this exhaustive access model, multiple meanings of ambiguous words are activated regardless of contextual cues. Simpson and Burgess (1988) proposed that all of the meanings of ambiguous words do not necessarily reach activation at the same time. However, when and how we ask subjects to access the meaning of a word in an experimental task becomes a critical variable in ambiguity research, as we see later (Simpson, 1994). The most frequent meaning or the meaning cued by the context may reach threshold before other meanings. The context of the ambiguous word can help resolve the appropriate meaning during a postlexical decision-making process. The exhaustive access model is not without opposition. There are theorists who think that only the appropriate meaning is cued by the context and that other meanings are not activated.

The alternative view of lexical ambiguity is one supporting **selective access** to meaning (Glucksberg, Kreuz, & Rho, 1986; Paul, Kellas, Martin, & Clark, 1992; Schvaneveldt, Meyer, & Becker, 1976; Simpson, 1981; Tabossi, 1988). According to the selective access point of view, the context provides sufficient cues to activate one interpretation of the ambiguous word that is appropriate. In the *carpenter* example, only the "boring holes" meaning is activated in consciousness. Does this mean that multiple activations could occur outside of awareness? How does context narrow down the possible interpretations? These questions made it clear that researchers needed to devise some method to measure if multiple meanings were available during processing. One way to do this was to manipulate how the context biases the interpretation of the ambiguous word.

Swinney (1979) used a *cross-modal priming task* to examine the problem of context effects. In this task, subjects have to listen to a sentence (auditory mode) that contains an ambiguous word, for example, *bug*. Immediately after the subjects hear the ambiguous word, they see (visual mode) one of the associates of the word (e.g., *ant* or *spy*) or an unrelated word (e.g., *sew*) projected on a screen. They must perform a lexical decision task on the projected word. The question is how the auditory prime will affect the visual target; hence "cross-modal" priming. Here is an example.

> The man was surprised when he found several spiders, roaches, and other *bugs* in the corner of his room.

Then the word *ant* or *spy* or *sew* was projected. Swinney found that both associates *ant* and *spy* were responded to more quickly than *sew* even when the context primed only the insect interpretation (*ant*) of *bug*. In this experiment, it appeared that both meanings of the ambiguous word were activated even though the context was biased toward one meaning.

Another way to look at ambiguity is that one meaning of the word is *dominant* over other interpretations, and this **dominant meaning** is the one that is usually activated. Onifer and Swinney (1981) produced results similar to those of Swinney (1979) using sentences that primed both *noisy* and *round* as associates of *ring*. They assumed that the noun version of *ring* was the dominant meaning and the verb meaning was the **subordinate meaning.** They used the lexical decision task with both dominant (*round*) and subordinate (*noisy*) associates of *ring* in both a dominant and a subordinate context:

> *Dominant:* The housewife's face literally lit up as a plumber extracted her lost wedding ring from the sink.

> *Subordinate:* The office walls were so thin that they could hear the ring of their neighbor's phone whenever a call came in.

The researchers found that both dominant and subordinate associates of the target word were primed regardless of the biasing context provided by the sentence. It did not make a difference whether the meaning was subordinate or dominant. Both subordinate and dominant associates were activated, supporting the exhaustive access view.

ACCESSING DOMINANT AND SUBORDINATE MEANINGS

Eye fixation methodology is becoming an increasingly popular means of studying lexical ambiguity because it has an advantage over the processing complexity methods. Eye fixation is less subject to postlexical decision-making processes. The eye-tracking task measures the amount of time a subject spends fixating on lexically ambiguous words. Duffy, Morris, and Rayner (1988) used the eye-tracking method to compare what they called *polarized* ambiguous words with *balanced* ambiguous words. *Polarized* words are those that have a meaning that dominates other interpretations or are used more frequently than other meanings. For example, the usual interpretation of *yarn* is that it is "for knitting." The interpretation as "folk tale" is subordinate and infrequent. *Balanced* ambiguous words do not have one dominant interpretation; for example, *right* is equally likely to mean "a direction" or "correct." The role of context in lexical access now becomes important because context can be used to cue balanced, polarized, or subordinate meanings of ambiguous words.

The context can be used to bias the interpretation of an ambiguous word when it is presented before the ambiguous word. Here is an example of a *before* bias context using the ambiguous word *scale* in a sentence:

The fish was no longer in pain once the scale was removed.

Presenting the context after the ambiguous word will not bias its meaning because no clues are presented before the word is accessed.

Once the scale was removed, the fish was no longer in pain.

The sentence context in both kinds of sentences is always biased toward the subordinate meaning ("skin") of the ambiguous word rather than the dominant meaning ("weighing device"). Duffy et al. (1988) found that eye gaze was longer on the balanced ambiguous words than on unambiguous words (control words) in the *after* condition, indicating that both meanings of the balanced words were accessed when there was no biasing context. The polarized words did *not* receive extra gaze times because their dominant meanings are activated immediately. In the *before* condition, eye gaze on the target word was longer only with polarized words. The dominant meaning of the polarized word ("weighing device") was activated along with the meaning activated by the biasing context ("skin"), which caused the additional gaze times. In the *before* condition, longer gaze times occur with polarized words because the dominant meaning was also activated, as if the polarized word were acting like a balanced ambiguous word. The bias context before the ambiguous word creates a *reordered access* to its meaning according to Rayner and his colleagues (Duffy et al., 1988; Rayner & Frazier, 1989; Rayner & Morris, 1991). The context raises activation level of subordinate meaning to such a level that it competes with the otherwise dominant meaning for access.

Lexically ambiguous words activate multiple meanings, and context also constrains activation. But activation depends on the **time course** of activation, that is, when the lexical activation is tested. The influence of context and dominance depend on *when* in the course of the on-line processing the decision has to be made.

TASK DEMANDS AND THE TIME COURSE OF MEANING ACTIVATION

One important experiment for demonstrating the time course of lexical access with ambiguous words was conducted by Simpson and Burgess (1985). They used a lexical decision task involving prime-target pairs (*bank-money*) with varying *interstimulus intervals* (ISIs) between the prime word and the target word. The lexically ambiguous primes like *bank* had dominant (*money*) and subordinate (*river*) associates. The assumption is that the dominant meaning is primed immediately but that other associates are activated over time. Varying the ISI should affect the decision time, depending on whether the target was a dominant or subordinate associate. In the study, there were three ISIs: immediate (16 ms between prime and target), moderate (300 ms), or long (750 ms). Simpson and Burgess found that the immediate interval primed only the dominant meaning (*money*). At the 300-ms ISI, both meanings were available because the subordinate meaning showed priming. However, at the 750-ms ISI, only the dominant meaning remained active, producing a priming effect. The subordinate meaning apparently faded because it did not show priming. In a follow-up study, Simpson and Burgess (1988) showed that if a low-frequency associate was not presented in the first 750 ms following lexically ambiguous primes (e.g., *ball*), the decision time was actually slower than if an unrelated word (e.g., *panel*) was presented first. In other words, the prime had the effect of inhibiting the less frequent associate.

Another task-related issue is the context produced by single words versus sentences. The sentence context may produce a different kind of bias relative to that induced in single-word prime-target studies. The sentence context may produce a bias that builds up prior to the ambiguous target word. We have evidence (Simpson & Burgess, 1985) that dominant meaning is available immediately after a prime but that multiple meanings are available after 200 ms. At 750 ms, only the context-induced meanings or primed meanings are activated. In contrast, Tanenhaus, Carlson, and Seidenberg (1984) and Swinney (1979) found that *multiple* meanings are activated immediately after a sentence context. After a 200-ms interval, only the contextually biased meaning remained. Expectancies built up in the sentence context before the ambiguous word work faster (at 200 ms) than contextually biased meanings from a word in isolation (at 750 ms).

One intriguing finding in the lexical ambiguity literature was a study done by Kellas, Ferraro, and Simpson (1988). They recognized that very few studies of word recognition directly examined the allocation of attention during word recognition tasks, so they designed a study to plot attention demands over the course of lexical decision making. In one study, they had subjects perform a lexical decision task while simultaneously listening for the presence of an auditory probe that occurred 90, 180, or 270 ms following the lexical decision target. They found that lexical decisions and probe responses were fastest for the ambiguous words, followed by unambiguous words and pseudowords. Ambiguous word processing required less attention, and the demands on attention decreased across the time course of the task. In a second experiment, subjects performed the lexical decision task simultaneously with a short-term memory task (recalling a list of seven digits after the lexical decision response). The results were similar to the first experiment in that attention demands were inversely related to the number of meanings associated with the stimulus word. Attention demands on lexical access are greatest after the presentation of the stimulus words but decrease over the time course of the task. The study showed that multiple-meaning words are less demanding of attention in a lexical decision task than words with only one meaning.

SUPPORT FOR THE SELECTIVE ACCESS MODEL

Tabossi (1988; Tabossi, Colombo, & Job, 1987) reported results that conflict with the conventional view of selective access. Using an immediate presentation method, Tabossi found that selective access might occur immediately when the context is sufficiently constraining toward one meaning. Subjects in her experiments performed lexical decisions immediately after an ambiguous word in a cross-modal presentation. She found that when sentences were biased toward a dominant meaning, only that meaning was activated, given that the context primed a pertinent feature of that meaning. Tabossi et al. (1987) presented sentences like this:

> The violent hurricane did not damage the ships that were in the port, one of the best equipped along the coast.

This type of sentence accentuates the pertinent feature of *port* as a safe haven. Targets appropriate to this feature were primed.

Paul et al. (1992) reported results similar to Tabossi's using a **Stroop task.** On the original Stroop task (Stroop, 1935), subjects were presented with words written in different colors of ink. The subjects' task is to say only the color of the ink as quickly as possible without making mistakes. If the item on the next line was the word *green*, the subject was to answer "black" because the word is printed in black ink. Our facility with lexical access is so overpracticed that it is difficult to suppress the meaning of the word and pay attention only to the color of the print. Paul et al. (1992) had subjects do the color-naming Stroop task after reading sentences that ended with ambiguous words. The sentence context activated semantic features of the word's dominant or of its subordinate meaning. Targets that were congruent or incongruent with the contextual meaning were presented at 0 ms, 300 ms, or 600 ms intervals after the sentence. Paul et al. found slower color-naming times for the contextually congruent targets than for the incongruent targets. It did not matter if sentences were biased toward the dominant meaning or the subordinate meaning, even with the immediate (0-ms) presentation. As in the Tabossi experiment, what affected Stroop task response time most was the contextually appropriate meaning that was activated.

Additional support for contextually appropriate meaning activation comes from research on *event-related potential* (ERP) by Van Petten and Kutas (1987; see also Chapter 2). Whereas Van Petten and Kutas found that naming latencies to either meaning of a homograph showed priming at 200 and 700 ms, in line with the multiple access view, the ERP data revealed otherwise. You will recall from Chapter 2 that the N400 is a language-related response that produces an electrical potential 400 ms after the onset of a stimulus. The onset of the N400 is a function of contextually appropriate meaning. The N400 response to target words related to homographs occurred *earlier* for contextually congruent targets than for incongruent or unrelated targets. Van Petten and Kutas concluded that the ERP data supported a role for context in the initial processing of the ambiguous homograph. However, the naming facilitation, they reasoned, was the product of backward priming, whereby the target reactivates the prime and both are processed in parallel.

CONCLUSIONS ABOUT LEXICAL AMBIGUITY

Simpson (1994) carefully reviewed studies on the topic of lexical ambiguity and examined the kinds of tasks used. He concluded that the time course of lexical access in a task is the critical variable. Simpson contrasted research with processing complexity tasks (e.g., sentence verification, sentence completion, phoneme monitoring) versus eye tracking, which is emerging as the preferred method of studying ambiguity. Processing-complexity-type tasks are those that infer that one or more meanings are activated, based on comparisons between sentences with ambiguous homographs and control sentences. These methods tap into the lexical accessing process at different points than eye tracking tasks do. Processing complexity tasks are off-line, indirect measures of lexical access, and it is not clear if their effects are traceable to initial lexical access or postaccess selection processes that occur after multiple meanings have been activated. To get a clear picture of the access process, it is essential to study the processes the lead up to activation rather than postselection processes. Gaze duration tasks (e.g., Duffy et al., 1988) are less vulnerable to the off-line criticism. Complexity tasks may be tapping into postlexical access stages, while eye tracking is a better measure of on-line attention demands of ambiguous words.

Now we move on to models of lexical access that can account for lexical access data.

Models of Lexical Access

The models of semantic memory presented earlier in the chapter were discussed in the context of accounting for research on word associations and sentence verification data. Models of lexical access, to which we now turn, attempt to describe how people access words in memory. Both structural and processing aspects of the lexicon are important to understanding what words mean and how words are recognized. Viable access models must be able to account for empirical data. In particular, they must account for why high-frequency words are accessed faster than low-frequency words (the frequency effect) and why activating one word facilitates the recognition of others that are similar in meaning (the semantic priming effect). One issue to be resolved is whether the word frequency and priming effects make use of top-down processes that interact with bottom-up processes. In the next section, we consider three models of lexical access: the autonomous search model, the logogen model, and the connectionist model.

THE AUTONOMOUS SEARCH MODEL

Forster's (1976, 1979, 1987, 1989) **autonomous search model** views the word recognition system as divided into several parts. The original form of the model is illustrated in Figure 4.10. One peripheral access file handles word orthography. A second file handles acoustic and phonetic input. The orthographic and phonological access files contain mostly information about the initial parts of words. The third file retrieves words according to their semantic and syntactic properties. Only one of these files can be activated at a time; hence it is a serial processor.

When a word is presented visually or auditorily, the input stimulus is converted to a perceptual representation and submitted to the appropriate file for analysis. Items in the file are arranged by frequency of usage, with high-frequency words at the top of the stack such that they are accessed before low-frequency words. The second stage of the process involves matching the input to entries in the

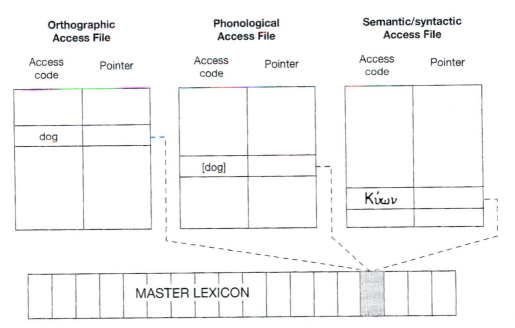

Figure 4.10. Architecture of Forster's Serial Search Model of Word Recognition
Note. Architecture of Forster's (1976) serial model of word recognition. Reprinted by permission of Kenneth Forster.

bins. When an entry in the files is matched to the input stimulus, a pointer to the entry in the *master lexicon* is retrieved. The master lexicon contains all linguistic information about a word (e.g., semantic, phonological, spelling, and grammatical class). After the pointer has been traced to the master lexicon, the syntactic and semantic information associated with the entry is integrated with output from other processors.

The master lexicon is arranged into bins with the most frequent entries on top. Entries are searched serially until an exact match is found. When the entry is retrieved, it is checked against the input. If the match is correct, the search is terminated. If the match is imperfect, most nonwords (e.g., *stlct*) will be rejected, unless they have properties (e.g., *shime*) similar to real words. The search will take longer for regular nonwords than for irregular nonwords.

The model has undergone extensive revisions, which make it more congruent with activation models, which will be discussed shortly. The newer model (Forster, 1989) has multiple comparators for each bin rather than trying to determine which bin to look in first. The revised model assumes different levels of activity for the entries, a change motivated by priming studies that showed priming based on the orthographic similarities between primes and targets. Priming would activate some entries more than others. This makes the search model more similar to activation models like the logogen model (discussed next). It should be mentioned that there are competing hybrid models of serial search that attempt to deal more efficiently with priming and frequency effects, including Becker's (1979) verification model and Glanzer and Ehrenreich's (1979) pocket dictionary model.

THE LOGOGEN MODEL

Morton (1969, 1970, 1979, 1982) developed a model of lexical access that would account for both priming and frequency effects. From its inception, the **logogen model** has influenced other conceptualizations of parallel word access. In the logogen model, each word is represented in memory by a *logogen*. Accessing the meaning of a logogen is done through the process of activation, not by searching. The logogen is like a meter that is counting up all the activity that points to it. Each logogen has a threshold level that must be reached for recognition to occur. When sufficient activity has accumulated, the logogen will trigger recognition of the word (e.g., *aluminum*). Logogens compete for recognition. Logogens that are not identified remain at a resting level of activation. After a logogen has been activated, its threshold will return to a resting state, but it will take some time to get there. Therefore, recently activated words will retain their lowered thresholds for a short period, making them more readily identifiable to repeated or related incoming stimuli.

Information arrives in the logogen system in parallel from orthographic, phonological, or semantic representations. Entries that are similar to the stimulus will be activated, but only one will be recognized. The recognition of one logogen will lower the threshold of words that are similar physically, visually, acoustically, or semantically. The effect of lowering the thresholds of similar words can account for the semantic priming effects and acoustic confusions with phonetically similar words.

Morton proposed that each logogen had a variable threshold. High-frequency words have lower activation thresholds than low-frequency words. The logogen model assumes that activation uses contextual information. Syntactic context (grammatical class or sentence location) and conversational topic can affect word recognition by assuming that there is a memory buffer that keeps a running tab of incoming information for comparison purposes. The buffer lowers the thresholds of logogens that are expected on the basis of syntactic and conversational input, which would account for semantic priming effects. This happens because the logogen system feeds information to a cognitive system, which feeds back into the logogen system.

The original model (Morton, 1969) assumed that it was possible for auditory information to prime visual information, but this assumption was not supported by subsequent research, and the model had to be revised. Morton (1979; Morton & Patterson, 1980) modified the model to constrain cross-modality priming. The updated version, shown in Figure 4.11, maintains separate channels and logogens for visual and auditory input. Another difficulty with the original model was how it dealt with nonwords, especially those that are similar to real words (e.g., *shime*). One suggestion was to create a deadline period for recognition, after which unrecognized candidates are rejected as real words (Coltheart, Davelaar, Jonasson, & Besner, 1977).

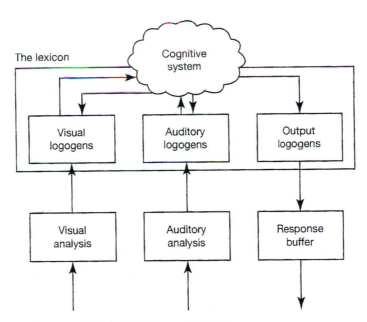

Figure 4.11. The Revised Logogen Model
Note. From Morton & Patterson (1998). Reprinted by permission of John Morton.

Activation models like the logogen model are good at accounting for *neighborhood* effects (Luce, Pisoni, & Goldinger, 1990). A word's **neighborhood** consists of all words that are similar in orthography or phonology. The neighborhood contains words that differ from the target word by one letter or one phoneme. Words are not recognized in isolation from related lexical items (neighbors). For example, neighbors of *hate* would include *late,* which is phonologically and orthographically related; *hale,* which is orthographically related; and *eight,* which is phonologically related. Some words have large neighborhoods, and others have small ones. Both neighborhood frequency and neighborhood size affect word recognition times (see Balota, 1994). Parallel activation models like Morton's predict that neighborhood size would not affect processing time, whereas serial search models would predict that search time would increase with size. The frequency of neighbors is also important and interacts with neighborhood size. Neighborhood size is not so important if all neighbors are high-frequency, but Morton's model would predict faster responses for high-frequency neighbors but not low-frequency neighbors.

The logogen model does have some problems. For example, what constitutes the perceptual unit that maps acoustic and phonetic input into the logogens is unclear. Since the model operates on words as units, it is not clear how sublexical units such as syllables are processed or how nonwords are processed. The model also does not specify how different sources of linguistic information are integrated, that is, how auditory inputs are synthesized with visual inputs. Finally, the model has difficulty accounting for similarity effects. If logogens are activated individually, how do they facilitate or inhibit activation of phonetically similar logogens?

THE CONNECTIONIST MODEL

Seidenberg and McClelland's (1989) connectionist model does an excellent job of accounting for data on word recognition. It was developed to account for lexical decision tasks and word-naming tasks. The Seidenberg and McClelland model is similar to the earlier TRACE model of recognition (see Chapter 3). However, this updated version does not have localized representations like its predecessor. There is no lexicon in the Seidenberg and McClelland model. It has distributed representations that do not have a single representation like a lexicon with lexemes that represents single words, for example, *dog.* There is no *dog* node; the word is recognized by its unique *pattern* of orthographic activation distributed in the network.

The model is largely determined by the characteristics of orthography. The model tries to show how a lexical processing system develops when influenced by a spelling-to-sound learning regime. Regular and irregular words are learned through experience with spelling-sound correspondences. There is no mechanism that looks up words, no lexicon, and no set of phonological rules. The key feature is that there is a single procedure for computing phonological representations from orthographic representations that works for regular words, exceptional words, and nonwords.

The Seidenberg and McClelland model is illustrated in Figure 4.12. It has a set of input units that translate the orthography of the stimulus along with a set of output units that represent the stimulus' phonology. The input units are connected to a group of *hidden units*. The hidden units' only inputs and outputs are within the system being modeled, and they are not contacted by external systems. The hidden units are connected to the phonological output units. The weights (strength of association) connecting input and output are adjusted according to a *back-propagation* rule that is adjusted to reduce the difference between output units and "correct" pronunciation. Feedback (correction) adjusts the association between the output and the correct target. There are no a priori weights between the input and output units before learning begins. The weights are established by feedback in the back-propagation process. In the training phase of the model's development, Seidenberg and McClelland fed the model 2,897 monosyllabic English words at a rate that reflected their frequency of usage in the language. The model produced phonology that corresponded to regular words, high-frequency exception words (e.g., *have*), and novel nonwords.

In an important way, this model captures the *frequency-by-regularity* interaction in lexical research. This interaction indicates that for high-frequency words, the correspondence between orthography and phonology is of little importance. However, for low-frequency words, the impact of spelling-to-sound correspondence is large. The dual-route model of lexical access accommodates this interaction, assuming that the direct path rather than the indirect path accesses high-frequency words (Andrews, 1982; Monsell, Patterson, Graham, Hughes, & Milroy, 1992; Paap & Noel, 1991; Seidenberg, Waters, Barnes, & Tanenhaus, 1984). That the word is not pronounced according to regular phonological rules overrides inconsistent correspondence between orthography and sound. For example, *have* has such a

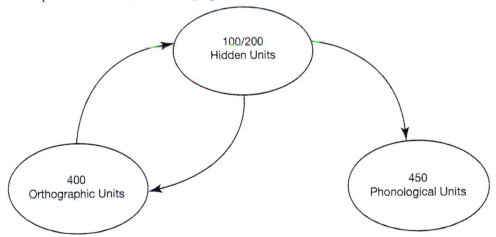

Figure 4.12. Structure of the Seidenberg and McClelland Model

Note. From "A distributed, developmental model of word recognition and naming" by M. S. Seidenberg & J. L. McClelland, *Psychological Review*, 96(4), p. 527. Copyright © 1989 by the American Psychological Association. Reprinted with permission.

high frequency of use that lexical access is achieved before incorrect pronunciation information ("Should it sound like *gave* or *wave*?") is overridden. Conversely, a low-frequency word slows up the lexical path and allows for interference from phonological mediation. The critical point for the dual-route model is that the output of low-frequency mediated responses can be overridden by the availability of phonological information produced by the indirect route.

In comparison, the Seidenberg and McClelland model does not assume separate (dual) paths to a lexicon or even the existence of a lexicon to account for the frequency-by-regularity interaction. The frequency-regularity relationship is produced by the correspondences between frequency and spelling-to-sound correspondence in the alphabetic system. With continued practice, the difference between target activation (the "right" pronunciation) and the actual activation computed by the network gets smaller and smaller. The activation of phonological units approximate the target values more and more, regardless of whether the word has regular correspondence (e.g., *gave*) or exceptional correspondence (e.g., *have*). For high-frequency words, regular correspondences do not make a difference. However, for low-frequency exceptional words, the magnitude of error between the target and activated units is larger than it is for low-frequency regular words.

This model also accounts for some interesting neighborhood effects on pronunciation. The consistency of spelling-to-sound correspondence in English is influenced by word neighborhood, words that differ by one letter or one phoneme, as mentioned earlier. Jared, McRae, and Seidenberg (1990) demonstrated that regular words (e.g., *mint*) show consistency effects, especially when high-frequency neighbors have consistent spelling-to-sound patterns (e.g., *lint*) more so than when neighbors have inconsistent spelling-to-sound patterns (e.g., *pint*). The neighborhood frequency effects are handled nicely by connectionist models like Seidenberg and McClelland's (1989), which predicts pronunciation on the basis of lexical frequency and correspondence.

> **Review Question**
> Given the work of Vakoch and Wurm (1997), how would you modify one of the models of semantic memory to include the emotional aspects of word meaning?

Key Terms

ACT model
ambiguity
autonomous search
   model
bound morpheme

closed-class words
complex
connectionist model
connotation
decomposition view

denotation
derivational
   morpheme
dominant meaning
exhaustive access

eye fixation
free association
free morpheme
gestures
imagery
inflectional morpheme
logogen model
morphology
neighborhood
open-class words

orthography
phoneme monitoring
Remote Associates
    Test (RAT)
reference
selective access
semantic differential
semantic feature
semantic memory
semantic priming

semantic verification
spreading activation
    model
Stroop task
subordinate meaning
time course
typicality
word association
WordNet
Zipf's law

What Lies Ahead

Chapter 5 follows the topics of word meaning and reference covered here but in a larger linguistic context. We move on to look at how we understand words in the context of sentences. Obviously, the lexical access and ambiguity issues addressed in this chapter overlap with the discussion of syntax that follows.

Suggested Web Sites

ACT: http://act.psy.cmu.edu
Cross-linguistic comparison of sound symbolism in animal names:
    http://www.percepp.demon.co.uk/animals.htm
Jung's word association lecture:
    http://psychclassics.yorku.ca/Jung/Association/lecture1.htm
WordNet: http://www.princeton.cogsci.edu/~wn/

Answers to the RAT: thief, memory, salt, window, lion, sick, street

Chapter 5
Sentence Processing

Critical Thinking Questions

1. What kinds of grammars do psycholinguists employ to describe sentence structure?

2. What parsing strategies have been proposed to show how sentences are understood?

3. How does working memory affect the sentence comprehension process?

4. How do emotional aspects of speech affect sentence comprehension?

5. How do the inferences we draw during the comprehension process influence understanding?

Exercise 5.1. **Sentence Comprehension**
In your notebook, write your interpretations of the following sentences before you begin reading this chapter.

1. Julie doused the bonfire.

2. Colorless green ideas sleep furiously.

3. The horse raced past the barn fell.

4. I saw the woman in the park with the binoculars.

5. Three turtles sat on a log, and a fish swam under them.

6. Are you going to take the train to school this week?

7. Dr. Pendragon is a boring lecturer and a nasty son of a bitch.

In Chapter 4, we addressed the issue of words and word recognition. In this chapter, we move on to consider how listeners and readers comprehend sequences of words in sentences. To produce a comprehensible sentence, a speaker or writer has to accomplish both semantic and syntactic goals. One must first find the words that represent the appropriate meanings and then place those words in the correct grammatical order. To comprehend what we read and hear, we also have to determine the grammatical structure of the sentence and what meaning it conveys. In this chapter, we are interested in how we derive meaning from sentences (comprehension) and what role memory plays in the process.

Sentences and Syntax

What is a sentence? A sentence consists of one or more propositions that represent a complete thought. A **proposition** is a factual claim. For example, *Ugly neighbors own dirty cats* contains three propositions: *the neighbors have cats, the neighbors are ugly,* and *the cats are dirty.* We can use syntax to assemble these propositions in different grammatical structures that express the same idea, for example, *Dirty cats are owned by ugly neighbors* or *The cats that ugly neighbors own are dirty* or *The neighbors who own dirty cats are ugly.* How do we analyze sentences like these to find their meanings? How do we know they have the same meaning?

There are three general factors that affect sentence processing: syntactic structure of the sentence, parsing strategies, and memory capacity. One task for psycholinguists is to describe sentences in structural or grammatical terms. Grammatically, there are different types of sentences: active, passive, relative-clause, embedded, and so on. The goal is to show how grammatical structure affects how people read and listen to sentences and to show where difficulties occur when listeners or readers try to find the intended meaning of the sentence.

A second task facing psycholinguists is to describe the strategies that listeners or readers use to parse sentences for meaning. **Parsing** is the assignment of the words in a sentence to their appropriate linguistic categories, also known as parts of speech, or constituents. Parsing is not merely diagramming sentences; it is finding out what they mean according to rules for syntax. Several questions must be addressed. How do we parse word sequences into meaningful propositions? What parsing strategies are available to us to find meaning? How do we select strategies to deal with syntactic complexity or ambiguity?

The third task for psycholinguists is to determine how memory capacity influences comprehension. Because our short-term memory capabilities are limited, there is a limit on how much information about a sentence can be kept in mind at the same time. Listeners or readers must quickly determine the meaning of a sentence and move on. Structural complexity and ambiguity can adversely affect the parsing process and force the listener or reader to backtrack. The memory issue raises questions about what kinds of information are being used to make sense of what is being processed. Variables that can be integrated in the parsing process include inferences, prosody, emotion, and context. Psycholinguists disagree on how and when these variables have their effects, and more questions arise: How does prior context help resolve ambiguity? How do the speaker's prosodic cues affect our comprehension of a sentence? What inferences do people draw and retain in memory? Obviously, this third area covers a wide variety of topics, some of which have to be addressed more fully in chapters that follow.

The rest of this chapter is dedicated to three major topics: sentence structure, sentence processing strategies, and working memory capacity. First, we look at sentence structure according to three competing points of view: the traditional linguistic approach, semantic-based grammars, and optimality theory.

Sentence Structure and Tree Diagrams: The Traditional View

Several problems have to be solved to understand a sentence. The individual words have to be identified and their meanings retained for higher-level processing. Contextual information, punctuation or intonation, and integrated information about thematic roles for people, objects, and events are useful in assigning an overall meaning to the words in the sentence. Psycholinguists who attempt to solve these problems have borrowed generously from linguistic theory developed by Chomsky (1957, 1965, 1981) and his colleagues. One standard tool to set out sentence structure and meaning was the **tree diagram** (also known as a *phrase marker*), which clarifies the relationships among the constituents of the sentence. The tree diagram or *constituent structure tree* captures the hierarchical structural relationships between the constituents in the sentence—the nouns, adjectives, verbs, noun phrases, and verb phrases. It is used to derive the major roles and actions within the sentence. Within this framework, the major problem is determining how people convert a sentence into a tree diagram representing the structure of the sentence.

The **phrase structure** tree indicates three aspects of the listener or speaker's syntactic knowledge: (1) the linear order of the words in the sentence, (2) the grouping of words into syntactic categories, and (3) the hierarchical structure of the categories. Every sentence in English can be represented by a phrase structure tree that reveals the constituent grouping or by a series of rewrite rules. The tree diagram on the left in Figure 5.1 shows a sentence in a simple sentence structure: adjective-adjective-noun-verb-adverb. We can also represent the structure with **rewrite rules**, which indicate how one constituent can be translated or rewritten into another constituent, as follows.

S → NP + VP

NP → adjective + adjective + noun

VP → verb + adverb

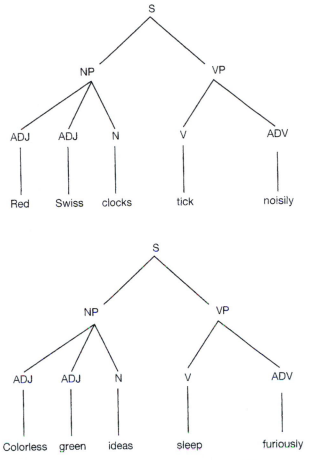

Figure 5.1. Tree Diagrams for a Simple Sentence Structure

This linguistic shorthand shows that the sentence (S) is rewritten (as indicated by the arrow) as a noun phrase (NP) plus a verb phrase (VP). The NP contains a noun with its modifiers, and the VP contains a verb and its modifiers. The meaning of the sentence is constructed as the words are added to the constituent slots. Adding semantically appropriate words to the terminal constituent slots makes one sentence meaningful (*Red Swiss watches tick noisily*) but another sequence of words (*Colorless green ideas sleep furiously*) meaningless, albeit syntactically well formed, as shown in Figure 5.1 (Chomsky, 1957).

One way to measure sentence complexity is to look at the number and types of nodes on the tree diagram. For example, the sentences in Figure 5.1 do not have as many nodes as the sentence in Figure 5.2. Complex sentences have complex tree structures (e.g., number of nodes and phrases nested within phrases). Complex sentences—for example, those with an embedded clause or phrase (a sentence within a sentence), like *The student that the teacher questioned passed the course*—and longer

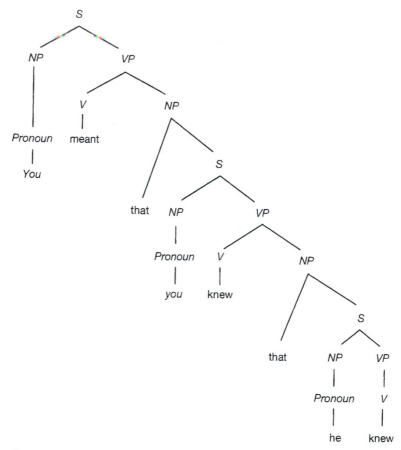

Figure 5.2. Tree Diagram for a More Complex Sentence Structure
Note. From *An Introduction to Language, 6th edition,* by V. Fromkin © 1998. Reprinted
with permission of Heinle & Heinle a division of Thomson Learning. Fax 800 730-2215.

sentences, like the one you are currently reading, place a burden on the memory capacity of readers and listeners (Kimball, 1973). Another factor that affects comprehension is the predictability of the constituents in the sentence being parsed. Some
word sequences are predictable and easily understood. Regularities in speech help
comprehension; for example, the rhythm and familiarity of *Mary had a little lamb; its
fleece was white as snow* make the sentence easy to understand. But everyday speech is
not as predictable as a memorized rhyme. Conversations are filled with sentences that
are unpredictable, complex, ungrammatical, incomplete, or out of context.

TRANSFORMATIONAL RULES

Chomsky (1965) developed *transformational generative grammar* (TGG) to account
for our understanding of the relationship between a set of sentences with the same
meaning or structure. Besides accounting for the relationship between constituents

within a sentence, TGG uses **transformational rules** to describe the relationships *between* sentences. The transformational rules specify the obligatory and optional constituent structures that transform one sentence into another. One could describe a "family" of sentences based on how the constituent repositioning transformed simple active affirmative declarative sentences into related sentences: passive, negative, interrogative, and relative-clause sentences. Consider the following family of sentences.

1. Mary gave a bouquet of daffodils to Pat.

2. Pat was given a bouquet of daffodils by Mary.

3. Did Mary give a bouquet of daffodils to Pat?

4. Was it not a bouquet of daffodils that Mary gave to Pat?

Each sentence expresses a similar idea through a different sequence of words. Our linguistic awareness tells us that they express the same underlying idea, although we cannot specify the linguistic rules involved. The underlying sentence is a simple active affirmative declarative sentence; it is the basis on which the passive, interrogative, relative-clause, or negation transformations are performed. The passive transformation in this instance, moving from sentence 1 to sentence 2, is achieved by reordering the noun phrases (*Mary, Pat*), changing the verb (*gave*) to the participle, adding the auxiliary verb *was*, and adding the preposition *by*. These rules will work on most active-to-passive transformations.

Transformational rules account for the reordering of constituents from one sentence form to another, that is, how one sentence can be rewritten as another. The rules represent the syntactic knowledge that underlies our understanding that the family of sentences is related. In other words, although sentences 1–4 have different surface orderings, the underlying meaning is the same, which brings us to the distinction of surface structure versus deep structure.

SENTENCES: SURFACE STRUCTURE AND DEEP STRUCTURE

We know that sentences 1–4 are related because they have the same *deep structure* expressed through different surface forms. The linear ordering that we read or hear is the **surface structure.** The underlying idea or meaning of the surface structure is its **deep structure.** The *surface structure* is a linear arrangement of constituents that reflect a complex set of ideas. The *deep structure* came to be regarded as the underlying meaning of the sentence. Deep-structure sentences are simple active sentences that are transformed into more complex linear surface orders (e.g., relative clauses are added, or sentences are embedded one inside another). The deep meaning is the same in sentences 1–4, while the surface arrangements are quite different. The sentences thus have the same deep structure but different surface structures. Sentences 5 and 6 have different surface structures but the same deep structure (Fromkin & Rodman, 1998), as can be seen in Figure 5.3.

5. The father wept silently.

6. The father silently wept.

The tree diagram for sentence 5 is the deep structure underlying both sentences. If no transformations apply, the surface and deep structure are the same. If transformations apply, then the surface structure is the result of transformations to the deep structure. Sentence 6 appears different on the surface because the deep structure has underdone an adverb-moving transformation. Figure 5.4 shows how transformational rules are applied to a deep-structure sentence (*The father is weeping silently*) to convert into a surface structure question (*Is the father silently weeping?*).

What the deep and surface structures mean to the psycholinguist is that sentence processing requires two stages. One stage operates to discover the surface structure of a sentence, and the second operates to discover the underlying meaning of a sentence. Consider sentence 7.

7. They are boiling potatoes.

The syntactic structure of this sentence is ambiguous. We can derive two deep structures from one surface structure. We see the different structures in the tree diagrams in Figure 5.5. How we parse the surface structure determines if *boiling* is a verb or an adjective, that is, whether potatoes are boiling in pots of water or not. The question we will return to later in the chapter is how syntactic structure as defined by tree structure affects sentence comprehension. Next we move on to look at alternative models of sentence structure.

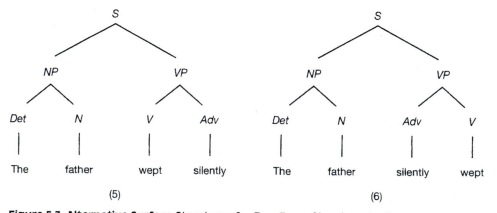

Figure 5.3. Alternative Surface Structures for Two Deep-Structure Sentences
Note. From *An Introduction to Language, 6th edition,* by V. Fromkin © 1998. Reprinted with permission of Heinle & Heinle a division of Thomson Learning. Fax 800 730-2215.

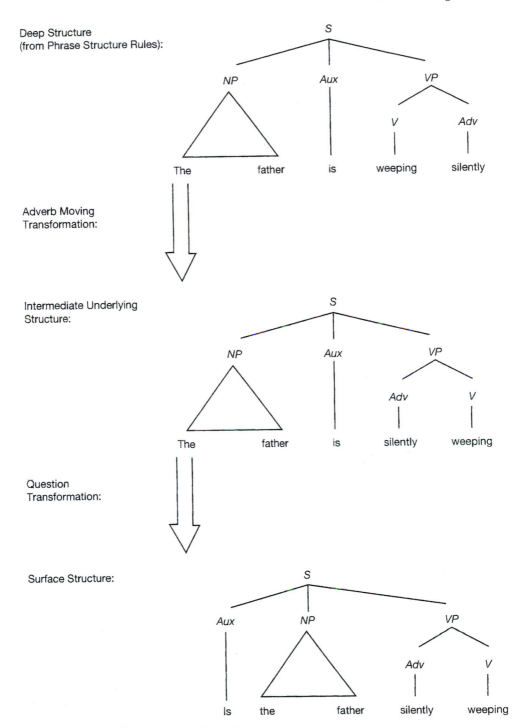

Deep Structure
(from Phrase Structure Rules):

Adverb Moving
Transformation:

Intermediate Underlying
Structure:

Question
Transformation:

Surface Structure:

Figure 5.4. Applying Transformational Rules

Note. From *An Introduction to Language, 6th edition,* by V. Fromkin © 1998. Reprinted with permission of Heinle & Heinle a division of Thomson Learning. Fax 800 730-2215.

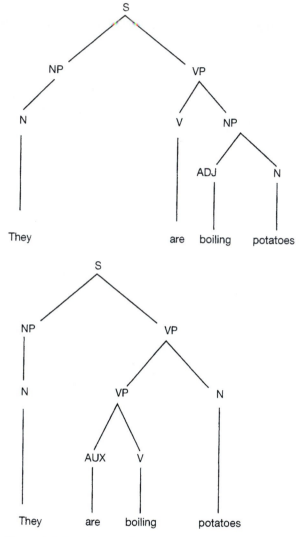

Figure 5.5. Ambiguous Surface Structure: Two Tree Structures

Semantic and Lexical-Based Grammars

Syntax-based grammars like Chomsky's were an attempt to derive meaning through syntactic structure. A semantics-based grammar is a theory of derived sentence meaning based on the semantic relationships between a verb and its associated nouns (cases). **Case grammar** (Fillmore, 1968) focuses on the verb in the sentence and the various arguments (nouns) that regularly occur with it to express an idea. Case grammar relies heavily on word meaning, as opposed to structural relationships in transformational grammar. The point of case grammar is to show that the underlying semantic relationships between the verb and its nouns remain stable even though surface structures differ. Consider the following set of sentences.

8. The vault opened.

9. The pass code opened the vault.

10. The teller opened the vault with the pass code.

11. The vault was opened with the pass code by the teller.

Teller is always the agentive case, *vault* is always the objective case, and *pass code* is always the instrumental case. Case grammar can explain the structural similarities between semantically similar verbs like *puncture* and *stab,* which both entail an instrument that cuts, an agent to do the damage, and an object that receives the action. TGG misses these semantic regularities. Although the theory of case grammar was never fully developed, it influenced the way psycholinguists described language acquisition by children and the way those working in artificial intelligence wrote programs that simulated human behaviors.

Mitchell and Holmes (1985) demonstrated that some verbs have a built-in or implicit syntax, as case grammar would imply. If some verbs constrain the words associated with them, these constraints must influence comprehension. For example, comprehension time should be facilitated by verbs that build expectations of associated nouns in a sentence. Providing readers with sentences containing nouns that do not fit their expectations should slow down reading times. This is what Mitchell and Holmes found. In sentences like the following, subjects took significantly longer to read the prepositional phrase *in his hand* in sentences like 12 than in those like 13.

12. The groundskeeper noticed the girl waving a stick in his hand.

13. The groundskeeper chased the girl waving a stick in his hand.

The verb in these sentences affects the reader's expectations: *Chased* accommodates the expectation of an instrumental case, *a stick in his hand,* but *noticed* does not accommodate, substantially slowing reading times for the unexpected phrase.

LEXICAL FRAME ANALYSIS

Another alternative to the parsing-by-trees view and similar to case grammar is **lexical frame analysis.** The lexical frame account (Ford, Bresnan, & Kaplan, 1982) parses sentences on the basis of properties of individual words in the sentence under construction. More specifically, stored information about the verb in the sentence incorporates information about the variety of ways it can be used. The frame of each of the forms of usage specifies the argument structure that the verb can enter into. A verb like *positioned* can enter into a structure in which it has a direct object NP and a prepositional phrase complement, such as

14. The saleswoman positioned the dress on the rack.

Each verb may have a preferred frame that is more salient than alternative frames. Lexical frame analysis proposes that the most salient form dictates parsing decisions. As soon as the reader or listener encounters the verb, the frame associated with it is activated. The activated frame is used for the basis of assigning structure to ambiguous constituents. What is critical here is that initial decisions about parsing are based on word-specific information from the reader's or listener's lexicon that is used to make structural assignments.

THEMATIC STRUCTURE ANALYSIS

A related view of the parsing mechanism, known as **thematic structure analysis,** focuses on lexical information, like frame analysis, but relies more heavily on deriving semantic interpretations of sentences (Pritchett, 1988; Tanenhaus, Carlson, & Trueswell, 1989). Ambiguities are resolved in light of moment-to-moment decisions about thematic structures of sentences. During the course of parsing, *thematic roles* (agent, patient, goal, proposition, etc.) are assigned to every noun phrase in conjunction with role assignors like verbs. Not unlike the frame analysis and case grammar, verbs determine the roles that need to be filled. So a sentence that begins *John put . . .* has two roles to be filled. To handle the incomplete information, Pritchett (1988) assumed that the parser selects a reading that imposes the lowest "cost" to the system incurred by linking roles with NPs. Tanenhaus et al. (1989) also emphasize the role of thematic structure in the process of parsing. They view the thematic process as one that links and coordinates semantic and discourse information, as well as lexical and syntactic information. In both cases, thematic structure analyses propose that initial parsing decisions are determined by thematic operations as opposed to tree-driven lexical decisions.

As was the case in Chapter 4 with respect to lexical access, the question of whether semantic or contextual information is used during the parsing process is a matter of controversy. It should be apparent that a parsing model that integrates semantic and discourse information into the parsing process does not operate on the modularity principle (see Chapter 3), that is, solely on the basis of an encapsulated syntactic module as proposed by Fodor (1983) and others (Ferreira & Clifton, 1986; Rayner, Carlson, & Frazier, 1983). As we see next, another issue that bridges lexical access and parsing literature is how well connectionist theories account for the data.

Review Question
What advantage do lexical or semantic-based grammars provide over the traditional syntax-based model?

Optimality Theory

The grammars discussed to this point represent attempts to describe linguistic knowledge and the role of semantics and syntactic rules in sentence processing. Optimization is a neural-network or connectionist-inspired perspective (cf. McClelland, Rumelhart, and the PDP Research Group, 1986) on the nature of linguistic knowledge and grammatical constraints (Prince & Smolensky, 1991, 1997). This constraint-based grammar is an alternative to Chomsky's tree-diagram approach. **Optimality theory** (OT) proposes that grammars contain constraints on the well-formedness (grammatical, sound fine, are usually well-attested) of linguistic structures. These constraints are in conflict with each other within one language and across languages. For example, English has a subject-verb-object (SVO) constraint on word order, but this constraint is not absolute, as can be demonstrated in the case of questions, such as *What did John see?* The object-question word *what* moves to the front of the string because the constraint on the question-initial word ordering dominates the SVO constraint in English. The ranking of constraints in OT grammar orders structures from those that best satisfy the **constraint hierarchy** to those that are least satisfying. The constraint ranking and ordering of structures represents the characterization of knowledge of grammar.

An example of cross-linguistic conflicting constraints can be found in the sentence *It rains* versus the Italian *Piove*. The constraint requiring all sentences to have subjects in English conflicts with the constraint requiring all words to contribute to the meaning of the sentence. *It* does not contribute to meaning in this usage. This and the SVO example point to the central element in the grammar, that is, a means for managing the pervasive conflicts between grammatical constraints. The key to the architecture of the OT grammar is in the strength asymmetry between two constraints. To return to the example, *It rains*—English weights the need to have a subject in the sentence over the constraint that all words contribute to the meaning of the sentence. This relationship between these constraints does not arise in Italian. The constraint against meaningless words dominates the subjectless sentence constraint. The resulting sentence in Italian, *Piove* (simply *Rains*), is well formed in Italian. Optimality theory can indicate what languages have in common and how they differ by showing how constraints are ranked within each language. Let's consider OT in more detail.

Where strength asymmetry exists between two constraints, no amount of success on the weaker constraint can outweigh for a failure of the stronger constraint.

In other words, the degree of failure in the weaker constraint is tolerated as long as it aids the success of the stronger one. The observed weight of any particular constraint ranges from "never violated" to "always violated," depending on the domination hierarchy for the language in question. Extending this idea, a grammar consists of a strict domination hierarchy of constraints. Each more important constraint takes priority over all constraints lower in the hierarchy. Only the ranking of constraints matters for determining optimality. Different rankings of the set of constraints give rise to different linguistic patterns. Optimality theory proposes that the set of well-formedness constraints is present in every language. The grammar for a particular language is the domination ranking for a particular set of constraints from a universal constraint set.

Within the constraint set, structural complexity is determined in part by *markedness*. An element of a structure is *marked* if it is more complex than an alternative structure on some relevant dimension. In English, as noted earlier, sentences lacking subjects are more marked than those with subjects. What is important here is that markedness may correlate with comprehension, production, and memory functions. Marked elements tend to be avoided, and children acquire them later than unmarked structures.

The neural network representation of a sentence like *Big dogs bite* is illustrated in Figure 5.6 as a pattern of activated nodes (an NP and VP in this case) in the neural network. The pattern associated with the sentence is a grid of activated and inactivated nodes. This is the neural-network alternative to tree diagrams of sentences created by linguists. The bottom part of the figure is the pattern of neural activity associated with the verb phrase (*bite*), and the middle grid the is pattern of activity associated with the noun phrase (*big dogs*). The uppermost grid is the pattern of neural activity associated with the complete sentence.

The network attempts to maximize the *harmony* of the pattern of activity creating a linguistic structure. The activity patterns—the patterns of inhibitory and excitatory connections in the network—define which structures have maximal harmony, that is, which are grammatical. The harmony function determines which conflicting constraints are respected when they are in conflict. The function seeks the grammatical structure that best satisfies the total set of constraints in the network. A pattern of activation that maximizes the harmony is the one that optimally balances the conflicting demands of all the constraints within the dominance hierarchy.

Using grammatical knowledge to comprehend language in OT involves listening or reading a string of words and finding the constraint structure associated with the string. Speaking is a different use of the same grammatical information. In the comprehension process, words are nested into phrases, and implied connections between words are filled. For example, in the sentence *John hopes George admires him*, the link is established between *John* and the pronoun *him*. Using linguistic knowledge involves finding optimal structures in the constraint hierarchy.

Although the details of the theory are beyond the scope of this book, connectionist constraint-based theories of language are emerging to challenge traditional structural linguistics–inspired approaches to comprehension. We move on from

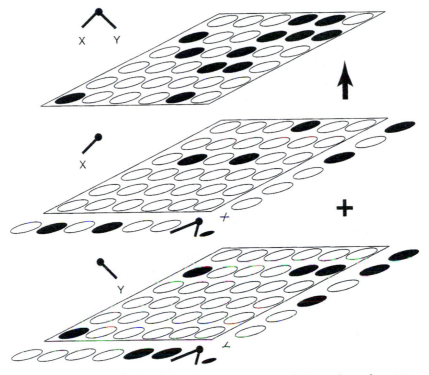

Figure 5.6. Patterns of Activity in Neural Networks The top plane shows a pattern of activity for the sentence *Big dogs bite*, in which *X* stands for the noun phrase (*Big dogs*) and *Y* for the verb phrase (*bite*). The activity levels of units in the neural network are shown as circles.
Note. Reprinted with permission from "Optimality: From neural networks to universal grammar" by A. Prince & P. Smolensky, *Science, 275(5306)*. Copyright 1997, American Association for the Advancement of Science.

grammars to look at the strategies that have been proposed to account for language comprehension processes and the models that incorporate these strategies.

Parsing Strategies and Models

How would you draw a tree diagram for a sentence that begins like sentence 15?

15a. Every night Kim bathes the cat . . .

This appears to be a simple SVO structure, one that begins Adj + N + V + NP. But what happens when the rest of the sentence is processed?

15b. . . . wants tasty food.

When we read *Every night Kim bathes the cat wants,* we realize that *cat* is not the object of *bathes* but the subject of the clause that follows. This realization causes us to construct a different tree in order to make sense of the sentence. The question to be answered is what happens when we encounter ambiguous strings like these *garden path sentences?*

GARDEN PATH SENTENCES

A **garden path sentence** (GPS) is a metaphor for being led down a linguistic path that takes us to the wrong meaning. This means that when we are presented with a tricky sentence that was created by researchers with a juncture where one or more interpretations are possible, we proceed down the path not knowing that we have constructed the wrong syntactic structure. In other words, the sentence starts off appearing to have one kind of syntactic structure that turns out to be incorrect based on information that comes later in the sentence. GP sentences are almost never encountered in real life but can be useful for revealing how the mind works. Here are some examples (from Pinker, 1994):

16. The horse raced past the barn fell.

17. The man who hunts ducks out on weekends.

18. The cotton clothing is usually made of grows in Mississippi.

19. The prime number few.

20. Fat people eat accumulates.

After reading sentence 16, ask yourself, who fell, the horse or the barn? When you get to the end of sentence 16, you realize that you have understood that a horse raced passed the barn, but you do not know what to do with *fell. The horse* is interpreted as a noun phrase and *raced* as the beginning of the verb phrase that completes the sentence. Everything is going fine until you get the to word *fell.* Then you realize that you have been led down the garden path, that *raced* is not part of the verb at all but rather a modifier applied to *horse.* Here is Pinker's clarification of the sentence: "The horse that was walked past the fence proceeded steadily, but the horse raced past the barn fell." Sentence 17 reveals a strong tendency to interpret *who hunts ducks* as a single clause because *hunts* usually has an object. In reality, *ducks out* is the main verb and *who hunts* modifies *the man.* Some of these GPSs can be disambiguated by adding a word or two or by pausing and word stress when we speak; for example:

The horse (that was) raced past the barn fell.

The cotton (that) clothing is usually made of grows in Mississippi.

(The) fat (that) people eat accumulates.

The interesting question is how we derive only one meaning and fail to realize that there are alternative interpretations of these sentences. What strategy allowed us to do this? The GPS is a nice linguistic trick, but why are we tricked by our parsing? We are tricked because we read with a parsing strategy that tells us to assume the simplest interpretation until we must do otherwise. We read past the possible clause boundary and do not close the clause until we have determined where the clause ends. The serial processing strategy predicts no difference between processing ambiguous and unambiguous material prior to the discovery of an inconsistency. The parser selects a preferred reading, which is abandoned only when it results in an anomaly or inconsistency.

There are, in principle, three alternative ways to develop a structural analysis of a GPS (Mitchell, 1994). First, the reader could assemble a structure for just one of the possible interpretations and ignore all others, as in the garden path model. Second, the reader could assemble a structure for all of the possible interpretations in parallel. Third, the reader could make a partial analysis with minimal commitment and wait to make a final decision when the relevant information is found later in the sentence. The literature has generated a variety of models to account for parsing ambiguous sentences. The following discussion is limited to the major provisions of the garden path model and competing views (minimal commitment and constraint satisfaction) with a focus on the models that have generated the most interest.

THE GARDEN PATH MODEL: MINIMAL ATTACHMENT AND LATE CLOSURE

The garden path model was proposed by Frazier (1979, 1987; Frazier & Rayner, 1982). It assumes that a reader builds an initial analysis of a sentence using syntactic information or phrase structure rules. Words in the sentence are assigned to phrasal constituents that are determined by parsing. When the text contains syntactic ambiguities, the reader abandons the initial analysis and revises the structure under construction.

Frazier and her colleagues (Frazier, 1979; Frazier & Rayner, 1982; see also Clifton & Ferreira, 1987) have proposed two parsing strategies that have received a good deal of attention: minimal attachment and late closure. Using the **minimal attachment** strategy, we attach each incoming lexical item into the existing structure, adding the fewest possible number of nodes to the tree. Using **late closure,** we attach incoming lexical items, when grammatically permissible, into the phrase being processed. Minimal attachment and late closure are general principles that can be applied to a number of syntactic constructions. They guide the reader in decisions about initial attachments, assuming that information about a word (e.g., part of speech, phrase structure rules associated with part of speech) are needed to fit the word into the sentence structure. Other researchers disagree with Frazier about how multiple sources of information such as argument structure or thematic role can constrain parsing decisions (Clifton, 1992; Mitchell, 1987; Tanenhaus et al., 1989), as we shall see shortly.

Frazier's late closure strategy predicts that reading times for passages that follow ambiguous noun phrases are greater in sentences that violate the strategy, like sentence 21, as opposed to passages that conform to it, as in sentence 22.

21. As soon as he had phoned his wife started to prepare for the journey.

22. As soon as he had phoned his wife she started to prepare for the journey.

The pattern of reading times predicted by late closure has been found in several studies (e.g., Frazier & Rayner, 1982; Mitchell & Holmes, 1985). The pattern suggests that more reanalysis is required when the ambiguous phrase *his wife* is the subject of the main clause in sentence 21 than when it is part of a preposed clause in sentence 22. This means that the preliminary parsing favored the latter interpretation, which is in line with attaching the new material to the tree structure under construction. Many studies have demonstrated that the simplest tree structure is favored over more complex ones, for example, in main-clause versus reduced-relative ambiguities (*The horse that was raced past the barn fell* versus *The horse raced past the barn fell*).

The late closure strategy reflects the tendency to attach incoming words to the current constituent under construction (Frazier, 1987). The alternative would be to keep our options open and consider all kinds of different interpretations. The problem with the open-options alternative is that it places a greater load on working memory than trying to retain one option at a time.

If parsing strategies are psychologically real, they should affect eye movement patterns during reading. For example, experiments should reveal that different patterns of eye fixations occur on GPSs relative to non-GP sentences. Evidence from a number of experiments that examine how readers usually scan GPSs supports the late closure strategy. Early studies using eye movement measures indicated that GPSs disrupted reading. Frazier and Rayner (1982) and Rayner et al. (1983) demonstrated garden path effects with sentences like 23 and 24, which both begin with *We knew John*.

23. We knew John well.

24. We knew John left.

The minimal attachment principle constructs *John* as the object of *knew*, which is consistent with *well* but inconsistent with *left*. In sentence 23, *John* is the subject of the clause, not the object of the main verb. When the reader processes *left*, having followed the GPS, the initial analysis has to be reconstructed. The disruption is indicated by the eye movement pattern. The initial fixation on *left* is significantly longer than it is on *well*. The tree structures for sentences 23 and 24 are illustrated in Figure 5.7. The minimal attachment principle suggests that sentence 23 is preferred to sentence 24 because fewer nodes are needed to attach *John* to the tree.

The garden path model states that we construct one interpretation until we realize that something is wrong (Ferreira & Clifton, 1986; Frazier & Clifton, 1996). The minimal attachment principle specifies that the reader or listener should apply

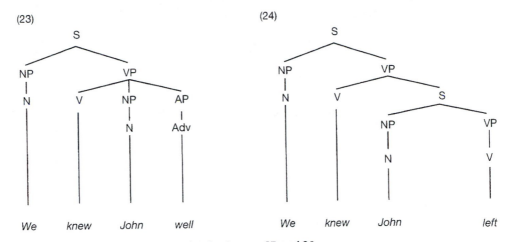

Figure 5.7. The Tree Structures for Sentences 23 and 24

Note. Figure from "The Interaction of Syntax and Semantics During Sentence Processing: Eye Movements in the Analysis of Semantically Biased Sentences" in *Journal of Verbal Learning and Verbal Behavior,* Volume 22, 358–374, copyright 1983, Elsevier Science (USA), reproduced by permission of the publisher.

the simplest structure to the sentence that is possible. This would mean assigning the least possible number of phrases to the string of words.

CONSTRAINT SATISFACTION MODELS

One area of debate in parsing studies is the degree to which lexical, semantic, and pragmatic information constrains initial parsing decisions or syntactic constructions. In contrast to the research that supports minimal attachment via syntactic processing, several studies have found support for the involvement of semantic information and nonminimal attachment. The notion of *constraint satisfaction* has been more recently incorporated into optimality theory.

Marslen-Wilson and Tyler (1980) provided evidence that processing time for sentences increases as the verb in the verb phrase moves semantically from normal to ungrammatical. They asked subjects to respond when they heard the word *guitar* in the following set of sentences, all of which followed the sentence *The crowd was waiting eagerly.*

25. The young man grabbed the guitar.

26. The young man buried the guitar.

27. The young man drank the guitar.

28. The young man slept the guitar.

Subjects took progressively more time to respond as they proceeded through sentences 25 to 28. The constraints on what people can and cannot do with guitars affects the processing of the sentences. Results like these have led some researchers to propose a **constraint satisfaction** explanation for sentence comprehension, contending that lexical and semantic information limits or constrains what structures can be parsed.

Constraint satisfaction models propose that multiple readings of a phrase are activated until the correct reading can be determined later in the sentence (MacDonald, Pearlmutter, & Seidenberg, 1994; Trueswell & Tanenhaus, 1994). This does not mean that all readings are activated but that context and expectations will prompt readers to anticipate multiple readings.

There is evidence that multiple interpretations are constructed for ambiguous sentences when the semantic features of a particular word constrain the interpretations of other words in the sentence (Trueswell, Tanenhaus, & Garnsey, 1994). To demonstrate the effect of semantic constraint, Trueswell et al. designed an experiment with verbs that semantically constrained the nouns associated with them. Subjects had to read sentences like the following while their reading times were recorded.

29. The witness examined by the lawyer was useless.

30. The evidence examined by the lawyer was useless.

Trueswell et al. proposed that constraint satisfaction parsing is necessary when more than one interpretation of a word can occur during sentence processing of ambiguous sentences. If the minimal attachment strategy works, then sentences 29 and 30 should be processed in the same manner while reading because they have the same syntactic structure. According to constraint satisfaction, these sentences should be difficult to read because the minimal attachment strategy will not work on either.

Results indicated that the reading speed for sentences like 30 were faster than those like 29 because of the semantic constraints of the sentence, not its syntax. *Examine* constrains the interpretation of *evidence* but not *witness*. Witnesses can examine things, but a noun like *evidence* cannot produce this expectation; it is more constrained in interpretation. The semantic constraints on *evidence* make it easier to process.

Taraban and McClelland (1988) created sentences that were semantically biased toward nonminimal attachment interpretations. They found faster reading times for nonminimal sentences like 31 than for minimal attachment sentences like 32.

31. The thieves stole all the paintings in the museum while the guard slept.

32. The thieves stole all the paintings in the night while the guard slept.

These data support the role of semantic information in sentence comprehension in line with predictions of the constraint model. However, Altmann and colleagues (Altmann, Garnham, & Dennis, 1992; Altmann & Steedman, 1988) have argued that parsing difficulty measured by reading time attributed to nonminimal attachment is actually a function of the number of propositions that must be added to the text to satisfy the semantic requirements. They claim that minimal and non-minimal sentences can be compared only when preceding contexts are referentially supportive. Clifton and Ferreira (1987) demonstrated that the problem of parsing a GPS is not eliminated by additional contextual information, and parsing seems to unfold on the basis of syntactic information (a tree diagram) without interacting with other knowledge. Studies that supported the nonminimal attachment advantage used self-paced reading and off-line methods, while other studies with different methods have not found contextual override effects (Ferreira & Clifton, 1986; Rayner & Morris, 1992).

CROSS-LINGUISTIC STUDIES: THE UNIVERSALITY OF PARSING STRATEGIES

Cross-linguistic studies provide data that distinguish general principles of comprehension from those that are language-specific, for example, limited to English syntax. Cuetos and Mitchell (1988) examined the principle of late closure parsing with English and Spanish speakers. Look at sentence 33:

33. Andrew had a dinner party yesterday with the niece of the teacher who belonged to the Communist Party.

The late closure principle states that when readers or listeners are presented with a sentence like 33, they attach the relative clause, *who belonged to the Communist Party,* to *the teacher* rather than *the niece.* Reading time data from English speakers support the late closure idea. However, Spanish speakers tended to attach the clause to the earlier noun phrase, *the niece.* The preference for early closure in Spanish indicates that late closure is not a universal comprehension principle.

MacWhinney and Bates (1989) studied how different cues are weighted in the comprehension process across a variety of languages. They suggested that comprehension involves the competition and convergence of multiple cues, including semantic, grammatical, and morphological cues, that are being concurrently processed. When these cues provide conflicting information regarding interpretation, the relative weights of the cues determine the final interpretation based on a constraint satisfaction algorithm. The weights associated with various cues differ from language to language. When subjects are asked to judge which noun phrase is the agent of a pseudosentence like *The pencils the cow are kicking,* which pits cues against each other, the weights among cues varies across languages. English listeners are influenced by word order, while Hungarian listeners rely heavily on inflectional morphemes. Chinese, which has little inflectional morphology, makes listeners rely on a variety of cues. The weights from strongest to weakest cues in Chinese are passive marker, animate noun, word order, object marker, and indefinite marker, respectively (Li, Bates, & MacWhinney, 1993). The model has been extended to a variety of language processes including language acquisition and aphasic breakdown (Bates, Wulfeck, & MacWhinney, 1991).

Comparing Parsing Strategies

Most of the models discussed so far agree about one aspect of parsing: When processing load increases, the parsing tactics used are restricted to a few words or phrases in the sentence under construction. The models make different assumptions about exactly how and where the load occurs.

In the *ambiguous region* of the sentence in question, evidence reveals that ambiguous material is not more difficult to process than in matched sentences that are not ambiguous. Processing equivalence in the ambiguous region has been demonstrated with eye-tracking methods (Frazier & Rayner, 1982) and in self-paced reading (Cuetos & Mitchell, 1988; Mitchell, Corley, & Garnham, 1992). Processing load in the ambiguous region of the sentence is no more difficult than in unambiguous sentences, a finding that is compatible with the serial garden path model.

In the *disambiguating region*, there are different views about what strategies are being used. There is strong support for models that predict an increase in processing load in the disambiguating region, such as the serial garden path model. The serial model makes one structural analysis through the ambiguous region and proceeds smoothly if the reading is compatible with the sentence under construction. Alternative interpretations are simply ignored. The model predicts that there will be difficulties when sentence continuation is at odds with the preferred analysis. The existing structure has to be abandoned and replaced, which is assumed to take time and effort (Frazier, 1987; Frazier & Rayner, 1982).

One alternative interpretation to the GP model of ambiguous sentences neither commits itself to a single structure nor builds all potential structures for ambiguous sentences. The *minimal commitment model* (Frazier & Rayner, 1982) and the *wait-and-see* version (Just & Carpenter, 1980) propose that certain aspects of processing can be temporarily suspended, producing an incomplete and low-level analysis of the sentence. The restricted form of the sentence is maintained until the reader processes information that is sufficient to resolve the original ambiguity. The details of the mechanism that triggers the full analysis were not made explicit in these early models, while other accounts (e.g., Frazier & Rayner, 1987) were more explicit about the syntactic triggering mechanisms.

In minimal commitment models, some (but not all) of the parsing decisions are postponed during the first pass through the ambiguous part of the sentence. If disambiguating information is identified, it can be used to reinstate all analyses and bring all processing up to date. The backlog of processing at this point leads to increments in processing time over the area of concern (Gorrell, 1987). Evidence shows that immediately following the ambiguous region, at least one continuation of the sentence will take longer to process than in the same region in an unambiguous context. The disambiguation effects occur for a variety of types of ambiguity—for example, when clauses without commas are compared to control sentences with commas, as in sentence 34.

34. After the young Londoner had visited(,) his parents prepared to celebrate their anniversary.

Disambiguation effects also have been found for reading times in disambiguating regions in reduced (35a) and unreduced (35b) relatives (Ferreira & Clifton, 1986).

35a. The defendant examined by the lawyer turned out to be unreliable.

35b. The defendant who was examined by the lawyer turned out to be unreliable.

These and other findings (see Mitchell, 1994) provide support for models that predict processing load increments in the disambiguating region. The evidence is compatible with the garden path model and the minimal commitment model. Constraint-based models (e.g., Prince & Smolensky, 1997; Taraban & McClelland, 1988; Trueswell & Tanenhaus, 1994) contrast with the serial processing model of parsing. They demonstrate how syntactic decisions are influenced by lexical and semantic information activated during the comprehension process.

> **Review Question**
> What are the strengths and weaknesses of the garden path model versus the constraint satisfaction model?

Working Memory and Sentence Comprehension

One question that has to be addressed is how parsing strategies influence memory constraints on what can be retained during the comprehension process. This approach examines how resource limitations in working memory affect comprehension (Carpenter, Miyake, & Just, 1994, 1995). The working memory capacity perspective shifts the emphasis from *structural* aspects of language processing to focus on the dynamics of language *processing*.

Working memory can be construed as a pool of resources that perform operations. Working memory is limited by the number of resource demands present and their levels of complexity. Because the pool of resources is limited, demanding sentences or tasks will manifest themselves in patterns of errors or increased processing times. The linearity of spoken and written language necessitates the temporary storage of readers' and listeners' computations.

The *working memory view* focuses on the task requirements of natural language processing (Carpenter & Just, 1989). Comprehension relies on computation of thematic role, syntactic structure, integration of information, inferences, comparisons, and other logical operations. Ongoing computations during the comprehension process require the maintenance of representations at multiple levels in memory. Kimball's (1973) influential parsing model was based on the assumption that the number of structural elements that can be maintained at one time during the parsing process is limited. Kimball's view of minimal attachment—introducing the fewest possible number of nodes into the sentence under construction—is predicated on the idea that simple trees can be retained in working memory more easily than more complex parsings. Kimball's notion of working memory is similar to more recent theories of working memory.

Traditional models of memory (see Willingham, 2001) have viewed short-term memory in a manner that has emphasized storage of limited amounts of information for brief intervals (e.g., remembering a telephone number). Short-term memory has also been regarded as a way station on the road to long-term memory. More recent models of memory (e.g., Cowan, 1988) have challenged the traditional model of short-term memory as a single buffer with a view espousing multiple working memory that handles different representations. The working memory view is compatible with Baddeley's proposal (1976, 1986) that traditional memory span measures include a peripheral phonological buffer called the *articulatory loop* and a (subvocal) rehearsal process. **Memory span** is based on performance in word or digit span tasks, which require the subject to recall a list of items (e.g., words or digits) in exact serial order. The goal of the parsing model from a working memory view is to provide an analysis of parsing that will explain why some syntactic structures are more difficult to understand than others and why readers and listeners prefer one interpretation of an ambiguous construction over another, as in garden path sentences.

Language comprehension is a task that requires extensive use of working memory with multiple levels of representation. Traditional structural models of short-term memory (Atkinson & Shiffrin, 1968) are inadequate to account for recent models of sentence parsing. In addition, traditional measures of structural capacity, such as digit span and word span, are not highly correlated with performance on language comprehension tasks that make extensive use of working memory (Baddeley, 1986; Baddeley & Hitch, 1974; also see Carpenter et al., 1994). Simple memory span does not predict individual differences among children's reading performance (Perfetti & Goldman, 1976). Also, analyses of aphasic processing have revealed that among patients with two- or three-item word or digit spans, these are not predictive of the patients' sentence comprehension performance (Caplan & Waters, 1990). The failure of traditional memory span to predict comprehension performance leaves the door open for alternative measures of working memory.

One alternative test devised to assess working memory is the **reading span** test (Daneman & Carpenter, 1980), which taps both processing and storage capacity. This test requires the subject to read a set of unrelated sentences and then recall the final word of each sentence. For example, after reading the sentences *When at last his eyes opened, there was no gleam of triumph, no shade of anger* and *The taxi turned up Michigan Avenue, where they had a clear view of the lake,* the subject would have to recall the words *anger* and *lake*. The set of sentences is increased until the maximum number of sentences that can be remembered is determined by the number of sentence-final words recalled. For college students, reading spans run from 2 to 5.5 words. Reading span is also highly correlated with listening span. Typically, one's reading span is lower for more complex sentences. Reading and listening spans also correlate highly with many other measures of reading comprehension, like the SAT (Masson & Miller, 1983). Tests that measure processing and storage demands reveal systematic individual differences that are not tapped by traditional memory span tests for the effect of aging (Babcock & Salthouse, 1990) or reading impairments where IQ scores are equated (Carr, 1991). Thus alternative working memory span tests (e.g., reading span) provide a valuable measure of language comprehension capacity and population differences.

INDIVIDUAL DIFFERENCES WITH SYNTACTIC COMPLEXITY

A central argument in the working memory model is that sentence comprehension tasks reveal systematic effects of working memory constraints. Working memory span can account for systematic differences among college students during the time course of comprehension and accuracy of processing. These differences are especially clear when sentences are highly demanding due to structural complexity or task demands (Carpenter & Just, 1989; Just & Carpenter, 1987, 1992).

One type of sentence structure that is difficult for skilled readers to comprehend is the center-embedded clause, for example, *The student that the teacher questioned passed the course.* The relative clause, *that the teacher questioned,* is embedded in the main clause and places a demand on working memory because it interrupts the constituents in the main clause, *the student passed the course.* Several studies have shown that some types of center-embedded clauses are less demanding than others. For example, subject-relative sentences like 36 are easier to process than object-relative sentences like 37.

36. The reporter who attacked the senator admitted the error.

37. The reporter who the senator attacked admitted the error.

King and Just (1991) had normal adult readers with low, medium, and high working memory spans read center-embedded sentences like 36 and 37 in a self-paced, word-by-word reading paradigm (Just, Carpenter, & Woolley, 1982). According to the working memory model, each reader's memory capacity influences the relative difficulty of center-embedded sentences. Readers with a lower capacity are expected to have more trouble with the more difficult object-relative sentences than readers with high capacity, especially in the region of the sentence where processing demands are high. The results of the King and Just study are illustrated in Figure 5.8. All groups took more time to process object-relative sentences compared to subject-relative sentences. However, notice the large individual differences in reading times localized to the object-relative sentences in the right panel of Figure 5.8. Working memory constraints are manifested when processing demands exceed capacity, as in objective-relative sentences. Note that the processing difficulties in these sentences occur at the point where critical syntactic information becomes available. Increased reading times occur at the verb of the embedded clause and at

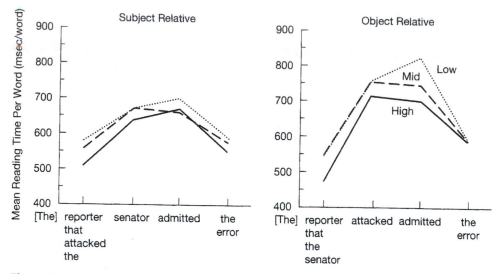

Figure 5.8. Reading Times for High-, Medium-, and Low-Span Readers

Note. From "A capacity theory of comprehension: Individual differences in working memory" by M. A. Just & P. A. Carpenter, *Psychological Review*, 99, p.130. Copyright © 1992 by the American Psychological Association. Reprinted with permission.

the verb in the main clause, but these times are longer for subjects with smaller spans. Thus working memory constraints are most evident when demands for capacity is high and resources are limited.

INDIVIDUAL DIFFERENCES WITH LINGUISTIC AMBIGUITY

Another factor that places demands on working memory is ambiguity. Lexical or syntactic ambiguity in the absence of context for disambiguation can require the reader to maintain multiple interpretations in working memory. The working memory model suggests that high-span readers are more able than low-span readers to maintain multiple interpretations. Several studies of syntactic and lexical ambiguity have supported this view (Carpenter, Miyake, & Just, 1995; MacDonald, Just, & Carpenter, 1992; Miyake, Just, & Carpenter, 1994). Miyake et al. (1994) constructed sentences with neutral introductions that contained a homograph, which was only disambiguated later in the sentence, for example:

38. Because Ken really liked the boxer, he took the bus to the nearest pet store to buy the animal.

39. Because Ken really liked the boxer, he took the bus to the nearest sports arena to see the match.

Boxer can be interpreted as a *dog* or a *pugilist* (the dominant meaning), but readers cannot determine which meaning is intended until they have read eight more words, arriving at *pet store* or *sports arena*. As noted in Chapter 4, both meanings of the ambiguous word are activated and maintained immediately after it is recognized, but the subordinate meaning (*dog*) fades over time. Results indicated that low-span readers spent a similar amount of time reading control and ambiguous sentences for the dominant resolution. However, for the subordinate resolution, low-span readers showed a large ambiguity effect; that is, they had much longer reading times for ambiguous than unambiguous sentences, especially at the final word. High-span readers, who supposedly have a larger pool of working resources, did not show reading time increases for either dominant or subordinate resolution.

MacDonald et al. (1992) demonstrated working memory effects in the maintenance of multiple syntactic interpretations. In this study, high- and low-span readers were presented with sentences like

> 40. The experienced soldiers warned about the dangers before the midnight raid.
>
> 41. The experienced soldiers warned about the dangers conducted the midnight *raid*.

These sentences are ambiguous because the initial verb can be interpreted as a main verb (sentence 40) or as a past participle (sentence 41). The working memory model predicts that syntactic representations are initially computed by all readers on the first encounter of the ambiguity (Gorrell, 1987). As was the case with lexical ambiguity, the model suggests that a reader's working memory capacity affects how much text the reader can cover and maintain multiple syntactic representations. MacDonald et al. (1992) found that low-span readers, who have limited capacity for multiple representations, abandoned the less preferred interpretation (the past participle) and consequently showed great difficulty when the disambiguation turned out to be consistent with that less preferred interpretation. The reading times and errors for the high-span readers supported the idea that they were able to maintain the subordinate representation over a longer distance, but with the added cost of postponing higher-level processes.

The working memory model also makes predictions on the basis of capacity restrictions for the comprehension of multisentence text and discourse (Carpenter et al., 1994, 1995). For example, Daneman and Carpenter (1980) found that reading span predicted the text distance over which a reader could find an antecedent for a pronoun. For short distances of a few words, differences in capacity were not important; however, when six or seven sentences intervened between the pronoun and its antecedent, large individual differences emerged. Readers with a reading span of five were able to identify the correct antecedent 100 percent of the time, but readers with a span of two did not connect the two references. These results are plotted in Figure 5.9. Although these studies take us beyond what can be addressed in this chapter, suffice it to say that high-capacity readers show better retention and integration over multisentence passages than low-capacity readers do.

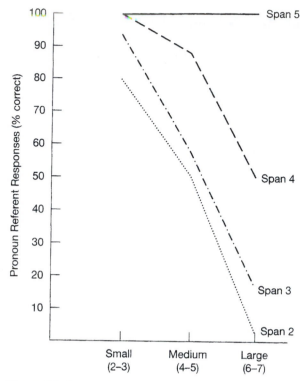

Figure 5.9. Correct Interpretation of Pronoun Antecedents as a Function of Number of Intervening Words

Note. Figure by Daneman & Carpenter in *Journal of Verbal Learning and Verbal Behavior,* Volume 19, page 456, copyright 1980, Elsevier Science (USA), reproduced by permission of the publisher.

WORKING MEMORY AND MODULARITY

The working memory constraints on interrelated levels of language processing create a new perspective on the question of syntactic **modularity.** Fodor (1983) conjectured that a fast, domain-specific encapsulated cognitive module performs syntactic processing. *Encapsulation* refers to the module's processes' being unaffected by other classes of information. The question of whether parsing operations are encapsulated or not have been addressed by some of the experiments described earlier (Rayner et al., 1983; Taraban & McClelland, 1988). Research focused on structurally ambiguous sentences in which readers could avoid being led down the garden path only by making immediate use of syntactic information. The study by Ferreira and Clifton (1986) favoring syntactic modularity used sentences like *The evidence examined by the lawyer shocked the jury.* Readers showed garden path effects when they reached the disambiguating *by* phrase, despite their knowledge that an inanimate noun, like *evidence,* could not be the agent of *examined.* The fixation times in the disambiguating region were just as long as when no disambiguating information was present (*The defendant examined by the lawyer. . . .*). The lack of influence by pragmatic information on the parsing process was attributed to the encapsulated syntactic module.

The working memory view offers a different explanation of this research, namely, that the interactive processes required to integrate syntactic and pragmatic information may require more processing resources and produce individual differences on the Ferreira and Clifton task. When Just and Carpenter (1992) reran the experiment, only low-span readers produced the GP effect, failing to use immediately available pragmatic information to guide parsing. Readers with limited capacity may not have the resources to activate additional sources of information during sentence processing to the degree that nonsyntactic information can affect comprehension. By contrast, high-span readers did not show GP effects, suggesting that they have the capacity to activate information about the inanimacy of the head noun. The modularity explanation does not fit the pattern of results unless syntactic processing is encapsulated for low-span readers. The working memory model posits that interaction requires capacity, and only readers with sufficient capacity have the resources to exploit immediate interaction.

Review Question
Why is the working memory view a necessary addition to the garden path and constraint satisfaction views of parsing?

Factors That Influence Sentence Comprehension

This section covers a variety of factors that affect sentence comprehension. These include affective prosody, emotional expression, emotional involvement, inferences, and long-term retention.

AFFECTIVE PROSODY AND EMOTIONAL EXPRESSION

When we are reading, punctuation lets us know when we have reached the end of a sentence or a clause, but this is not so obvious when we are listening to spoken speech. It is important that we look at prosodic aspects of sentences because the manner in which a sentence is spoken affects its interpretation (Bachorowski, 1999; Bachorowski & Owren, 1995; Beach, 1991; Ferreira, 1993). It is important to make the distinction between affective prosody and the vocal expression of emotion. **Affective prosody** is primarily concerned with suprasegmental aspects of the speech signal that contain emotional as well as linguistic information. **Vocal expression of**

emotion, by contrast, includes acoustic cues that do not require suprasegmental integration and play no major linguistic role. Both qualities of spoken speech affect communication, but in different ways.

We rely on the affective prosodic features of speech—intonation, stress, tempo, pauses, and vowel lengthening—to provide cues to assist syntactic and semantic parsing. Changes in intonation signal whether the speaker is making a statement or asking a question. Questions are marked with a rising intonation at the end of the sentence. To mark the end of a sentence, speakers pause. Pausing and vowel lengthening also mark clausal boundaries (Ferreira, 1993); so do intonation, stress, and timing. If you say this sentence aloud to yourself, you will hear what I mean: *In order to pass the test, she had to study very hard.* The clausal boundary in the text is marked by the presence of the comma for the reader, but this cue is not present for the listener, who is relying on **prosody.** Notice that you lengthen the vowel in the word *test* at the clause boundary. Pausing and stress are helpful in disambiguating garden path sentences like *The man who hunts ducks out on weekends,* lengthening the vowel in *hunts* and pausing before *ducks.* In experiments where sentences are created so that the prosodic cues conflict with the syntactic boundary of the clause, in some cases the prosodic information in the sentence outweighs conflicting syntactic cues (Wingfield & Klein, 1971).

Speakers use word stress or emphasis to direct listeners to the important syntactic and thematic information in a sentence. Word stress or emphasis can be used to help disambiguate a structurally ambiguous sentence like sentence 42 (Ferreira, Henderson, Anes, Weeks, & McFarlane, 1996).

42. I saw the woman in the park with the binoculars.

Consider what happens when you shift the word stress and pausing from one underlined word to another word in sentence 43.

43. Are <u>you</u> going to take the <u>train</u> back to <u>school</u> <u>this week</u>?

By shifting the word stress and pausing to a different thematic role, the speaker gives a clue to what noun is most important in the question. Say the sentence to yourself aloud several times, shifting the stress and pause to one of the underlined words or expressions. Understanding of sentence 43 is influenced by the affective prosodic cues produced by the speaker, even though the syntactic structure of the sentence remains unchanged.

The second type of emotional cues in speech provide information about the speaker's emotional state. The vocal expression of emotion and the perception of emotion are fundamental qualities of human communication. Prosody is used to make affective judgments about a speaker's mood (Bachorowski, 1999). It can indicate if the speaker is happy, sad, angry, or sarcastic, affecting how the sentence is understood. Listeners associate particular patterns of acoustic cues with discrete emotional states. In experimental studies where actors attempt to portray various emotions (Scherer, Banse, Wallbott, & Goldbeck, 1991), listeners have been able to perceive emotions significantly better than they would by chance. Cross-linguistic studies have shown similarities in perceptual accuracy, suggesting that the ability to comprehend emotional aspects of speech is universal (Scherer, Banse, & Wallbott, 2001).

EMOTIONAL INVOLVEMENT DURING THE COMPREHENSION PROCESS

Throughout this chapter, we have seen that sentence comprehension relies heavily on parsing strategies that determine the syntactic relationships and semantic features of sentences. We have also seen that factors such as ambiguity, prosody, and memory play a critical role in our understanding of sentences we read and hear.

Laboratory studies of the verbatim retention of surface structure paint a bleak picture of our ability to recall exactly what someone said. J. S. Sachs (1967) demonstrated how quickly **verbatim memory** for sentences fades. She presented subjects with a tape-recorded paragraph that contained a target sentence, *He sent a letter about it to Galileo, the great Italian scientist,* that would later be used in a surprise memory test. Subjects were tested on the target sentence at different time intervals to measure the retention of details. The test could occur at one of three intervals: immediately after the target sentence, 80 syllables (about 27 seconds) after the sentence, or 160 syllables after the target sentence. Subjects had to respond "yes" if the test sentence was identical to the target or "no" if it differed in any way from the target.

Of interest was the type of detail that would be retained over longer retention intervals. One test sentence changed both the word order and the meaning of the original sentence: *Galileo, the great Italian scientist, sent him a letter about it.* Another test retained the meaning of the original but changed it from the active to the passive voice: *A letter about it was sent to Galileo, the great Italian scientist.* The third version retained the meaning but changed the order of the phrases: *He sent Galileo, the great Italian scientist, a letter about it.* The test pitted memory for syntax against memory for meaning. If the testing occurred immediately after the target sentences, subjects were fairly accurate. At 80 and 160 syllables, they performed no better than chance on the sentences with syntactic changes but were much more accurate (80 percent) at detecting changes in meaning. The results indicate that that subjects rapidly lose the surface details of the sentence but retain the gist of it. The longer the retention interval, the stronger the effect. This **gist effect** has also been demonstrated using American Sign Language (Hanson & Bellugi, 1982).

But how do verbatim memory studies compare to memory for emotional material? What do you remember about Dr. Pendragon and his lectures from Exercise 5.1? Recall as accurately as possible the sentence that described Dr. Pendragon. If someone tells you an obscene joke, insults you deeply, or tells you some juicy gossip about a mutual friend, how likely is it that you can remember the words and phrases that you heard or read?

Generally speaking, the listener's **emotional involvement** (the activation of emotions during comprehension or production) in speech makes it more memorable. For example, what do we remember from the lectures we hear? Some comments stick in memory better than others, and unfortunately, the remembered comments may have nothing to do with the material on which we are tested. Although their lecture materials did not include emotional or offensive speech, Kintsch and Bates (1977) showed that students listening to college lectures had good memory for jokes and announcements conveying lecture-relevant information. Murphy and Shapiro (1994) found that listeners take special care to focus on the surface details of jokes and insults. In a related study on memory for conversations, MacWhinney, Keenan, and Reinke (1982) found impressive accuracy for memory for the surface structure and meaning of sentences that contained profanity and sexually suggestive language. Ironically, their memory was so good for these items that the researchers expurgated the profanity and sexually suggestive items from their final statistical analysis because the memory was unlike that for other materials they were studying!

In a study of conversational memory for sexual content, Pezdek and Prull (1993) had their subjects listen to recorded conversations between a man and a woman. These sexual materials contained scenarios similar to the Clarence Thomas and Anita Hill hearings, during which Hill accused Supreme Court Justice nominee Thomas of making sexually harassing remarks at the office. When tested for retention five weeks later, sexually explicit items were recognized and recalled more accurately than nonsexual items for both verbatim and gist memory. Memory was more accurate when the sexual suggestions were inconsistent with the context (e.g., in an office setting) than when suggestions were consistent (e.g., in a singles bar). The sexual speech stood out more when it was out of context. The authors concluded, "This study extends our understanding of eyewitness memory to memory for information in conversations. Given the importance of being able to assess memory for sexual language, we look forward to additional research elucidating memory differences between sexual and nonsexual material" (p. 309). These studies suggest that memory for surface details of the sentences we comprehend are less important than the overall meaning of the sentence, unless the material evokes an emotional reading, which in many cases leads to superior memory for the original constituents.

We have addressed how emotional properties of speech are used for comprehension and how they reveal information about the emotional state of the speaker. One issue we have yet to address is how sentence parsing is realized at the neurological level. An area of research that is evolving here is the monitoring of brain wave activity as a correlate of the comprehension process.

EVENT-RELATED POTENTIALS DURING THE COMPREHENSION PROCESS

There is ample evidence that cognitive activity is mirrored by modulations in electrical activity in the brain in the form of event-related brain potentials (ERPs; see Chapters 2 and 4). The N400 research (Kutas & Hillyard, 1980, 1983) was originally viewed as a *semantic* violation detector, but since then studies have shown that semantic effects interact with lexical, contextual, and discourse levels. These methods are being refined to address violations of syntactic structure that occur during on-line processing, a topic that is directly related to the subject of this chapter.

In an early study by Kutas and Hillyard (1983), ERP data were recorded to monitor semantic deviations as well as morphological text violations in verb number, noun number, and verb tense. The N400 response to a semantic violation can be seen in the top half of Figure 5.10. Deviation in verb number, illustrated in the bottom of the figure, indicates enhanced late positivity to the syntactic violation. More recently, Osterhout (1990; Osterhout & Holcomb, 1992) looked for ERPs and syntactic violations by manipulating verb argument structure. In one study, Osterhout compared sentences like these:

44. The broker hoped to sell the stock.

45. The broker persuaded to sell the stock.

Although sentence 44 is a common construction, sentence 45 becomes unusual at *to* because *persuaded* in its active form requires an object. The ERP data indicated that between 300 and 900 ms after the onset of the word *to*, the reading was more positive in sentence 45. This response was labeled **P600.** Note the similarity between these data and those from Kutas and Hillyard (1983) illustrated in Figure 5.10.

Semantic Deviation

Grammatical Deviation

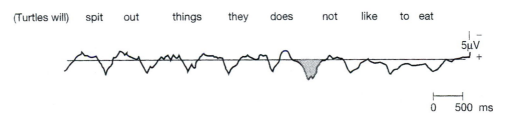

Figure 5.10. Average ERPs in Response to Semantic and Grammatical Violations in Sentences

Note. From "Event-Related Brain Potentials to Grammatical Errors and Semantic Anomalies" by M. Kutas & S. A. Hillyard, *Memory and Cognition, 11,* 539–550. Reprinted by permission of the Psychonomic Society.

In a subsequent experiment, Osterhout (1990; Osterhout & Holcomb, 1992) presented subjects with verbs that varied in their preference to take an object, as in the following sentences:

46. The doctor hoped the patient was lying. (*pure intransitive*)

47. The doctor believed the patient was lying. (*biased intransitive*)

48. The doctor charged the patient was lying. (*biased transitive*)

49. The doctor forced the patient was lying. (*pure transitive*)

The subjects rated the acceptability of sentences 46–49, revealing the gradient of acceptability: 91, 84, 66, and 4 percent, respectively. The ERPs elicited by these sentences followed the gradient of acceptability. The highest positive amplitude of P600 was sentence 49, with intermediate amplitude for sentence 48. There was little difference between the amplitudes of the intransitive sentences 46 and 47. Although ERP studies used to examine sentence parsing do not get the attention that more popular reaction time and eye movement methods do, there is clearly ERP variability associated with syntactic violations analogous to timing and fixation data (Kutas & Van Petten, 1994). A clearer picture of ERP correlates of sentence parsing will emerge as the body of research expands and matures.

Review Questions

Time flies like arrows. How many meanings does the sentence have? How can you use prosody to help disambiguate the sentence?

INFERENCES

An **inference** refers to information that is activated during the listening or reading process that is not explicitly stated. One way to represent the activated information is in terms of propositions (Kintsch, 1974; Singer & Ferreira, 1983). For example, when we read *Julie doused the bonfire. It went out*, we activate *water* as the instrument and realize a proposition such as *Julie doused the fire with water*. An alternative view of inferencing is that it happens at the level of features of meaning (McKoon & Ratcliff, 1989). According to this view, the bonfire passage would activate features of *water* such as liquid. One issue in the inference literature is whether these kinds of activations are transient and short-lived, like the multiple meanings of ambiguous words that are activated during lexical access (Swinney, 1979), or whether the activations are encoded into a more permanent sentence representation. One might resolve the problem by assuming that depth of encoding of inferences can be viewed as a matter of degree and depends on the nature of the text and the capacity of the comprehender. The point is that information that is not explicit in a text may be inferred by a reader through *elaborative inference* (Rayner & Sereno, 1994) in order to comprehend text. The representation of the text would include what the reader infers as well as what is explicit in the text.

Chapter 4 contained numerous examples of how multiple meanings of words are activated in the comprehension process, even though some are short-lived. Here the question is how and when inferential information is activated. Till, Mross, and Kintsch (1988) studied the activation of semantic associates and nonassociates of discourse using the lexical decision task (see Chapter 4). Subjects were presented with sentences such as this one:

> 50. The townspeople were amazed to find that all the buildings had collapsed except the mint.

Lexical decision words were presented immediately after the sentence at different delays following *mint*. The test words included relevant associates (*money*), irrelevant associates (*candy*), and relevant inferences (*earthquake*). The lexical decision times were assumed to reflect activation strength. Results showed that the irrelevant associates (*candy*) were facilitated, but only for 300 ms. Relevant associates (*money*) showed facilitation at 200 ms and persistent facilitation to 1.5 s. Nonassociated inferences were facilitated too, but only after a delay of 1 s, indicating some enduring role during the comprehension process. It is not clear, however, where the inference is activated in the experiment. It could be a postlexical access activation rather than one that occurs immediately during comprehension of the text. Clearer evidence for the time course of inferencing can be found in another study.

McKoon and Ratcliff (1989) had subjects read pairs of passages and answer questions after each pair. During the answering phase, relevant associates (*money*) were facilitated by prime words from the same text and by the use of neutral primes (e.g., *ready*). However, inference words (*earthquake*) were facilitated only by primes from the text. The conclusion is that associative elaborations are encoded during the comprehension process, but inferences are only weakly encoded. In a related study, McKoon and Ratcliff (1988) indicated how inferences activate semantic features of words in the text. They had subjects read passages such as sentence 51:

> 51. The still life would require great accuracy. The painter searched many days to find the color most suited to use in the painting of the ripe tomato.

Notice that the second sentence accentuates the color of the tomato. After reading the passage, subjects performed a primed verification task. Some statements matched the emphasized feature in the passage—for example, *Tomatoes are red*—or mismatched the emphasized feature—for example, *Tomatoes are round*. When primed by a statement from the passage, matched sentences (. . . *red*) were verified faster than mismatched sentences (. . . *round*). The authors concluded that relevant features were encoded into the representation of the text.

Another means of looking at inferential processes during sentence comprehension has been through the study of *anaphor* (Van den Broek, 1994). Anaphor is a pronominal or similar expression such as a reflexive pronoun whose reference is determined by a previous sentence or discourse, such that the anaphor is coreferential with its antecedent. For example, in *Jim hit himself, himself* refers to *Jim*. Reading time measures have shown that reading slows down when anaphors have to be resolved (Garrod & Sanford, 1990). After reading a sentence with an unresolved anaphoric reference, the antecedent will be more available compared to a sentence that does not contain the antecedent. However, inappropriate referents will not be available at the end of either kind of sentence (Gernsbacher, 1989). So readers slow down when they have to search for the anaphoric referent. Gernsbacher (1989, 1990, 1991b) describes the establishment of anaphoric coherence with two mechanisms, one that *enhances* the antecedent and one that *suppresses* the "other" concepts.

Comprehension involves the constant activation of concepts. Anaphors play an important role by activating the referent's identity and suppressing or decreasing the nonreferential concepts. The implication is that anaphors differ in their effectiveness in alternating activation. The more specific the anaphor linking the referent to its identity, the quicker it enhances the antecedent and suppresses nonreferential concepts (Gernsbacher, 1989, 1990). In a well-structured text, the antecedent is usually part of the concepts that are activated. Sometimes the two are separated from each other, and the antecedent is not activated. If the appropriate antecedent is not currently activated when the reader processes the anaphor, a memory search via a spreading activation process ensues (O'Brien, 1987; O'Brien & Albrecht, 1991; O'Brien, Plewes, & Albrecht, 1990). O'Brien et al. (1990; O'Brien & Albrecht, 1991) found that antecedents that occur late in the text and close to the anaphor are accessed more quickly than antecedents that appear early on. Also, the speed with which the antecedent can be activated depends on the number of concepts associated with it. The more highly elaborated antecedent is activated more quickly than the less elaborated antecedents. The results indicate that anaphoric resolution is a function of the distance between the anaphor and the referent and also of the number of paths linked to it.

As noted in our discussion of working memory, one of the factors that affects inference processing and text integration processes, like those used in anaphoric reference, is working memory capacity. The greater the on-line working memory capacity or reading span, the more likely it is that elaborative inferences can be made during the comprehension process. The relationship between reading span and pronoun resolution is supported by the study by Daneman and Carpenter (1980) discussed earlier and illustrated in Figure 5.10. Like drawing an inference, the reader must identify the antecedent concept and link it to the current sentence being processed. People differ in their ability to make these kinds of bridging links. Singer, Andrusiak, Reisdorf, and Black (1992) found that reading span was a significant predictor of one's accuracy at judging inference test statements that bridged to nonadjacent ideas.

Eye movement research has been used to study inferencing. The results of eye movement research confirm the idea that elaborative inferences occur on-line. The data can be used to differentiate between instances of inference making and instances in which the reader awaits explicit information. O'Brien, Shank, Myers, and

Rayner (1988) measured fixation times on the final sentence of a passage: *He threw the knife into the bushes, took her money, and ran away.* Of interest was the amount of time on the target word, *knife,* which was previously either explicitly mentioned in the text (. . . *stabbed with his knife*) or strongly implied (. . . *stabbed her with his weapon*). They found no difference between fixation times across these conditions, suggesting that the concept of *knife* had been activated from the prior context. However, when the text did not strongly imply *knife* (. . . *assaulted her with his weapon*), fixation time on *knife* in the final sentence was longer than the explicit or strongly implied condition, suggesting a memory search for the antecedent.

There has been a great deal of research on the question of inference processing as it relates to sentence comprehension, discourse processing, and reading comprehension (see Gernsbacher, 1994). I have limited the discussion here to aspects of inferencing that are related to aspects of sentence comprehension without covering the overlapping body of research on reading and discourse processes, which we will delve into in Chapters 7 and 8. What we have covered here reflects two trends in inference processing research (Singer, 1994). One trend attempts to find language and listener or reader characteristics that guide inference activation, and the second attempts to identify connections between concepts that help preserve text coherence. Research has shown that inferences, featural information, and relevant concepts are activated and encoded during the comprehension process.

COMPREHENSION AND LONG-TERM RETENTION

As we noted with respect to verbatim memory (J. S. Sachs, 1967), the surface details of a sentence give way to false but reasonable inferences about what was heard or read. Consider a sentence you read earlier in the chapter. Which sentence of the four below do you remember reading in Exercise 5.1?

    a. Three turtles sat on a log, and a fish swam under them.

    b. Three turtles sat by the log, and a fish swam under it.

    c. Three turtles sat on a log, and a fish swam under it.

    d. Three turtles sat by a log, and a fish swam under them.

Pick the sentence that is worded exactly the same as the one you read at the beginning of the chapter. It is interesting how quickly our memories for the little details fade. But this example is not about memory so much as it is about the inferences we draw from sentences. We go beyond the facts and use our knowledge of the world to figure out what people say to us. (I'll reveal the answer shortly.)

When Bransford, Barclay, and Franks (1972) asked subjects to make old-new judgments about the *turtle* sentences they had seen earlier, knowledge of spatial relationships caused them to make erroneous inferences about sentences they had never seen. Subjects thought they had seen sentence (b) when they had actually seen sentence (a). Subjects inferred quite logically that if the fish swam under the turtles, it must have swum under the log as well. Listeners and readers use generalized world knowledge to make sense of sentences. Many times this knowledge leads to poor judgments about the exact details of a statement.

False recognition errors for sentences are not particularly problematic in psycholinguistic experiments, but they are problematic in a court of law, as research by Loftus and her associates has demonstrated (Loftus & Palmer, 1974; Loftus, Schooler, & Wagenaar, 1985). In her experiments, subjects are shown a film depicting a traffic accident in which one automobile crashes into another. Subjects are later interrogated about the film in a manner that influences their later recall of the incident. Some subjects are asked, "How fast were the cars going when they *smashed* into each other?" Another group is asked, "How fast were the cars going when they *hit* each other?" The verb *smashed* implies more damage than a verb like *hit* does. In their responses to the biasing question with *smashed,* subjects not only made higher speed estimates of the accident but also added erroneous details, such as broken glass, that did not appear in the film. These results have important implications for the quality of eyewitness testimony. Misleading inferences can have both immediate and long-lasting effects. We examine psycholinguistic research in courtroom settings and in police interrogations in more detail in Chapter 13.

Review Question
During eyewitness testimony, how do cognitive factors like memory and inferences constrain long-term memory for the details of conversation?

Key Terms

affective prosody	lexical frame analysis	rewrite rule
case grammar	memory span	surface structure
constraint hierarchy	minimal attachment	thematic structure
constraint satisfaction	modularity	analysis
deep structure	optimality theory	transformational
emotional	P600	rules
involvement	parsing	tree diagram
garden path sentence	phrase structure	verbatim memory
gist effect	proposition	vocal expression of
inference	prosody	emotion
late closure	reading span	working memory

What Lies Ahead

Chapter 6 looks at the process of speech production and models of speech production. Speech production follows on the heels of what we have covered about the perception and comprehension of language in Chapters 3, 4, and 5. It also sets the stage for Chapter 7 on writing and reading processes.

Suggested Web Site

Rutgers Optimality Theory Archive: http://ruccs.rutgers.edu/roa-nog.html

Chapter 6
Speech Production

Critical Thinking Questions

1. What are the basic stages of speech production?

2. How do people find words to express their thoughts?

3. What kinds of speech errors do speakers make?

4. What do speech errors reveal about the stages of speech production?

5. How do people implement their speech plans?

6. What happens when people realize they have made a mistake?

7. What models have been developed to describe speech production?

Exercise 6.1. **Speech Errors**
Listen to someone reading the news on the radio or television and record any speech errors (e.g., slips of the tongue) that you hear. Compare your findings to speech errors covered later in the chapter. Using an audio or video recorder will make this exercise easier.

In Chapter 5, we were interested in how listeners and readers comprehend sentences. In this chapter, we are interested in how speakers translate thoughts into sentences. Research on comprehension processes has revealed that we process speech at multiple levels to derive meaning, operating on phonemes, words, phrases, and sentence units. The idea of language levels is useful here as we explore how speech is produced. However, do not infer that speech production is merely the reversal of comprehension processes, because comprehension and production use different neural and anatomical structures.

Whereas psychologists have a considerable body of research on comprehension processes, how sentences are produced is less well understood. One difficulty regarding natural speech production is that most of the process goes on outside of conscious awareness, making it hard to pin down what is happening and when. We are left with many questions about the process and a need to devise methods to elucidate the production process (see Bowers, Vigliocco, Stadthagen-Gonzalez, & Vinson, 1999; Griffin & Bock, 2000). We consider some of the major speech production questions in this chapter. For example, how do we conceptualize what we are going to say? How do we find the "right" words to express our conceptualizations? What are the "units" or building blocks of speech production? What are the "stages" of assembling speech units? What kinds of errors do people make while speaking, and what do the errors tell us about speech production? What factors affect speech production, such as speaking rate and pausing? How are gestures and emotions integrated into the speech stream? What models have been proposed to account for the data?

A comprehensive approach to speech production attempts to account for how people integrate speech, emotions, and gestures to affect listeners. One challenge for a comprehensive view is to show how words and other components associated with them are planned and combined during the speech production process. This is a difficult undertaking because most influential theories of speech production are restricted in scope to linguistic components (syntax, morphology, semantics, phonology). However, we addressed in Chapters 4 and 5 the notion that nonlinguistic components of communication are activated with words. For example, the meaning of a verb like *stab* contains its syntactic and semantic constraints, as well as a gesture for the stabbing motion. There is no reason to doubt that *stab* also activates emotional information about what it feels like to stab something or to be stabbed. To be successful, a comprehensive model of speech production will have to show that speaking "stab" activates links to lexical, emotional, motoric, semantic, phonological, and syntactic representations, some of which will be represented in sentence and gestural forms (McNeill & Duncan, 2000). We need to show that speaking a word like *stab* allows for the activation of any or all of these verbal and nonverbal links.

The production process outlined in this chapter has four parts, which form the plan for the chapter itself: conceptualizing the message, forming a linguistic plan, implementing the plan, and self-monitoring for errors.

Conceptualizing an Intended Message

More than a century ago, William James (1890) provided a useful analysis of the speech production process. James envisioned speech production as involving two simultaneous processes: (1) the thought process, which is global and holistic, involving a type of thinking in **mentalese** that is not yet speech, and (2) the speech process, which is serial and linear assemblage of the units of language. Wundt (1900/1970) also recognized this dualistic nature of speaking. Wundt saw the sentence as both simultaneous and linear, existing in totality in consciousness but changing from moment to moment as constituents moved in and out of one's attention. McNeill (1987, 1999, 2000) and others (see Bock & Levelt, 1994) have used the ideas of James and Wundt as a working model of speech production, one that simultaneously operated on a holistic, private, inner speech level and on a second level that is a serial or linear linguistic process involved with "unpacking" the inner speech content.

McNeill views the two production processes as intertwined, feeding off of the same initial thought. As a thought is unpacked, speech symbolically represents the important aspects of the original idea. The linear expression, a string of words, is synchronized with gestures, global symbols that "mean" the same thing as the words do. McNeill (1999; McNeill & Duncan, 2000) uses the term **growth point** to describe the beginning of conceptualization, which combines imagery with linguistic categorical content before the output stages unpack the synchronized speech and gestures.

EYE MOVEMENTS DURING SPEECH PLANNING

One means of examining the holistic-to-sequential transition of speech production described by psychologists such as Wundt, James, and McNeill is to elucidate the events that give rise to simple sentences. If we assume that people look at what they are thinking, as we did when we considered eye movement as a correlate of parsing strategies in Chapter 5, then we can use eye movements here to look at what people are thinking about as they prepare a sentence describing what they see.

To study the time course of sentence production, Griffin and Bock (2000) monitored **eye movements** of speakers as they described events depicted in pictures. Eye movements are used to diagnose the temporal relationships between extracting an understanding of the event as a whole, formulating a sentence by retrieving and arranging words, and finally by articulating the sentence. Griffin and Bock used picture sets that portrayed active events (*The mouse is squirting the turtle with water*) like those depicted at the top of Figure 6.1 and pictures that portrayed active-passive events (*The mailman is being chased by the dog* versus *The mailman is chasing the dog*), depending on whether the human is the agent or the patient in the scene. One group of subjects describes the events pictured as they are being viewed (extemporaneous speech). A second group viewed the same events while preparing their descriptions, which were produced after the picture disappeared from view (prepared speech). A third group viewed pictures with the purpose of finding the person or thing being acted upon, known as the *patient,* and then pressing a button (patient detection), a task that cannot be accomplished without understanding the causal structure of the event. A fourth group (inspection) viewed the pictures without any particular task to gauge how picture elements attract attention. If the

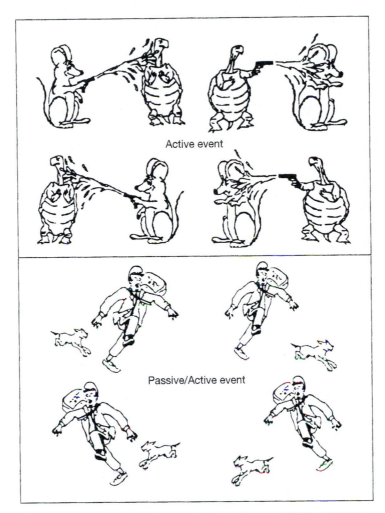

Figure 6.1. Examples of Picture Sets Used in the Griffin and Bock Experiments The top panel shows an active picture set, typically described in the active voice in all four versions. The bottom panel shows a passive-active picture set, typically described in the active voice if the human is performing the action and in the passive if the human is acted upon.

Note. From Griffin, Z., & Bock, K. (2000). What the eyes say about speaking. *Psychological Science, 11(4),* 274–279. Reprinted by permission of Blackwell Publishers.

holistic stage precedes sequential formulation, speakers should inspect events enough to code them prior to speaking.

The viewing times of the elements of the picture over the time course of the four different viewing conditions are plotted in Figure 6.2. Several points are noteworthy about the figure. Griffin and Bock (2000) found that when speaking extemporaneously, speakers begin fixating on the pictured elements less than a second

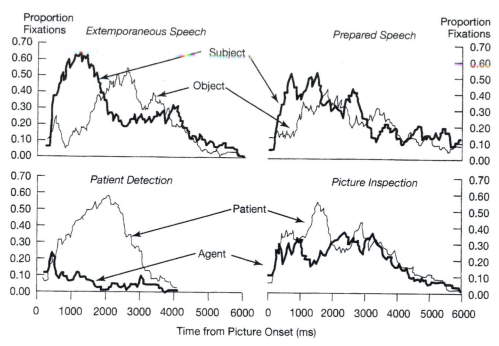

Figure 6.2. Eye Movements during the Griffin and Bock Experiment The curves plot changes in viewing in successive 4-ms intervals during the four types of tasks. Results for all picture types and versions are combined.

Note. From Griffin, Z., and Bock, K. (2000). What the eyes say about speaking. *Psychological Science, 11(4),* 274–279. Reprinted by permission of Blackwell Publishers.

before naming them in their descriptions, consistent with sequential encoding. Eye movements also anticipate the order of mention despite changes in picture orientation, in who did what to whom, and in sentence structure. Speakers' initial eye movements and those of subjects performing the nonspeaking patient detection task suggest that response-relevant information is rapidly extracted from the pictures, permitting them to select grammatical subjects based on their comprehension of the event rather than salience (the inspection task). The inspectors did not systematically fixate on one region of the picture during the first 1200 ms after the picture onset when they fixated on the patient. Extemporaneous speakers began fixating on pictured elements less than a second before naming the actors in their descriptions, the subject first and then the object.

To determine if extemporaneous speakers extract the event structure prior to speaking, points of divergence between agent and patient regions in the patient detection task, which demands comprehension of the event, are compared to corresponding divergence for the subject and object noun phrases in extemporaneous speech. During detection, divergence is significantly different at 456 ms after onset. For extemporaneous speakers, divergence reached significance at 336 ms. The overt response times of these two groups are comparable as detectors took 1690 ms to indicate that they found the patient (pressed the button), while speakers describe the subject and then the object at 1686 ms after the picture onset. These comparisons suggest that speakers rapidly extracted the event structure and that there is a very orderly linkage between successive fixations during event viewing and word order in speaking.

Griffin and Bock have designed a clever method to examine what people are thinking about prior to speaking about what they see. Although we cannot see the holistic mentalese prior to speaking, eye movements reliably show what speakers are going to talk about and in what order, before they speak in this event description task.

Formulating a Linguistic Plan

Another component of the speech production process is generating a framework on which to hang the units of speech. This component has three phases: identifying the meaning, selecting a syntactic structure, and generating an intonation contour. The framework begins with a thought you want to express and the searches for definitions that best match the thought, like consulting a dictionary in reverse—defining the meaning and then finding the word to match it. The next step involves finding the appropriate syntactic structure.

We used tree diagrams in Chapter 5 to show how people parse sentences with a phrase structure grammar. One could assume that we use them here to generate sentences, starting with a sentence-level representation (S) and fleshing out the phrases (NP + VP), then the constituents within phrases (N, V, Adv, Adj, etc.). An alternative conceptualization, also discussed in Chapter 5, relies on a semantics-based framework using not tree diagrams but cases, themes, or roles assigned to the main verbs and nouns in the sentence. Here we would find the appropriate nouns and verbs that describe the actions, actors, and objects in the conceptualization. The verb *stab* would activate agent, patient, and instrument roles. A third alternative would be the connectionist model. A sentence to be spoken would be represented by spreading activation through a network of nodes representing phonological, lexical, and morphological levels. Finding the syntactic frame could be described using any of these three models.

The intonation contour indicates whether you are going to ask a question or make a statement. The constituents in the utterance that need to be emphasized or stressed have to be tagged at this point. Here is where we lay out the stress pattern in the sentence to be produced. For example, I might want to say "*Here* is where we lay out the stress pattern" to emphasize *where* we are in the production process. Alternatively, I might say "Here is where we layout the *stress pattern*" to emphasize *which component* is involved at this particular stage. Why is the intonation important so early in the plan? Because it represents fairly global features of what is going to be said. Intonation contour is a broad plan for the sentence or question under construction. The prosodic structure is created from the sentence's syntax but without knowledge of its phonemic contents (Ferreira, 1993). The prosodic structure of a sentence can be thought of as a tree diagram with constituents arranged in a hierarchy. Branches of the prosodic tree do not cross, meaning that a prosodic word can fit in only one phonological phrase. The utterance is the highest level in the hierarchy.

The utterance *As Jim knows, Mary became a psychologist* divides into two intonational phrases, *As Jim knows* and *Mary became a psychologist*. Below the level of the intonational phrase is the phonological phrase. In the example, these would be *As Jim, knows, Mary, became a psychologist*. Below the phonological phrase is the prosodic word level, consisting mainly of content, not function, words. These would be *As Jim, knows, Mary, became, a psychologist*, since *as* and *a* are not phonological words. Ferreira (1993) demonstrated that syntactic structure by itself in not necessary or sufficient to account for prosodic aspects of word duration and pausing. Word and pause durations are explained successfully from the hierarchical structure just suggested here. The hierarchical structure is used to create timing intervals for the utterance. After we have assembled the overall prosodic properties of the sentence, we have to go about finding the right words to fit the frame.

Finding Words

At some point in the speech production process, we have to find the right content words to express our thoughts, and the words have to be inserted into the sentence frame. The word-finding component is instigated after we have conceptualized what we want to say, generated a framework, and determined its prosodic properties. The word-finding component relies on the process of lexical access, a process we addressed in Chapters 4 and 5. It refers to finding the right content words, the right function words, and also the appropriate prefixes and suffixes in languages that have inflections. The affixes and inflectional morphemes are selected after the content words, as we will soon see. It is only after we have the right words and affixes that we can determine how the word is going to be pronounced, that is, the word's *phonetic segmentation*.

PICTURE NAMING

Lexical selection has a long history of experimentation, dating back to Cattell (1885). Cattell discovered that people were slower at naming pictures than at reading words because written words have a more direct access to the lexicon than pictures, which have to be interpreted conceptually. These kinds of results have been studied extensively (see Glaser, 1992, for a review), and one line of research informative about speech production is known as the *picture-naming interference paradigm*.

This research into **picture naming** involves the presentation of two stimuli. The primary stimulus is a picture, which the subject has to name as quickly as possible.

The secondary stimulus is a spoken or printed distractor word that the subject is supposed to ignore. This is a difficult task because subjects have trouble completely ignoring the distractors, and that distraction slows down the picture-naming times. There are usually two variables that are of interest in these experiments. The first is the relationship between the picture's name (target word) and the distractor. The second is the asynchrony between presentation of the distractor and presentation of the picture. If the picture is of a sheep, the distractor could be semantically related *(goat)* or unrelated *(house),* or it could be phonologically related *(sheet).* Using distractors that are semantically related to the picture versus those that are phonologically related, we can make inferences about where in the lexical access process semantic and phonological information becomes activated.

Glaser and Dungelhoff (1984) conducted a classic study of picture-naming interference. They presented distractors in a range from 400 ms before the picture to 400 ms after the picture. The printed distractor was either semantically related (e.g., *goat*) or unrelated (e.g., *house*) to the target word (e.g., *sheep*). All distractor words were names of pictures used in the experiment. Results indicated that the naming response was delayed when semantically related distractors were presented, relative to unrelated distractors. This effect has been referred to as **semantic inhibition:** The related distractor inhibits the activation of the target word, which is similar in meaning.

In the Glaser and Dungelhoff study, we could see the naming effect but could not tell which cues were selected first, semantic or phonological. Schriefers, Meyer, and Levelt (1990) conducted an alternative picture-naming experiment to deal with this issue. The question of interest was whether people first retrieve the semantics of lexical items and then later retrieve the phonology or whether they retrieve these aspects simultaneously. In other words, is a **serial model** for language production accurate?

In this study, subjects were engaged in a picture-naming task during which they were presented with distracting auditory stimuli. The distractors were semantically related, phonologically related, or unrelated. Distractors were presented at different times: 150 ms before the picture, concurrently with the picture, or 150 ms after the picture. Results indicated that *early* distractors slowed down semantic reaction times but phonological distractors had no effect. With *concurrent* presentation, semantic distractors had no effect but phonological distractors speeded up reaction times. At the *delayed* interval, semantic distractors had no effect but phonological distractors speeded up reaction times even more. The interpretation is that semantics are activated during lexical access before phonological aspects are activated, confirming the serial model.

NOT FINDING A WORD: THE TIP-OF-THE-TONGUE PHENOMENON

Brown and McNeill (1966) devised a method to reveal how lexical access is conducted. Subjects are given the definition of an unusual word and are asked to name what word fits the definition. When subjects were given a definition such as "a flat-bottomed boat used in Asia," a predictable pattern of responses occurred. Some of the subjects knew the target word, *sampan,* but others did not. Subjects who thought they could find the word even though it was not immediately available were in the **tip-of-the-tongue state (TOT).** TOT subjects guessed at the target word. The list of guesses generated in TOT showed how subjects searched memory. A list of guesses that includes *sampoon, sarong, cheyenne,* and *shang pan* reveals the semantic nature (something from Asia) and the phonological nature (two syllables, first accented) of the target word. The TOT study shows that people have a feeling that a word is within reach even when direct access fails.

The TOT phenomenon happens frequently when we try to remember the name of a somewhat familiar person (e.g., *Dan*). We generate a list of likely guesses that are similar to the target (*Doug, Dave, Don, Dean,* etc.) much like the subjects in TOT. TOT has been studied extensively (see A. S. Brown, 1991, for a review), and it is a topic of interest in the research on aging and memory (Burke, MacKay, Worthley, & Wade, 1991) because it is frequently experienced in the elderly population. Brown summarized some of the most consistent findings of numerous TOT studies as follows:

- The phenomenon is universal, spanning all ages.

- TOT can be induced in many ways, such as by giving a definition and seeking the proper words, showing a face and seeking names, or asking people to label odors.

- Based on diary studies, it is estimated that a TOT occurs about once a week, and the rate increases as we age.

- Everyday TOTs are most often triggered by names of acquaintances.

- Words related to the target often come to mind and are usually similar in meaning or sound to the target word.

- In TOT, people can guess the first letter about 50 percent of the time, and they can guess the number of syllables 50 to 80 percent of the time.

- About 50 percent of TOTs are successfully resolved within about one minute.

The traditional view of TOT is that the speaker cannot access a retrievable memory. Recently, B. L. Schwartz and his colleagues (Schwartz, Benjamin, & Bjork, 1997; Schwartz & Smith, 1997; Schwartz, Travis, Castro, & Smith, 2000) proposed that such states reflect an inferential process in which subjects experience difficulty generating an answer because they have incomplete information about the target. Schwartz and Smith (1977) found that TOTs are more likely to occur when the subject has a medium or maximum amount of information about the target; minimal information is insufficient to trigger a TOT. Further Schwartz et al. (2000) found that TOTs were more likely to be resolved and recognized for emotional than for nonemotional TOTs. The TOT is a phenomenological state that is correlated with the person's sense of emotionality, memory strength, and imminence of resolving the TOT.

Research covered to this point is predicated on the idea that lexical access is a two-stage process wherein conceptual semantic and syntactic sources of information about the target words are retrieved prior to phonological information about the target. The TOT experience can be described as a failure to retrieve the full phonological word form even though the more abstract semantic features of the word have been selected (Garrett, 1984; Levelt, 1989). However, this conceptualization does not distinguish semantic activation at the conceptual level from that at the lexical level. The existence of an abstract lexical representation independent of the conceptual level, however, has not been determined by these kinds of studies in English.

People in the tip-of-the-tongue state should be able to report specific syntactic information about the target they cannot name, and they should be able to know these features even when they have little phonological information about it. Vigliocco, Antonini, and Garrett (1997) tested these two hypotheses using information about **grammatical gender** during tip-of-the-tongue experiences in Italian. Grammatical gender assignment is important because it is used to compute agreement between nouns and determiners (e.g., *la penna* versus *il libro*), between nouns and adjectives (e.g., *la penna colorata* versus *il libro colorato*), and other links between nouns and pronouns and between nouns and predicates. Grammatical gender is assigned to every noun in Italian in a seemingly arbitrary fashion. Italian nouns are classified strictly on the basis of linguistic properties, not conceptual properties.

Vigliocco et al. (1997) presented subjects with definitions and examined when they were unable to provide the target word (the TOT experience). Subjects were asked to guess the gender of the noun, the number of syllables, and other aspects (letters, other words that come to mind). After answering these questions, subjects were presented with the target and asked if they knew the word and if it was the one they were thinking of. Responses were divided into *positive* and *negative* TOTs. A positive TOT was scored if the subject could not say the word but did provide more complete information in the questionnaire and answered the recognition question in the affirmative. A negative TOT was scored if the subject did not recognize the word, gave more information, but did not affirm the target word at recognition.

The overall distribution of masculine and feminine guesses for positive and negative TOTs is presented in Figure 6.3. Speakers in the positive TOT do have access to syntactic features of targets for which they cannot generate a phonological representation. Grammatical gender is dissociated from the conceptual representation in Italian, allowing for the distinction between lexical and conceptual information. This study provides the first clear evidence for a lexical stage that includes syntax and is separate from both conceptual and phonological correlates of syntactic features. It adds to the picture-naming literature with respect to how words are accessed. Next we look at implementing the speech plan.

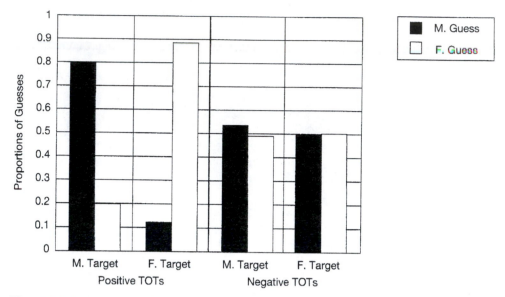

Figure 6.3. Guesses Regarding the Gender of Italian Words in the Tip-of-the-Tongue State

Note. From Vigliocco, G., Antonini, T., & Garrett, M. F. (1997). Grammatical gender is on the tip of Italian tongues. *Psychological Science, 8(4),* 314–317. Reprinted by permission of Blackwell Publishers.

Implementing the Plan

Now we have reached the point where the speaker has to implement the speech plan by saying what he or she has been intending to say. Just because one has a plan does not mean it's going to be carried out fluently or correctly; the speech error data have been informative on that account. There are some additional factors that need to be addressed.

In this section, we consider the flow or stream of words that are produced to express the speaker's intentions. Here is where the speaker implements the plan that has been constructed. Some comparisons between speaking and signing are made.

SPEECH HESITATIONS, PAUSES, AND FILLERS

Speakers produce **pauses** in order to be understood. We also use pauses to produce an "idealized" representation of a sentence, especially when we are reading. For example, pausing is used to set off one clause from another so that the listener does not string all the words together into the same clause. Speakers also pause in an attempt to control their speech rates, not talking too fast or too slowly. One factor that contributes to the perception of high speech rate is that the speaker does not pause very frequently or for very long durations when he or she does pause. Sometimes the perception of speeded speech is merely the reduced amount of pausing and not an increased number of words. Pauses are important to speech production and speech comprehension processes.

Goldman-Eisler (1968) has made an extensive analysis of the role of pausing in spontaneous speech. She found that most normal, unprepared speech consists of three-word phrases. Long, ten-word phrases occur in only 10 percent of unpracticed speech. Even if a speaker practices the text several times, ten-word phrases occur at a rate of only 15 percent. With practice, pausing will diminish, and smoother production will occur. When discourse is prepared in advance, smooth transitions will occur when the speaker shifts from one idea to another. Without preparation, disfluencies and pauses occur when the speaker shifts ideas while talking (Greene & Cappella, 1986).

The locations of pauses in speech are fairly predictable. Most pausing occurs before content words rather than before function words. Most pausing (55 percent) occurs at a grammatical boundary, but the remaining body of pauses does not appear at predictable grammatical junctures. The effect of pausing as a function of grammatical structure is particularly obvious when speakers are reading text, where most of their pausing will occur at the sentence and phrase boundaries. When the sentence constituents are large, speakers will pause at the boundary, but when constituents are small, pauses will occur at the end of a group of constituents (Grosjean, Grosjean, & Lane, 1979).

In conversations, pauses generally take one of two forms. They can be silent or filled. **Filled pauses** can take one of several forms. Many filled pauses take the form of nonword sounds (e.g., *um, er, ah*) or interjections (e.g., *well, say*). DuBois (1974) found that speakers filled pauses with connection phrases such as *that is, rather,* and *I mean* in order to correct an error in the previous clause. These fillers are an indication that the speaker is interrupting his or her speech to repair a previous statement. We look at different kinds of repairs in the following section.

One of the variables that influences pausing in speech is the number of potential word candidates from which the speaker can draw. Schachter, Christenfeld, Ravina, and Bilous (1991) counted the number of filled pauses during lectures given by speakers from different academic disciplines. They found that humanists used more fillers than social scientists or natural science lecturers. Schacter et al. proposed that this was because the humanities lecture with a richer pool of words and synonyms relative to natural science lectures, which offer few alternative words for concepts such as "molecule," "atom," or "electron." In a follow-up study, Schachter, Rauscher, Christenfeld, and Crone (1994) counted the number of different words used in lectures and in professional publications. They found that humanists used a greater variety of words relative to social scientists and natural scientists, supporting their original claim.

This brings us to the point where we consider what happens when the speech plan goes awry.

Errors in Speech Production

You might be asking yourself, how do we know that the speech production process unfolds in the order in which it has been presented here? The answer is that evidence from speech error data supports dividing the process into these stages. For example, if you say, "Stop beating your brick against the head wall," when you intended to say, "Stop beating your head against a brick wall," we know that the error occurred when words were being inserted into the sentence frame because otherwise the overall plan seems to be fine.

As mentioned, the major obstacle to understanding the initial stages of speech production is that we cannot directly access the production of speech. What we can observe about speech are the outputs of the linear symbolic process. Speech errors are the most widely used source of evidence for speech production. Psycholinguists have been attracted to speech errors because they can be used to speculate about the order of planning processes that precede articulation. Speech errors represent failed processes. Because speech errors occur at different levels of organization (phonemic, syntactic, or semantic), they have been used to describe speech production as a series of planning stages.

TYPES OF SPEECH ERRORS

Lashley (1951) suggested that speech errors were a valuable source of evidence for a speech plan that ultimately directs the speech muscles to move. Speech errors provide evidence that the final execution of a sentence engages different levels or units of planning. Previous analyses of speech errors (Dell, 1986; Fromkin, 1971, 1973; Garrett, 1975, 1976) provide ample evidence that errors occur primarily within one production level (semantic, lexical, morphological, or phonological) rather than across levels. Speech units exchange with each other on the same level of analysis—that is, phonemes changes places with phonemes; they do not change places with syllables. Fromkin (1973) and others (Dell, 1986) have noted that most speech errors could be described by a few types of persistent errors. Here are a few examples.

Blend: two speech units are combined	*grizzly + ghastly → grastly*
Anticipation: a speech unit is activated too early	*take my bike → bake my bike*
Perseveration: a speech unit is activated too late	*pulled a tantrum → pulled a pantrum*
Substitution: a unit is changed into a different unit	*the place opens → the place closes*

Misdeviation: the wrong unit is attached to a word

intervening node → *intervenient node*

Shift: the speech unit (an affix here) moves to a different location

she decides to hit it → *she decide to hits it*

Exchange: two units swap positions

Katz and Fodor → *Fats and Kodor*

Addition: a unit is added

carefully enough → *clarefully enough*

Deletion: a unit is deleted

plastic → *plattic*

Note the different units affected in these kinds of examples: features, syllables, morphemes, affixes, words, and syntactic phrases. Some kinds of errors are difficult to classify. For example, if the error was *I won't ask any flavors* (intending *favors*), is this a phoneme addition or a word substitution? Is *Why is natural glass* (for *gas*) *so expensive?* a phoneme addition or a perseveration of the /l/ in *natural?* These problems aside, natural language errors are evidence of speech planning units and of stages of speech production. First we examine how speech errors occur within similar units of speech, and then we draw some conclusions about the stages of speech planning.

In our discussion of speech perception and comprehension, there was a need to posit a hierarchy of speech units, building from the smallest to the largest, that is,

distinctive features → phonetic segments → syllables → words → phrases → . . .

How does this order apply to speech articulation? Slip-of-the-tongue errors suggest that articulatory units for speech production can be found at each of these levels of speech.

DISTINCTIVE FEATURE ERRORS

The phonological rules for speech were presented in Chapter 3. You might recall that phonemes, which are classes of sounds, consist of bundles of distinctive features (e.g., voicing) that are used to make contrasts with a target phone and other phonemes. Errors at the distinctive feature level will change the phonemic representation of the word. For example, the following phrases reflect errors based on *voicing* (movement of the vocal cords). They appear as exchanges where the unvoiced phoneme is mistakenly voiced and vice versa (Fromkin, 1971; Fromkin and Ratner, 1998):

big and fat → pig and vat

Is pat a girl? → Is bat a curl?

clear blue sky → glear plue sky

The phonetic segments or distinctive features appear to switch places in the final speech plan. Errors at this level provide evidence that the speech plan operates on units smaller than phonemes. Notice that if distinctive feature errors occur at the last moment, the sentence structure and the words in it must have already been selected for the plan.

PHONEME ERRORS

Interest in phonological errors goes back at least to the Meringer and Mayer study (1895) of anticipation and perseveration errors. These kinds of errors are very common, and there are many examples of them. Errors of phoneme **anticipation** occur when a speaker produces too early a sound that should properly occur later in the sentence, as in these phrases from Fromkin and Ratner (1998):

reading list → leading list

Sue weeded → See weeded

Errors of phoneme **perseveration** occur when the speaker continues to produce a phoneme that was used earlier in the sentence, as in the following from Fromkin and Ratner (1998):

phonological rule → phonological fool

annotated bibliography → annotated babliography

Anticipations and perseverations provide evidence that speakers formulate a speech plan. Sometimes the processing works forward, and sometimes it works backward. There must be a stage in production that is suspended where earlier and later words are mutually available within the same representation. Overall, speech error patterns of anticipations and perseverations depend on precipitating variables (Dell, Burger, & Svec, 1997). When speech error rates are high, errors are usually of the perseverative type. Perseverations are common when speakers produce novel phrases, but anticipations are more common when speakers produce practiced phrases. Perseverations are also more common in children and some aphasics than in normal adult speakers.

Phonemes, like distinctive features, can also exchange places in the phrase, as in the following examples of **exchanges** from Fromkin (1973):

left hemisphere → heft lemisphere

feed the pooch → food the peach

brake fluid → blake fruid

Phonemic errors include the *additions* of phonemes to words (*box → blocks*), the deletions of phonemes (*speech → peach*), the exchange of phonemes (*bird watcher → word botcher*), and exchanges of clusters of phonemes (*stick in the mud* → *smuck in the tid*). Notice that vowels exchange with vowels and consonants with consonants. There are no cases where vowels and consonants exchange. Only like units exchange. Again, phonological errors occur after syntax and lexical plans have been made.

LABORATORY-INDUCED PHONEME EXCHANGES

Baars, Motley, and MacKay (1975) created a method to induce slips of the tongue in a laboratory situation. Subjects had to read pairs of words silently until they were signaled to respond by speaking aloud. For example, the subject reads silently

ball doze

bash door

bean deck

bell dark

darn bore

(*signal to speak aloud*)

The pairs were designed to induce an exchange of syllable initial consonants. On 30 percent of the trials, subjects made exchange errors, saying *barn door* instead of articulating the pair as presented.

One important issue was whether it made any difference if the final spoken pair consisted of real words or not. To test this question, a nonlexical condition presented pairs of words, but if the induced exchange error occurred, the subject would have to produce nonwords (e.g., *bart doard*). A nonlexical trial might look like this:

big dutch

bang doll

bill deal

bark dog

bart board

(*signal to speak aloud*)

The nonlexical condition produced errors on only 10 percent of the trials. Baars et al. referred to this difference between the lexical and nonlexical exchanges as a **lexical bias effect.** Subjects are more likely to make an exchange error if it creates real words. This suggests that there is a means of separating words from nonwords during the planning or articulation process. The nature of the lexical editing process has been a subject of much debate. How one would account for the lexical bias effect (with a serial versus interactive process) depends on the particular model of speech production in question, as we will see at the end of the chapter.

SYLLABLE ERRORS

Speech errors that are larger than features or phonemes also occur during speech production. These kinds of errors swap syllables that do not involve morphemes. In many cases, according to MacKay (1969), syllable exchanges involve the same syllabic positions within the affected words; that is, a word-initial segment swaps with another word-initial segment, and a word-final segment swaps with another word-final segment. Here is a case where the final syllables are exchanged:

Merrill and Fenner → Merrer and Fennill

Syllables are also involved in *blends* (MacKay, 1972). Notice how the first syllable blends with the final syllable:

shout + yell → shell

grizzly + ghastly → grastly

WORD AND MORPHEME ERRORS

Word errors generally occur after the overall syntactic structure of the sentence has been planned. The analysis of errors in lexical selection remains one of the most active areas in speech production research (Bock & Levelt, 1994), and it provides some of the most interesting kinds of errors, as we shall see. Words can be exchanged, perseverated, or exchanged, as demonstrated by Fromkin (1973) and discussed earlier. Here are some examples:

tank of gas → gas of tank

lighter for every purse → purse for every lighter

Substitutions of whole words indicate that speech production includes planning for constituents within sentence frames. Words tend to exchange with like constituents—nouns for nouns, verbs for verbs, and adjectives for adjectives. Content words and function words do not exchange with each other.

In our examples, words as whole units change places. But units of meaning are not limited to words; they also include morphemes (see Chapter 4). Fromkin and Ratner (1998) reported speech errors with both derivational and inflectional morphemes. Some examples of errors with inflectional morphemes follow. Notice that the root words were exchanged but not the morphemes. The morphemes stayed where they were in the speech plan.

rules of word formation → words of rule formation

cow tracks → track cows

have screws loose → have screw looses

Derivational morpheme errors occur in these examples:

easily enough → easy enoughly

there's a good likelihood → there's a good likeliness

can't quite make it → can't quietly make it

Word substitutes are often related semantically to intended words (Garrett, 1988), as in *He is too old, I mean, he is too young* or *I wanted to take my daughter, er, my wife.* These errors indicate that the speaker is in the right semantic ballpark but has chosen a word with the wrong semantic feature. Word errors can also involve the substitution of a word that is similar to the one intended but with a different meaning. These substitutions are called *malapropisms.* An example from Fromkin (1973) is *white Anglo-Saxon prostitute* for *white Anglo-Saxon Protestant.* The psychological meaning of these kinds of lexical selection errors that involve emotion-laden semantics has been studied in the guise of "Freudian slips."

FREUDIAN SLIPS

Freud (1916/1963) lectured extensively about the mistakes people make in everyday situations—forgetting to do a task, forgetting someone's name, hearing the "wrong" word or name in a sentence, saying or writing the "wrong" word or name in a sentence. Freud referred to such everyday mistakes as *parapraxes,* but the verbal ones have come to be known as **Freudian slips.** Here are examples from his work and others (Meringer & Mayer, 1895; see also Ellis, 1980):

> A president of the House of Parliament who wanted to open the meeting said, *"Gentlemen, I take notice that a full quorum of members is present and herewith declare the sitting closed."*

> A professor says, *"In the case of the female genitalia, in spite of temptations [Versuchungen], I beg your pardon, experiments [Versuche] . . ."*

> *Eiweiß-scheibchen* (small slices of white bread) → *Eischeißweibchen* (literally, "egg shit female")

> *Alabasterbüchse* (alabaster box) → *Alabüsterbachse* (*Büste* = "woman's bust")

There are several difficulties involved in using parapraxes as data for a model of speech production. First, the "unconscious" thought stage of speech production has proved impenetrable with linguistic tools. Second, the emotional meaning of any slip requires knowledge about the speaker and the context in which the slip occurs. We must know what the person intended to do in order to interpret the meaning of the slip. Third, the analysis of behavioral or verbal slips is by nature post hoc because one cannot predict when these are going to occur. Fourth, the personal significance of a Freudian slip may require a detailed knowledge of the inner life of the speaker, as in psychoanalysis.

We do know that one cause of speech errors is situational anxiety (Clark & Clark, 1977). When people speak about topics that cause anxiety, they produce more pausing and speech errors. Anxiety disrupts the planning and articulation stages of speech production because speakers become tense. For example, a man becomes angry at his new partner and calls the partner by his ex-partner's name. Another disruptive factor is that anxiety-provoking topics may be more difficult to approach cognitively; that is, unpacking complex emotional topics may take more time and more planning to meet the intentions of the speaker. Verbalization during anxiety-producing situations may require greater demands on lexical selection processes in order to express the "right" thoughts. So the anxiety of the topic or the anxiety in the social situation affects speech planning and articulation.

The laboratory study of forbidden words can only partially touch on our linguistic self-censorship. Induced-slip experiments have been done with anxiety-provoking stimuli. Studies by Motley, Camden, and Baars (1981, 1982) used a method of inducing slips to examine stages of speech production discussed earlier. They wanted to determine whether subjects were editing speech during sentence formulation prior to articulation. As a means of measuring the speaker's awareness of the emotional slip, they recorded the **galvanic skin response** (GSR), an indication of emotional arousal. If a subject was aware that he or she was going to say a taboo word pair (e.g., *cool-tits*), higher GSR readings should occur relative to GSRs before nontaboo pairs (e.g., *tool-kits*). The experimentally induced slip technique presented subjects with preliminary pairs of words (e.g., *cool-tarts*) to be read silently. After silently reading the preliminary pairs, subjects had to speak the target pair (e.g., *tool-kits*) to see if this pair would produce a taboo pair (e.g., *cool-tits*), which should be primed by the preliminary pairs.

Results indicated that the slips did undergo some form of censorship. Subjects produced more neutral-error slips (e.g., *cool-kits*) than taboo slips (e.g., *cool-tits*). Target pairs associated with large GSRs (that is, taboos) took longer to say (had longer utterance latency) than small GSR-evoking targets. Pairs with large GSRs took more processing time than pairs with small GSRs. Apparently, the words activated emotional arousal, causing subjects' elevated GSRs. The inappropriate emotional words (remember, they have to say them) required subjects to spend time censoring them prior to speaking.

Motley (1980) found that he could induce more sexually loaded slips (e.g., *fine body*) by making sexuality more salient in the laboratory setting. Using all male subjects and a provocatively dressed female experimenter, Motley found that sexual slips were more common than when a male experimenter conducted the same experiment. We know that speakers are aware of the emotionality of what they are going to say because previous studies revealed elevated GSRs. Self-censorship was part of the speech production process because speakers delayed what they were about to say. These effects are in line with our discussion regarding situational anxiety and the lexical bias effect. What the laboratory-induced-slip studies suggest is that the emotionality of the speech situation and the speaker's awareness of taboo words should be incorporated into models of speech production.

Freudian Slips: A New Look?

Psychologists since Freud have grappled with the nature or existence of the unconscious. It might be prudent for psycholinguists to abandon that idea and find an alternative explanation for errors with emotional content. The notion should also be expanded to include sign language slips. If a word or sign contains information about its semantic, syntactic, and morphophonemic properties, perhaps it also links to information about its emotional content (discussed in Chapter 4). If a word is tagged with emotional information as to its activity, potency, and evaluation features (aspects of the semantic differential), then these features could form the basis for a censorship decision. We need some mechanism that censors emotional speech production in contexts where emotional words are inappropriate. The classical notion of the Freudian slip can be replaced by the emotional tagging hypothesis. A Freudian slip would occur in a situation where the *inappropriate* emotional tags slip through the censor along with *appropriate* semantic, syntactic, and phonological properties. Otherwise, the sentence frame of a Freudian slip is fine. It is the emotional information connoted by the word chosen that is the problem. Freudian slips contain words accessed during the word-finding stage that have the wrong emotional properties. The key is tagging lexical items with emotional information. We cover emotions more in detail in Chapter 11.

Before leaving the topic of speech errors, one way to further buttress the reality of planning units and planning stages during speech is to compare errors in speaking to errors that occur in the production of sign language.

SLIPS OF THE HAND

The signs used in ASL are not the kind of holistic gestures that McNeill described. ASL signs are subdivided into an internal structure that unfolds in a stagelike fashion similar to spoken sentences. The stagelike production of signed speech opens it up to errors or **slips of the hand** that are functionally equivalent to slips of the tongue.

Newkirk, Klima, Pedersen, and Bellugi (1980) found that slips of the hand by deaf signers were remarkably similar to slips of the tongue. American Sign Language combines three basic components: hand configurations, the placement of articulation, and movement. The patterns of speech errors that unfold in signing suggest that signing occurs over a series of planning stages much like speech. For example, a signer who intends to sign *sick* may produce the sign for *sick* with the hand configuration for *bored*, or vice versa, while the placement and movement components are not altered. This type of error is illustrated in Figure 6.4. Many of the errors Newkirk et al. recorded were like this example, involving only one component of the three components in the slip of the hand.

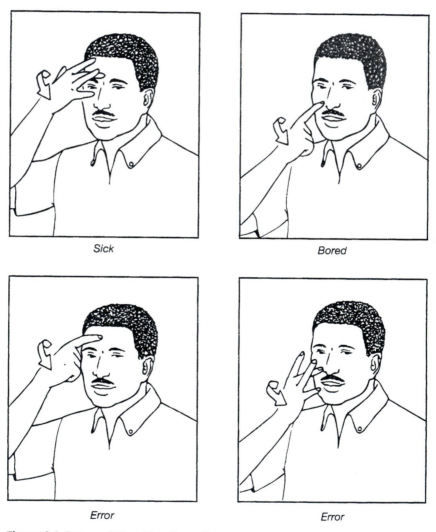

Sick   *Bored*

Error   *Error*

Figure 6.4. Errors of Hand Configurations
Note. From D. Newkirk, E.S. Klima, C.C. Pedersen, & U. Bellugi, in *Errors in Linguistic Performance: Slips of the Tongue, Ear, Pen, and Hand,* edited by Victoria A. Fromkin, copyright 1980, Elsevier Science (USA), reproduced by permission of the publisher.

The production of signed speech involves a series of stages that occur independently. Signed errors engage similar components that exchange with each other, not across components, much like spoken components (words, phonemes, syllables), which likewise exchange with analogous components. Signing errors may involve exchanging or substituting components such as distinctive features of signs (e.g., a bent finger or an unbent finger) or morphological features of signs. For example, in Figure 6.5, the signer intends to sign *must see*, which includes a hand configuration with a bent index finger. The sign for *see* has a hand configuration that

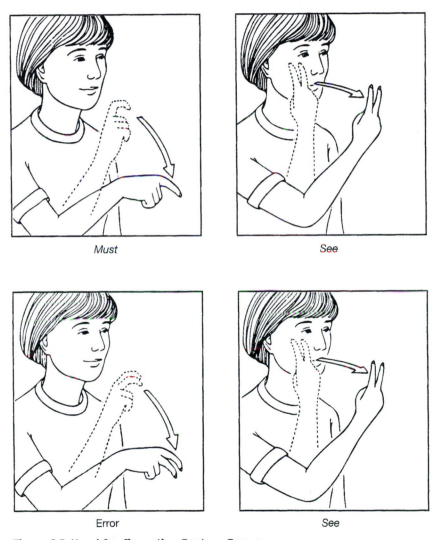

Must

See

Error

See

Figure 6.5. Hand Configuration Feature Errors

Note. From D. Newkirk, E.S. Klima, C.C. Pedersen, & U. Bellugi, in *Errors in Linguistic Performance: Slips of the Tongue, Ear, Pen, and Hand,* edited by Victoria A. Fromkin, copyright 1980, Elsevier Science (USA), reproduced by permission of the publisher.

makes a V like the "peace sign." The error illustrated in Figure 6.5 has the signer anticipating the two-fingered V sign in *see* by erroneously using two fingers to make the *must* sign.

Newkirk et al. (1980) found that when signers make errors that produced novel signs, the novel signs obeyed the rules of ASL much like blends and substitutions in speech obey the phonological rules of speech (Dell, Read, Adams, & Meyer, 2000). If speech errors are seen as functionally equivalent to errors made in ASL, this is further evidence that language production processes are based on the underlying plans for those for oral speaking.

CONCLUSIONS ABOUT SPEECH ERRORS

Generally speaking, the order of emergence of speech errors shows that planning occurs first with semantic information and sentence framing, then moves into lexical and morphological stages, which are followed finally by phonological information. Garrett (1975) proposed that speech errors could be characterized by four common properties:

- Elements that interact come from similar environments.

- Elements that interact tend to be similar: consonants with consonants and vowels with vowels.

- Slips that create novel words generally obey the phonological rules of language (see Dell et al., 2000).

- Stress patterns in production are consistent. Swapped segments usually come from stressed components of words or phrases or from components that are marked for minor stress features.

Exercise 6.2. **Speech Errors**
Can you put what you've just read about speech errors to use? The task is to record and analyze errors in spontaneous speech (not reading a text or a news report). Listen to someone speaking spontaneously. This could be done during a course discussion or by eavesdropping on everyday conversations on campus. It is easier with a tape recorder if one is handy. Thirty minutes or so should suffice. In your notebook, indicate the errors, slips of the tongue, mispronunciations, and omissions that were made. Note where the speaker made self-corrections. We'll talk about them later in the chapter. Compare your recordings to what you've just read about speech errors. What conclusions can you draw?

Production Monitoring and Editing

Once we have a plan in mind, we have to say what we intended to say. The Freudian slip research supports the notion that speakers monitor their speech for socially inappropriate taboo words. Speakers produced more neutral slips than errors that resulted in taboo words. The planning and production phases of speech would seem to run in interwoven cycles (see Danks, 1977): making a plan, saying something, planning some more, saying some more. Sometimes the production cycle will produce fluent speech, and other times there will be hesitations and pauses, as noted earlier. Each phase of the cycle will take time and use working memory resources. A complex and lengthy plan cannot be generated and carried out due to working memory limitations. We addressed working memory limitation in Chapter 5 in connection with sentence comprehension. Similar working memory limitations constrain sentence production processes.

It is possible that self-monitoring occurs at two points in the speech production process. One type of editing could occur as a form of *covert* self-monitoring during the planning stage and the other, a type of *overt* monitoring, during speaking. The lexical bias effect (slips produce more word than nonword errors) has been suggested (Garrett, 1980) as evidence that covert editing eliminates the nonword errors during the planning process. The raised GSR readings prior to the production of taboo slips seems to suggest that there is a level of awareness of the emotionality of the to-be-articulated word before it is spoken.

The data supporting a covert level of monitoring are more convincing. Nooteboom (1980) found that roughly two-thirds of speech errors are corrected shortly after the error, usually at the first word boundary after the error. But different types of errors produce different levels of detection. Anticipations (e.g., *she shells* instead of *seashells*) were repaired more often than perseverations (e.g., *sea sells* instead of *seashells*). Nooteboom thought that the urge to correct the error was immediate but that the speaker had to wait until a constituent boundary was reached in order to fulfill the urge to repair.

Levelt (1983, 1989) developed one of the most influential classification systems for **self-repairs** on the basis of self-repair behavior of adult speakers of Dutch. Subjects were presented with complex sets of color patterns that are connected with lines, as depicted in Figure 6.6. The subject has to describe the layout of colors, starting at the point designated by the arrow. Consider configuration (a) in the figure. The subject has to describe the arrangement of colors, for example, "Above

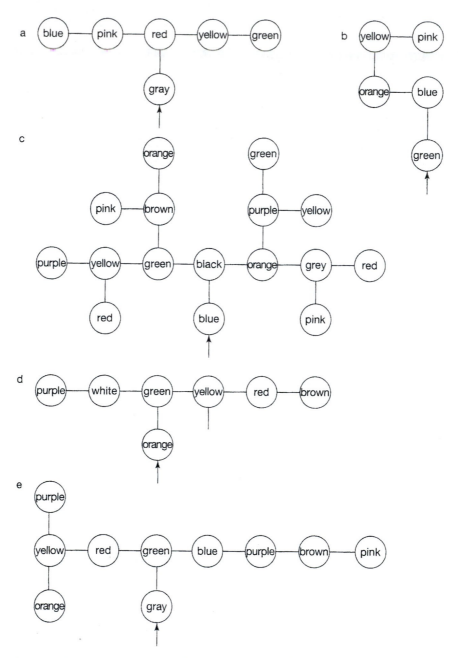

Figure 6.6 Patterns to Be Described in Levelt's Self-Repair Experiment
Note. From Levelt, Willem, *Speaking: From Intention to Articulation*. Reprinted by permission of MIT Press.

the gray patch is a red one. To the right of the red patch is a yellow one . . . ," as if a hypothetical listener has to reproduce the layout from the subject's description. The task results in speech errors and interruptions that can be analyzed. Levelt found that 18 percent of the errors were repaired *within* the troublesome word.

Most of the errors (51 percent) were corrected immediately *after* the error, and 31 percent were delayed one or more words. These results were similar to what Nooteboom (1980) found with spontaneous speech errors.

Levelt (1983) noted that we interrupt speech after error detection in order to make an **editing expression** (*I mean, uh,* etc.) and then continue with the self-repair. Each editing expression signals a different kind of trouble. *Uh* is the most common and is used when speakers get stuck searching for information in the middle of an utterance. *I mean* indicates that the speaker needs to add a word or substitute a different item for the one spoken.

Levelt proposed that self-repairs occurred at both the covert and overt levels. Again, the notion of covert repairs is difficult to verify because the troublesome item is not open to inspection. The overt error repairs are further classified according to the reason for the repair. Overt error repairs are instigated to correct phonological, morphological, lexical, syntactic, and inappropriateness (e.g., imprecise terms or lack of specification) problems. Here is an example of each kind of repair, where ^ marks the point of repair:

Phonological	They have a /naɪš/ ^ nice boat.
Morphological	So the man have ^ has got his hats back.
Lexical	If you must read ^ uh write the English word . . .
Syntactic	It's not you do ^ something you do every day.
Inappropriate with replacement	It turns out to be a film ^ a movie scene . . .
Inappropriate with insertion	You see a policemen ^ an English policeman . . .

Self-repairs, according to Levelt (1983, 1989), also come in three types. *Instant repairs* occur when the speaker traces back to the mistake, which is then replaced, for example: *the blank crossing point* ^ *white crossing point.* Anticipatory *retracings* occur as the speaker returns to a point in the sentence *before* the error, for example: *to the purple crossing point* ^ *to the red crossing point.* And in the third form, *fresh starts,* the speaker abandons the original sentence and starts over, for example: *from yellow down to brown* ^ *no, that's red.* Levelt (1989) found that most self-repairs were instant repairs (51 percent) and anticipatory retracings (41 percent); only 8 percent were fresh starts. Repairs tend to be targeted to the troublesome area, and speakers generally fix the problem without repeating the entire utterance. However, fresh starts are most likely when the original item is contextually inappropriate. What was said is not an error, strictly speaking, the phrase that gets a fresh start is correct; however, it is awkward or inappropriate and therefore needs to be rephrased.

Given the evidence, one cannot avoid the conclusion that speech production incorporates simultaneous comprehension monitoring and correction strategies.

We turn now to models of speech production. These generally come in two types, those that envision production as a serial process and those that envision production as a parallel process, for example, spreading activation of nodes in a network. Following these are models that integrate gesturing into the production process.

Models of Speech Production

Speech production models need to account for evidence from natural language and from experimental analyses of speech production. Laboratory research and studies of speech errors show speech production as a sequence of independent stages. Errors tend to occur at a particular level of production. For example, most phonological speech errors have been recorded to occur within the same clause, but word exchanges can occur across clauses. This gives the impression that word selection and phonological representations are established at different points in the speech production process. These are some of the facts that require explanation. The next four traditional models are outlined.

THE FROMKIN MODEL

In her pioneering effort, Fromkin (1971) proposed that planning stages or representations are created in order from meaning to syntax and then to phonological representation, as follows:

1. Propositional representations are chosen.
2. Syntactic frame is created.
3. Intonation contour is matched to syntactic frame.
4. Content words are inserted into the syntactic frame.
5. Function words and affixes are inserted.
6. Phonemic representations are added.
7. Phonological rules are applied.

One conclusive piece of evidence for this order comes from errors that involve moving an inflectional plural morpheme (/s/ or /z/) from one word to another. The final placement accommodates to the phonological rule for voicing such that the voiced version /z/ attaches to words ending with voiced consonants and the unvoiced version /s/ attaches to words ending with unvoiced consonants. The phonological rules accommodate to the errors by applying the rules to produce outputs that are consistent with the phonological rules of the language. Phonological rules have to be applied after the morpheme shift (Dell et al., 2000).

The supporting evidence for Fromkin's model is derived from speech error data as you can see from our earlier discussions. Other supporting evidence reveals that in the midst of "late" speech errors, intonation contour will remain the same. For example, even when the words or sounds are switched from one place to another in the string, the intonation pattern of the intended string remains intact. This means that the intonation contour must be activated before words are inserted, for example, *hammer and SICKLE* → *sickle and HAMMER*, or *a computer in our own LABoratory* → *a laboratory in our own comPUter.* At the level of function words, affixes and function words can shift, indicating that the function word inserter can misidentify the appropriate location in the frame, as noted—for example, *have screws loose* → *have screw looses.* The ordering of production supports the point made in the picture-naming literature that semantics are processed before phonology (Schriefers et al., 1990). Fromkin's conceptualization of the speech production process is similar to a model proposed by Garrett.

THE GARRETT MODEL

The Fromkin and Garrett models represent speech production as a series of stages that unfold from early (syntax) to late (phonology) processes. Based on speech error evidence, Fromkin (1971, 1973) and Garrett (1975) proposed models that consist of roughly six stages from the early units to the later. The models can be summarized as follows:

1. Meaning to be conveyed and intentions of a speaker are chosen.

2. Syntactic structure of the sentence and its constituent slots is created.

3. Intonation contour and what word slots are stressed.

4. Lexical selection of content words (e.g., adjectives, nouns, and verbs) are selected.

5. Affixes (prefixes and suffixes) and function words are selected.

6. Phonological segments are selected according to phonological rules.

Garrett's 1984 model is illustrated in Figure 6.7. Like Fromkin, Garrett distinguishes between three different levels of production: conceptual, sentence, and articulatory. The conceptual meaning to be conveyed is represented as an "inferential processes" in the model. At the sentence level in the model, Garrett makes a distinction between a *functional level* and a *positional level.* The functional level involves planning with multiphrasal units where the assignment of lexical-class items to their phrasal roles takes place. Here is the stage where word exchanges occur that involve words that play the same grammatical role.

The positional level is pronunciation-oriented. Here the sounds in words and sentence elements are assigned to locations in the output string. This is the stage

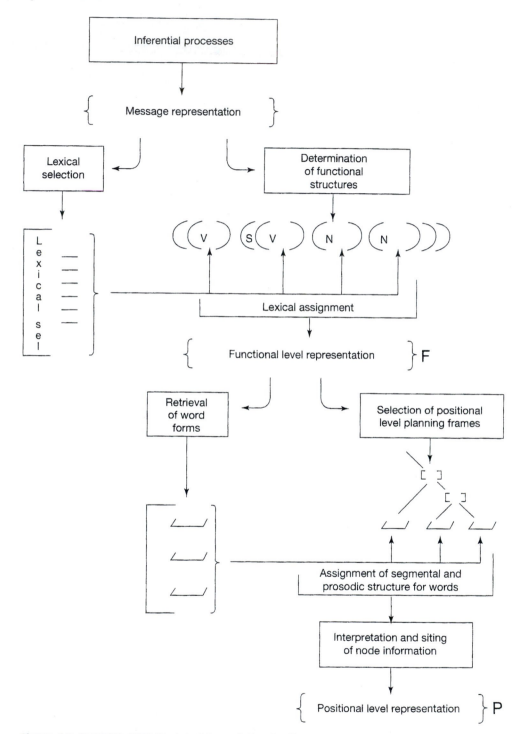

Figure 6.7. Garrett's 1975 Model of Speech Production
Note. Fromkin, V., & Bernstein Ratner, N. (1998). Speech production. In J. Berko Gleason and N. Bernstein Ratner (Eds.). *Psycholinguistics (2e),* (pp. 309–346). Reprinted from *Cognition,* Vol 42, M. F. Garrett, "Disorders of lexical selection," pp. 143–180, copyright 1984, with permission from Elsevier Science.

where errors that involve sound exchanges, word substitutions that are similar in form (but not meaning), and morpheme shifts take place. The phonologization of grammatical morphemes occurs at the phonetic representation level, which accounts for errors that show that the final output string conforms to the language's phonological constraints.

The final stage of the model (similar to Fromkin's) is the articulatory level. Here the motor program sends commands to the organs of speech, producing the acoustic patterns in the message.

Garrett's model accounts for much of the speech error data. His explanation of the lexical bias effect, which posits an editing stage prior to articulation that monitors for nonwords, contrasts with parallel models described next, which account for lexical bias through spreading activation.

THE BOCK AND LEVELT MODEL

Willem Levelt and colleagues have written extensively about the stages of the speech production process (Levelt, 1989; Bock & Levelt, 1994; Levelt, Roelofs, & Meyer, 2000). Figure 6.8 presents an overview of this model, showing four levels of processing: message, functional, positional, and phonological. The *message* captures the intended meaning and provides output for grammatical encoding. *Grammatical encoding* combines functional and positional sets of information. *Functional processing* uses lexical selection, which captures the lexical concepts that are appropriate to convey the speaker's meaning, and function assignment, which involves assignment of grammatical roles or syntactic functions. *Positional processing* creates an ordered set of word slots—the "constituent assembly" box in Figure 6.8—and inflection or morphological slots. The *phonological encoding* stage creates the phonological structure of the message in terms of phonological units of words along with prosodic features of larger units.

Bock and Levelt (1994) described the stage of grammatical encoding in the production process, which they characterized as those that create the "skeleton" of the speech and those that "flesh the skeleton out." Grammatical encoding involves the selection of the appropriate lexical units and assembling them in a syntactic frame. In contrast, phonological encoding involves the assembly of sound units and intonation contour. Grammatical encoding is impenetrable to consciousness, but speech errors provide clues to how language production works. The products of the functional processing stage of Bock and Levelt's model are illustrated in Figure 6.9, which shows how a speaker would assemble the sentence *She was handing him some broccoli.*

The word as a grammatical entity is referred to as a **lemma.** Lexical selection begins with finding the lexical concepts and lemmas appropriate for the message. Lemmas contain the grammatical information for a lexical concept, for example, whether it is a noun, a verb, and so on. Lemmas contrast with *lexemes,* which capture a word's morphological and phonological shape. A common speech error at the lemma level might result in substituting *cauliflower* for *broccoli,* which preserves both the general features of the intended word and its grammatical form (see Stemberger, 1985).

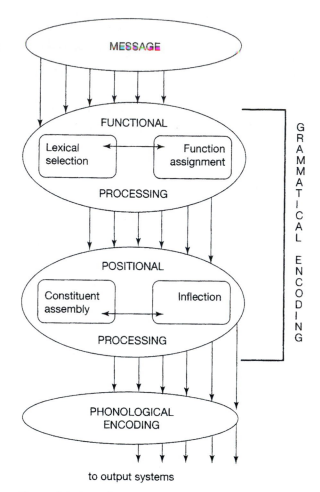

Figure 6.8. Overview of the Language Production Process

Note. Figure from "Language production: Grammatical encoding" by Bock, K., & Levelt, W., in *Handbook of Psycholinguistics,* edited by Morton A. Gernsbacher, copyright 1994, Elsevier Science (USA), reproduced by permission of the publisher.

Function assignment, the next step, involves the assignment of grammatical functions such as subject, object, or pronoun. An error at this stage might involve exchanging the feminine and masculine pronouns, resulting in *He handed her some broccoli.* The stage of propositional processing fixes the order of units in the utterance by assigning phrasal constituents according to their syntactic dependencies. If we conceptualize this stage as a tree diagram, the product of the positional processing, on the basis of the previous functional processing, would look something like Figure 6.10, which shows how the two stages unfold. The final stage of grammatical encoding involves the generation of affixes regarding number, tense, and aspect that are bound to

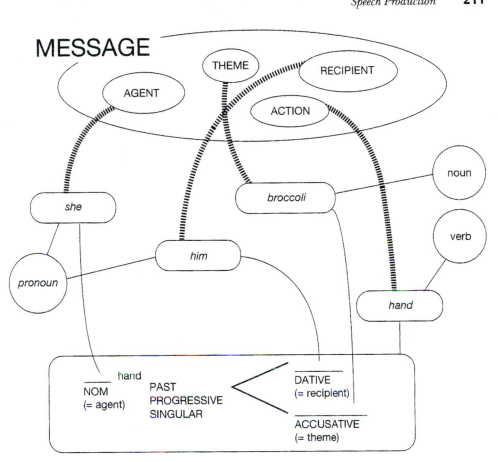

Figure 6.9. The Products of Functional Processing

Note. Figure from "Language production: Grammatical encoding" by Bock, K., & Levelt, W., in *Handbook of Psycholinguistics,* edited by Morton A. Gernsbacher, copyright 1994, Elsevier Science (USA), reproduced by permission of the publisher.

other words. Here is the point where *-ing* is added to the verb *hand.* Here is the stage where lexeme-level or morpheme errors occur whereby inflections are misallocated, shifted, or stranded. The relationship among the conceptual, lemma, and lexeme levels of the lexical access model are illustrated in Figure 6.11.

Bock and Levelt (1994) and Levelt et al. (2000) have marshaled a great deal of evidence (more than can be detailed here) in the form of errors, experimental research, and computer modeling to support their model of speech production. Levelt et al. focus on the lexical access aspect of speech production, assuming that conceptualizing and producing names is one of the most critical aspects of the production process. An outline of the new lexical access process is shown in Figure 6.12. Notice the inclusion of a multilevel *self-monitoring process,* which is necessary to account for evidence regarding hesitation, pauses, self-editing, and repair strategies discussed earlier.

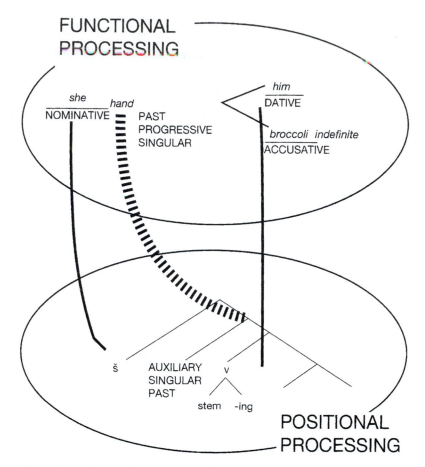

Figure 6.10. The Events of Grammatical Encoding

Note. Figure from "Language production: Grammatical encoding" by Bock, K., & Levelt, W., in *Handbook of Psycholinguistics,* edited by Morton A. Gernsbacher, copyright 1994, Elsevier Science (USA), reproduced by permission of the publisher.

THE DELL MODEL

Dell's connectionist model of speech production (Dell, 1986; Dell, Chang, & Griffin, 1999) is predicated on the notion of spreading activation over multiple levels of nodes. Words are the main nodes in the network, with connections to conceptual units and to phonetic units. The order of operations proceeds from concepts to words and then to sounds, that is, from semantic nodes to syntactic, morphological, and phonological nodes. The spreading activation principle is bidirectional, permitting interactions between semantic and phonological units. Activation at syntactic nodes spreads to morphemes, which spread to phonemes. Morphological nodes also activate syntactic nodes. Figure 6.13 shows Dell's network version for the sentence *Some swimmers sink.* Concepts activate lexical units that share semantic

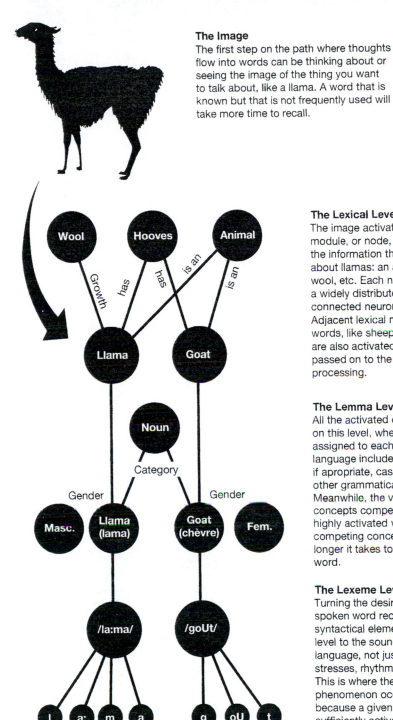

The Image
The first step on the path where thoughts flow into words can be thinking about or seeing the image of the thing you want to talk about, like a llama. A word that is known but that is not frequently used will take more time to recall.

The Lexical Level, or Concept
The image activates the lexical module, or node, for llama, carrying all the information the brain has stored about llamas: an animal with hooves, wool, etc. Each node is believed to be a widely distributed network of connected neurons in the brain. Adjacent lexical nodes for related words, like sheep, goat, animal, etc., are also activated, the information is passed on to the next module for processing.

The Lemma Level
All the activated concepts are passed on this level, where proper syntax is assigned to each one. These rules of language include word order, gender if apropriate, case markings, and other grammatical features. Meanwhile, the various activated concepts compete; usually the most highly activated wins, but the more competing concepts interfere, the longer it takes to generate the desired word.

The Lexeme Level
Turning the desired concept into a spoken word requires matching the syntactical elements from the lemma level to the sounds that make up a language, not just syllables but stresses, rhythms, and intonation. This is where the tip-of-the-tongue phenomenon occurs, perhaps because a given lexical node was not sufficiently activated to make it to the lexeme level.

Figure 6.11. Levels of Speech Production
Note. Figure from "Language production: Grammatical encoding" by Bock, K., & Levelt, W., in *Handbook of Psycholinguistics*, edited by Morton A. Gernsbacher, copyright 1994, Elsevier Science (USA), reproduced by permission of the publisher.

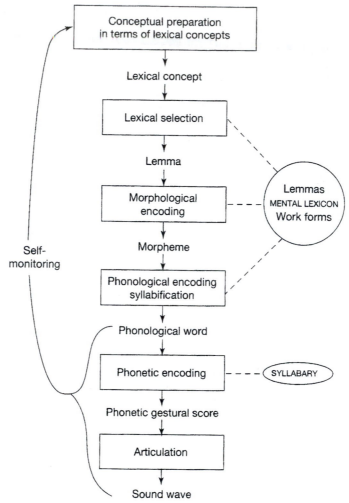

Figure 6.12. Stages of Speech Production

Note. "A Theory of Lexical Access in Speech Production" by Levelt, W.J.M., Roelofs, A., and Meyer, A.S., in *Behavioral and Brain Sciences,* Vol. 22, No. 1 (2000): 1–75. Reprinted with permission of Cambridge University Press.

features; for example, *swimmer* will activate units like *drown, sink,* and *swim.* It will also activate a syntactic class of nouns, affixes (the plural), and a class of verbs.

During the planning of a sentence, several nodes will be activated at the four different levels. They will remain activated for a while but will eventually degrade to zero activation. Because activation fans out in all directions, words related to the meaning of an activated node will be activated, as will words related to the phonetic structure. The cohort of activated nodes can be considered the basis for speech errors (Dell, 1995). Figure 6.14 illustrates a hypothetical slip where the speaker articulates *prevent* instead of the intended word, *present.* Whether such slips are semantic or phonological is indeterminate. Activated nodes become the potential candidates

LEXICAL NETWORK

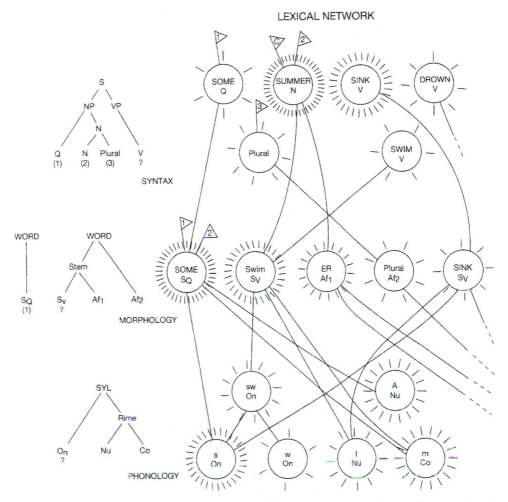

Figure 6.13. Network Model of Speech Production Tactic frames (left) specify an ordered set of categorically labeled slots. The question mark indicates the slot in each frame that is presently being filled. The highlighting surrounding the nodes reflects activation level, and the flag marked "C" indicates the current node at each level. Each node is labeled for membership in some syntactic or morphological category.

Note. From "A spreading activation theory of retrieval in sentence production" by G. S. Dell, *Psychological Review*, 93, p. 290. Copyright © 1986 by the American Psychological Association. Reprinted with permission.

for erroneous use in the final production of the sentence, with nodes exchanging within node levels but not across node levels. Words, morphemes, or phonemes swap with each other because they have high activation levels. Dell, like Levelt, proposes a speech comprehension component that monitors for errors and accounts for self-repairs and corrections.

Dell's model accounts for several kinds of evidence. It can explain slips that are phonemically similar by the notion that each phoneme activates phonemes with corresponding distinctive features. This increases the likelihood that a slip will be phonologically similar to the intended target. The spreading activation model can

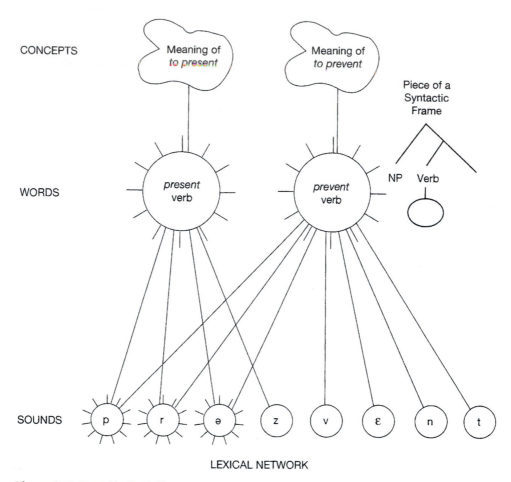

Figure 6.14. Hypothetical Slip

Note. From Osherson, Gleitman, Liberman, *An Invitation to Cognitive Science*, Vol. 1. Reprinted by permission of the MIT Press.

account for the finding that speakers are likely to create slips with semantic associations to words presented earlier in the phonetic bias procedure (Motley & Baars, 1976). For example, after reading a set of *g-w* word pairs, the slip *wet gun* will occur, replacing *get one*, if a semantically similar phrase, like *damp rifle* occurred before the target pair. The model also accounts for the lexical bias effect discussed previously. Here errors favoring "true" words occur due to backward spreading activation. This does not occur for nonwords because nonwords do not have morphological nodes like true words. The backward spreading process allows the model to account for lexical bias without assuming a special editing or monitoring function (Baars et al., 1975).

The spreading activation model of speech production effectively accounts for production phenomena related to speaking rates. The spreading and decay of activation during slow speaking accounts for the lower rate of errors because there is ample time to activate correct sounds and time for the previously activated units to decay. Speeding up the rate of speech production creates a situation where previously activated units remain active and incorrect but similar units compete for activation. In addition, Dell (1985) found that when speakers are asked to speak quickly, lexical bias effects are attenuated because the effect is based on backward activation, which takes time to occur. Slower speaking rates result in more errors because there is more time for backward activation.

The serial model contrasts well with parallel spreading activation models such as Dell's. A good way to show the difference would be to look at the lexical bias effect. The lexical bias effect generated a lot of interest, and psycholinguists divided on how to account for the data. The gist of the problem was whether speakers were monitoring and filtering out the nonwords (a serial view of speech production) or whether the lexical bias effect is due to top-down processing caused by the simultaneous activation of words and phonemes (a **parallel model**). In line with the parallel activation view, Dell (1985, 1986) proposed that activation spreads backward in the network from phonemes to words, which takes time. The effect occurs only when subjects are allowed time to respond (Dell, 1985). Garrett (1980) argued that there was no lexical bias effect in naturally occurring speech and that it was more likely caused experimentally. Garrett believed that the effect was due to self-monitoring and that it was the covert monitoring process that took more time, not spreading activation. So both models made identical predictions but on different grounds.

Next we consider models that address the role of gesturing during speech production, a level of processing that the previous models have ignored.

Gesture-Inclusive Models

Comprehensive views of speech production integrate speaking with nonverbal expression (e.g., gestures). The traditional models covered so far do not incorporate gestures into the speech stream. Speech production includes spoken and signed modes—vocalizations and hand symbols are human speech. Further, oral speech production occurs with synchronous gesture components. The relationship of the spoken word to the gesture is a matter for debate. Two main approaches are apparent in the gesture and language literature: one that views the two forms of expression as independent and the other that views them as integrated.

Types of Gestures Coordinated with Speech Production

Iconic gestures occur when the hands are symbols in form and manner of meaning that co-occurs with linguistic meaning. For example, "up inside the drainpipe" co-occurs with a pointed finger and hand moving upward in a single movement. Iconics have their own content and accompany narrative speech. In

Box Continues

contrast, **beats** are concurrent with speech but emphasize the discourse function of the speech with up and down or back-and-forth movements, usually with clauses that introduce new information or sum up or anticipate the narrative content. Beats are extranarrative gestures with minimal content that emphasize the relational functions of the speech. **Cohesive gestures** make use of iconics to tie together different parts of the narrative. A speaker might move the hand and wrist from the lap backward toward the ear to indicate that the current reference is linked to a previous statement. **Deictic gestures** are pointing gestures that occur at the beginning of a conversation or the beginning of a new topic, which may or may not be aimed at a real or imagined physical target. For example, a speaker may point off into the distance with the word *there*, which could refer to a point in physical context or to a past place or time. **Metaphorics** are images of abstract concepts that are not picturable themselves. For example, a "mathematical dual" might be represented by a gesture of a closed hand and wrist rotating upward, then downward. Gestures are differentiated from **emblematics,** which are recognized as having meaning, such as "the finger," the "thumbs up" sign, and the "OK" sign.

THE McNEILL INTEGRATED MODEL

In the **integrated model,** gestures are a component of the production process for the speaker and at the same time part of the comprehension process for the listener (Goldin-Meadow, 1999; McNeill, 1999). Goldin-Meadow has written extensively about how children's early gestures precede and then coordinate with spoken speech over time. In the early stages of language acquisition, children's gestures and speech are part of a unified system where the gestures convey the same information that is contained in their speech. As children develop spoken language, gestures are maintained, but they play a less comprehensive role, albeit an important one, especially in narrative stories.

One difficulty for speech production and for gesture research is that both speech and gesture are post hoc representations of thought. McNeill (1987, 1992, 1999) proposed that the *iconic gesture* is a holistic representation of what was to be expressed linearly with words, such that the gestures in essence meant the same thing as the thought and the sentence. According to McNeill (1987, 1992, 1999; McNeill & Duncan, 2000), gestures and sentences share a common mental source that precedes the socially constituted (spoken) form. I noted at the beginning of this chapter that the synchronous gesture and linguistic unit was called the *growth point.* Whereas speech, to be produced orally, must undergo morphological and phonological stages, gestures are more direct. Gestures lack the social constraints placed on speaking, as they unfold from the growth point. Therefore, spontaneous gestures anticipate speech and are synchronized with it, representing the speaker's mental operations in an undistorted form. We can see the synchronization of

he tries going up the inside of the drainpipe

he tries climbing up the drainspout of the building

and he goes up through the pipe this time

this time he tries to go up inside the raingutter

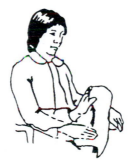

as he tries climbing up the rain barrel

Figure 6.15. Gestures Used by Five Speakers Describing the Same Drawing
Note. From McNeill, D., *Hand and mind: What gestures reveal about thought,* 1992, University of Chicago Press. Reprinted by permission.

speech and gesture in Figure 6.15, which shows five different speakers describing the same cartoon that each has seen. Notice that each person points upward with the fingers and each uses the word *up*. The gesture is not a translation of the sentence but a parallel internal mental representation of the sentence. In this way, speech and gestures are generated from the same internal plan, but they do not necessarily express identical features of the conceptualization of an event. We can see these relationships in some recent research.

McNeill and Duncan (2000) studied **motion events** in Spanish, English, and Chinese to show how gestures are integrated with linguistic forms. A motion event consists of a moving object (e.g., bowling ball), a reference object where the trajectory occurs (e.g., drainpipe), a trajectory or **path** (e.g., down), and the **manner** in which the motion is performed (e.g., rolls), as in *The bowling ball rolls down the drainpipe.* Each language has a characteristic way of conceptualizing the components of a motion event. In English, the path is encoded outside of the main verb in an adjunct to the verb, such as *down.* Spanish is verb-framed, and the path information is assigned to the verb itself. Chinese frames the path information more like English than Spanish. In contrast to path information, manner is encoded in the verb in English and Chinese (e.g., *walk, stroll, run*). Alternatively, in Spanish, path is encoded in the verb but manner is often introduced outside the verb, for example, *sale volando* ("exits flying"), where the path is the verb and the manner is a gerund.

In English, a speaker can emphasize manner through gesture or not emphasize manner. For example, the verb *rolls* may co-occur with a wiggling hand gesture emphasizing manner, or it may co-occur with a hand-plunging-down gesture, emphasizing path information. In Spanish, speakers often omit manner from their speech, while including it abundantly in their gesturing. For example, a speaker who says, "goes into" in Spanish might raise both hands simultaneously or show a corkscrewing motion, indicating manner and path. In English, gestural manner focuses at the verb if manner is an important part of the idea. In Spanish, gestural manner can appear in the absence of spoken manner and can provide path information.

In contrast, in Chinese, gestural information occurs earlier in the temporal sequence than in either English or Spanish. While English and Spanish gestures focus on the subject-verb transformation, Chinese speakers often shift the focus forward in the surface speech. For example, when a Chinese speaker said what could be translated as *The old lady with a big stick knocked him down,* she performed a downward-blow gesture as she said "big stick" (*da bang*), not when she uttered the verb "hit down" (*da xia*). McNeill and Duncan (2000) interpret this as evidence of imagery that determines which idea-speech units are going to be upcoming references before they are articulated in speech.

In a related study on gesture and language, Kita (2000) described an experiment comparing Japanese and English speakers' descriptions of an animated cartoon. The cartoon scene shows a cat and a bird across from one another in the windows of different buildings. The cat swings out across the street on a rope, hanging from somewhere above, attempting to catch the bird. The scene involves spatial information that is difficult to describe in Japanese because there is no word like *swing* in the language that encodes the agentive change of location and there is no easy way to paraphrase. All English speakers in the experiment used the word *swing,* but none of the Japanese speakers lexically encoded the arc trajectory; instead they made descriptions like, *tried to jump over to* or *go to the direction of the bird.*

The participants' gestures revealed cross-linguistic similarities and differences. Japanese speakers made twice as many gestures as English speakers, but they also produced more speech to describe the scene. Most strikingly, Japanese speakers produced a large number of gestures depicting straight paths rather than arc-shaped paths. Half of the Japanese speakers produced at least one straight gesture, whereas only one English speaker in fourteen made a straight gesture; the rest made arcs. However, most of the Japanese speakers also produced arc gestures, accurately depicting the path. The study suggests that both spatiomotoric representation of the event and the linguistic encoding of the event shape representational gestures. In this example, the two forces are coexpressive in English, whereas they are in competition in Japanese. The spatiomotoric organization represented in gesture provides an alternative to the less informative speech message in Japanese.

A different form of evidence supporting the integrated view of speech and gesture comes from the examination of gesture production during stuttered speech. Mayberry and Jaques (2000) elicited extemporaneous speech during a cartoon narration task from stutterers and compared their responses with nonstuttering subjects. The narration task was open-ended, and speakers could say as much as they wished. Control subjects said 35 percent more words in 50 percent less time than those who stuttered, underscoring the fact that stuttering makes spoken expression difficult. The reduced output of the subjects who stuttered was accompanied by only half the number of gestures produced by control subjects (82 versus 152 total gestures). The controls accompanied 78 percent of their words with gestures, compared to only 30 percent of the words accompanied with gestures by stutterers.

Over the time course of the narration, control subjects gestured for 70 percent of the time they spoke, versus stutterers, who gestured for 20 percent of the time. More important, the gestures that accompany gestured speech, rather than compensating for reduced content, show a marked reduction; that is, stuttered speech is marked by *fewer* gestures than fluent speech. Moreover, gestures are rarely coproduced with stuttered disfluencies. The hands can be observed to fall during the stuttering and rise again and resume gesturing when the speech becomes fluent. The stutterers' sound repetitions and prolongations almost never co-occurred with the initiation of a gesture. The results suggest that the onset of a representational gesture requires fluent word production and that gesture production is halted during stuttering.

The *sketch model* developed by de Ruiter (2000) illustrates the temporal synchronization of gesture and speech as suggested by McNeill and others. The model is shown in Figure 6.16. What is important to note is that the conceptualizer spins out a gestural sketch for the gesture planner at the same stage where it spins out a message for the formulator. Notice that the formulator in the model is essentially Levelt's (1989) conceptualization of the speech production process outlined before. The congruence between the sketch model and Levelt's model is particularly appealing for psycholinguists who want to integrate the literature on articulated speech with that on gestures. A great deal of evidence already supports Levelt's model. To support a role for gestures in the production process, one has to demonstrate how and where

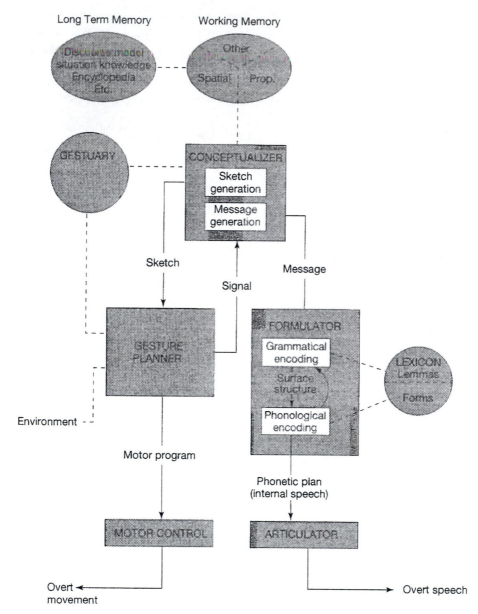

Figure 6.16. The Sketch Model

Note. From *Language and Gesture,* David McNeill (ed.). Reprinted with permission of Cambridge University Press.

this integration takes place. The sketch model can account for the evidence presented on the synchronization of speech and gesture by using the conceptualizer to synchronize both plans. A different view of the relationship between gestures and speech is addressed next.

THE KRAUSS AUTONOMOUS MODEL

A contrasting nonintegrated view of gestures and speech proposes that gestures primarily serve the lexical access needs of the speaker, at least according to Krauss and his associates (Krauss, Chen, & Gottesman, 2000; Krauss & Hadar, 1999; Rauscher, Krauss, & Chen, 1996). In the Krauss **autonomous model,** speech and gesture systems are connected at the working memory level, but they quickly diverge and do not share a mutual conceptualization stage, as they do in the sketch model. The purpose of the information encoded in the gesture is to facilitate lexical retrieval by cross-modal priming during phonological encoding. The choice of the phonological encoder, rather than semantics, was based on evidence from the research using the TOT paradigm that retrieval failures were primarily phonological and not semantic (see A. S. Brown, 1991). The gesture facilitates word retrieval through cross-modal priming. The conceptual features encoded in the gesture help narrow the search for the target words. Like the sketch model, the Krauss model is an extension of the Levelt (1989) model of speech production. The Krauss model is outlined in Figure 6.17. Notice that the gesture system runs in parallel to the speech system rather than being integrated or synchronized with speech.

Krauss et al. (2000) assume that memory employs a number of formats to encode different representations of an event. The activation of a concept in one format tends to activate related concepts in other formats. Concepts differ in how efficiently and completely they can be represented in one format or another. A comprehensive mental representation of some concepts requires input from other representational formats. Some representations in one format can be translated into another format such that a verbal description can translated into a visual image and vice versa. This quality of feature overlap in propositional and spatial representations is illustrated in Figure 6.18. The conceptualization of an event may also produce features that are encoded in one format but not the other. In other words, gestures may encode aspects of an event that are not encoded propositionally.

Krauss et al. (2000) cite an example of a speaker saying *with a big cake on it* while making a series of circular motions of the forearm with the index finger pointing downward. In this case, the conceptualization of the cake did not encode size and shape of the cake propositionally; that information, however, is encoded with the spatiodynamic aspect of the gesturing. Importantly, Krauss et al. assume that the size and shape were not part of the speaker's communicative intention. They believe that the function of the gesture was to facilitate lexical retrieval by feeding information into the phonological encoder where it can have its effect. The "round" gesture helps retrieve *cake* because roundness is a semantic feature that it shares with *cake*, a property that is illustrated in Figure 6.18.

The central hypothesis of the Krauss model is that gestures derive from nonpropositional representations of the source concept in order to assist lexical access. Gestures are not integrated and synchronized with speaking from the same growth point, as is suggested in the McNeill model. As Krauss et al. (2000) describe the process, "gestures are the product of the same conceptual processes that ultimately result in speech, but the two productions diverge early on" (p. 272). Although they

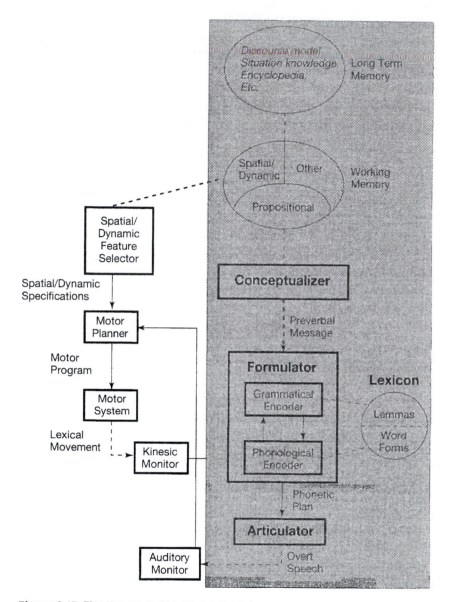

Figure 6.17. The Krauss Autonomous Model
Note. From *Language and Gesture*, David McNeill (ed.). Reprinted with permission of
Cambridge University Press.

recognize that some gestures are communicatively intended and coordinated with
speaking, Krauss et al. see no reason to assume that most gestures are of this nature.
They cite as evidence the fact that speakers gesture while speaking on the telephone and the listener cannot see them. Their view of the McNeill model is that although it is plausible that gestures and words are integrated during speech
production, there is little unequivocal evidence to support that claim. The literature
on how gestures facilitate lexical access is likewise less than clear.

Lexical gestures and lexical access

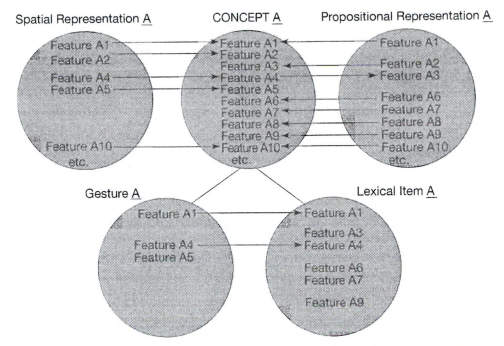

Figure 6.18. Mental Representation of a Hypothetical Source Concept and Its Reflection in Speech and Gesture

Note. From *Language and Gesture*, David McNeill (ed.). Reprinted with permission of Cambridge University Press.

Beattie and Coughlan (1999) induced the tip-of-the-tongue state with participants who were either free to gesture or had to do the task with their arms folded. They found that gestures were associated with lexical search and that sometimes the gestures were detailed enough that naive judges could discriminate which lexical item was the target from a set of alternatives. However, other gestures associated with the task were not informative, and there was no evidence that the presence of the gesture actually helped the person find the target item. This gesture-TOT methodology contrasts with the spontaneous use of gestures in fluent sentence-sized descriptions, as studied by McNeill. It focuses on the search aspects in TOT alone without manipulating a speaker's communicative intention to be understood by another.

Key Terms

anticipations	deictic gesture	eye movements
autonomous model	emblematic	filled pause
beat	exchanges	Freudian slip

galvanic skin response
grammatical gender
growth point
iconic gesture
integrated model
lemma
lexical bias effect

manner
mentalese
motion event
parallel model
path
pause
perseverations

picture naming
self-repairs
semantic inhibition
serial model
slips of the hand
tip-of-the-tongue
  (TOT) state

What Lies Ahead

We continue the discussion of speech production into the next chapter, where we cover the production of written speech. In addition, the complex psycholinguistic processes underlying reading are also addressed. Naturally, these two topics are intimately tied to the question of literacy and education, opening the door to applications of psycholinguistic research to everyday language problems in Part Two of the book.

Suggested Web Site

Slips: http://personal.bgsu.edu/~swellsj/slips/

Chapter 7
Writing and Reading Processes

Critical Thinking Questions

1. What does the term *literacy* mean?

2. How have writing systems evolved?

3. What are the major components of the Flower and Hayes model of writing?

4. How are writing components engaged over the course of writing?

5. What distinguishes good writers from poor writers?

6. How does phonological awareness affect reading?

7. What distinguishes good readers from poor readers?

8. What are the major components of reading?

9. How does deafness affect reading?

10. What are four models of reading presented in this chapter?

Exercise 7.1. **The Psychology of Writing**
Write a paragraph about something funny that happened to you. Take a few minutes to reflect on how you constructed your text. When did the planning occur? What about the revising stage? Did you get stuck at any point? Did your writing flow along effortlessly? How much time do you think you spent revising? Compare your answers to the research on the time course of writing.

This chapter outlines the basic processes underlying skilled reading and writing. Psychologists have been interested in the process of reading and the teaching of reading for more than a century (Huey, 1908/1968). At present, the amount of research on reading far outweighs the body of research on writing. These two processes represent incredibly important aspects of being an educated person. Reading and writing are the basis of literacy.

Literacy

Not everyone who can speak is literate. Understanding spoken language does not guarantee that one can produce or comprehend text. **Literacy** is the ability to read and write functionally, that is, to achieve everyday living goals through reading or producing text. Functional literacy involves a complex set of skills that include the ability to focus one's attention and to recognize language patterns, a knowledge of words and word meanings, holding information in working memory, retrieving and storing information in long-term memory, knowledge about the world and one's culture, and knowledge of emotional expression. A failure to successfully engage any skill (e.g., word recognition) may result in reading and writing difficulty.

Scribner and Cole (1981) demonstrated that the intellectual and cognitive consequences of literacy arise out of the ways literate practices are used in social situations. They see literacy as a set of socially organized practices such that it is not simply knowing how to read and write but applying knowledge in specific contexts. Scribner and Cole studied the Vai people of Liberia, who have three kinds of literary practices: Arabic-language literacy used for reading the Koran; English-language literacy for business and government use; and Vai-language literacy, which involves a unique writing system learned in adulthood, for personal correspondence and personal business transactions. The consequences for each literary practice were dissociated from the school setting and were traceable to practices of each of the literacies. The consequences of each literacy were not generalizable. This view stands in contrast to those who see social situations as a function of literacy practices (Havelock, 1986). Instead of literacy as the context for social stability needed to be accomplished by all, Scribner and Cole see that literacy is useful in specific contexts and for particular purposes that are constrained by sociocultural forces.

Achieving literacy has personal consequences. Athey (1970) argued for a personal affective component of literacy that accompanies cognitive and linguistic processes. She has presented evidence for several affective correlates of the comprehension process. **Good readers** have better self-concepts—feelings of adequacy, self-worth, and self-reliance that are important factors in reading achievement. **Poor readers** lack independence, leadership, and responsibility skills. More important, Athey noted that anxiety is an important dimension of reading disability, which excites fluency but depresses word recognition and memory processes. Negative correlations between reading comprehension and anxiety have been found in several studies, which show that anxiety may interact with intelligence, neuroticism, introversion, and socioeconomic status (SES).

Whatever the relationship of affective variables and reading ability might be, we cannot ignore the fact that literacy takes place in a variety of social contexts among people who possess different personalities and intellectual skills. Learning to read is a demand imposed by a culture at a certain age. Knowing how to read satisfies the adults concerned about literacy and gives the child a tool to solve problems. Knowing how to read thus contributes in no small measure to the child's feeling of environmental mastery (Athey, 1970).

Speaking and Writing

The anatomic capability for speaking has been estimated to have evolved one hundred thousand years ago (Lieberman, 1991). Writing, in contrast, has evolved much more recently, within the past ten thousand years. Unlike our proclivity for speech, we have no natural predisposition for reading or writing. And whereas infants readily acquire the use of speech in their environments, children need explicit instruction and modeling to become proficient at reading and writing. Speech and text are different media. Speech is dynamic and continuous, and it unfolds quickly in time. Compared to speech, text is static and discrete, and it unfolds over space, not time.

Since the time of Aristotle, it has been assumed that writing is a graphic method of transcribing speech (Harris, 1986). Traditionally, it has been assumed that since children already speak the language, they learn to read it—in other words, that learning to read is a matter of finding out how to represent speech graphically. The emphasis falls on the child's learning of letters, *not* on analyzing his or her speech. Olson (1996) has challenged this "romantic view" of the relationship between language and writing. Recent work with preliterate children and nonliterate adults shows that reading requires a form of knowledge distinct from oral competence. Olson suggests that the relationship between speech and reading is the opposite of the romantic view. Learning to read involves the discovery of the structures of language rather than their transcription. Through writing one learns about the units of language involved in speaking.

Review Question
How do emotion and culture affect literacy?

Writing Systems

The production of text systems is built on a method for representing units of speech (e.g., phonemes) through units of writing (e.g., alphabet). English text is based on an alphabetical **orthography,** which relates graphemes to phonemes. The **grapheme** is the smallest unit of writing that makes a difference in meaning. It is similar structurally to the phoneme in that both are the building blocks of language. In English, there are twenty-six grapheme units, in addition to punctuation marks and other meaningful symbols that are used in text (e.g., @, &). The major breakthrough in writing literacy was the establishment of the alphabet, a system that represented speech sounds with a small set of phonetic symbols. Symbols and iconography, the precursors of alphabets, were too idiosyncratic and not systematic or efficient enough to do what alphabets do.

Historians of writing (e.g., Havelock, 1982) distinguish four stages in the evolution of writing, beginning with picture writing, then word-based writing, followed by sound-based syllabic writing, and ending with the Greek alphabetic system. Scholars (Harris, 1986; Olson, 1996) argue that the evolution of these systems reflects evolving concepts and categories for thinking about the structure of spoken language. The development of the use of visible marks to represent speech was at the same time an attempt to represent the structure of speech. In this way, writing is a way of discovering language.

GRAPHICS

The Neolithic period, ten to twenty thousand years ago, marked the beginning of pottery making, food preservation, and ornamentation of the dead, a period contemporaneous with drawing and the use of tallies (Schmandt-Bessarat, 1986, 1987, 1992). Graphic representations, signs, and token systems where used to keep records of debts, mark ownership, and represent religious concepts. Figure 7.1 shows an example of these kinds of **pictograms.** Similarly, **ideograms** are symbols with abstract or conventional meanings but have no immediate links to recognizable objects or referents, as is the case with pictograms. The links between the ideogram and its meaning are abstract, not intended for literal visual interpretation; for example, the ideogram for a bison would look nothing like a bison. Although graphic systems served as memory devices, allowing one to bring the cultural meanings into memory, little in these systems can be understood as linguistic constituents.

WORDS

Western linguistically based writing systems apparently evolved from token accounting systems in Mesopotamia around the ninth millennium B.C. by the Sumerians living in modern-day Iraq (Schmandt-Bessarat, 1992). The tokens were impressed into clay

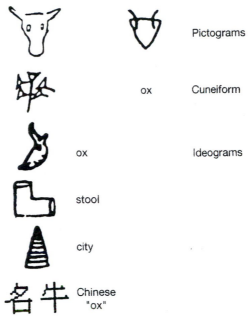

Pictograms

ox   Cuneiform

ox   Ideograms

stool

city

Chinese
"ox"

Figure 7.1. Different Forms of Writing

tablets to denote commodities such as grain, oil, or animals. About the fourth millennium B.C., the variety of tokens increased greatly, and these records are regarded as the first true writing (Schmandt-Bessarat, 1986, 1987, 1992). Harris (1986) questioned whether these tokens represented words or things. He argued that the critical step occurred when the token system acquired syntax. For example, instead of using three tokens to represent *three sheep,* two tokens were used, one to represent *three* and another to represent *sheep.* The two signs are now syntactically related, giving the token system a generative quality, permitting the combination and recombination of symbols. These types of syntactic scripts appeared about 3000 B.C. in the Near East.

The Sumerian script remained *logographic,* like many Asian languages that are based on **logograms,** which employ word-sized graphemes, as exemplified in the Japanese *kanji* systems and in Chinese (see Figure 7.1). When the Semitic speaking Akkadians adapted the Sumerian system, they added phonographic properties to the script, giving rise to **cuneiform** systems that are based on pressing a wedge-shaped stylus into a soft clay tablet. These scripts give the first clear example of the linguistic knowledge of the writer (Nissen, 1986).

SYLLABLES

A **syllabary,** such as the Japanese *kana* system, uses syllable-sized graphemes that represent spoken syllables, not whole words. They are not like logograms or phonemes (alphabetic letters) but syllables consisting of consonant–vowel clusters.

The Akkadians borrowed logographic signs for one-syllable words from the Sumerians and treated them as pronounced syllables. For example, the Akkadians took the Sumerian graphs for *a, wi, lu,* and *um* to represent the Akkadian word *a-wi-lu-um,* or "man," ignoring the fact that each Sumerian graph represented a different word. To read Akkadian would amount to pronouncing a series of sounds and graphs that now represented the syllables of Akkadian rather than the words in Sumerian.

PHONEMES

The story of borrowing has been suggested to account for the discovery of subsyllabic units of speech, or phonemes. The real conceptual leap in writing systems occurred with **alphabetic systems.** The syllabic script used by the Akkadians was apparently borrowed by the Phoenicians to form a representation of consonants. The Greeks then borrowed the Semitic script to represent the Greek language (Havelock, 1982). The earliest alphabetic system appeared around 1700 B.C. in Palestine and Syria. These alphabets soon evolved through Phoenician and then Greek into the Etruscan and finally the Roman alphabet. The Phoenician script had twenty-two graphic signs (*aleph, bet, gemel,* etc.), all representing consonants. The final transition to alphabetic writing came from the Greeks, who adapted the Semitic script about 750 B.C. and added vowel sounds (Harris, 1986; Havelock, 1982). In Greek as in English, vowel differences provide linguistic constrast, for example, *bed* versus *bad.* The Greeks were now in a position to "hear" the sounds in their language represented by written signs.

Modern-day alphabetic systems usually have twenty to thirty symbols but range from eleven (in Rotokas) to seventy-four symbols (in Khmer; see Crystal, 1987). Some systems are very regular, like Spanish and Finnish, where the **grapheme-to-phoneme correspondence (GPC)** is fairly predictable. But English and Gaelic are irregular, showing inconsistent GPC. For example, consider how many ways we can pronounce the letter *o,* as in *throw, fought, out, now,* or *not,* indicating an irregular relationship between the grapheme and its phonemes. Some of the irregularities in English spelling derive from having borrowed words from other languages. English has kept the etymological roots (spelling patterns) of many of the words it has adopted, rather than converting foreign spelling patterns to English orthography. This allows English speakers to realize the relationships between words like *sign* and *signature* or *bomb* and *bombardier* that have similar meanings but different pronunciations. The other cause of low GPC in English is that spelling rarely changes as pronunciation changes; hence many older words in English are spelled in a way that preserves a historical pronunciation rather than a current one.

Writing Processes

Whereas leaving a simple note or message requires minimal effort, composing a long narrative is a complex task. The composition process relies on a pool of mental and physical resources; it requires a medium for production (e.g., handwriting or typing), the conventions of the medium (e.g., font, punctuation, and symbols), and a composition plan for laying out the text in the appropriate format. Unlike speaking, writing includes a stage for rewriting and revision. Writing also includes a method of allowing the writer to see, as a hard copy, what is being written and what has been written. The process of writing can be understood as a linear process that unfolds over time. Like the production of speech, writing involves a series of overarching stages.

One way to understand writing is to look at the process as a cognitive skill that draws equally on language resources and general cognitive resources such as working memory and attention. The degree to which one becomes accomplished at writing depends on the development of these cognitive and language resources. One such cognitive model of the stages and components of writing is discussed next.

THE FLOWER AND HAYES MODEL

Since writing tasks are so varied in content, purpose, and scope, it is important to conceptualize the processes and components involved in writing very broadly. Such a conception is offered by Flower and Hayes (1984; Hayes & Flower, 1986; see also Bruning, Schraw, & Ronning, 1995). In this model, writing is viewed as a form of problem solving that has three major features: a task environment, a long-term memory component, and a working memory component. These three components become interactive when writers compose text (see Figure 7.2). Let us look more closely at its components.

Task Environment

The **task environment** consists of two main factors: the writing assignment and a means of storing the writing. The *writing assignment* refers to the writer's framework and goal, including the topic, scope, and intended audience of the text. The writer's initial conception of the assignment or purpose of the writing is a crucial stage in the writing process. The writer's initial conceptualization determines how he or she sets up the overall writing plan and subgoals. Misconceptions about the nature or scope of the purpose of the text often produce assignment failures.

The format of the text is used to produce an external representation of the assignment. This may include handwritten notes or drafts of the assignment or computer versions of it. These external formats allow the writer to view the text, and they provide a working copy on which revisions and additions can be made. The ability to generate an external representation reduces demands on long-term memory for information about the assignment. Imagine how difficult it is to keep the writing plans "in your head" without committing them to an external copy.

Long-Term Memory

Writing relies on two major resources in long-term memory: knowledge about the topic under discussion and knowledge about how readers respond to text. Writers need to know general strategies, such as what kinds of writing techniques work best under a given set of circumstances, how to structure an argument, how to create

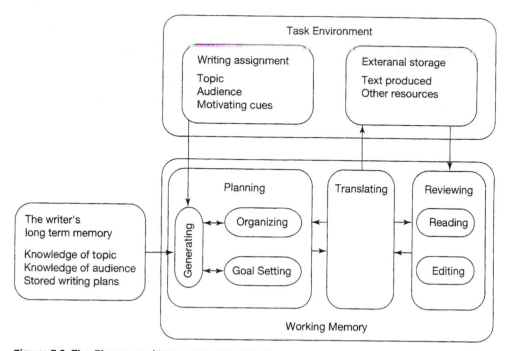

Figure 7.2. The Flower and Hayes Model of Writing

Note. The Hayes & Flower model of writing. Adapted from L. W. Gregg & E. R. Steinberg, *Cognitive Processes in Writing*, p. 11. Reprinted by permission of Lawrence Erlbaum Associates.

suspense, or how to get the reader emotionally involved with the text. A writer also needs to know a large number of facts and ideas about the subject of the writing assignment. Subject matter knowledge requires a sufficient level of prior familiarity with the topic under construction, either through reading about the topic and related matters or by participating in the actual experiences that constitute the topic. Bereiter and Scardamalia (1987) suggested that with increasing experience at writing, better writers raise the difficulty level of writing by changing from a simple reproduction of the facts, or a *knowledge-telling* approach, to one that involves more complex reformulation of the facts, or *knowledge transformation*. Knowledge transformation produces better documents than knowledge telling when writing time is held constant. Long-term memory is essential to writing, and so is the manner in which it is used to improve writing.

Working Memory

There are numerous demands on working memory during the writing process. Writers must balance in working memory several competing sources of information regarding the planning, translating, and reviewing of ideas. Failure to balance the competing memory demands can cause writing difficulties, which interfere with the writer's overall writing plan. Thus writing failures may be predicated on flawed information processing as much as on poor compositional skills. Kellogg (1987) used a *workload hypothesis* to suggest that better writers should exert less effort during writing than poor writers who have less topic knowledge. Better writers can allocate less time and effort to text generation and devote the time gained to revising, where it is of greater utility.

The *planning process* refers to the process for generating and organizing information for the text. Writers must conceptualize a plan, which includes an overall goal and subgoals to be achieved with the text. The overall format of the text must be conceptualized along with the substages or outline of the overall text. Writers have to plan a text sequence (e.g., chronological order) and the steps within the sequence (e.g., what happened specifically at different points in the chronology).

The *generation process* is difficult for many writers. Here is where the writer must produce ideas to be laid out as sentences and paragraphs. A writer needs to focus on the topic and not wander in thought, as well as have the motivation to stick to the physical task of writing itself (e.g., staying in the chair and generating words and sentences). The ideas the writer generates for the text may originate from information in long-term memory or from searching for new information through reading, collecting data, or synthesizing bits of information.

The ideas must undergo a translation process from the writer's long-term memory to the text under construction. The translation process requires the writer to convert his or her ideas into meaningful and grammatically correct sentences. Powerful ideas must be translated into equally compelling text. The translation process draws on the writer's knowledge of words, sentence types, and paragraph structures.

The *review process* forces the writer to revisit the text that has been externally stored. After some text has been constructed, the writer can monitor and evaluate what has been produced and make revisions. The quality of the text will reflect the writer's understanding of what makes a piece of writing good or not. Qualities like cohesion, clarity, conciseness, reference, vocabulary, and discourse processes are important. For the evaluation process to be effective, the writer must understand the difference between good writing and ineffective writing.

Reviewing the text requires that it be revised on the basis of the outcomes of the monitoring and evaluation stages. This **revision** process is difficult for some writers because it forces them to destroy or change existing external representations on which thought and labor have already been expended. Ultimately, writers learn that revision produces improved texts. Editing will help almost any piece of writing, but not all writers' attempts at editing are equal. **Poor writers** focus on making mechanical changes, whereas **good writers** pay more attention to the overall message and content of the text. Poor writers' mechanical changes are of little consequence if the overall presentation is flawed. Changing the minor details of a text does not improve problems in its overall structure.

INDIVIDUAL DIFFERENCES IN WRITING

What differentiates a good writer from a poor one is not intelligence, academic achievement, or the motivation to write (Benton, Kraft, Glover, & Plake, 1984). Differences in ability are a matter of how writers use the components and processes (e.g., revision) of writing. What has emerged in the research about writing is that good and poor writers differ in their reading, amount of writing, information processing, planning, and organizational skills. A significant body of literature indicates that good and poor writers differ on how these components are used. This can be summarized as follows.

Analyzing the Writing Task

Good writers comprehend their assignments as rhetorical problems determined by the subject matter, purpose, and audience (Carey, Flower, Hayes, Schriver, & Haas, 1989). Benton et al. (1984) found that good writers were better than poor writers at information processing tasks related to reading. Better writers are faster and more accurate at reordering a string of letters or a list of words in working memory. Better writers are also more capable of constructing a sentence out of a randomized list of words. Older writers and better writers also pay more attention to the ideas they are expressing relative to the mechanical features of what they are writing (e.g., spelling, punctuation, or capitalization). Good writers also have more practice at the process of writing than poor writers do.

Generating Ideas

Good writers get a wide range of ideas from the rhetorical problem and add their own ideas (Flower & Hayes, 1980).

Incorporating Documentation

Good writers tend to process and integrate documentation sources into their ideas before they begin writing, whereas less skilled writers turn to documentation when their own ideas are exhausted (Kennedy, 1985).

Organizing

Poor writers do not construct an outline in advance, even though outlining leads to higher text quality (Kellogg, 1987). They seldom plan the text as a whole. Organizationally speaking, poor writers tend to be **knowledge tellers** rather than **knowledge restructurers** (Bereiter & Scardamalia, 1987). Poor writers spit out what they know without carefully assessing its importance to or cohesion with the overall structure of the text. In other words, knowledge tellers produce text without much attention to how they are reporting the details. Good writers (knowledge restructurers) are better storytellers. They are more attentive to the structure of text; they tie ideas together within paragraphs and make transitions that bridge paragraphs. Good writers make better use of cohesive ties (e.g., conjunctions, reference, lexical ties) and produce more of them than poor writers do (Butterfield, 1986). Good writers carefully examine what they have written to make sure the text says what they intended to say and that it uses the right words.

Revising

Good writers revise more, and their revisions improve the meaning of the text (Flower, Hayes, Carey, Schriver, & Stratman, 1986), but less skilled writers concentrate on mechanical errors (e.g., spelling), the correction of which does not increase the quality of the text as a whole.

Employing Writing Strategies

Good writers shift their strategies as the writing task changes (Kennedy, 1985). Processes that are useful at the beginning of the writing task—for example, reading the assignment—become less useful later on. Revising the text is not as important at the beginning of the task as it is at the end.

Reading and Writing

Good writers are usually good readers, and reading comprehension is positively correlated with writing ability (Shell, Colvin, & Bruning, 1995). Root (1985) found that professional writers spent a large part of their time engaged in reading about a wide variety of topics. The ideas that are to be generated by the writer come from his or her vast pool of information that is gained from a diverse and sustained reading program.

WRITING AND EMOTION

Brand (1991) noted that although psychologists have addressed social and emotional factors that affect interpersonal behavior, little has been done to study the relationship between these variables in composition studies, where they might play a significant role. According to Kellogg (1994), many accomplished writers have attested to their need for routine, ritual, and the proper emotional and supportive environment for writing. For many famous writers, the absence of these situational and emotional supports will interfere with their writing. Other writers are able to write almost on demand regardless of contextual or emotional constraints. Some professional writers feel that they are writing and composing all the time, whether they are in front of a word processor or not. Others admit that they must wait until the mood to write strikes them.

One experience common to writers of all types is the phenomenon known as **writer's block,** when writing goals cannot be accomplished for one reason or another or perhaps no good reason at all. We cannot fully understand the process of writing without addressing the emotional factors that motivate and block its course. By its very personal nature, writing performance should depend at least in part on emotional factors; writing should relate directly to the degree of positive affect associated with it. The writer who likes writing and finds emotional fulfillment in completing documents that are enjoyed by others ought to spend the most time engaged in writing. Writers who suffer anxiety about writing and about having others read the resulting product probably avoid the task or experience bouts of writer's block (Kellogg, 1994).

For both professional and casual writers, the act of writing meets many emotional needs; in fact, writing has a variety of positive effects on affect and mental heath. Writing about traumatic events has been shown to have a beneficial effect on individuals who have been through tough times. Pennebaker (1990) found that having people write about their personal traumas in diaries improves their mental health. He studied a sample of fifty healthy undergraduates who were randomly assigned to write for twenty minutes on four consecutive days about either trivial topics or about traumatic and upsetting events. Blood samples were taken at the beginning of the study, on the final day of the study, and six weeks after the writing stopped. Students who revealed personal traumas in writing exercises showed evidence of more positive immune systems (lymphocyte response), and they visited the campus health facilities for illnesses less than students in the trivial writing condition (Pennebaker, Kiecolt-Glaser, & Glaser, 1988).

THE TIME COURSE OF WRITING

Breetvelt, van den Bergh, and Rijlaarsdam (1994) investigated the relationship between cognitive activities (e.g., goal setting, writing, revising) and text quality. Using the Flower and Hayes (1983) reading model, eleven different cognitive activities were defined. They are listed in Table 7.1 along with a brief description of each. The authors wanted to plot how the activities unfolded over the course of a writing assignment and how they correlated with text quality.

To study how these strategies shifted over the time course of writing compositions, Breetvelt et al. (1994) asked a group of above-average ninth-grade students to write two essays within a 150-minute time limit and at the same time to verbalize everything they thought while writing, that is, to provide a **verbal protocol.** Most experiments on writing do not use direct behavioral measures like reaction time; instead, they rely on verbal protocol analysis (Bereiter & Scardamalia, 1987). Here the verbal protocols provided the data for determining which cognitive activity was occurring, its frequency, and its duration. The protocol of the writing process was divided into thirds, each episode containing one-third of the cognitive activities from the protocol.

As for text quality, none of the eleven cognitive activities had a constant effect on text quality over the time course of the writing process. Table 7.2 summarizes the positive and negative influences on quality of writing. It can be seen that the frequency of the cognitive activity influences quality differently, depending on which episode is examined. During the initial episode, reading the assignment and evaluating had a positive influence, but goal setting, structuring, and revising had a negative effect. The effects of the other activities were not significant. At the second episode of the process, goal setting and structuring had a positive effect, while reading the assignment, giving comments, pausing, and revising had a negative effect. In the final phase of writing, self-instruction, goal setting, writing, and rereading

Table 7.1. Eleven Cognitive Activities and Their Descriptions

Cognitive Activity	Description	Examples from Protocols
Reading the writing assignment	(Re)reading the writing assignment or quotations	
Self-instruction	Self-instruction concerning some of the activities from this scheme	"First I have to order this" "Let's read what I have written so far" "The issue is . . ."
Goal setting	Formulating task demands derived from the assignment or self-devised	"I have to adduce more arguments in support of this"
Generating	Generating ideas, propositions, or only the next few words	
Structuring	Selecting, evaluating, ordering, or outlining of ideas	"first . . . , then . . ." ". . . is related to . . ."
Giving comments	Reflecting on or evaluating the writing assignment or one's own writing process	"I agree with this" "I should have . . ."
Pausing	Silence or sounds or words indicating thoughtfulness	"hm, hm"
Writing	Dictating to oneself or copying	
Rereading	Rereading the outline, fragments, or sentences one has already written	
Evaluating	Evaluating formal aspects (e.g., grammar) or aspects having to do with the meaning of the written text	"Here I should put a comma" "The issue at stake remains unclear"
Revising	Revising formal aspects or aspects of text meaning by addition, deletion, or transposition	

positively influenced text quality. The other activities did not have a negative effect on text quality in the final stage.

The relationships between cognitive activities in the writing process are time-dependent, and their effect on text quality changes over time. Therefore, time is an essential variable in writing research. In contrast to research by Flower and Hayes (1983), revising the text did not have a uniform effect on text quality; in fact, it had a negative effect in the early stages. Whereas Flower and Hayes found that evaluating is a prerequisite for revising, evaluating was positively related to quality in the Breetvelt et al. (1994) trials but negatively related to revising. Some notes of caution are warranted here, however. First of all, Breetvelt et al. sampled students who were good writers. Second, writers had access to documentation materials, which is not the case in most writing assignments. Third, the writers produced text over a single session, and we do not see how the allocation of effort shifts with practice.

Table 7.2. A Summary of Regression Weights by Episode Showing the Influence of Cognitive Activities on Text Quality

Cognitive Activity	Episode in the Writing Process		
	1	2	3
Reading the writing assignment	+	−	
Self-instruction			+
Goal setting	−	+	+
Generating ideas		+	
Structuring	−	+	
Giving comments		−	
Pausing		−	
Writing			+
Rereading			+
Evaluating	+	−	
Revising	−	−	

+ indicates a positive influence; − indicates a negative influence.

Note. From Breetvelt, I., van den Bergh, H., & Rijlaarsdam, G. (1994). Relations between writing processes and text quality: When and how? *Cognition and Instruction, 12(2),* 103–123. Reprinted by permission of Lawrence Erlbaum Associates.

This final criticism was addressed in a study by Levy and Ransdell (1995), who studied writers over the course of ten weekly writing sessions. These researchers assessed the time and effort allocated to cognitive activities or writing subprocesses. Like Flower and Hayes (1980), they construed writing as a threefold process: planning, generating text, and revising and reviewing. Undergraduates were asked to write high-quality documents on a regular basis during which three types of data were recorded following four training sessions (weeks 1 to 4): verbal protocols of what they were doing, an on-line record of the actual text as it was written and revised in a Windows word processing environment, and interference reaction times (IRT) to a secondary interference task. For the IRT measure, subjects had to press a button when they heard a tone during their writing. The IRT was used to measure the allocation of cognitive effort across the subcomponents of the writing task. The advantage here is that not only were subprocesses monitored and timed but also a measure of cognitive effort on each task was available. The result is a time and effort measure of the writing process. Each essay was evaluated for quality, and in a follow-up experiment subjects were asked to estimate how much time they spent engaged in each of the subprocesses.

The results of measures of cognitive effort over the course of writing during weeks 5 through 10 indicated that subjects exhibited longer IRTs during revising and generating text than during the planning stage. These IRTs were very stable within and across writing sessions and did not show differences over time. We can interpret these as an indication that planning requires less effort than revising or generating.

As for the time on subprocesses, the allocation of time varied systematically within sessions. Subjects spent about 45 percent of the time *planning* during the first five minutes but gradually stabilized to 35 percent thereafter. Over the ten-week period, they devoted less time to planning, dropping from 40 to 30 percent. The time spent generating text increased within sessions but not across the course of the experiment. Writers spent 40 percent of their time *generating text* during the first five minutes and increased it to 50 percent before returning to 40 percent during the last five minutes of the session. In the first five minutes, *reviewing* time occurred only about 3 percent of the time but rose to 5 percent for the duration of the sessions. A bit less overall time was spent *revising*, and the pattern was very similar to that for reviewing.

During weeks 5 through 10, subjects spent about 40 percent of the time planning and 45 percent of the time generating text, with only 8 percent of the time going to reviewing, 6 percent to revising, and 1 percent to other activities. But as just mentioned, these patterns shift within and across sessions, as can be seen by looking at the interaction of subprocess, week, and five-minute sessions in Figure 7.3. The upward-sloping lines (from left to right) show more time spent on a process within a specific time block; the steeper the line, the greater the relative increase in time allocated. Notice that *planning* shows progressive decreases within sessions across the course of the experiment. However, *text generation* time increases

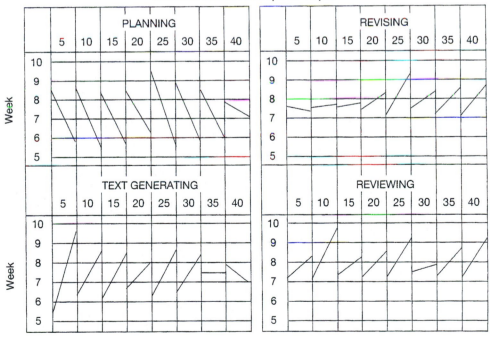

TIME ON WRITING PROCESS

Figure 7.3. Writing Times for Subprocesses

Note. From Levy, C. M., & Ransdell, S. (1995). Is writing as difficult as it seems? *Memory and Cognition, 23(6),* 767–779. Reprinted by permission of the Psychonomic Society.

sharply in the first five minutes but increases slowly across weeks for the latter time blocks. *Revising* time showed little change during early time blocks but increased during later time blocks as the experiment progressed. *Reviewing* time across the weeks increased at three points: after the first five minutes, after twenty minutes, and after thirty minutes of writing. These differential allocation times remained very stable for writers from week to week.

The time allocation indicates that writers trade off *planning* time for text generation about two-thirds of the way through a writing session. Here they increase their *text-generating* time until about 85 percent of the session is over. From that point, text generation decreases to allow more time for *revision*, which accounts for only 2 to 3 percent of the processing time until this last time block, where it accounts for 10 percent. *Reviewing* is very similar to this pattern.

Quality scores were moderately high (74 percent of the maximum points possible) but less than scores for comparison articles excerpted from the high-quality *New Yorker* magazine (82 percent). High-quality student documents had been subjected to more revising and reviewing periods than low-quality documents but roughly the same number of planning and text-generating periods. The highest-quality essays were written by people who spent 40 percent more time revising and reviewing than the writers of low-quality documents. The difference on these measures was 9.1 percent for the high-quality essays versus 6.5 percent for the low-quality ones. The revising that occurs in the later part of the writing session, after a significant amount of writing has been generated, contributes the most to the quality of the document.

As for the time estimations of percentage of time on task, the most dramatic finding was the large discrepancy between estimated and actual times spent revising and reviewing. Writers initially estimated that they were spending one-third of their time doing these tasks when in actuality they spent only about 5 percent of the time during week 5. The subjects were vastly overestimating how much time they spent revising and reviewing. After the experiment, they still believed they spent one-third of their time revising when it had only risen to 10 percent of the writing process. Ten weeks of self-monitoring and thinking aloud did not bring the writers' beliefs about their efforts closer to reality.

This experiment allows for the measurement of resources over the course of a writing session and across a ten-week period of writing, providing more detailed data than most writing research. The positive relationship between IRT and document quality is consistent with Bereiter and Scardamalia's (1987) knowledge-transforming view of writing, that better writers put greater cognitive effort into writing because they are not just telling what they know. This is particularly important during the revision cycles, which are most important to producing a high-quality text. Revision takes less total time than other subprocesses, but it disproportionately contributes to writing quality. It would seem that in order to produce better outcomes, writing programs and writing research should give greater weight to subjects' substantial overestimation of revising efforts relative to the effort they expend in planning and generating text.

WRITING STRATEGIES AND TECHNOLOGY

The statement that not all editing leads to improvements in the overall text indicates that writing meets with a variety of successes and failures. Kellogg (1994) has conducted extensive research on the psychology of writing and evaluated the effectiveness of writing strategies and writing technologies such as **word processors** (e.g., Word, WordPerfect). He noted that the final draft of a document is improved if writers engage in prewriting strategies. These might include making lists, finding clusters of ideas that are related, or constructing outlines. Outlines tend to be helpful if the writer has a grasp of the knowledge domain associated with the topic. However, an outline can limit the scope or overall schema of a writing plan if the writer has limited domain knowledge.

Kellogg suggests that writers adopt a strategy of writing a series of drafts of a document. By separating the document into stages of writing that can be revised and updated, the writer can separate the overall plan from idea translation and review stages. Separating writing stages over a series of drafts reduces the burden of trying to maintain several goals in working memory.

Modern writing technology in Kellogg's view deserves only lukewarm praise. For example, the results of college students' use of word processors versus writing compositions by hand for composition courses are mixed. Although students who use word processors produce longer texts with fewer technical errors, there is no significant difference in overall writing quality. Word processors cause some difficulties, too. It is hard to apprehend the scope of a long paper stored in a word processor, which allows only a page-by-page view. The word processor does not simply make the handwriting task easier; it entirely shifts the demands of the task, according to Norman (1989). Word processors restructure the memory and attention demands of handwriting.

> **Review Question**
> How could you use your knowledge of writing processes and good versus poor writers to improve your own writing?

Learning to Read

The task of the young reader is to identify in a new visual code words that have become familiar in speech. One skill that is of critical importance to reading is the ability to link graphemes (printed letters) to phonemes, as we see next. Two factors that are predictive of reading achievement are phonological skills and letter recognition (Bradley & Bryant, 1983; Bryant & Bradley, 1985; Liberman, Shankweiler, Fischer, & Carter, 1974; Vellutino & Scanlon, 1987; Vellutino, Scanlon, & Spearing, 1995).

PHONOLOGICAL AWARENESS

Phonological awareness is the conscious awareness of the phonological features of speech, such as the ability to count the number of syllables in a word or to name other words that rhyme with it. We read earlier that grapheme-to-phoneme correspondence in English is somewhat irregular relative to languages like Finnish or Spanish. Because English does not have a one-to-one letter-to-sound correspondence, children have difficulty mastering the code for letters that have more than one pronunciation. For example, *c* is pronounced /s/ in *certain* but /k/ in *cat*. They also have to learn that some letters are not pronounced at all, like *e* in the word *mouse*, and that some pronunciations depend on the adjacent letters, like *-gh* in *enough* and *eight*. The child's success in early reading relies on how readily he or she develops a metalinguistic awareness of phonemes.

Reading to preliterate children has a significant impact on their awareness of printed language. Reading helps them understand that what is on the page can be spoken. It introduces phonological qualities such as rhyme, alliteration, and sound segmentation—in other words, it teaches them that words have phonological components. Early reading experiences may encourage a child to attempt to make sense of what is on the page of an illustrated text independently (Marsh & Desberg, 1983), guessing at what is in picture and print. Another reading connection comes through the child's early attempts at spelling. Read (1981) found that early spelling attempts show what children hear in speech. Some phonemes are deleted, for example, when the child writes *nubrs* for *numbers*. Children also spell words by using the letters' names, such as spelling *lady* as *lade* (Treiman, 1993). For example, in a local essay contest, a 5-year-old wrote, *My Gramu is famrs. She hohpt dring the woor* ("My Grandma is famous. She helped during the war . . .").

Children vary in the their awareness of linguistic units. Rozin, Bressman, and Taft (1974) showed how shallow this awareness can be. They showed preliterate kindergartners pairs of words like *mow* and *motorcycle* and asked them which one was *mow*. Only 1 in 10 performed to their criterion of 7 out of 8 correct. The kindergartners seemed unaware of the relationship between sound and writing, that is, that words that take a longer time to pronounce have more letters.

Research by Liberman et al. (1974) found that phonemic awareness is particularly difficult for some. They examined 4-, 5-, and 6-year-olds' awareness of phonemes and syllables. One group of children had to listen to words and then tap on the table with a wooden stick one, two, or three times to indicate the number of syllables in each word. A different group had to use the tapping task to identify the number of phonemes in each word. A word like *hospital* should have received three taps by the first group; a word like *dog* should receive three taps by the second. The results indicated that the phoneme task was much more difficult than the syllable task for all age groups. None of the 4-year-olds and only 17 percent of the 5-year-olds could perform the phonemic segmentation task. But almost half of the 5-year-olds could segment words into the correct number of syllables.

Phonological awareness in a spoken language depends on the degree of regularity in the language and the kinds of phonological rules in the language being learned. When the development of phonological awareness was compared between Turkish- and English-speaking kindergarten and first-grade children, the Turkish speakers were more proficient in handling the syllables and deleting final phonemes of words (Durgunoglu & Oeney, 1999). These patterns are related to the characteristics of the respective spoken languages, such as the salience of the syllable, familiarity of the nonword patterns, importance of onset or final phoneme deletion, and importance of vowel harmony. Phonological awareness depends on the characteristics of the spoken language, its orthography, and literacy instruction.

That phonological awareness is clearly related to success in reading has been demonstrated many times (Bradley & Bryant, 1983; Rieben & Perfetti, 1991; Stanovich, Cunningham, & Cramer, 1984; Tunmer, Herriman, & Neesdale, 1988). Training in metalinguistic awareness has been found to improve reading performance (Ball & Blachman, 1991). For example, Lundberg, Frost, and Petersen (1988) developed a successful program for Danish preschoolers that used games and exercises to improve phonological awareness over an eight-month period. Children in the program achieved significant improvement on several tasks and sustained these gains over a period of time. This kind of research indicates that phonological awareness mediates how to read in an alphabetic writing system.

The relationship between phonological awareness and reading also receives support from studies with adult illiterates (Morais, Bertelson, Cary, & Alegria, 1986). Adult illiterates are weak on tasks requiring the analysis of phonemic structure, but they do better with syllabic-level and rhyming tasks. It may be that awareness can develop outside literacy contexts. For example, there are opportunities to engage in syllabic and rhyming ability that can draw attention to the existence of phonemes.

One additional way to understand phonological awareness is to contrast alphabetic and nonalphabetic writing systems. Chinese is logographic rather than alphabetic, so Chinese children must learn to read characters that are related more by meaning than by phonology (Perfetti, Zhang, & Berent, 1992). Chinese children are expected to master 3,500 characters during their six years in elementary school. Whereas alphabetic systems are ruled-based, logographic systems require associative learning. If phonological awareness depends on alphabetic rules, readers of Chinese should score low on that parameter.

Chinese readers also have available an alphabetic system, the *pinyin* system, which uses alphabetic symbols to guide the pronunciation of characters. Read, Zhang, Nie, and Ding (1986) tested performance on a phoneme analysis task with two groups of adult Chinese readers. One group learned traditional characters, and the other learned pinyin. Only the pinyin group performed the task successfully. The character group performed on the par of a group of illiterates. Weighing the evidence from writing systems, the picture regarding phonemic awareness is clearer. Phonological awareness is limited as a spontaneous cognitive ability but important for reading in an alphabetic system. Learning to read promotes the awareness of phonemes and depends on the emergence of this awareness.

Although still a matter for dispute, reading researchers suggest that reading acquisition goes through a series of stages, as has been intimated in the discussion so far (Barron, 1992; Chall, 1983; Ehri, 1985; Firth, 1985). These can be summarized roughly as follows:

1. Letter recognition and knowledge

2. Logographic recognition of familiar words with semiphonetic reading

3. Alphabetic reading through GPC rules

4. Word recognition by whole word or phonological strategy (or both)

5. Orthographic fluency, with analogies, pronunciation, morphemic strategies, and inference

The processes of reading have an interactive or bidirectional relationship with each of these stages. For example, letter naming has been the subject of much interest in research because it has been found to be predictive of later word recognition ability (Wolf, 1991). When average readers acquire reading, one result is that their letter-naming speech quickly reaches adult levels. Another important interactive aspect of the acquisition of reading includes vocabulary knowledge, which has a bidirectional relationship with letter recognition and naming skills (Beck, Perfetti, & McKeown, 1982). Knowing more words helps build letter skills, and better letter skills aid the discovery of new words. The successful attainment of adult fluency in reading, however, evades some readers, as we see next.

INDIVIDUAL DIFFERENCES IN READING

One might look at reading ability as the acquisition of expertise at the task. Efficient readers use highly automated skills of decoding orthographic information into phonological codes that can then be used to access lexical information. Wagner and Stanovich (1996) proposed that reading skill is the product of two processes, one that converts letters into sounds and a second that recognizes words on the basis of phonological codes. Extensive reading practice will help automatize the conversion of letters to sounds.

One way to differentiate efficient readers from poor readers is on the basis of the automatization of reading. Wagner and Stanovich (1996) thought that differences in reading ability were in part genetic. Although practice would help orthographic-to-phonological conversions, some aspects of phonological awareness cannot be increased with practice. Reading disabilities may originate in part from differences in phonological awareness.

Shankweiler et al. (1995) made a comprehensive comparison of schoolchildren with learning disabilities and found that deficits associated with reading were selective. Syntactic abilities did not differentiate poor from average readers even when IQ was factored out. Syntactic ability did not differentiate children with reading disabilities from children with other learning disabilities. They found that phonological skills were the most likely mediators of genetically based differences in reading ability. Poor readers have difficulty generating appropriate derived forms due to limitations on their phonological skills. Poor readers' difficulties with parsing words phonetically interfere with the ability to acquire the alphabetic principle (i.e., grapheme-phoneme correspondences) and the acquisition of word recognition skills. Reading comprehension difficulty stems from the poor readers' insufficient word recognition skills, which prevent rapid transitions from lower-level to higher-level units of reading.

Not only do less skilled readers have difficulty finding the appropriate meanings of words in an efficient manner, but they also have difficulty suppressing inappropriate meanings (Gernsbacher, Varner, & Faust, 1990). Subjects had to read sentences, for example, *He dug with the spade*, followed by test words, such as *ace*, and then decide whether the test word fit the sentence. The unskilled readers were slower than the skilled readers on these trials. Gernsbacher and Robertson (1995) proposed that unskilled readers are slower to accept inappropriate meanings because they are less able to suppress the appropriate meanings in some contexts. They devised a task that measured how quickly subjects could reject appropriate meanings. The subjects' task was to judge whether the test word was related to the sentence's final word but *not* to the sentence. Subjects had to reject *ace* after reading *He dealt the spade*. Unskilled readers reacted more slowly than skilled readers on these trials, in which they had to reject the appropriate meaning of a homonym. Efficient reading relies not only on finding the appropriate information to establish lexical meaning but also on ignoring irrelevant information (Gibson & Levin, 1975).

Review Question
How could the parent of a young child use the information in this section to help the child to learn to read?

Reading Processes

The components we use for reading are in part structural; they depend on the text being read. We use the structural aspects of text for word recognition purposes; that is, we use letters to identify words and their meanings. The structural aspects of text include punctuation, symbols, and the medium of writing, be it handwritten, typed, or computer-generated. Structural aspects define the set of distinctive features that allow us to distinguish one letter from another. Structure also refers to discrete words, which vary in length individually and in location within sentences. These sentences are in turn further embedded in an overall text structure. These structural aspects of the text interact with cognitive processes.

Cognitive resources include working memory, parsing strategies, word recognition, semantic memory, world knowledge, and knowledge of discourse. Some cognitive components of reading may be inferred by looking at eye movement patterns. For example, we can see what text is the focus of visual attention when the eye is fixated. What text is important to the reader will be brought into his or her view. Effective reading requires the ability to selectively attend to text and find what is important. As reading becomes more skilled and the reader more experienced, reading processes become automated. Reading also requires the ability for the cross-modal transfer of information. Readers must be able to efficiently integrate words from spoken and written modalities, and they must be able to translate written ideas into speech and vice versa. Modalities and sources must be combined to make a coherent emotional and culturally relevant reading of a text.

EYE MOVEMENTS DURING READING

The eyeball makes two kinds of processing movements during reading. First there are movements in the form of rapid lateral **saccades,** which usually jump from seven to nine letters at a time. **Fixations** are the points where the eye stops moving, focuses on a stationary section of text, and picks up visual data from the text. Psychologists have referred to the period of visual fixation on visual information as the **span of perception,** which amounts to a perceptual input stage. Perceptual span occurs in every sensory system. In reading, the perceptual span is roughly two to three words per fixation. Each fixation can be divided into three regions, *foveal, parafoveal,* and *peripheral,* based on the reader's acuity. The **foveal region,** specialized for detail, includes 2 degrees of visual angle around the fixation point. The farther from the fovea, the less details are picked up. The **parafoveal region** extends from the foveal region to about 5 degrees of visual angle on each side of the fixation. Some useful details can be captured here, such as the first few letters of the parafoveal word, which provide some information to help guide the reader to the next fixation. The **peripheral region** includes everything beyond the parafoveal region.

Another metaphor for the perceptual span is that of the perceptual window or **visual window.** The visual window for reading is not a symmetrical distribution of attention because it includes more letters to the right of the fixation (ten to fifteen) than to the left (four). The visual asymmetry occurs in English readers because reading in English progresses from left to right (Rayner & McConkie, 1976; Rayner & Pollatsek, 1989). Hebrew shows the alternative pattern, reading from right to left, and the span of perception in Hebrew is consequently asymmetrical to the left of the fixation (Pollatsek, Bolozky, Well, & Rayner, 1981). Perceptual span also depends on orthography and is smaller for readers of Japanese and Chinese, which are largely logographic (Ikeda & Saida, 1978; Osaka, 1987).

The fixation period provides for a visual "snapshot" of the text (Rayner & Pollatsek, 1989). But as the structural features of the text vary, so will the nature of the fixations and snapshots. Longer words get more attention than shorter words; unfamiliar words get more attention than familiar ones. Subjects will also fixate longer on the final word of a sentence to "wrap up" the meaning of the sentence (Just & Carpenter, 1980).

About 80 percent of the fixation times are used to pick up content word information, as opposed to information about function words. Within each fixation, a reader is attempting to do a number of things: wrap up the information from the previous scan, focus on the important information ahead, relate the new information to the old, anticipate what might come next, make sense of words from distinctive features, and derive an overall gist of the text. The fixation involves not merely extracting from text but also incorporating information from past inspections and anticipations of what is to come.

Figure 7.4 shows a reader's eye movement patterns on a page of text (Rayner & Pollatsek, 1989). The average saccade length is 8.5 characters, ranging from 1 to 18 characters. The average fixation duration is 218 ms, with a range of 66 to 416 ms. Most words are fixated only once; however, *enough* is fixated twice, and *pain* and *least* are not fixated at all. Eye movements bring all words close to the fovea. Fixation durations are variable, and we can speculate that longer times indicate that the reader is taking more time processing the fixated word. There are several measures of fixation time that can be compared. Consider the time spent looking at *brainstorm*, for example. One is the length of time spent on the *first fixation;* that would be 277 ms. Another measure is **gaze duration**, the total fixation time before moving off, which assumes that the second fixation was needed to complete processing; that would be 277 + 120 = 397 ms. The third measure is *total viewing time*, which includes later fixations that result from regressive movements; that would be a total of 576 ms for *brainstorm*.

Eye movements depend on the topic of discussion and the print typography—such things as letter size, font, and line length (see Morrison & Imhoff, 1981). More difficult texts require longer fixations. Table 7.3 indicates how fixation times, regressions, and reading speed (words per minute) change as a function of what subject matter is being read. Eye movements are also related to orthography. For English, difficult text increases the average fixation duration. Fixation durations also tend to be longer for readers of Japanese, Chinese, and Hebrew than for readers of English. For example, the average fixation duration for Chinese readers is about 300 ms and for Israeli readers around 265 ms (see Rayner & Pollatsek, 1989). However, when measured in amounts of meaning extracted per unit of time, reading in different languages seems to be equivalent.

Eye movement studies are among the most popular ways to look at the reading process. Other methods of studying reading include reading aloud, proofreading, visual search, experimentally controlled text presentation, subject-controlled presentations of text, word identification, and naming strategies (see Just & Carpenter, 1987; Rayner & Pollatsek, 1989). Space limits an analysis of each of these in detail. The remainder of this discussion will concentrate on the role of phonology in reading. Most of the time, we can clearly hear our voice saying the words we read, in a sort of **inner speech.** What is the role of phonological coding in reading? Of the several techniques that can be used to study phonological coding, we look at tongue twisters and then at a comparison of normal and deaf reading techniques.

Roadside joggers endure sweat, pain and angry drivers in the name of

1	2		3	4		5	6	7		8
286	221		246	277		256	233	216		188

fitness. A healthy body may seem reward enough for most people. However,

9	10	12	13	11	14	15	16	17	18	19
301	177	196	175	244	302	112	177	266	188	199

for all those who question the payoff, some recent research on physical

21	20	22	23	24	25	26	27
216	212	179	109	266	245	188	205

activity and creativity has provided some surprisingly good news. Regular

29	28	30	31	32	33	34	35	36	37
201	66	201	188	203	220	217	288	212	75

bouts of aerobic exercise may also help spark a brainstorm of creative

38	39	42	40	43	41	44	45	46	47	48
312	260	271	188	350	215	221	266	277	120	219
								50		
								179		

thinking. At least, this is the conclusion that was reached in a study that

49	51	52	53	54	57	55	56	60	59
266	213	210	216	416	200	177	113	206	220
						58			
						218			

Figure 7.4. Text Excerpt with Fixation Sequence and Fixation Durations Indicated
Note. From Rayner, K., & Pollatsek, A. (1989). *The Psychology of Reading.* Reprinted by permission.

READING TONGUE TWISTERS

This technique for studying reading processes involves having subjects read **tongue twisters,** sentences that are difficult to enunciate because they contain repetitions of the same or similar sounds in different configurations, for example, *Peter Piper picked*

Table 7.3. Details of Eye Movements in Ten Good Readers Reading Different Types of Texts

Topic	Fixation Duration (ms)	Saccade Length (characters)	Regressions (% of total fixations)	Reading Speed (words per minute)
Light fiction	202	9.2	3	365
Newspaper article	209	8.3	6	321
History	222	8.3	4	313
Psychology	216	8.1	11	308
English literature	220	7.9	10	305
Economics	233	7.0	11	268
Mathematics	254	7.3	18	243
Physics	261	6.9	17	238
Biology	264	6.8	18	233
Mean	231	7.8	11	288

From Rayner, K. & Pollatsek, A. (1989). *The Psychology of Reading.* Reprinted by permission.

a peck of pickled peppers. Oral reading of tongue twisters is slowed by the same articulatory processes that makes saying tongue twisters difficult when no reading is involved. Of interest here is a comparison of oral versus silent reading of tongue twisters.

Haber and Haber (1982) gave subjects control sentences and tongue twisters (e.g., *Samuel caught the high ball neatly* versus *Barbara burned the brown bread badly*). They found that tongue twisters took longer than controls, and the differences between the two types of sentences were the same in both silent and oral reading. Of course silent reading was faster than oral reading. Ayers (1984) replicated these results by embedding tongue twisters in paragraphs. Paragraphs with tongue twisters took longer to read both silently and orally because extra articulatory programming is required in silent reading and is not suppressed, relative to the control paragraphs.

McCutchen and Perfetti (1982) had subjects silently read sentences and make semantic acceptability judgments. Some of the sentences had tongue twisters with similar initial consonants. Other sentences were matched with phonetically neutral sentences with a mix of initial phonemes. The semantic judgments were longer for the tongue twister sentences than the neutral sentences. These tongue twister studies show that silent reading times for tongue twisters are slowed relative to control sentences. The interference appears to be based on the phonetic similarity of representations activated during reading. McCutchen and Perfetti argued that this occurs postlexically.

A paradigm very similar to the tongue twister effect is the *phonemic similarity effect.* Baddeley and Hitch (1974) asked subjects to make semantic acceptability judgments of sentences made of phonemically similar words—for example, *Crude rude Jude chewed stewed food* versus *Crude rude chewed Jude stewed food*. Subjects took longer to reject or accept sentences like these compared to sentences that contained words that were not phonemically similar. Later, Baddeley and Lewis (1981) had subjects make acceptability judgments while continually counting aloud. They found that this form of articulatory suppression produced an increase in errors but did not influence the size of the phonemic similarity effect.

These studies on inner speech suggest that the sounds of words influence the speed and accuracy of silent reading. Subjects have a harder time rejecting a phrase or sentence when it has words with similar sounds relative to sentences with words that are not phonemically similar. Sentences with words that are similar are more difficult to read both orally and silently.

DEAF READING AND CHINESE READING

In the preceding section, we looked at research that manipulated variables related to inner speech. Another way to pursue the issue is to look at **deaf reading;** that is, subjects who cannot engage in speech recoding because they are profoundly deaf. Although most deaf children learn to read, they do not do so very well (R. Conrad, 1972). R. Conrad (1972) and Treiman and Hirsh-Pasek (1983) concluded that on average, adult deaf readers read at about the fourth- or fifth-grade level. About half of deaf people with a hearing loss of 85 dB have virtually no reading comprehension at all (R. Conrad, 1977).

The profoundly deaf do not learn the sound structure of English because they do not learn English through the alphabetic channel. Spoken language for them is American Sign Language (ASL), which is signed with the hands. These deaf subjects have to learn with an additional handicap; they learn to read a language that is different from the one they sign. Interestingly, some profoundly deaf people can read fairly well. R. Conrad (1977) estimated that 4.5 percent of hearing-impaired students with formal school training in England and Wales could read at a level commensurate with their age. Good readers among the profoundly deaf are less common than among students with some residual hearing. Children with exposure to spoken language tend to be better readers.

Research with profoundly deaf readers indicates that phonological recoding does not occur. Treiman and Hirsh-Pasek (1983) studied a group of congenitally and profoundly deaf adult ASL native signers, comparing them to hearing subjects with comparable reading levels. Experimental materials included **homophones** (e.g., *their-there*) and tongue twisters. They found that deaf subjects did not have difficulty with homophones but the normal subjects did, ruling out the recoding to articulation. There was scant evidence that subjects recoded words into finger spelling. However, deaf subjects had considerable difficulty with sentences that had similar signs—"hand twisters," if you will. This indicates that they did recode words into signs. Signers also had trouble reading tongue twisters, suggesting that the effect may be due to visual similarity.

Profoundly deaf readers seem to recode to their native language in ASL when reading English. Although ASL has no direct relation to print, access to an inner form seems to aid reading performance, which may assist memory and comprehension processes, according to Treiman and Hirsh-Pasek (1983).

These results raise the issue of orthography and inner speech. Because some reading systems like Chinese rely less heavily on sound recoding than alphabetic systems do, one might suspect that logographic systems are more likely to go from print to meaning without inner speech. Research indicates that speech recoding does occur in Chinese because Chinese readers make confusion errors in working memory for characters with similar-sounding names (Tzeng & Hung, 1980; Tzeng, Hung, & Wang, 1977) but probably resulting in less recoding than occurs in English (Treiman, Baron, & Luk, 1981). It appears that once logographic characters are learned, they are phonetically recoded in working memory like English words.

Phonological effects are less expected in Chinese than in alphabetic languages like English because the basic units of written Chinese (characters) map directly into units of meaning. Phonology could be bypassed altogether in reading Chinese, but this is not the case. Recent research by Ziegler, Tan, Perry, and Montant (2000) confirms the role of phonology in Chinese silent reading. They presented subjects with characters with no homophone mates, few (less than six) homophone mates, and many (more than seven) homophone mates. Subjects were timed for naming, delayed naming, and lexical decision. The more homophones a word has, the higher its phonological frequency. If phonological frequency plays a role in reading over and above a character's surface frequency, then characters with many homophone mates should benefit from having higher phonological frequencies.

The results of Ziegler et al. (2000) provided evidence for a phonological frequency effect in reading. Characters with few or many homophone mates were named faster and produced quicker lexical decision times than characters with no homophone mates. The identical patterns were obtained in naming and lexical decision but not delayed naming, which shows that the phonological frequency effect is not restricted to tasks that require explicit computation of phonology but seems to underlie lexical processing in general. Since the effect was not present in delayed naming, it cannot be explained by articulatory differences between stimulus groups. Phonological frequency could be seen as a signature of accessing phonological representations in the mental lexicon. Phonological word forms seem to be routinely activated in word recognition, even in logographic language like Chinese. These results support a more universal phonological principle that emphasizes the dependence of writing systems on spoken language and a preference for speech coding over visual coding.

Deaf readers recode printed information into ASL for comprehension purposes. One interpretation is that profoundly deaf people have difficulty reading due in part to inner speech being more efficient than recoding that involves manual gestures. Readers of logographic systems like Chinese can most likely access meaning visually, but associations between printed words and pronunciation are activated during reading because they are important in comprehending texts.

Models of Reading

Space does not permit an exhaustive treatment of models of reading. We focus on four different models, two that concentrate on word recognition and two that take a more comprehensive approach. How do we get from print to meaning? The most important process in reading is *word recognition*. All models of reading attempt to account for the process of decoding text through word recognition.

All reading models begin with an initial input stage where graphic information is processed, but models differ on what happens after that. **Top-down processing** models (Goodman, 1970; F. Smith, 1971) emphasize how higher-order conceptual information in memory (world knowledge, context, discourse structure) guides the reading at lower levels (letters, syllables, words). **Bottom-up processing** models (Gough, 1972; La Berge & Samuels, 1974; Massaro, 1975) argue that processing is fast and information flows through a series of stages. Visual information sampled from print is transformed through a series of stages with little influence from general world information, contextual information, or other higher-order processing strategies (e.g., discourse structure). **Interactive models** (Just & Carpenter, 1987; Rayner & Pollatsek, 1989; Seidenberg & McClelland, 1989), which have garnered a lot of attention in psycholinguistics, draw on both top-down and bottom-up processing in the interpretation of a text. Bottom-up and interactive models rely heavily on the stage of graphophonemic decoding as a means to obtain lexical meaning. All models rely heavily on a stage of lexical access and word recognition to account for how we read.

It is not clear how much information beyond words (i.e., phrases, clauses, or sentences) is held and integrated in memory. Parsing strategies and limitations on parsing are not specified. It is not clear what happens to the current information in memory when the reader scans a new section of text, for example. What happens when the same letters are processed on subsequent fixations? Most problematic for all models are the higher-order processes. Little is clear about how inference, prior sentence knowledge, text macrostructure, or general world knowledge influence perceptual processes. It is unclear how higher-order information is integrated with information coming in to working memory. Although perceptual and visual information input is critical to translating text into meaning, how higher-order processes guide these preliminary stages is not clear. Initial stages operate on more than letters and words alone, but how and why fixation points and perceptual span shift within texts is not clear.

DUAL-ROUTE MODEL OF WORD RECOGNITION

Word recognition models describe how to find word meanings in memory. We discussed these extensively in Chapter 4, but they are obviously pertinent to the process of reading since word recognition is the most important part of the reading process. The starting point in the reading process is the visual input stage; but from there tracks to meaning diverge, depending on the model in question. The **dual-route model** assumes that meaning can be accessed directly from visual input or indirectly through a phonological recoding stage.

The classic dual-route model (Coltheart, 1978; Coltheart, Curtis, Atkins, & Haller, 1993; Coltheart, Rastle, Perry, Langdon, & Ziegler, 2001) proposes two independent coding systems that access word meaning. One route uses words to directly access lexical representation, and the second uses GPC rules to access them indirectly. The direct and indirect routes are also referred to as lexical (whole word) and phonological or sublexical access. In other words, after the reader fixates on a letter string, access to the word meaning can occur directly from the whole word or indirectly through letter-sound decoding, which is assumed to take longer than the direct path. A recent version of the Dual-Route Cascaded (DRC) model of visual word recognition and reading aloud is illustrated in Figure 7.5. The indirect grapheme-to-phoneme system is shown on the right of the figure, and the direct path to the lexicon, with or without meaning activation, is on the left.

Evidence supporting the direct access path comes from our ability to readily find different meanings for *homophones,* words that sound the same, like *there* and

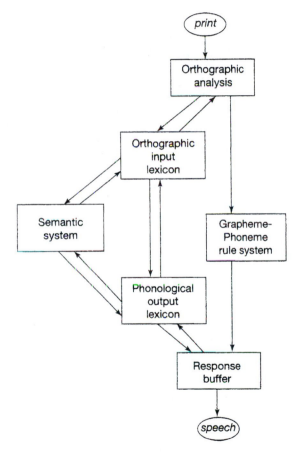

Figure 7.5. Basic Architecture of the Dual-Route Cascaded Model of Visual Word Recognition and Reading Aloud

Note. From "Basic architecture of the Dual Route Cascaded model of visual word recognition and reading aloud" by M. Coltheart, et al., *Psychological Review,* 108, p. 213. Copyright © 2001 by the American Psychological Association. Reprinted with permission.

their (Baron, 1973). In addition, people with some forms of dyslexia can access word meanings directly without translating single letters into phonemes. Also, children who are deaf from birth learn to read without knowing the sounds of the words they are reading, as discussed earlier.

The indirect hypothesis proposes that readers find sounds that letters represent in order to find the meaning of the words made up of those letters. Supporting evidence includes the fact that many people move their lips when they read and that they sound out new words and infrequent words.

Another line of support for the dual-route model comes from research with people with language disorders. Research on readers with different forms of acquired dyslexia seems to support the dual-route model of lexical access. Interest in acquired dyslexia can be traced to an important paper on the topic by Marshall and Newcombe (1973) in which they contrasted differences between *surface* and *deep* forms of acquired dyslexia.

Readers with **deep dyslexia** have impaired phonological decoding. They still can read words by finding them directly in semantic memory without relying on phonological decoding. Deep dyslexics can also read real words (e.g., *paper*) but not pseudowords (e.g., *trape*), indicating that the direct route is available. The errors produced in deep dyslexia are obviously of a semantic nature, and sometimes they are a combination of semantic and visual errors. The visual concreteness of the word is also important. Deep dyslexics can identify concrete words better than words that are abstract or low in imageability. Along this line of reasoning, they are better at identifying content words than function words (Rayner & Pollatsek, 1989). The pattern of semantic and combined errors in deep dyslexia might look like the following (target word → word as read):

$$ape \rightarrow monkey$$

$$forest \rightarrow trees$$

$$signal \rightarrow single \text{ (visual error)}$$

$$sympathy \text{ (via } symphony\text{)} \rightarrow orchestra \text{ (semantic and visual error)}$$

The deep dyslexic finds these kinds of concrete words without taking a phonological route. For them, it is as if the phonological route is not functional. Patients with deep dyslexia have reading problems that are the opposite of those experienced in surface dyslexia. Deep dyslexics have damage to the phonological pathway, resulting in their inability to read simple pronounceable nonwords (e.g., *tave*). The classic symptom is the presence of semantic errors in oral reading, for example, reading "dog" for *cat*. Semantic errors can be visual in nature, for example, "cot" for *cat,* or mixed visual-and-semantic errors, for example, "orchestra" for *sympathy.* Performance in deep dyslexia also depends on part of speech (nouns > adjectives > verbs > function words) and word concreteness (concrete > abstract).

Readers with **surface dyslexia** show a different pattern of reading errors. They rely almost entirely on phonological recoding to find word meaning. Surface dyslexics can decode pseudowords and regularly spelled words; however, they have trouble with irregular words (e.g., *epoch*) and those with unusual pronunciation patterns (e.g., *sew*). The pattern of errors in surface dyslexics shows that they are trying to find the relationships between graphemes and phonemes. Their errors look like these examples:

$$island \rightarrow izland$$

$$sugar \rightarrow sudger$$

$$disease \rightarrow decease$$

$$guest \rightarrow just$$

The words that the dyslexic pronounces are phonologically approximate to the target words. The research on dyslexia is equivocal on the question of whether lexical access is a direct or an indirect process because it can be used to support both routes.

Forster and Chambers (1973) proposed that we may use the direct route for familiar words and the indirect route and sounding out for words that are less familiar. Naming tasks have been used to show that skilled readers can name printed words more quickly than they can sound out pseudowords. What is suggested is that familiar words are recognized by the direct route but pseudowords and unfamiliar words are recognized by sounding them out. Another consistent finding is that orthographically regular words are named faster than irregular or exception words (Baron & Strawson, 1976). However, high-frequency exception words are named as fast as regular high-frequency words, and low-frequency regular words are named faster than low-frequency exception words (Seidenberg, Waters, Barnes, & Tanenhaus, 1984). This suggests that high-frequency words are recognized directly whether they are regular or not. Both paths are competitive with low-frequency words, where exceptions are more likely to be recognized indirectly.

Glushko (1979) presented evidence that the dual route may be somewhat oversimplified. Glushko found that a pseudoword like *tave* (orthographically similar to the high-frequency exception word *have*) takes longer to name than a pseudoword like *feal*, which has regularly pronounced neighbors, such as *meal* or *real* (see Chapter 4 on neighborhood effects). Also, regular words with consistent neighborhoods are named faster than regular words with inconsistent neighborhoods. Seidenberg et al. (1984) found that low-frequency regular and consistent words were named faster than low-frequency regular and inconsistent words. These findings suggest that a single mechanism that recognizes words with similar spellings may be an alternative to the dual-route model.

CONNECTIONIST MODEL OF READING

As an alternative to the dual-route model, connectionist models propose a single mechanism for recognizing words. You might recall that we looked at this model in Chapter 4 when we examined lexical access. Here we concentrate on the oral reading of single words and recent revisions in the model, especially as they relate to word reading and dyslexia (Plaut, 1999; Plaut, McClelland, Seidenberg, & Patterson, 1996).

Connectionist theories eschew the notion that language performance takes the form of "rules." They deny a strict dichotomy between "regular" words that obey rules and "exception" words that violate rules. They claim that language knowledge is graded, based on a learning device that gradually picks up the statistical structure among written and spoken words. The connectionist framework for lexical processing is illustrated in Figure 7.6. Orthography, phonology, and semantics are represented by patterns of activity in the network. Similar words have similar patterns of activity. Relationships among orthography, phonology, and semantics are learned through experience and accomplished through the simultaneous interaction of numerous units in the network. Repeated processing patterns form stable "attractors," or patterns of activity. Reading aloud requires that the orthographic pattern for a word generate a phonological pattern.

Skilled reading in connectionism takes place without what amounts to individual words or lexical entries. Skilled reading requires the combined support of semantic and phonological pathways, and readers may differ in their competence with each. Words and nonwords are distinguished by their unique patterns of activation at the semantic, phonological, and orthographic nodes. There are no separate mechanisms for lexical and sublexical processes, in contrast to Coltheart et al. (1993). All parts of the network participate in processing all types of input, but to different degrees. Plaut et al. (1996) offered a mathematical analysis of how skilled readers pronounce regular

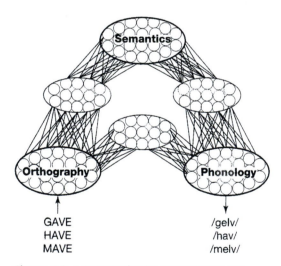

Figure 7.6. A Connectionist Framework for Lexical Processing

Note. From "A Connectionist Approach to Word Reading and Acquired Dyslexia: Extension to Sequential Processing," by Plaut, D. C., *Cognitive Science,* Vol. 23 (4), pp. 543–568. © Cognitive Science Society. Reprinted by permission of Cognitive Science Society and the author.

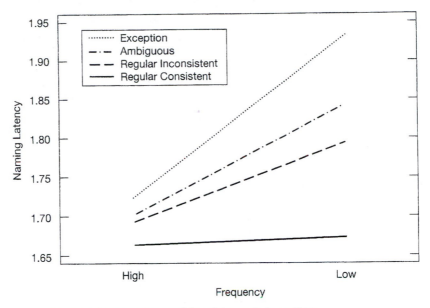

Figure 7.7. Word Frequency and Consistency Interaction

Note. From "A Connectionist Approach to Word Reading and Acquired Dyslexia: Extension to Sequential Processing," by Plaut, D. C., *Cognitive Science*, Vol. 23 (4), pp. 543–568. © Cognitive Science Society. Reprinted by permission of Cognitive Science Society and the author.

words, exception words, and nonwords. They replicated frequency-by-consistency interaction patterns found in word naming research, as can be seen in Figure 7.7. The word types matter little if the words are high-frequency. Inconsistencies and exception words have their effects when words are infrequent.

The semantic pathway is important to account for the pattern of problems that arise in surface dyslexia. Here patients can read nonwords and regular words with normal speech and accuracy. An interaction of frequency and consistency in reading accuracy occurs, such that infrequent exception words are pronounced poorly, often resulting in a **regularization error**—for example, enunciating *sew* as *sue*. Surface dyslexia is based on the interaction of the semantic and phonological pathways. The semantic pathway reduces errors by contributing the correct pronunciation, lessening the pressure on the phonological pathway to pronounce all words itself. The semantic pathway will learn to pronounce words that are frequent or consistent but will not master infrequent words or exception words. Brain damage impairing the semantic pathway reveals the limitations of the intact but isolated phonological pathway, giving rise to the pattern of errors in surface dyslexia. Surface dyslexia seems to involve reading primarily via the phonological pathway because of an impairment of the semantic pathway.

The relevance of semantic impairment in surface dyslexia is supported by cases of semantic dementia (the inability to match words to their meanings) and Alzheimer's-type dementia (Graham, Hodges, & Patterson, 1994; Plaut et al., 1996).

The surface-dyslexic reading pattern emerges as the semantic dementia patient's lexical semantic knowledge deteriorates and the disease progresses. The severity of their reading difficulties is correlated with the degree of semantic deterioration. A similar pattern applies to Alzheimer's patients (Patterson, Graham, & Hodges, 1994). The interpretation is that the network is performing with partial elimination of the semantic pathway. As semantics are degraded, performance on low-frequency exceptions is affected first and high-frequency exceptions after that. Performance on regular words and nonwords is relatively unaffected by semantic deterioration. Dementia patients exhibit a drop in performance on low-frequency regular words when their semantic impairment is very severe. Dementia patients also show deterioration on the phonological pathway, degrading performance on exception words more than performance on regular words.

Phonological dyslexia is closely related to deep dyslexia involving selective problems reading nonwords compared to words but without concomitant semantic errors. Phonological dyslexic patients read words, both regular and exception, much better than nonwords, whereas surface dyslexic patients read nonwords much better than exception words. Phonological dyslexia is interpreted as the result of selective damage to the phonological pathway such that reading is accomplished primarily in the semantic pathway.

Hinton and Shallice (1991) were able to reproduce that pattern of errors found in deep dyslexia by damaging the part of the network that mapped orthography onto semantics. The initial input gave rise to errors that were semantically related to nearby attractors, as well as errors that were visually related to the semantic pattern.

In sum, connectionist models use a single mechanism to account for all input items. This mechanism does not distinguish between regular and exception words. Impaired performance as the result of brain damage reflects the underlying division of labor among multiple resources of information. The semantic and visual errors in deep dyslexia are a consequence of how the network learns to map orthography onto semantics. Surface dyslexia errors occur when the phonological pathway, trained in the context of semantic support, loses the support of semantics. The performance of dementia patients is similar to the performance of surface dyslexics.

We shift from the two models of reading that concentrate on the word recognition process to examine more comprehensive accounts of the reading process. Comprehensive interactive models of reading that go beyond word recognition have been proposed by Just and Carpenter (1980, 1987), Rayner and Pollatsek (1989), and others (Gibson & Levin, 1975; Goodman, 1970; Gough, 1972; La Berge & Samuels, 1974; F. Smith, 1971). For a more complete treatment of models of reading theories, see Rayner and Pollatsek (1989) or Just and Carpenter (1987).

JUST AND CARPENTER MODEL

The Just and Carpenter model (1980) is outlined in Figure 7.8. This model is primarily interactive, relying on both bottom-up analyses of letters and letter features and top-down influences from long-term memory. The reading process begins with information obtained during an eye fixation on the text. This process begins with physical

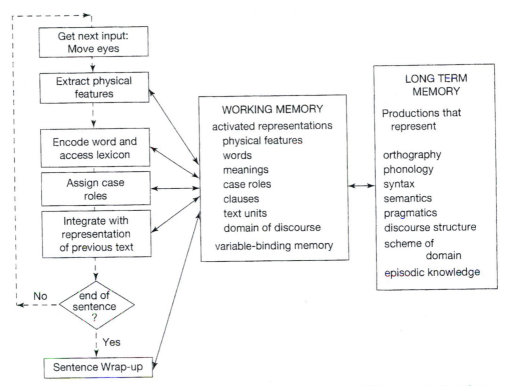

Figure 7.8. The Just and Carpenter Model of Major Processes and Structures in Reading Comprehension Solid lines denote data paths, and dashed lines indicate canonical flow of control (serial order).

Note. From "A theory of reading from eye fixations to comprehension" by M. A. Just & P. A. Carpenter, *Psychological Review*, 87, p. 331. Copyright © 1980 by the American Psychological Association. Reprinted with permission.

features being extracted from the input. The eyes remain fixated until the "get next input" step is engaged, after the collection of necessary information has been completed, which takes about 50 ms. Before new information is input, the reader must access the meaning of words in the fixation span and transfer the meanings to working memory. The "get next input" stage moves the eyes forward one or two words.

During the "encode word and access lexicon" stage, the word is perceptually encoded and its underlying concept is activated. The conceptual representation serves as a "pointer" to a more precise meaning representation. The "assign case roles" stage is used to determine the syntactic function of a word. Here is the first point where a word is related to other words being processed in working memory. Words have to be integrated with other words. The clauses in which the identified words appear have to be updated, since case assignment is made within clauses.

The integration stage is important because the reader has to relate clauses and sentences with each other in order to appreciate the coherence of the larger text. Integration occurs when each word is encountered and the attempt is made to relate the new word to previous information. The second level of integration is a running clause interpretation, an attempt to update the clause information with each word being read.

The integration of new and old information occurs through one of two strategies. First, readers check to see if the new information is related to the topic in the working memory buffer. The second strategy, which takes longer than the first, is to search for explicitly marked old information in working memory, for example, from a clause being read. The reader resolves inconsistencies with sentences and clauses and searches for referents that have not been assigned roles in the "sentence wrap-up" stage.

Top-down processing occurs through a "production system" that is stored in permanent memory. This is one of the most important aspects of the model. The production system is used to specify what information should be present in working memory to enable the actions to be produced, through a series of **condition-action rules.** The condition specifies what should be present or absent in working memory to enable an action. For example, one parsing production specifies that if an article (*a, an, the*) has been encoded (condition), a slot for a noun phrase should be established (action).

Productions are executed through *recognize-act cycles*. During each cycle, the contents of working memory are evaluated, and productions whose contents have been satisfied are executed, modifying and updating the contents of working memory. Now new contents of working memory can be evaluated. When the contents of working memory satisfy the production system, another reading cycle can begin.

The model is driven primarily by bottom-up processes unless errors in processing are detected. However, top-down processes do influence the bottom-up processes. The model allows for any stage to be influenced by any other stage, and it executes multiple productions simultaneously, giving it the quality of being interactive.

This model is able to explain many reading phenomena, as outlined in Just and Carpenter (1987), but it also has some weaknesses pointed out by eye movement researchers (e.g., Fisher & Shebilske, 1984; Slowiaczek, 1983). One criticism is that the models do not fully explain control of eye movements or the parafoveal processing of text. Another objection is that the 50-ms duration of the "get next input" stage is too brief. The major criticism of the model is that it is not clear what it would predict in advance about the kinds of processes that occur during reading. The model accounts for reading performance but does not point to clear predictions of an experiment, in contrast to bottom-up models proposed by La Berge and Samuels (1974) or Gough (1972). For example, bottom-up models argue that visual information is sampled from the printed page and transformed through a series of stages with little or no interaction with general word knowledge, contextual information, or higher-order processing. In other words, a good model of reading both accounts for reading performance and makes predictions about experimental conditions.

RAYNER AND POLLATSEK MODEL

Like the Just and Carpenter model, the Rayner and Pollatsek (1989) model is driven primarily by bottom-up processes that also interact with top-down processes. The authors presented it as a work in progress that would account for major evidence about reading rather than make explicit predictions about reading.

The components and process of reading are shown in Figure 7.9. Saccade and eye fixation are in circles to indicate that they are observable behaviors that are

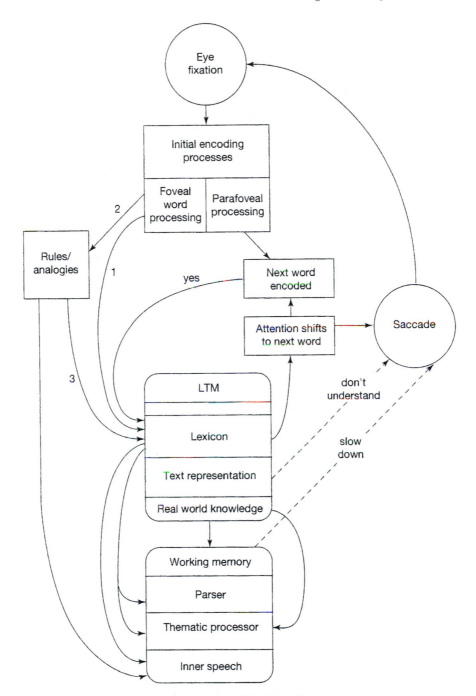

Figure 7.9. The Rayner and Pollatsek Model of Reading
Note. From Rayner, K., & Pollatsek, A. (1989). *The Psychology of Reading.* Reprinted by permission.

distinguishable from processing activities, represented by boxes, or memory structures (long-term memory, LTM; and working memory). LTM has three components: the lexicon, real-world knowledge, and text representations of what has been read. The working memory has components: inner speech, a syntactic parser, and a thematic processing module.

The reading sequence begins with an eye fixation. The initial encoding has two separate processes that occur simultaneously: foveal word processing and parafoveal processing. Foveal processing is concerned with processing letters in parallel in the word on which the eyes are fixated. Parafoveal processing involves extracting information (word, letter, and word length information) to the right of the word on which the eyes are fixated and is used to determine where to look next. Fixation on a word allows for lexical access, which can occur by indirect auditory code route (2–3 in the figure) or through a direct route (1). The meaning of the word and its syntactic information is derived from the lexicon. Both routes to the lexicon help activate an acoustic representation of the word characterized by the concept of "inner speech."

The idea that meaning is derived from a phonological representation of a printed word has given rise to the controversial notion that readers read through a process of silent inner speech, a kind of talking to oneself during reading, which may be viewed as an essential component of the indirect route of reading. The presence of inner speech could merely be a result of learning to read aloud, or it could play a more important role in comprehending what we read. Rayner and Pollatsek (1989) argue that the most convincing theory of inner speech is that inner speech aids comprehension by constructing a more durable trace of the printed material to be used in working memory. The phonological image can be held in working memory until the semantic and syntactic features of the text can be determined.

When lexical access is completed, the process shifts to the next word to the right of the fixation point. The previous word is integrated with the meaning of the text being constructed in working memory. Prior to the change in fixation point, the letters that begin the next word have been processed and identified in an abstract code, which speeds up its subsequent identification. When a word is difficult to identify or integrate, the eye will remain fixated on it. The reader may also make a second fixation on the word, disrupting the normal processing cycle. Readers having trouble making sense of a text can either consult their inner speech representation of a word or look back in the text.

The parser assigns strings of words to syntactic constituents using strategies like minimal attachment and late closure discussed in Chapter 5. It will sometimes get "garden-pathed" when it ignores important contextual and pragmatic information. The reader will have to backtrack to the point where things went wrong. The thematic processor monitors the semantic content of the text and weighs alternative interpretations of it in order to find the most plausible one. Meaning construction also involves inferences, text structures, anaphor, the use of context, and cohesive devices. Exactly what happens after the reader leaves the lexicon in this model is a bit murky.

The model can account for individual differences in reading and differences in direct versus indirect word recognition. Rayner and Pollatsek (1989) think that there is little difference between skilled readers in the early processes in this model (perceptual span). Differences in reading speed will show up during word recognition, direct processing being faster than indirect processing. Also, what readers know about the world and the topic of the text will clearly affect comprehension. It is less clear how readers choose parsing strategies when they read text.

Key Terms

alphabetic system	homophone	pictogram
bottom-up processing	ideogram	poor readers
condition-action rules	inner speech	poor writers
cuneiform	interactive models	regularization error
deaf reading	IRT	revision
deep dyslexia	knowledge	saccade
dual-route model	restructurer	span of perception
fixation	knowledge teller	surface dyslexia
foveal region	literacy	syllabary
gaze duration	logogram	task environment
good readers	orthography	tongue twister
good writers	parafoveal region	top-down processing
grapheme	peripheral region	verbal protocol
grapheme-to-phoneme	phonological	visual window
correspondence	awareness	word processor
(GPC)	phonological dyslexia	writer's block

What Lies Ahead

Chapter 8 continues our analysis of reading but does so in the context of discourse, narratives, stories, and scripts. We also consider the social context in which we understand discourse and how relationships between speakers and listeners affect what they are talking about and what goals they are trying to achieve by talking to each other.

Suggested Web Sites

Writing links: http://www.depts.washington.edu/psywc/links.html
Reading and literacy link: http://stills.nap.edu/html/sor/sor-7.htm

PART 2
Applied Psycholinguistics

Chapter 8
Discourse: Text and Conversation

Critical Thinking Questions

1. What devices do writers use to make a text cohesive?

2. Why do texts require multiple representations (surface, network, mental model)?

3. What is the role of inferencing in text comprehension?

4. How do readers use schemas to comprehend text?

5. How does culture affect discourse processes?

6. What role do gestures play in conversations?

7. What is the joint project view of discourse?

8. How are conversations opened and closed? How are turns taken?

9. What is the nature of personal narratives and storytelling?

Exercise 8.1. **Conversations**

Before you begin reading the material in this chapter, take a few minutes to record in your notebook a conversation that you have had recently. Identify the who, what, where, and when information. What was the purpose of the conversation? Were you catching up on old times, purchasing an item, requesting information over the phone, or complaining about your professors? Finally, do you think there are rules for conversations? If yes, what are they?

Discourse

We communicate with each other through conversations and written texts, using multisentence segments of connected discourse. *Discourse* refers to a sequence of written sentences or spoken utterances that attempts to achieve some goal (e.g., borrowing notes from a friend, placing a bet). In this chapter, we shift away from the sentence as a unit of analysis to look at multisentence discourse. Discourse occurs in diverse situations; it can take the form of a telephone conversation, courtroom testimony, psychotherapy, parent-child dialogue, leisure conversation, business transaction, or classroom instruction. It is important for psycholinguists to focus on many forms of discourse to understand speech comprehension and production processes. One goal of the chapter is to describe discourse as a structured system and as a speech process. I elucidate the nature of discourse structures and the discourse strategies that are used to produce and comprehend them. The first half of the chapter covers text; the second half, conversation.

IS DISCOURSE A PRODUCT OR A PROCESS?

One issue in discourse processing is whether the topic of interest is the product of linguistic behavior or a process of communication (H. H. Clark, 1994; Kintsch, 1994; Sanford & Garrod, 1994). The *product* or *text view* is that discourse is an object that is produced by people speaking or by writing text. Here discourse is a text or sequence of sentences that obtains coherence through its internal linguistic structure (Halliday & Hasan, 1976; van Dijk, 1972). Coherence refers to a person's mental representation of discourse in an organized and meaningful way. From this point of view, the following small bit of discourse can be considered coherent due to the relationships between words in the two-sentence text: *My uncle drank too much last night. He lost his job yesterday.* These two sentences form a coherent segment of text from a structural point of view. The text view evolved among linguists and philosophers from the study of sentence grammar. The unit of analysis is larger than a sentence but more like a sentence than an utterance. However, the text view fails to address the particular speakers, listeners, or context involved.

The *process view,* developed by sociologists and anthropologists, looks at what people actually do in the communication process. Here we are concerned with the nature of the activity between two or more people who are trying to achieve some outcomes together (H. H. Clark, 1996; Goffman, 1971; Sacks, Schegloff, & Jefferson, 1974). The process orientation has produced a *joint activity view* of discourse, which examines what people are doing with conversations, stories, or narratives, which are storylike accounts of events. From this view, we cannot understand what a given piece of discourse means as an object without comprehending the process that created it (H. H. Clark, 1996).

The text view has produced competing systems to describe intratext relationships and also different levels of analysis (see van den Broek, 1994, or Kintsch, 1994). I will not provide an exhaustive review of competing systems but will focus instead on those that have captured the most attention. As for different levels of analysis, it has become apparent that a text cannot be understood by a single-sentence level of analysis (Kintsch, 1994). Both the structure of the text as a whole and the understanding of it, as created in the mind of the reader, are critically important. Discourse studies have produced the idea that conventions or rules guide conversations, for example, about taking turns in conversations or how to respond to questions. The formulaic level of analysis (e.g., grammatical rules) used in sentential syntax has not been achieved in discourse research. A standard unit of discourse analysis has not been found, primarily because discourse contexts are so varied and one formula cannot apply to all. There is, however, an in-depth understanding of discourse within specific situations, such as person-to-person conversations, stories, and narratives. Discourse is a function of the participants' attitudes, knowledge, and cultural background. Cross-cultural differences in discourse also emerge. The ultimate meaning of any piece of discourse depends on and is derived from social interaction. The meaning and structure of discourse can be realized by analyzing what goes on in different speech contexts. We begin our analysis of discourse by asking some questions about text and text comprehension.

Text Structure and Comprehension

How are texts structured? How do we form a mental representation of a text? These are two basic issues in discourse, and as you can imagine, the answers depend on who one asks. One straightforward approach to text is to describe the features of it that make it coherent. *Coherence* refers to the linkages among propositions in the reader's mental representation of the text. We read about *cohesion* next.

Cohesion is the connection among the sentences in discourse. Cohesion depends on linguistic devices in the text that establish linkages. Writers and readers use several linguistic devices to keep a conversation cohesive (Halliday & Hasan, 1976). Some cohesive devices change the way a referent is described. In our example (*My uncle drank too much . . .*), reference shifted from a noun (*uncle*) to a pronoun (*he*). *Anaphora* is the general term used for cohesive references that link past statements to current statements. Let us look at some examples of anaphora using pronouns, demonstratives, and comparatives.

Pronouns are inserted in discourse to replace referents that have already been established. If the text reads *My brother is an inventor,* soon thereafter it can continue *He invented the machine that prints payroll checks.* The reader understands that the pronoun *he* refers to *my brother. Demonstratives* are pronouns such as *this, these, that, those, here,* or *there.* If I read *That was the worst movie I've seen this year,* I know that *that . . . movie* refers to a movie mentioned previously in the text. *Comparatives* contrast one referent in the text with another through the use of words like *same* or *different*, as in *It's a different menu from the one we had last week.*

Substitutions are made so that one does not have to keep repeating the same word or phrase in a narrative. If we read *He knew he was going to get drunk before he went to the party,* a substitution might be *and that is what he did,* where *that* substitutes for the proposition *get drunk at the party.* Similarly, when the topic or referent is understood, ellipsis can be used. *Ellipsis* is the substitution of "nothing" for a thought that is understood. The narration might continue with *He always seems to make the most of these boring office parties, but his wife can't. . . .* The information omitted from the end of this sentence but understood is *make the most of these boring office parties.* The information can be omitted because the reader understands that ellipsis is a cohesive device that requires that he or she fill in the missing information.

One of the most common forms of anaphora is the use of *conjunctions* such as *and, because, but, then,* or *so.* These conjunctions form additive (*and*), causative (*because*), adversative (*but*), and temporal (*then, so*) links to other statements in a text. One example of the use of a conjunction might be something like the following, *She was hoping that her boss would not see that she had too much to drink, but she was not so lucky.* The *but* sets in opposition what the woman hoped for and what actually occurred.

Cohesion can also be maintained at the lexical level with reiteration, synonymy, and hyponymy. *Reiteration* uses the same word in related sentences such as *I saw a boy win the spelling bee. The boy was delighted afterward. Synonymy* uses a synonym of the first referent in the second mention, as in *I saw a boy win the spelling bee. The lad was delighted afterward. Hyponymy* uses a hyponym in the second mention in place of the original word, as in *I saw a boy win the spelling bee. The child was delighted afterward.* Associating a current reference to one made earlier in the text creates cohesion in these anaphoric references. The current expression links back to the previous one. There is a second way to establish cohesion with *cataphors,* which link forward instead of backward. A cataphoric reference looks ahead in the discourse, as *This* does in *This is what I told you: Never throw good money after bad.*

There is plenty of evidence (see Chapters 5 and 7) that coherence in the reader's mind is established when **anaphors** are resolved during reading. Readers slow down when they have to resolve anaphors (Garrod & Sanford, 1990). Antecedents are more available after resolving an anaphoric reference than when a sentence does not contain an anaphoric reference. Inappropriate referents are not available in either of these cases (Gernsbacher, 1989; McKoon & Ratcliff, 1980; van den Broek, 1994). This means that when readers encounter statements that require searches for antecedents, the readers slow down and reactivate the antecedents. Next we examine the structure of text at three different levels. These are (1) the surface propositions in the text; (2) the text as a text base, propositional network, or story grammar; and (3) the mental model the reader builds from the text.

Macrostructure, Microstructure, and Mental Model

In Chapter 5, we covered the understanding of individual sentences; here we address the global text structure. Discourse is structured at three levels. A text is a set of individual sentences, but the sentences produce overarching themes and relationships, as our discussion of cohesion made clear. Understanding each individual sentence operates on a *local* level, that is, on the sentence currently in working memory. But if we think of a text as a string of interrelated sentences that have some general purpose, we have to analyze the text structure on a *global* level. We can look at how the individual sentences or propositions are linked to or help achieve the main points of the text. The global structure or theme is called the **macrostructure,** which forms the general meaning of the whole text. The **microstructures** are the local propositions (in sentences) in the text, which are used to support the macrostructure and add meaning to it (Kintsch & van Dijk, 1978). The theme of the text appears to us when we establish the connections between the macro and micro levels of the text. We have to comprehend the microstructures and at the same time use them to understand how they construct the macrostructure of the text.

Text comprehension is a strategic and constructive process whereby the reader uses information in the text as cues to the structure of the events, images, and inferences drawn from the text. One of the major issues in discourse comprehension concerns the need for a situational representation, in addition to a representation of the text itself. During the discourse comprehension process, readers actively construct a **mental model** of what they are processing (Johnson-Laird, 1983; van Dijk & Kintsch, 1983). The comprehension of the text depends not only on a mental representation of the text but also on a mental representation of the situation described by the text. The text and mental models will be similar in many instances, but often they are not, as in cases where the reader updates an older mental model or where stored knowledge conflicts with information in the text structure chosen by the author. Bits of information, which may be out of sequence and scattered throughout a story, are brought together and reorganized into a representation that makes more sense to the reader. The mental model becomes a rich global representation based on reasoning that goes beyond the mere parsing and comprehension of sentences. A mental model is under continuous construction and revision as incoming information and inferences about the text are processed.

The mental model represents what the text has conveyed to the reader, it is used to understand what has been read and what is still to come. If you can imagine yourself reading a detective novel, trying to figure out "who done it" by piecing together all the clues given, you would be constructing a mental model of the novel. One author may intentionally mislead you or leave out important details, requiring you to reconstruct the crime and make inferences about the perpetrator. Mental models are currently popular in cognitive psychology and in the discourse processing literature. Research on mental models confirms that discourse representations exist on the three levels we have identified: microstructures, macrostructures, and the mental models constructed by readers.

Inferences

All discourse attempts to produce and maintain a coherent global structure. Inferences help do this. Akin to the construction of a mental model, an *inference* is an attempt to fill in what is not explicitly stated in a text. We discussed *elaborative inferences* in Chapter 5. Elaborative inferences are not necessary; they may or may not accompany discourse comprehension. For example, *robin* might be activated after reading *The red-breasted bird pecked the ground;* on a higher level of text inference, *Pete played a prank* might be activated after reading *Pete positioned the thumbtack on the chair* (Singer, 1994). These inferences are not necessary to comprehend the text, even though the reader activates them. In contrast, other types of inference are essential to comprehend what is happening in the text.

BRIDGING INFERENCES

Bridging inferences are necessary for comprehension because discourse coherence is impaired if they are not drawn (H. H. Clark, 1977; Haviland & Clark, 1974). For example, these two sentences need a bridging inference: *The spy quickly threw his report in the fire. The ashes floated up the chimney.* Here the reader must make a bridging inference such as *The report burned to ashes* to comprehend what is going on in these two sentences. Although elaborative inferences are not necessary for coherence, bridging inferences are. It is worth noting that bridging inferences are thought to be automatic, whereas elaborative inferences are thought to be more deliberate and controlled (St. George, Mannes, & Hoffman, 1997).

To understand a passage, the reader has to identify relationships between current sentences and what has preceded them. The words in a current sentence may or may not be coreferential with a word from a previous sentence. In addition, coreference can be direct or indirect (H. H. Clark, 1977), as the next four sentences illustrate.

1. We got the beer out of the car. The beer was warm.

2. We got the brew out of the car. The beer was warm.

3. We got the beverage out of the car. The beer was warm.

4. We got the beer out of the car. It was warm.

Beer in the second sentence of 1 is coreferential with the first sentence. However, in 2 through 4, coreference of *beer* is established through synonym, category name, and pronoun. The reader has to resolve the anaphoric reference, *the beer*, in the second sentence. If a lot of text intervenes between the anaphor and its referent, the referent has to be reinstated in working memory before coreference is determined (Haviland & Clark, 1974). In contrast, sentences like 5 have no referent to *beer* in the antecedent sentence.

> 5. We got the picnic supplies out of the car. The beer was warm.

Here the reader must make a bridging inference between the two sentences that the supplies included beer. This kind of bridging is necessary when anaphoric resolution fails.

If only bridging inferences are necessary for coherence, they should be more likely to occur on-line relative to elaborative inferences. Singer (1980) examined inferences about concepts that filled agent, instrument, and patient roles. Subjects had to read the sentences and then verify if *A dentist pulled the tooth* was true. Examples 6 through 8 illustrate the agent sentences.

> 6. The dentist pulled the tooth painlessly. The patient liked the new method. (*explicit*)
>
> 7. The tooth was pulled painlessly. The dentist used a new method. (*bridging*)
>
> 8. The tooth was pulled painlessly. The patient liked the new method. (*elaborative*)

Discourse segment 6 mentions the dentist explicitly. Coherence in 7 depends on the bridging inference that the dentist pulled the tooth. Segment 8 allows an elaborative inference, but coherence does not rely on it. Each sentence pair was followed by the verification sentence. Verification times were about equal in the explicit and bridging situations. However, readers were 0.25 s slower with the elaborative sentences. Verification times supported the notion that only bridging inferences are reliably activated during comprehension.

Inferential reasoning is a concept central to the mental work needed to construct a model of a text. Inferences are used to make bridges from one proposition to another. They are part of the active constructive process of comprehension. The inference fills in what is missing but necessary to construct a more complete mental model of what is being discussed. Readers have to make inferences in order to comprehend what has not been stated explicitly because no author or storyteller provides all of the facts, details, and information in a story. Authors do not have to give all the facts because readers draw heavily on inferential processes to comprehend what they read. An author can rely on readers to make the inference that when told that *the birdhouse was painted blue*, they will infer that a human being did the painting. If we read, for example, *He lost the keys to his house*, we infer that he will have to find another means to get into his house.

CAUSAL INFERENCES

The study of bridging inferences has addressed the issue of causal links between segments of text. In *John cashed his paycheck. He spent the next hour shopping for an anniversary gift*, we understand the motivation or cause of the check cashing as necessary to do the shopping. **Causal inferences** can be framed as physical, psychological, and motivational causes. The study of causal inferences can be understood in the context of models of representations and process underlying causal relations. A network model of the causal structure of narratives has been detailed by Trabasso and van den Broek (1985; Trabasso, van den Broek, & Suh, 1989; van den Broek, 1990).

Causal bridging inferences are drawn during text comprehension according to research using on-line and memory measures. For example, the bridging process is affected by the degree of causal relatedness (Myers, Shinjo, & Duffy, 1987). Segments 9, 10, and 11 illustrate sequences of high, medium, and low relatedness, respectively. When subjects read these sentences, the reading times for the second sentence of the pair decrease systematically with increasing causal relatedness (i.e., $9 < 10 < 11$).

9. Tony's friend suddenly pushed him into a pond.
   He walked home, soaking wet, to change his clothes.

10. Tony met his friend near a pond in the park.
    He walked home, soaking wet, to change his clothes.

11. Tony sat under a tree reading a good book.
    He walked home, soaking wet, to change his clothes.

The reading times are interpreted as reflecting the ease of drawing causal bridging inferences where the text outcome is linked to its cause.

The point is that the causal relationships are important components of a narrative text. **Narratives** usually describe how actions and events change the state of objects and people. Causal relationships play an important role in the comprehension of the text (Bartlett, 1932). They are also central components of the reader's mental representation of the text, what the reader constructs as a model of it (see van den Broek, 1994). Statements that are part of the causal network of a story are recalled more frequently than statements that are not (Trabasso & van den Broek, 1985; Trabasso et al., 1984). Let's look at the sample story in Table 8.1. A **causal chain** can describe this story by showing how each statement is related, leading to the next statement. His going to the store causes the outcome that Brian is buying a CD player. Notice that statement 9 is a *dead end*, not part of the causal chain. However, to capture the multiple sources of causality, the simple serial chain of events with one dead end at 9 is inadequate.

The multiple causes or consequences in narratives have led to the development of the notion of text as a **causal network.** In the network view, events in the story are the result of combinations of causal antecedents as opposed to single causes. Brian's acquisition of the CD player is motivated by wanting it and enabled

Table 8.1. Sample Narrative

Story Grammar Category	Statement Number	Statement
Setting	1	One day, Brian was looking through the newspaper.
Initiating event	2	He saw an ad for some fancy CD players.
Internal response	3	He really liked the way they looked.
Goal	4	Brian decided he wanted to buy one.
Attempt	5	He called the store for the price of a nice model.
Outcome	6	He did not have enough money.
Goal	7	He decided to work a paper route.
Attempt	8	For months he got up early
Outcome	9	so that he had his afternoons free
Attempt	10	and delivered the newspapers.
Outcome	11	He quickly earned the $300 that he needed.
Attempt	12	On his first day off, he went to the store.
Outcome	13	He bought the CD player that he had wanted for so long.
Consequence	14	He was so happy that he immediately organized a party.

Table from "Comprehension and memory of narrative texts: Inferences and coherence" by van den Broek, P., in *Handbook of Psycholinguistics*, edited by Morton A. Gernsbacher, copyright 1994, Elsevier Science (USA), reproduced by permission of the publisher.

by having the money to buy it when he visited the store. If any of these conditions did not obtain, the outcome would not have occurred. Networks capture complex relationships; in fact, the model incorporates the causal chain idea but more elaborately, with interconnections. The chain version and the network version are compared in Figure 8.1. The interconnectedness of the statements also allows for alternate paths to the outcome. For example, Brian's wanting the CD player and the outcome of buying it can be connected by a path that excludes his getting a paper route—in other words, jumping from 4 to 12 or 13 and bypassing 7–11. Statements with multiple connections play an important role in the structure of the text. If statements differ as to their importance to the story, then the statements have a *hierarchical structure*. *Superordinate* chains describe the events of the narrative at a general, abstract level. *Subordinate* levels provide increasingly more details. These hierarchical levels are represented as the vertical dimension of the bottom part of Figure 8.1. Notice that the dead end (9) is at the bottom of the hierarchy.

One might wonder how interconnectedness would affect memory representation of the text. It would seem plausible that statements with multiple connections would be remembered better than those with few connections. Results of studies of memory for narrative content have shown that statements with many connections play a prominent role in the memory representation of the narrative. Highly connected statements are recalled more frequently than statements with few connections (Fletcher & Bloom, 1988; Graesser & Clark, 1985; Trabasso & van den Broek, 1985; Trabasso et al., 1984). This pattern has been found with both laboratory-constructed narratives and with naturally constructed literary texts (van den Broek, Rohleder, & Narvaez, 1996). Highly connected segments also occur more frequently than less

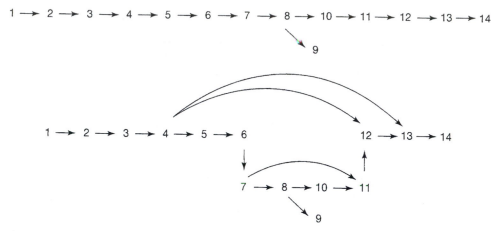

Figure 8.1. Causal Chain *(top)* and Causal Network *(bottom)* Representations of the Sample Narrative in Table 8.1

Note. Figure from "Comprehension and memory of narrative texts: Inferences and coherence" by van den Broek, P., in *Handbook of Psycholinguistics*, edited by Morton A. Gernsbacher, copyright 1994, Elsevier Science (USA), reproduced by permission of the publisher.

connected ones in summarization protocols (van den Broek & Trabasso, 1986). One final observation is that highly connected statements are judged to be more important than those with few connections (O'Brien & Myers, 1987; Trabasso & Sperry, 1985). The conclusion to be drawn is that a statement's importance to the reader's memory representation of the text is heavily influenced by its causal connections.

Causal relationships play an important role in the memory representation of a narrative. The representation of the text can be construed as a network of interconnected events with multiple antecedents and consequences. The psychological validity of networks has been validated by research on causal chain status, hierarchical position, and number of causal relationships to other segments. Retrieval of narrative information has been demonstrated to be a function of the relational qualities of the text, that is, whether there are causal links from activated information to information to be retrieved and how far apart these segments are in the network.

PARTIAL PROCESSING

Sanford and Garrod (1994) argued that coherence is not so much a property of a text as it is a property of the mental representation or interpretation of a text. A text can be interpreted coherently without appropriate cohesive devices. Coherence is constructed in the mind of the reader through the establishment of an interconnected mental representation. Sanford and Garrod believe that coherence can be shallow or deep, depending on how the text is processed. Johnson-Laird (1981) examined how readers fail to notice anomalies in text such as 12.

12. This book fills a much-needed gap.

Readers do not necessarily notice that this sentence asserts that it is not the book but the gap that is needed. Readers give the sentence a pragmatic interpretation, only partially analyzing its syntax. This might be an indication that they are attempting to match the input to a familiar frame, for example, that books are written to fill gaps in the literature. In this case, the reader's stored knowledge overrides detailed processing and permits the anomaly to go unnoticed.

Erickson and Mattson (1981) demonstrated a poignant example of **partial processing,** which they dubbed the "Moses illusion." They asked subjects to answer the question in 13.

13. How many animals of each sort did Moses put on the Ark?

A large number of them answer "two," only later to realize that it was Noah who put animals on the Ark, not Moses. Erickson and Mattson presumed that the failure to detect the anomaly was due to the semantic relatedness between the two biblical figures. Moses mistakes are not due to sensory-level misperceptions of the two names. Participants will make the Moses mistake even after correctly reading the questions aloud (Reder & Kusbit, 1991).

Shafto and MacKay (2000) propose a different line of reasoning to account for partial processing. They replicated the Moses illusion and another one, the *Armstrong illusion.* The Armstrong illusion involved questions such as this one: *What was the famous line uttered by Louis Armstrong when he first set foot on the moon?* Subjects usually respond to this as if it is a valid question, even though they realize that *Louis Armstrong* was a jazz musician who never made a trip to the moon. This does not occur because the subjects ignore the names but because the name *Louis Armstrong* and *Neil Armstrong* are phonologically related, according to Shafto and MacKay. They explained these illusions through *node structure theory* (NST), which postulates a network of interconnected representational units or nodes on a "most primed wins" basis. The bottom-up plus top-down activation mechanism activates whatever node has the most priming at any given time. Figures 8.2 and 8.3 illustrate how the Moses and Armstrong illusions arise from different forms of node activation. Moses mistakes are due to convergent priming through bottom-up priming and semantic priming. *Moses* indirectly primes *Noah,* which receives more convergent sources of semantic priming and is miscomprehended as *Noah,* as is illustrated in Figure 8.2.

Armstrong questions produce convergent priming in part through shared phonology. *Neil Armstrong* receives phonological activation from *Louis Armstrong* plus semantic activation from the sentence context via *astronaut, first man on the moon,* and *famous line.* The network is illustrated in Figure 8.3. Therefore, *Neil Armstrong* accumulates more convergent priming than *Louis Armstrong,* causing the miscomprehension. NST establishes a single unified answer to these kinds of illusions. They occur because a specious name receives more priming than the presented but invalid name. But then what accounts for subjects who are able to detect the incongruities in these questions? Shafto and MacKay (2000) suggest that participants detect anomalies when they become aware that the novel information conflicts with simultaneously activated information in semantic memory. The name node (e.g.,

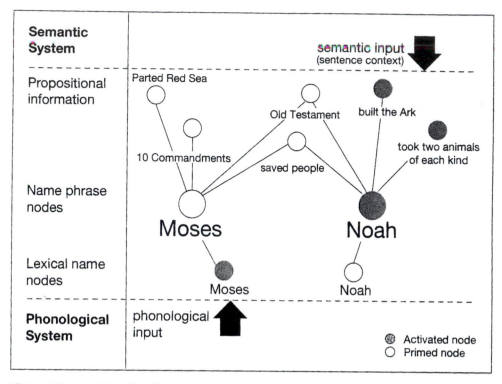

Figure 8.2. Explaining the Moses Illusion

Note. From Shafto, M., & MacKay, D. (2000). The Moses, Mega-Moses, and Armstrong Illlusions: Integrating language comprehension and semantic memory. *Psychological Science, 11(5)*, 372–378. Reprinted by permission of Blackwell Publishers.

Louis Armstrong) conflicts with question-based information (e.g., *an astronaut*). The occurrence of partial processing effects reinforces the idea that coherence is in the mind of the reader.

THE STORY GRAMMAR

Thorndyke (1977) and others (Mandler & Johnson, 1977; Rumelhart, 1975; Stein & Glenn, 1979) have described how rules used during reading could be applied to understanding story structures. In simple terms, a **story grammar** consists of a *setting* (time and location) and one or more *episodes*. Story grammars differ in their details and structural categories. The setting provides background for the story about to unfold through references to characters and objects and through temporal and geographical information. Episodes are organized around a goal and its outcome. Table 8.1 indicates how each segment of the CD player story is categorized in the story grammar. Each episode has a different function in the story. The *initiating event* sets a train of action in motion. The initiating event results in reaction by the protagonist, an *internal response,* which causes the explicit or implicit establishment

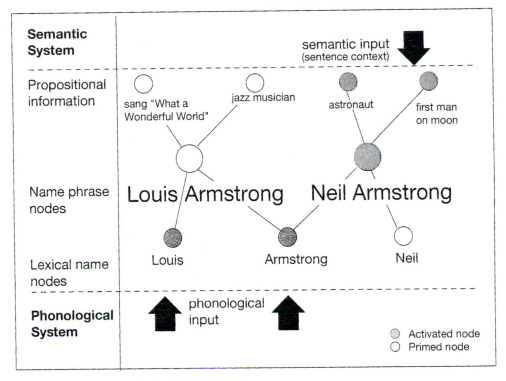

Figure 8.3. Explaining the Armstrong Illusion
Note. From Shafto, M., & MacKay, D. (2000). The Moses, Mega-Moses, and Armstrong Illlusions: Integrating language comprehension and semantic memory. *Psychological Science, 11(5)*, 372–378. Reprinted by permission of Blackwell Publishers.

of his or her *goal*. The goal motivates one or more *attempts* that lead the story's *outcome*. Finally, the outcome produces a *reaction*.

Thorndyke (1977) found that memory for propositions in a story was related to the centrality of the information to the overall structure. Facts directly related to the macrostructure were remembered better than unrelated micropropositions. More specifically, initiating events, outcomes, major settings, and some goals are recalled better than minor settings, internal responses, attempts, and reactions (Mandler & Johnson, 1977; Stein & Glenn, 1979; Trabasso et al., 1984). Readers recall categories in the order suggested by the grammar. If goal information is displaced in various positions in the text, subjects will recall the information in the predicted location, and when texts are scrambled, the episodic structure is restored during recall (Mandler, 1984). Also, readers draw inferences more easily within an episode than across episodes (Beeman & Gernsbacher, 1992). The reader's memory reflects the episodic structure of the text.

Statements in the story are differentiated into categories, each with its own function. Initiating events (IE), outcomes (O), and goals (G) play a more prominent role in the representation of the text than attempts (A), internal responses (IR), and reactions (R). Segments of the text are organized as episodes with separate goals. Interdependent episodes may form a hierarchy, with the highest levels more central to the representation of the story than lower levels. Figure 8.4 illustrates a network that represents the causal and categorical properties of the CD player story. Each event is labeled with the category of its content. Subscripts for each event refer first to its position in the surface structure in the text and second to its level in the hierarchical structure of the story. Note that some categories have more causal connections than others. The hierarchical levels are defined by the causal relationships between episodes. One can identify factors that influence memory for texts, namely, causal relationships, causal chains, hierarchical structure, and categorical function.

SCHEMAS AND SCRIPTS

A **schema** in the discourse literature is a mental framework used to organize meaningful material on the basis of prior experience with an event or a social situation. The schema guides our understanding of the global outline of the story on which the particular details of propositions are hung. Rather than building a text structure from scratch, schemas function as control structures that ensure the operation of the appropriate context-sensitive construction rules for the text. This situation is a bit different when compared to the reading of a text, in which no schema is activated and the reader constructs a representation of it with weak and sloppy construction rules (Kintsch, 1994). Schemas are culturally constructed, and they affect our understanding as well as our memory for a story. The relevant schema also guides the production of discourse as in a conversation or a storytelling episode.

    Scripts are shorter and more specific than schemas. Scripts provide the details of a sequence of events that unfold chronologically in particular settings and under particular circumstances. Take the "restaurant script" as an example. The restaurant script specifies the who, what, where, and when of dining. The script indicates that participants wait to be seated, they look at menus, they order food, they wait for the food, which is delivered in a particular order, and they eat the food, wait for

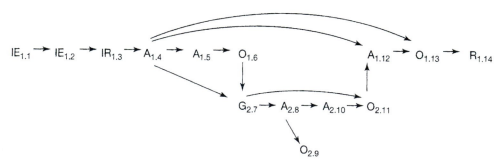

Figure 8.4. Causal, Hierarchical, and Story Grammar Properties of the Sample Narrative in Table 8.1

Note. Figure from "Comprehension and memory of narrative texts: Inferences and coherence" by P. van den Broek, in *Handbook of Psycholinguistics*, edited by Morton A. Gernsbacher, copyright 1984, Elsevier Science (USA), reproduced by permission of the publisher.

the check, pay the check, and leave a tip before departing. The order of the script is not very flexible, but its generality provides a basis for behaving in unfamiliar restaurant settings. Once you know the script, you know what to do and when to do it in the restaurant. The script provides a basis for behaving in the real world as well as a basis for understanding restaurants and generating stories about restaurants.

Building a schematic representation of a narrative involves activating the relevant information for the text structure and at the same time not activating what is inappropriate. The process of building a framework for a narrative proposed by Gernsbacher (1990) assigns a major role to both facilitatory and inhibitory mechanisms that control the formation of mental representations of discourse. In addition to finding the right and not the wrong framework, discourse comprehension models also have to address individual differences in reading ability. For example, Perfetti (1985) outlined a framework for discourse comprehension that focuses on the role of verbal skills and abilities involved in reading. Just and Carpenter (1987) also point out the role of working memory, especially memory span, in the processing of text. We covered some of these limitations in Chapter 7, and they are also pertinent here.

What happens when text does not make sense—for example, when a piece of discourse seems to have no clear topic or no background information against which the listener or reader can make a judgment? This question was addressed by Dooling and Lachman (1971). They presented subjects with the following passage. Read it and try to make some sense of it before reading further.

> With hocked gems financing him, our hero bravely defied all scornful laughter that tried to prevent his scheme. Your eyes deceive you, he said; an egg, not a table, correctly typifies this unexplored planet. Now three sturdy sisters sought proof, forging along sometimes through calm vastness yet more often over turbulent peaks and valleys. Days became weeks as many doubters spread fearful rumors about the edge. At last, from nowhere, welcome winged creatures appeared signifying momentous success.

What did you construct on the first pass? Someone landing on another planet? A crazy man wandering in the mountains? The prose passage is intentionally difficult to read and remember, and that was in part the point of the experiment, to see what people would remember if they were not given a schema for the story. Few people could determine the point of the passage. It is difficult to draw inferences or build a mental model from the text.

However, when subjects were given the title "Christopher Columbus Discovering America" prior to reading, the title worked as a schema providing a structure in which to interpret the confusing sentences, make inferences, and construct a mental representation of Columbus's journey. Subjects not given the title have difficulty constructing a coherent representation of the story, as you probably did. Return to the passage and notice how much more sense it makes with the relevant schema. Notice that you can interpret and link what were on the first pass ambiguous and figurative phrases into a coherent mental model.

Situational Mental Models

Comprehension researchers during the 1980s realized that constructing a propositional text base was not the end of the comprehension process (see Fletcher, 1994). The propositional text base is a mental representation of what the sentences in the text mean as a whole. Two people can interpret the same discourse very differently. People often update their understanding of a text or conversation. New information modifies our representation of a situation or text as a whole without necessarily altering our earlier memories for narratives and conversations. Some types of discourse give the reader or listener a clear feeling about spatial and sensory properties that go beyond the propositional text base. The result of these findings is that a large volume of research has been generated to account for how prior knowledge is incorporated with current propositional content to construct a mental representation of a discourse situation. Many experiments focus on differences in representations without systematically comparing them.

Fletcher and Chrysler (1990) were among the first to conduct research on all three levels (surface, text base, and situational model) within the context of a single experimental design using recognition memory. Subjects read a set of texts that describe a different ordering among a set of objects, as in the following passage:

> George likes to flaunt his wealth by purchasing rare art treasures. He has a Persian rug worth as much as my car and it's the cheapest thing he owns. Last week he bought a French oil painting for $12,000 and an Indian necklace for $13,500. George says that his wife was angry when she found out that the necklace cost more than the carpet. His most expensive "treasures" are a Ming vase and a Greek statue. The statue is the only thing he ever spent more than $50,000 for. It's hard to believe that the statue cost George five times what he paid for the beautiful Persian carpet. (pp. 175–190)

If they are able to differentiate between target sentences from an earlier text and meaning-preserving paraphrases of those same sentences, the differences are taken to be a measure of memory for **surface** representation (or microstructure). The surface test would present a choice between two words that occurred in the discourse, as in 14.

14. George says that his wife was angry when she found out that the necklace cost more than the carpet/rug.

On another level, if recognition performance improves when distractors alter the meaning of the test sentence but not the underlying situation, performance is taken as a measure of the influence of the **text base** (macrostructure), as in sentence 15.

15. George says that his wife was angry when she found out that the necklace cost more than the carpet/painting.

On the third level, if performance improves further when distractor sentences are inconsistent with the situation described, this is taken as a measure of the influence of the **situational model,** as in sentence 16.

> 16. George says that his wife was angry when she found out that the necklace cost more than the lamp/vase.

Fletcher and Chrysler found that when the words were synonymous with the test text (14), performance was 71 percent correct. When distractors altered a proposition in the test sentence but not the underlying order of the five objects (15), performance improved to 87 percent correct. Finally, when distractors were inconsistent with the order described by the text (16), performance increased to 98 percent correct. They argued that this order of improvement was evidence for three separate levels of mental representation of text.

Kintsch, Welsch, Schmalhofer, and Zinny (1990) demonstrated that the three levels of text representation have different rates of memory decay. Subjects were presented with brief narrative descriptions of highly scripted activities such as going to a movie. Subjects had to complete recognition memory tests at delays ranging from 0 minutes to 4 days. The recognition test used sentences taken *verbatim* from the stories, *paraphrases* of story sentences, sentences easily *inferred* from one of the stories, *new sentences consistent* with scripted activities, and *new sentences not consistent* with activities in any stories. The recognition differences between verbatim and paraphrased sentences was used to measure the strength of surface representations. The differences between paraphrases and inferences were used to measure text base strength. Differences between inferences and consistent new sentences were used to measure the strength of the situational model. The measures of memory strength for the three text levels as a function of delay interval are illustrated in Figure 8.5. The strength of the memory trace was calculated (using a signal detection equation) for each level; the higher the scale value, the better the memory. A score of zero on the vertical axis represents a lack of memory. The three levels show dramatically different decay rates. Surface memory was significant only when tested immediately after the stories. Memory for propositional text base started high and then decayed quickly. The situational information began high but did not decay over the four-day delay interval. Comprehension of discourse results in different representations for the discourse, its meaning, and the situation to which it refers. Each level of representation results from a different type of language processing.

Memory experiments show that each level has a different decay function. Research on mental models has also been conducted to account for spatial, temporal, and causal aspects of situational models. We turn to spatial models next.

SPATIAL MODELS

Not all discourses can be represented completely as a network of propositions. Perhaps the most obvious exceptions involve descriptions of space. Mani and Johnson-Laird (1982) provided a demonstration of spatial situations. Subjects were presented

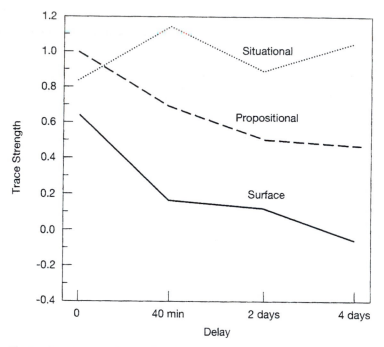

Figure 8.5. Memory Decay for Text Representations

Note. Figure from "Sentence Recognition: A Theoretical Analysis" by W. Kintsch, et al., from *Journal of Memory and Language,* Volume 29, 133–159, copyright 1990, Elsevier Science (USA), reproduced by permission of the publisher.

with texts describing the spatial arrangement of four objects in two different formats. *Determinate* descriptions were consistent with a single arrangement of the four objects, for example: *The bookshelf is to the right of the chair. The chair is in front of the table. The bed is behind the table.* This spatial description is consistent with the layout

bed

table

chair   bookshelf

In contrast, *indeterminate* descriptions reversed the arguments to produce the same kind of text base but one that was spatially ambiguous. These texts were consistent with two spatial layouts, for example: *The bookshelf is to the right of the chair. The chair is in front of the table. The bed is behind the chair.* This description is consistent with two layouts:

bed   table

table   bed

chair   bookshelf   chair   bookshelf

Mani and Johnson-Laird found that recognition memory was better for the determinate descriptions, which they attributed to subjects' inability to construct **spatial models** from the ambiguous descriptions. Research on spatial models continues to be one of the most active areas of situational modeling.

Perrig and Kintsch (1985) dissociated the propositional text base from the situational model by creating two texts of a hypothetical town. The "survey" text version was written from the perspective of an observer taking a bird's-eye view of the town from above. This version included topographical statements such as *North of the highway just east of the river is a gas station.* The "route" text version presented the same information in the form of driving directions, such as *On your left after you cross the river you see a gas station.* Perrig and Kintsch found that subjects who read the survey text had an easier time drawing a map of the town compared to remembering the text. They argued that these differences occur because the survey text, not the route text, facilitates the construction of a spatial model. The route view, in contrast, simplifies the construction of a coherent propositional text base because coreferential propositions occur near each other in the route text.

It would seem that comprehension usually results in the construction of a spatial model. However, Zwaan and van Oostendorp (1993) argued that constructing, maintaining, and updating a spatial model is not a priority during normal comprehension of narratives. They presented subjects with text from a real mystery novel describing the details of a murder scene, which included the location of the body and other clues. The text was modified to make spatial modeling easy by making all the locations determinate. But regardless of these modifications to make spatial modeling easy, subjects had trouble verifying spatial references when they were asked to read the text normally. When instructions placed emphasis on constructing a spatial representation, their performance improved, but they spent considerably more time reading the text.

Along with the construction of a spatial model of a text, readers also construct temporal and causal models of the episodes in a text. These were outlined in the section on causal inferences. We now leave our discussion of the printed word to consider spoken discourse.

Conversation

The primary form of discourse, spontaneous face-to-face conversation, is universal. The purpose of language is very simple, according to H. H. Clark (1996): "Language is for doing things" (p. 1). We do not produce speech for its own sake; we speak to affect listeners and to accomplish personal goals. In contrast, the text view, evolved to account for written discourse in stories, essays, descriptions, and novels, is contrived. Most conversations are used to make statements (assertions), ask questions, or tell people to do things. Although discourse goals may seem simple (e.g., asking someone to do something), what we end up doing in a conversation may not be clear or obvious. A structural analysis of discourse describes the series of sentences that are exchanged between participants. But structure alone cannot reveal the depth of psychological, cultural, and emotional work being accomplished between speakers and listeners.

The psycholinguist's task in discourse analysis is to monitor both linguistic structure and psychological motives that are present. Thus discourse analysis requires the tools of the social sciences and the cognitive sciences. We should see discourse as a system of linguistic exchanges embedded in social activity. We begin by asking some simple questions about how people talk to each other and what guides their talk.

Any conversation, whatever its goal, exists as a system of rules and conventions. The patterns of conversation emerge upon analysis by looking at what participants are doing when they talk. One early approach was to look for some simple rules, or **conversational maxims** (Grice, 1975), that are used to guide our conduct while speaking. Another approach was to look at these exchanges as **speech acts** or routines wherein people try to accomplish simple conversational and personal goals (Searle, 1969, 1975b).

CONVERSATIONAL MAXIMS

The work of Paul Grice (1975) was the starting point to elucidate conversational postulates, which could reveal what conversation was ideally to achieve. Grice viewed conversation as a cooperative effort with a common purpose guided by unwritten rules. The common priorities are implicit rules or shared beliefs that participants follow so that they would not lie, deceive, obfuscate, monopolize, or waste each other's time. These simple cooperative rules amount to a set of guidelines that participants try to follow without violation. We realize that the rules exist when violations of them result in concerted efforts to restore the conversation to the right form; for example, if one person dominates a conversation, he or she will be urged to allow someone else to talk. The four maxims governing the cooperative principle, according to Grice, involve quantity, quality, manner, and relevance.

- *Quantity:* The speaker should make complete statements covering the necessary information. The speaker should tell just enough, not too much or too little.

- *Quality:* The speaker should be truthful. The listener relies on the speaker to provide information that is accurate. Sometimes speakers bend the rules of quality when they use certain forms of speech, such as metaphor, hyperbole, or sarcastic irony (as we consider in Chapter 9). The listener should know that these exceptions are not meant to be factual statements and that bending the truth, as in hyperbole, has a different intended purpose.

- *Manner:* The speaker should be clear and concise and should not obscure the information in the conversation. The speaker should avoid ambiguity and vagueness.

- *Relevance:* What the speaker says should be relevant to the topic at hand. The information should be useful and related to what is being discussed. Conversations are not about speaking; they are about making contributions to the ongoing discussion.

Although Grice's work provided the starting point for discourse analysis, it needed to be expanded and revised. Grice's guidelines are centered on the speaker's role; the listener's needs are less clear. Grice did not describe the shared knowledge that exists between speakers and listeners that make conversations work. For the guidelines to function, they must exist as mutual speaker and listener goals. In other words, we need to answer a different set of questions about conversations. What are the outcomes of conversations; what do they produce? If conversational guidelines have mutual force, we might view conversations not so much as cooperation but as acts in which dialogue is used to achieve a speaker's intentions, as we consider next and in Chapter 9.

SPEECH ACTS

Austin (1962) originated a speech act theory, which was later revised and elaborated by Searle (1969, 1975b). The speaker's intention is the speech act. It is with the intention that we see "how to do things with words." Austin (1962) outlined five kinds of speech acts.

Commisives commit the speaker to do something—for example, *I promise, I swear, I vow.*

Verdictives represent some truth—for example, *I acquit, I calculated, I will describe.*

Expositives elaborate the speaker's views—for example, *I emphasize, I illustrate, I deny that . . .*

Behabitives are reactions—for example, *I applaud, I hate, I congratulate you.*

Exercitives advocate or decide actions—for example, *I order, I nominate, I remove you.*

These speech acts focus primarily on the speaker's goals. What about the listener? When we talk, we expect something to happen as a result of what we have said. We ask for information, tell someone to do something, or promise to do something. Each of these speech acts will affect the listener in different ways. Ideally, asking someone for information should produce that information, but this does not always happen. The real impact of the speech act depends on what the listener does in response.

Austin's speech acts focus on the surface form of the utterance and what it means to the speaker. The original system was somewhat limited in scope; conversations were not analyzed beyond these simple forms. What was needed was an analysis of what ultimately happens as a result of a statement, request, or question, not merely what is intended. We need to understand what is the *force* of the speaker's utterance on the behavior of the listeners. Searle (1975b) offered such a shift in emphasis. In Searle's system, every utterance serves some purpose for the speaker. He proposed a five-category system:

Representatives convey the speaker's belief that an utterance is true—for example, *There's a red-bellied woodpecker on the feeder.*

Directives try to get the listener to do something or answer a question—for example, *Can you help me clean?*

Commissives commit the speaker to do something in the future—for example, *I'll help you clean tomorrow.*

Expressives refer to the speaker's state of mind—for example, *I'm tired of your not helping with the chores.*

Performatives create a new condition—for example, *You're under arrest.*

The most common types of speech acts are commanding people to do things, asking questions, and making assertions. The point of speech act theory for Searle is to describe how speakers use conventional utterance forms to elicit reactions from listeners. Whether listeners do what is expected is another matter to which we will turn shortly.

In addition to the speech acts described by Austin and Searle, other forms are possible. Some acts are less direct than those listed here. For example, to get what they want and appear polite rather than blunt, speakers may make requests in an indirect fashion. For example, I can tell my partner in a very direct manner, *Clean the house.* An indirect request would sound more like *Would you mind picking up the house a bit today?* The intended goal is the same in both instances (get the house cleaned), but the indirect method is perceived as more polite and will meet with a more favorable response. The issue of indirect speech acts is addressed in Chapter 9.

Discourse as a Joint Project

As we have seen, there are several ways to characterize conversations. The unfolding structure of a conversation depends on the participants' goals, shared background knowledge, and what new information needs to be added to that shared information to achieve the goals. The structure of a conversation can be described as a series of turns between speakers and listeners. While looking at turn taking, we must also understand the importance of the topic of conversation—what is being talked about—and how to adhere to the topic and enhance it, as well as shift away from the topic when necessary. The approach I outline is one taken by H. H. Clark (1996). In Clark's view, conversation exists as a *joint activity*, like a dance, between participants where a cohesive and purposeful exchange takes place. Here we do not look at what speakers are saying; instead we look at what conversants are doing together. A conversation requires the coordinated activity of two or more people taking on different roles to accomplish public and personal goals. The conversants participate in a **joint project,** the coordination of joint actions (e.g., a request followed by a compliant response). A joint project would be what is happening in the conversational activities that constitute acts such as marrying, appointing, or betting.

To elucidate the components and strategies used in conversations, let's look a sample of a telephone conversation from H. H. Clark (1994) between Alice, who is Professor Dwight's secretary, and Benjamin, who is Professor Dwight's student. Conversations often unfold in bursts about six words long referred to as *intonation units* (Chafe, 1992; H. H. Clark, 1994). Each unit has a single intonation contour that ends with a terminal contour, and it has a point of accent, usually near the end of the unit. Intonation units are sometimes interrupted at the beginning with pauses, hesitations, repeats, and repairs. Units often begin with *and, and then, but,* or *so.* They are more than just units of linguistic formulation because they represent the way the narrator thinks about what is being described. Alice (A) initiates the call to complete a joint project, that is, to give Benjamin (B) a message from the professor. The conversation can be used to illustrate elements of joint projects (personnel, common ground, action sequences, and grounding). In the example, a comma indicates the end of an intonation unit, a dash indicates a long pause, a spaced hyphen indicates a short pause, a colon indicates a stretched vowel sound, and partially overlapping pairs are surrounded by asterisks (e.g., **seminar** and **yes**). *It* in sentence 9 refers to attending the seminar.

1. A. (*rings*)

2. B. Benjamin Holloway

3. A. this is Professor Dwight's secretary, from Polymania College,

4. B. ooh yes,—

5. A. uh:m—about the: lexicology **seminar**

6. B. **yes**

7. A. actually Professor Dwight says in fact they've only got two more m—uh:m sessions to go, because I didn't realize it it—finishes at Easter,

8. B. I see, yes, **uh:um**

9. A. **so** it—wouldn't really be—

10. B. much point,—**no**

11. A. **no,**—(*laughs*)

12. B. OK right, thanks very much,

13. A. OK—**bye**

14. B. **bye,**

PERSONNEL

A joint activity needs at least two participants. In the conversation example, Alice and Benjamin alternate between participant roles of addressee and speaker. Participant roles expand when there are more than two people in a conversational setting (Goffman, 1976). One contrast is between participants and nonparticipants or overhearers. Participants can be divided into speakers, addressees, and side participants, who are not anticipated to answer the speaker. Overhearers include two roles, bystanders and eavesdroppers. Bystanders are recognized as present and have access to what the speaker says. Eavesdroppers have access to what the speaker is saying but are not fully recognized as present. These roles are illustrated in Figure 8.6.

Participants in conversations also have their own identities, feelings, and needs or *personal roles*. They also have professional identities. Alice is the professor's secretary, and Benjamin is one of his students. When Benjamin answers the phone, she responds in her professional role, not her personal role.

COMMON GROUND

Common ground refers to mutual shared beliefs, knowledge, and understandings. Common ground exists on more than one level. On one level, it refers to my awareness of our shared knowledge—I am aware of what we have in common. On another

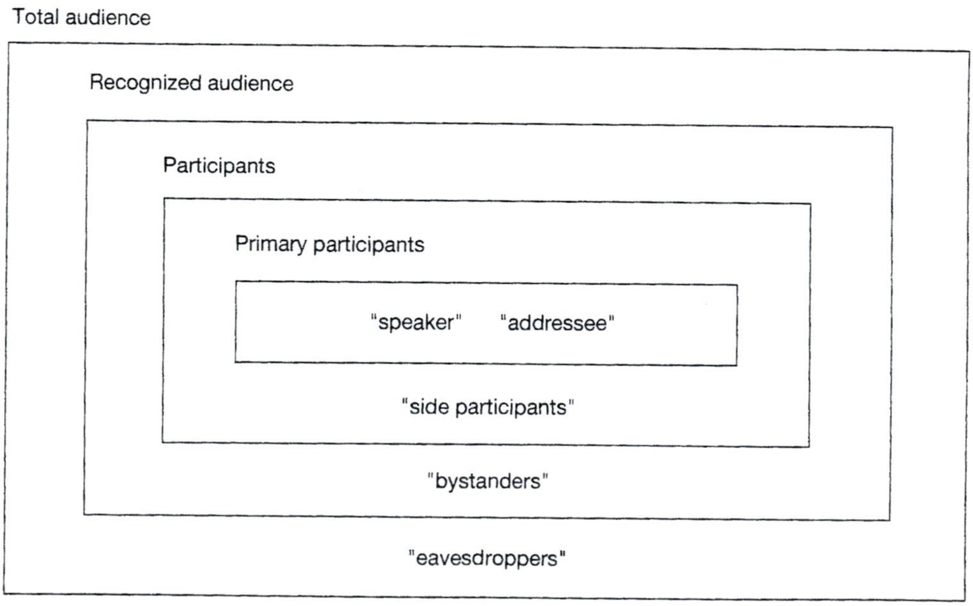

Figure 8.6. Roles in Conversation
Note. From *Using Language* by Herbert Clark, Figure 1 on p. 14, 1996. Reprinted with permission of Cambridge University Press.

level, common ground represents what all members of the community have in common. So as a member of a speech community (e.g., a profession, demographic group, religious order, or ethnic group), I have a level of consciousness of what is common group knowledge and can assume that others in the group have the same knowledge. For example, the community of college students knows what "the GREs" are, and the community of psycholinguists knows what "descriptive grammar" means; these would not have to be explained explicitly. During a conversation, new information is added to both levels of the participants' common ground.

Common ground is essential for any form of joint activity. Participants must be aware of their common knowledge and use it to formulate expressions for joint activities or problems. It is common ground that allows a speaker to expect that a listener will understand what is said or requested and will respond in a predictable manner. Common ground guides all social conversations. The shared knowledge we construct allows us to develop a personal sense of common ground and a communal common ground with others. The *personal* knowledge reflects what we know and what information is or is not important. The *communal* knowledge allows us to communicate to other members of the community with a set of shared expectations or shared expertise on the basis of language, nationality, residence, education, occupation, hobby, politics, ethnicity, subculture, or gender (see H. H. Clark, 1996). This shared expertise not only defines our friends and strangers but is also the basis for our engaging in and accomplishing joint activities.

In the sample conversation, Alice and Benjamin have a diverse set of groups, systems, and networks to which they belong—for example, musicians, Catholics, soccer fans, British subjects, and members of Polymania College. When Alice introduces herself as the professor's secretary and Benjamin indicates that he understands, they assume that this information is part of their common ground. Common ground will accumulate with each turn of the conversation. Each public move in the conversation is interpreted against the common ground between the participants.

ACTION SEQUENCES AND ADJACENCY PAIRS

The joint projects that participants attempt in discourse can be divided into smaller joint actions that are performed in sequence. Alice and Benjamin participate in three broad actions in sequence. They open the conversation in lines 1–4, exchange information in lines 5–12, and close the conversation in lines 13 and 14. Each of these broad actions divides into smaller joint actions. For example, the opening action consists of opening the telephone channel in lines 1 and 2. Then Benjamin identifies himself to Alice and Alice identifies herself to Benjamin. The exchange and closing actions can be divided as well. This phone conversation is a joint project that consists of multiple joint actions.

Another way to understand conversation as multiple joint action is to approach conversational activity as pairs of utterances. **Adjacency pairs** (Schegloff & Sacks, 1973) refer to conventional patterns that unfold in a stimulus-response format; the speaker makes one utterance that results in a conventional response. H. H. Clark (1994, 1996) refers to these pairs as *minimal joint projects*. Here are some examples of common joint projects.

1. The speaker complains; the listener apologizes.

2. The speaker summons, the listener answers.

3. The speaker invites; the listener accepts or declines.

4. The speaker compliments; the listener acknowledges.

5. The speaker greets; the listener greets in kind.

Adjacency pairs work at two levels: The first expression reveals what the speaker needs or has in mind. The second level of work comes from the addressee, who must first construe what is meant or requested and then formulate a reply.

The adjacency pairs operate as a joint action mutually engaged in by the speaker and the addressee, who resolve two problems at once by engaging in the joint project (H. H. Clark, 1996). The formulation of the adjacency pair as a joint project produces a comprehensive analysis that shows what the speaker and listener are doing *together*. Unlike speech act analysis, it does not limit analysis to the surface forms of speakers' expressions. As a joint project, the adjacency pair requires a mutual understanding of what is being requested or expressed. Further, the effect of the speaker's statements or requests depends on the listener's compliance on the project. Unfortunately, some listeners will not comply. For example, a request for assistance in some matter can be met with resistance or refusal to take part, terminating the joint project. *Can you help me with the cleaning?* might be met with an outraged, *No, I can't. Do it yourself.*

In the sample conversation, there are many adjacency pairs, as there are in many conversations. They act as building blocks for the dialogue. There is a summons-response in 1–2, followed by assertion-assent pairs in 3–4, 5–6, and 7–8. The conversation ends with a thanks-response pair, followed by the closing good-bye pair.

GROUNDING AND CONTRIBUTIONS

Statements do not appear out of thin air. In a conversation, a speaker has to produce sentences that fit with the common ground; they must add to the participants' shared knowledge. Clark and Haviland (1977) called this fit the *given-new contract*, which specifies that the speaker relies on the listener to compare the new information (unknown to the listener) that the speaker produces to the old shared (given) information. For example, if I tell my roommate *The mouse was the one who ate the cat's food*, the given information is that something has been eating the cat's food, but it was not my cat. The new information is that the mouse is the perpetrator. The speaker and listener have already shared the given information, but this new information about the mouse was not known by my roommate until I said it.

In the example, Alice and Benjamin have to attend to, identify, and comprehend each other's comments. They have to keep track of the changing common ground and to believe that they have sufficiently understood what each other meant (Clark & Schaefer, 1989). **Grounding** is the process of reaching this criterion of understanding; speakers and listeners must *ground* each utterance. When an utterance is grounded, a *contribution* has been made. Contributions involve a *presentation* phase and an *acceptance* phase. The speaker presents a comment to be understood in the presentation phase. The addressees provide evidence that they understand in the acceptance phase. At 2, Benjamin states his name to identify himself, and then Alice identifies herself. When Benjamin says *ooh yes,—* he signals that he understood her contribution, completing the adjacency pair. The minimal joint project is accomplished through contributions, and Alice and Benjamin ground it before moving on.

CONVERSATIONAL TURN TAKING

We rarely engage in conversational free for all, with several speakers talking simultaneously. In general conversation, there are times when conversants overlap, as in family arguments, but these overlaps occur for only very brief periods. Conversations are ordinarily systematic sets of exchanges where one person talks and others listen, waiting for their turn to speak. This give-and-take format occurs in a formal conversation such as a debate or in a courtroom setting. Landmark research by Sacks, Schegloff, and Jefferson (1974) found that some but not all forms of conversations are controlled by three simple implicit turn-taking rules:

1. The speaker can pick the next speaker.

2. If the speaker does not pick the next speaker, someone else can speak.

3. The speaker may continue but does not have to.

Rules for speaking are predicated on the idea that while one person is speaking, another person is waiting to talk. The next speaker waits until the current speaker is finished. If it is not clear who will be the next speaker, a self-selection process occurs. The current speaker can continue until another speaker self-selects. Conversation and turn taking unfold in a multilayered social setting where verbal and nonverbal information is exchanged.

Sacks et al. (1974) observed that conversations produce predictable behaviors. Speakers take turns; usually one person speaks at a time. Speakers time their turn to begin when the current speaker ends, with a minimal gap. In many cases, this is less than 0.2 s from the end of the previous speaker's speech (Beattie & Barnard, 1979). If there is overlap, it is brief. In formal conversation (e.g., debate), turn ordering varies, as does turn duration, and conversation times can be specified or fixed. The distribution of turns varies, depending on the group makeup. Turns can be elaborate and long, or they can be as brief as one word. Taking turns relies on making transitions from one speaker to the next.

Schank (1977) thought that when speakers stick to a project at hand, the propositions that they produce will *intersect* with each other often through reiteration. These reiterations appear to conjoin concepts of the underlying ideas, beliefs, or actions related to the project. For example, a listener relates the action described in a speaker's sentence to the follow-up statement. The verb used in one sentence would be intersected by a related verb in a subsequent comment. The intersections would form a chain of cohesive concepts running throughout the conversation.

The presence of intersections or reiterations of propositions in a joint project maintains the chain of statements as coherent and relevant. At a new turn, the speaker can make references to previous topics, more specific references, or more general references to something in the propositional chain. Within the ensuing chain of propositions, any constituent in a statement could be used to start a new joint activity. An example of intersecting chains of propositions within dialogue can be found in the work of playwright David Mamet. Consider this exchange involving a professor named John and his student, Carol, from the play *Oleanna* (Mamet).*

CAROL: How can I go back and tell them the grades that I . . .

JOHN: . . . what can I do . . . ?

CAROL: Teach me. Teach me.

JOHN: . . . I'm trying to teach you.

CAROL: I read your book. I read it. I don't under . . .

JOHN: . . . you don't understand it.

CAROL: No.

JOHN: Well, perhaps it's not well written. . . .

CAROL: (*simultaneously with* written) No. No. No. I want to understand it.

JOHN: What don't you understand? (*Pause*)

CAROL: Any of it. What you're trying to say. When you talk about . . .

JOHN: . . . yes . . . ? (*She consults her notes.*)

CAROL: Virtual warehousing of the young . . .

JOHN: Virtual warehousing of the young. If we artificially prolong adolescence . . .

You can hear how the words *teach, virtual warehousing,* and *understand* in one statement are appropriated by the speaker in the next turn. These intersections of

---

*Excerpt From *Oleanna* by David Mamet, copyright © 1992 by David Mamet. Used by permission of Pantheon Books, a division of Random House, Inc.

concepts link parts of the dialogue about classroom culture to the preceding and following statements. Although this is drama, it does represent how speakers and listeners make discourse coherent by restating the concepts of the project under discussion.

A number of strategies that occur in conversations do not follow turn-taking rules (H. H. Clark, 1994). For example, Benjamin's acknowledgement in line 6 is timed to overlap the end of Alice's statement about the seminar. He is not taking a turn; he is acknowledging her comment. Lines 9 and 10 amount to collaborative completions, contrary to turn-taking rules. Sometimes speakers invite the addressees to interrupt the turn whether or not the turn has ended—asking a question can do this—and continuing the turn after the addressee answers it. Speakers waiting their turn also interrupt when they believe that the interruption will get to something more important than what the current speaker is contributing. Nonlinguistic signals are used in face-to-face conversations that are not easily classified as turns. The addressee can answer with overlapping nodding or shaking of the head while the speaker is talking. In a related matter, the assertion for a turn or the yielding of a turn can often be coordinated with stereotyped gesturing.

> **Review Question**
> Apply the notions of intersection, turn taking, cohesion, common ground, and joint project to Mamet's *Oleanna* quote.

TURN TAKING AND COHESIVE GESTURES

Duncan and Fiske (1985) studied how gestures are used to maintain turns, to signal that the speaker is about to end, or to signal that a new turn is about to begin. Turn-taking gestures include the use of gaze, hand gestures, gesticulation, head turning, body posture, and vocalizations. The cues for yielding the speaker position to become a listener are unfilled pauses, a trailing off of voice intensity, cessation of gesticulations, relaxation of the body, looking at the next intended speaker, or the utterance of some stereotypical expression. The cues for taking up the new speaker position are marked with at least two of the following signals: shifting head direction away from the partner, moving the head forward, initiating gesticulations, tensing the body, or pointing a finger.

Nonverbal and verbal signals are also used to maintain the ongoing discussion. Listeners will nod their heads, gaze at the speaker, and fill in the gaps with *mm-hmm, uh-huh,* or *right.* When they are following the conversation, listeners will repeat part of a speaker's utterance or complete a sentence when the end is anticipated. When confused by conversation, listeners will ask for clarification, indicating that both the speaker and listener are cooperating to keep the conversation cohesive.

Gesturing during conversation also plays a role in making the narrative more coherent. **Cohesive gestures** (McNeill, 1987) play a role similar to cohesive pronouns; they make reference to previously presented information. Cohesive gestures are also known as *anaphoric gestures* because they operate similarly to the anaphoric pronouns by referring to a previous concept. A speaker will not begin a conversation with a cohesive gesture; these come later. The turn begins with a pointing gesture, which marks the beginning of the turn. As the speaker continues, he or she will utter a word that is accompanied by a gesture that represents the utterance; for example, a stabbing motion accompanies the word *stabbed* in a description of a knife assault, *She stabbed him with a knife.* The cohesive gesture occurs when the speaker continues, *She did it just like that,* repeating the stabbing gesture on the word *that.*

Here's another example of cohesive gesturing. A speaker telling about his family living in Boston rotates his left hand away from his body as he pronounces the word *Boston.* He later makes a reference to his wife's family living in South Carolina, rotating his right hand away from his body when saying *South Carolina.* When he then says, *But we are going to visit them over vacation,* rotating his right hand away from his body, we know that *them* refers to his wife's family because the right hand gesture is the same one used for the first reference to *South Carolina.* Anaphoric reference has been established here verbally and nonverbally through the use of both *them* and the cohesive right hand gesture.

OPENING A CONVERSATION

How do we start a conversation? The participants need to coordinate an entry into the joint activity, produce the body of conversation for the activity, and exit from the conversation. The participants must be willing and able to enter the conversation with each other and work on the current project. It might begin with a simple conventional statement like *Hello* or *What's up?* or a statement about the weather to establish common ground: *Nice day, eh?* We can open conversations with an offer to help someone: *Can I help you?* We also open conversations with questions such as *Can you tell me how to get to Beacon Street?* Once we get the conversation going, the project can be pursued in more detail, or a new project can be introduced. The speaker engineers the addressee's entry into the conversation through a series of steps. Summons and response was used in the example, lines 1–2. By line 4, the conversants have established that they are willing and able to continue. The joint project is introduced in line 5, and in line 6 it is acknowledged and open for further consideration.

Telephone conversations often open through a series of steps similar to those just described. First a common channel is established. Next the participants establish mutual knowledge of their identities. They also have to establish a joint willingness to participate in the conversation. If they are both willing, then the first joint project can be opened for further consideration (Schegloff, 1968, 1979).

CLOSING A CONVERSATION

We do not end conversations by walking away from our listeners or by bluntly stopping our contribution to the conversation. Conversations end through the use of predictable transitions. Conversations more or less wind down step by step. When participants believe that they have completed their last topic, they prepare to exit and then do so. In many conversations, we give off signals that the dialogue is about to end before it does. These signals may come in the form of **preclosing statements** such as *I guess I'll have to let you go, Let's do lunch sometime, That's about it,* or *OK.* These comments tell the listener that the speaker is about to stop talking. Benjamin thanks Alice at the end of the phone call and she says *OK*-, indicating that the last topic has been completed. They then end the conversation with a mutual good-bye. Sometimes before ending a conversation, acquaintances will reassure each other that they will talk again to reaffirm their relationship; that is, the break is not a permanent one.

Sometimes we have business that requires immediate attention so we have to make statements like *I have another call* or *I'm late for my appointment.* These interruptive statements have the effect of justifying the early closure, according to Albert and Kessler (1978). They found that speakers have several conventional strategies to end conversations. Some will summarize the conversation; others express pleasure about the relationship, plan for future conversations, or wish the listener well. These closing strategies tend to follow a linear sequence. People make the summary statements early in the closing sequence and then do the well-wishing at the end of the sequence. As such, the ending sequence and the reciprocal statements between the participants produce a mutual conversational dance to the end. The conversation winds down instead of ending abruptly. If a conversation must end abruptly, an explanation is warranted.

CONVERSATIONAL LAYERS

H. H. Clark (1996) viewed verbal interactions as taking place in different **conversational layers,** as if each layer were a different theatrical stage with different participants and contexts. Each time we shift from one layer to another, we enter a new domain with new participants and a new conversational context. Clark used the example of two modern-day children pretending to be living during the gold rush days in Dakota Territory. One layer of conversation involves the domain of life in gold rush era Deadwood and the behaviors, attitudes, and actions that were imagined and pretended. In the gold rush domain, the children exist not as children but as Wild Bill and Calamity Jane. The second domain is the modern-day relationship between the two children (e.g., that they are neighbors and friends) and the knowledge that what they were doing was acting as if they were in the past. Here they exist in the modern-day domain as playmates, not as Wild Bill and Calamity Jane.

A conversation between two people can slip in and out of two or more layers. The concept of layers is important because it construes speech as nonlinear and allows participants to make meaningful shifts from one domain to another. The joint activities of one domain shift to different set of joint activities in the other. What might appear as discontinuity makes more sense when viewed as layers. Layers unfold when we introduce narratives, stories, or jokes into an ongoing conversation. Participants can switch from the conversation to a second layer and then to a third in the same physical setting. Within the course of a conversation, joint projects in layers can shift frequently, as we see in Chapter 9.

Review Question

By looking at conversants' gestures and nonverbal behavior, how could you tell who was talking and who was signaling for a turn?

TOPICS

It is simple to say that the **topic** is what the conversation is about. But what does that mean? Exactly what constitutes what the conversation is about is not clear. What is clear is that a conversation concentrates on a so-called topic and then it moves on to another project. Conversations are fluid, and what is or what will be the topic is not tightly controlled or determined as it is in a written essay. The topic of a text is planned and directed by a sequence of assertions made to support a general theme. The notion of a topic seems well suited to describe text, but it does not apply so well to a multilayered conversation.

It might be better to replace the idea of a topic with the idea of a joint activity, which describes what the participants are working on together rather than what they are talking about. A conversation is under joint control; it is not like a text. Conversants are doing more than making assertions around one topic. Each person's turn changes the joint project in some way, usually driving it closer to the goal of the conversation.

Not all potential joint projects are equally interesting, due to differences in common ground. Common ground will help select the project, but it will not guarantee that at any one point in time what someone wants to talk about will be appropriate for all listeners. The topic or project under discussion may begin as soon as a speaker makes an opening statement, *I never did like golf,* or opening request, *Where did you buy your Honda?* From there the project should follow some guidelines; it should be relevant and clear and not waste the listener's time.

UNSAFE TOPICS

Choosing a project for mutual discussion is also a means of avoiding or negotiating around unsafe topics. But what is an *unsafe topic?* Establishing common ground also establishes a set of taboos, topics that are inappropriate or even intolerable.

Sometimes participants mutually agree to avoid a source of conflict (e.g., in-laws or ex-partners); that is, their common ground includes its taboos. At other times guidelines are clear; a professor cannot talk about a student's grade with other people, and a physician must protect a patient's confidentiality. In many situations, unsafe topics are culturally defined as taboo or dangerous.

Unsafe topics traditionally include religion, sex, politics, income, disease, body products, body processes, and mental health. The joint project in polite settings would avoid unsafe topics as one would avoid cones on an automotive test track. One good way to determine what constitute unsafe or taboo topics is to look for the presence of *euphemisms*. Allan and Burridge (1991) provide a detailed analysis of euphemisms, which are safe words that are used as substitutes for more emotional, offensive, or inappropriate words. For example, the term *working girl* is a euphemism for *whore*. This euphemism belies our anxiety around conversations about sexuality while at the same time allowing us to approach the taboo topic in guarded terms.

Narratives

As noted earlier, a *narrative* is a storylike account of an event from the past. Narratives differ from conversations in that they are produced by an individual speaking alone. In a conversation, participants must mutually believe that they want the speaker to tell a narrative. It usually unfolds in a chronological sequence, although flashbacks and foreshadowing can occur. However, changing the sequence of events will make it more difficult for the listener to understand what happened. Narrative content includes a variety of information about the setting, the participants, sensory qualities and experiences, emotional reactions, and perceptions, along with quotations and meaningful sound effects. The intonation units that form building blocks of the narrative are also shaped by audience reactions. The audience can produce or withhold nods, smiles, *yeahs*, and *uh-huhs*. In fact, many narratives are produced piece by piece through audience prompts (Falk, 1980; Polanyi, 1989; Tannen, 1984).

McCabe (1996) believed that narratives functioned to make past events and memories more vivid and present. They help establish intimacy with listeners by connecting them to the events of one's life. The narrative presents the narrator in a certain role, for example, as a risk taker, scoundrel, hero, bystander, or victim. The narrative genre helps the speaker understand his or her experiences through the recounting of the past in a context where listeners can ask questions and make comments about the significance of the speaker's experiences. As the facts are recounted and reinterpreted, the speaker's story becomes more coherent, and the speaker comes to better understand what has happened in a richer personal and cultural context. Narratives are frequently used as research tools by journalists, historians, and social workers, who ask their informants to recount the past.

A narrative is frequently told from a certain perspective so that the listener can create a situational model of it. Spatial perspective provides the physical point of view that the observer takes on the scene—are we in a room? over a town? walking on a beach? Temporal perspective views the events over time—current, past, future, or imaginary. A figure-ground perspective sets off something that is the focus of attention, the figure (e.g., a shiny object), against a background (e.g., a crowded beach), depending on what the narrator selects as the focus of attention. The stance that the narrator takes toward the scene, the objects, and the people in it is the conceptual perspective. For example, the people at the beach could be "intruders" or "fellow sunbathers." The narrator works in the past much of the time but can start in the past and move into the present, making the scene more vivid (Shiffrin, 1981).

PERSONAL NARRATIVES AND SPEAKER GENDER

Labov (1972c) proposed that narratives of personal experience be divided into six parts:

1. An abstract or summary of the entire story:

   I had a problem with a retired professor at the grocery store the other day.

2. An orientation about the who, what, where, and when of the story, somewhat like stage directions:

   I was waiting in line with a basketful of groceries for dinner in front of old Professor Fedders from Williams.

3. A complicating action; a statement or description about what happened:

   I realized that I had forgotten the brown rice, which I had to have for the stew. I said, "I'll be right back." I got out of line and ran back to the rice shelf, but when I came back, Professor Fedders was putting his stuff on the belt. I picked up my basket, but he ignored me and kept putting his stuff on the belt. I said, "Hello, Professor Fedders? How are you enjoying your retirement?"

4. An evaluation of the narrative; the point of telling the narrative or what the narrator is getting at:

   I like to talk to people in line. If you're nice, they're nice too.

5. The result of or resolution to the complicating action:

   When he saw it was me, he asked me to get ahead of him, which I did—the old fart.

6. A coda or signal that the narrative is finished:

   So that's what happens when you're nice to people in line.

These parts reflect what narrators are trying to do in their narratives. Each contribution enables the listeners to adjust their situational models at the right time. It also enables them to add new elements to the situation in relation to what is already there in the model. The narrator guides the audience from the here-and-now through the story, moving from one event to another, focusing on what is important until the event is resolved. Each of the six points is used to connect the elements of the story to the model. Finally, at the end of the story, it is back to the here-and-now.

There is ample evidence that the speaker's gender plays a significant role in personal narratives. When adults are asked to talk about their recent past experiences, females focus on the importance of other people in their lives and struggles with intimacy. Their childhood narratives are details about people such as sibling rivalry, childhood playmates, and their parents' misunderstandings (Schwartz, 1984). Males tell about experiences of approval or praise from others or themes of youthful recreation. They report more stories about mastery, fulfilling a desire, successful performance, and people who urged them to succeed (Schwartz, 1984; Thorne, 1995). Thorne (1995) asked adults to recount memories from various points in time. Males frequently reported the desire to avoid others and to seek autonomy or independence. Females spoke more often than males about wanting love, seeking approval, and needing help. Gender differences are also evident in the organization of the narratives. Females' narratives are longer, more detailed, and rated by both males and females as more accurate than males' narratives (de Vries, Blando, & Walker, 1995).

These gender differences take a developmental course. Buckner and Fivush (1998) found gender differences in the personal narratives of 7-year-olds. Boys and girls differed significantly in narrative content and organization. Girls' narratives were longer, more temporally and causally connected, and embellished with more details than boys' narratives. Girls' narratives were more likely to be set in an interpersonal context and to include more affiliation themes, emotion, and references to others. These differences are not due to literacy skills (Reese, 1995). Stapely and Haviland (1989) found that by adolescence, boys' stories focused on situations involving autonomy and activity, while girls were more likely to highlight affiliative aspects of experience. These studies support the idea that females explicitly "people" their narratives more than males do. These are not just differences in structure but substantial differences in what girls and boys choose to converse about.

STORYTELLING

Narrative segments in conversation are very similar to storytelling. Cassady (1990) defined **storytelling** as an oral art form that provides a means of preserving and transmitting ideas, images, motives, and emotions that are universal. Storytelling exists at a formal level where an audience assembles for the purpose of listening to a storyteller tell a story such as a folktale. Less formal storytelling also exists when speakers shift conversational layers to recount an interesting or exciting episode from the past. Storytelling, both formal and informal, is universal. It allows us to share experiences, pass on historical events, and instruct children. Gender differences are apparent in the stories people choose to tell, indicating that they may serve different purposes. For example, more males than females tend to tell boastful or self-aggrandizing stories in which they get the better of their fellows (Buckner & Fivush, 1998; Johnstone, 1993). Most storytellers shy away from boastful stories and rely more on humorous stories, stories about troubles or problems they have experienced, and stories about embarrassing events from the past (Norrick, 2000).

In oral storytelling, specialized formulas and repetitions will cluster around openings and codas, transition points, and resolutions. To draw an audience into a story, tellers use formulas. Sacks (1972) pointed out how effective saying *"Guess what?"* is to coercing the addressee to set the stage for a story by responding *"What?"* Norrick (2000) provided examples of stories that began with introductory statements like *"I remember the most embarrassing moment of my life . . . I was so embarrassed."* Another speaker started a narrative by stating, *"This is the latest thing. This just happened today."* One formulaic introduction for a familiar story is *"Remember the time . . . ?"* or *"Remember when . . . ?"*

Formulas are also used within the narrative once the introduction has been established. Sometimes these take the form of a formulaic phrase at the middle or end of the story that can be used to draw the threads of the narrative together. For example, the figurative *"I was just like a leaf in the wind"* draws the episodes that precede it into a single image. Other phrases can take on a local formulaicity if they are repeated (Tannen, 1987). For example, *"It was really weird"* can be used to introduce an episode. Then, through its repetition after the episode, the final mention of *weird* signals that the recounting of the weird episode is finished.

Research on repetitions in stories has demonstrated that they play a key role in setting up patterns that help build a situational model (Norrick, 1987, 1993b; Tannen, 1989). Repetitions divide the story into equal parts or help impose a hierarchical structure from one portion of the narrative to another. Restarting a story beginning occurs frequently as tellers need to revise their false starts with backtracks. Here is an example from Norrick (2000, p. 118):

We had a—

My mom always had like a dish cloth

That had holes in it

Repetitions at transitions can heighten the dramatic effect of the story and stress the teller's evaluation of the story. Consider the following (from Norrick, 2000, p. 63):

WOODY: And I mean what is the likelihood of that thing—
That damn shovel came right down on his head

GRANT & GINGER: (*laughing*)

WOODY: I mean—I mean it came down and it flattened him (*punctuates with a hand-clap*)

The repetition can be used to heighten or highlight evaluations in narratives. Notice how the repetition of *horrid* and *blinded* reinforces how bad and tragic Mark's accident story is:

MARK: and one girl pulled her headgear off her mouth
       and let it snap back
       and it slid up her face
       and stuck in her eyes
       and blinded her

JACOB: Wow

MARK: isn't that horrid?
       That's horrid.

JACOB: **when my—**

MARK: **blinded her** for life
       Isn't that just horrid?

Mark uses the repetition to underline the bizarreness of the accident and how terrible it was, repeating phrases to accentuate his evaluation.

Formulaic story conclusions are also frequently used. Formulaic story closings like those noted are more varied than story openers. Sacks (1992) noted the use of proverbs and clichés as story conclusions. Norrick (2000), for example, noted how the stock phrase *And I lived to tell the story* as a coda works particularly well. One of his storytellers ended a story about accepting his early retirement money with *grabbing the money and running with it,* based on the *grab the money and run* cliché. The formulaic finish *Here I am* or *I lived to tell the story* brings the audience back to the here-and-now.

RETELLING AND RETOLD STORIES

Retellings, or **retold stories,** offer important evidence about narrative structure. Multiple performances reveal the elements of the narrative that are stable and those that vary from context to context. With the exception of Chafe's (1998) work, previous studies have generally ignored retold stories. Chafe describes storytelling as if the narrator is retrieving information from memory, selecting from it, and verbalizing. Norrick (2000) views the story as a reconstruction rather than a recall, a reconstruction that is tailored to fit the needs of the current listeners. It is important to separate the story from the narrative performance of it. By separating the story structure from a real-time performance, one can be said to be telling the same story (Polanyi, 1981). Sacks (1972, 1992) argues that each narrative performance is a separate story tied to a local context. Alternatively, Labov (1972c; Labov & Waletzky, 1967) think that separate tellings of a single story do occur. Only by examining retellings in different contexts can we see how the individual storyteller varies the narrative structure to fit a specific context.

A common form of retelling is instigated by elicited retellings; for example, one of the conversants asks another to tell a particular story. Another reason to retell a story is when a new hearer enters the context. Norrick (2000) provides the example of a woman telling a story about a bag left in a turkey. She then retells the story on the same topic for another woman who arrives on the scene from another room asking "*Who?*" and thereby instigating a retelling in the same context. When Norrick examined retelling in different contexts, he found a wide range of permutations and paraphrases. He also noted numerous similarities and parallel elements. The closest similarities often appeared among nonnarrative elements in evaluation, background information, and dialogue. The identical phrases in subsequent tellings suggest a verbatim recall of whole chunks of narrative or the use of specific narrative techniques at critical points in a story. Telling the same stories again and again allows tellers to recycle and crystallize stories and parts of stories as complete chunks. However, when narrators are asked to write their narratives, passages that were repeated verbatim in oral narratives were deleted in written ones (Norrick, 2000).

One dynamic that unfolds in a conversational context is that once one speaker has told a story, another speaker may respond with a *response story*. There are multiple motivations to tell a parallel story. The new teller may want to indicate that the first story was understood or to make comments about it. Retelling stories provides for building rapport between conversants. The give-and-take in storytelling interactions raises questions about who has the right to tell a story, of what kind, and to whom in the real-time conversational situation. The next storyteller may seek alignment with the speaker or take a stance for or against its characters and contents. It should also be mentioned that familiar stories are often conarrated. Telling a familiar story can entice listeners to participate or become a conarrator (Labov, 1972c; Polanyi, 1979; Sacks, 1992). These kinds of conarrations are common as *family lore*, stories that are often recalled and repeated during family interactions.

HUMOR AND JOKING NARRATIVES

Humor refers generally to anything that is funny. A joke is more specific; it is self-contained, context-free discourse that is intended to provide amusement to listeners (Long & Graesser, 1988). Jokes are structured, with conversational markers that set them off from the previous conversational layer. The joke frame may employ fixed openings—*Did I tell you the one about* . . .—which opens a new layer of conversation with a new project, the joke. The speaker can continue telling jokes or can return to the previous conversational layer. Hockett (1977) developed a convincing analysis of **joking narratives,** noting that most jokes consist of a *buildup* phase in the body of the joke and a *punch line* that closes the joke. The punch line reverses in some sense what we expect to hear. Hockett demonstrated that we can often recognize a *pivot* word or phrase in which a semantic duality lies. Here is a famous one-liner that can serve as an example:

A panhandler came up to me today and said he hadn't had a bite in weeks, so I bit him.

We can schematize it as follows:

Buildup	A panhandler came up to me today and said he hadn't
Pivot	*had a bite* in weeks,
Punch line	so I bit him.

Following Sacks (1974), Norrick (1993a) used conversation analysis to study successful and unsuccessful narrative joke performances. Jokes are designed to elicit a laugh from the audience. To do this, they require special prefaces to produce a sense of newness. There is usually a pivotal point in the buildup that may require verbatim wording, a point on which the response to the joke turns. Unlike other forms of narrative, jokes are not so amenable to conarration. Joke telling can be competitive, like other forms of humor. When the audience fails to understand a joking narrative, tellers are frequently at a loss to produce a satisfactory version.

Unlike the context-free joke, *wit* relies heavily on the context where it occurs, which includes shared knowledge and the current topic. The use of wit fits the statement *You had to be there to get it.* For example, while I was conducting a professional development workshop for schoolteachers on students' "dirty word" problems, I asked the participants how they would react if a student came into the classroom and said, "I didn't finish the fucking homework." A seasoned teacher raised his hand and replied, "I'd say, 'That's not the kind of homework I assigned,'" causing spasms of laughter. The humor in wit emerges out of the teller's relationship to people and events in the conversational context.

Riddles, like wit, have been around a long time. They have been found in Anglo-Saxon written texts dating from as early as the eighth century. A riddle is a puzzling question that is posed for solution, as a linguistic game or contest. An example of a riddle is *They are two brothers, but however much they run, they never reach each other.* (Answer: bicycle wheels). Riddles have been used as tests of wisdom and sense of humor (Crystal, 1987).

One way to understand humor is as a joint project that is intended to achieve public and private goals. For humor to work, the speaker and listener have to cooperate in one domain and understand that the humor is intended to achieve goals. Alternatively, the forms of humor mentioned here can be understood within the strictures of speech act theory according to Long and Graesser (1988). As a speech act, humor can be seen as a discourse tool used to achieve a speaker's intentions. Some of the discourse intentions, or joint projects, for humor are as follows:

- *Self-disclosure* through revealing information about what constitutes shared knowledge. The listener has to work to discover the irony in the speaker's humor and find the important information about the context at hand.

- *Decommitment* through turning a faux pas into jest.

- *Social control* by establishing in-group solidarity through the disparagement of an out-group.

- *Conveying social norms* to people with equal status by using humor to tell them in an indirect way what is inappropriate.

- *Ingratiation* by producing liking through mirth.

- *Discourse management* by controlling the topic and flow.

- *Social play* through discourse.

Understanding humor is an essential aspect of human communication. It is difficult to imagine getting through a day without encountering some form of humor in informal conversations or in text. Humor, as we have just read, is not merely emotionally satisfying; it is also used to achieve social goals.

> **Review Questions**
> Are there rules for joke telling? What kinds of jokes would be considered inappropriate in the classroom?

Culture and Discourse

All conversations occur in social and physical contexts, but exactly what is constructed mentally in these settings depends in part on a cultural viewpoint. All cultures use folk tales to impart wisdom and cultural knowledge to children. However, the structure and expectations in folk stories depend on who is doing the telling and who is doing the listening. We look briefly at cultural differences in folk tales and narratives.

Dooling and Lachman's (1971) Christopher Columbus experiment draws on a tradition of studying memory for prose in natural settings that began with the work of British psychologist Frederick Bartlett (1932). Bartlett was intently interested in how people remembered the details of the stories and reports that they heard in everyday life. He also delighted in giving his British students Amerindian folk tales in order to see what they would remember. One of his selections was "The War of the Ghosts," a folk story in Kwakiutl, the language of natives of Vancouver Island, British Columbia.

"The War of the Ghosts" differs in structure and detail from typical British and American folk tales. Bartlett found that on remembering the tale, his British students would leave out details and make the story more congruent with their own familiar folk schemas. Most students' recall reflects not a reproduction of the facts but a *reconstruction* of the tale that fits their own expectations and cultural values. For instance, after a few weeks, many students erroneously recall that an Indian died at sunset, which is congruent with Western tales but not the actual setting in the story. Without the background knowledge of the Kwakiutl culture, readers construct a mental model of the story that fits their own experience. Details that are important to Kwakiutl natives might not be represented in your mental model. Cultural differences in comprehension and recall of narratives are also found in the way different cultures tell stories.

CROSS-CULTURAL DIFFERENCES IN NARRATIVES AND STORIES

In our discussion of narrative, we observed that the style of narrative reporting is a developmental phenomenon. Children begin telling primitive narratives around 2 years of age, and they get progressively better until age 6, when they produce a story that contains the basic requirements of the narrative according to their culture (Berko-Gleason & Melzi, 1997; McCabe, 1998). At age 6, what one hears as narrative depends on which culture is speaking. Cultural preferences affect both the storytelling schema and the schema regarding how to listen to or interpret the narratives. Miller, Wiley, Fung, and Liang (1997) found that the acquisition of a culture's schema for storytelling begins as early as age 2. They compared Taiwanese and European American families' stories, where past experiences of the focal child (2 years old) were narrated. Chinese families, in keeping with the high value placed on didactic narrative in the Confucian tradition, were more likely to use personal storytelling to convey moral and social standards. European American narrators used stories as a medium of entertainment and affirmation. Storytelling operates as a socializing practice that differs widely across cultures and can be differentiated as early an age as 2 years.

In a related study, Samuelsson, Mauritzson, Carlsson, and Ueda (1998) found that a narrative like the popular children's book "The Giving Tree" can be interpreted in a number of ways by people from different cultures. This study asked mothers from Japan and Sweden what they felt as they heard the tale, what the tale was about, and what children would learn from the tale. Japanese mothers saw a hierarchical relationship in the tale. Swedish mothers saw a mutual relationship. Interestingly, a comparison between Swedish mothers and Swedish children showed dramatic similarities between interpretations. Samuelsson et al. argue that the differences in interpretations of the tale can be related to differences in Japanese and Swedish children's life-world. This study reinforces the point made by Bartlett's (1932) research.

Cultural values readily affect narrative structures. For example, in Japan, wordiness is viewed negatively. The personal narratives of Japanese children, not surprisingly, are brief and unembellished accounts of the past (Minami & McCabe, 1995). Japanese children are taught to rely on their listeners for empathy, and in doing so, some of the details can be omitted or not made explicit because the listeners will fill in the blanks. Japanese mothers' interactions with their children foster this style. They request less description from their children, and they frequently interrupt their children to utter brief acknowledgments. The interruptions have the effect of stopping the children from talking at length. In contrast,

American mothers work to develop an elaborative narrative style in their children's utterances.

Family members play important character roles in the children's narratives, especially those of Spanish-speaking narrators (Silva & McCabe, 1996). When asked to tell a story from a wordless picture book, Spanish-speaking children and adults produced more details, describing the setting of the story, its landmarks, and its location, than speakers from other cultures (Berman & Slobin, 1994). Details about landmarks and locations are more prominent in their stories relative to African American and North American children, who tend to focus more on actions than setting the scene of the story.

African American narratives tend to link several related experiences as they are performed. Their stories are therefore lengthy and include many details and personal anecdotes to establish the main point of the narrative. Michaels (1983) described the differences between African American and white children as follows. The narratives among white, middle-class groups tended to be lengthy and tightly organized around a single topic. These were referred to as **topic-centered stories.** The narratives told by African Americans are referred to as **topic-associated stories.** S. B. Heath (1983) suggested that the narratives told by African Americans in the rural southeastern United States were also performances. Verbal narrators in this community were skilled at telling stories that sustained the audience's attention. Sometimes these were poetic in structure and used nonverbal embellishments or exaggerations of the facts to produce a good performance.

Narrative style and structure are not innate. Children acquire their culture's style early in development and use it to reinforce cultural values, as these studies have shown. Cross-cultural differences in narrative have obvious applications to educational, counseling, and clinical conversational contexts (Berko-Gleason & Melzi, 1997). One of the limitations of discourse theory is that there have been too few attempts to incorporate nonverbal, emotional, and offensive aspects of conversations into theoretical models. For instance, there are few "dark topics" addressed in discourse processing, leaving us to believe that conversations produce little in the way of emotional reactions. This belies the prevalence of family arguments, harassment, hate speech, blaming and accusing, and verbal abuse. We have faced this form of emotional void before; psychologists need to investigate the emotional repercussions of conversations and text before our picture will be complete (Jay, 2000).

Key Terms

adjacency pair	causal network	conversational maxims
anaphor	cohesion	grounding
bridging inference	cohesive gestures	joint project
causal chain	common ground	joking narrative
causal inference	conversational layers	macrostructure

mental model
microstructure
narrative
partial processing
preclosing statement
retold story

schema
script
situational model
spatial model
speech acts
story grammar

storytelling
surface memory
text base
topic
topic-centered story
turn taking

What Lies Ahead

Chapter 9 covers the topic of nonliteral speech and includes metaphors, politeness, sarcasm, name-calling, and idioms. These figures of speech are common in discourse and narratives, and an understanding of them is critical to understanding what people are trying to accomplish in discourse settings. In many cases, figures of speech permit people to reduce complicated constructs to more concrete terms or to express emotional content in more guarded terms.

Suggested Web Site

Discourse processes: http://www.psyc.memphis.edu/st&d/st&d.htm

Chapter 9
Figurative Speech and Thought

Critical Thinking Questions

1. What is the standard pragmatic view of figurative language?

2. What processing models have evolved to account for how we comprehend figurative language?

3. How are metaphorical and metonymic expressions processed?

4. What kinds of emotional work do we accomplish with figurative language?

5. What are indirect requests, and why do we use them?

6. How do we process conventionalized expressions like idioms?

7. Why do we use figurative language?

Exercise 9.1. **Figurative Speech**
Figurative speech is common in everyday conversation. How do you interpret it? What does each of the following phrases mean? Write down your interpretation in your notebook. Contrast the figurative meanings of these phrases with their literal meanings.

1. My roommate is a pig.

2. I thought I was going to kick the bucket.

3. I have a million things to do.

4. Do you know the time?

5. How many times have I told you to wipe your feet before entering the house?

Figurative speech is not intended to be interpreted literally. Speech is filled with nonliteral phrases in the form of idioms, insults, sarcasm, irony, hyperbole, metaphor, simile, metonymy, teasing, and put-ons. Figurative speech can use imagery to describe something or compare two different things to make the situation clearer or more interesting. Like the examples in Exercise 9.1, it is pervasive in everyday speech and written discourse (Gibbs, 1994; Kreuz, Roberts, Johnson, & Bertus, 1996; Pollio, Smith, & Pollio, 1990). Figurative comments can appear ambiguous, and their meanings can be difficult to pin down out of context. The meanings we construct for a given comment can rely heavily on context and prior discourse. The meaning ascribed to *That chicken is too hot to eat* depends on whether *chicken* refers to a human or a bird, whether the referent is alive or dead, and whether *hot* refers to temperature or spiciness. If *chicken* refers to a human, the meaning is figurative and insulting. Common idioms like *kick the bucket* are figurative, and so are comments like *your house is a pigpen*. We understand that the *house* is not literally a pigpen but it is messy like one. This chapter focuses on figurative expressions and the cognitive processes used to understand them. Examples of some of the figures of speech that will be considered appear in Table 9.1.

There has been a great deal of research over the past twenty years in psycholinguistics and related disciplines on the issue of how people interpret figurative language. This research has focused more on comprehension processes than on production processes. The questions about figurative language overlap with several general issues in psycholinguistics, including those surrounding word meaning (Chapter 4), sentence comprehension (Chapter 5), and discourse processes (Chapter 8). One controversy in the literature is whether we construct both literal and figurative interpretations of figurative speech during comprehension and if we do, which has predominance. Another question is whether figurative speech is anomalous, requiring special mechanisms to account for how it is comprehended. Grice's (1978) view of conversational cooperation (recall his maxims, outlined in Chapter 8) represented figurative language as though it violated the principals of cooperation, requiring the listener to make inferences or implications when a literal understanding was found to be defective. For example, if John asks Mary, *Can you take me to the airport?* and Mary

Table 9.1. Eight Forms of Nonliteral Language

Type	Definition	Example
Hyperbole	Deliberate exaggeration	*The cafeteria line was a mile long.*
Idiom	Conventionalized nonliteral expression	*He kicked the bucket.*
Indirect request	Request for actions stated obliquely	*Can you pass the salt?*
Irony	Opposite meaning intended	*What gorgeous weather!* (spoken during a thunderstorm)
Metaphor	Implicit comparison	*The road was a snake.*
Rhetorical question	Assertion framed as question	*Who do you think you are?*
Simile	Explicit comparison	*My job is like a jail.*
Understatement	Deliberate underemphasis	*Mozart wrote some decent music.*

Note. Reprinted from *Poetics, 22,* R. J. Kreuz and R. M. Roberts, "The Empirical Study of Figurative Language in Literature," pp. 151–169. Copyright 1993 with permission from Elsevier Science.

replies, *Do I look like a taxi?* her sarcastic comment violates the cooperative principle by answering a question with another question, and it requires John to make an inference that she means "no." Does this extra work require more processing time?

Grice (1978) assumed that the listener has to do extra cognitive work to figure out the meaning of this response. In other words, figurative language requires a special process that occurs only after the literal fails. This would suggest that the literal reading of speech is obligatory and derived prior to a figurative interpretation. However, a good deal of research contradicts what has been called the **standard pragmatic view** of figurative language. Many studies have revealed that it takes no longer to comprehend figurative expressions than it does literal ones (see Blasko, 1999; McElree & Nordlie, 1999; Ortony, Schallert, Reynolds, & Antos, 1978). Other researchers have demonstrated that people do not need to detect a defective literal interpretation before constructing a figurative one (Glucksberg, Gildea, & Bookin, 1982; Shinjo & Myers, 1987). Individual differences also play a role in figurative language comprehension and interpretation; not everyone "gets it" the same way (Blasko, 1999). These studies have led some researchers (Gibbs, 1984, 1989) to suggest that we abandon the distinction of literal versus nonliteral and study how participants comprehend utterances based on more general principles of common ground and knowledge of each other's discourse goals. The literal-nonliteral issue is far from settled, and we will have to address different processing models of figurative language.

The meaning of a segment of speech combines what a speaker intends with what a listener understands. To be insulted by being called a *redneck,* you have to know what it means figuratively. A foreign visitor or a young child does not immediately grasp the intricacies of insults in English. Understanding insulting language requires some experience with how emotional information is marked in native speech. To ascribe a figurative meaning to words requires us to look at the use of words in discourse. In many conversations, the dictionary meanings of a word is not what is intended or understood. For example, the literal meaning of an idiom like *bite the bullet* might be what a foreigner or a child might comprehend, but that is not what the speaker intended. One has to activate the figurative meaning and suppress the irrelevant literal meaning to get the speaker's intended meaning. Before we look at figures of speech, it is important to make a common distinction between *connotative meaning* and *denotative meaning,* which allows us to describe the emotional force of figurative language.

Denotative and Connotative Aspects of Meaning

Denotation deals with the literal referential aspects of word meaning. We covered this in Chapter 4. **Connotation** refers to the affective meaning and culturally supported assumptions that are associated with the denotative meaning of a word. One approach to constructing meaning used *semantic features*—associated facts and characteristics—to get a sense of the word. Semantic features indicate whether the concept is a living thing (e.g., an animal or a plant) and such aspects as its age (e.g., maturity or antiquity), size (e.g., large, medium, or small), or origin (e.g., Swiss or Australian). An alternative method of marking the sense of a word is reviewing the different interpretations of the word, which produces a list of definitions or usages. For example, the meaning of *plant* is "a living organism that makes its own food," "vegetation smaller than a shrub," "a factory or its machinery," or "set in the ground." Each usage of *plant* is a separate way to interpret the word. The literal meaning of the word is usually one of these interpretations.

Figurative language can be analyzed in feature or interpretive terms, but not without some difficulty. The problem with novel, made-up-on-the-spot figurative language is that the listener cannot activate stored interpretations because the novel interpretations are not stored in memory. New figurative meanings have to be *constructed* in the speech context. Consider *Your roommate is an animal.* Literally, the statement is true. Looking for shared features, however, for *roommate* and *animal* will not make much sense without knowledge of what has taken place in the context of the comment—is this about messiness, rudeness, sexuality, or physical characteristics? The *emotional* aspects that accompany meanings of *animal* are different from what might be associated with the term used literally. The emotional meaning of *animal* depends on context and usage. In this instance, *animal* might mean "large," "brutish," "mean," "ignorant," or "slovenly," evoking negative affect. But it could be used to refer to sexual behavior in an emotionally positive way, for example, meaning "lusty," "insatiable," "wild," "uninhibited," or "out of control." Thus like *animal,* a word can take on positive and negative connotative aspects of its literal meaning, depending on how it is used in a context and the participants' common ground (Jay & Danks, 1977).

The meaning of the remark about the roommate is constructed in the minds of the participants in the conversation. Whether a positive or a negative reading is constructed depends on what the participants share as common ground about the roommate. Their common ground includes their attitudes, beliefs, perceptions, and knowledge about the roommate. Common ground provides the information and context in which figurative speech can be produced fluently and understood easily.

The remainder of this chapter explores the nature of figurative speech, the kind used in connotation, metaphor, irony, sarcasm, teasing, idioms, hyperbole, and understatement.

> **Review Question**
> Describe the denotative and connotative meanings of animal names.

Metaphor

One of the most common forms of figurative speech is the *metaphor.* A **metaphor** makes an implicit comparison between two concepts, as in *Cigarettes are time bombs.* Metaphors are similar to **similes,** which make explicit comparisons using *like* or *as,* as in *Cigarettes are like time bombs.* Each expression relates our understanding of one thing (cigarettes) to another (time bombs). Metaphors can be *conventionalized,* or "frozen" in meaning, as in the expression *he's living on borrowed time.* Other metaphors are made up on the spot, for example, *Bob is a big tub of pus.* Ortony (1975) argued that metaphors work because they use a simple idea to express a more complex thought. In metaphor, a complex concept is grounded in something known. Consider these:

You are wasting time.

We are running out of time.

He's living on borrowed time.

I've invested a lot of time in this relationship.

Spend your time wisely.

Through metaphor, the abstract and confusing can be made more concrete and meaningful. "Time" is difficult for us to understand because it has no concrete physical or spatial reality. The money expressions on the list might appear to be literal, but a closer look reveals a systematic metaphorical structure. They reveal how we think about time in relationship to money. Each is a metaphorical entailment of the **conceptual metaphor** TIME IS MONEY. Conceptual metaphors are part of our unconscious everyday conceptual system. Conceptual metaphors reflect how people in our culture think about some object or situation, according to Lakoff and Johnson (1980). It is the conceptual representation that gives rise to the spoken metaphor and its *entailments,* other statements that follow from the main metaphor. In other words, in this view, metaphors are derived from the structure of thought. People think of *time* as they do *money,* which can be won or lost, spent, borrowed, saved, or wasted. So we say things like *don't waste my time.* For comparison, another common conceptual metaphor is ARGUMENTS ARE WARS. This thought will be the conceptual basis for expressions such as *I won the argument, He shot down my argument, His criticisms were right on target,* and *He demolished my argument.* This reflects a systematic mental structuring: people conceptualize arguments in terms of wars.

Metaphors are important in conversations because they facilitate understanding. They are used in politics, science, and psychotherapy to aid comprehension and understanding of complex, intense, or confusing thoughts and feelings. Metaphors for feelings are common in psychology and psychotherapy. A patient might say to the therapist something like *When my son comes home late, I feel like exploding.* The comparison of the patient's stored up feelings to a bomb has an important figurative meaning. The patient feels volatile, dangerous, unpredictable, ready to release his accumulated anger. His metaphor encapsulates his complex feelings of anger toward his son in a simple conceptual metaphor: ANGER IS A BOMB. This is a common way to conceptualize anger. Another is as a heated fluid: ANGER IS A HEATED FLUID IN A CONTAINER. We talk of *boiling with anger, reaching the boiling point, feeling hot under the collar.* Many of our basic emotion concepts like anger are understood metaphorically in terms of motion, space, and force.

COMPREHENDING METAPHORS

A metaphor, for example, ANGER IS A BOMB, consists of three elements, a *topic*, a *vehicle*, and a *ground*. The **topic** of the metaphor is generally the subject of the sentence (*anger*) and is more complex than the concept to which it is being compared (*bomb*). The **vehicle** is a simple concrete or mutually known concept. The **ground** is the similarity that exists between the topic and vehicle (e.g., dangerous, volatile, stored energy, unpredictable). A listener has to construct a relationship or comparison (ground) between the two concepts to see where they overlap. The problem is to find out how the topic is related to the vehicle. In the metaphor *Bob is a big tub of pus, Bob* is the topic and *big tub of pus* is the vehicle. The ground is established by analysis: Like the tub of pus, Bob is large, fat, passive, and disgusting. Through the ground, we construct a relationship between the topic and vehicle and in this case an emotional evaluation. The meaning of the metaphor does not exist in the word meaning; it emerges as we construct the ground.

To date, no single theory has evolved to account for how people process metaphors. In fact, several views have emerged. The *comparison view* suggests that metaphors are understood through the process of comparing the topic and vehicle in order to find the semantic similarities between them (Ortony, 1979) or to find semantic anomalies between them (Clark & Lucy, 1975). I used the comparison view to compare *Bob* to the *big tub of pus* to find the overlapping features in the example. Some observers argue that metaphors are understood through their connection to an underlying *conceptual structure* that represents the world in general terms, similar to the view espoused by Lakoff and Johnson (1980). The *domain interaction view* (Tourangeau & Sternberg, 1982) integrates the similarity and semantic anomaly comparisons within a broader domain of knowledge about the concepts that are being compared. For example, how can we consider people to be like containers? Meaning construction is not limited to concepts ("Bob," "tub") used in the metaphor. In the Bob metaphor, we would look for similarities between people and containers, not just tubs. Alternatively, Glucksberg and Keysar (1990) view metaphors as figurative *class-inclusion statements* in which the topic of the metaphor can be considered as a member of the class of concepts implied by the vehicle of the metaphor. The meaning of the metaphor is determined by deciding how the topic fits as a member of the category defined by the vehicle. For example, in what way is Bob (the human body) a member of the container category? Both hold healthy or disgusting contents, can rest passively, can vary in size from large to small, or can be overfilled. The class-inclusion view constructs meaning through class-inclusion statements whereby *Bob* and *tub* are members of a category "container" that does not have a category name (Cacciari & Glucksberg, 1994).

One model of figurative language processing currently gaining attention is Giora's **graded salience** model (Giora, 1999; Giora & Fein, 1999a, 1999b; Giora, Fein, & Schwartz, 1998). Giora has argued against the selective access view of context, that is, that context tells us how to read the metaphoricity of an expression. The main idea behind graded salience is that people give priority to the salient meaning of a word regardless of context. The salient meaning of a word or expression is its lexicalized meaning, the meaning that is retrieved from memory rather than from the context. The salient meaning is the literal meaning of a novel metaphor but not the intended nonliteral meaning made available by the context. The familiarity, availability, frequency, and conventionality of an expression contribute to its salient meaning and give it privileged status. Therefore, the salient meanings of unfamiliar metaphoric, ironic, or idiomatic expressions are always accessed initially, regardless of context. For familiar metaphors, the literal and nonliteral meanings are activated at the same time, regardless of whether the context is biased in favor of one reading or the other.

How, then, do we understand metaphors? How do we figure out the ground when we hear a metaphor? One answer is that it depends on what processing model you believe. Let's start with a simple experiment that demonstrates the psychological reality of metaphor comprehension. A cued recall paradigm was used to demonstrate that a person does construct the ground relationship for comprehension purposes. Verbugge and McCarrell (1977) presented subjects with metaphors and later prompted their memory using the topic, the ground, or the vehicle of the metaphor as a recall cue. If we construct the ground, then it should work as well as the vehicle or the topic as a cue to the entire metaphor, and that is what they found. The listener must construct the ground, which is unstated in the literal meaning of the words, because the ground works equally well as a prompt for recall. The study shows that although the comparison (ground) between the topic and vehicle is not stated in the metaphor, subjects nonetheless activated it or figured it out and later used it in the memory task.

The result of the recall study leaves us wondering *how* listeners construct the ground. Do we construct a metaphorical comparison immediately, or do we construct the literal meaning and then the metaphorical? Or do we compute the literal and figurative meanings simultaneously? Consider the *Bob* and *bomb* metaphors. How readily we comprehend the metaphors and to what degree they make sense to us depends on how much we know about the topics. With some background information or context with respect to the topics, the meanings are more readily available relative to metaphors taken out of context. Ortony et al. (1978) found that how we comprehend metaphors depends on the context in which they are presented. Context provides cues for making the comparison between topic and vehicle that help construct meaning. Without contextual cues, metaphors take longer than literal statements to comprehend. But with contextual cues, metaphors and literal statements take the same amount of time to comprehend, indicating that no secondary translation stage is necessary to understand the metaphor if it has the appropriate cues.

Do the results of the Ortony et al. (1978) experiment mean that metaphorical meaning is immediately available in the right context? If a *metaphorical* meaning were readily available, would it get in the way of making judgments about the *literal* meaning of a metaphor? Glucksberg et al. (1982) asked subjects to judge whether presented sentences were literally true. Some of the sentences were true metaphors but were not literally true—for example, *All jobs are jails.* The logic behind the experiment was as follows: Metaphorically true but literally false sentences are more difficult to judge than metaphorically false sentences because the metaphorical truth interferes with judging its literal falsity. When sentences are both literally and metaphorically false— for example, *All desks are roads*—they are easy to judge. That is what the researchers found: The judgments of metaphorically true sentences that were literally false took longer than judgments of sentences that were not metaphorically true. The metaphorical meaning added to judgment times regarding literality.

In a follow-up study, Gildea and Glucksberg (1983) presented subjects with metaphors that could be understood in isolation, such as *All jobs are jails.* They compared these metaphors to ones that were contextually dependent, such as *All hands are medicine. All hands are medicine* makes figurative sense if we are given some background information like *Some songs are soothing,* which is literally true. When *All hands are medicine* was preceded by a *literal* prime, like *Some songs are soothing,* judgments about the literal truth of the sentence were slowed relative to giving no prime. Priming the *metaphorical* meanings interfered with making *literal* judgments because the activation of the metaphorical reading competed with the literal interpretation. Like literal statements, metaphorical readings are facilitated by contextually relevant information that activates the relevant meaning of the words in the sentence. Asking subjects to make *literal* readings of sentences that are *metaphorically* primed adds another burden to the process, that of deriving a competing alternative meaning, which slows judgment times.

Contrary to Grice's standard pragmatic view, we have seen that in Glucksberg's research, both literal and metaphorical meanings require activation and construction of the appropriate meanings. Both the literal meaning and the metaphorical meaning require the activation of information that links word meaning to what is happening in a broader context. The literal and metaphorical readings depend on the context in which they occur. A metaphorical reading has to relate the salient features of words being compared. Glucksberg et al. (1982) found that how we interpret a metaphor like *My surgeon is a butcher* depends on the topic. *My surgeon is a butcher* activates a different set of features relative to those features used to make sense of *My copyeditor is a butcher.* Even though both are metaphors, the constructed senses depend on context. One feature that both metaphors have in common is that they both make negative evaluative statements about the topics of the metaphor. We understand that the surgeon and the editor are not doing a good job. Consider the interpretation of *Your roommate is an animal* in these two contexts.

The bathroom was a mess. Your roommate is an animal.

The noises in the bedroom kept me awake all night. Your roommate is an animal.

The interpretation depends on the context in which it occurs, each with a different connotation.

Metaphor understanding, especially in the case of novel figures of speech, extends the sense of words used in context (Cacciari & Glucksberg, 1994). When words are used in novel ways, we do not look for the new meaning in the mental lexicon because it has not been constructed yet, and the sense of the topic has to be extended to the new context. Metaphors are one of the most powerful sources of creating new meanings and sense, both on the spot and over time. Recently, dictionaries have been updated to indicate that *butcher* has the sense of "clumsy, awkward, unskillful." But new meanings like these do not occur randomly; they are motivated by the nature of our cognitive structures. Ullmann (1962) proposed that metaphors follow four patterns:

1. *Anthropomorphization,* using part of the human body to make a reference to other objects—for example, *the heart of the matter*

2. Using concrete and experiential words to make references to the abstract— for example, *shed some light on; had bitter feelings about*

3. Using animals—for example, *monkey around with*

4. *Synesthesia,* using one sense to describe another sense—for example, *her voice sounded so sweet*

The innovative use of metaphors made up on the spot require listeners to go beyond the literal lexical meanings involved and create a new sense or a new combination of meanings, based on world knowledge, discourse principles, and contextual information (Cacciari & Glucksberg, 1994). For example, *Send him home with a couple of uniforms* has a different contextual interpretation than the one about clothing. If the context makes you realize the man has just been involved in a barroom brawl, you might understand that the speaker intended the phrase to mean "Send him home with a couple of uniformed officers" (after Gerrig, 1989). The point of this line of reasoning, according to Glucksberg and colleagues (Cacciari & Glucksberg, 1994; Glucksberg & Keysar, 1990; Glucksberg, Keysar, & McGlone, 1992), is that the moment-to-moment process of creating meaning and the interpretation of words whether literal or figurative always involves a mixture of sense selection and sense creation. This view of figurative speech has had considerable appeal (see H. H. Clark, 1983; Clark & Gerrig, 1983; Gerrig, 1989; Gerrig & Murphy, 1992).

In the *butcher* examples, we understand that the metaphors convey connotative information about how poorly the surgeon and the copyeditor do their work. The speaker's attitude toward the person is implied. We take up the issue of affective readings of metaphors next as we look at metaphors for love.

LOVE AND LUST METAPHORS

The concept of "love" is exceedingly complex and therefore ripe for the use of metaphor (Kövecses, 1988). Certainly playwrights and poets throughout history have created many metaphors to express love. Researchers who have compiled lists of love metaphors find that they reflect the culture's model of love (Jay, 2000; Kövecses, 1988; Lakoff & Johnson, 1980). The words used to describe male and female relationships are based on cultural models of appropriate and inappropriate gender-related behaviors like sexual looseness or attractiveness (see Holland & Quinn, 1987; Jay, 2000). These kinds of gender-related terms (e.g., *bitch, wolf, hunk, honey, knockout*) come from constructs that also define romantic love and sexual desire. Romantic metaphors are based on the conceptual metaphors like these:

LOVE IS A JOURNEY:
We are going together.
Look how far we've come.
We had to go our separate ways.
We can't turn back now.
This relationship isn't going anywhere.

LOVE IS A GROWING PLANT:
Their love blossomed.
Our relationship withered.
Love is in blooming.

THE SEAT OF LOVE IS THE HEART:
I gave her my heart.
She broke my heart.
He won my heart.
She is my sweetheart.

Although language scholars have studied romantic love by looking at metaphors, less attention has been paid to metaphors that involve sexual desire or lust as an aspect of love (Jay, 2000). How do metaphors represent sexual desire? The use of figurative language to describe sexual desire has a long history. But because sex is a taboo topic, academic analyses of sexual metaphors have been sparse. What data we have about sexual metaphors (Jay, 1991, 2000) show that as with romantic metaphors, sexual metaphors are not literally true, but there is a cultural basis for them. Pragmatically speaking, sex metaphors allow us to talk about sexual desire without literally talking about sex. For example, figurative sexual language has been used in African American folk blues lyrics to disguise the singer's sexual desire (Titon, 1994). Sex references to animals, machines, automobiles, and magic are common. When bluesman Slim Harpo sings, "*I'm a king bee buzzin' around your hive,*" he is not singing about apiculture. The song is about sexual desire, and the sexual imagery becomes obvious in the context of the entire song. Sexual metaphors like this present attitudes about sexual relationships that are culturally based.

Lakoff and Johnson (1980) suggested that metaphors are based on simple cultural models of the world like GOOD IS UP and BAD IS DOWN. How does this apply to love metaphors? Well, because of our puritanical roots in America, we have construed romantic love to be lofty and ideal and have construed sexuality to be low and evil. Sexual metaphors conform to these general cultural models. "Good" love would be represented by a metaphor LOVE IS A DEITY, as in *He put her on a pedestal* or *I worship the ground you walk on.* Negative attitudes about sexual desire are represented by *She is a fallen angel, He soiled her reputation,* or *He's a lowdown dirty dog.* One widely used metaphor is that THE SEAT OF ROMANCE IS THE HEART. References to different parts of the body are used for sexual desire, for example, *sins of the flesh, burning in my loins,* or *piece of ass.* Because our culture construes different kinds of love, speakers produce metaphors that express these views. We should have separate metaphors to express sexual desire (lust), affection, and romantic love, if these are culturally experienced as different attitudes. Here are some samples (Jay, 2000):

Lust: *You have hot pants. They were bedbunnies. He has good buns.*

Love: *You are my heartthrob. I worship the ground you walk on. You have my heart.*

Affection: *You are my kitten. You are my peachy pie.*

Research supports the view that we use love metaphors and lust metaphors for different purposes. Readers can readily sort a list of love metaphors into lust, affection, or love categories with a great deal of intersubject agreement (Jay, 1991; Jay & Richard, 1995). As expected, the semantics of each category were different.

Lust—references to heat, beds, meat, wild animals, sex, games, and cheapness

Affection—references to domestic animals, closeness, plants, fruit, and sweet deserts

Love—references to heart, unity, and deity

One application of metaphor judgments to the real world of adult sexuality is to the problem of sexual harassment. Jay and Richard (1995) assumed that the metaphors would be positively arousing between partners in a mutual relationship, but that the sexual component in the lust metaphors was inappropriate in employer and employee talk in a workplace setting. We asked men and women to rate how offensive the metaphors were and how likely they were to constitute sexual harassment if used at work. The differential impact of these categories was clear. The lust metaphors were significantly more offensive and more harassing than love or affection metaphors, and not unexpectedly, women found them significantly more offensive and more harassing than men did (Jay, 2000). This was the kind of validation we needed to demonstrate the comprehension of different forms of figurative reference to love. Figurative statements about relationships carry a salient cultural and emotional message about the nature of intimacy, whether it is pointedly sexual or romantic. Verbal sexual harassment research has rarely included figurative statements about sexual desire, as if they do not exist. We will return to the use of emotion metaphors in Chapter 13, where we consider their use in therapeutic contexts.

Metaphorical expressions are very common in speech and text. They serve the purpose of relating something that is difficult or abstract to something that is more concrete or imaginable. Besides encapsulating the overall meaning of something in more concrete terms, they also help us describe and convey our feelings and attitudes about people and situations. Next we consider how we can understand the overall meaning of something by reference to one aspect of the situation.

Review Questions
Could you determine how a couple related to each other on the basis of the love metaphors they use? Why?

Metonymy

Metonymy is the tactic of using a familiar or easily perceived aspect of an object or situation to stand for the thing as a whole (Lakoff & Johnson, 1980). One hears metonymic references in the news—for example, *The Kremlin denied accusations of arms dealing* or *Wall Street reacted favorably to the interest rate cut*. In these two examples, a place is used to stand for an institution located at that place. Our conceptual system is full of metonymic models of various types:

Object used for user: *The taxis are on strike.*

Place used for the event: *Watergate changed American politics.*

Controller used for the controlled: *Bush bombed Iraq.*

The ability to conceptualize objects and events in metonymic terms provides a basis for making inferences. For example, if Mary asks John, *How did you get to the airport?* and John replies *I stuck out my thumb,* John means to inform her that he hitchhiked. Mary's successful interpretation of John's answer requires her to make an inference about what he meant. John might have also answered the question with, *I drove the car, I called my neighbor,* or *I rode the bus.* In each case, a subpart of a travel script stands for the whole script. Mary understood that John wanted her to comprehend the entire travel script when he mentioned the subpart, *stuck out my thumb.*

Frisson and Pickering (1999) used eye-tracking methodology to investigate the time course of processing of metonymic expressions, comparing them to literal expressions. Again the question of interest is whether literal and figurative meanings are activated at the same time. In one study, they examined place-for-institution metonymies such as *the convent* in *That blasphemous woman had to answer to the convent.* Eye movement times for metonymies were similar to those for sentences with literal interpretations, indicating that the figurative reading was readily available with the literal. A second study produced similar results using place-for-event sentences such as *A lot of Americans protested during Vietnam.* In this experiment, a similar pattern of results was obtained regarding the availability of the figurative meanings. Frisson and Pickering suggested that the results support an account of processing in which both literal and figurative senses are accessed immediately, rather than a model where literal or figurative sense is accessed first.

Gernsbacher (1991b) provided evidence that people reason metonymically when understanding discourse. They interpret syntactically anomalous references in a manner that produces a coherent figurative reading of them. Consider these pairs:

I need to call the garage. *They* said they'd have my car ready by five o'clock.

I think I'll order a frozen margarita. I just love *them.*

In each case, a plural pronoun is used following a singular noun antecedent, violating the prescription that pronoun and antecedent must agree. Gernsbacher demonstrated that people rate these conceptual anaphors as more natural and read them faster than they do sentences with grammatically correct pronouns. Comprehending conceptual metaphors relies on singular entities mentioned (e.g., *the garage*) to stand for a conceptual set (e.g., the garage employees). Our ability to think metonymically allows us to understand easily and quickly these "illegal" plural pronouns. The listener must activate the appropriate antecedent information about the referent and link it to the anaphor. More recently, Gernsbacher and Robertson (1999) have demonstrated the importance of suppression in figurative language comprehension. Making the appropriate figurative or metonymic inferences also means *not* activating extraneous, unnecessary, or inappropriate information in metaphors and idioms.

Conventional metonymic expression such as *Wall Street reacted favorably* . . . may appear to us as literal statements rather than figurative expressions because they are so common. However, less conventional expressions, such as *The ham on rye is getting impatient for his check,* make little sense when taken out of context (in this case, on the lips of one waitress speaking to another in a diner). With these kinds of **contextual expressions** (Gerrig, 1986), the meaning of the words and phrases depend on the context. Gibbs (1990b) demonstrated that readers could determine the appropriate referents for metonymic expressions in discourse. He showed that readers recognized that *tuxedo* in *John fired the tuxedo because he kept dropping the tray* referred to a butler, despite its literal incongruity in the sentence. In these cases, people must create a new sense to supplement or extend the ordinary sense of words in the metonymies.

Context facilitates sense creation in novel metonymies, but common ground— the participants' shared beliefs, knowledge, and attitudes—is also critical (Clark & Gerrig, 1983). In other words, a metonymic reference makes sense if it is part of the shared knowledge between speaker and listener. For example, *While I was taking his picture, Steve did a Napoleon for the camera* requires shared knowledge of the famous painting of Napoleon with his hand in his vest. The expression is understood if the knowledge of Napoleon's portrait is common ground. An expression like *I met a girl at the coffeehouse who did an Elizabeth Taylor while I was talking to her* is difficult to understand. The listener does not know which bit of information about Elizabeth Taylor is the common ground, making it difficult to understand what *did an Elizabeth Taylor* meant. These studies of metonymic expressions substantiate the importance of common ground information in our understanding of them.

In the opening section of this chapter, I tried to show how and why metaphors appear in speech. This research emphasizes how we comprehend figurative speech, and several processing models have emerged. One issue is whether literal and non-literal meanings are both activated during the comprehension process. It seems clear that during comprehension, both figurative and literal information is available, but which reading is given priority is a matter of current dispute. Figurative language has the effect (or the goal) of making the abstract more concrete. Figurative language also provides emotional information about the speaker and his or her attitudes. We will see this emotional aspect as we continue to look at different forms of figurative speech.

Figurative Language in Discourse

The common theme in this section on discourse is that the meaning of figurative statements involves two or more layers of conversation; one is literal, and the others are pretense (H. H. Clark, 1996). In Chapter 8, the concept of layering was introduced. If you will recall, I presented an example from Clark where two children were pretending to be living in the gold rush days in the Dakota Territory. The conversation that unfolded existed at two layers or domains, one in the present day and the other in the gold rush era. Layering is essential to understanding figurative uses of speech, according to Clark. In case of sarcasm, irony, or metaphor, for example, there is always more than one conversational layer. One layer can be viewed as literal or serious, and the second layer is figurative. The second layer may be humorous, imaginary, or insulting relative to the first layer. Figurative speech relies on the coexistence of meanings, that is, the incongruity of meaning in two layers. Speakers and listeners use the shared background knowledge in the conversation and knowledge of the how figurative meaning works to derive figurative meaning. Conversants recognize the coexistence of at least two layers of joint activity to produce the figurative, which requires some pretense.

JOINT PRETENSE

Joint pretense means that when the speaker and the listener participate in a figurative layer, they are both aware that they are acting in a different domain. They also both realize that literal and figurative domains coexist. Consider the layering that goes on in psychotherapy as people describe the internal and external worlds in a therapeutic dialogue. Consider a couple who have an abusive relationship at home. How can this turmoil be understood and conveyed in therapy? In one session, the counselor may have the couple role-play or act out problems with hand puppets. What happens when they use puppets to role-play problems in the marriage for the therapist? We hear the couple speaking about their problems through the puppets as characters in puppet voices.

HER PUPPET: You're clamming up again! I hate it when you do that.

HIS PUPPET: You just pissed me off again. Why should I talk to you? It doesn't really matter.

The conflicts and problems portrayed by the puppets are derived from the couple's communication problems in everyday life, where they live out their real problems. A third layer involves the therapeutic setting in the therapist's office where the couple are neither at home nor in the puppet domain. The layering idea is appropriate for describing how patients narrate and describe what is happening in their everyday lives.

Layer	Domain	Relationship	Social Setting	Dialogue
1	home	partners	intimate	fighting, arguing
2	counseling	clients	therapy	reporting, telling
3	imagined	puppets	roles	portraying

In figurative situations, joint pretense relies on the processes of imagination and appreciation. The participants have to imagine a domain of conversation other than a serious one. Through joint pretense comes the emotional work of producing a sense of humor, anger, or suspense. In the example, participants must appreciate what they are doing on three levels. One layer is where the puppets are talking, one is a couple describing everyday life in therapy, and the third layer is the relationship of the partners at home. The husband and wife can pretend to live in a puppet world with one puppet saying, "*You're clamming up again.*" They are showing the counselor that they have communication problems through the puppet dialogue, but this is not exactly what happened at home; it is a *representation* of it. Maybe the husband does not express his anger at home or in the therapist's office the way he did with the puppet.

We will see that sarcasm, irony, teasing, and other forms of figurative speech all require joint pretense and layering, according to H. H. Clark (1996). For example, figurative statements have both serious and figurative meanings, depending on what layer is observed. The literal and its alternative exist in different domains. At the core of figurative speech, like irony, is the fact that the imagined layer is incongruous with what is happening in the serious layer. We also use layering to tease people, to kid them. You might have had a conversation that went like this:

KAY: How do I look?

TOM: You look, hmm, plain, sorta plain.

KAY: What do you mean, "plain"?

TOM: Plain, like Amish plain.

KAY: (*staring*)

TOM: I was just kidding.

KAY: (*shaking her head*)

Tom tells Kay that she looks "plain" in an attempt to be honest or even to pay Kay a compliment. However, Kay does not take it as a compliment. When Tom realizes that he has offended her, he suggests that the previous comment was pretense, a tease. Was it really pretense, or did Tom just say that after she showed offense? People do kid each other from time to time. The "just kidding" reply marks the existence of a nonserious layer (Kowalski, 2000). Similarly, the appreciation and imagination processes involved in layering are similar to what is needed in narratives, stories, jokes, and folk tales discussed in Chapter 8. Note that the device used to open a story for a child, *Once upon a time . . .* , takes the listener to an imaginary layer, a new domain with different settings, speakers, and plots. The dialogue between Tom and Kay shows that different kinds of emotional and social goals exist across layers of conversation. We can also see this kind of social and emotional work when we look at how people ask each other for help.

INDIRECT REQUESTS

Speech act theory was introduced in Chapter 8 as a means of describing conversational structure. Our analysis there indicated that conversation can be understood as an attempt to achieve a speaker's intentions. The overall evaluation of speech act theory was deemed insufficient to account for all types of dialogue because the speaker's intentions were not measured against the listener's understanding of them. Speech acts are better understood as joint activities in which people work toward a particular goal (H. H. Clark, 1996). A direct speech act involving a declaration such as *I appoint you our new vice president* depends on the speaker's authority and the listener's compliance. Even a direct simple request such as *Please tell me the time* works only if both speaker and listener cooperate.

Metonymic reasoning can be used when speakers make requests of others. The speaker has to provide enough information to enable the addressee to recognize what has to be done. The project should be accomplished without making the addressee feel imposed on. When Americans make requests, we tend to employ indirect speech (for example, *Can you pass me the salt?*) because it seems more polite than direct speech (for example, *Give me the salt*). **Indirect requests** are not literally meant to do what is expressed on the surface layer. The intended meaning of an indirect request does not correspond to the literal meaning, so another layer of understanding is required to derive the intended figurative meaning. A good deal of research on indirect speech has focused on indirect requests (H. H. Clark, 1996; Clark & Clark, 1977; Gibbs, 1986c, 1994).

For the request to work, the listener has to understand that the literal meaning of the request is not what is intended and must comply with the indirect meaning. Answering literally *Sure I can!* to *Can you pass the salt?* would be rude (or humorous) and uncooperative. Searle (1975a) used the term *felicity conditions* to describe the listener's cooperation here. Felicity conditions are the prerequisites that the listener must meet in order to comply. The listener must have the ability to comply, the desire to comply (immediately or in the future), and a good reason to comply. If one of these felicity conditions is not present, the indirect request will not be honored. Various sorts of indirect requests are commonly employed:

Ability: *Can you drive me to the airport? Will you be able to lend us a hand?*

Wish or need: *I would like you to help us out. We need your help.*

Possession: *Do you have change for a dollar?*

Permission: *May I see your lecture notes for a minute?*

Willingness: *Would you mind helping us out?*

Stating a relevant fact: *I have twenty boxes to move.*

Asking a favor: *How about helping us set up the buffet?*

Reason: *You really should pitch in, you know.*

Personality or character: *Can we count on you? You're always so helpful!*

Joint projects use both conceptual and pragmatic information in the production and understanding of indirect requests. Gibbs (1986c) proposed that speakers design their requests to specify the greatest obstacle to compliance for the listener. In mentioning the real or apparent obstacles, the speaker assumes that the listener can metonymically infer the entire sequence of events necessary for compliance. Gibbs demonstrated that when participants read stories where the addressee possessed an object that was desired by the speaker, 68 percent of the time they generated possession utterances—for example, *Do you have change for a dollar?* Possession requests occur when the addressee has something the speaker wants. In comparison, possession requests occurred in only 6 percent of the cases where the obstacle was the addressee's ability. Ability requests, as noted, are framed in terms such as *Can you . . .* or *Are you able to . . .* Possession utterances were never generated when the addressee was unaware of any need for action. People made permission utterances—*May I see your lecture notes for a minute?*—in permission contexts. Permission contexts involve asking the addressee for permission to do or say something. Permission utterances were used only 10 percent of the time in possession contexts, since most of these requests are going to come in the form of possession requests. Gibbs believes that speakers are sensitive to obstacles in situations and couch their indirect requests in those terms. His research demonstrates how metonymic reasoning influences the pragmatics underlying indirect requests.

Since requests come in positive (*Can you . . . ?*) and negative (*Why not . . . ?*) forms, we might wonder which is easier to process. Clark and Lucy (1975) studied the time it takes to process negative and positive requests, comparing three different types. One type takes a positive literal and positive indirect form: *Can you open the door?* Another type has a positive literal but negative indirect form: *Must you open the door?* The third type has a negative literal form but a positive indirect form: *Why not open the door?* Comparing reaction times across the three forms, results indicated that the easiest (quickest) type to compute was the first type, the one with both positive literal and figurative forms. The longest to compute was the second type, with a positive literal form but a negative indirect form. We seem to be more prepared to process positive indirect requests than negative ones.

Although early models of indirect request comprehension supported the idea that both direct and indirect versions are accessed during comprehension (Clark & Lucy, 1975), Gibbs's (1979) view is that a literal interpretation of an indirect request is accessed only when there is insufficient information in the context to formulate the indirect meaning. Generally speaking, conventional indirect requests—for example, *Do you know the time?*—are understood as indirect requests without accessing the intervening direct interpretation. This finding is in line with other research on figurative speech; that is, it is immediately understood without being translated from a literal reading first (Shinjo & Myers, 1987; Sperber & Wilson, 1981).

One interesting addition to the traditional line of research on indirect requests focused on the role of **gestures** in indirect request processing. Kelly, Barr, Church, and Lynch (1999) noted that most theories of pragmatics look at the verbal content of indirect requests and ignore information about the utterance that may be conveyed nonverbally. They found that people were more likely to interpret an utterance as an indirect request when the speech was accompanied by a relevant pointing gesture compared to speech or gesture alone. They believed that gestures and speech help disambiguate meanings. This kind of research supports the idea that psycholinguists need to take a more comprehensive look at verbal and nonverbal information used in pragmatic understanding. I would add that the social and emotional information in the speech context also plays an important role in figurative speech comprehension. The incongruity between the two layers of literal and figurative meaning creates the emotional or connotative meaning of the statement. The degree of discrepancy is a means of showing us the speaker's attitude about the subject. Emotionality is a critical element of indirect requests, as we shall see when we consider our need to maintain a sense of politeness.

POLITENESS

One popular way to understand the function of indirect speech is through Brown and Levinson's (1987) theory of politeness, which was based on Goffman's (1967) influential writings on *face* and *face-work* (also see Holtgraves, 1998). Goffman described face as the public display of one's identity. Face-work describes the communication in almost every interaction that is used to create, support, or challenge face. Through face-work, people can show respect or cooperation, reaffirm a relationship, or insult and challenge each other. Brown and Levinson (1987) divided face into two forms of desire: **negative face,** the desire to be free and autonomous, and **positive face,** the desire to be connected with others. Requests for assistance threaten the addressee's negative face because they impose on the need for autonomy. Insults and disagreements threaten positive face for both speaker and addressee. Social interactions constantly present dilemmas for participants who need to work together to accomplish goals and at the same time not threaten each other's face.

One solution to social dilemmas is to make a request of another person without threatening his or her face. Indirect requests—for example, *It's a bit drafty in here*—are especially effective because they are less imposing than imperatives, such as *Close the door.* The operative factor is to make a request so as to redress negative face. The speaker can do this by using negative politeness to address the listener's ability or willingness to fulfill the request—for example, *Can you shut the door?* or *Would you shut the door?* Research indicates that the perceived politeness of negatively polite requests varies with the implied effort for the addressee (Clark & Schunk, 1980, 1981). Requests show how politeness can be maintained by violating Grice's cooperative principle by making the request indirectly. Face can also be maintained without indirectness by using a prerequest such as *Are you busy?* that raises the addressee's potential inability to comply with the request (S. Levinson, 1983). If the addressee is not able to comply with the prerequest, the speaker manages face by not making the real request.

Interpersonal variables are also important in politeness. People are more polite to those who have more power (Brown & Gilman, 1989; Holtgraves & Yang, 1990, 1992). The social relationship or closeness between participants has brought mixed results in research on politeness. There appears to be a positive correlation between politeness and liking but a negative one between familiarity and politeness (Brown & Gilman, 1989; Slugoski & Turnbull, 1988). The fact that you know someone does not directly lead to politeness. So making indirect requests conveys the speaker's concern for the face of the addressee and also implicates varying degrees of status and interpersonal relationship between the two parties.

Review Question
Differentiate between direct and indirect requests and indicate how listeners comprehend them.

IRONY AND SARCASM

Irony has traditionally been interpreted as the use of figurative speech to produce the "opposite" of its literal meaning—for example, saying *This is a tough life* when you are basking in the sun on your vacation. One problem with this definition is that in many cases of irony, the opposite of a literal meaning is unclear. It might be better to look at irony as another form of figurative language, where one thing is stated but something else is intended. Irony can appear as *ironic criticism,* where a positive literal statement is understood negatively. Another view of irony is that it is like storytelling because it relies on joint pretense (Clark & Gerrig, 1984). The speaker and listener understand that what is spoken literally has a different meaning on a second figurative level. When a mother says *I love children who keep their rooms clean,* she is pretending to be an invisible mother who really believes that children really keep their bedrooms tidy all the time. Her children, if they understand irony, should recognize her comment as pretense, understanding that she is speaking ironically and expressing a derogatory attitude.

Another view is that irony requires the listener to substitute a new meaning for the literal meaning (Dews et al., 1996). Like other forms of figurative language, ironic utterances can be tested for how literal and figurative meanings are activated. Dews and Winner (1999; see also Schwoebel, Dews, Winner & Srinivas, 2000) tested the hypothesis that some portion of the literal meaning of an ironic expression is activated with the intended meaning. They found that it took subjects longer to judge the positive or negative tone of expressions used ironically than when used literally, supporting the idea that the literal meaning of the ironic expression was activated and it interfered with the figurative meaning judgment. In a second experiment, subjects took longer to judge the tone of the literal meaning of expressions used ironically, supporting the idea that that figurative meaning of the ironic expressions was activated and it interfered with the literal meaning judgment. These experiments support the multiple-meaning approach to irony processing, which holds that both literal and figurative meanings are processed (Dews & Winner, 1997). They are also consistent with the idea that the literal meaning of the expression mutes the evaluative tone of the intended figurative meaning.

But the expression of an ironic view of a situation does not necessarily have to be constructed figuratively in language. The speaker may say what is meant in a literal fashion that produces an ironic reading (Sperber & Wilson, 1981). If someone runs a red light ahead of my car and I respond by saying *I love people who obey traffic laws,* I produce a sarcastic reading of the situation in the mind of the listener even though the statement reflected my true literal attitude.

Sarcasm operates very much like irony, but with more emotional punch. *Sarcasm* refers to a satirical or ironic utterance that is intended to convey a negative attitude, insult, or offend (Haiman, 1998). The point of sarcasm goes beyond the ironic; it is to produce a negative feeling or attitude. Consider a father's response to his child in the following:

CHILD: (*spilling milk on the kitchen floor*) Oops!

FATHER: That was very nice.

The father's response is both ironic and sarcastic. The father meant to convey his disapproval for what the child has done. The sarcasm will work as a rebuke here only if the child understands the figurative meaning of the father's statement. He may mark the sarcasm directly by emphasizing the word *nice,* prolonging its pronunciation, or making incongruous facial gestures such as grimacing or wincing.

Often sarcasm produces negative tone or even contempt through the incongruity between what is said and what is felt. This might be more obvious between two adults:

JOE: (*home from a golf outing*) Boy, did I have a rough day.

SALLY: (*mockingly*) Po-oo-or baby.

The sarcastic tone is enhanced and intensified by the way *poor baby* is enunciated. A mocking, false sympathetic tone will make it more sarcastic. What is said and how it is said produce an affective tone entirely the opposite of what is literally present in the surface layer. Again, for sarcasm to work, the participants must appreciate both levels of conversation.

In forms of sarcastic irony, the listener must substitute the speaker's implied or true beliefs for those professed. Let's consider the ironic meaning of the following exchange between two disgruntled office workers:

MARY: Tomorrow is our manager's birthday.

JOAN: Why, I think I'll bake her a great big cake.

If we assume that Mary and Joan do not like their manager, we can see the exchange operating on two levels. One is a serious, literal level, where what is said is true. On the second level, they make it clear that they do not like the manager and that Joan would never bake a cake for her birthday. The irony relies on their shared knowledge about work and their dislike of the boss. What appears to be positive on the surface is the opposite of what is intended. Neither of them likes the manager nor would ever celebrate her birthday. The meaning of the irony depends on the intimacy and shared knowledge between Joan and Mary. Irony produces information about the speaker's emotions, attitudes, and feelings. The nonverbal and prosodic elements reinforce the incongruity between the literal and the ironic. It is in the incongruity between what is stated and what is known that irony works. What is stated literally can exaggerate the opposite of what is felt emotionally. For example, eavesdroppers will not easily sense the irony if they do not know how Joan and Mary feel about their boss. What is stated is actually false in relation to their feelings about the manager. By making a statement of support that they both know is false, they reveal their true feelings and attitudes about the work environment.

Another way to mark the irony is through **echoic mention,** which occurs when a listener repeats a word or phrase from the ironic statement to emphasize its incongruity. This could be done in the example above if Mary were to echo at some point later in their conversation *Don't forget, it must be a really big cake.* Echoic mention theory (Jorgensen, Miller, & Sperber, 1984; Sperber & Wilson, 1981) states that ironic expressions are about speakers' attitudes. The goal of irony is achieved when the listener is reminded (through echoic mention) about the speaker's real attitude about a situation. Mentioning the cake reactivates Mary's and Joan's attitudes about their boss. Research on echoic mention has revealed that people rate explicit ironic mentions as more ironic than expressions that were not echoed explicitly (Gibbs, 1986b; Jorgensen et al., 1984). In other words, a comment about the cake will be perceived as more ironic if there has been a prior comment about the cake in relation to the boss's birthday. Research on sarcasm indicates that people comprehend sarcasm in explicit echoes faster than they comprehend expressions based on less explicit echoes or no echoes (Gibbs, 1986b).

An echo need not refer anyone's expression, attitude, or opinions to be ironic (Kreuz & Glucksberg, 1989). When I say to a colleague *What a nice day* in the middle of a snowstorm, my comment will be received as sarcastic irony. The expression reminds us of our expectations for good weather and expresses my negative feelings about the storm. Positive statements do not require explicit prior mention because they allude to social norms and expectations. For example, when someone says *What a nice friend you are* to someone who did something unfriendly, the comment is judged more sarcastic than a negative statement like *You are a terrible friend* (Kreuz & Glucksberg, 1989). However, negative expressions such as *You are a terrible friend* when someone has been friendly do not implicitly allude to positive social norms. This kind of negative expression would require an explicit antecedent to be understood easily. Irony through echoic mention is a reminder to a prior situation or a conventional state of affairs.

Gibbs (2000) examined irony in talk among friends during ten-minute conversations. He found five kinds of irony that accounted for 8 percent of all conversational turns: jocularity, sarcasm, hyperbole, rhetorical questions, and understatements. Kreuz, Kassler, Coppenrath, and Allen (1999) found that verbal irony is used with friends as well as strangers, including tag questions like, *You think you're really something, don't you?* They studied the role of shared common ground and tag questions in the perception of irony and found that the common ground and tag manipulations did not affect the degree of perceived irony, however, common ground did influence the perception of the appropriateness of the ironic expressions. We have seen how people comprehend irony, leading us to wonder how people react emotionally to irony and sarcasm.

REACTIONS TO IRONY

Imagine how you would react to finding a long line at the theater when you expected a short line. How would you react verbally to your friends? Colston and O'Brien (2000) noted that irony (*Oh, fantastic, there's no line at all*) and understatement (*There seems to be a bit of a line*) perform similar pragmatic functions since they both make use of a potential contrast between expected and experienced events. Both refer to an expected event, no line or a short line at the theater. This contrast will make irony and understatement funnier, more critical, and more expressive of the difference between expected and found events than literal remarks like *This line is very long.* Colston and O'Brien found that irony made a stronger contrast than understatement did. Irony is better at being funny, critical, and expressive of a difference than understatement. Understatement is more protective of the speaker than irony is. Generally speaking, this study shows that irony operates better pragmatically than understatement does at achieving emotional and social goals.

In a related study, Leggitt and Gibbs (2000) examined people's emotional reactions to ironic and nonironic expressions. In a series of experiments, subjects rated their own reactions, the emotional state of the speaker, and how they thought the speaker wanted them to feel. The kind of statement affected addressees' emotions, especially when it involved irony, rhetorical questions, understatement, and nonironic statements. Sarcasm and satire may reveal the speaker's own emotions while paying little attention to addressees' emotions. This study argues that theories of figurative language comprehension need to address how figurative language affects speakers and listeners at a social and emotional level. Many cases of sarcasm and irony are marked by nonverbal information such as rolling eyes, winking, a mocking intonation, or emphasis on one of the incongruous words in the literal statement. In the Mary-Joan example, stressing *a great big cake* would do this. There is some evidence that the use of nonverbal cues (e.g., sneers or rolling eyeballs) to emphasize irony and sarcasm is common, if not universal (Haiman, 1998). All languages have available paralinguistic cues like exaggeration and prolongation to mark that the figurative is intended. Japanese, German, English, Russian, Greek, and Tagalog mark sarcasm with the use of simple prolongation (Adachi, 1996; Haiman, 1998; Jonsson, 1995). Other studies indicate that irony does not necessarily require special intonation to be effective (Gibbs, 1986a, 1986b).

Irony does not require special cognitive processing to be understood because figurative modes of thought are commonplace, according to Gibbs (1994). In fact, people can give an ironic reading to statements that were not intended to be ironic. If a student tells the professor about a crush on the professor and sometime later, when they are discussing the writings of Freud, the professor says *Tell me what you find about breaking taboos,* the student may understand the professor's comment ironically even if the literal was intended. Following the ironic reading of the comment about taboos, the student may experience positive (humor) or negative (insult) emotions about the situation. The professor may not realize that the comment was ironic even though knowledge of the student's crush is part of their common ground.

Lee and Katz (1997) conducted research to explore the relationships among ridicule, irony, and sarcasm. In two different experiments, subjects had to read a series of passages. One group had to rate a target expression in terms of the extent to which it represented a good example of sarcasm. The second group rated the expression in terms of the extent to which it represented a good example of irony. A manipulation involving ridicule was found to affect subjects' rating of sarcasm but not their ratings of irony. Lee and Katz found that ratings of the degree to which a victim was ridiculed were correlated with sarcasm to a greater degree than with irony. These results support the idea that sarcasm and irony differ on the degree to which they ridicule a victim. In a related study, Gerrig and Goldvarg (2000) had subjects read stories that varied in situational disparity (what is expected to happen versus what really happens) or by virtue of the characters' emotional involvement in the situation. They found that the perception of sarcasm increases with the size of situational disparity between the speakers' beliefs, desires, or expectations and the actual outcomes in the stories.

Irony calls attention to the incongruity between the two conversational layers. This serves two functions emotionally. First, irony has a **muting function** whereby the ironic criticism is attenuated by the literal praise. In this case, the ironic expression will come off as less critical than a direct attack. Second, irony has a **humor function** whereby the incongruity produces a humorous response that mutes the upset that may be generated by a literal statement (Dews et al., 1996). The ironic mutes the negative attitude by causing laughter. The use of irony is a way for the speaker to express strong negative feelings or attitudes without mentioning them literally. There are other forms of figurative language that express negative attitudes in terms that produce an offensive reaction rather than laughter.

DIRTY WORDS, NAME-CALLING, AND INSULTS

Figurative language employing taboo words is primarily for the purpose of providing emotional information about a situation or person (Jay, 1996, 2000). These emotional uses of words are not simple acts of blowing off some steam (to use the *anger* metaphor). They are highly conventionalized and culturally determined, like other forms of figurative language (Jay, 1992a, 2000; Leach, 1966). *Insults* are direct verbal attacks, and as such, they threaten the face of both the speaker and the addressee. Insults and **name-calling** can also take a form of metonymic reference (e.g., *piece of ass*). Here are some examples of figurative uses of dirty words (Jay, 1992a):

Now you're gonna smell like a shithouse when you get home.

She looks like a horse's ass.

He did a half-ass job.

You bet your ass.

He's going to get his ass kicked.

Typical pain in the ass.

You are such a lying sack of shit.

Kiss my ass.

I've got a shitload of work to do.

The way we talk about taboo words belies conceptual metaphors that GOOD IS CLEAN or GOOD IS UP. Hence we can refer to taboo language as *dirty, filthy, toilet language, bathroom language, gutter talk, smut, foul language,* and *scatological.* The scatological is evidenced by references to *shit* and *ass* in the examples. As you can imagine, the use of references to the body in insults is different from their use in love and affection metaphors. The cultural taboos on the body and body products are the source of figurative expressions that make reference to the taboos. References to the genitalia can be particularly insulting. These kinds of figurative references to taboos are common and are influenced by social factors such as context and gender norms (Jay, 1992a, 2000). Taboo words like *ass*, *shit*, and *fuck* have multiple connotative and literal meanings, but men and women use them differently in public. Females use the word *ass* to connote a social deviation or a body part; but males use *ass* mainly to refer to a body part, as in *She has a nice ass*, and not to note deviation from a norm (e.g., *dumbass* or *silly ass*). Men also use other body part words this way; using *cock*, *cunt*, and *dick* to refer to body parts more so than to connote social deviations. Women make these kinds of metonymic references to body parts, but in general they are less likely to use taboo words to express emotions in public (Jay, 1992b).

A good example of figurative connotation is what we hear in insulting and name-calling episodes. Consider one type of insult, the use of animal names to refer to people. All cultures have folklore, superstitions, and taboos regarding animals and animal names. We can see these clearly through cultural and religious dietary practices and religious customs involving animals. The use of animal names as insults must fit the culture's representation of the animal's traits, behaviors, and characteristics. What is insulting or taboo depends on how the culture defines the animal in question; it is not necessarily intrinsic to the animal. We have to be familiar with the culture's view of the animal in order to know its positive and negative qualities. Barnyard animals and pets are a good source of animal name insults because we know a lot about them (e.g., *cock*, *cow*, *swine*, or *ass*). Children learn these animal name insults early in the acquisition of vocabulary, and elderly Americans retain the use of them even in the midst of dementia (Jay, 1992a, 1996, 2000).

I used several examples of animal name insults earlier in the chapter. *Pig* is a good example of an insulting name because we think of pigs as fat, dirty, and lazy. In fact, it is difficult to think of anything associated with the word *pig* that is not insulting. When we call someone a *pig*, we evoke these negative features in the name and attribute them to the person. We do not call people *marmots* or *toucans* because our culture has not marked them conceptually or figuratively as possessing positive or negative characteristics. Name-calling and insulting is not limited to sexual, scatological, and animal semantics. The considerable lexicon of figurative insulting language includes the semantics of mental health, social deviance, ethnic origin, age, religion, disease, body parts, body products, body processes, and social economic status (see Jay, 2000).

TEASING AND PUT-ONS

Teasing operates much like name-calling, irony, and sarcasm in the sense that they all produce emotional information and attitudes about something. A tease is a playful provocation in which one person comments on something relevant to the victim. Teasing has an element of humor that masks the underlying negative attitude. Imagine a couple in a restaurant:

BUD: I think this place is kind of expensive. Well, I'll order a salad or something.

HILDA: (*in a mocking tone*) Waitress, can we look at the children's menu?

Teasing allows a speaker to imply something offensive or negative without explicitly saying it. The tease also produces a humorous reaction, which helps mute the criticism. Hilda is telling Bud that he is cheap, that he's there to have a real meal but he's too cheap to pay what it costs. A tease is a *reaction* to something that has happened or was said. Going to a figurative layer allows the infraction to be addressed indirectly. Teasing and sarcasm work only when both parties are privy to multiple layers of meaning. A teasing remark is made because it will be understood figuratively and because it is less harsh than an insult—for example, Hilda could have said *You sure are a cheap bastard!*

BUD: I can't find my screwdriver. Have you seen it?

HILDA: (*in a childish voice*) Mommy, Billy hid my tools.

Without telling Bud he is bothering her, Hilda's tease tells him to go get the tools himself. By using a childish voice and complaining as if a child is talking to his mother, Hilda tells Bud that he is being childish and lazy without saying *You're lazy and you're bothering me.* Hilda's voicing will mark and intensify the statement as a tease, but Bud has to understand it as a tease and not a non sequitur. Going to the new childish layer produces a new meaning about how Bud and Hilda interact and the undesirability of his original question.

How do people react to being teased? Alberts, Kellar-Guenther, and Corman (1996) examined factors that influenced victims' responses to being teased, teasing topics, and perceptions of the perpetrator's intent. Victims reported that they experienced a limited range of teasing: things said, appearance, romance or sex, ability, and identity. They reported that they focused on four kinds of cues to determine the perpetrator's intent: background knowledge, context, paralinguistic cues, and self. Victims were more likely to perceive humorous intent overall, and they were more likely to react positively if they perceived humorous intent. However, if they perceived a more serious intent, they were more likely to respond negatively. More recently, Kowalski (2000) examined victims' and perpetrators' autobiographical narratives describing instances of being teased and teasing. Perpetrators perceived these events as more humorous and less damaging than victims perceived them. However, perpetrators reported more guilt than victims did. Similar to the results of Alberts et al. (1996), most of the incidents that victims reported focused on physical appearance, relationships, and behavior. Perpetrators' narratives focused on behavior, body parts, and appearance.

In a recent review, Keltner, Capps, Kring, Young, and Heerey (2001) suggested an approach to encompass the diverse behaviors labeled as teasing, indicating how teasing can lead to affiliative outcomes (e.g., humor) or hostile outcomes (e.g., anger). Most of the studies reviewed indicate that norm violation or conflict prompts teasing. Teasing was found to be more frequent and hostile when initiated by high-status, familiar others and by men, not unlike the findings related to sexual harassment and insults (Jay, 2000). These studies make it clear that teasing, as a conventionalized form of figurative language, frequently has as its implicit or explicit goal a negative impact on the victim's emotional well-being.

A **put-on** works like a tease, but it is not a reaction to a specific event; it is more generally motivated like a prank (H. H. Clark, 1996). Consider one partner trying to fool the other by creating an imaginary layer for the purpose of teasing about his work habits. Like the tease, this relies on common ground and is done to make an emotional statement or convey the perpetrator's attitude:

KAY: Honey, the office called. They're waiting for you to help with the scheduling problem.

TOM: Really? Gee, I'd better get over to the office this morning!

KAY: No one called. I was just pushing your buttons. Why don't you stay at home and help me paint today?

Kay, for the purpose of exaggerating Tom's work habits, is putting Tom on. She has to make him think she is serious about the phone call in the first place. Her put-on is a figurative comment about Tom's undesirable work habits. Kay sets up a false situation as if it were real. The put-on relies on Tom's taking it seriously momentarily, acting out the undesirable response in some way. Tom acts on the serious layer until the incongruity indicates that this is a put-on. The incongruity realization resolves the tension when Tom understands the figurative meaning—in this case, that no one cares whether Tom goes into the office or not. Kay also points out the incongruity by saying *I was just pushing your buttons*, indicating her emotional intent. Rather than telling Tom not to worry about work, the put-on brings this meaning when the second layer is entered. Here the figurative emotional meaning is that Tom works too much. Rather than saying that literally, Kay is putting him on. If he acted offended or became angered by the put-on, Kay can always say *I was just kidding* to mute some of the criticism in the put-on layer (Kowalski, 2000).

Review Question
How does humor mask negative attitudes in sarcasm, irony, teasing, and put-ons?

HYPERBOLE AND MEIOSIS

Hyperbole and **meiosis** refer to exaggeration and understatement, respectively. The purpose of overstating or understating a literal truth is to make an emotional statement. The mother who tells her teenage child *I can't see the floor because of your* *clothing* is not making a statement of fact. The hyperbole is meant to direct the child to clean up the room. A neighbor once said to me while I was working in the garden, *I've got tons of peat moss!* He meant to convey that he had enough peat moss to share with me, though he probably had no more than a few dozen pounds. This is how some Americans exaggerate in everyday speech. Meiosis, on the other hand, is meant to minimize the importance or impact of something. This might happen for the child who tells his mother *I had a little cake* means to minimize the fact that he ate a big piece. You have probably fallen more than once for the promise that *This will only take a second.* Minimization also occurs in medical and therapeutic settings, where patients have to talk about their feelings or problems. Minimization works here to make the problems not seem so bad, but it also undermines addressing the real nature of the problems at hand.

Both hyperbole and meiosis violate Grice's cooperative principle in that they are not truthful. Both hyperbole and meiosis are a matter of degree, depending on the words used and how much they depart from the truth. For example, one can exaggerate about the amount of time spent waiting in a line in varying degrees by different amounts of time. For example, *I waited in line for (hours, days, weeks, months, years).* Although hyperbole is one of the most common forms of figurative language, little research has been done on the phenomenon relative to other forms of figurative speech (Kreuz et al., 1996). Even less research exists on meiosis. Roberts and Kreuz (1994) found that the major reasons for using hyperbole were to be humorous, to emphasize something, or to be more clear. Recent research has confirmed some of these motivations.

Colston and Keller (1998) studied how irony and hyperbole were used to express surprise. They found that when both irony and hyperbole are used together, they express more surprise than if either is used alone. They found no difference between levels of surprise for irony versus hyperbole, however. Both forms were more surprising than literal expressions. When a speaker exaggerates an unexpected event, as much surprise is expressed by slightly realistic hyperbole as by some outlandish, improbable hyperbole. It might be that we achieve optimum surprise at a given level of exaggeration and that exaggerating further will not increase surprise. In contrast to earlier studies, Kreuz, Kassler, and Coppenrath (1998) obtained less convincing results about the discourse goal of hyperbole. They found the hyperbolic statements were less believable, were less likely to be used, and were less appropriate than the use of nonexaggerations. However, problems with the clarity of the materials in their study may have caused the hyperbolic statements to be less effective. For example, in this study, they used exaggerated statements about the weight of a *grand piano*, which requires knowledge about the size of the piano. The exact size of a grand would need to be mutually shared by subjects in order to grasp where the exaggeration begins about its weight. Some might not have known much about the size of a grand piano.

More research on exaggeration and understatement is warranted, with the express purpose of better understanding the discourse status of these figures of speech. A better understanding of meiosis and hyperbole has applications in children's language development (Varga, 2000) and in doctor-patient discourse in medical and therapeutic settings (Zanarini & Frankenburg, 1994).

IDIOMATIC EXPRESSIONS

Idioms are conventionalized expressions that have figurative meanings that cannot be derived from the literal meaning of the phrase. Here are some common idioms (from Fromkin & Rodman, 1998, p. 189).

I'll eat my hat.

He put his foot in his mouth.

She threw her weight around.

Cut it out.

I like to keep tabs on my neighbor.

I'm going to rake him over the coals.

Common idioms become conventionalized or frozen in usage, and they resist changes in syntactic structure. Whereas one can say *The FBI kept tabs on the radicals,* one cannot say *Tabs were kept on the radicals by the FBI* without sounding strange and destroying the idiomatic meaning. In this sense, the idiom is nondecomposable. Cutler (1982) found that the longer an idiom has been in use, the greater the number of transformations it will resist, indicating that expressions take on idiomatic meaning over a period of time, gradually withdrawing from their literal interpretations. Swinney and Cutler (1979) showed that idioms (e.g., *bite the bullet*) are processed like complex single words rather than phrases. Within sentences, idioms are judged to be acceptable more quickly than nonidiomatic phrases (e.g., *bite the sandwich*). However, the notion that idioms are frozen and resistant to transformation has been challenged.

Gibbs (1990a, 1994; Gibbs & Nayak, 1989) argued that idioms are not all that frozen and do require some analysis. His research shows that individual words in idioms systematically contribute to the figurative meaning of the idiom, contrary to a noncompositional or frozen view. *Spill the beans* is an analyzable idiom, not a single word. *Beans* refers to some idea or secret. *Spill* refers to the act of revealing it. Gibbs and Nayak demonstrated that people find semantically decomposable idioms more flexible than nondecomposable ones. For example, *John laid down the law* can be altered to *The law was laid down by John* without disrupting the figurative meaning. By contrast, nondecomposable idioms like the *keeping tabs* example cannot be changed without disrupting its figurative meaning. Further, Gibbs, Nayak, Bolton, and Keppel (1989) showed that decomposable idioms could be altered at the lexical level without disrupting their figurative meaning. For example, *button your lips* can be changed to *fasten your lips.* Lexical substitutions in nondecomposable idioms cannot do this without disrupting figurative meaning. For example, we cannot change *kick the bucket* to *punt the bucket.*

The decomposable aspect of idioms affects their on-line comprehension. A compositional analysis of nondecomposable idioms (*kick the bucket*) provides little information about their figurative meaning. However, since the individual components of the decomposable idioms (*lay down the law*) each play a role in figurative meaning, people process these idioms in a compositional manner, assessing and combining each component according to grammatical rules. Gibbs, Nayak, and Cutting (1989) demonstrated that people take significantly longer to read decomposable idioms than to read nondecomposable expressions, suggesting that readers attempt some form of compositional analysis of idiomatic phrases. This finding should not be taken to mean that readers automatically compute literal meanings of idioms (Gibbs, 1980, 1985), only that some componential processing assigns figurative meanings to individual components of the idiom.

Hamblin and Gibbs (1999) demonstrated that the meanings of nondecomposable idioms are determined in part by the meaning of the main verbs in the idiom. In other words, the verbs contribute subtle but important influences on what frozen phrases like *kick the bucket* mean. The verb *kick* refers to a single, swift ballistic movement; therefore, you cannot *kick the bucket* if you are in the process of slowly dying. Three experiments using subjects' ratings of how well definitions and the last lines of stories fit the meaning of original idioms suggest that even nondecomposable idioms are not frozen because part of their overall meaning depends on the meaning of the particular verb in the expression, as in the case of *kick* in *kick the bucket*.

People may analyze idioms in a manner similar to analyzing metaphors by mapping related information from two different domains (Gibbs, 1994). *Spilled the beans* relates the knowledge of knocking over a container of beans to a person revealing a secret. In this example, *spill the beans* is understood as revealing a secret based on the underlying conceptual metaphors THE MIND IS A CONTAINER and IDEAS ARE PHYSICAL ENTITIES (Lakoff & Johnson, 1980). Revealing a secret is associated with some internal pressure, causing the speaker to unintentionally let loose with the secret (Gibbs & O'Brien, 1990). This interpretation is congruent with imagery associated with idioms, in this case about what *spilling the beans* looks like in the minds of the listeners. When Gibbs and O'Brien asked subjects to form images of groups of idioms with similar figurative meanings (e.g., *let the cat out of the bag, blow the lid off, spill the beans*), their descriptions were strikingly consistent. Knowledge about containers under pressure helps structure the comprehension of revealing secrets; that is, the internal pressure causes the container to burst, producing the unintentional release of its contents.

People can make sense of idioms on the basis of their metaphorical knowledge, according to Gibbs's views on the conceptual structure underlying figurative language. Gibbs, Bogdanovich, Sykes, and Barr (1997) examined the role of conceptual metaphors in immediate idiom comprehension using a priming method. Subjects were engaged in a self-paced reading task followed by a visual lexical decision task. One experiment showed that readers accessed conceptual metaphors when understanding idioms and to a lesser extent when processing literal paraphrases of the idioms. Subjects accessed the appropriate conceptual metaphors such as ANGER IS HEAT when processing an idiom like *blow your stack*. Subjects did not access that conceptual metaphor when they read *jump down your throat*, which is an idiom with similar figurative meaning but associated with a different conceptual metaphor, ANGER IS ANIMAL BEHAVIOR. These findings support the constraining role that common patterns of metaphorical thought have in idiom understanding.

Gibbs's view of idioms does not appeal to everyone. Glucksberg and Keysar (1990) suggested a different way to understand figurative language and idioms without using conceptual structure. They argued that metaphors are what they appear to be: class-inclusion assertions in which the topic of the metaphor is assigned to a diagnostic category. Similarly, Keysar and Bly (1999) argued that idioms couldn't be used to argue for the existence of conceptual structures that are independent of language. They used idioms that are not in common use to test the hypothesis that the relative transparency of an idiom's real or alternative meaning is a function of what the meaning of the idiom is believed to be in the mind of the subject. They found that when people learn an idiom's meaning, they attempt to map aspects of that meaning onto the linguistic components of the idiom, which makes the stipulated meaning of the idiom seem transparent. What happens when people are given different meanings for the same idiom? Do they rely on conceptual structure or the stipulated meaning? People who learned that the expression *The goose hangs high* means "the situation bodes well" have difficulty conceiving of a negative interpretation. Those who learned that the idiom means "we face impending doom" have difficulty conceiving of a positive interpretation. In this way, a person's knowledge of the meaning of the idiom constrains the way he or she uses the idiom. One's intuitions about the transparency of the idiom reflect the interpretive strategies at work and not so much an independent conceptual structure.

This research is congruent with the graded salience view of figurative processing (Giora, 1999; Giora & Fein, 1999a, 1999b; Giora, Fein, & Schwartz, 1998). The salient meaning of the idiom (or metaphor or irony) is processed first and more quickly than the figurative meaning regardless of context, especially for less familiar expressions, which are more difficult to grasp figuratively (Giora & Fein, 1999a). This was the point of the Keysar and Bly (1999) study. We do not access the conceptual metaphorical structure underlying a metaphor independently of the lexical properties of the words involved. The most salient meanings of the words and expression are those that arise early in the comprehension process.

There is a third view, a compromise view, of what happens when we process idiomatic expressions. Research shows that idiomatic expressions have been viewed in two general ways. The noncompositional approach represents idioms and idiom processing as similar to long words. The compositional approach emphasizes the semantic contribution of idioms' component word meanings in interpretation. After reviewing linguistic and psycholinguistic perspectives in idiom representation and idiom processing, Titone and Connine (1999) argued that neither approach alone adequately captures the existing research on idiom processing. They proposed a hybrid model of idiom representation and processing based on eye-tracking studies. This model ascribes compositional and noncompositional aspects to idiomatic speech. In this approach, idioms function simultaneously as compositional phrases and as arbitrary word sequences. The eye-tracking data showed that idiom reading rates differ as a function of the inherent decomposability of the idiom being tracked.

RHETORICAL QUESTIONS

Rhetorical questions are exemplified by comments like these.

How many times have I told you?

Who do you think you are?

How should I know?

Rhetorical questions are not meant to be answered. A rhetorical question operates more like a statement. Take the case of the disgruntled worker who says *Who cares if I go to work?* This rhetorical question means something figurative, *No one cares if I go to work; I am not needed and I will not be missed.* Roberts and Kreuz (1994) found that rhetorical questions mainly serve the purposes of making clarifications and expressing negative emotions. The rhetorical question about work certainly reflects a negative attitude. The speaker wishes this were not the case; it would be nice to feel needed and missed at work. This figurative meaning reveals that the question is a lament about working conditions, not a question to be answered. The mother who says *How many times have I told you to wash your hands before dinner?* does not want a number in response; she wants the child to wash and at the same time understand that she is upset at the child's noncompliance.

Rhetorical questions, like hyperbolic statements, are common in speech but underresearched by psycholinguists. Research in child development (Sell, Kreuz, & Coppenrath, 1997; Winner et al., 1987) has shown that children are exposed to many different forms of figurative language, especially rhetorical questions. Winner et al. (1987) found that the younger the child, the more likely figurative language would be interpreted as a lie. Sell et al. (1997) showed that even though children are not successful at interpreting all forms of figurative language, they are exposed to it quite often. An analysis of seventeen half-hour videotaped interactions with parents and their children revealed a high rate of rhetorical questions and idioms, more so than hyperbole and metaphors, which were also common. It may be the case, as in the examples, that parents use rhetorical questions (and sarcasm) to manage children's behavior and to make negative comments about their behavior or express negative attitudes to them. Apparently, more work needs to be done on the comprehension side of rhetorical questions.

WHY DO WE USE FIGURATIVE LANGUAGE?

Why do we construct figures of speech rather than saying what we mean more literally? Most of the research on figurative language is aimed at comprehension rather than the factors that produce it. Metaphors are not created as fancy linguistic devices (Black, 1962, 1979). Ortony (1980) suggested that metaphors perform three functions in language very proficiently: expressing the inexpressible, allowing vividness of expression, and providing a compact means of expression for complex ideas. These functions may serve as clues as to why figurative language is so prevalent in everyday talk—because it does what literal language struggles to do. Metaphors are often constructed to frame something new or unknown in terms of something known or familiar, as when a concept that is difficult to comprehend, like "time," is framed in terms of money or physical space. Metaphors are used to communicate complex properties in a kind of shorthand that is understood by a speech community (Glucksberg & Keysar, 1990). One of the areas of knowledge that metaphors serve best is providing a concrete and detailed representation of our internal states, especially emotional states (Fussell & Moss, 1998; Ortony & Fainsilber, 1987). The facilitation of understanding of emotion states through metaphor accounts for why there are so many figurative expressions for love and sexual desire (Kövecses, 1988; Jay, 2000).

Ortony (1975, 1980) argued that metaphors are important to understand subjective experiences that are difficult to capture in literal terms. Emotional experiences are also complex and in many cases very intense. Figurative expression can capture some of these aspects of emotions. Ortony and Fainsilber (1987) examined figurative speech in oral descriptions of emotional experiences. They found that metaphor is more often used to describe feelings than to describe overt actions that result from these feelings. Figurative language is used to express intense emotions more than mild ones. Fussell (1992; Fussell & Moss, 1998) has made an extensive analysis of the use of figurative language in descriptions of emotional situations. Fussell (1992) asked undergraduates to write descriptions of instances in which they experienced intense feelings of anger, sadness, happiness, and pride. Figure 9.1 shows metaphor use as a

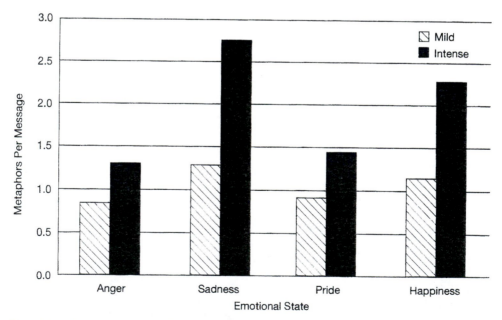

Figure 9.1. Metaphors for Feelings as a Function of Intensity of Emotional State
Note. From Fussell, S., & Moss, M. (1998). Figurative language in emotional communication. In S. Fussell and R. Kreuz (Eds.), *Social and cognitive approaches to interpersonal communication* (pp. 113–141). Mahwah, NJ: Erlbaum. Reprinted by permission.

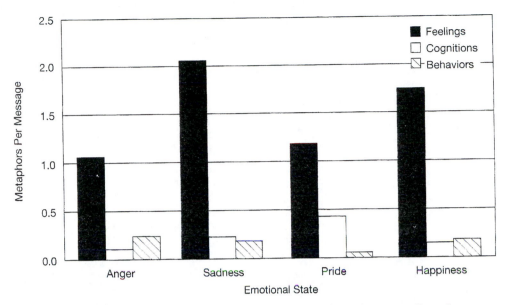

Figure 9.2. Affective, Cognitive, and Bodily Response Metaphors as a Function of Emotional State

Note. From Fussell, S., & Moss, M. (1998). Figurative language in emotional communication. In S. Fussell and R. Kreuz (Eds.), Social and cognitive approaches to interpersonal communication (pp. 113–141). Mahwah, NJ: Erlbaum. Reprinted by permission.

function of the nature and intensity of these emotional states. Figurative language use varied with the type of emotion and its intensity. Like Ortony and Fainsilber, Fussell found that narrators used more figurative language when they described intense experiences than when they described mild experiences. Fussell also found that metaphors are used more to describe feelings than to express cognitions or behaviors associated with their emotional experiences. These data are illustrated in Figure 9.2.

The use of figurative expressions when describing feelings, cognitions, and behaviors associated with *anger* are listed in Table 9.2 (Fussell & Moss, 1998). These statements are consistent with previous research on metaphorical statements about anger. For example, narrators made statements like *I felt trapped by emotion* and *My mind was seething and boiling*. Some of their expressions were frozen or conventional statements, but a number of them were also novel, for example, *My mind was seething and boiling* or *My insides seemed ready to hurt*. Emotion expressions reflect different underlying representations of *anger* when compared to *sadness*. Expressions of sadness had different themes, such as something being "missing." For example, sadness expressions included images like *hollowness, emptiness, having a piece missing,* or *a hole in the heart*. In a similar fashion, in expressions underlying the feeling of *pride*, the narrators mentioned that they felt *larger* or *bigger* in these situations. These kinds of studies, which focus on the production side of figurative language, provide a better understanding of what social and emotional factors give rise to the use of figurative expressions instead of literal ones.

Earlier we read that figurative language affects participants on emotional and social levels. In other words, figurative language serves the purpose of informing

Table 9.2. Figurative Expressions for Affective, Cognitive, and Bodily Responses in Descriptions of Personal Experiences of Anger

---

Affective Responses

I felt like a coiled spring.
Trapped by emotion.
Don't want to blow my top.
I felt "dark" and mean.
My temper burst.
I was *red hot* with anger.
My mind was seething and boiling.

Cognitive Reactions

I'd like to dismember him and keep him in my drawers.
I want to put somebody through the wall into the next planet.
[I had a] desire to crush the other.

Bodily Responses

My stomach was twisted in knots.
My entire insides seemed ready to hurt.
My insides feel all hot.
I feel like I'm going to burst.

Note. From *The Uses of Metaphor in Written Description of Emotional States* by S. R. Fussell, 1992. Unpublished manuscript, Carnegie Mellon University. Reprinted in Fussell & Moss, 1998. Copyright 1992 by Susan R. Fussell. Reprinted by permission.

addressees about social and emotional states. If figurative language helps inform listeners, it could play an important role in educational settings. Recent research has delved into the pragmatic functions of figurative language and the gestures that accompany it in lectures. Corts and Pollio (1999) studied the relationship between figurative language and gesturing in college lectures and found that both gestures and figurative language came in *bursts*. Both novel figures of speech and iconic gestures were found to concern the central topic of the lecture. They were likely to occur when the lecture dealt with topics that were beyond the students' common knowledge and experience, for example, "what it is like to be old." Figures of speech and gestures were also likely when the lecture presented a new understanding of a familiar topic, for example, that "alcoholism is a game, not a disease." Sometimes the figures of speech and gestures overlapped. The gesture served to enhance the metaphor rather than provide an alternative representation of it. In all occurrences, the gesture concerned the vehicle, not the topic of the metaphor. Other cases of deictic gesturing and clichéd figures of speech appeared to relate more to the flow of the lecture than to its informational content. The role of the gesturing and figurative language on the part of the speaker in this study fits well the research on gestures in earlier chapters that showed the facilitative effect of gestures on comprehension. As Corts and Pollio suggest, they add to or enhance the imagery suggested by the figurative speech; and according to research by Kelly et al. (1999), gestures may help disambiguate the meaning of indirect speech.

Finally, in a set of studies on the use of figurative language, Roberts and Kreuz (1994) gave undergraduates examples of eight different kinds of figurative expressions (see Table 9.1) and asked them to provide three additional examples of each figure and the reasons why an individual would use that figure of speech. From their responses, a goal taxonomy was constructed, based on the goal statements that the subjects generated. For example, if a subject wrote *to be funny, to be comical,* or *to be a clown,* these statements were categorized as *to be humorous* as a discourse goal. The analyses were based on the number of unique discourse goals in the taxonomy, not the number of responses. The discourse goal taxonomy, along with the percentages of subjects reporting each goal, is presented in Table 9.3. These results suggest that different discourse goals are achieved with different figures of speech. Only indirect requests fulfilled the goal *to be polite,* as much previous research would suggest. Other goals can be filled with alternative figures of speech; for example, speakers can be humorous with hyperbole, irony, simile, or idioms.

The goals fulfilled by metaphor and simile show the most overlap in discourse goals, both being used *to compare similarities, to provoke thought,* and *to clarify.* However, they do differ on the goals *to be humorous* and *to deemphasize.* Metaphors also seem to be much more likely to be used *to add interest* compared to similes. These results are in line with Glucksberg and Keysar's (1990) suggestion that metaphors are more forceful comparisons than similes. This may account for why metaphors are comprehended more quickly than similes (A. Johnson, 1996). Converting a comparison from a metaphor to a simile weakens or hedges the comparison. For example, *Sam is a pig* is stronger than *Sam is like a pig.* If a simile is considered weaker than a metaphor, the addressee may consider that by using a simile, the speaker does not intend to be so insulting. Although studies have demonstrated strength differences between similes and metaphors—for example, when a simile is changed into a metaphor—some recent laboratory research (Chiappe & Kennedy, 2000) suggests that these differences are largely eliminated when metaphors and similes are used on their own without a supporting context.

The taxonomy can also be used to make claims about figures of speech individually. For example, indirect requests overlap least with other kinds of figurative speech. The main goals of indirect requests, *to be polite, to protect the self,* and *to guide another's actions,* were not supplied by very many subjects in any other condition. They act more like expressions of veridical information than other figures of speech, and they operate pragmatically very differently from other figures of speech. One additional comment is necessary to be consistent with the comprehensive theme of this text. What is missing in this final analysis is the examination of the more negative side of figurative speech. These studies do not reveal much about the bad things people do with figurative language. If Roberts and Kreuz (1994) had included taboo figurative speech, such as insults, teasing, or put-ons, they perhaps would have added discourse goals such as *to be impolite, to diminish or belittle,* or *to offend.* Their analysis seems to have erased the negative use of figurative language that is so troublesome in contemporary everyday life.

Table 9.3. The Discourse Goal Taxonomy with Percentages of Subjects Reporting Each Goal

Discourse Goal	Figure of Speech							
	Hyperbole	Under-statement	Irony	Metaphor	Simile	Idiom	Indirect Request	Rhetorical Question
To be conventional	22	13	06	24	06	**38**	14	11
To be unconventional		13	06			13		06
To be eloquent	06	06	06	**35**	22	19	07	
To be humorous	**61**	25	**65**		**33**	**44**	07	
To protect the self		31	06			06	**57**	17
To compare similarities				**35**	**33**			
To contrast differences		06	18	06				
To emphasize	**67**	31	**35**	24	11	31	07	28
To deemphasize		**75**			11	06	07	
To add interest	33	06	24	**71**	22	31		
To provoke thought	22	06	29	**35**	**39**	06		22
To differentiate groups		06	12		06	13		
To clarify	**83**	13	**35**	**82**	**94**	**38**	07	**72**
To be polite		06				06	**64**	
To get attention	11	25	18	12	11	13		17
To show positive emotion	11	31	18	06	06	19	21	28
To show negative emotion	17	**69**	**94**		17	31		**56**
To guide another's actions			06			06	**64**	06
To manage the discourse	06	13	18	06			21	**39**
Other		19	06	12	06		14	17
Disagreements	11		12	18		06		11

Note. Percentages in boldface indicate goals listed by at least one-third of the subjects in that condition. From Roberts, R., & Kreuz, R. (1994). Why do people use figurative language? *Psychological Science, 5(3),* 159–163. Reprinted by permission of Blackwell Publishers.

Key Terms

conceptual metaphor
connotation
contextual expression
denotation

echoic mention
gestures
graded salience
ground

hyperbole
idiom
indirect request
irony

joint pretense
meiosis
metaphor
metonymy
muting function
name-calling

negative face
positive face
put-on
rhetorical question
sarcasm
simile

standard pragmatic
  view
teasing
topic
vehicle

What Lies Ahead

The next two chapters are dedicated to the topic of language acquisition. The first, Chapter 10, covers phonological, lexical, and grammatical development. This is a lively area of research in psycholinguistics, and several theories have emerged that explore the social, cognitive, and behavioral underpinnings of language learning. These theories address age-old debates in psychology, such as the nature-nurture controversy.

Suggested Readings Web Site

Conceptual metaphors: http://cogsci.berkeley.edu/MetaphorHome.html

Chapter 10

Language Development I: Phonology, Lexicon, and Grammar

Critical Thinking Questions

1. What are the predominant contemporary theories of language development?

2. What are the major controversies in developmental research?

3. What is the course of phonological development?

4. How do lexical and semantic aspects of language unfold through childhood?

5. Describe the course of grammatical and morphological development.

6. What have cross-linguistic studies revealed about language development?

7. How does bilingual language acquisition compare to the monolingual situation?

Exercise 10.1. **Child Language: What Have You Read so Far?**
Before you begin reading this chapter, scan your notes and skim the first nine chapters of text for information about how children use language. Make a list of what we have discussed so far. What are some questions about children's speech that have not been addressed?

To this point, we have examined aspects of human language without expending much effort on the questions of how and why language is acquired. Yet the answers are crucial to the elaboration of psychological theories about the nature of language and the human mind. First there is the question of function: Why do children talk? Or conversely, why do parents talk to children? The answer is closely tied to social interaction and biological development. Then there is the question of structure: What do children acquire? This answer is critically important because it defines the boundaries of language. Traditional components include morphology, syntax, and phonology, but we cannot ignore pragmatics, emotion, and culture because every human who acquires language does so as an emotional being in a culture. Finally, there is the nature-nurture question: How do children acquire language? In the end, the questions about language acquisition lead us to broader theories of language. From the psychological point of view, human cognition and neurological development set the limits on what can be acquired and when and how it can be acquired. What children say and when it happens is of crucial importance.

The questions we ask about development determine the scope of investigation as well as what we think children are doing when they acquire language. If we assume that language is merely semantics, syntax, and morphology, then that is what will be studied. How we define language affects what we think children are doing and how we design research to study children. If culture and emotion are critical aspects of language, then these factors have to be incorporated into research methods.

Studying child language is predicated on a few simple goals. First, we want to know what "normal" language development is. Then we can compare the abnormal, delayed, or accelerated speech to the normal course. Second, we want to know what the milestones, or stages of development, are. Third, we want to compare language development across languages. Some simple strategies are used to achieve these goals. **Cross-sectional studies** look at different age groups of children at the same time on the same task in order to plot task performance as a function of age. **Longitudinal studies** follow one child or group of children over an extended period of time. Although expensive and time-consuming, longitudinal studies offer more reliable data than cross-sectional studies. When we have established normative data, we can make cross-linguistic comparisons to answer questions about universal features of language acquisition and universal properties of language as well as cross-linguistic differences in languages. Many experiments use time-tested research procedures (e.g., preferential looking), but others use procedures unique to psycholinguistics (e.g., enacting or role-playing a sentence).

CHILDES

One resource that has proved especially valuable to many developmental psychologists is the extensive electronic computer-based child language archive known as **CHILDES** (Child Language Data Exchange System). The standardized database contains child language transcripts in many languages from many different projects. It also contains child-directed speech. All transcripts are formatted for easy searching. Brian MacWhinney and Catherine Snow

Box Continues

started the CHILDES project with the help of funds from the MacArthur Foundation. Roger Brown and others have contributed their transcripts of child speech to the project, which now has over one hundred speech samples in more than twenty languages. MacWhinney monitors the system at Carnegie Mellon University. CHILDES also maintain an up-to-date bibliography of research on child language.

Theories of Language Development

Whether you interact with children regularly or not, you know that young children are not as skilled at language or aware of language as older children and adults. How do children obtain the adult level of competence? Assuming that simple imitation or practice explains their increasing linguistic sophistication overlooks the uniformity and universality of language acquisition. A simple learning explanation is insufficient because linguistic parameters are numerous and complex. The theories and approaches that are currently popular are reviewed here. As you will see, trying to account for child language development draws on some familiar psychological debates: the nature-nurture controversy, the relationship between language and thought, and the relative importance of linguistic structure and the social functions of speech.

NATIVIST-LINGUIST THEORY

The nativist-linguist approach is most closely tied with the work of Noam Chomsky (1982, 1988), who proposed that infants are born with a *language acquisition device* (**LAD**) that makes each child biologically prepared to acquire language regardless of setting. Children must acquire language within a critical developmental period because language is determined by a biological timetable (see Figure 10.1). One of the main tasks for the growing child is to figure out meaning from the surface structure samples provided by the environment (Pinker, 1994). The nativist view assumes that language is species-specific and unique to humans, which has a strong genetic basis that makes language development look very similar across different languages and cultures. Another major assumption is that the language environment does not provide sufficient samples from which to discover the complex adult grammar using learning mechanisms. What the child hears is only indirectly related to the formal grammatical rules that are the ultimate goal of language acquisition. The child acquires language by developing a succession of hypotheses about grammar. In addition, nativist-linguists (Morgan, Bonamo, & Travis, 1995; Pinker, 1994) argue that children are rarely told whether their sentences are correct or not.

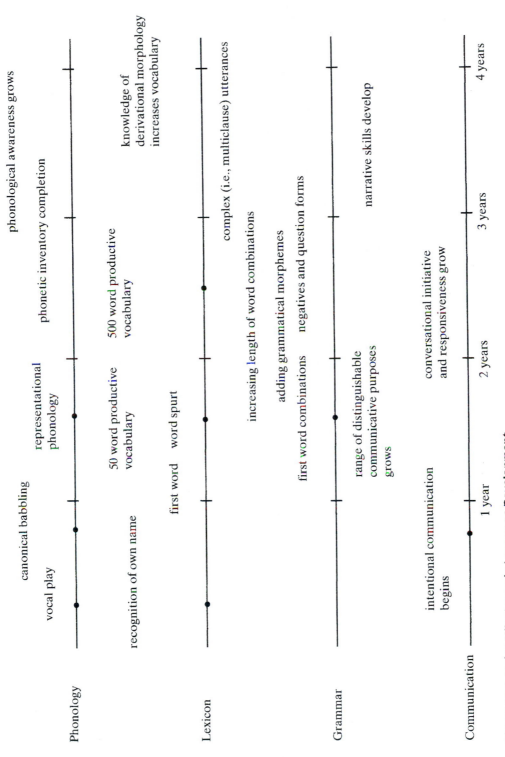

Figure 10.1. Major Milestones in Language Development

Note. From *Language Development, 2nd edition*, by E. Hoff © 2001. Reprinted with permission of Brooks/Cole, an imprint of the Wadsworth Group, a division of Thomson Learning. Fax 800-730-2215.

That is, children are not given **negative evidence,** feedback about ungrammatical strings. It is assumed that without some innate rules, children would never figure out the correct rules because they receive insufficient data from the environment (Pinker, 1984; Wexler & Culicover, 1980).

The child acquires grammar because it is a universal property of language, and all a child need do is hear enough language to impute the rules of language. The LAD uses the raw linguistic data to abstract the grammatical rules of the native language. The uniformity and regularity of language are due to the development of an inborn **universal grammar** (UG), accomplished in part by parameter setting. **Parameters** in the UG are regular features of a language, such as word order. Setting these parameters leads to acquisition of the local language. For example, a child acquiring English has to set the parameter for word order to mark the relationships between words in a sentence. Word order is strict in English, relaxed in Russian, and free in Warlpiri. Another parameter is whether sentences require explicit subjects or not. Sentences in English require an explicit subject, while Spanish and Italian do not. The child operates like a codebreaker who uses the LAD to decode the native language.

Cross-cultural studies have provided a good deal of support for the linguistic approach (Slobin, 1985), for example, children learn a subject-object word order regardless of the order used by older speakers around them. The universality of language and the regularity of the order of emergence of grammatical aspects of language argue against a strict learning approach. Alternatively, there are plenty of studies that are problematic for the nativist view. Several studies have questioned the idea of no negative evidence, for example (Bohannon, MacWhinney, & Snow, 1990). Bohannon and Stanowicz (1988) found that over 90 percent of adult imitations of child speech followed well-formed utterances; however, 70 percent of adult replies recast or expanded imitations following errors. Parents and nonparents rarely repeated the child's errors but instead changed the child's utterance to a correct alternative. Probably the most frequent criticism of the nativist-linguist approach is the tendency to use innateness as an explanation for language development whenever an environmental factor has a weak effect on the child's speech.

BEHAVIORIST-LEARNING THEORY

The behaviorist's learning approach relies on the components of classical and operant conditioning; these are the bedrock of the behaviorist tradition of mid-twentieth-century psychology (Mowrer, 1960; Osgood, 1953; Skinner, 1957; Staats, 1971). **Classical conditioning** pairs neutral stimuli to reflexes, as in the original Pavlovian paradigm, where the dog would salivate (reflex) when presented with a tone (stimulus) that signaled that food was coming. As for language, associations would be formed between words and their internal responses. For example, when the child says *milk* prior to feeding, the word becomes associated with the milk. Once *milk* reliably elicits a response, it can be conditioned to another word like *bottle.* **Operant conditioning** refers to how we use behavior to obtain consequences, such that the behavior operates on the environment to bring about favorable consequences or avoid adverse ones. Children utter words because they cause adults to give them things they want. For example, a child learns to say *more* because saying it ordinarily gets the child more food. Behaviorists assume that the child's speech will be rewarded the more it sounds like adult speech. Adultlike utterances get rewarded, and inappropriate or meaningless speech does not. More recently, social learning theory has been used to explain the role of imitation, vicarious learning (observing what happens to others), and modeling (imitating others' speech) as components of language learning. Adults provide a model of speaking that the child can imitate and expand on. Adults teach or train the child how to speak through reinforcement and *shaping*, rewarding closer and closer approximations of adult speech.

SOCIAL INTERACTION THEORY

The social interactionist approach (Berko-Gleason, Hay, & Cain, 1989; Bruner, 1983, 1995; Snow, 1981, 1999; Snow & Ferguson, 1977; Tomasello, 1995) proposes that children acquire language through close interaction with adults and older children. A social interactionist believes that the structure of language arises out of the social and communicative functions that language plays in human interaction (Bates & MacWhinney, 1982). The child acts more as a social agent, learning language through social interaction, than as a language acquisition device, acquiring hypotheses about the rules of language. A more adultlike form of speech will produce a more sophisticated social life for the child. Children learn language only by hearing others use it; they do not pick up language passively from television or radio because language learning relies on frequent one-on-one contact with an older speaker who provides questions, comments, and speech to be listened to. The social interactionist approach anticipates language differences based on gender, culture, and class.

Tomasello (1995; Tomasello, Kruger, & Ratner, 1993) focused on the early social and pragmatic skills and their relationship to language acquisition. What is important here is the infant's understanding that other people are intentional agents, which is the forerunner of lexical development. From that point, infants begin to communicate to ensure mutual attention with people (e.g., pointing and gesturing) prior to uttering their first words. They interact in speech games and routines like peek-a-boo and naming body parts for the purpose of social goals (Bruner, 1983; Ninio & Bruner, 1978; Ninio & Snow, 1996). The vocal language that emerges thereafter is predicated on social interaction, not the need to convey information to others. What motivates language acquisition is social precocity (Snow, 1999).

The social interactionist assumes that language development is about acquiring grammatical rules, similar to the linguistic view. But one can assume that these rules have evolved from associations and imitations in a social context (Moerk, 1991). Language rules are important here, but interactionists are less dedicated to structure than linguists are. The function of language in social communication is the central theme because grammatical structures are immaterial if they do not have a practical function such as comprehension and making oneself understood. The social interactionist attempts to account for grammatical development by looking at how the changes function in social communication (Berko-Gleason, 1977).

Parents and caregivers bear the onus of communication, accentuating important words, repeating them, and pronouncing them slowly. In fact, **child-directed speech** (CDS) plays a crucial role in the social interactionist explanation for language development, as we will see. Individuals who take care of children must comprehend the meaning of a child's speech regardless of what the child says. These episodes take the form of consultation between the caregiver and the child (Golinkoff, 1983). If the child is hungry and says *mutz* to his mother in the kitchen, the mother, who has spent a good deal of time with her hungry child, will respond by giving the child some milk, understanding that *mutz* means "milk" to the child. One of the benefits of social interaction on the part of caregivers is that this attention promotes language development. For example, Tomasello and Farrar (1986) found that mothers who spend more time conversing about an object of the child's gaze raised babies who spoke their first words earlier and had larger vocabularies than other children.

Like the other theories, social interactionism is not without its critics. Newport, Gleitman, and Gleitman (1977) argued that CDS is not a simpler subset of speech because the imperatives and questions directed to children are more complex than simple active, declarative sentences. Also, not all features of CDS are universal (Bohannon & Warren-Leubecker, 1988), and it is not exactly clear which features are necessary for development. Consider the case of delayed development and CDS. This is a correlational problem: In cases of child language neglect, it is not possible to tell whether the child is not picking up the cues from parents or the parents are not providing the cues because the child is not optimally responsive (Baker & Nelson, 1984). Methodological issues like these aside, social interactionists employ both behaviorists' empirical perspective and the idea that children acquire a language code that is conveyed through dialogue.

CONNECTIONIST THEORY

The *parallel distributed process* (PDP) or *connectionist* approach is a neurolinguistic-inspired account for how children learn phonology, grammar, and morphological properties of words and word endings (McClelland, Rumelhart, & the PDP Research Group, 1986). **Connectionism** holds that language exists in a neuronlike network of nodes or processing units on phonological, morphological, and syntactic levels. PDP is predicated on the information processing paradigm where language is input, stored, and retrieved to be used by neurons in the brain. The child learns associations between sound sequences, words, and meanings by hearing them in the environment. Each neural processing unit (e.g., sound, word, concept) is activated or strengthened by hearing or using it. The child learns that the inflection *-ed* is added to verbs to produce the past tense by hearing people talk about things that have already happened. The meaning of a word would amount to what nodes were activated at any one given time. In this way, meaning is distributed throughout the network. What the child does in learning language is build a network of nodes based on language input. Learning is a matter of associations and node strengths rather than rule learning. Children do not learn rules; they do not need rules to learn language. Phonological, morphological, and syntactic nodes are concurrently activated, that is, acting in parallel with each other and affecting the activation thresholds of nodes involved or anticipated.

One of the clearest differences between nativist and connectionist views of language is at the morphological level of past tense formation in English. The connectionist model of past tense learning (Daugherty & Seidenberg, 1994) initially contains verb stem phonology and verb ending phonology. Through experience, children learn that some stems and some endings co-occur, strengthening their relationship. Novel verb forms will activate the most frequent word endings on the basis of sound; for example, if *lick* becomes *licked*, then *knick* will become *knicked*. In contrast, the nativist (Pinker & Prince, 1994) version does not rely on phonological similarity of the old to the novel but the learning of a rule, for example, "add *-ed.*" So if you gave a child a nonsense word like *The mouse is dorfing,* the child would apply the rule and respond *The mouse dorfed* when asked *What did the mouse do yesterday?* The attraction to connectionism is that it has the potential to account for language acquisition with a simple, general-purpose learning mechanism.

COGNITIVE THEORY

Is language an autonomous, modularized function or merely a part of our general cognitive functions? The cognitive approach views language as a general ability that emerges within the context of other general cognitive abilities like memory, attention, and problem solving (Bates, 1979; Macnamara, 1972; Piaget, 1926, 1954). Piaget's theory of cognitive development, especially his notion of the sensorimotor stage, describes much of what is happening in early child language: a focus on objects in the world and how they operate. Is this a fact of language or of general cognitive growth? Piaget's (1954) assumption is that language is not a separate facility but one of several cognitive abilities. Language is structured or constrained by the changes in cognition. For example, the reason nouns occur early in linguistic development (Nelson, 1973) is because they are the center of attention during the sensorimotor stage. The child's first word combinations depend on perceptions of semantic relations between people and objects in the environment (Bowerman, 1982). The development of disappearance utterances such as *allgone* is related to the idea of *object permanence,* that objects still exist even if they are out of sight.

Unlike the nativists, who are waiting for the adult grammar to emerge and are not so much interested in performance errors, Piagetians find errors a source of useful data because they reveal limitations in cognitive capacity. One thing that seems clear about child language learning from the cognitive point of view is that infants have to know what people are talking about before they learn the precise words. Macnamara (1972) stated that children must know what others are talking about before they realize what each word means. This is the first step in language acquisition: figuring out what people are talking about. Piaget (1926) believed that language use comes about after the child has figured out what the world is all about. This position is somewhat perplexing to the nativists, who view language as a special and independent process, not one subservient to cognition. However, age-related correlations and the co-occurrence of words and perceptions (e.g., *allgone*) are not necessarily causal relations (Curtiss, 1981; Newport et al., 1977). There are some developments that precede others, but that does not mean that one is *necessary* for the other (Bates & Snyder, 1987). The broader claims by Piaget and others that cognitive development determines language acquisition is more or less untested.

Language and Communication: Formalist and Functionalist Views

How important is communication to language and to language acquisition? Children learn a complex system that they can use to communicate. Is that what language is for, communication? Or is language divorced from its role in communication? These questions draw on the distinction between *formalism* and *functionalism*. **Formalism** is the view that language and language acquisition have nothing to do with communication. **Functionalism** is the view that both language and the process of language acquisition are governed and shaped by the communication functions that language serves. The clearest statement of formalism comes from Chomsky (1991), who argues that the faculty of language as a computational-representation system can be used in communication but is not intrinsically a system of communication. For the formalists, language is an arbitrary and autonomous system independent of its function.

The functionalist position is that language is a system constructed from the communication functions it serves. Children discover language by using it to communicate. In other words, the form of language is created by or constrained by communicative functions (MacWhinney, Bates, & Kliegl, 1984). There are a number of functionalist models, which range in how deeply they link language to communication. Snow (1999) argues that the child's social capacities are the launch pad for language, with the key to language acquisition being children's realization that people are trying to communicate with them. L. Bloom's (1991) view is that the desire to communicate one's thoughts and emotions to others is the force underlying language acquisition. Tomasello and associates (Tomasello, 1992; Carpenter, Nagell, & Tomasello, 1998) state the functionalist position most strongly by defining the language acquisition process as a social skill. The components of language that children learn, such as words and sentences, are structured by the social functions they serve. Tomasello's view denies nativisitic formal linguistic theories that rely on abstract rules and portrays language as a set of social conventions that function to enable one person to manipulate another person.

STATISTICAL LEARNING VERSUS RULE LEARNING

One of the central controversies in language learning is whether the child is learning the statistical patterns and regularities in a language community or learning the rules of language. In many ways, this is the nature-versus-nurture debate, the question of whether language is learned or innate.

Saffran, Aslin, & Newport (1996) presented 8-month-old babies to two minutes of tape-recorded "words" that were combined randomly in a single stream of speech. The words were strings like *tupiro, golabu, bidaku,* and *padoti.* The babies would hear something like this: *tupirogolabubidakupadotibidakutupiro.* Following this exposure, the babies were presented either with the same "words" again or on other trials with strings of "nonwords" made up of the same syllables but in different orders. The major finding was that the infants listened longer to the nonwords than they did to the words, which is consistent with the findings that children prefer novel stimuli to familiar ones. The explanation for how they knew the difference lies in learning the statistical probabilities of syllables in the words: *tu* is followed by *pi, pi* is followed by *ro,* and so on. The nonword strings had different transitional probabilities, even though the syllables in the words and nonwords were the same. What the babies were doing was counting the statistical frequency of one particular syllable's being followed by another. The study provided evidence that babies can learn language (Bates & Elman, 1996). But Pinker (1999) argued that language learning is more than identifying words in the speech stream.

An alternative view is that babies do not learn probabilities; they learn algebraic rules. Marcus, Vijayan, Bandi, Rao, & Vishton (1999) presented babies with two-minute sequences that either followed an ABA pattern (e.g., *gatiga, linali*) or an ABB pattern (e.g., *gatiti, linana*). Next babies heard sequences of new syllables that either matched the one they heard previously or matched the alternative pattern. In this second phase, for example, the ABA sequence was a word like *wofewo* and the ABB pattern was a word like *wofefe.* When the babies heard the new (second) pattern, they were able to differentiate between the pattern they heard and the alternative pattern even though they had never heard any of the new syllables in the second phase. Marcus et al. argued that the babies learned a pattern where symbols or variables can stand for any sound. Babies learn regularities that go beyond the actual stimuli presented and abstract patterns among the variables that can refer to old or new stimuli. This argument about word rules versus a word's statistical probabilities extends to broader issues about whether language knowledge can be characterized as knowing rules versus knowing statistics (Pinker, 1999); that is, what kind of rules does the child acquire? This is a question that will arise at several points in this chapter and the next.

DEVELOPMENTAL AND LEARNABILITY APPROACHES

Differences between the developmental learning and rules viewpoints lead to differences in theoretical approaches to doing research on child language. The major difference can be construed as a *development* (of knowledge) versus *learnability* (of rules) debate. It should be noted that neither approach offers a complete account of the process.

The goal of the **developmental approach** to psycholinguistics is to account for the course of language development. The developmentalist wants to know, What course does language development take, and how can we explain it? Investigating these questions begins by collecting data about what children do. From the data, the developmentalist makes inferences about what children know. The developmental shifts in what children know form the foundation for explaining the process of child development (L. Bloom, 1991). A good example of this approach is Roger Brown's (1973) study of grammatical inflections and why some inflections emerge before others. For example, children say *Mommy go* and *Daddy sock* before they say *Mommy is going* and *Daddy's sock.* Brown tried to explain the order of emergence of inflections by looking at their frequency as input, their semantic complexity, their meaning, and the strategies used to encode them. He found that simple frequency was insufficient to explain their developmental course. Semantic and grammatical complexity were more important. Children did not go from a state of not knowing when to inflect verbs to a state of inflecting all verbs correctly, as one would suspect if they simply had to learn the rule. Instead they seemed to produce inflections on a probabilistic basis. More recent research has found essentially the same thing, as children learned inflections for some forms as separate words (Bloom, Lifter, & Hafitz, 1980). The rules that adults use for inflecting verbs came later. Here we see inflections learned by rote, bit by bit, with the rule being induced toward the end of the course.

The **learnability approach** to language acquisition does not focus on the developmental course of language acquisition. Instead, the goal of learnability is to start with a theory of adult language to account for how it was learnable by children, that is, what processes were used to achieve the adult state. This approach relies on the use of innate knowledge of language to account for language acquisition. A complete account of language acquisition can be put forth with a linguistic theory and a willingness to rely on innate knowledge for explaining the gaps (Wexler & Culicover, 1980). Learnability produces a different account for the emergence of grammatical morphemes. Initially, children do not know how to mark verb tense. However, the rule to mark tense is universal, and therefore part of the innate universal grammar that is part of every child's genetic endowment. Why, then, don't children use inflections appropriately? Wexler (1996) argues that the explanation is based on the logical deduction that some parts of the UG mature later than others. Children do not inflect verbs because they do not have that part of the UG yet. Some learnability theorists would suggest a different explanation, based on a strong continuity hypothesis, that changes in the child's use of inflections is not based on developmental changes in linguistic knowledge but rather on changes in performance limitations such as those imposed by a limited memory span.

Now that we have an outline of the differences in the two major theories of language development and have learned to approach language development from a methodological point of view, it is time to look at how language acquisition unfolds on the phonological, lexical, morphological, and syntactic levels of analysis.

Phonological Development

One of the first tasks for the neonate is to figure out what the phonological building blocks are in the native language. To do this, the infant must learn how to segment the speech stream and determine which sounds are meaningful (the ones that make a difference) and those that are not part of the native language.

PRELINGUISTIC SPEECH PERCEPTION

The newborn comes into the world with the ability to hear and, evidence tells us, some memory of what was heard in the uterus (Kuhl, 1987). DeCasper and Fifer (1980) found that newborns less than one day old preferred hearing their mother's voice over listening to an unfamiliar female voice, suggesting that prenatal auditory experience was involved. DeCasper and Spence (1986) expanded on this idea, demonstrating that newborns remembered what they heard prenatally. They asked pregnant women to read a specific passage aloud every day for the last six weeks of their pregnancies. Babies were tested a few days after birth, listening to the passage that was read prenatally and another novel passage. They showed a preference for the familiar passage over the new one. A control group of babies whose mothers did not read aloud prenatally showed no preference for the two passages.

Adding to the evidence for prenatal learning, Jacques Mehler and his colleagues (1988) found that babies born to French-speaking mothers preferred listening to tapes in French over tapes in Russian. Babies whose mothers spoke a language other than Russian or French did not show a preference for one or the other. Like the previous studies, this evidence suggests that infants prefer listening to a language with which they are familiar—the one their mothers spoke—over one that is novel. As to what they are hearing prenatally that provides these preferences, the evidence seems to suggest that the prosodic contours of their mothers' speech is the cue. When Mehler et al. filtered the French and Russian speech segments so that only the prosodic cues were left, the results of the previous study were replicated, demonstrating the potency of prosodic cues as the variable of interest.

You may be wondering just how newborn babies can demonstrate a preference for one type of speech over another. The answer comes from methodology we introduced in Chapter 3 on speech perception.

High-Amplitude Sucking and Head-Turning Procedures

Developmentalists have to make inferences about what preverbal children are learning because they cannot speak. To see what they could perceive, infants can be hooked up to a device that records how vigorously they are sucking on an artificial nipple to receive formula. This is called the **high-amplitude sucking procedure (HAS).** The sucking response is a good indicator of the infant's arousal level, since sucking rate increases when changes in environmental stimuli are detected. Infants will increase their sucking rates to novel stimuli and decrease their rates when they become habituated or bored. Babies lose interest when a sound is constantly repeated, but they will increase their interest when a new sound is presented, indicating a shift in arousal via sucking rate.

A second way to obtain evidence of sound preference is through the *head-turn* technique (Brody, Zelazo, & Chaika, 1984). One procedure tests for habituation simply by recording how the newborn orients to new stimuli. Another procedure capitalizes on the older infant's tendency to listen to something new or to look at something interesting like a moving toy. This procedure is used with infants between 5 months and 1 year of age. For example, using the moving toy as a reward, infants can be trained to turn their heads when sounds they are listening to change in some way. At first, the sound is played repeatedly and then changed, at which point the moving toy is presented. After several of these trials, the baby will turn to where the moving toy appears before it is activated, when the sound is changed. Babies are presented with sound pairs to see if they can discriminate between them.

Infant Speech Discrimination

The high-amplitude sucking procedure and the head-turning procedure can be used to determine when infants detect changes in phonetic features (e.g., voice onset time) of their native language or in other languages. Infants can discriminate speech contrasts that occur in all languages. As early as 4 weeks of age, infants can discriminate between /p/, /b/, and /d/, for example. They can detect differences that are not part of their native language, for example, discriminating between vowel contrasts that occur in French but not in English (Trehub, 1976). Infants can discriminate between consonant contrasts in Hindi that do not occur in English (Werker, Gilbert, Humphrey, & Tees, 1981).

Infants up to about 12 months have the ability to perceive differences in phonemes that adults cannot perceive. For example, English-speaking infants can discriminate between two phonemes in Czech or between phonemes used in Hindi or in Salish that are not phonemes in English (Werker & Tees, 1984). After 12 months, these discriminatory capabilities weaken. Many studies have documented the range of speech perception abilities in infants, and several summaries are available (Goodman & Nusbaum, 1994; Kuhl & Meltzoff, 1997; Werker & Polka, 1993). These findings indicate that the child comes into the world ready to learn any human language but that the perceptual abilities adjust to his or her native speech environment within the first year.

Kuhl (1993; Kuhl & Meltzoff, 1997) proposed the *native language magnet* model of speech development to account for the influence of linguistic environment on speech perception. Infants start out sensitive to all forms of phonetic contrast but lose this level of discrimination by the end of the first year. It is as if they are shifting their discriminatory abilities to fit the central tendencies of vowel sounds in their native-language environments. The native-language exposure draws the infant closer and closer to the central vowel magnets in their language. The infant does not lose the ability to make discriminations; nonnative discriminations can be retaught in adulthood to adults learning foreign languages. These contrasts also improve over the course of training (Best, 1994).

In Chapter 3, we discussed the **categorical perception** of consonants. Children, like adults, have poor discrimination within a phoneme category but good discrimination across phoneme categories. At the age of 1 month, infants can discriminate between /b/ and /p/ and syllables /ba/ and /pa/ (Eimas, Siqueland, Jusczyk, & Vigorito, 1971). We noted that voice onset time (VOT) is a distinctive feature of English consonants; for example, /b/ is perceived if the VOT of the bilabial consonant is less than 25 ms, but /p/ is perceived if the VOT is between 25 and 60 ms. Varying the VOT showed that children had poor discrimination within categories but good discrimination across phoneme boundaries. Using the sucking technique, we noted that infants habituate to sounds within a category but would increase sucking rate (dishabituation) when the sounds shifted categories (/b/ to /p/).

The child's ability to discriminate phonemes and the evidence of categorical perception does not rely on perceptual skills that are particular to speech sounds. Two lines of evidence support this view. First, nonspeech sounds are also perceived categorically (Miller, Wier, Pastore, Kelley, & Dooling, 1976). Second, nonhumans (chinchillas) also exhibit categorical perception, that is, a phoneme boundary effect for /p/ and /b/ (Kuhl & Miller, 1975). The phoneme boundary effect is apparently the property of mammalian audition that language uses. In other words, it is not property unique to human perception because we have language.

Although the research to this point indicates that infants have the ability to distinguish different phonemes, this does not mean that they perceive speech as a series of different phonemes. One proposal is that infants use syllables in perceptual and memory processes. For example, using the HAS, Jusczyk and Derrah (1987) presented 2-month-old infants with a series of syllables (/bi/, /bo/, /ba/). In the next phase of the experiment, they added syllables (/bu/, /du/, /da/) to the set or they changed the initial set by beginning each with /d/. What happened in the second phase was that no matter how much the initial set of syllables was altered, the infants increased their sucking rates. The degree of change did not affect sucking rate. In a related study (Bijeljac-Babic, Bertoncini, & Mehler, 1993), 4-day-old infants were able to distinguish between two-syllable sounds (e.g., *rifo, ublo*) from three-syllable sounds (e.g., *rekivu, kesopa*). However, they were not able to discriminate a two-syllable sequence with four phonemes from one with six phonemes (e.g., *treklu, suldri*). The infants in these studies process the speech in terms of syllables, not phonemes, even though they have the ability to make phoneme-level discriminations.

Child-Directed Speech

Children, generally speaking, hear speech that is different than adult speech because speech is tailored to their needs. The CDS, also known as "motherese," is a slower, more stressed, simplified, and repetitive version of an adult sentence in the native language (Snow & Ferguson, 1977). In English, relative to adult-directed speech, CDS has a higher frequency or pitch than adult speech, a wider range of pitches, longer pauses, and shorter phrases (Fernald, et al., 1989). CDS is produced at a slower rate than adult speech, and it has the effect of prolonging the vowel sounds, which produces better examples of the vowel being produced (Kuhl & Meltzoff, 1997). However, this particular pattern of pronunciation is not universal. In Quiche Mayan, CDS is characterized by *low* frequency, and *high* frequency occurs in the speech directed to social superiors. Quiche Mayan produces its own brand of CDS that draws the child's attention to a means of producing well-formed utterances. Mothers (and fathers) provide a relatively clean and clear database for their children who attend to it. Experimental studies have demonstrated that infants prefer to listen to CDS compared to adult-directed speech, a preference that may be seen in newborns and 1-month-olds (Cooper & Aslin, 1990; Fernald, 1985; Fernald & Kuhl, 1987). If you have watched children's television, you may have noticed the use of CDS on *Teletubbies,* which is written for the express purpose of appealing to children.

Why is CDS so interesting to infants? Fernald and Kuhl (1987) found that it might have something to do with prosody. They found that 4-month-old infants preferred it to adult-directed speech even when everything but the speech contour or melody had been filtered out of the speech stream. Cooper and Aslin (1990) found something different with 1-month-olds; they preferred only the full speech stream, and the prosody alone was not enough. It may be that infants start out preferring the entire signal but later prefer the prosodic cues alone because the cues are what get associated with positive social interactions with caregivers. Fernald (1992) suggested that CDS might have an emotional effect on the child independent of the words employed. She pointed out the universal correlation between intonation contour and the emotion behind what is being said. For example, intonation patterns for prohibitions (e.g., *no, don't*) and for praise (e.g., *good girl, fine*) are much the same across different languages. Fernald (1989) also demonstrated that parents could discriminate between approval and prohibition statements to babies on the basis of prosody alone.

Hirsh-Pasek and associates (1987) have suggested that CDS may be the pathway to language acquisition. They presented 7- to 10-month-old infants with speech samples that had pauses added at clausal boundaries or within clauses. They found that children preferred listening to the samples with the pauses at the boundary, indicating that these were perceptual units for them. Kemler-Nelson, Hirsh-Pasek, Jusczyk, and Wright-Cassidy (1989) repeated the procedure with one set of CDS samples and another set of adult-directed samples with added pauses. Again the infants preferred the pauses at the boundaries in the CDS samples, but they did not show a preference with the adult-directed samples. The infants were sensitive to clausal units in CDS but not in the adult sample. Findings like these have led to the development of a *prosodic bootstrapping hypothesis,* which states that infants use prosodic structure to find the clues to language structure. This is a more particular variant of the *phonological bootstrapping hypothesis,* which states that speech properties other than prosody are the important cues to language structure (Morgan & Demuth, 1996). We will return to bootstrapping hypotheses when we attempt to account for how children learn words and grammar by using phonological cues.

Before we leave this discussion, it should be mentioned that adults in some cultures do not direct speech to prelinguistic infants. Samoans (Ochs, 1982), Papua New Guineans (Schieffelin & Ochs, 1986), and African Americans in the rural southern United States (S. B. Heath, 1983) do not talk to prelinguistic infants, even though they love, hold, and care for them. Therefore, CDS has properties that make it interesting, provides a clear database or sample of speech, and helps the infant identify the important units of speech.

PRELINGUISTIC SPEECH PRODUCTION

During infancy, the child's speech production will undergo a predictable sequence of changes (Oller, 1980). These are shown in Table 10.1. The normal newborn produces nonlinguistic fussing and crying sounds and vegetative sounds (e.g., sneezing and burping). Around 2 to 4 months, infants begin to signal comfort states through cooing sounds, and crying occurs less frequently. *Vocal play* occurs between 4 and 6 months and is thought to be a period when infants are working with their vocal apparatus to see what kinds of sounds they can produce. **Babbling** begins at about 6 months of age and undergoes a series of simple stages. It begins with the production of simple syllables and ends up becoming finely tuned to the sounds that will

Table 10.1. Emergence of Responses and Vocalizations in the First Year of Life

Age Group	Responses	Vocalizations
Newborns	Startles Is calmed by voice Prefers mother's voice	Crying Vegetative sounds
1–3 months	Laughs Smiles at speaker	Cooing sounds Crying Vowel sounds
3–7 months	Responds to emotional intonation (e.g., friendly, angry)	Speechlike sounds Syllables Reduplicated babbling: *ba, ga, bababa*
8–12 months	Responds to name Responds to *no* Recognizes games and routines like peek-a-boo or bye-bye Recognizes some words	Variegated babbling: *gadabaga* Sentence intonations Protowords

be used in the child's first words. While the original speech sounds are somewhat sloppy, they become closer to ideal phonemes with practice. The babbling rate can be operantly increased through parental attention; however, the types of sounds babbled are less influenced by attention. Multisyllabic babbling can take one of two forms, *reduplications,* which are repetitions of the same syllable (e.g., *bababa*), or *variegated babbling,* which consists of strings of different syllables, such as *badagaba.* Reduplications dominate the earlier stages of babbling until variegated forms become more frequent at the end of the babbling stage.

Deaf children enter the babbling stages later than hearing children. The variety of sounds in the deaf child's consonant and vowel repertoire decreases over time, while the variety of sounds in hearing children's babbling increases (Oller & Eilers, 1988; Stoel-Gammon & Otomo, 1986).

Intonation contours, modulations, and stress patterns appear in what might be called a *conversational babbling stage* or a *jargon stage.* At about 10 months, we begin to hear the initiation of meaningful speech. Adults around children at this stage will get the impression that they are trying to talk in complete sentences, especially because children also integrate gestures, eye movement, and intonation contours into their babbling.

Much prespeech vocalization seems to be universal, as babies produce similar sounds in different language environments. However, as early as 6 months of age, the specific language environment influences the sounds that are produced. Competent adult speakers can hear the difference between babblings of babies learning different languages (de Boysson-Bardies, Sagart, & Durand, 1984). In this research, French speakers could discriminate between 15-s segments of French babbling when compared to Arabic or Chinese babbling. Listeners could tell the differences in this study without having to specify how they were different. Another approach to these differences searches for particular differences in parental speech and infant babbling in babies as young as 9 months old who are learning different languages (de Boysson-Bardies, Halle, Sagart, & Durant, 1989; de Boysson-Bardies et al., 1992). For example, adults who speak Japanese or French produce words that contain more nasal sounds than adults speaking Swedish or English. An analysis of babies' babbling demonstrated that Japanese and French infants babble more nasal sounds than Swedish or English babies do. It would seem that infants pay attention to slight differences in sounds that are frequent in their native languages, although babies from different cultures make speech sounds that generally sound very much alike (Oller & Eilers, 1998)

PERCEPTION AND PRODUCTION DIFFERENCES: THE *FIS* PHENOMENON

The fact that children cannot produce all phonemes in their native language does not mean they cannot hear them. Children can hear differences that they cannot produce; in other words, their reception of speech outstrips their expression of it. This phenomenon was described by Berko and Brown (1960), who reported on a child who could not say *fish;* she said *fis.* But when her mother said *fis,* the little girl would get upset, knowing that her mother was mispronouncing the word. The child's perception was better than her production. This has come to be known as the *fis* **phenomenon.**

Lexical and Semantic Development

Having looked at phonological development, we turn to the words that children learn. I aim to look at the words that are produced and their possible meanings, which in many cases are not equivalent to adult meanings or usages. It is not possible to draw a distinction about where phonology ends and semantics begins. Semantics does not develop independently from syntax. Phonology, semantic, and syntactic development overlap a great deal, and the child's semantic learning must be understood in the context in which it occurs. We have to understand what the child is trying to do with words in context and how what seems like nonsense (e.g., *mutz*) to the uninitiated represents a consistent usage of an idiosyncratic word or "protoword" for the child. Should we count these as words or not? These idiosyncratic forms are used like real words (e.g., when the kid wants milk), but we would have to know a good deal about the history of the child's use of them to count them as something other than gibberish.

FIRST WORDS

Many children go through a transitional phase between babbling and their first real words. The first "real" words appear at the end of the first year for the normal child. But as just mentioned, these real words are preceded by *protowords* or idiomorphs, which are personally meaningful or relevant strings of sounds that are not real words (Bates, 1976). The child may consistently respond *mutz* when given milk. In essence, although *mutz* is not a word, it is used consistently as if it were. But because it functions within a limited range of contexts and not with other speakers, it remains a protoword.

The single-word stage has been called the *holophrastic* ("entire expression") *phase* because children use single words to express a complete thought to a listener. For example, when the child says *Milk,* the holophrase could mean a number of things—for example, *I want milk, I spilled the milk, Mom has milk,* or *That's milk.* Like the protoword, the holophrase derives its meaning in part from the context in which it occurs. Adults in the situation work to figure out what the child's intention is on hearing the single word. Exactly what the word means depends on what is happening in the context and how the adult and child have used the word previously.

Many of the child's **first words** are **context-bound words,** used in one particular setting. Barrett (1986) described how 12-month-old Adam used the word *duck* only when he was hitting his yellow ducks off the edge of the bathtub. Playing with the ducks in other situations or looking at real ducks never elicited the word *duck*. The word, at this point, was tied to the bathtub experience and not extended to other uses of his toy ducks or real ducks. In this case, like the protoword, the context-bound word does not operate fully like adult words and seems to be associated with a particular goal. Similarly, Caselli et al. (1995), after studying hundreds of Italian and American children, found that a child's first words are tied to specific language games or routines and are situation-specific. Other evidence suggests that first words can also be referential (Harris, Barrett, Jones, & Brookes, 1988).

Harris et al. (1988) recorded the first ten words produced by four children and found that most of them (22 of 40) were context-bound. There were also nominal words (14 of 40), which were names for things (e.g., *doggy*) and nonnominal words like *more, yes,* and *no*. The nonnominal words were not context-bound but were used more flexibly. Children seem to ascribe narrower meanings of words than would be supported by their experiences hearing words in different contexts. But these narrow meanings do not remain fixed. Words that are originally bound eventually become decontextualized. For example, Barrett's son began using the word *duck* in other settings two weeks after he restricted the word to the bathtub situation. Children seem to start talking with some words that are bound to the situations that instigate them and another set of words that are more adultlike in use.

Common nouns make up the largest class of words in the initial vocabulary. The first fifty words of the initial vocabulary are from all major grammatical cases that adults use (Nelson, 1973). Verbs, adjectives, and function words only account for 10 percent of the early vocabulary (Bates et al., 1994; Dromi, 1987). Nouns predominate in the vocabulary until the child has acquired over two hundred words. What do children talk about with this limited lexicon? Semantically speaking, early words include terms for foods, drinks, animals, body parts, clothing, household items, people, toys, vehicles, actions, games (e.g., *peek-a-boo*), childhood routines (e.g., *bye-bye*), and descriptions (e.g., *allgone, hot*). Nelson (1973) found that children use general nouns (e.g., *ball, car*) more than specific nouns (e.g., *Daddy*), action words, modifiers, politeness words (e.g., *please*), or function words. Nelson categorized the nouns into six types:

Specific nominals: *mommy, daddy, Rover*

General nominals: *dog, ball, milk, he, this*

Action words: *go, up, look*

Modifiers: *big, allgone, outside, mine*

Personal social words: *no, want, please*

Grammatical junction words: *what, is, for*

Gopnik and Choi (1995) and others (Fernald & Morikawa, 1993) questioned the universality of the noun-dominated lexicon, noting that it may be more particular to English than to other languages. For example, verbs appear earlier and predominate in the vocabularies of Korean children. Tardif (1996) found that children learning Mandarin Chinese acquire verbs at a rate equal to or greater than that for nouns. It is possible that Asian languages do not produce the noun bias that is present in English because in Asian languages, the verb often comes at the end of a sentence, which makes it very prominent to children.

After this noun-dominated period in English, children begin to add verbs, adjectives, and to a lesser degree, function words, until they have accumulated about six hundred words. This period of rapid vocabulary acquisition has been dubbed the **word spurt.**

THE WORD SPURT

One of the reasons Nelson (1973) ended her study at the fifty-word level had to do with the word spurt. Mothers in the study had a good deal of difficulty keeping up with their children's lexical acquisitions beginning around the age of 18 months. Several researchers have reported on this phenomenon (Benedict, 1979; P. Bloom, 1993; McShane, 1980; Nelson, 1973), but all do not agree about why it occurs or whether all children experience the word spurt. For example, Goldfield and Reznick (1990) found that thirteen of eighteen children they studied did show a spurt, but some children are gradual word learners who do not forge ahead in word acquisition. Individual differences between gradual learners and spurters are apparent in Figure 10.2. But maybe Goldfield and Reznick stopped collecting data before the gradual learners went through their surges. Mervis and Bertrand (1995) followed some gradual learners and observed that they did eventually go through a word spurt.

Why is there a word spurt? One of the interesting observations about the words acquired during the rapid increase in vocabulary is that most of these words are labels for objects. The gradual learners in Goldfield and Reznick's (1990) study maintained a constant rate of noun learning and hence showed no surge. Children under the age of 18 months seem unable to learn words as efficiently as their older counterparts with larger vocabularies (Lucariello, 1987). One explanation is that children prior to the fifty-word level have word-learning constraints (Mervis & Bertrand, 1994). Another explanation is that they lack the "naming insight" for labeling (i.e., everything has a name) prior to the spurt (L. Smith, 1995). Vihman (1996) argued that it was the limitations on the child's phonological system that constrained word learning. Finally, Gopnik and Meltzoff (1986) proposed that one part of word learning depends on cognitive development, and prior to the word spurt, children do not understand that objects can be assembled into groups or categorized. One question that arises from the growth in vocabulary is whether children are using their new labels appropriately. The answer seems to be not always, because sometimes they overextend or underextend their meanings.

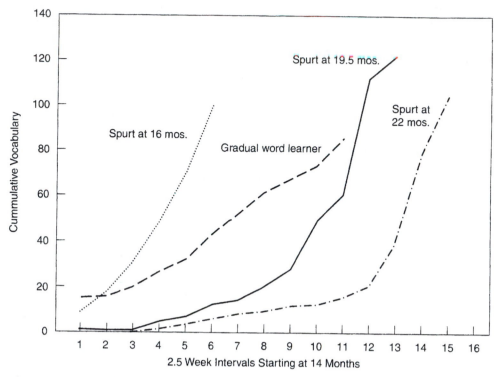

Figure 10.2. Lexical Growth in Four Children

Note. "Early Lexical Acquisition: Rate, Content, and the Vocabulary Spurt," Goldfield, B. and Reznick, J. in *Journal of Child Language,* Vol. 17 (1990): 171–184. Reprinted with permission of Cambridge University Press.

OVEREXTENSION AND UNDEREXTENSION

Overextension and **underextension** refer to children's use of words that are either too broad or too restrictive relative to adult use. An example of an overextension of an adult word would be when a child refers to all four-legged animals as *cows* or when all beverages are called *juice.* Underextension occurs when children use words too narrowly, as when referring to only the family dog as *dog* but never using *dog* to refer to other dogs in the neighborhood. I once observed two toddlers arguing over the word *daddy* when their fathers arrived to pick them up at day care. When one child called his father "Daddy," the other said, *"That's* not daddy. *Daddy's* my daddy!"

Overextension and underextension occur for several reasons. Children may perceptually know the differences between different objects but not have acquired the word or label for other objects. Children might overextend words in order to express the similarities between the objects they labeled. Underextension might result when the child does not realize that the label refers to a class of objects and is not restricted to the originally named object.

Children also construct novel uses of words. *Novel words* are words and word forms from the adult lexicon that children give a novel but consistent meaning.

E. Clark (1982, 1993) noted that children sometimes invent words to fill in what is missing in their lexicons. My neighbor called his hot dog bun a *holder;* another example would be using the word *pourer* for a cup. These kinds of inventions are somewhat regular and simple, as when a child uses *pillow* to mean "to throw a pillow at." They are also transparent—for example, *plant-man* for gardener—and they are productive or creative, adding *-er* to names for people who do things, like *cooker* for one who grills hamburgers (E. Clark, 1993).

Interestingly, Nelson (1973) and Reich (1986) noted that an object's movements and whether the child can manipulate the object affect whether the child learns the object's name. Children learn names for clothing they can manipulate before those for clothing they cannot handle. Similarly, words for objects that move (e.g., *truck*) are learned before objects that do not move (e.g., *rug*). Children are interested in objects that do things. They learn about the world by interacting in it, not by being passive observers. Keep in mind that children learn words that help them perform functions and operate on the world around them (Nelson, 1973). The child uses words like *more* and *allgone* in order to get things, not just to make comments on the state of the surroundings.

Children live in a world of named objects and named actions. The typical child will know six thousand words by 6 years of age (Carey, 1978). But in the named world, not everything is named. Parents and older children construct a linguistic reality through the importance they give to the objects and actions that are named and taught to the child. The child's goal is to learn words and how to do things with words. Words do not merely name things; they do things to other people that satisfy the emotional and social needs of the child. The child learns language and at the same time how to interact with others through language. The infant's cry of hunger is replaced by a plea for "*food.*" Through words, children can represent and misrepresent themselves to their parents. *Mommy, I'm hungry* will get the child a cookie, whether the child is hungry or not. The child learns that saying *I'm hungry* is a way to interact and get something at the same time.

HOW DO CHILDREN LEARN NEW WORDS?

Let us now address the mechanisms that have been proposed to account for how words are learned. It is one problem to collect examples of child speech and another to explain why you found what you did. As you will see, there are several competing views of word learning that align themselves with different theories of language acquisition discussed earlier.

The Segmentation and Mapping Problems

The **segmentation problem** refers to the child's difficulty, when listening to a continuous chain of speech, of figuring out where the words start and end. Here is an example of the segmentation that occurred during a conversation with my 4-year-old nephew, Patrick:

PATRICK: Where are you going?

TIM: I have to go back to Miami.

PATRICK: (*to his mother*) Mom, where's Tim's "ami"?

Children have to find the word boundaries. How do they do this? They can use *stress* or *rhythm* to mark word boundaries (Cutler, 1994; Jusczyk, 1999). Stressed syllables usually fall at the beginnings of words, allowing the child to check for the contrast between the ending of one word and the beginning of another. Another candidate for word boundaries could be phonotactic rules of the language that specify legal sequences of phonemes. Babies at the age of 9 months are sensitive to the rules of their native language; we know this because they prefer to listen to the sound patterns that follow the rules of their native language rather than those of a foreign language (Jusczyk, Friederici, Wessels, & Svenkerud, 1993).

Having determined that a particular sound sequence constitutes a word, the child has to conceptualize what the word means or what it refers to. When Dad walks by and Mom says, "New shoes?" does the child think Mom is talking about how Dad is walking, what's on his feet, or where he is headed? This has been called the **mapping problem.** Quine (1960) characterized the problem by noting that there are an infinite number of hypotheses about a word's meaning that are possible given the data; however, the child tends to figure out the meanings of the words they hear. Are we to assume that when a child says the word *shoe*, the word is a referent to the category of shoes? Are we sure the child is referring to the shoe as an object and not an aspect of it, such as the lace or the tongue of the shoe? Maybe when the child hears the word *shoe*, he or she thinks the word means *put on your shoe*.

Carey (1978) found that children who hear a new word will develop a hypothesis about what the word means. She referred to this as *fast mapping*. An interesting procedure has been developed to show how readily fast mapping occurs. In an experimental setting, children are given four objects, of which three are known objects (e.g., ball, bottle, cup) and one is unfamiliar (e.g., honey dipper). The child is then asked, *Can I have the cup?* The child usually indicates which one it is. The experimenter asks, *Can I have the zib?* By the age of 20 months, most children can figure out that the unfamiliar object is the one with the new name (Mervis & Bertrand, 1994). The next question is how they do this: How do they know that the unfamiliar object is the one with the unfamiliar name?

Markman (1991, 1994) proposed that children operate on new words with a set of three constraints on possible interpretations.

- *Whole object assumption:* The new word refers to the entire object, not a part of the object. For example, when I pointed to the stove and told my daughter, "That is hot," she thought *hot* was the label for the stove.

- *Taxonomic assumption:* Words refer to things that are of the same type. In other words, labels refer to a category of objects. *Dog* refers to the category of dogs, not things that go with dogs, such as bones, leashes, or dog beds.

- *Mutual exclusivity assumption:* Different words refer to different types of things, and these kinds of things do not overlap with other categories. *Dog* is a label for dog kinds of things, which do not include cats or gerbils.

Pragmatic Strategies

A different approach to word learning, based on pragmatic variables, has been proposed by E. Clark (1993, 1995). **Pragmatic strategies** focus on how language is used in a speech community. For example, the *principle of conventionality* states that word meanings are determined by convention. Speakers agree about words for things; individuals cannot make up words as they please because communication would fail for lack of mutual understanding. The *principle of contrast* states that different words have different meanings, which is similar to the mutual exclusivity assumption except that the principle of contrast would allow for objects to have more than one label were it not prohibited by the idea of mutual exclusivity. Consider that the object labeled *cat* can also be labeled *animal.*

The pragmatic view of word learning has not proved satisfying for all. V. Gathercole (1989) suggested a different set of operating principles. For example, novel words do not have novel meaning because of some linguistic principle but because children assume that the speaker is trying to tell them something new and the use of a known word would not convey this. This produces a simple operating principle that a new thing has a new name and indeed the new things might also have other names (Mervis & Bertrand, 1994).

The pragmatic approach emphasizes how people talk to children, that is, the input that children receive from others. People tend to project a local focus when talking to children, perhaps realizing that they have limited memory capabilities. One way to do this is to monitor what the child is looking at or playing with. Children will learn new labels better when the labels refer to what they are attending to, rather that labels that require the child to redirect attention to something that is not in their field of focus (Tomasello & Todd, 1983). In this way, there is a match between what the child looks at and what the adult talks about, making it easier to figure out the meanings of new words. Another way to derive meanings of new words is through sentence structure.

Syntactic Bootstrapping

The approaches to word learning we have considered so far have compared what the child already knows about words and things to what is being presented in the social and physical context. A different approach to word meaning focuses on syntax or sentence structure. The methodology differs somewhat from pragmatic approaches. For example, Naigles (1990) showed that 2-year-olds used sentence structure and verb meaning to develop the new meaning of verbs. They were shown videotapes (of actors in costumes) depicting a novel action, for example, a rabbit repeatedly pushing a duck into a squatting position while at the same time the rabbit and the duck are making circles in the air with their right hands. One of these actions was described with a novel verb, for example, *The rabbit is gorping the duck* (for the pushing) or *The rabbit and duck are gorping* (for the hand circling). If children are ascribing the meaning of the new verbs from syntax, the children who hear the first sentence should think *gorping* refers to what the rabbit is doing to the duck, while the other children should think it refers to what they are both doing.

When children were then presented with each action on its own, they picked the meaning that was congruent with the sentence they had originally heard. When each action was shown on a different TV screen, children looked longer at the scene depicting the action they heard described before. Naigles (1990, 1995; Naigles & Hoff-Ginsberg, 1998) has proposed that knowledge of grammatical structure is used to learn new verbs via **syntactic bootstrapping.** In other words, children solve the mapping problem using language-specific innate information, not communicative intentions, or else by paying attention to what the speakers are looking at.

Thus several views have emerged to account for the process of learning words. It may be that each of these strategies is used to some extent to learn what new words mean. It is probably also true that fast mappings are only partially correct and that more experience from multiple exposures will expand on the meaning of the new word (Hoff & Naigles, 1999). Now we move on to address the issue of grammatical and morphological development.

Review Questions
What words are in the child's early lexicon? Why?

Grammatical and Morphological Development

As the child adds more words to the lexicon, he or she learns to use them in progressively more complex ways on the path to producing adultlike speech. Children do not just learn to add endings on a particular word; they acquire general syntactic rules or statistical regularities that allow them to generate new words by adding the appropriate grammatical morphemes to mark possession, pluralization, or tense. The child arrives at a point where learning words means learning grammatical constraints on words, word endings, and word order. One source of insight into the child's grammatical development was a study by Roger Brown.

ROGER BROWN'S OBSERVATIONAL STUDY

Roger Brown (1973) pioneered the extensive use of the longitudinal observational method in psycholinguistics by watching and recording three children, Adam, Eve, and Sarah, on a monthly basis in their homes. Observation is conceptually simple: Find a child, and record what he or she says. But observation presents problems with recording and notation. One has to record all of the contextual details affecting speech as well as what the child said or was trying to say.

At this point, we are ready to consider the emergence of multiword production and comprehension. When children start using two-word utterances, it is necessary to account for how they order words. What is the basis for regularity in word ordering? Whereas the holophrastic stage relies heavily on context to determine what single words mean, two-word sentences fall into patterns that are less contextually bound. We see the patterns once we examine a corpus of two-word phrases or "sentences."

Telegraphic Speech

Brown and Fraser (1963) called two-word utterances **telegraphic speech** because they resembled the sparse syntax used in the telegrams that people sent before e-mail and fax technology. Because the cost of the telegram was based on the number of words used, people cut out all words that seemed unnecessary, ending up with terse statements like "Arriving Sunday, Grand Central, 2 p.m." Prepositions, articles, and functions words were omitted, producing a sentence much like the young child's sentences devoid of everything but content words, like *Mommy sock.*

Semantically, the first two-word phrases represent different kinds of intentions, according to Brown (1973). Children produce **negations** when they say no to something (e.g., *no nap*), recurrences when they ask for more of something (e.g., *more candy*), nonexistence to comment that something has disappeared (e.g., *all-gone daddy*), and notices where they call attention to something or someone (e.g., *hi doggie*). Brown preferred to look at the relationships between the two words in the sentence. He described the semantic relationships expressed in the advanced two-word stage with a set of eight relationships, which reflect the semantic roles of the words in the sentences. The relational meaning of the sentence refers to the relationship between the referents in the sentence. For example, sentences with *my*, like *My doggie*, express a possessor-possession relationship. Here are the eight advanced two-word patterns that Brown recorded:

Agent + action	*Mommy come.*
Action + object	*Drive car.*
Agent + object	*Mommy sock.*
Action + location	*Sit chair.*
Entity + location	*Cup table.*
Possessor + possession	*My doggie.*
Entity + attribute	*Crayon big.*
Demonstrative + entity	*Dat money.*

At this **two-word stage,** Brown found that children do a great deal of talking about objects, where objects are located, what they are like, and who owns them. Children also talk about the behaviors and actions of people and objects.

Table 10.2. Children's Complex Sentences, in Order of Development

Type	Examples
1. Object complementation	*Watch me draw circles.*
	I see you sit down.
2. *Wh-* embedded clauses	*Can I do it when we get home?*
	I show you how to do it.
3. Coordinating conjunctions	*He was stuck, and I got him out.*
	When I was a little girl I could go "geek-geek"
	like that, but now I can go "this is a chair."
4. Subordinating conjunctions	*Here's a set. It must be mine if it's a little one.*
	I want this doll because she's big.

Note. Table from "The genesis of complex sentences" by J. Limber, in *Cognitive Development and the Acquisition of Language*, edited by T. E. Moore, copyright 1973, Elsevier Science (USA), reproduced by permission of the publisher.

As the child develops a more sophisticated view of the world and a broader verbal repertoire, the complexity of the sentences produced also increases. The level of sophistication depends on the type of utterance. Syntactically complex utterances appear later in the production sequence. Questions, negations, passive sentences, compound sentences, and complementary sentences do not emerge all at once; they go through a predictable sequence of development based on their semantic and syntactic complexity. Table 10.2 lists some examples of complex sentences in roughly their order of emergence.

Notice that what is missing in these two-word, telegraphic phases is grammatical morphemes, the words and word endings that mark grammatical information. Morphemes like -*ing* are generally attached to verbs; and words like *a* and *the* appear at the beginning of a noun phrase. These morphemes carry less meaning relative to the nouns and verbs that children use. Exactly why children omit them is open to question. They may be less essential to the meaning. They may also be deleted because of working memory or cognitive limitations. Another explanation is that these aspects of the language are not often stressed in adult speech (Demuth, 1994). Let us look next at how grammatical morphemes are used when they begin to appear.

> **Review Question**
> What do the child's one-word and two-word sentences reveal about the child's view of the world?

Grammatical Morpheme Development

One can study morphological development by observation or through controlled experimental methods. The **elicitation method** has been used to determine if children can produce grammatical morphemes (or inflections), for example, adding proper endings when nouns are plurals. The experimenter elicits a response by asking the child to fill in missing information. What the child says indicates his or her level of comprehension. Berko (1958) used the elicitation technique to see if children could apply a plural morpheme to a novel word. In this case, the experimenter asks, "*This is a wug. Now here are two* _____." The child fills in the blank with a word that he or she has never heard. The child must know that the grammatical morpheme for plurals is –*s* and that /z/, not /s/, is the right form of the morpheme because the preceding consonant is voiced.

Morphological development has also been plotted observationally (R. Brown, 1973). As children's utterances increase in length and become semantically more complex, another aspect of grammar develops, the use of *grammatical morphemes*. Grammatical morphemes include possessives, plurals, and past tense inflections as well as prepositions, articles, and auxiliary verbs, which change the meaning of the utterances in which they occur in subtle ways. One of the remarkable findings that Roger Brown reported was the emergence of fourteen grammatical morphemes in the speech of the children he studied. Today it is generally accepted that grammatical morphemes emerge in a fairly predictable order (see Table 10.3). The children learned the morphemes in similar order but at varying rates. De Villiers and de Villiers (1973) replicated the order of emergence data with a larger sample of children who were at different levels of language development.

Cross-Linguistic Differences

The order of emergence of grammatical morphemes is particular to children learning English, a language where inflections are less important than word order. Children learning English have to learn that subjects precede and objects follow the verb in a sentence. However, a child learning Hungarian has to make many distinctions

Table 10.3. Order of Acquisition of Grammatical Morphemes

1. Present progressive	*Adam is eating.*
2. Preposition *in*	*Eve sit in chair.*
3. Preposition *on*	*Sweater is on chair.*
4. Plurals	*books*
5. Irregular past tenses	*went, come, ate*
6. Possessives	*Adam's chair.*
7. Uncontracted copula	*Cowboy is big.*
8. Articles	*the doggie, a cookie*
9. Regular past tenses	*Eve walked home.*
10. Third person present regular	*He plays.*
11. Third person present irregular	*He has some toys.*
12. Uncontracted auxiliary	*He was going to work.*
13. Contracted copula	*I'm happy.*
14. Contracted auxiliary	*Mommy's going shopping.*

Note. Reprinted by permission of the publisher from *A First Language: The Early Stages* by Roger Brown, p. 57, Cambridge, Mass.: Harvard University Press, Copyright © 1973 by the President and Fellows of Harvard College.

among the nouns and have to add a different suffix to it depending on the role it serves. English-speaking children may learn morphology later than Hungarian children because inflections are not as salient or important in English. In languages where morphology is more salient, children learn it earlier (Peters, 1995). For example, children learning Turkish have been found to produce inflected forms of words before they learn how to combine them (Aksu-Koc & Slobin, 1985). The order of emergence of grammatical morphemes in English may have given the impression that they are difficult to learn. However, a study of cross-linguistic comparisons indicates that inflection learning depends on the language in question.

MEASURING GRAMMATICAL DEVELOPMENT: MLU

One might think that the course of syntactic development after the holophrastic stage is correlated with age, but that is not so. Roger Brown (1973) found that age was not a good indicator of grammatical sophistication, so he created a method that relied on the length of the utterances that the child produced. He called this measure the *mean length of utterance* (**MLU**), which simply measures the average length of the phrases counted in terms of morphemes that the child produces over a span of time. Children tend to increase the grammatical complexity of their utterances over time. The length of morphemes is a good measure of how grammatically complex an utterance is. MLU has become the conventional measure of syntactic sophistication. We can see in Figure 10.3 how MLU progressed among Brown's three subjects. Notice that the shape of the function is roughly the same in all cases and that the ultimate acquisition is not strictly bound by chronological age.

The MLU measurement has also been used to divide grammatical development into a series of five stages (Miller & Chapman, 1981). These stages and age ranges derived from a sample of 123 children are listed in Table 10.4, which also provides a convenient outline of grammatical development. During stage I, children begin to combine words. Children begin to add grammatical morphemes to utterances in stage II. They begin to use negation and question forms in stage III. Complex sentences emerge in stage IV. Finally, new forms of complex sentences appear in stage V.

COMPLEX SENTENCE FORMS

After achieving the two-word sentence phase, children add grammatical morphemes to their sentences, and the form of the sentences evolves from active and declarative utterances to questions, negations, and compound sentences. These forms take on a predictable pattern in English.

Learning to Ask Questions

In English, the interrogative is marked by intonation pattern, a rising intonation at the end of the utterance, as well as a reordering of the word pattern in the active sentence (Klima & Bellugi, 1966). At first, children rely on rising intonation to

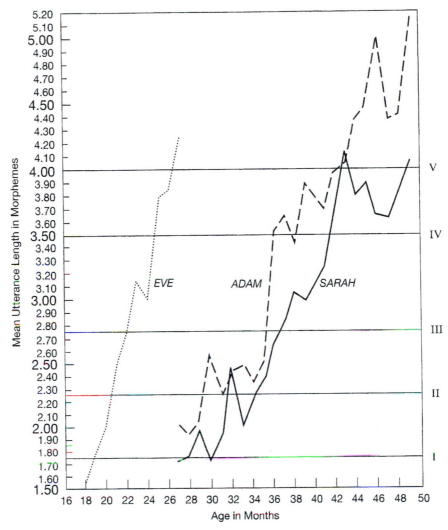

Figure 10.3. Mean Utterance Length and Age in Three Children

Note. Reprinted by permission of the publisher from *A First Language: The Early Stages,* by Roger Brown, p. 57, Cambridge, Mass.: Harvard University Press. Copyright © 1973 by the President and Fellows of Harvard College.

mark their questions, for example, *Daddy's home?* Early on, children learn to ask simple yes-or-no questions by reversing the ordering of the subject and verb, as in *Is daddy home?* Obviously, they require only a yes or no response. The yes-no questions are fairly simple, and they emerge before children ask *wh- questions,* which are more complex in terms of transformational rules.

The *wh-* questions are *who, what, where, when, which, whose, why,* and *how.* Children tend to produce questions with *what, where,* and *who* before the other forms. After these emerge, *when, how,* and *why* appear. *Wh-* questions require the reordering principle, like yes-no questions, in addition to putting the appropriate *wh-* word

Table 10.4. Stages of Grammatical Development and Normative Age Ranges

Stage	Mean Length of Utterance (words)	Age Range (months)
Early I	1.01–1.49	16–26
Late I	1.50–1.99	18–31
II	2.00–2.49	21–35
III	2.50–2.99	24–41
Early IV	3.00–3.49	28–45
Late IV/Early V	3.50–3.99	31–50
Late V	4.00–4.49	37–52
Post V	4.5+	41–

Note. From Miller, J. & Chapman, R. (1981). The relation between age and mean length of utterance. *Journal of Speech and Hearing Research, 24,* 154–161. Reprinted by permission of American Speech-Language-Hearing Association.

in the initial slot in the sentence. Children begin producing *wh-* questions by omitting the auxiliaries, for example, *Who that?* When they start using auxiliaries, they may place them in different slots, for example, *Where Tim is going?* De Villiers, Roeper, and Vainikka (1990) found that the inversion of auxiliaries is a function of the type of *wh-* question used. Auxiliaries appear at different times with different forms. One explanation for the differences in order of emergence may be demands for cognitive resources. *How, when,* and *why* questions are cognitively abstract and syntactically complex. Questions emerge in a manner that fits explanations for how children view the world (Wootten, Merkin, Hood, & Bloom, 1979); that is, children ask about objects, people, and locations before they ask about other aspects of cognition, such as manner, time, or causality.

Learning to Say *No* and *Not*

Children produce affirmative sentences before negative sentences. According to Bellugi (1967; Klima & Bellugi, 1966), children progress through three phases of producing negative sentences. In the first stage, the child merely puts *no* or *not* at the beginning of a simple sentence. This will produce sentences like *No doggie run.* Some researchers, such as de Villiers and de Villiers (1985), believe that this early use of negatives at the beginning of a sentence is not a universal aspect of negative development but merely a pattern that some children developed.

At around the 3.0 MLU level, children will place the negative before the verb, resulting in sentences like *Doggie no run.* They will begin to use contractions such as *don't* and *can't* in their sentences and not just as one-word negations. At around 3.5 to 4.0 MLU, they enter the third phase, when they can add negative markers to the auxiliary verbs in the sentence. This will result in sentences like *Doggie doesn't run.* Adult feedback will not have much effect if the child is not cognitively ready to use negations, as McNeill's (1966, p. 69) example makes clear.

CHILD: Nobody doesn't like me.

MOTHER: No, say, "Nobody likes me."

CHILD: Nobody doesn't like me. (*repeated eight times*)

MOTHER: No, now listen carefully: Say, "Nobody likes me."

CHILD: Oh, nobody don't likes me.

Complex and Compound Sentences

Following the emergence of grammatical morphemes, negations, and question forms, sentences that contain more than one clause begin to appear. These complex sentences take a variety of forms. The first appearance of complex sentences comes after children are producing four-word utterances at a regular rate, which is usually around age 2 years. The order of emergence is object complementation, then *wh-* embedded clauses, coordinating conjunctions, and finally subordinating conjunctions. They will produce most of the complex sentence forms by the age of 4 years (Bowerman, 1976, 1979; Limber, 1973).

Review Questions
What are the stages of asking questions? Negations?

DEVELOPMENT OF COMPREHENSION

To this point, we have been concentrating on speech production capacities. Now we shift to the question of comprehension. It would seem reasonable that children must first know what is going on in the world before they try to connect the language they hear to the situation. In other words, their knowledge of the world in many cases precedes their language about the world. Consider an adult in a foreign country: He or she would have to figure out what was happening in a given context and then map the foreign words to the events. We saw something like this with the *fis* phenomenon. Children cannot say the correct pronunciation, although they understand the correct version when they hear it. We can ask the same question about the relationship between what children produce and what they understand but cannot produce.

How well do children understand the subject-verb-object (SVO) ordering in English? One way to test whether the child understands SVO order is to have them act out different sentences such as *The boy kissed the girl* or *The cat was chased by the dog*. Another technique is to ask the child to point to a picture that represents the sentence. Notice that in these examples, a child might get the right answer through a word order strategy (SVO) or by knowing what the nouns mean and guessing at what the sentences mean (e.g., dogs chase cats, not vice versa) without knowing the passive voice. One way to determine what the child comprehends is through the **preferential looking** method. Preferential looking relies on a simple behavior: The infant gazes at one of two images projected on a screen while seated in the lap of his or her blindfolded parent. The technique eliminates the production requirement by measuring if the infant can gaze at the correct visual representation of a sentence (e.g., *Big Bird pushes Cookie Monster*). The advantage of the looking method is that it does not require the child to produce a sentence or produce difficult motor movements; for example, the child does not have to demonstrate *The cat was chased by the dog* with toy animals.

With the looking method, we can ask a number of questions about comprehension. Golinkoff, Hirsh-Pasek, Cauley, and Gordon (1987) got around the guessing and performance criticisms by showing the child two video screens that portrayed two actions that were equally likely (e.g., *Big Bird pushes Cookie Monster* or *Cookie Monster pushes Big Bird*). While the child was looking at the screens, he or she heard a sentence that referred to one of the videos but not the other. As early as 17 months of age, children responded correctly by looking at the scene described in the sentence. This act of comprehension comes before the child can produce the sentence in question, indicating that young children comprehend simple sentences before they can produce them.

Hirsh-Pasek and Golinkoff (1991) demonstrated comprehension with a group of 13- to 15-month-old children using the preferential looking method. Children were shown two scenes: one with a woman kissing keys and holding a ball in the other hand and another with a woman kissing the ball and holding the keys in her other hand. Children heard a sentence such as *She's kissing the keys,* a sentence that contains referents in both videos but describes an action taking place in only one video. The children looked longer at the scene that matched the sentence they heard than they looked at the nonmatching scene. Here we have evidence that they comprehended the meaning of the sentence and not just the words in the sentence. In this case, comprehension preceded production. But sometimes the relationship between comprehension and production is reversed.

There are cases where a child is not able to comprehend the utterances they produce. For example, children can produce if-then utterances without understanding the logic of the form. A child might say, "*If I am a good boy, then I get some ice cream*" without understanding the nature of conditional logic. We would not expect the child to understand syllogistic reasoning just because he or she uttered an if-then sentence. Another methodological issue about testing for comprehension is that the results are inconsistent: Children who demonstrated comprehension in a supportive environment failed when tested for the same level of comprehension in a laboratory setting (French, Lucariello, Seidman, & Nelson, 1985). The failure at comprehension may occur because the child needs the supportive contextual cues for comprehension and cannot understand the sentence in isolation from them in the laboratory (de Villiers & Roeper, 1995).

We move next to one of the most hotly debated questions in the developmental literature: Why do young children regularize irregular verbs?

OVERREGULARIZATION

How do children learning English deal with irregular words like the verbs *go-went, break-broke,* which differ from regular verbs that just add *-ed* in the past tense? This area of morphological and semantic development has received a great deal of attention (Allen & Seidenberg, 1999; Pinker, 1999; Pinker & Prince, 1988; Rumelhart, McClelland, & the PDP Research Group, 1986; Slobin, 1973). The problem is called **overregularization** because children (and adults from time to time) treat irregular verbs as regular by placing standard *-ed* past tense endings on them, resulting in words like *goed* or *breaked.* As we observe the child learning verb morphology, we see three different phases. First, the irregular words are used correctly, probably by rote. Next children overregularize their verbs, indicating that they have learned that past events are associated with verbs that end in *-ed.* Here they will misapply the rule or the statistical regularity to the irregular. Finally, the correct irregular form is used, but it is recognized as an exception to the past tense rule or the statistical regularity of verbs.

Two of the stronger general theories about how regularization occurs are the nativist-linguist view and the connectionist view. The nativist view (Pinker, 1999) is that children are learning morphological rules like the past tense inflection, and they have to learn the rule before they learn the exceptions to it. Overregularization would represent a failure to access the irregular forms of verbs. The final stage would have the children accessing the irregular verbs because they do not classify it as a regular verb but as an exception. In a procedure similar to the *wug* test, Pinker and associates (Pinker, Lebeaux, & Frost, 1987; Gropen, Pinker, Hollander, & Goldberg, 1991) demonstrated the rule-based strategy by presenting children with novel verbs, which they had to use in a different sentence structure. For example, the child presented with *The pig is pilking the horse* can later say *The horse is being pilked by the pig.* The child presented with *I'm mooping the ball to the mouse* can later say *I'm mooping the mouse a ball.*

Rumelhart et al. (1986) and others (Allen & Seidenberg, 1999; Bates & Goodman, 1999) provide an alternative view of regularization based on the tenets of *parallel distributed processing* or *connectionism,* discussed earlier in this chapter. The argument here is that the knowledge underlying the regularities of children's speech comes from stored memories derived from statistical regularities from previous language input. In the connectionists' view, verbs and their tenses are a set of interconnected nodes within a larger neurolinguistic network of phonemes, word endings, and meanings.

Review Question
Describe the order of acquisition of grammatical morphemes.

Enduring Issues in Grammatical Development

We end our exploration of grammatical development by looking at some enduring issues on the topic. This is not a comprehensive or exhaustive treatment, and more complete analyses are available elsewhere (e.g., Berko-Gleason, 1997; P. Bloom, 1994; Hoff, 2001).

CONNECTIONISM VERSUS NATIVISM

Connectionists believe that children in a language-rich environment learn grammar through a general learning mechanism (Plunkett & Schafer, 1999). The proof of this claim has been established by building a computer program that will operate on language input and eventually produce humanlike utterances by refining its language functions. One problem with this approach is that it has not been conducted in a comprehensive fashion but instead works on language output piecemeal, one topic at a time. Recent evidence of children's learning of the distributional regularities of speech has buttressed the language learning view (Saffran et al., 1996).

One argument offered by the nativists like Chomsky to support the idea of an innate grammar is that the language a child hears is filled with errors—this is known as the **poverty of stimulus** argument. Chomsky claimed that children could not learn the rules of language from input that is filled with errors, false starts, and slips of the tongue. Therefore, the logical conclusion was that the child used an innate grammar to circumvent the poor database.

But how does the child know an overregularization (e.g., *drinked, gooses*) is wrong? One way a child could do this would be to say the word and see if it elicits negative **parental feedback**—a frown, a puzzled look, or a correction. This argument (similar to the poverty of stimulus argument) is the *negative evidence* argument. What is not in the language is considered negative evidence. In other words, hearing grammatical sentences is not enough to reveal all of the rules of language; the child also has to get negative evidence. Pinker (1999) argues that children do not solve the language acquisition problem by depending on parental feedback. Rather they start with a mechanism or principle that blocks overregularization. For example, when a child hears his parents say *broke* instead of *breaked*, he stores *broke* in memory, and the blocking mechanism represses the tendency to say *breaked*. The reason children overregularize is that they have not yet accumulated enough evidence to build the correct memory trace. Blocking and using memory traces may be sufficient to account for irregular verb development and explain why children get worse at it before they get better.

The final issue is to look at how parents and other adults interact with children before making a final decision about whether negative evidence helps grammatical development.

ADULT AND PARENTAL FEEDBACK

Do parents correct their children's speech or not? Pinker (1999) has argued that children are not given much corrective feedback and do not need much because the child is operating with an innate grammar. Earlier Brown and Hanlon (1970) analyzed the mothers' responses to Adam, Sarah, and Eve. Their mothers did correct factual errors, mispronunciations, naughty words, and some overregulated verbs, but grammatical errors generally received little comment. More recently, however, a different picture has emerged.

First of all, Newport et al. (1977) demonstrated that when adults talk to children, they produce very few grammatical errors; this differs from the Chomskian contention that language input is unreliable and full of errors. As for the issue of whether parents correct ungrammatical sentences, Bohannon and Stanowicz (1988) discovered that parents were more likely to repeat children's grammatical sentences verbatim than they were to repeat sentences with mistakes. Adults were more likely to repeat with corrections the sentences that contained mistakes. They were also more likely to ask the child for clarification for sentences with errors. This is not the only experiment to demonstrate that parents respond differently to the grammaticality of their children's speech (see Demetras, Post, & Snow, 1986). Maybe the more interesting question is how children use their parents' responses to help them learn the native language. It is not clear how children would make grammatical sense of a mistake they made in the first place. The parents provide a rich linguistic environment from which the child can operate. There is evidence that the frequency with which parents produce auxiliary verb questions (e.g., *Can you bounce the ball?*) determine the child's acquisition of the form (Newport et al., 1977; Shatz, Hoff-Ginsberg, & MacIver, 1989). So the feedback does have some effect on grammatical development.

Cross-Linguistic Comparisons, Sign Language, and Bilingualism

We now turn to a discussion of some important research on language learning. These issues include the child's awareness of language as an object, strategies for language learning, cross-linguistic comparisons, bilingualism, and sign language learning.

Learning two languages helps promote *metalinguistic awareness*, which refers to the child's awareness of the components and features of language. This is where language can be viewed as an object. The age when metalinguistic awareness begins depends on how success is measured. Two-year-olds can tell that ungrammatical sentences sound "silly." The knowledge that what we call an object is arbitrary or that we can say the same thing with different sentences emerges around the age of 6.

Children learning two languages usually have a more advanced metalinguistic awareness of language in general than monolingual children do because they are forced to think about language structure and rules in more than one way. The bilingual environment presents the child with evidence that the relationship between words and the objects to which they refer is arbitrary (Reynolds, 1990). Other issues in language learning focus on cross-linguistic comparisons.

Cross-linguistic comparisons have lead some researchers to look for common acquisition strategies. Slobin (1985) proposed that children around the world operate on language using a limited set of strategies to figure out what is important about their native language. The language a child produces is a function of the pervasiveness and regularity of the grammatical constructions. Slobin (1973) suggested the following strategies or **operating principles** for children who are learning a language:

1. Pay attention to the end of words.

2. The phonological forms of words can be systematically modified.

3. Pay attention to the order of words and morphemes.

4. Avoid interruption or rearrangement of linguistic units.

5. Underlying semantic relations should be marked overtly and clearly.

6. Avoid exceptions.

7. The use of grammatical markers should make semantic sense.

Slobin and others have used these strategies to explain the emergence of language in childhood, as well as universal properties of language acquisition. In the cross-linguistic comparisons we will examine, we see that there is a tendency for children to not break up syntactic units when negatives are first learned. For example, they just tack the negative on the beginning or end of the utterance. This tendency is based on operating principle 4, which also applies to how children first produce relative clauses—by tacking them onto the end of a sentence (e.g., *The boy gave the apple to the horse who is pulling the wagon*) rather than embedding them in the middle (e.g., *The boy who is pulling the wagon gave the apple to the horse*).

Morphological rules (e.g., how to add morphemes on the end of words) have to be salient in speech to the child, and they have to be understood prior to producing utterances with them. The salience of a language rule depends in part on how frequently and clearly speakers in the child's learning environment express it. In any language, the grammatical forms that are stressed are always acquired before the less stressed forms. For example, in Hebrew, gender must be marked in every sentence, but in French, gender is not so clearly marked. Not surprisingly, children learning Hebrew acquire the concept of gender marking before children learning French.

Cross-linguistic comparisons permit psycholinguists to search for linguistic universals that occur in all languages (Slobin, 1982). Universal features are the product of children's general language-learning abilities and universal strategies used to learn language in the physical world. The English-speaking child's tendency to put negative morphemes at the beginning or end of a phrase is employed in other languages where children move negative morphemes to keep word order intact. It has been found in Japanese (Clancy, 1985), Polish (Smoczynska, 1985), and Turkish (Aksu-Koc & Slobin, 1985), suggesting that negation in any language may be easier to learn when it does not break up intact syntactic groupings.

The way children learn to express locative properties of objects is suggestive of a general cognitive orientation to objects in the world, a facility that exists independently of learning the syntax needed to express location. Children around the world between ages 2 and 5 tend to talk about the location of objects in a fairly predictable sequence. They start with *in* and *on*, then *under, beside, between, front,* and finally *back* (Johnston & Slobin, 1979), even when the syntactic difficulty for expressing the locative varies from language to language. This sequence suggests that language is adjusted to how the child relates personally to objects in the world. Children begin with familiar, simple relationships and end with those more difficult to understand conceptually.

Because language can be produced in several modes (gestured, written, and spoken), we expect to find linguistic milestones both across languages and across modalities. Cross-linguistic universals should have correlates in signed languages. In this sense, the comparison of English to ASL is a cross-linguistic comparison.

> **Review Question**
> What methods are used to study child language learning?

SIGN LANGUAGE

Children who learn sign languages are not all on equal ground. Many deaf children with hearing parents are not discovered to be deaf until months after birth. This is different from a situation in which the parents know the child is deaf and begin signing immediately or where the child can hear but his or her parents use sign language. It would seem that the proper comparison of ASL learning to normal learning would be to select a sample of hearing children of deaf parents who were exposed to sign language as their first language from day one. Deaf children who learn ASL from either deaf signing parents or hearing signing parents represent a less comparable set of circumstances. In fact, our comparison group will not extrapolate to deaf children generally, but it will allow us to compare the acquisition of signed versus spoken speech.

One obvious question is whether signing children go through the same stages of language acquisition as speaking children. Petitto and Marentette (1991) found that manual babbling by children learning ASL as a first language was roughly similar to vocal babbling. Signed syllables contained elements of ASL (e.g., location, hand shape, and movement) but were not in themselves meaningful signs. Compared to hearing infants who also produce manual babbling, deaf infants produced far more of it.

Prinz and Prinz (1979) observed a bilingual hearing and signing child. She produced her first sign at 7 months and five different signs at 12 months, one of which was a word. Bonvillian, Orlansky, and Novack (1983) found similar results with a broader sample of hearing and signing children who produced their first signs around 8.5 months, about three months before their first words. Folven and Bonvillian (1991) qualified the earlier studies by noting that although children's initial signs appear at approximately 8 months, they do not use these signs to refer to objects until around 1 year. The earlier use of signs was generally imitations of adult signs and those used in signing routines or asking for familiar objects.

At the two-word stage, signers operate similarly to children learning to speak English, according to Newport and Ashbrook (1977). The semantic relationships are similar to those listed earlier by R. Brown (1973), and they emerge in roughly the same order as spoken two-word sentences. Both speaking and signing children at this stage use word order as a cue to meaning, rather than using morphological suffixes. Both hearing and signing children fail to use morphology when putting their two words together. We can conclude that speaking and signing, at least through the two-word stage, are somewhat similar, which is what we would expect if language acquisition had a strong biological or cognitive component.

The comparison of children who learned ASL in infancy with those who learned ASL later in childhood provides a good test of the critical period hypothesis for language learning. If delayed learners perform worse than early learners do, this would support the critical period idea. Newport (1990; see also Mayberry & Eichen, 1991) conducted such an experiment by giving a battery of language tests to adults who had been signing for more than thirty years. Some of them had been signing since infancy, and others were not exposed to ASL until mid to late childhood. Newport's results were fairly clear: Those who learned ASL earlier performed better than those who learned later. Even after thirty years of signing, the late learners were not as proficient as the signers who learned ASL in infancy.

Review Question
Describe some cross-linguistic differences and similarities in child language learning.

BILINGUAL LANGUAGE DEVELOPMENT

Although we have read a lot about monolingual language development, we have not addressed the child who learns more than one language. There is a considerable amount of literature on bilingual language learning and at least two scientific journals dedicated to the subject—more literature than can be covered here. Bilingual research covers children learning two languages simultaneously or sequentially and adults learning a second language (L2) later in life (Bhatia & Ritchie, 1999; de Houwer, 1995; Kilborn, 1994; Oller & Eilers, 2002). In the space available, my aim is to cover some basic research questions: How does language develop in children who are learning two languages simultaneously? And what does bilingual development tell us about language development generally?

Is the bilingual child better off or worse off for having two languages within one mind? The answer depends on how the languages are organized. The positive view is known as *additive bilingualism*, which holds that the second language merely adds to the native one. The negative view, *subtractive bilingualism*, is the notion that learning a second language subtracts from fluency in the native language (Bialystok & Hakuta, 1994). Children who grow up learning two languages usually do so without much trouble. Relative to their agemates, they might show a slower rate of vocabulary in one language because they are learning vocabulary in two languages. Let's look at the situation in more detail.

Language Differentiation

One of the first questions we have to address is whether simultaneous bilingualism produces different language systems for each language or one undifferentiated system. From the differentiation question comes another issue, whether bilingualism affects the rate and course of language development. Research has developed around phonological, lexical, and morphosyntactic differentiation.

Researchers suggested that bilingual **differentiation** would emerge earliest in the phonological system. De Houwer (1995) reviewed cases of phonological development and decided that they provided evidence of early phonological differentiation. In these cases and others (C. Hoffman, 1991), children did not exhibit confusion between the phonological systems of the two languages. But it could be the case that these 18- to 24-month-olds started out with one system that later diverge into differentiated systems. Navarro (1998) approached the problem experimentally, as opposed to the earlier case studies. He taped bilingual Spanish-English children and played the tapes to adults who were to judge if they could identify the target language or not. Although they could judge the words at a little better than chance, over 30 percent of the bilinguals' words were unassignable to a target language based on phonological cues. From this evidence, Navarro concluded that the lexical and grammatical systems seemed to be processed through a single undifferentiated, dominant-language-based system.

Lexical differentiation is determined in part by the degree of overlap in the lexicons of the bilingual child, although this is a somewhat controversial assumption. The idea is that the lack of synonyms is evidence of a single system. It is not clear how much overlap would be needed as evidence of different systems. Another problem is that children generally learn one language from one parent and the second from a different parent or a grandparent. Arguments have been mounted for both separate and undifferentiated systems (de Houwer, 1995). Pearson, Fernandez, and Oller

(1995) conducted a large-scale study of Spanish-English bilinguals between 8 and 30 months and found that there was a 30 percent overlap in vocabularies. They concluded that this was sufficient to support the idea of two separate lexical systems.

The real test of bilingual differentiation is whether the child has different morphosyntactic systems; that is, is the child building two grammatical systems or one? If the child confuses or intermixes grammatical rules (e.g., word ordering) from both languages, this would be evidence of a single system. After examining the relevant literature, de Houwer (1995) concluded that children were keeping their syntactic systems separate. In other words, children learning two languages such as French and English do not confound English words with French rules of word order.

> **Review Question**
> What evidence supports the idea that language is innate?

Development in Two Languages

How does bilingual development compare with monolingual development? There is not much of a database to answer this question, and what evidence exists is not particularly clear. Investigators who have reviewed the relevant literature, comparing bilingual case studies with different studies of monolingual development (de Houwer, 1995; Lindholm, 1980), judged that both the rate and the course of development in monolingual and bilingual children are similar. To be more definitive, however, research needs to directly compare monolingual and bilingual development. These kinds of studies are being developed in the literature. For example, Oller, Eilers, Urbano, and Cobo-Lewis (1997) found that babies exposed to a monolingual or a bilingual setting started babbling on the same schedule. Studies of later phonological development in a bilingual setting have provided evidence of minor delays for the bilingual child. Ardila (in press) showed that Spanish-English bilinguals were delayed in producing the Spanish *r* when compared to children learning Spanish only. But this is not strong evidence about phonological development because it only looked at speech production delay and not the underlying phonological comprehension abilities.

There is some evidence of delay if one looks at the lexical development in monolingual and bilingual child populations. Pearson, Fernandez, and Oller (1993) looked at children aged 8 to 30 months and found that bilinguals have similar comprehension lexicons but smaller production lexicons than monolinguals. It has also been demonstrated that bilinguals aged 5 and older have smaller comprehension lexicons than monolinguals (e.g., Umbel, Pearson, Fernandez, & Oller, 1992). Interestingly, bilingual children usually know words in one language that they do not know in the other. In other words, their overall lexicon is larger than the lexicon of one language alone.

Research on grammatical development and bilingualism is deficient on direct comparisons between bilingual and monolingual populations, but what has been reviewed suggests that the course and rate of development in bilinguals is roughly the same as for monolinguals (de Houwer, 1995). More recently, V. Gathercole (2002) compared the development of three morphosyntactic properties (mass versus count nouns in English, gender in Spanish, and *that*-trace in both languages), two specific to one language and the other used in both. The *that*-trace is the important comparison. In English, one can say *Who do you think has big feet* but not *Who do you think that has big feet,* but in Spanish, the opposite is true. Gathercole found that all three properties were acquired faster by monolinguals than by bilinguals. But the course of their development was no different. In addition, by the age of 10, the differences disappeared. In a task on which children had to identify ungrammatical sentences in English, knowing Spanish did not seem to affect these judgments. However, knowing both languages affects language production in Spanish (Ardila, in press). Bilingual children will sometimes use English adjective order (e.g., *a big house*) when speaking Spanish, saying **la grande casa,* which is ungrammatical in Spanish. The research to this point indicates that simultaneous bilingual language learning is possible, but with some minor costs.

Other Issues in Bilingualism

The question of bilingualism cannot be separated from the social and political climate in which the learning takes place. In addition, the personality and cognitive abilities of the child are also important. One of the crucial variables is the acceptance of the different languages in both cultures (Glick, 1987), a problem we will address in Chapter 13.

One issue in multiple language learning is whether the native language and languages learned later are acquired by the same processes. Does one just transfer the learning mechanisms and strategies used in the native language to L2? If language acquisition involves the UG, do the native grammar's parameters have to be reset? Certainly the input conditions are different in learning the second language because the learned language can be used as a database for inspecting the new input. Wong-Fillmore (1991) described learning a second language as a process that consists of learning large chunks of speech that are used for communication purposes. Only later are the chunks analyzed into components. One has to wonder how this strategy is influenced by the cognitive abilities of the learner. In other words, what kinds of cognitive characteristics aid in the acquisition process?

Is there an aptitude for learning a second language? One skill that does seem critical is *phonological memory*. Service (1992; Service & Kohonen, 1995) demonstrated that children who were better at repeating a novel sound sequence after a single presentation were better able to learn a second language. Along with phonological awareness, some social personality variables may be necessary. The L2 learner cannot be overloaded by the presence of second-language speakers. Wong-Fillmore (1991) noted that children who are shy and withdrawn learn more slowly than those who are socially adept. Children who have low anxiety and have a willingness to communicate are also more successful than anxious, unwilling learners (Segalowitz, 1997). Age is also an important factor. Older children make rapid progress initially in comparison to younger L2 learners (Snow & Hoefnagel-Hohle, 1978). However, the ability to speak L2 without an accent is more likely to be achieved by younger learners (Flege, 1995). Crystal (1987) noted that there is no need for pessimism or doubt about bilingual children because millions of them around the world develop language proficiency with little difficulty, reaching school age with linguistic abilities equivalent to those of their monolingual classmates. We return to the social and cognitive issues involved in bilingualism in Chapter 12.

Review Question
Compare the bilingual child to the monolingual child.

Key Terms

babbling	functionalism	parameters
categorical perception	high-amplitude	parental feedback
child-directed speech	sucking procedure	poverty of stimulus
CHILDES	(HAS)	pragmatic strategies
classical conditioning	LAD	preferential looking
connectionism	learnability approach	segmentation problem
context-bound word	longitudinal study	statistical learning
cross-sectional study	mapping problem	syntactic
developmental	MLU	bootstrapping
approach	negation	telegraphic speech
differentiation	negative evidence	two-word stage
elicitation method	operant conditioning	universal grammar
first words	operating principles	underextension
fis phenomenon	overextension	word spurt
formalism	overregularization	

What Lies Ahead

Chapter 11 complements this chapter by addressing how emergence, emotion, and embodiment play a role in language learning and comprehension. We look at how the prelinguistic child expresses knowledge of the world without speaking and how that knowledge changes when words are acquired. These issues address how the physical world is constructed for the child through language and how emotion is constructed with and through language.

Suggested Web Sites

CHILDES: http://poppy.psy.cmu.edu/childes/index.hmtl (or e-mail Brian MacWhinney at macw@cmu.edu)

Teletubbies speech: http://www.pbskids.org/teletubbies/

Chapter 11

Language Development II: Emergence, Emotion, and Embodiment

Critical Thinking Questions

1. Describe the cognitive and interactionist views of language development.

2. How does language emerge from embodiment?

3. How do gestures reflect embodiment?

4. What role do instrumental and classical conditioning play in language development?

5. What is the relationship between language and emotion?

6. How does multiple code theory account for emotional language processing?

7. Are individual differences in language learning important?

Exercise 11.1. **Language and Emotion**

Imagine these situations. Record in your notebook how you would respond verbally and emotionally in each case.

1. You have been waiting for thirty minutes for the concert hall to open. As the door finally opens, a young man darts in front of you and knocks you out of line.

2. Your mother calls and tells you that she has won a sweepstakes prize of $1 million.

3. It is fifteen minutes before class, and you have just finished your twenty-page term paper on your computer. When you give the command to print the file, you get an error message indicating that the file does not exist and you are unable to access any earlier version of it.

Traditional views of language acquisition, with the exception of the social interaction approach, describe language without relating it to our emotional lives. Furthermore, traditional approaches downplay individual differences in speech that stem from personal learning experiences. A number of questions about language development remain. How do language and emotion become linked? How do children express themselves emotionally in the preverbal stage? How do children express emotions verbally? What role do classical and operant conditioning play in word meaning? What is the embodiment of language? How are words and emotions represented "in" us? We need to account for differences in emotional language appraisal and production. These questions also anticipate the social and cultural aspects of language discussed in the next two chapters.

In this chapter, we consider how we acquire language on a personal level. We construct a "self" and a view of the world through language. Each of us acquires language in response to our unique social learning history and psychological temperament. The learning view opposes nativist theory, which focuses on disembodied language universals. Nativism treats language and body as separate entities; the embodiment view does not. The goal in this chapter is to describe language *learning* and to link language to emotional experiences. We focus on six topics: social and physical interaction, emergence, embodiment, behaviorism, emotion, and symbolism.

Language from Interaction

In Chapter 10, we learned that children come into the world ready to acquire any language but that what they learn is shaped by the environment. I want to continue the analysis of language development in this chapter but shift away from the nativist argument to consider in more detail the interactionist and behaviorist points of view. Interactionists acknowledge that there are innate properties of the mind that allow language to develop from experience. The emphasis in interactionism and behaviorism is on the child's language-learning experiences. What is most relevant to interactionists and behaviorists is the nature of the input that children receive from others as they interact with the environment (see Braine, 1994; Snow, 1999). The first perspective of language acquisition we consider is the *constructionist* position espoused by Piaget and Bruner. I contrast this view with the inner speech view from the writings of Vygotsky and Luria.

LANGUAGE CONSTRUCTION: PIAGET AND BRUNER

Swiss psychologist Jean Piaget (1926) envisioned language acquisition as part of a larger cognitive enterprise that begins with sensorimotor representations of the world and ends with abstract hypothetical reasoning or *formal operational thought.* Piaget referred to the period between birth and 2 years as the *sensorimotor period,* during which the child learns that the world is made of stable objects with different shapes, sizes, and movements. It is no wonder that the child produces the names for objects, physical states, and actions with the first fifty words (Nelson, 1973), because these are the focus of sensorimotor thinking.

According to Piaget, the hallmark of the sensorimotor period is the attainment of **object permanence,** the belief that objects exist even when they are out of sight. Until object permanence is attained, the infant operates on a different principle, that of "out of sight, out of mind." Objects removed from view are not pursued visually or physically. Baillargeon, Spelke, and Wasserman (1985) demonstrated object permanence in infants 4½ months old, five months earlier than Piaget's theory predicts. At any rate, the development of object names allow the child to think about objects in their absence. The use of words reflecting object permanence include references to disappearances, saying *allgone* when an object disappears, and references to success and failure by saying *there* when strategies work out or *uh-oh* when they fail. These early sensorimotor verbal references reveal a type of means-ends understanding that coordinates linguistic usage with a view of the physical world.

Concomitant with object permanence is the development of **pretend play,** during which the child uses toys and other objects symbolically, and **deferred imitation,** in which the child imitates a behavior that was viewed on a previous occasion. The ability to represent objects symbolically in the mind and to repeat the actions of another person from a previous occasion indicate that these concepts have been "embodied," that is, stored in memories as bodily actions and motor movements. The child can now act out objects' meanings by imitating what has been observed about objects and their actions. One frequently cited example of imitation comes from Piaget (1962), who observed his daughter throw a tantrum that very closely repeated what she had seen a playmate do on the previous day. To do this requires a memory representation of the tantrum that activates gestures, referencing what she had seen. How do these types of concrete thinking and imitation relate to language processes?

How does the belief in a world of stable objects and actions affect the child's language comprehension? Shatz (1978) noted that young children 19 to 34 months old respond to sentences using a verb-object (VO) comprehension strategy. The **VO strategy** provides a correct response for statements like *Why don't you put the doll on the swing* but not to interrogatives such as *Do you want to put the doll on the swing?* To the latter, the child should not perform an action but instead answer the question. Shatz found that 65 to 70 percent of the responses to a variety of sentence types were VO action responses, as predicted. Children responded to complex sentences by relying on simple VO strategies focused on the objects and verbs named in an utterance. This VO strategy will lead to accurate performance with active sentences and assertions but not passive statements or interrogatives. The point is that the child has a limited concrete view of the world, which affects language processing, according to Piaget.

Children's limited cognitive spans affect their communication skills. Piaget (1926) compared children's dialogues with each other to adult-adult dialogues to show how children develop discourse competence and why. In his view, spontaneous "conversations" between preschool children give the illusion of turn-taking and social interaction. But under the surface, they are more accurately viewed as **collective monologues.** The preschooler cannot participate in a true dialogue because he or she cannot take the point of view of the listener. In Piaget's terms, the child is egocentric or self-centered, a general cognitive characteristic not limited to language. The child cannot engage in true dialogue because he or she lacks the cognitive skill to do so and is too egocentric. Piaget also suggested that children do not try to participate in conversations either. In other words, the preschooler lacks both the skill and the will to participate in dialogue.

Jerome Bruner's theory (1990) is similar to Piaget's in that he proposes that children develop cognitively and linguistically through a series of three stages: *enactive, iconic,* and *symbolic*. During the *enactive* mode, children learn how to perform actions or operations. Images, words, and symbols are not significantly involved. Later, thinking becomes less context- and object-bound. In the *iconic* stage, children are capable of understanding pictures, memories, and images of objects they have previously dealt with. It is not until late childhood that children begin to represent the world as an abstract entity in the *symbolic* stage, where they can manipulate and appreciate purely abstract concepts. Bruner's symbolic stage is comparable to Piaget's formal operational thought.

What do these theories indicate about language development? Both propose that children's early reasoning is based on motor-body references, which later defer to the hypothetical abstract world. The point is that early language is mapped onto the child's conceptualization of a physical world filled with people, objects, and the actions they take. Only later can symbolic and abstract thought emerge on the basis of the earlier embodiment of thought. The progression to abstraction does not mean that sensorimotor representations are overwritten by language but rather that they are *supplemented* by language. In adulthood, *on* still means *on* and *in* still means *in* regardless of the level of cognitive thinking because these are embodied physical symbols.

LANGUAGE AS INNER SPEECH: VYGOTSKY AND LURIA

A different view of language development has emerged in Russian psychology. The Russian psychologist L. S. Vygotsky's (1962) concept of language internalization is the reverse of Piaget's. Whereas Piaget thought that language started out as egocentric and then turned social, Vygotsky thought that it was the other way around. Only after playing with social speech for some time could the child embody language internally and use it to control thought and direct behavior. Vygotsky thought that language was acquired through social interaction. Within this interaction were embodied social roles and cultural norms. The child through social interaction constructs a general view of the world. Vygotsky studied how egocentric speech evolved as thinking developed. When children become operational (to use Piaget's terminology), their egocentric speech goes "underground," according to Vygotsky, in the form of **inner speech.** Inner speech is verbalized thought or self-talk that accompanies thinking. This kind of "thinking out loud" occurs for the same reasons that children initially count on their fingers. Both are temporary aids that help make the transition to thinking silently; they operate as surrogates between the physical and the abstract. Eventually the self-talk fades into muttering and finally thinking silently.

Luria (1964) developed a view of language and thought similar to Vygotsky's. Luria was interested in the regulatory function of speech, that is, how speech is used to instigate, monitor, and guide behavior. To Luria, speech can be regarded as an internal instruction, which is the core of regulating voluntary behaviors. In this paradigm, the child learns self-regulation (e.g., to stop or go in response to *stop* or *go*) by internalizing someone's verbal command. Initially, the parent gives a command like *stop!* to the child, for example, as he approaches a hot stove. The parent has to repeat the command from time to time. The child progressively internalizes speech by first saying commands out loud, saying *stop!* himself when approaching the stove, and finally, according to Vygotsky and Luria, simply thinking the commands to himself silently.

This progression from social control to internalization is the opposite of the scheme that Piaget envisioned. For Luria and Vygotsky, speech begins as an external social symbol that is progressively internalized to serve self-regulatory needs. These two views are not necessarily incompatible. Children may engage in monologue for self-direction and also participate in dialogue for different reasons, such as obtaining food or attention. One of the central ideas here is that language develops out of interactions with people and objects in context. Language starts out bound to these concrete representations but later becomes more abstract and less context-bound.

A recent development in language learning is *emergentism* (MacWhinney, 1999a). These new models focus on language learning through interaction with the physical world and with people in the context of connectionist models of language development. We consider emergence next.

EMERGENCE FROM EMBODIMENT

A main concern in this chapter is the emotional and behavioral underpinnings of language. From this point of view, speech is more than saying words; it expresses and represents emotional states, and it manipulates listeners. Emotional aspects of speech are represented as physiological and behavioral correlates of meaning. Activating a word's meaning activates its behavioral and emotional components. The child's view of the world is *embodied* in language that emerges with development. **Embodiment** is both developmental and ongoing. Developmentally, prelinguistic children cannot represent the world abstractly; they rely on gestural and behavioral representations. Lexical development allows the child to store experiences in the world in the form of verbal symbols. From childhood through adulthood, embodiment is ongoing as new learning creates memories of experiences on a daily basis.

The traditional view of human communication is that comprehension of spoken speech is successful when the listener decodes what the speaker intended through propositional representation (Clark & Clark, 1977). The listener constructs a tree diagram of how the words in the sentence are related to each other. But this account of depicting communication through the connectedness of words fails in a deep way according to the **emergence** view of language development (MacWhinney, 1999a). According to the emergence view, language develops out of the child's social and physical interactions in the physical world, through which a model of the self, objects, actions, and social roles are created and used to comprehend and produce speech. Rather than being innate or hard-wired, language structure emerges and becomes embodied through environmental interactions.

Emergence is a different view of language processing; it looks carefully at what the speaker and listener are trying to accomplish. The traditional approach to comprehending a sentence, such as *The boy took off the lid and let the frog out of the glass jar,* is to graph the relationship between the words in the sentence. But this fails to represent its deeper meanings. That is, we do not appreciate the flow of action, the unity of the scene, the physical sense of unscrewing the lid, or how the frog behaved when released from the jar. MacWhinney (1999b) proposes emergence as an alternative to the standard view; it regards language as a process of **perspective taking.** The listener understands the sentence by taking the *speaker's* perspective of the scene to make sense of what is happening in the utterance.

According to MacWhinney's perspective-taking account, language comprehension and production are embodied processes. The purpose of language processes is to convey embodied meanings through various perspectives and shifts in perspective. To understand a sentence like the frog example, the listener has to become actively involved, imagining the boy unscrewing the lid, feeling the weight of the frog in the jar, feeling the frog shifting from place to place, and seeing it spring onto green grass. Even if we have little firsthand experience with frogs, we can imagine this. The extent to which we understand the sentence is a function of our ability to assume a perspective from which the scene can be enacted.

EMBODIMENT AND MEMORY

In a related line of research, Glenberg (1997) attempted to construct a theory of memory that was based on an embodied internal representation of the world derived from physical and perceptual interaction with the world. He proposed that embodiment was also the basis for language comprehension. That is, memory and language comprehension arise from bodily interaction with the world. Glenberg sees language as a symbolic system that acts as a surrogate for direct interaction with the world. The meaning of a word for an object or event or the meaning of a spoken sentence depends on what the person can do with the object, event, or sentence.

According to Glenberg (1997), the world is conceptualized as patterns of bodily movements we use to deal with it. The meaning of an object, event, or sentence is therefore personal, reflecting what that person can do with the object, event, or sentence. Conceptualization is concrete and reflects how bodies interact with objects. The meaning of an object is a pattern of possible actions or "projectable features" of the object determined by our bodily movements and memories of previous actions. The meaning of my coffee cup is influenced by how far it is from me (Can I reach it?), its shape and size, the orientation of its handle (How do I get my fingers into it?), and the force I must exert to lift it. Its meaning is built on memories of previous interactions with it. These memories make it mine.

For language to be a useful surrogate of the world, it must make contact with embodied representations that we use to represent the world. According to Glenberg, we understand language by creating embodied representations of situations that language describes. This is how we learn about the world from language. This account works when language is being used as a surrogate for events that are not being witnessed at the moment or when it is used to enhance current experience, for example, when a mother instructs her child that something is "hot." The representations derived from her language must integrate or "mesh" with the child's representations of the environment. When being told "That plate is hot," the child must modify his or her embodied representation of the plate in order to modify interactions with the plate and not get burned (Don't touch it for a while).

Glenberg claims that meaning and symbolic representation are "in" us; this is what he means by embodiment. The emotional representations of a word's meaning are activated by what is associated with the word. One of the critical ideas for emergence is Glenberg's notion of "**mesh.**" This concept emphasizes the degree to which properties stored in memory interact with new embodied perceptions in a manner that give rise to subjective experience and new learning. When we read the frog sentence, we imagine and we feel the frog in the jar through our past experiences with objects in small containers. We go beyond the relationship of the words in the surface structure and take a richer perspective on what the words mean as embodied from experience. The word *twisting* meshes with our memories of opening jars.

What is important here is the role of embodiment in language acquisition, that is, how memories are created through multiple levels of encoding. Properties of objects, events, and social roles stored in memory interact with new embodied perceptions, giving birth to new subjective experiences and new learning. Embodiment unifies our flesh-and-blood emotional and instinctual affordances with less concrete linguistic structures and social relations. By its embodied nature, language acquisition is understood as a multilayered process of words, emotions, and experiences. The emergence of language through embodiment provides a rich account of language, one compatible with the role of individual differences in language learning, personality, and worldview, as we see next.

INTERACTION WITH LANGUAGE: EXPRESSIVE AND REFERENTIAL LANGUAGE LEARNERS

Children start talking by referencing objects and people from their physical sensorimotor view and social surroundings. The path to symbolism differs from child to child. Children have been labeled **referential learners** if their vocabulary contains a high percentage of nominals or labels (nouns, verbs, proper names, and descriptive adjectives) to refer to their immediate environment. Children who use language to emphasize social interaction through comments like *gimme* or *stop it* are labeled **expressive learners** (Nelson, 1973). Expressive children have a similar number of words but a lower proportion of nominals. The expressive-referential difference is a matter of degree. All children make references to the environment and make comments regarding social interactions. Most children exhibit a mixture of these kinds of references.

The distinction has led to a debate about the origin and meaning of these different styles of reference. Interestingly, as referential and expressive children develop, their styles seem to merge into a more adultlike production. Expressive children learn more nouns and descriptors for objects, and referential children come to use longer sentencelike utterances. It is as if the expressives are working from whole utterances and then learning the parts, while the referentials learn the parts and later assemble the wholes.

Expressive children tend to have bigger vocabularies of words used to manipulate others' attention. Referential children tend to have a vocabulary that is used to name objects rather than manipulate interpersonal relations. Nelson (1981) and others (Della Corte, Benedict, & Klein, 1983) searched for the causes of these individual differences and found that the mother's speech patterns were part of the cause. Referential children had mothers who uttered descriptive statements to the child more often than expressive mothers did. Expressive children had mothers who produced more prescriptive statements, telling them what to do (Pine, 1994). Referential children, demographically speaking, are more likely to be firstborns and have college-educated parents, who might be more likely to label objects than less educated parents (Goldfield & Reznick, 1990). Later-born children may get less attention and become more likely to learn more language from the environment.

What developmentalists have shown is that language is coemergent with an understanding of the physical and social world. However, the understanding of the world depends in part on the mother's interactions with the child, implicating the role of learning and teaching strategies. Nelson thought referential differences came from the child's view of the function of language: labeling or referencing objects versus a means for interacting with other people. The point is that children take different paths to language learning not predicted by the nativist view. They develop a view of language that emerges from social interactions in the physical world.

Before children begin speaking, we have to pay attention to how they use their bodies to communicate. In particular, we look at how children use gestures to communicate before they can speak. The body is the sole medium of prelinguistic communication. Language emerges later and is coordinated with gesturing.

PRELINGUISTIC GESTURES AND COMMUNICATIVE INTENT

Prelinguistic gestures are hand movements (e.g., pointing) that precede speech and are used to communicate to others. Gestures are evidence that a child has an intention that he or she cannot express verbally. Infants begin to use gestures around 8 months of age, but how do we know they are intentional? Crying, fussing, and smiling can be used by parents to infer intention, but they in themselves do not constitute intent.

Bruner (1975) suggested that we impose three criteria on gesturing to determine if the gestures are intentional: waiting, persistence, and the use of alternative strategies. For example, if a child wants Dad to fetch a toy, gesturing to him might not be sufficient if Dad is not looking. She will have to wait until Dad is paying attention. If Dad looks but does not fetch, she will have to persist in pointing at the toy. If this does not work, she might have to do something else to get the toy, perhaps screaming, crying, or whining. Prelinguistic gestures rely on the parent to infer that the child's pointing and fussing are signs of desire. Also note that one cannot tell what the child is doing with the pointing gesture by looking at the gesture alone. We have to watch the child, the parents' reactions, and the child's response to the parents' behaviors.

The pattern of gesturing to get a parental response suggests goal-directed or means-ends behavior on the part of the child. Children use gestures because of what the gestures produce. In this way, children intentionally use gestures to express desires that cannot be expressed orally. Bates, Camaioni, and Volterra (1975) found that prelinguistic gesturing filled two desires: assertions used to get adults' attention and requests of adults to obtain objects. The child's gesture pattern, coordinated with the parental responses, teaches the child that communicating involves a series of discrete behavior segments that are interdependent and instrumental to obtaining goals (Bruner, 1975). The parent may mark the beginning of the segment by asking *Do you want the toy?* and end the segment by saying *There you are.* The child learns that the gestures are part of a bigger routine.

Merely making a requesting gesture does not fill intentions; it depends on how adults respond to the request. A child will respond to others' gestures based on this coordinated strategy. When an adult points to an object, the child will look in the direction of the object and not at the adult's face (Clark & Clark, 1977). The child comes to realize that communication involves a set of physical behaviors and interactions that can be instigated by her or by others. As Snow (1977) suggests, babies are treated as conversational partners from the moment of birth. Mothers respond to a child's vocalizations and noises as if they were part of a conversational dialogue. For example, the child smiles, and the mother says *What a nice smile;* the child makes a noise, and the mother responds *There's a nice noise.*

Intentionality, according to Bates et al. (1975), becomes evident around 9 to 10 months of age, when children begin to fuss to elicit aid from others to obtain objects. The child may say *mmm* and at the same time use a pointing gesture to make a request. Bates et al. labeled these kinds of requests as *protoimperatives* because they served as primitive commands. Another form of intentional behavior, which occurs later, is the *protodeclarative:* The child points to an object and vocalizes in order to get the adult to pay attention to the object. The child achieves the goal when the adult looks at the object. Another term for what is happening in these instances is **joint attention** (Carpenter, Nagell, & Tomasello, 1998). The child and adult are paying attention to a third object. The main idea underlying joint attention is that the child can follow the gaze of another person and at the same time try to direct the other's attention to something of interest. In a way, the child is assuming that the other person has a mind and can think of what he or she is thinking, forming the basis for communication. Interestingly, Tomasello and colleagues (Carpenter et al., 1998; Tomasello, 1995; Tomasello & Todd, 1983) found that the more effort put into joint attention, the faster the development of language.

TYPES OF GESTURES

Children's gestures differ in both form and function. Around the age of 12 months, gestures are often coordinated with eye contact with another person or an alternating pattern of looking at the person, then looking at an object (Tomasello, 1995). We focus on two kinds of gestures: *deictic* and *representational* gestures (see Iverson & Thal, 1998). **Deictic gestures** establish reference by calling attention to an object or event through *showing* an object to another person; *pointing* with the index finger; *reaching,* often opening and closing the hand; or *giving* an object to another person. Symbolic or **representational gestures** have referential and semantic content. They can be *object-related*—for example, opening and closing the mouth for *fish*—or they can be *culturally defined* conventional gestures such as waving bye-bye or nodding the head for *yes* (Acredolo & Goodwyn, 1985, 1988).

The gestures for giving, showing, and reaching emerge between 8 and 14 months of age as a means of focusing the child's attention and drawing the adults' attention (Bates, 1976). These form the basis for establishing reference, indicating a new level of communicative competence. These gestures seem to occur first in response to adult behavior, but over time they become less linked to a specific context. Bates, O'Connell, and Shore (1987) suggested that giving, showing, and reaching were necessary prerequisites for pointing since they allow the child to establish a base for referential communication on a simple level. Pointing appears just a bit later in the developmental sequence, between 12 and 14 months. Pointing occurs before this, but not in an interactive pattern with an adult, coordinated with gazing at the object and the adult. After 12 months, the pointing takes on a social status because it is used to direct attention.

Gestures Coordinated with Speech

Werner and Kaplan (1963) argued that children's referential behavior is derived within a social context where children share the objects and events they think about. They suggested that gestures are the outgrowth of sensorimotor thinking and eventually become symbols for referents. In this way, the gesture as a symbol has the effect of decontextualizing the referent. The early action-based gestures emerge from games and routines children learn to perform. These are often repeated and become further and further displaced from their referents. What is important here is how gestures develop in conjunction with words.

The developmental pattern of language and gesture is one of mutual exchange. That is, gestures and words show little semantic overlap, and children interchange them in a context to refer to objects and events therein. But what happens to gesturing when the child's vocabulary expands? Do words replace referential gestures?

Iverson, Capirci, and Caselli (1994) explored the interplay between gestures and words in 16- and 20-month-old children. They reported that gesturing occurred extensively in both age groups. The younger children had more gestures than words and showed a clear preference for using gestures over words. Importantly, the number of gestures they used at this stage was highly correlated with their oral performance later in development. In speech, they used more representational than deictic *words*, but in gesturing, they used more deictic than representational *gestures*. However, the older children had more words than gestures and used words more frequently than gestures. Here we see a shift in the composition of gestures versus words in the older children. Older children clearly prefer to communicate vocally, and there is a significant increase in deictic words and deictic gestures. The production of representational gestures declined.

In younger children, the gestures seem to permit communication with elements that are not available in speech. The gestures tend to complement rather than overlap their words, semantically speaking. As the children transition to a more verbal system, they change the way gesturing is used. Older children tend to increase their pointing gestures and decrease their representational gestures, preferring to replace them with words, as predicted earlier by Werner and Kaplan (1963). The gesture plays a central role in making the transition to abstract articulation, and once the word becomes predominant, the representational gesture becomes less necessary for communication.

Gesture-Word Combinations

Children produce word-gesture combinations months before they begin producing two-word utterances. In other words, the child who used only one word or one gesture at a time shifts to two different kinds of combinations of word and gesture as a single utterance (Bates, Benigni, Bretherton, Camaioni, & Volterra, 1979). **Complementary gestures** combined with words, which occur between 14 and 16 months of age, are often redundant, such as pointing to a cup and saying *cup* at the same time. **Supplementary gestures** combined with words unfold between 16 and 18 months and convey different but related information, such as pointing to a cup and saying *mommy* at the same time, indicating that it is Mom's cup.

In a later study, Capirci, Iverson, Pizzuto, and Volterra (1996) explored the use of gestures and words during transition from one-word to two-word speech. Results supported the notion that children move from complementary to supplementary combinations before two-word utterances emerge. The use of gestural and gesture-word combinations appears to be a robust developmental phenomenon. The most frequent two-element combinations tend to be deictic gestures and representational words. No child produced two referential gestures in combination. The transition period prior to two-word utterances seems to represent a two-element cross-modal stage where the child uses what works best in each mode of communication. Children can combine two ideas (one word and one gesture) prior to combining two ideas with words alone. Although deictic gestures occur frequently here, deictic words do not. E. Clark (1978) suggested that deictic words are more cognitively complex than their gestural counterparts, perhaps overburdening the child's limited cognitive capacity. Gestures play an important role in the child's communicative and abstract-symbolic development. Children exhibit communicative intent with two-element cross-modal utterances prior to two-word speech.

GESTURES FROM BILINGUAL CHILDREN

One way to demonstrate the interdependence of gesture and language is to show how gesturing emerges for a bilingual child when the two languages develop at an uneven pace. Bilingual children often develop their languages at different rates because one parent interacts with the child in one language more than the other parent does in the second language (Nicoladis & Genesee, 1997). If gestures are linked to cognitive skills that are independent of language, then gesturing in two languages should be identical, and the frequency of gesturing would be independent of the rate of development in either language. However, if bilingual gesturing were specifically linked to the growth of language, then the rate of development would be contingent on the rate at which each language develops.

Mayberry and Nicoladis (2000) conducted a longitudinal investigation of gesture and language development in French-English bilinguals between the ages of 2 and 3½ years. They counted the number of pointing gestures, iconics (representational images), and beats (hand and arm movements that mark the structure of discourse) that the children used while communicating with their mothers.

The children produced 81 percent of their gestures while speaking at age 2 and 90 percent while speaking at age 3½, ruling out the notion that gestures compensate for the inability to speak. Most of the children's gesturing relied on pointing. Importantly, the kinds of gestures the children used depended on the language they were speaking. They began speaking using iconic and beat gestures only after they reached the two-word stage. Therefore, the utterances that co-occurred with iconics and beats were more complex than those with points or no gesturing. This relationship is illustrated in Figure 11.1. For children who spoke multiword utterances in one language (English) but not the other (French), the presence of iconics and beats occurred only with the more developed language (English) and never with the less developed language (French). Mayberry and Nicoladis's experiment provides a clear picture of how gesturing emerges with language development. When children mature to multiword utterances, they shift to

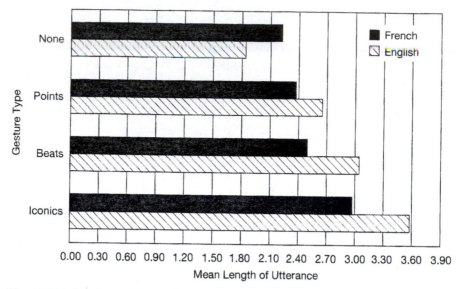

Figure 11.1. Average Length of Spoken Utterances with and without Accompanying Gestures in Bilingual Children

Note. From Mayberry, R. I., & Nicoladis, E. (2000). Gesture reflects language development: Evidence from bilingual children. *Current Directions in Psychological Science, 9(6),* 192–199. Reprinted by permission of Blackwell Publishers.

new and more language-related types of gestures (iconics and beats). Gesturing reflects the child's understanding of the physical world, how to interact with others to obtain objects, and once speech emerges, how to coordinate gesturing with linguistic structure.

Review Question
How could parenting style affect children's communication style?

Language and Learning

Children use language to do things to other people. This is the *instrumentality* of language, the use of language as an instrument to achieve personal and social intentions. Skinner's theory of language was based on the tenets of **instrumental conditioning** as outlined in *Verbal Behavior* (1957). Skinner used instrumental or operant conditioning to show how we use language to manipulate others. While the theory falls short of accounting for grammar, it does address some the functions of language. Instrumentality is important to social interactionists because language intentions form the purpose of speaking to others.

The role of parental feedback becomes an important variable from a learning perspective because feedback plays a role in shaping how children speak. Here we ask what it is that parents intend when they correct their children. Even if parents are not able to teach past tense inflections for regular verbs before children are ready, as we read in Chapter 10, parents remain deeply involved with language learning on a social level. Reconsider the example from McNeill (1966, p. 69).

CHILD: Nobody doesn't like me.

MOTHER: No, say, "Nobody likes me."

CHILD: Nobody doesn't like me. *(repeated eight times)*

MOTHER: No, now listen carefully: Say, "Nobody likes me."

CHILD: Oh, nobody don't likes me.

What is the mother trying to do here? From an instrumental view, she is trying to shape the child's language. Through interaction, the child learns that his or her mother is concerned with the way language is used.

Roger Brown (1965, 1968) described the growth of language within the dynamics of mother-child interaction. He argued that these exchanges provided a rich set of data for the child to discover grammar. For example, mothers use questions to help the child learn the grammatical form of questions. The child says something like *I want milk* and the mother asks *You want what?* Another type of helpful maternal interaction involves what Brown called **expansions.** These occurred in 30 percent of Brown's data. When Adam said *Throw Daddy,* his mother expanded the sentence, saying *Throw it to Daddy.* The expansion provides Adam with a well-formed version of his probable syntax. The feedback and expansion of children's speech provides a database from which the child can learn. This is not to say that the parent is explicitly instructing the child (although this does occur); it is more likely that the parent is trying to verify the child's intentions. Most of the time, parents are not trying to correct syntax but rather to determine the truth or falsity of children's statements. Brown, Cazden, and Bellugi (1967) proposed that truth-value and not grammatical well-formedness governed the explicit verbal reinforcement from parents.

More recently, Moerk (1989, 1990) has argued forcefully that mother-child interactions are sufficient to enable a child to learn language skills. The LAD and innate knowledge postulated by Chomsky are not necessary to explain language acquisition, according to Moerk. He suggests that no child learns "a language"; what children do learn is how to incrementally improve their communication skills. Moerk (1989) suggests that language learning is a set of learning processes and skills that exist on different levels of complexity. Maternal rewards and corrections are integrated with perceptual, cognitive, and social learning concepts in order to explain the complexity of language learning (Moerk, 1990). Moerk (1990) published data establishing the effectiveness of reinforcers for language learning. He found that the child in the study repeated part or all of her rewarded utterances.

These data challenge the poverty of stimulus argument (Chomsky, 1959), which states that parents provide insufficient data for the child to learn grammar.

On a more practical social level, parents monitor their children's language for inappropriate words and phrases. Parents are concerned about what their children say and where they say it (Berges, Neiderbach, Rubin, Sharpe, & Tesler, 1983). Parental feedback clearly operates on social aspects of language production. American children are punished for saying "bad" words with the soap-in-the-mouth routine, physical punishments, and mild reprimands (Jay, King, & Duncan, 2002). In the parents' mind, they are correcting the social misuse of language. Herein the meaning of "bad" or "dirty" words becomes associated with their instrumental consequences. Words, which are linked to punishment, are inhibited. The instrumental history of the bad word is part of its meaning, as we shall see.

The conclusion from the instrumental conditioning point of view is that what is effective in achieving the speaker's personal and social goals will be repeated and what does not work will be dropped. This means that the consequences of word usage are stored along with the word in memory. But as we have seen in McNeill's example, instrumentality may not affect the child's inflections before the child is ready.

LEARNING AND EMOTIONS RECONSIDERED

In the late 1960s, psycholinguists abandoned the learning point of view and took up the information processing metaphor for language use. The problem with the computer-inspired metaphor is that it erased the emotional aspect of thinking and speaking. Social milieu and emotion are essential to language learning. Speech cannot be deemotionalized or decontextualized. This mind-without-emotion view is what Damasio (1994) called **Descartes' error.** Damasio (1994) and Pinker (1997) have made the case that we cannot separate affect from intellect. We cannot divorce the affect in speech or the motivation to speak from the system of language. Why? Speech creates arousal and allows us to appraise arousal. Speech causes emotional reactions and allows us to name what we feel.

Early versions of Chomsky's grammar (1957, 1965) took a structural approach, and meaning was secondary. Emotional aspects of sentence production, such as stress, intensity, intonation, and rhythm, were not considered part of the paradigm. These features express emotion without being verbally coded (Haiman, 1998). Linguists considered suprasegmental aspects of speaking as the "music" that comes with the words. Following on this figure, the music, the stress, the rhythm, the pitch, and the loudness of language are all embodied representations that create emotional meaning. These representations are part of the message; they are the emotional aspects of the message. When we comprehend *what* people say, we comprehend *how* they say it.

Few researchers have studied how emotion influences structure. How do the emotional aspects of an utterance influence surface structure? Using a preferred adjective ordering technique, Jay and Danks (1977) demonstrated that the affective meaning of a sentence does become represented through syntax. When connotative meaning was to be expressed, subjects preferred taboo adjectives to be farther from the noun they modified, for example, *shitty little boy*. When denotative meaning was to be expressed, subjects preferred the taboo adjectives placed closer to the noun, for example, *little shitty boy*. This experiment demonstrated how emotional meanings affect surface structure. Different emotional intentions are marked by different preferred adjective orderings, which ultimately affect the listener's comprehension of the utterance and attitudes about the person described (Jay, 1981).

The relationship between emotion and speech is a matter of degree, ranging from speech that is controlled and deliberate to reflexive or **automatic speech** (Jay, 2000). With reflexive emotional speech, the emotion and words are coemergent. At the reflexive end of the continuum, there is the involuntary production of emotional speech, as when someone crashes into your car and you say *damned Nazi*. In the deliberate case, the emotion is less immediate and obvious; there is a conscious effortful guided search for emotional meaning, as when a politician must find the right phrase, for example, *Hitler was a damned Nazi*. The point is that there are different levels of neural involvement and emotionality motivating the utterance *damned Nazi*. While the surface structure is the same, the underlying emotional meaning is not. In one case it is deliberate and denotative, but in the other it is reflexive and emotionally inspired (Van Lancker, 1987). How emotional aspects of words are learned is covered next.

CLASSICALLY CONDITIONED WORD MEANING

A word's meaning is complex, as we have noted repeatedly. Here the discussion is limited to the emotional aspects of meaning. It is difficult to discuss emotional meaning without considering learning. Children learn semantic meaning through a variety of strategies (discussed in Chapter 10). We will address some of the affective correlates of words, the idea that words have emotional meaning. How does this happen? One explanation comes from the **classical conditioning** (CC) paradigm, which is based on the simple contiguity of word with affect.

Consider the CC paradigm from Pavlov's research on the physiology of digestion. Pavlov noted that dogs normally salivate (unconditioned response, UR) to the smell and sight of food (unconditioned stimulus, US). If an originally neutral signal such as a bell (conditioned stimulus, CS) repeatedly precedes the food, the dog associates the bell with the food. After a few pairings, the dog salivates (conditioned response, CR) to the sound of the bell without the food. Although the bell is physically separated from the food in the real world, in the dog's brain they are intimately tied. The originally neutral bell now evokes a physiological reaction to the food, as if it were the food. As a bell evokes the physiological reactions associated with it, so can a word as a conditioned stimulus evoke visceral reactions associated with it for humans. This paradigm is outlined in Figure 11.2.

When children learn words, they learn their connotations. Toddlers' reactions to interjections like *No! Good! Stop!* or *Hot!* reveal observable physiological and

Before conditioning

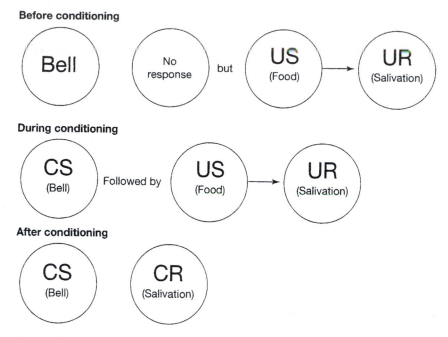

Figure 11.2. A Paradigm of the Classical Conditioning Process

Note. Psychology: An Introduction 10/E by Morris/Maisto, © 1999. Reprinted by permission of Pearson Education, Inc., Upper Saddle River, NJ.

emotional components. These interjections evoke **approach** or **avoidance** behavior and emotional reactions. The child's attention shifts to the adult in the situation. Arousal becomes part of the meaning of each expression. The toddler is trained how to behave (avoid or approach) in response to interjections and commands. The link between the emotional word and its physiological component is as real for the child as the bell-food link is for the dog. Through classical conditioning, the child embodies visceral and behavioral meanings of words. *Good!* evokes behavior and affect. Initially, the word elicits little response from the child. Like the CS prior to conditioning, the word is neutral. But when the mother says *good* and hugs the child, unconditioned responses are elicited, including feeling warm, squirming, cuddling closer, tossing the head back, and pleasant sensations. *Good* repeated with hugs over time will elicit a pleasant feeling (conditioned response), one of well-being. The sequence of events is depicted in the top part of Figure 11.3.

The word *good* produces external and internal responses. These responses are depicted in the bottom part of Figure 11.3. The new partial response to the word, r_m, is internal and unobservable. The subscript m refers to the *meaning* function in behavioral terms. *Good* is now a stimulus that evokes a conditioned r_{m+}, the pleasant feeling, which evokes a stimulus pattern s_m, which produces external responses R_1, $R_2, \ldots, R_n$—in this case, approach behaviors. We can establish a meaning for *bad* with classical conditioning using a negative US, such as restraining, grabbing, or hurting the child. But *bad* will then evoke an unpleasant internal response r_{m-} from

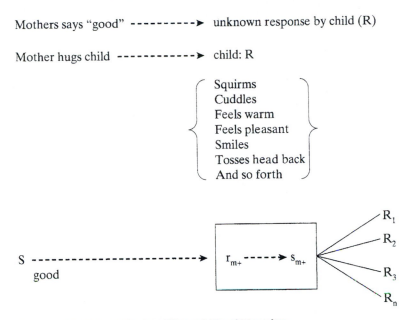

Figure 11.3. Classically Conditioned Word Meaning
Note. From Pollio, H. R. (1974). *The Psychology of Symbolic Activity.* Reading, MA: Addison-Wesley. Reprinted by permission.

unpleasant feelings caused by aversive stimuli (e.g., grabbing). Rather than producing approach behavior, *bad* will produce avoidance behaviors such as moving away or cowering.

A word acquires emotional meaning through physical-emotional association, as illustrated in the *good* example. Words also acquire emotional meaning through association with other emotional words. Pollio (1974) illustrated how one could condition the word *communism* to evoke a negative r_{m-} by pairing it with other negatively toned words (e.g., *bad, disease*). This is illustrated in Figure 11.4. *Communism* as illustrated in this example becomes "contaminated" with negative connotative meaning. A sequence of exchanges about communism is depicted in the top part of the figure. The conditioning stages are depicted in the bottom part.

LABORATORY STUDIES OF VERBAL CONDITIONING

To understand how conditioned meaning is established in a laboratory setting, we have to create a situation with people that is analogous to Pavlov's original study. Razran (1939, 1961) did this when he demonstrated that human subjects could be trained to salivate to the denotative or connotative aspects of a word. In the denotative study, Razran (1939) trained subjects to salivate to a word like *freeze*. He later exposed them to words that were structurally similar, such as *frieze*, or semantically similar, such as *chill*. One would expect the strongest response to the test word most similar to the original word, according to a generalization hypothesis. Razran found

David: What is Communism?
Enlightened Social Studies Teacher: Communism is Bad.
David: Is it Bad like Measles?
Teacher: In a way—it's sort of a Disease.
David: Is it worse than Mumps?
Teacher: Yes, it's very Bad, more like a Cancer.
David: Oh, that's funny—I thought it was an economic system.

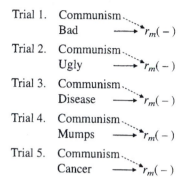

Trial 1.   Communism
          Bad $\longrightarrow$ $r_m(-)$

Trial 2.   Communism
          Ugly $\longrightarrow$ $r_m(-)$

Trial 3.   Communism
          Disease $\longrightarrow$ $r_m(-)$

Trial 4.   Communism
          Mumps $\longrightarrow$ $r_m(-)$

Trial 5.   Communism
          Cancer $\longrightarrow$ $r_m(-)$

Figure 11.4. Conditioning for Negative Connotative Meaning *Note. From Pollio, H. R. (1974). The Psychology of Symbolic Activity.* Reading, MA: Addison-Wesley. Reprinted by permission.

that subjects responded most to the semantically similar word rather than the structurally similar one, indicating that they were storing the denotative meaning of the word in memory. Since he used the salivary reflex and not an avoidance reflex (e.g., fear or anxiety), we cannot observe the feeling component here. However, we do see the conditioned physiological response (salivating) similar to what Pavlov achieved with a nonverbal signal (bell).

The connotative aspects of conditioned meaning are more apparent in another study in which Razran (1961) conditioned a subject to salivate to the Russian word for *good* (*khorosho*) and to inhibit salivating to the word *bad* (*plokho*). After the subject was presented with good and bad words in acquisition trials, the subject generalized the responses to "good news" sentences (e.g., *The pupil studies excellently*) and "bad news" sentences (e.g., *My friend is seriously ill*). Although the methodology is somewhat odd, it proves a point: Emotional reactions can be elicited by word meanings, and the physiological response generalizes to sentences similar in affective meaning. Razran demonstrated an important link between an abstract word and an emotional response to it.

There is additional evidence that the associations between internal activation and external verbal responses are established through classical conditioning as reported by Staats (1968) and his colleagues. In these studies, classical conditioning was used to link one verbal item to a second verbal item, confirming **word association** on the basis of affective meaning. Staats and Staats (1957, 1959, 1963; see also Staats, 1964) have demonstrated conditioned meaning through a series of experiments. In the learning phase, subjects are presented with neutral nonsense syllables (e.g., *xof*, *wem*) that are paired with either positively rated words or negatively rated words. Subjects are then asked to provide evaluative ratings for each nonsense syllable. The nonsense syllables paired with positively rated words evoke positive ratings. Nonsense syllables paired with negatively rated words take on negative meaning.

The classically conditioned effect extends beyond nonsense syllables. It has been demonstrated with positive and negative ratings of names of national groups (Staats & Staats, 1958). Association with names for social groups that are liked or disliked will evoke positive and negative reactions. Now you can imagine why the words used to discuss an emotionally loaded political topic like abortion are determined by the speaker's political agenda. Those who advocate women's rights to determine reproductive health use the positive term *choice*. Those arguing against these choices associate abortion with the negative word *murder*. One group associates abortion with a positive word and behavior, *choice*, while the opposition focuses on a negative word and behavior, *murder*. These pairings will produce positive and negative connotative meanings, according to the Staats' research. Words like *abortion* become emotionally contaminated through association with positive or negative words.

AFFECT AND BEHAVIOR

Some emotional word associations can be established through association to aversive stimuli. If nonsense syllables or names are conditioned to unpleasant noises or shocks, the nonsense syllables produce a **galvanic skin response** (GSR), an indication of arousal (see Chapter 6). The greater the intensity of the original shock or noise, the greater the size of the GSR. GSR levels are also correlated with negative word ratings (Staats, Staats, & Crawford, 1962). The GSR concomitant with negative ratings shows that words produce physiological reactions and negative affect. Negative connotation can produce a behavioral response in the form of an avoidance reaction. The important point is that evoking the meaning of the word (saying or hearing it) produces a physiological response and emotional feeling caused by the original aversive stimulus (e.g., shock). The word, behavior, and feeling aspects become linked, like nodes in a connectionist network. One aspect or component of meaning (e.g., word) activates the other components (e.g., feelings and behaviors).

In a classic paper on conditioned meaning, Corteen and Wood (1972) demonstrated that a conditioned GSR to city names, presented over earphones, can be elicited without the subject's being aware of the presentation. In the initial stage of the experiment, city names heard over earphones are paired with an electric shock (US). The second stage of the experiment is a dichotic shadowing task in which the subjects are told to monitor a prose passage in the right ear and ignore the speech in the left ear (the city names). The city names paired with shock elicit greater GSRs than control words when presented in the nonattended ear. Subjects reported that they were unaware of the words in the nonattended ear. What is significant here is the subjects' emotional response to previously conditioned words that were outside of their consciousness. We return to this idea later in this chapter.

Psychologists have demonstrated many times that word meaning evokes some simple approach-avoidance tendencies on the part of human subjects. "Pleasant" words evoke approach or movements toward the stimulus, and "unpleasant" words evoke avoidance or movements away. Pollio and Gerow (1968) elucidated these tendencies by measuring the time it took subjects to name word associates in positive and negative contexts. Here context meant word lists containing positive or negative words. The rationale was that a negative word from a list of other negative words would evoke the greatest avoidance or longest reaction times. Positive words from a list of other positive words would evoke the fastest reaction times due to approach tendencies. A negative word in the context of positive words or a positive word in the context of negative words would fall somewhere in between, depending on the number of positive or negative words in the contexts.

As you can see in Figure 11.5, the results unfold as predicted. Subjects provided longer reaction times to negative words in negative contexts (–, –) and shorter reaction times to positive words in positive contexts (+, +). The reaction times also depend on the context of the negative and positive stimulus words. Reaction time to a positive stimulus word slows down as the number of negative words in the context increases (–, +). Conversely, the reaction time to a negative target word quickens as the number of positive words in its context increases (+, –). Pleasant

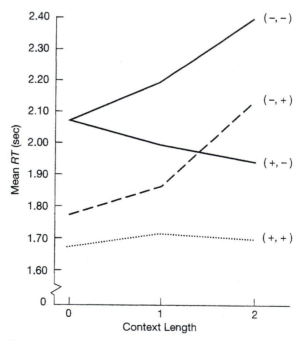

Figure 11.5. Associative Reaction Times to Pleasant (+) and Unpleasant (–) Stimuli as a Function of Context Length and Type *Note.* From *American Journal of Psychology.* Copyright 1968 by the Board of Trustees of the University of Illinois. Used with permission of the University of Illinois Press.

words produce quick associative (approach) responses, and adding pleasant words to the list increases the speed. Adding unpleasant words to the list slows the response speed (avoidance). These studies show that emotional words affect physiological reactions and guide approach-avoidance behaviors.

Another question remains: How do we measure affective differences across word meanings?

MEASURING AFFECT WITH THE SEMANTIC DIFFERENTIAL

Behaviorists suggest that the fractional meaning responses r_m become associates of words. One way to tap these emotional meanings is through the **semantic differential** (SD) (Osgood, Suci, & Tannenbaum, 1957; see also Chapter 4). Osgood (1953, 1963) viewed meaning as an internal response in the absence of a concrete referent. We associate verbal symbols with our memories from personal experience. These associations affect the SD ratings.

As you may recall from Chapter 4, the SD consists of a series of 7-point bipolar rating scales (*good-bad, weak-strong,* etc.) on which words are rated. The affective dimensions of the scales are Evaluation, Potency, and Activity. Although *communism* will feel different to a member of the Chinese Communist Party, its ratings might look something like the following to a conservative and loyal American:

communism

fair	1	2	3	4	5	⑥	7	unfair
strong	1	2	3	4	⑤	6	7	weak
active	1	2	③	4	5	6	7	passive

This would produce a triad that was 6 on the Evaluation scale, 5 on Potency, and 3 on Activity. The word *communism* would occupy this point in three-dimensional emotional space. One could distinguish the emotional meaning of a word like *communism* from other words, like *love* or *democracy,* by its location in semantic space, according to Osgood. The SD has been used reliably as a measure of connotation; but it is not clear how this analysis would apply to denotative meaning.

DEVELOPMENT OF EMOTIONAL ASSOCIATIONS

The emergence of meaning is both developmental and ongoing. Learning theory predicts that children produce a different pattern of associations with emotional words than adults do because adults have more diverse semantic memories and emotional experiences. The adult asked to provide an associate to *mother* will generally name a semantic opposite, *father.* But the young child might respond with *hug* because the child relies more on the internal mediators of the stimulus word. The child also does not have a well-developed concept of "semantic opposite" yet. In the same way, the child is more likely to associate *stove* with *hot* than with another kitchen appliance.

Osgood's analysis of emotional meaning and semantic space provides a framework for understanding how words are linked to emotions and physical reactions. A meaningful word activates its semantic and emotional associates. The emotional associates of a word are the various r_{ms}, and the semantic associates of the word are r_{as}. The hypothetical pattern of associations is depicted in Figure 11.6. Note that the word associates r_a and internal emotional responses r_m are linked. One word can evoke another word as a response either through learning (r_m) or semantic similarity (r_a). For example, the word *woman* will evoke other associative words like *man*, and it will evoke emotional responses that reflect the listener's learning history. Through the concept of classical conditioning we can appreciate why word association and free association are valuable tools in psychoanalysis. Words activate the emotional meanings that were conditioned earlier in life. We explore these applications further in the next section.

Conditioned-meaning studies show that we develop physiological reactions to denotative and connotative properties of words. These reactions are not experimental artifacts; they are part of a word's embodied meaning. Words are inseparable from their emotional consequences. Hearing and producing emotional words

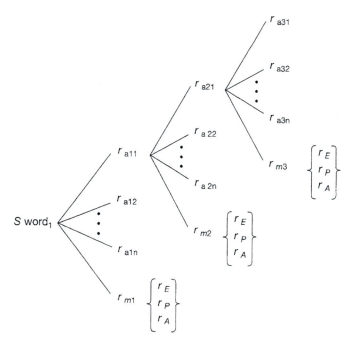

Figure 11.6. Hypothetical Pattern of Semantic (r_a) and Emotional (r_m) Responses Evoked by a Single Stimulus Word (S word₁) *Note.* From Pollio, H. R. (1974). *The Psychology of Symbolic Activity.* Reading, MA: Addison-Wesley.

evokes approach or avoidance responses. The discussion of learning in this chapter is meant to stimulate interest in emotional aspects of language, not a return to behaviorism. Modern theories of language need to address some of these issues. One cannot say or hear powerful words without activating some emotional reaction linked to them. We can see this more clearly in patients with emotional disorders.

Review Question

Speculate about the use of emotional language as political rhetoric. How would you "contaminate" the philosophies of members of an opposing political party through the use of negatively toned language?

Language and Emotion

Normal people have emotional reactions to emotional words. We have conditioned reactions to **taboo words** in our native language, but we do not have strong emotional reactions to taboo words in a foreign language. We understand the word *shit*, and hearing or saying it is generally associated with some physiological arousal. One can know denotatively that the word for *shit* in French is *merde*. While *shit* is emotionally arousing for most Americans, *merde* will be connotatively and physiologically unarousing (Jay, 1992a, 2000). When we hear or say *merde* there is little or no arousal, even though we know it is offensive in French. *Merde* has not been classically conditioned. With enough classical conditioning, *merde* can become emotionally loaded, and this is the point: Connotation comes out of learning.

People with emotional disturbances, such as spider phobics, respond very differently to spider words than normal people do. The behaviorist approach provides part of the answer through an analysis of how spiders, the word *spider*, and anxiety are associated. Normal people form emotional reactions to words, but not like those formed by people with phobic concerns. Emotional aspects of speech processing originate subcortically in the limbic system and are lateralized in the right cerebral hemisphere. Psycholinguists acknowledge an emotion-language link but do not go on to integrate a theory of language with a theory of emotion (Adolphs, Russell, & Tranel, 1999, Lamendella, 1977; Ross, Thompson, & Yenkosky, 1997; Van Lancker, 1987; Van Lancker & Cummings, 1999). The lack of integration produces an **emotion gap** in psycholinguistic theory (Jay, 2000). We need to establish links to the two types of processing to bridge the emotion gap.

Maybe we can understand the link better through an analogy. The function of emotional speech is similar to the function of the horn in an automobile (Jay, 2000). It alerts others to how we feel. All cars are wired with a horn, but how we use this warning system is a personal matter. The horn can be used to express a wide variety of emotions (e.g., surprise, joy, fear, anger, or frustration). Notice that aside from emoting with the entire automobile, the horn is the main mechanism for expressing emotions in the car. Our subcortical emotional system is built in and becomes linked to language. Emotional language is one way we express emotions. Verbally, only deeply emotional language is able to express deeply felt emotions.

Cleansing the Lexicon of Dirty Words

What would happen if we erased our deep emotional words from official dictionaries? Would it be like taking the horn from the car? Consider this example. During the Holocaust and World War II, the Nazi regime consciously removed from its official documents emotionally loaded words tied to the extermination of Jews. They replaced emotional words with neutral ones. For example, *gas chamber* was replaced by a word like *equipment,* and *extermination* was replaced by a word like *action.* Without deeply disturbing words, deeply disturbing emotions are attenuated. The cleansed language facilitated the Nazi bureaucrats' denial of what was going on and removed the guilt that is created by the more emotional words.

DESCARTES' ERROR

How we learn to link emotions to speech is a matter of great personal and social significance. The emotional architecture of the brain is primary in providing the emotional shadings for words. Expressed emotions and felt emotions rely in part on language, and language relies on emotional words to convey emotions verbally. Only humans have the ability to express emotions symbolically. Psychologists are currently being persuaded to integrate emotion into models of thinking and reasoning by such prominent authors as Damasio (1994) and Pinker (1997). In *Descartes' Error,* Damasio (1994) argues persuasively that mind and body operate as one. Emotion guides cognition; cognition affects emotion. The emotional embodiment of language philosophy argues that decision making and communication are derived from an embodied sense of self. Our selves do things with language that reflect our emotional, social, and physiological goals. Language and communication cannot be divorced from these goals.

What is important for Pinker (1997) is the fact that emotion guides intelligent behavior and communication. Emotion motivates decision making. The importance of language, especially emotional language, is that it achieves goals for people. Language may produce negative emotions like anger and shame, but it also produces positive emotions like romantic love and gratitude. Emotions play two roles in a theory of language. On one hand, they are an aspect of a word's meaning; on the other hand, they are important in the achievement of pragmatic goals of speech. We use language to manipulate others. The manipulative intentions are what Pinker would describe as communication goals and subgoals, which always include an emotional component. One way to look at how we manipulate each other with emotional words is through name-calling

CHILDREN, TABOO WORDS, AND NAME-CALLING

Emotional language is central to the expression of emotions (affect) and to the appraisal of affect. Drawing on our life experiences, emotional language makes us angry, upset, happy, sad, and surprised, and we use it to make others angry, upset, happy, sad, and surprised. Emotional language both expresses and identifies our emotional state to others. Think of hearing your most despised nickname—were you called *Carrot Top* or *Jerry the Fairy* or *Bubble Butt*? Or consider the profanity you use or think about using when you experience frustration, like when someone pushes in front of you in a line or pulls out in front of your car. Consider your answers to Exercise 11.1. What do these responses reveal about your own links between emotion and language?

Every child in every culture acquires a forbidden lexicon that once learned, must not be used. To the child, no other words are quite like these. The child's taboo lexicon has not been identified and discussed openly in psycholinguistics (Jay, 2000). One prime reason is the nature of current methodology. Adults observing children in home settings and laboratory settings are not as likely to hear forbidden speech as they would in more relaxed play settings. Parents have problems with forbidden words that children use for body parts, body products, sexuality, ethnic names, names, or insults (Berges et al., 1983). Roger Brown (1973) opens his landmark study of language development with a quote from Eve, "I hafta pee-pee just to pass the time away." These kinds of toilet references are common in early childhood, as any parent can attest. What is interesting is that taboo words like *pee-pee, poop, shit,* or *turd* do not appear in Brown's book. With one exception (Berko-Gleason, 1997), the discussion of childhood cursing never appears in psychology textbooks about child language. Taboo words appear in the lexicon within the first two years, and they persist throughout childhood and adolescence into senility (Berges et al., 1983; Jay, 1992a, 1996).

In an extensive study of preteenagers' speech in public places (Jay, 1992a), we recorded 1- and 2-year-olds using *ass, asshole, bum (buttocks), Christ, Jesus, puke, shit,* and *ugly.* The early production vocabulary continues to grow each year for boys but not for girls. Although girls outswear boys publicly between the ages of 3 to 6 years, their production vocabulary declines as they enter grade school. The boys, by contrast, continue to add forbidden words to their lexicon, reaching a production vocabulary of about thirty-five words at age 10. These trends are pictured in Figure 11.7. So it is clear that children acquire emotional words early on. How these words relate to their emotional lives is not so clear. The point at which children understand cursing in an adultlike fashion is unknown.

The relationship between language and emotion extends to research on children's appreciation of social humor (McGhee, 1979) and their **name-calling** routines (see Jay, 1992a; Winslow, 1969). A child's sense of humor progresses with

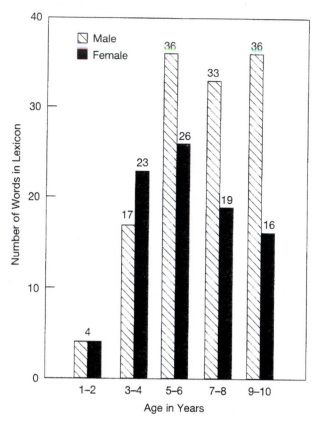

Figure 11.7. Lexicon Size as a Function of Sex and Age
Note. From Jay, T. B. (1992). *Cursing in America*. Reprinted by
permission of John Benjamins N.A. Inc.

changes in cognitive reasoning and social perception. They make the transition
from a focus on the concrete physical world to social references that rely on abstract thinking. Name-calling progresses from the visually concrete (e.g., *Bubble
Butt*) to later refer to the intricacies of social and political life (e.g., *damned Nazi,
communist*). Most cursing (roughly two-thirds) is associated with the expression of
anger and frustration. This function holds from childhood through old age (Jay,
1992a, 1996). Curse words are associated with experiences of prohibitions on them
in early childhood.

The use of emotional language marks an incident as an emotional one. Emotional language comes packed with the speaker's and listener's personal experiences. Emotional words also reference their social and cultural history. Consider
these: *darling, Jew, babe, queer, loverboy, fat ass, bigot, pumpkin, Nazi, hunk, cheater, honey,*
and *stupid*. These kinds of words have personal significance. Saying these words
does more than activate their denotative meanings. These words are offensive or
endearing due to their emotional associations. To say or hear them is to evoke the
emotional and visceral responses attached to them. What is important is how the
language learner connects words with the body, a relationship explored next.

THE EMOTIONAL STROOP TASK

Experimentally, how can we demonstrate that the semantic meaning of a word has emotional consequences? We have seen how word meaning affects SD ratings and increases GSR. What about the effect of meaning on cognitive processing? One method that has proved informative is the **emotional Stroop task,** which can show a link between the conditioned meaning of words and processing disruption.

In the original *Stroop task* (Stroop, 1935), first mentioned in Chapter 4, subjects name the color of ink in which a word is printed, trying to ignore the word itself. Usually the word produces lexical activation, which interferes with or disrupts the color-naming task. What would happen if we did the task using emotionally loaded words with subjects with emotional disorders? One of the central features of cognitive theories of psychopathology is *attentional bias.* People with anxiety and depressive disorders exhibit a sensitivity to and preoccupation with stimuli in the environment related to their concerns. Depressives are preoccupied with past loss and ruminations (e.g., *I lost my friend; I am a failure*). Anxious people are hyperviligilant regarding dangerous cues. People with panic disorders are preoccupied with their bodily sensations. Patients with posttraumatic stress disorder (PTSD) look for stimuli that remind them of the past trauma.

One method of demonstrating these attentional biases is by showing that selective attention to pertinent stimuli causes disruption. Many studies have shown that color naming with emotional words is slowed in people with emotional disorders compared to their nonemotional-word color naming. Control groups of normal people do not exhibit these attentional biases when naming emotional color words (see Williams, Mathews, & MacLeod, 1996). In their review of the literature, Williams et al. found that when patients with emotional disturbances perform the emotional Stroop task, their performance is disrupted by words that are related specifically to their current interests. Patients with anxieties about health exhibit disruption on physically threatening words such as *cancer* or *blood.* Spider phobics show interference (in the range of 190 ms) for words like *hairy* and *crawl.* Rape victims with PTSD show disruptions for words related to the rape theme. Students with high anxiety when tested before an examination show significant naming interference for threat words like *stupidity* or *lonely.* Patients with obsessive-compulsive disorder (OCD) who engage in washing rituals are disrupted by words related to contamination (e.g., *filth*). Finally, mildly depressed patients, when presented with neutral, positive, and negative words, are significantly slower in naming the colors of negative words than those of positive or neutral words.

What is important in these studies is *not* the emotional valence of the words per se but how words relate to an individual's current concerns. The connection must be between the person's pathology and words specifically related to those concerns. This research provides a framework for understanding attentional biases for emotional stimuli. The problems and the words associated with them are embodied through personal experience. From here one can also determine if psychotherapy reduces interference on the Stroop task. This line of research makes sense only if we acknowledge and understand that words are connected to emotional reactions.

THE MULTIPLE CODE THEORY OF
EMOTIONAL INFORMATION PROCESSING

The dual or multiple code analysis of language and emotion dates back notably to the writings of Freud (1940). Freud described a primary level of processing that is emotional and out of awareness (in the unconscious). In addition, there is a secondary level of processing that is conscious and self-aware. One goal in psychoanalysis was to bring the client through free association and dream analysis to the point where the connection between self-aware thoughts and motivations were connected with their emotional and unconscious counterparts.

The information processing aspects of primary- and secondary-level processing might prove important for psycholinguists if they are translatable to and compatible with cognitive science. Recently, Bucci (1993, 1997, 2000) has developed the **multiple code theory** (MCT) of language and emotion that attempts to update Freudian psychology in cognitive science terms. This is one of the few contemporary theories that attempts to link the emotional aspects of language addressed earlier in the chapter with information processing models of language (e.g., PDP). The multiple code theory is important here because it links language to emotion in a manner similar to the way cognitive psychologists link different modes of information processing, for example, language and visual imagery (e.g., Kosslyn, 1987; Paivio, 1986). In the case of MCT, the verbal and emotional representations have multiple links, as do the verbal and visual in dual code theory.

Information in the human mind exists in both *verbal* form and in multiple *nonverbal* channels. The verbal code is dominant in our conscious state and is what we use to regulate and direct ourselves. The verbal code can activate imagery, emotions, and actions. The nonverbal system has multiple channels that have representations in all sensory modalities along with motoric and bodily schemas. The nonverbal system has both symbolic (e.g., images) and subsymbolic representations. The subsymbolic representations are very important in the current discussion because they hearken to what we mean by embodiment. Subsymbolic representations underlie our capacity to move about in the world (e.g., ski down a hill) and predict the movements and changes of objects in the environment (e.g., arc of a baseball, aroma of different kinds of foods). We use subsymbolic representations to help distinguish when changes occur in facial expression, prosody, and one's own body. MCT in effect expands Freud's system into three levels of awareness: a verbal level, a nonverbal symbolic level, and a nonverbal subsymbolic level of representation.

Emotional schemas—for example, terror, helplessness, pleasure, or desire—operate within and outside of awareness. Emotional schemas are dominated by motoric and visceral processing (e.g., fight-or-flight response, autonomic nervous system activation). In contrast, cognitive schemas rely on linguistic and symbolic thought (e.g., what to do in a restaurant). Emotions comprise our desires, expectations, and notions derived through social interaction about other people. They include representations of objects in all sensory modalities and images of objects of emotions, which include approach and avoidance tendencies with patterns of motoric and visceral experience. Plutchik (2001) has recently developed the idea that emotions are feedback processes, not simple linear events. Information from the environment is evaluated in terms of needs, and a cognitive experience is connected with an emotional reaction. Cognition works to help predict the future more effectively. The relationships are illustrated in Figure 11.8.

Emotional schemas, according to Bucci (1993, 2000), can be activated by memory images or by language that has similar physiological dynamics as the experiences themselves. Any component of an emotional schema can activate another component or be activated by another component. Some external stimuli may not reliably activate an emotional schema, and some emotional schemas may occur without awareness of external causality. The ability of words that are outside of a person's awareness to activate an emotional response was mentioned earlier (Corteen & Woods, 1972). The Corteen and Woods study proved that we can have emotional reactions that are outside of awareness but linked to verbal stimuli, a conclusion that has been drawn by many others (e.g., Damasio, 1994; Hugdahl, 1995; Plutchik, 2001; Stein, 1991, Ch. 7).

The links between emotional and linguistic aspects of experience are bidirectional. They are assumed to be compatible with connectionist theory (Seidenberg & McClelland, 1989; Smolensky, 1988). Different levels of representation can activate each other. Words (although connectionist networks usually do not have "word" nodes) evoke emotions, and emotions are describable in words, although not completely. An example of one of these multilevel links is illustrated in Figure 11.9. The act of linking or associating one level of representation to another level is called **referential activity** (RA). RA helps establish connections between the verbal and the nonverbal. The referential process is multichanneled and develops initially in infant-mother interactions. In childhood, references expand to include other people and objects. Children learn to label entities and their properties, as discussed previously in the chapter. References and imagery vary from concrete (e.g., *hot, sweet*) to abstract representations (e.g., *justice, communism*). Similarly, emotional schemas are verbally labeled. They vary in their ability to be described in words; some are quite difficult to express verbally. People also exhibit wide individual differences in their ability to link the verbal to the nonverbal. What is important is how we learn to link mental representations of words onto emotional schemas.

Bucci (1984; Bucci & Freedman, 1978) examined the ability of people to "find the words" to express experience, that is, to link verbal and nonverbal emotional representations in the mind. She asked participants to generate a brief spoken narrative of a personal experience. Some people were able to quickly label an experience or perception. Others struggled to complete the referential task. Bucci divided narrators into two categories on the basis of their referential activity. People with quick naming speeds were described as high in referential activity (**high RA**). High RA's selected more specific episodes, produced a single elaborate theme, and used fewer first person and third person pronouns. They used literary devices (e.g., quotations and present tense descriptions of the past) that created vivid and immediate descriptions. High-RA subjects linked the verbal to the motoric representations, gesticulating while speaking and linking their gestures to the rhythm of their speech.

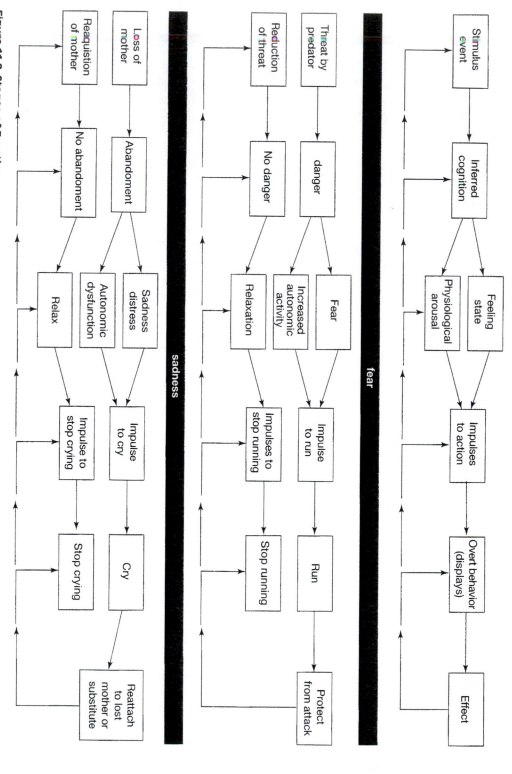

Figure 11.8. Stages of Emotion

Note. Figure from "The Nature of Emotions" by Annette de Ferrari, *American Scientist, 89,* pp. 344–350. Reprinted by permission of Annette de Ferrari.

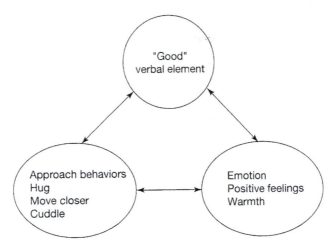

Figure 11.9. An Emotion-Word-Behavior Unit in Memory

In contrast, subjects low in referential activity (**low RA**) have difficulty linking emotional experiences to verbal representations. Their narratives were diffuse and general, and they focused on general personal reactions rather than on detailed descriptions of the incidents. These kinds of differences were also found on different referential tasks, such as simple tasks involving labeling color patches (Bucci, 1984). The level of RA reflects the degree to which a person is able to connect words to nonverbal (e.g., emotional) representations and the nature of the internal or external state being described. Here is an example of the high-RA and low-RA styles (Bucci, 1995, p. 109).

> *High RA:* I can't stand fruit with bad spots in it. It gives me the creeps. So I picked up that pineapple and it looked so nice, and then my finger went right through inside it. Into this brown, slimy, mushy stuff, and my stomach just turned over.

> *Low RA:* I love people and I like to be with people. And right now I feel very bad because I can't be with them and do the things I would like to do. But I'm looking forward to a happier and healthier future and— I don't know what else to say. What else can I talk about? Well— I've had a very eventful life, I think, I've worked practically all my life and I love people.

MCT is a framework that makes it possible to bridge the emotion gap between the verbal and the nonverbal. One of the important applications of multiple code theory is to the therapeutic context. People with high-RA abilities are better able to talk about their emotions, describe their dreams, describe their problems with other people, talk about their problems, and participate in free association. These functions all rely on the ability to translate emotional subsymbolic content into words. The problematic notion of repression of memory can be reformulated in MCT. Repression is defined as the unconscious blocking of anxiety-provoking memories. In MCT, repression can be understood as a blocking of connections between verbal and nonverbal representations or a blocking of links within emotional schemas (Bucci, 1993). These kinds of referential problems are not limited to people in therapy but occur in people talking about their emotions generally. MCT provides psycholinguists with a means of linking emotion to language through connectionism.

MCT was designed to be compatible with connectionist models of language processing. We can understand the verbal, symbolic, and subsymbolic aspects of experience as interconnected nodes in a parallel-distributed processing network that are associated with each other on the basis of frequency of occurrence and feedback (Anderson 1983; Seidenberg & McClelland, 1989; Smolensky, 1988). The aspects of language that connect emotion and context to verbal representation can be understood as a neural network-type model like ACT or PDP, as discussed in Chapter 4. Speech production, speech comprehension, and cognitive processes are assumed to link to emotion architecture in the neural network. What needs to be added to the traditional models are nodes representing emotional aspects of words. Nodes are established on the basis of what is learned from the environment.

The resultant architecture of emotions, words, and behavior, which incorporates classical conditioning, MCT, and connectionism, is suggested in Figures 11.8 and simplified in 11.9. Figure 11.9 could be one unit in the network that links the word *good* to approach behaviors and positive emotional feelings. Any element in the unit can activate any other element in the unit. The word can activate an emotional experience or behavior. An emotional experience can activate a verbal label for it.

From Physical to Symbolic

All that we have read in this chapter points to a relationship between speech and the environment. Speech uses arbitrary symbols to mark objects and abstract states in context. Speech is always alienated from but associated with experience (see Haiman, 1998). In this way, speech embodies what it encapsulates. The alienation of word from deed is a matter of degree. Euphemism, lying, sarcasm, hyperbole, and irony are figures of speech that take advantage of the ambiguity of language to portray one state of affairs as another (see Chapter 9). Sarcastic irony poses an utterance on one level that means the opposite in the second communication layer (H. H. Clark, 1996). I have illustrated a continuum of representation from the physical to the symbolic in Table 11.1. These can be understood as different layers of emotional expression.

The table running from left to right suggests the development of emotional symbolism. The table depicts, in the first column, conditions in the physical world that give rise to primitive physical reactions in the second column. The oral physical, emotional symbolic, and layered speech columns depict three different forms of oral reaction, which become more abstract moving from left to right. As children develop, they replace physical reactions (such as screaming) with symbolic ones

Table 11.1. Emotional Expressions: Physical and Layered

Physical World	→	Physical Reaction	→	Oral Physical Expression	→	Emotional Symbolic Expression	→	Layered Speech
Pain		hit		scream		slur		lie
Danger		bite		yell		curse		euphemism
Fear		tantrum		refuse		insult		sarcasm
Cold		run		laugh		names		hyperbole

(cursing). The layered speech level is the most abstract and cognitively complex form of emotional response. Layered speech mutes or veils a primitive emotional reaction with indirect or figurative speech (such as sarcasm).

Feelings are initially expressed nonverbally though screaming, crying, and the like. As adults, we end up with the facility to use figurative language in a way that hides or veils the underlying emotion in a different layer. Cursing and the use of strong emotional words lies in between the physical and the abstract. Whereas cursing closely represents an emotional experience like anger, irony veils an emotional experience by placing it in a second conversational layer. Cursing in anger is an obvious emotional statement. Sarcastic irony hides anger or frustration a layer away from the words on the surface of the utterance. Prelinguistic children express emotional states physically through behaviors like tantrums and screaming. A symbolic version of these emotions, as shown in Table 11.1, does not yet exist for the infant. Eventually these behaviors are replaced by emotional verbal symbols (words or signs) such as those used in cursing and swearing. Notice that the symbolic must emerge after the physical. Emotional symbols obtain their physiological associations through learning.

How does having an emotional lexicon affect the experience of emotion? The infant's cry for hunger is replaced later by a verbal request for food. The child learns that emotional states and desires can be represented with words (F. L. Goodenough, 1931; Haiman, 1998; Lamendella, 1977). Anger can be expressed through name-calling and making threats. Adults, but not young children, can veil negative emotional states in order to achieve communication goals (H. H. Clark, 1996; Haiman, 1998; Lamendella; 1977). In childhood, we observe a progression from the physical and emotional expression to the verbal and abstract representation of emotional meaning. Language starts out tied to the physical world but later becomes decontextualized.

How does speech embody the physically real? We see embodiment early in childhood when children represent the world in physical terms, first with gestures and then with names for objects, people, and the actions they take. At birth, an intense emotional experience can only be expressed through the body by laughing, crying, facial expression, screaming, and flailing the arms. Onto these physical representations are mapped verbal symbols. As the child grows, the ability to use symbols not bound by the immediate present evolves. The preverbal child will yell and scream when upset, and the school-aged child will say, "Mommy, I hate you." In adolescence, we might hear a teenager speaking sarcastically: "Oh, yes, I love my mother so-o-o much." The intensity of the felt emotion can be attenuated, alienated, and distorted by language.

The emotional language of insult, swearing, epithets, and profanity lies very close to vivid emotions, closer than euphemism, metaphor, ritual language, and politeness, which are constructed as socially acceptable replacements for emotional words. The reflexive use of profanity belies a close relationship.

The point of Table 11.1 is that some words, especially emotional words, lie closer to the emotional experience than other words. We could see this with spider phobics and emotionally disturbed people. Phobic words touch the phobic experience. This relationship between the felt emotional world and the emotional word representing feelings is what is central to this chapter. It is important to recognize that words are tied to our experiences of using them. In this way, emotions become embodied physically in words that are associated with experiences. The 2-year-old who is laughed at or scolded for saying *shit* cannot disassociate his arousal from the meaning of the word. The emotional consequence of saying *shit* is linked to its meaning. Emotional speech activates its connection to the right hemisphere and limbic areas, giving it a physiological meaning that is very vivid, more vivid than neutral language. Emotional speech exemplifies the physicality of speech. Another view of the physicality of language—how children learn to express anger symbolically—is covered in the accompanying excerpt from *Anger in Young Children*, by Florence L. Goodenough (1931).

---

*Anger in Young Children**

With the beginning of speech, verbal rejoinders used as least in part as substitutes for some of the more overt motor expressions of anger become increasingly prevalent. **Verbal refusal** either with or without motor accompaniment is reported in 3.3 per cent of the outbursts occurring among two-year-old children. The proportion increases steadily at each age until among the children of four or over it occurs in 35.1 per cent of all cases. Sex differences are small and inconsistent. **Threatening** appears first among children between the ages of two and three, when it is reported in 1.6 per cent of all outbursts. A year later the proportion has increased to 5.4 percent. Among children over four it occurs in 9.7 per cent of all cases. **Calling names** first appears at about the same time as threatening. It is reported in 1.4 per cent of the outbursts occurring among children between the ages of two and three, in 6.0 per cent of those reported for three-year-olds, and in 18.0 per cent of those reported for children over four. In both these forms of behavior, the growth in the power of symbolism is clearly shown. Again, sex differences are negligible. **Arguing** and **insisting** first appear at the age of three, when they are reported for 4.8 per cent of all cases. The proportion increases to 18.3 per cent among children over the age of four. . . .

In summary, then, one may say that with advancing age the forms of be-havior displayed during anger become more definitely directed toward a given end, while the primitive bodily responses of the infant and young child are gradually replaced by substitute reactions commonly of a somewhat less vi-olent and more symbolic character. This is most clearly shown in the steady increase in the proportion of retaliative behavior with age and the corre-sponding decrease in displays of simple undirected energy. Although incom-pleteness of report renders a precise quantitative analysis impossible, there is evidence that with advancing age an increasing proportion of the outbursts approach more nearly the forms described . . . as "learned varieties acquired in the sentiments." There is more evidence of the persistence of generalized reactions toward an individual and of increasing attempts to retaliate by indi-rect means designed to hurt the feelings rather than to injure the body of the offender. The cumulative effect both of increasing maturity and of specific training is clearly portrayed. (Goodenough, 1931, pp. 65–66, 69)

*From *Anger in Young Children* by Florence Laura Goodenough. Copyright 1931 by the University of Minnesota Press. Renewed 1959. Reprinted by permission.

To the child and to many adult speakers, the idea that a word can actually harm another person by the mere saying of it amounts to a form of "**word magic**" (Jay, 2000; Terwilliger, 1968). The idea that we can make people do things by say-ing words to them is not magic. In fact, we would not speak to people if we thought our speech had no effect on them. The Goodenough excerpt demonstrates three aspects of embodiment: (1) Emotional expression is coded in reference to physical external behavior and through repetition becomes internalized in language, (2) words associated with affect are imbued deeply with physiological and emotional meaning, and (3) emotions are activated by speech. The idea that words can insult, discriminate, harass, or intimidate people is predicated on the emotional impact of hearing words that are emotionally laden. The physiological and emotional mean-ing that words acquire is learned through experience or observation. The emo-tional power of hearing and saying such words must be embodied so as to produce arousal. Recall the *shit*-versus-*merde* and *equipment*-versus-*gas chamber* examples.

Key Terms

approach or avoidance	collective monologue	deictic gesture
arguing	complementary	Descartes' error
automatic speech	gesture	embodiment
classical conditioning	deferred imitation	emergence

emotional Stroop task
emotion gap
expansion
expressive learner
galvanic skin response
high RA
inner speech
insisting
instrumental
  conditioning
joint attention
low RA

mesh
multiple code theory
name-calling
object permanence
perspective taking
pretend play
r_m
referential activity
referential learner
representational
  gesture
semantic differential

sensorimotor thinking
supplementary gesture
taboo words
threatening
verbal refusal
VO strategy
word association
word magic

What Lies Ahead

Chapter 12 addresses the relationship of language to thought. Does the language we speak in any way limit the way we think about the world? Put another way, do the words we use constrain the way we perceive the world? We look at some traditional issues, such as the relationship between color terminology and perception, as well as some more contemporary and controversial topics. For example, how does our participation in social groups affect our language use; or how do dialects affect speech comprehension and production processes? Is one dialect better than another? Do men and women speak different "languages"?

Chapter 12
Language and Thought in a Social Context

Critical Thinking Questions

1. How are color words related to color perception?

2. In what ways is color terminology different from odor terminology?

3. How do we construct categories for food and disgust?

4. Describe Americans' model of intimacy.

5. What gender differences emerge in conversations?

6. What are communities of practice, and how do they influence speech?

7. What is the cultural basis for name-calling and insulting?

8. What are speech registers?

9. How is dialect use related to racism?

10. Describe the state of bilingualism and second language acquisition research.

11. How does language use promote solidarity or social distance?

Exercise 12.1. **College Slang**
Make a list of slang words that are in common use among college students in the United States. Now make a second list of words that would be understood only by someone at your school—for example, a name for a particular person, place, or situation on your campus. Do you use college slang with your parents, your siblings, and your professors? Why or why not?

Language, Thought, and Society

Questions about the relationship between language and thought are timeless; they pervade this text. We have seen that language has lasting effects on cognitive processes involving eyewitness testimony (Loftus, Schooler, & Wagenaar, 1985), inferential reasoning (Bransford, Barclay, & Franks, 1972), and imagery (Paivio, 1969), to name a few. In general, we discovered that words have a lasting effect on memory, perception, and mental tasks.

Carmichael, Hogan, and Walter (1932) demonstrated a classic example of the power of language on perceptual processes. Subjects were presented with simple line drawings one at a time like this 0—0 with different sets of labels. For example, one group of subjects was given the label *dumbbells* and the other *eyeglasses* for this figure. Later, when they were asked to draw the set of figures from memory, they drew objects that looked like the referents of the labels provided earlier. The *eyeglasses* became oval-shaped with a nosepiece, and the *dumbbells* became rounded with a thick handle. As originally presented, the line drawings were ambiguous, needing some interpretation. The labels offered a context or point of view that enabled the subject to store a representation of the object. This experiment provided evidence that words influence our choice of mental representation and memory for past experience.

In a problem-solving situation, Glucksberg & Danks (1968) demonstrated that the labels we give to objects in the problem affect its ultimate solution. In their experiment, subjects had to complete an electrical circuit by using the blade of a screwdriver to bridge a gap in the circuitry. Subjects were better able to solve the problem if the screwdriver was given a nonsense name like *peem*. Glucksberg and Danks reasoned that the nonsense term broke the tool's association with the predetermined function of turning screws. The nonsense term did not name the function it usually performed, freeing problem solvers to think about the object in a different way. The more flexible thinkers could see that all they needed was a piece of metal to complete the circuit, a goal accomplished with the blade of the tool.

What we address in this chapter is how the social context of communication affects what is said and understood. Communication always takes place in a cultural context, which influences what we say and hear. How do factors such as power, status, gender, race, occupation, and dialect determine speech? Speakers must have a model of social contexts to make changes in communication patterns when the social variables change. The question of socialization allows us to peer into the "dark side" of human communication to look at social problems like verbal abuse and racial, ethnic, and class discrimination. We consider the linguistic side of sexism, racism, classism, and ethnocentrism because they are ubiquitous social psychological issues.

The importance of culture in psycholinguistic theory depends on how broadly we define *language*. This text defines *language* to include the social and emotional aspects of speech. Defining *language* within a discipline is in important ways a social process itself, one with adherents and opponents (Kuhn, 1962). Culture is important to psycholinguistics. Currently, we are accumulating a good deal of cultural evidence through cross-linguistic and cross-cultural comparisons. That these studies exist implies that language does depend on culture in some ways. Cross-linguistic studies provide evidence for differences across languages and evidence for universal features of language.

An important conclusion of this chapter is that speech communities differ and that these differences affect cognition and social interaction. We will view language through social organization. How we talk and what we understand are the products of social references. These references are local, community, national, ethnic, and occupational lenses through which we look at a situation, and they form the basis for how we talk about a situation (H. H. Clark, 1996). We cannot address all the social and cultural variables that affect speech in one chapter. The topics to be addressed here include linguistic relativity, categorical references, food and disgust, cultural models, gender, communities of practice, language standards, and language solidarity. The first order of business is to address a traditional question about language and thought: How does vocabulary affect thought?

Linguistic Relativity

Language universals are aspects of language that are built-in or innate. For example, all languages have nouns and verbs. The LAD and universal grammar speak to the universal qualities of languages. The nativist approach as represented by the work of Pinker and Chomsky supports idea that language variation has natural limits. An opposing viewpoint (e.g., McClelland, Rumelhart, and the PDP Research Group, 1986) is that language is learned. The regularities in language are not built in but are patterns that emerge from learning. The question of the linguistic universal seems most appropriate to describe how we talk about our embodied representation of the physical world. How humans represent colors, objects, shapes, relative distance, and spatial relationships in language appears to be universal (Clark & Clark, 1977). Spatial prepositions (e.g., *near, next to, above, behind*) occur in every language and emerge in a orderly manner, although the way spatial prepositions are *grouped* varies from language to language. Other aspects of thought, such as gender identity or social class, appear to be the products of learning.

One of the main questions here is what happens when different languages have different representations of a concept. For example, do the many words one culture has for color cause that culture to see the world of color differently than a culture whose language contains only two or three words to describe the color spectrum? Does thinking about colors depend on what kinds of words we have for colors? The questions about universal and relative features of language can be traced to the linguistic relativity principle.

WHORF'S HYPOTHESIS

The classic approach to the relationship between language and thought is spelled out in the notion of **linguistic relativity.** Linguistic relativity suggests that the words and syntax that are used in our native language influence the way we think about the world. Here is the classic problem as posed by Whorf (1956, pp. 213–214), sometimes referred to as **Whorf's hypothesis:**

> We dissect nature along lines laid down by our native languages. The categories and types that we isolate from the world of phenomena we do not find there because they stare every observer in the face; on the contrary, the world is presented in a kaleidoscope flux of impressions which has to be organized by our minds—and this means largely by the linguistic systems in our minds. We cut up nature, organize it into concepts, and ascribe significances as we do, largely because we are parties to an agreement to organize it in this way—an agreement that holds through our speech community and is codified in the patterns of our language. The agreement is, of course, an implicit and unstated one, but its terms are absolutely obligatory; we cannot talk at all except by subscribing to the organization and classification of data, which the agreement decrees.

Whorf suggested that the words we use determine the way we think. His conclusions were based in part on his experience as an insurance investigator. Whorf studied how a cigarette smoker could toss a burning cigarette into a fuel drum, if the smoker thought the drum was "empty," ignoring the fact that the fumes would ignite violently. Whorf was convinced that language influenced our thought, perception, and behavior.

In another classic and often-cited example, Whorf reported that Eskimos have many words to describe different kinds of snow, whereas speakers of English only use *snow.* Therefore, according to the theory, Eskimos see the world of snow much differently than speakers of English do. Recent evidence suggests that Whorf's snow example is a myth. Martin (1986) and Pullum (1991) have found that Whorf failed to delve into the rich morphology of snow in English, which is not necessarily reflected by the number of lexemes. As it turns out, both English and Eskimo have many words for snow—including *sleet, slush, powder, packed powder, flakes,* and *flurries*—and we do not have drastically different worldviews of snow.

Whorf's argument has a strong and a weak version. The weak version is *linguistic relativism,* which posits that language comparisons constructed in one language cannot exist in other languages; they vary from language to language. A stronger form of the language and thought argument, **linguistic determinism,** posits that language determines the way we think. Cognitive processes such as shape perception and color perception are determined by the language we use. To study linguistic relativity, Whorf and his contemporaries would look at different cultures for evidence that language restricted thinking. However, the evidence has never unequivocally supported a strict deterministic position. By contrast, there is some evidence to support linguistic relativity.

COLOR TERMINOLOGY

Since its inception, the linguistic relativity hypothesis has generated a great deal of discussion. One area of interest to psychologists has been the question of how color terminology influences color perception. As it turns out, many languages have names for the primary colors (e.g., *red, yellow,* and *blue*). But not all languages have a rich color vocabulary like English. In fact, some languages have terms only for the primary colors (Berlin & Kay, 1969). How does a limited vocabulary affect perception? Perceptually, the best example of a primary color is called a **focal color** because it is the most central or most typical example of the entire range color. Red is the focal color of all reddish colors and blue is the focal color of all bluish colors. Focal colors affect cognitive process; they are named faster and with fewer words, and they are remembered better in memory tasks than nonfocal colors. What does this mean for Whorf's hypothesis?

Brown and Lenneberg (1954) conducted one of the original studies on color naming. They showed one group of subjects a set of colors and asked them to name them. The colors that were readily identified with names that the subjects agreed on were termed **codable colors.** In the second phase of the experiment, subjects examined codable and noncodable colors and were later given a recognition text. Their memory proved better for the codable colors relative to the noncodable ones. The study was interpreted as providing weak evidence in support of Whorf's hypothesis. Memory was related to ease of naming.

Heider (1972) presented a different view of language and color naming. She studied New Guinea speakers of Dani, a language that has only two color terms. *Mola* is for light colors like white, yellow, or orange, and *mili* is for dark colors like black, blue, and purple. The participants were asked to provide names for forty color chips. Dani and English speakers performed this task differently. The Dani agreed on very light colors and very dark colors but disagreed on colors in the middle of the spectrum. Individuals had different criteria for where the dividing line should fall. The English-speaking subjects had more agreement about how to categorize the color chips. On a recognition task, it was expected that the Dani would confuse the *mola* colors if the Whorfian hypothesis was true. However, the Dani made the same kinds of mistakes that the English speakers made. The Dani's performance was a bit worse than the English speakers', but they both performed well on the same kinds of chips, for example, the best example of red. Language did not seem so important here.

Heider and Oliver (1972) conducted a forced-choice recognition test with Dani and English speakers. The subjects had to choose between two chips, identifying which they had seen earlier. The critical question was whether the choices crossed a color line or not. Was one chip green and the other blue; or were they just different but both shades of blue? The interesting finding was that both the Dani and English speakers performed similarly whether the colors were from the same side of the color line or different sides of the color line. The number of color terms in the language did not make a difference—more evidence against the Whorfian hypothesis.

More recent experiments confirming the Heider and Oliver findings have been conducted by Davies and Corbett (1997). They studied speakers of English, Russian, and Setswana (from Botswana). Russian has two terms for blue that roughly correspond to light blue and dark blue. The Setswana language has one term that covers both green and blue. All participants were asked to sort a sample of sixty-five chips into groups, the number of which was not important. Davies and Corbett found that all three groups sorted the chips into similar groupings. Russians did not tend to separate light and dark blue. However, the Setswana speakers put more green chips in with the blue, as was expected.

Davies, Sowden, Jerrett, Jerrett and Corbett (1998) repeated the experiment, but this time they assigned the sorting task to a fixed number of categories. What they expected to find was that the Setswana speakers would agree when there was small number of groups because they only have six color terms. They expected greater agreement between Russian and English speakers with a large number of groups, since these languages have twelve and eleven basic color terms, respectively. What they found was surprising. Subjects from all three language groups performed remarkably similarly. There were differences that supported the Whorfian hypothesis, but they were small.

If we look across languages at how color terms emerge as a function of color vocabulary size, we find a very systematic evolution. Distinctions always begin at the black and white level, and then terms emerge in an orderly fashion, depending on the number of color words in the vocabulary. From first to emerge to last, the system looks like this:

1. black, white

2. red

3. yellow, green, blue

4. brown

5. purple, pink, orange, gray

A culture with three color terms would have *black, white,* and *red.* A culture with six color terms would in addition use *yellow, green,* and *blue.* Are these systematic distinctions the products of language? Probably not. Focal colors are predominant because of the architecture of color vision. The human visual system has evolved to perceive primary colors: The system of rods and cones in the retina work as opponent processes, for example, red-green, black-white, and yellow-blue. The three types of cones are tuned to perceiving the red, green, and blue portions of the spectrum. The rods code achromatic luminance (black or white). Milliseconds later in the vision process, at the level of ganglion cells and the lateral geniculate nucleus, the three color-opponent processes are merged into a color image (see Matlin & Foley, 1997). This sensory system produces color perception, not language.

Over the years, a great deal of work with different languages and different cultures has provided only weak evidence that language influences thinking about colors.

But color is a perceptual category, one that might not be appropriate for testing Whorf's hypothesis. We can see even more problems for a perceptual category that is very disorganized—odor.

Perhaps a better way to look at the relationship between language and perception is with something English speakers have difficulty with—labeling odors. Colors are easy to compare and contrast because they vary along linear dimensions of wavelength (hue), saturation (purity), and brightness (lightness). These are dimensions of the color wheel, which portrays variation in these three aspects of color in a three-dimensional space. But there is no device like a color wheel for odors that indicates how colors are related along a single dimension like wavelength. It is difficult to relate one odor to another analytically in the manner that colors can be related on the basis of wavelength.

ODOR TERMINOLOGY

It might be difficult for speakers of English to imagine a culture with only a few words for colors because we have so many words for colors. But what about labeling odors? We have limited means of describing odors. Unlike sounds and colors, odors are difficult to isolate and identify by name. Odor is part of a larger context. The smell of garlic makes you think of spices or pizza, not other plants or vegetables. Usually, we name odors by associating them with another object, for example, *pine-scented* or *lemon-scented*. The odor is described as "lemon," not "fruity" or "citrus." There are no "focal odors" or basic odor terms. It is therefore difficult to develop an unambiguous lexicon for odors—a problem that affects perceptual and memory processes.

To show how **odor names** affect memory processes, Desor and Beauchamp (1974) presented subjects with everyday odors of things like popcorn, motor oil, and chocolate. While subjects were good at identifying some odors, such as coffee, banana, and chocolate, only 20 percent could identify other smells, such as cat feces, ham, or sawdust. These familiar items elicited a wide range of labels. The important question was how labeling would affect memory for these items. Subjects were later given a recognition task for the items in the identification phase. Memory was not uniformly good. Subjects made recognition mistakes because they could not produce the correct labels for what they were sniffing. They could distinguish that the odors they were sniffing were different, but they could not name what they were discriminating.

Something like this identification failure might happen if a person who does not know anything about music is asked to identify notes on the music scale. One can be able to discriminate notes on a piano without knowing their names. You can tell that one note is higher than another when played on the piano without being able to name it (e.g., B or F). The subjects in the odor experiment could tell the odors were different but could not recognize them from the earlier presentation very well. Odors differ from one another in complex ways not like sounds or colors.

Cain (1979) demonstrated how the name given to a substance affects subsequent performance in recognition tasks. The more specific the name is for the substance, the better the retrieval. So a label like "chocolate" is better than a label like "candy." In a related odor study, Rabin and Cain (1986) presented subjects with twenty common odorants and asked them to rate how familiar they were with the odors and to supply names for odors. Subjects were able to name more than 50 percent of the test items. But when asked to complete a recognition task one day or seven days later, accuracy decreased with low-familiarity odors. Subjects did poorly with odors they could not name in the initial study. In this study and others, language strongly influenced odor identification and memory.

Naming odors and trying to remember them later is a typical language and perception problem. One experiment conducted in Italy showed that when strawberry and apple odorants were mislabeled as banana and apricot, respectively, they were remembered in that way—the label determined the memory representation. Apparently, extraneous cues like language dominate the description of the odor sensation (Batic & Gabassi, 1987). Research has shown that people commonly misidentify similar odors. Here is a good example. Engen (1991) reported that when it was discovered that a large beverage company had mislabeled thousands of cartons of strawberry drinks as raspberry and vice versa, the company expected to receive many complaints. But there were very few. In fact, there was little evidence that the mislabeling had been detected. If the beverage is labeled "raspberry," consumers assume that it smells and tastes like raspberry.

In the odor perception studies, we see the effect of labeling on memory. What can't be named is difficult to remember, as was seen in some of the color-coding studies. Further, what label we do give to a stimulus affects the way the item is represented in memory, as was evidenced in the Carmichael et al. (1932) study. Children's inclination and ability to describe olfactory preferences take a developmental course closely aligned with language development (Engen & Engen, 1997). Children's ability to describe odor experiences is a function of language development, according to Engen (1991). Children generally do not spontaneously talk about odor experiences during early stages of language acquisition, in part because these experiences are not so salient for them and they lack an odor-naming strategy. Sensory experiences with taste and smell are usually interrelated.

You might have wondered about the nature of the examples used so far in this chapter. Do you see any biases at work in the tests of Whorf's hypothesis? Whorf's examples tend to come from perceptual categories like colors, geometric shapes, or numbers. It may be the case that these are not good categories in which to test the Whorfian hypothesis because the categories are so closely tied to the physical world and the sensory systems that analyze it. What we label colors, shapes, and odors is heavily dependent on the sensory architecture we work with. Perceptual categories like color rely heavily on biology and are not constructed like categories that are used to describe the social world. Sociocognitive categories like family, food, and gender orientation are different than perceptual categories. It may be that Whorf would have been better advised to prove his point with nonperceptual, social categories.

Categorical Language

Some perceptual experiences, such as color naming, can rely on grouping examples on the basis of a single dimension like wavelength. Other perceptual experiences, such as odor naming, are difficult to group or categorize reliably (Engen, 1991). When Berlin and Kay (1969) asked subjects to group color chips, they found wide variability in boundary lines as a function of culture. When they asked subjects to find the best example of a color, there was general agreement on the exemplary or prototypical member of each basic color. The semantic space for basic color terms is built around a core **prototype,** which is the most codable or recognizable member of the category. Moving from the core to the boundary of the category, members exhibit a graded relationship to the core. Those near the center are more codable and recognizable. Before we address cultural effects on categorization and labeling, let's look at some fundamental properties of categorization.

Rosch (1974; Mervis & Rosch, 1981) studied extensively how we communicate about the world using concepts and categories. A **concept** is a set of properties that we ascribe to a class of objects; for example, "birds" have feathers, sing, lay eggs, and fly. Our concepts are hierarchical constructs with superordinate concepts and subordinate concepts (as mentioned in Chapter 4). Consider a superordinate concept like "animal"; it has a lower or **basic level** of classification, like *bird,* and more specific subordinate concepts, like *hummingbird.* Social communication occurs most often through the use of basic levels of concepts, those that are not too general (e.g., *food*) or too specific (e.g., *golden delicious apple*). Basic level concepts are those that are the most informative. *Categorization* is the process of assigning an object to a concept, as in "That is a bird" or "This is a banana." Much of the time, labeling and requesting are done at the basic level. A child who wants an apple will say, "I want an apple," not "I want a golden delicious apple" or "I want a fruit."

Categories can be normative and graded, or they can be made up on the spot (Barsalou, 1983). *Ad hoc* categories are made up on the spot to meet particular functions. An example of an ad hoc category might be something like *things to take on a camping trip.* There is no universal rule that will tell us what fits in this ad hoc category. Some categories, such as *odd numbers,* are **well-defined categories.** We know what concepts fit in this category—all numbers not divisible by 2. Many other categories are **fuzzy categories,** like *chairs.* Well-defined categories have clear boundaries; the boundaries of fuzzy categories are unclear. For example, don't you think a bean bag chair is an odd kind of chair? A bean bag chair could be a large pillow in another context; its categorization is not absolute because the boundary between large pillows and bean bag chairs is fuzzy.

Thus categorization can be imposed on thought by the language we use in a given situation. Linguistic relativity research has focused on perceptual categories. It might be more helpful, however, to make the case for linguistic relativity by focusing on social categories, which are constructed to meet socio-organizational goals. Social categories are culture-dependent, and this is the important point. What we need to communicate in terms of specificity depends on the context. For example, if there are several varieties of apples and I want a specific type, then I must ask for a "Granny Smith." One's specificity also takes a developmental course. Adults are good at taking the listeners' needs and context into consideration, but children need to learn language and learn about their culture; they take some time to develop the appropriate level of specification in communication tasks (Glucksberg, Krauss, & Weisberg, 1966; Keysar, Barr, & Horton, 1998). Let's look at a socially constructed category for comparison—food.

FOOD

A good example of a socially constructed category is *food*. Maybe you never thought about it because you learned about what is proper food when you were so young. The concept of what is edible and what constitutes good or bad food varies from culture to culture. What humans eat depends more on environment, family habits, religious customs, and social norms than it does on the human digestive system. Children are taught what is edible and what is not, a learning process that takes several years to complete. Humans eat a lot of different things, but not everything that is edible is defined as a potential food source. Grass is edible but is not put in the *food* category. Humans don't eat grass unless they are starving. We can see the effect of culture on food and language referring to food by looking at how we talk about beer.

Beer Categories

Every culture has some domains of life that are more important than others. The elevated importance of a category results in a lexicon that is more differentiated or extensive than less important categories. This is one of the ideas underlying linguistic relativity. Differentiation can be observed in cross-cultural food preferences. It might be informative to look at a category of food for which Americans have a limited number of words or semantic dimensions but other cultures have more words.

Over the years, I have asked many Americans about different kinds of beer. Most of my informants indicate that they call different kinds of malt beverages *beer*. Although some of them know the terms *ale* and *lager*, they cannot differentiate them. Most of them think I am asking for brand names like Budweiser or Coors. In reality, there are many kinds of malt beverages brewed around the world. Where other cultures might draw fine distinctions, Americans generally think in terms of "beer" or "light beer."

Unlike Americans, Germans and Austrians have an elaborate vocabulary for different kinds of beer (Hage, 1972). For example, the city of Munich (München in German) has a culture where beer is exalted. Beer drinking is symbolic of social solidarity in this city—witness the importance of the Oktoberfest, where Münchners reaffirm their values. First we look at the universe of beer in Munich, that is, the taxonomic and semantic structure of beer categories. Later we describe the motives for consuming the different kinds of beers. We start with the core terms for Munich beer and then add connoisseur terms.

Core Munich Beer Types

Wiesenbier—"meadow beer" for the annual Oktoberfest

Märzenbier—"March beer"

Heller Bock—a light strong beer

Salvator—a dark strong beer

Helles—light beer

Dunkles—dark beer

Weißes—white beer

Russ—white beer mixed with sweet lemonade

Radlermaß—dark beer with sweet lemonade

Nährbier—nourishing beer

Connoisseur Beer Types

Voll-Helles—full light beer

Export-Helles—export light beer

Voll-Dunkles—full dark beer

Export-Dunkles—export dark beer

Champagner-Weißes—champagne white beer

Weißer Bock—white bock

Lunchbier—lunch beer

Nährweizenbier—nourishing wheat beer

The connoisseur terms are built on the core terms, elaborating them in terms of exportation and other enhancements. The core beer terms evolve around five semantic dimensions, which are most critical for categorizing beer types:

1. Strength (strong, normal, weak)

2. Color (light, dark, brownish)

3. Fizziness (fizzy, not fizzy)

4. Aging (aged, unaged)

5. Clarity (clear, cloudy)

Table 12.1. Componential Definition of Munich Beers

Type of Beer	Strength	Color	Fizziness	Aging	Clarity
Wiesenbier	S	B	NF	A	
Märzenbier	S	B	NF	U	
Heller Bock	S	L	NF	A	
Salvator	S	D	NF	A	
Aventinus	N+	L	F	U	
Export-Helles	N+	L	NF	U	
Voll-Helles	N	L	NF	U	
Export-Dunkles	N+	D	NF	U	
Voll-Dunkles	N	D	NF	U	
Export-Weißes	N+	L	F	U	C
Champagner-Weißes	N	L	F	U	K
Normal-Weißes	N	L	F	U	C
Russ	W	L	F	U	
Radlermaß	W	D	F–	U	
Lunchbier	W	L	NF	U	
Nährbier	O	D	NF	U	
Nährwiesenbier	O	L	F	U	

Note. S = strong, N = normal, N+ = stronger than normal, W = weak, O = alcohol-free, L = light, B = brownish, D = dark, F = fizzy, F– = less fizzy, NF = nonfizzy, A = aged, U = unaged, C = clear, K = cloudy.
Reprinted by permission of Barbara Spradley from J. P. Spradley (Ed.) 1972. *Culture & Cognition:* Rules, maps, and plans (263–278). Waveland Press, Inc., Prospect Heights, IL.

The types of beer and their properties are listed in Table 12.1. This is a taxonomy of sorts. Which beer one drinks depends on where one drinks and who buys the drinks. The motivation to drink one particular type of beer over another is another matter. Some of the cognitive and behavioral implications for drinking the different styles of beer are listed in Table 12.2. For example, if the aim is refreshment, fizzy beers are ideal, especially if one wants to avoid intoxication. Strong beers are consumed in part for the intoxicating effects. Weak beers are for children, the elderly, and pregnant women.

With the consumption of different types of beer, there are different behavioral and social expectations. Beer drinking in Munich is mainly expected to facilitate social interaction and integration. The large beer halls make it difficult for people to drink alone or remain aloof. Various levels of intoxication and different kinds of beer drinkers emerge in the beer hall. These are listed in Tables 12.3 and 12.4, respectively. Intoxication levels range from slight to extreme, which produces a range of behavior from gaiety to loss of control. The behavior of beer drinking results in different types of beer drinker categories, or social roles involving beer drinking. The kinds of beer drinkers in Munich evolve through social and personal preferences. The approved style is communal, moderate drinking. The disapproved style is heaving drinking in isolation.

The purpose of elaborating Munich beer and drinking styles is to elucidate the features of semantic structure and their relationship to behavior and cognition (see Hage, 1972). I think this kind of analysis is more in line with Whorf's original

Table 12.2. Behavioral and Cognitive Implications of the Dimensions of Discrimination

Dimensions of Discrimination	Semantic Implications	Behavioral and Cognitive Implications		
		Culturally Defined Motives	Spatiotemporal	Status
1. The domain *beer*	beer versus other beverage domains	facilitation of social interaction, integration and:	defining value for Munich and Bavaria	
2. Strength	subset of strong beers	strong beers for (rapid) intoxication, for meals	strong beers constitute the Munich *Bierkalender* historical origin as a food substitute	for normal adults
	subset of normal beers	normal beers for meals, for intoxication		for normal adults
	subset of weak beers	weak beers to avoid intoxication or keep it minimal		
	subset of non-alcoholic beers	nonalcoholic beers for the avoidance of intoxication		for children, the aged, ill, and pregnant
3. Color	light versus dark subsets of beer	dark beers stimulate growth and health	Münchner see displacement of dark by light beers as index of culture change	
4. Fizziness	fizzy versus non-fizzy	fizzy beers for refreshment		
5. Aging	aged versus un-aged subsets of beer		aged beers have festive significance	for normal adults

Reprinted by permission of Barbara Spradley from J. P. Spradley (Ed.) 1972. *Culture & Cognition:* Rules, maps, and plans (263–278). Waveland Press, Inc., Prospect Heights, IL.

idea—that language is correlated with worldview and behavior. The language does not cause people to drink beer or think about beer in a particular way. The language of beer emerges from the way people in Munich socialize.

Munich beer categories are typical of other kinds of folk taxonomies. Not everyone in Munich will know all of these terms or make all of these distinctions beyond the core terms. However, like a culture with few color terms, most Americans talk about the universe of beer with a less elaborate lexicon than that of the Münchner. We turn now to a less palatable topic, disgust.

Table 12.3. Categories of Intoxication

Stages	*Einen Rausch haben* (to be drunk)					
	einen leichten Rausch haben (to be slightly drunk)		*einen Rausch haben* (to be drunk)		*einen schweren Rausch haben* (to be very drunk)	
	angeheitert sein	*ogstocha sein*	*betrunken sein*	*bsuffa sein*	*einen Vollrausch haben*	*einen Saurausch haben*
Emotional disposition	gay	gay or irritated	"neutral"			
Amount consumed	slight		moderate–great	very great		enormous
Self-control	present		diminished	to		absent

Reprinted by permission of Barbara Spradley from J. P. Spradley (Ed.) 1972. *Culture & Cognition:* Rules, maps, and plans (263–278). Waveland Press, Inc., Prospect Heights, IL.

Table 12.4. Categories of Munich Beer Drinkers

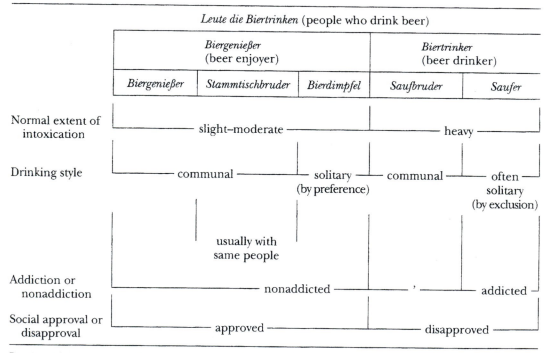

	Leute die Biertrinken (people who drink beer)				
	Biergenießer (beer enjoyer)			*Biertrinker* (beer drinker)	
	Biergenießer	*Stammtischbruder*	*Bierdimpfel*	*Saufbruder*	*Saufer*
Normal extent of intoxication	slight–moderate			heavy	
Drinking style	communal		solitary (by preference)	communal	often solitary (by exclusion)
		usually with same people			
Addiction or nonaddiction	nonaddicted			,	addicted
Social approval or disapproval	approved			disapproved	

Reprinted by permission of Barbara Spradley from J. P. Spradley (Ed.) 1972. *Culture & Cognition:* Rules, maps, and plans (263–278). Waveland Press, Inc., Prospect Heights, IL.

Disgust

The companion category to food is the category of *disgust* (Rozin & Fallon, 1987). In many cases, what is not edible is disgusting. But we are not born with knowledge of disgust items; we have to learn them. Infants will eat dirt, paint, and other indigestibles. For children, the boundary between food and disgust must be learned through classical and operant conditioning. The disgust response (e.g., opening mouth, gaping, restricting nostrils) is innate, but the items that elicit the disgust response must be learned or associated with it. The disgust response is classically conditioned to many specific objects within the first six years of development, but conditioning continues throughout the life span. Disgust takes a developmental course. A child will eat smelly cheese molded in the shape of dog feces, but an adult will not—not because of what the molded cheese *is* but because of what it *symbolizes*.

Food preferences and disgust, as products of learning, result in cross-cultural differences. Some children will grow up believing that insects are food; others will find them revolting. One culture finds raw fish edible; another defines it as inedible. What we eat, according to Rozin and Fallon, depends on our concepts of "body," "self," and "food." Good food we incorporate into our bodies to make ourselves healthy. Disgusting items are not good for the body or the self. Some nonfood items also elicit a disgust response, indicating oral rejection. Disgust is basically the failure of oral incorporation. Not all rejections are based on disgust. There are items that we do not eat not because they are disgusting but because they are harmful, such as bleach or glass. Other items depend on socialization; for example, grasshoppers, which have nutritional value, will be rejected by most American adults because of what we have learned. We think that a grasshopper is not food. We will also refuse to eat items that have been contaminated by disgust items or that look like disgust items (e.g., cheese shaped as dog feces). We don't eat the soup if we see a fly in the kettle.

The concept of "food" encapsulates our view of who we are and what we want in our bodies. Consider the concept of food through the philosophy of vegetarianism. Not unlike the conceptualization underlying beer and beer drinking, vegetarianism produces its own set of cognitions and behaviors. Vegetarianism, like beer drinking, is not a single unified doctrine; it can take different forms. One simple distinction is between *health vegetarians* and *moral vegetarians* (Brandt & Rozin, 1997). Each vegetarian construct produces different cognitions and behaviors regarding food. **Health vegetarians** do not eat meat or other animal products because they believe that these items are not healthy for them personally. **Moral vegetarians** do not eat animal products because they believe that animal life is sacred. At a dinner party where beef chili is served, the health vegetarian will be more likely than the moral vegetarian to eat some chili with meat in it. The health vegetarian realizes that diet rules can be broken; eating meat once will not make one unhealthy. The moral vegetarian cannot eat the chili because his or her diet rules are part of a broader ethical code of conduct, which cannot be compromised. Both philosophies define what is edible but whether these rules are compromised depends on one's moral reasoning.

In regard to the embodiment of language, words associated with edibility and disgust produce physical reactions and emotional feelings. Words can make us feel hungry or nauseated. These reactions vary among individuals depending on prior learning. Words associated with disgusting items (e.g., *puke*) produce a disgust response. Words become physically represented or embodied through association with food or disgust items. Conversations that include words like *snot, pus,* or *dog feces* will evoke disgust responses in some participants. The point is that our perception of "food" is not natural or innate; it is learned. Our relationships to food, food words, and disgust words are experienced through our bodies. We can see this with anyone who has developed a taste aversion. People who have become ill and vomited after eating a particular food, for example, steamed clams, will react negatively to clams, memories of clams, and the word *clams.* Victims will experience a classically conditioned visceral response to *steamed clams,* and the term will become embodied eliciting disgust. Talking about clams will produce the disgust response.

Review Questions

What foods do you find disgusting? Do you find some words disgusting? Is there a relationship between disgusting words and foods?

DETERMINING CATEGORICAL STRUCTURE BY MULTIDIMENSIONAL SCALING

One statistical method used to determine the organizational principles underlying a culture's semantic domain uses judgments of similarity of individual concepts. Participants are given a list of words and asked to judge on a scale of 1 to 9 how similar one word is to another on the list. This kind of **multidimensional scaling** (MDS) is a set of data analysis techniques that display the structure of similarity judgments as a geometric picture. MDS depicts the structure of the data by plotting the distances between pairs of concepts. Thus each concept is represented as a point in multidimensional space. Points that are close together represent concepts that are more similar than those spaced farther apart. The plot can be two- or three-dimensional.

Fillenbaum and Rapoport (1971) found that English speakers related colors on the basis of a two-dimensional color space that roughly corresponds to a color wheel, which is a circular arrangement of red-orange-yellow-green-indigo-violet. The semantic relationships between the items rated by MDS are revealed by their physical locations. The colors that have similar ratings are located near each other in multidimensional space (see Figure 12.1). The MDS technique depends on both perception and a culture's model of a particular category of thought. In this case, semantic space is similar to the perception of wavelength. Categories with more complex relationships produce a more diverse use of multidimensional space.

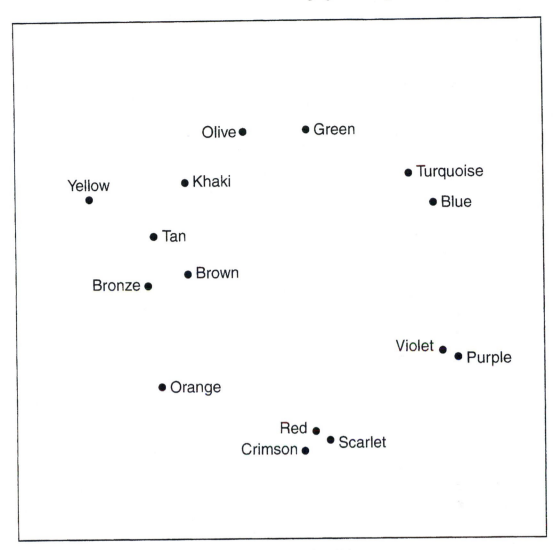

Figure 12.1. Semantic Space for Colors, as Determined by MDS

Note. Figure from *Structures in the Subjective Lexicon,* by Samuel Fillenbaum & Amnon Rapoport, copyright 1971, Elsevier Science (USA), reproduced by permission of the publisher.

Consider an MDS for the animal kingdom. In what ways are animals similar to each other? You might get a cluster of similarity for wild animals (*bear, lion*) that are spatially separated from ratings of domesticated animals (*goat, sheep*), depending on a culture's farming practices. You might see that small animals (*cat, mouse*) are semantically distant from large animals (*cow, pig*). Rips, Shoben, and Smith (1973) studied the semantic space for animals with MDS and obtained the results displayed in Figure 12.2. This is not as orderly as color space. There are clusters of animals that

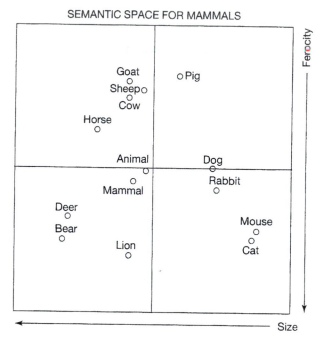

Figure 12.2. Semantic Space for Animals, as Determined by MDS *Note.* Figure from "Semantic Distance and the Verification of Semantic Relations" by L. J. Rips, E. J. Shoben & E. E. Smith in *Journal of Verbal Learning and Verbal Behavior*, Volume 12, 1–20, copyright 1973, Elsevier Science (USA), reproduced by permission of the publisher.

are similar to each other. The horizontal axis represents *size*, with animals getting larger as you proceed toward the left. The vertical represents a factor like *ferocity* that increases as you move down the axis. MDS reveals that our cultural model of animals focuses on their size and ferocity.

Without asking people how they think about the structure of color terms or the nature of the animal kingdom, the similarity ratings reveal the structure of semantic space. One's associations and scaling also depend on the category being studied because each category has its own structure (Fillenbaum & Rapoport, 1971). MDS methodology can be used for semantic domains that are more culturally complex than colors, such as *love* or *intimacy*, as we see in the next section.

What you might have previously understood as natural concepts like "food," "beer," and "disgust" are in reality social constructions. The analysis of both color terms and beer terms can be understood in terms of a paradigm that generates labels for members of a category. Both perceptual and social categories provide evidence of the power of the mind to impose classification on diverse sets of objects and events. If there is a case where language influences how we think about the world, it is in these kinds of social conceptualizations. We continue the discussion of categorization with a look at psychological and cultural foundations from which language emerges.

Cultural Models and Language

Linguistic relativity explores the relationship between the way a culture "thinks" and the words in its language. Our interest is in the cultural lexicon as it relates to psychological processes, social processes, and affective meaning. We are interested in how thought is influenced by a culture's lexicon. The organizational principles for knowledge depend on the semantic domain in question, as well as the culture under study. One culture might have a small vocabulary for colors but a large one for flowers. What would this level of differentiation mean? Differentiated categories like Munich beer types reflect the level of importance in the culture and how people socialize. The next topic explores how language, intimacy, and gender are related. What is our culture's model of intimacy?

GENDER, LANGUAGE, AND INTIMACY

Emotion-laden topics like intimacy, marriage, and family present a rich source of words for every culture. The structure of semantic knowledge about terms for sexuality and intimacy, of course, depend on culture and other factors such as the age, education, and gender of the speaker. Can the lexicon for talking about relationships between men and women be used to construct a cultural **model of intimacy?** This is a question posed by Holland and Skinner (1987), who studied language, intimacy, and prestige. Based on data collected from extensive interviews with college students regarding the nature of intimate relationships, Holland and Skinner constructed a list of words that men and women use to describe each other. Subjects were then asked to relate the set of male terms and the set female terms on whatever basis they thought was appropriate. Men rated the female terms and women rated the male terms. The words were then scaled using an MDS analysis. The output of the two scalings appears in Figures 12.3 and 12.4.

The main question of interest is, what are the dimensions that emerge from the scalings? On what basis do women and men relate to each other? Both male and female terms were associated on the basis of what might be called likability. Likability is a consistent dimension for describing both men and women socially. Likable men and women are referred to with terms of endearment (e.g., *girlfriend, boyfriend, lover, sweetheart*). Unlikable men are referred to with insults that indicate their ineffectiveness, ineptness, or selfishness (e.g., *bastard, jerk, nerd, prick*). Unlikable women are referred to with terms that reflect their overdemanding qualities (e.g., *bitch, cat, dog, nag*). Beyond likability, men and women construct different dimensions of intimacy. Men regard women as attractive possessions; the higher a woman's status, the more she enhances the man's reputation (e.g., *fox, doll, cute girl, dish*). At the other end of the dimension are low-status women who are sexually loose or lesbians (e.g., *whore, slut, dyke, butch*). Women do not view men as possessions but in terms of how they emphasize or exploit **gender differences.** At one end

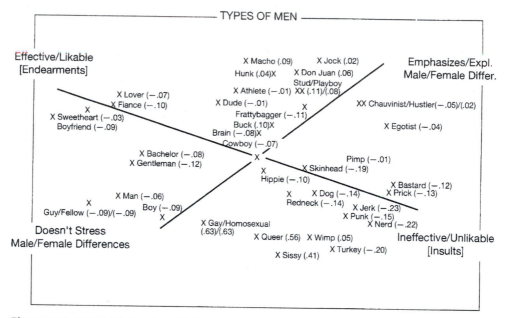

Figure 12.3. Three-Dimensional Representation of Male Social Types

Note. Stress = .147. From *Cultural Models in Language and Thought*, Dorothy Holland and Naomi Quinn. Reprinted with the permission of Cambridge University Press.

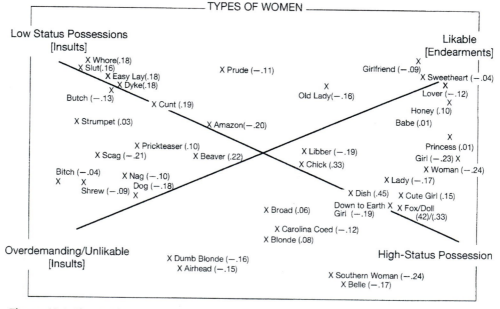

Figure 12.4. Three-Dimensional Representation of Female Social Types

Note. Stress = .138. From *Cultural Models in Language and Thought*, Dorothy Holland and Naomi Quinn. Reprinted with the permission of Cambridge University Press.

of this dimension are clustered attractive men who try to exploit women (e.g., *jock, stud, Don Juan, playboy*). At the other end of the dimension are less attractive men who do not stress male and female differences (e.g., *boy, guy, gay, queer*).

The MDS technique revealed how the lexicon for social intimacy is influenced by a culture's values regarding prestige, emotional maturity, and likability. These aspects of knowledge must not be regarded as essential aspects of the lexicon. They come from gender-related attitudes. We need to see these differences in intimacy in terms of cultural differences, not simple language differences. The semantic world is constructed by a culture to meet its social needs and values.

What the cultural model tells us is that we cannot divorce the lexicon of intimacy from cultural or subjective organization. Human language evolves through individuals who live in cultures.

COMMUNICATION AND CONTEXT

The topic of discussion in a conversation, what H. H. Clark (1996) called the *joint project*, is what people are talking about and what they are trying to achieve by conversing. Joint projects exist in conversational layers that can shift and establish a new common ground. Common ground shifts to accommodate the circumstances and the parties with whom we are conversing. The way we learn to converse is also a cultural model that specifies the who, what, where, and when of speaking.

Conversations rely on the establishment of common ground, which, you will recall from Chapter 8, is the conversants' mutual shared beliefs, knowledge, and values. This ground shifts when we move from one setting to another. H. H. Clark (1996) differentiated conversations in personal settings from those in institutional settings. *Personal conversations* include gossip, gab sessions, family matters, and romance. Conversations in *institutional settings* such as courts, church ceremonies, and business transactions rely more on explicit roles and rules specific to the context. These social practices include rigid rules for speaking, for example, in a courtroom trial. The institutional-personal distinction exists on a continuum because there are categories of speech that are simultaneously personal and institutional, such as a personalized wedding ceremony. Along with the rules of conversational patterning, every social context activates awareness about personal space, status, and dominance relationships that affect what can and cannot be said.

Social and personal variables determine a range of restrictions on speech. **Appropriate speech** is what is permissible and expected in a given situation. *Inappropriate speech* is impermissible in that situation (Jay, 2000). Appropriateness also affects turn taking, speech acts, given-new contracts, and intimacy. Breaking social rules can lead to social sanctions, which range from dirty looks or mild disapprobations to penalties described in civil, criminal, or business law (e.g., disorderly conduct or libel). But just because some language is forbidden does not mean that it will never be heard. The sanctions on speech are a sign that speech restrictions will be broken. If everyone were obedient, we would not need criminal and civil laws.

To demonstrate the power of context on appropriateness, I designed an experiment to measure how the likelihood of using taboo words depended on who was speaking and where they were speaking (Jay, 1992a). Imagine how college students' speech changes from context to context. What college students talk about on campus depends on who is listening (e.g., student, janitor, professors) and who is talking. Where the conversation takes place (e.g., dean's office, parking lot, dorm room) is also important. College students talk about college matters with friends at a party, but at home, the grounds for discussion change (see Exercise 12.1).

To get a sense of how students decide what is appropriate and what is not, they were asked to rate how likely they were to hear taboo words in various campus locations and how likely people in various campus occupations were to use taboo words (Jay, 1992a). These data appear in Tables 12.5 and 12.6, respectively. We can see wide variability in terms of both location and occupation, with a noticeable difference between expectations for male and female speakers. Male-dominated locales and male occupations were more likely to be associated with cursing than female-dominated locales and occupations.

Using the speaker and location data obtained earlier, I designed a second experiment. Subjects were presented with scenarios to be evaluated, such as *The dean said* hell *in the parking lot* or *The student said* shit *in the dean's office*. Subjects rated each

Table 12.5. Mean Likelihood of Hearing a Dirty Word in Various Campus Locations

Taconic Dorm (male)	90.32	Mail Room	35.31
Pub	89.25	Student Senate Office	35.31
Berkshire Dorm (coed)	88.75	Radio Station	34.69
Athletic Field	88.37	Student Affairs Office	34.38
Townhouse Apartments	86.25	Bookstore	33.44
Hoosac Dorm (female)	83.32	Veterans' Affairs Office	32.50
Greylock Dorm (female)	82.19	Swimming Pool	31.56
Game Room	79.63	Media Center	29.69
Gymnasium	78.94	Supply Room	28.75
Training Room	63.25	Piano Lab	23.44
Athletic Office	62.12	Copy Center	20.94
Maintenance Room	57.13	Payroll Office	19.38
Newspaper Office	55.31	Campus School	18.75
Parking Lot	54.06	Registrar's Office	16.62
Sidewalk	53.13	Health Center	15.31
Security Office	44.37	President's Office	14.50
Library	43.44	Financial Aid Office	12.06
Biology Lab	40.94	Career Planning Office	11.69
Theater	40.94	Placement Office	10.63
Resourceful Living Center	39.69	Admissions Office	7.25
Computer Center	37.81	Dean's Office	7.25
Chemistry Lab	37.81	Day Care Center	1.44
Faculty Lounge	35.88		

Note. Scale values are 0 = not likely at all, 100 = most likely/possible.
From Jay, T. B. (1992). *Cursing in America.* Reprinted by permission of John Benjamins N.A. Inc.

Table 12.6. Mean Likelihood of Using Dirty Words for Various Campus Occupations

Male Occupation	Rating	Female Occupation	Rating
Athletic Coach	82.50	Athletic Coach	49.37
Janitor	62.81	Cook	36.88
Policeman	62.50	Maid	33.44
Groundkeeper	58.13	Secretary	31.87
Building Superintendent	57.50	Bookstore Employee	28.44
Cook	51.88	Business Office Clerk	27.56
Teacher	44.50	Cashier	26.25
Mail Carrier	37.50	Teacher	24.69
Bookstore Employee	36.87	Admissions Officer	20.62
Business Office Clerk	32.81	Receptionist	20.06
Dean	28.75	Guidance Counselor	20.00
President	26.56	Nurse	19.37
Admissions Officer	25.00	Dean	14.38
Registrar	23.44	Librarian	7.87

Note. Scale values are 0 = not likely at all, 100 = most likely/possible.

From Jay, T. B. (1992). *Cursing in America.* Reprinted by permission of John Benjamins N.A. Inc.

scenario on a 1-to-100 scale, judging how likely it was to occur and how offensive it would be if it did occur. The mean offensiveness ratings are diagramed in Figure 12.5. These data are very orderly, and they show that students carry a mental model for appropriateness used to weigh the who, where, what, and when of taboo words in public. Notice the effect of ownership or dominance over territory, that is, one's own room or office. This is an implicit variable referred to as **turf** (Jay, 1992a). Turf represents the speaker's freedom and power within his or her own territory. Speakers are more likely to use taboo words and find it less offensive when they do use taboo words on their own turf.

The topics of intimacy and taboo are cultural constructions that impose constraints on how people talk and the words they use in a given situation. Men and women conceive of intimacy in both similar and different ways. The freedom to use taboo words is also constrained by contextual and personal factors in which gender plays no small role. We continue to explore gender and context in the next section.

Gender Differences in Conversations

Speaker gender has been clearly implicated in Americans' mental model of public cursing (Jay, 1992a, 2000), as can be seen in Tables 12.5 and 12.6. Male occupations and male locations are rated more likely to feature taboo words than female occupations or female locations. A consistent result over decades of research with taboo words is that women and men, boys and girls, and elderly men and elderly women

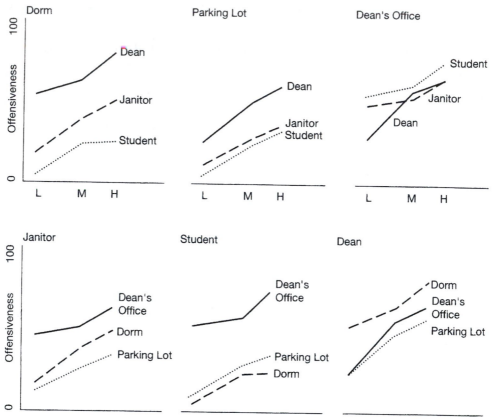

Figure 12.5. Mean Offensiveness Ratings as a Function of Speaker, Location, and Word

Note. Scale values are 0 = not offensive at all, 100 = most offensive possible. Offensiveness ratings are plotted vertically. The horizontal plot is obtained word offensiveness: L = low, M = medium, H = high. Both upper and lower graphs present the same data. However, data in the lower graphs are plotted as a function of the location noted at the top of the upper graphs. *Note.* From Jay, T. B. (1992). *Cursing in America.* Reprinted by permission of John Benjamins N.A. Inc.

use taboo words differently in public (de Klerk, 1990, 1991, 1992; Hughes, 1992; Jay, 1980, 1992a, 1996, 2000). Men have a larger production vocabulary than women, men use more offensive words than women, and men use offensive language more frequently in public than women. Note that these are relative contextual differences. One can find women using more offensive words and using them more frequently in female-dominant contexts like female dorm rooms or elderly nursing homes (Jay, 1992b, 1996). This makes sense as an effect of context on taboo language and reaffirms the common finding that women use more emotional language than men in conversations when conversations are decoupled from verbally aggressive and taboo topics (e.g., Goldshmidt & Weller, 2000). It is evident that gender differences in taboo language use have diminished in recent years (Jay, 2000). Taboo word use raises more general questions about men and women's speech.

The gender and language question was brought to the forefront during the women's movement in the 1970s. Thorne and Henley (1975) published a collection of important papers from this era. Another influential analysis of gender and language is Carol Gilligan's *In a Different Voice* (1982). Gilligan challenged the prejudice against women's speech and reframed what were regarded as weaknesses, criticizing the use of men's speech as the standard for all experiences. Gilligan showed that the strength of women's speech lies in the creation of connections between conversants. She explored social issues such as political order and the psychology of women's and men's lives. These early perspectives form the basis for contemporary questions regarding gender and language.

What do the terms *sex* and *gender* mean? In the 1970s, psycholinguists asked about sex and language. Now the debate has shifted away from biology to one about gender, culture, and language. I am suggesting a shift in thinking about what gender and language issues represent. Earlier research on **sex differences** has been replaced by questions about *gender differences, gender identity,* or *gender schemas.* While the earlier studies of sex differences represented speech differences as a matter of biology, contemporary gender studies recognize that one's gender role is a social construct wherein speech differences are proscribed. In other words, gender roles are learned and repeated in order to maintain gender constancy over situations.

By no means is the following a comprehensive analysis of gender and language research. We consider research on conversational interruptions and tag questions. We covered some of these issues when we discussed turn taking in Chapter 8. Research by Zimmerman and West (1975) reported that males do the most interrupting, 96 percent of the occurrences, in conversations between men and women. **Interruptions** have the effect of violating a speaker's turn. In same-sex conversations, turn taking and interruptions were more equal between participants. Men also frequently respond to female topics with delayed minimal responses. Minimal responses are remarks like *uh-huh* or *um-hmm,* which indicate some interest in the speaker's topic. In this case, several seconds elapsed before such responses were made. Zimmerman and West thought that these behaviors were attempts by men to deny women equal status in conversations and suggested that they reflected differences in power.

At the time, Zimmerman and West's research seemed to confirm what others were finding with regard to sex differences. In the case of research on tag questions, Lakoff (1975) found that women conveyed more uncertainty in their speech. Women also use more tag questions than men do. A **tag question** is an interrogative tacked on to a statement like *I think it's a bit stuffy in here, don't you?* or *It's getting late, don't you think?* Women also often use a rising intonation at the end of a statement, which has the effect of marking it as uncertain and unassertive. These studies of tag questions and interruptions portrayed women's speech as inferior to men's. In addition, other studies indicated that women use more questions, minimal responses, and attention-getting comments (e.g., *guess what*) than men do (Fishman, 1978). These data led researchers to believe that women do most of the work to keep conversations interactive in part because they have less power than men do in conversations.

These early studies of gender and conversational patterns have since been called into question. When McMullen, Vernon, and Murton (1995) repeated Fishman's (1978) study, they obtained a very different pattern of results. They found no differences between men and women in terms of questions, tag questions, and minimal responses. They did not find that women do more interactional work than men do. This is probably because men and women find different strategies to share power. Kollock, Blumstein, and Schwartz (1985) found that in couples with differential power, the more powerful partner interrupted more, and the less powerful person produced more tag questions and minimal responses, regardless of the gender of the partner.

People take turns in conversations, and that turn taking follows conversational rules, but we need to ask what is really happening in these speech contexts. Gilligan suggested that these early studies had many theoretical and methodological flaws. Gilligan (1982) and Tannen (1994) suggested that women and men have different approaches to discourse. One is not inferior to the other; they just reflect different conversational goals. Tannen used sociolinguistic discourse analysis to establish a basis for gender differences. From her point of view, men and women have different **communication goals** and so employ different strategies in conversations. Tannen suggested that men viewed conversations as hierarchical constructs where they try to "win" the conversation. A man attempts to establish his status and independence through talk. A woman, by contrast, views conversation as an opportunity to establish consensus through negotiating and building rapport.

What do these observed gender differences really mean? We must reformulate what men and women are doing in conversations. For example, one way to interpret tag questions is that tags are cohesive and facilitative devices in a conversation (Holmes, 1984). Tag questions do not reflect uncertainty; they signal that the speaker wants to include others in the dialogue. And interruptions, what do they mean? Several things, it turns out; they do not all function in the same way. Some interruptions occur or overlap speech in order for the interrupter to encourage the speaker or to support what the speaker is saying. In this way, the interruption functions as a cohesive device rather than an interruption. Men may swear publicly to be assertive, while women do not because swearing interferes with building rapport. Finally, we can see that earlier studies took place in formal situations. Formal situations accentuate motives for power or dominance, and they encourage speakers to represent their statuses within conversations (Tannen, 1994). Relaxed informal settings do not encourage speakers to present conversational markers of status. They make conversants feel relaxed. In part, earlier gender differences were the products of demand characteristics of the formal situations, which promoted male conversational patterns.

There is evidence that gender differences in language use take a developmental course. Preschool girls, for example, are more likely to ask an adult for help completing a puzzle than preschool boys are, even when they have the same level of need (Thompson, 1999). At this age, boys are more assertive and demanding, while preschool girls are more polite and cooperative (Esposito, 1979). Boys interrupt girls twice as frequently as girls interrupt boys. According to J. Sachs (1987), preschool boys tend to use imperatives (e.g., *gimme your arm, lie down*), while girls in the same situation use fewer imperatives and more inclusive language (e.g., *let's sit down; I'll be the doctor for my baby, and you be the doctor for your baby*). Sheldon (1990) found that in same-sex triads, boys gave directives and issued threats, while girls tended to negotiate settlements. Killen and Naigles (1995) found similar tactics in single-sex and mixed-sex triads, but the mixed groups produced less sex-stereotyped communication than same-sex groups. This latter result would indicate that preschoolers have the ability to adapt their communication style to their partners. The gender-stereotyped differences continue into middle childhood, where they diverge into styles similar to adult men's and women's styles, primarily because boys and girls participate in different cultures with different practices (Maltz & Borker, 1982). Boys work in large groups where dominance is important; girls work in small homogenous groups or pairs where play is more cooperative.

Gender identity is a social category that evolves over time, forcing psycholinguists to reexamine basic assumptions about conversational strategies. Recent reviews of research on the topic of sex differences and similarities in communication have revealed that women and men continue to be similar in some social domains and different in others (Canary & Dindia, 1998). Also, what is considered normal or permissible depends on the time frame. What was normal for women to do and to say in public in the 1950s does not translate directly to the present-day speech. One inherent difficulty with much of the research on gender is that the studies confound gender with race. Henley (1995b) pointed out the failure of early studies to include a comprehensive sample of women of color, instead relying on reports mainly from white middle-class women. Are these studies reflective of all women? All statuses? All races? The answer, of course, is that they are not. Extrapolations to other subject populations are not always valid.

Questions about what *women* say and how they speak are generally answered by what white middle-class women say and do. The results of gender research may represent middle-class women, but it does not necessarily apply to nonnormative samples. For example, college-aged white women use profanity frequently, but working-class white women are more conservative (Hughes, 1992). Henley's work on gender and dominance (1995a, 1995b; Thorne & Henley, 1975) reminds us that we must look at conversation as a function of context and status. Gender and status account for nonverbal factors such as posture, personal space, use of time, eye contact, touching, facial expression, and emotional expressions. Obviously, we need more comprehensive research before generalizations about gender can be validated.

Communities of Practice

Psycholinguists have been slow to examine how gender identity affects language use. **Gender identity** is the degree to which a person regards himself or herself as a male, female, lesbian, gay male, bisexual, or transgender. Can we use the notion of gender identity to ask how one's gender affects lexical choices? In what ways are male, female, gay male, and lesbian "sex talk" similar? In what ways are they different? How does context affect sex talk? Because gender is a socially constructed role, there should be differences in the sexual lexicon.

A recent development in sociolinguistics on the issue of language and gender generalizations is to look at **communities of practice** (CoPs). An understanding of gendered language requires an understanding of where speech practices take place. A CoP is a group whose joint interaction in some activity is intensive enough to give rise to a repertoire of shared practices (see Eckert, 1989; Eckert & McConnell-Ginet, 1999; Lave & Wenger, 1991; Wenger, 1998). When people engage in social practices, gendered language practices are developed that construct participants as girls or boys, men or women, Asian Americans, homosexuals, or rugby players, for example. Through these social and linguistic practices, gender and identity are co-constructed. We see these practices at work when we consider how people talk about sex as a function of who is in the audience. CoP is a reformulation of class differences and learning. The emphasis is on the social nature of learning, which is viewed as a situated activity. Learners participate in CoPs, where they master knowledge and skill in order to move toward full participation. This process produces an intersection of community, social practice, meaning, and identity (Wenger, 1998).

People adjust their language to fit the situation. Gender-preferential language will be most obvious in same-sex groups and weaker in mixed-sex groups. Both men and women make these kinds of accommodations (see Fitzpatrick, Mulac, & Dindia, 1995). These trends hold for interpersonal communication in face-to-face situations. However, the effects of CoP on language practices shift when the context moves to e-mail communication via computer. Without physical cues to identity, one is left with the content and style of the message in e-mail.

Thomson, Murachver, and Green (2001) examined how men and women react and accommodate to gender-preferential language in e-mail messages. College students were asked to write e-mail messages over a two-week period to two **"Netpals."** Both Netpals, Jane and Peter, were the same person, an experimenter, who used female-style language when writing as Jane and male-style language when writing as Peter. The gendered styles were based on previously identified qualities in e-mail messages; for example, females use more emotion words than males do. The template used for the Netpals' messages appears in Table 12.7. Thomson et al. were interested in how the participants would accommodate to the styles presented in the Netpals' messages. The participants' messages were coded on thirteen variables: adjectives, intensive adverbs, subordinating conjunctions, opinions, compliments, hedges, apologies, insults, questions, references to previous messages, self-derogatory comments, emotion words, and personal information.

The results indicated a strong effect for the Netpal's style of writing but no effect for the participants' gender. More adjectives, opinions, and insults were used when participants thought they were writing to the male Netpal. The other variables, with the exception of apologies, were used more frequently when participants thought they were writing to the female. The participants in the study changed their

Table 12.7. Frequencies of Language Features in the Netpals' Messages

Language Feature	Netpal Style	Message Number				
		1	2	3	4	5
Adjectives	Male	5	5	6	4	6
	Female	2	1	3	2	1
Emotion	Male	0	1	0	0	0
	Female	1	3	2	1	2
Intensive adverbs	Male	1	0	1	0	1
	Female	3	2	2	3	2
Questions	Male	2	1	1	0	0
	Female	3	2	3	2	1
Insults	Male	0	1	1	1	0
	Female	0	0	0	0	0
Opinions	Male	2	2	2	2	1
	Female	0	1	0	0	1
Self-derogatory comments	Male	0	0	0	0	0
	Female	1	2	0	1	1
Subordinating conjunctions	Male	0	1	1	0	0
	Female	2	2	2	1	1
Personal information	Male	2	3	1	0	1
	Female	6	5	4	3	2
Compliments	Male	0	0	0	0	0
	Female	0	2	0	1	0
References to previous message	Male	0	1	0	1	1
	Female	2	3	2	3	2

Note. From Thomson, R., Murachver, T., & Green, J. (2001). Where is the gender in gendered language? *Psychological Science, 12(2),* 171–175. Reprinted by permission of Blackwell Publishers.

writing style depending on which Netpal they were writing to, even if they wrote to both Netpals in the same writing session. The participant's gender had little to do with gendered speech. Since it was unclear whether participants were responding on the basis of style or name (Jane versus Peter), Thomson et al. ran a second experiment in which styles and names were manipulated independently. This time, the gender of the participant made some difference. Female participants produced more self-derogations and emotion words than males, who stated more opinions than female participants did. The Netpals' styles turned out to be more important than their names. Both male and female participants directed more opinions at male-style Netpals regardless of name. Also, both male and female participants used adverbs, hedges, derogations, emotions, personal information, and references to previous messages with female-style Netpals regardless of name.

Both males and females were able to shift their styles to accommodate to the style of their Netpals. Gender-preferential styles are not fixed but are constructed within a communication situation. Same-sex contexts in normal communications elicit styles that are more extreme than mixed-sex conversations because we shift the style of our speech to fit the situation and the participants in the conversation. Culture affects language use on several levels—codes, dialect, topic, common ground, and even, as we see next, the words we choose in conversations. CoP is a convenient label for social situations where the words we use mark us as members of a particular social group. CoPs are used in social, ethnic, educational, occupational, religious, governmental, military, and gender identity groups (Jay, 2000). The use of the CoP lexicon indicates that the speaker is a member of the group. Misuse of the specialized lexicon marks one as an outsider or a neophyte. In this way, lexical choices produce solidarity and distance. In this section, we consider the use of jargon, slang, sex talk, and name-calling as examples of lexical choice within CoPs.

JARGON

Jargon is the idiomatic speech of a special activity or social group. Knowledge of jargon identifies one as an "insider," a member of the group. Jargons are created to facilitate within-group communication, especially in a work setting; it makes communication clearer and more efficient. Many specialized jargons reduce words to abbreviations or truncated versions of longer words. *Oral examination* is reduced to *oral, postoperative recovery* becomes *postop; pregnant* becomes *PG;* and *rest and relaxation becomes R&R.* Abbreviated terms facilitate or solidify communication between members of an occupational group, saving time and energy and communicating in a precise and efficient way on the job.

Members of a group can use jargon to distance themselves from others or to make themselves feel superior to non–group members. College students experience the distancing effect of jargon in a discipline or facility that they are not familiar with. My students who are not familiar with computer jargon complain that the computer center staff try to confuse them with computer and Internet jargon. This may or may not be intentional. This confusion can induce a sense of inferiority on the part of outsiders or newcomers. They wonder, why would people use jargon around me if they know that I don't understand it? Jargon can in this way create social distance, if the speaker seeks it.

SLANG

Slang is an informal, nonstandard lexicon used between members of a speech community to mark membership in that community, to affront authority, to lower speech standards, or to preserve secrecy. Slang does not necessarily promote occupational communication efficiency in the way that jargon does. Eble (1996) and Partridge (1984) have described the function and vitality of slang in detail. Slang users constantly refresh the lexicon by creating new words. The creation of slang within a speech community supports the claim that languages are evolutionary. All languages evolve, making some words obsolete or archaic (e.g., *behold, hither, forsooth*). Slang speeds up the evolutionary process, actively exhausting meanings and reinventing new ones when mainstream culture appropriates slang terms.

Slang use is deliberate. Speakers know when and why they use it. Slang is common among college students, laborers, drug users, prostitutes, nurses, military personnel, and musicians. People use slang to mark the important social and functional aspects of their worldview (Jay, 2000). As a social marker, slang contributes to one's personal identity and group identity. But these identities are not fixed; they change with settings and personnel in settings. Personal identity is critically bound with issues surrounding sexuality, as we see next. How we reveal our sexual identities depends on who is listening.

SEXUAL TALK

Sexuality is a personally relevant but socially taboo topic in formal settings. The use of sexual slang is closely related to one's gender identity. Since sexuality is a taboo topic, many of us resort to the use of slang and euphemism in everyday conversations. Clinical terms (e.g., *penis* and *vagina*) seem too formal and do not evoke the deeper emotional reactions associated with slang and obscenity. Emotionally powerful obscene words are used to express our deepest emotional feelings. No other terminology can express these strong feelings as well (Jay, 2000). Wells's research (1989, 1990) is instructive on how closely **sexual talk** is integrated into identity.

How we talk about sex depends on who is listening. Wells (1989, 1990) examined how sex talk shifts as a function of gender and speech context by asking his subjects what words they would use in particular circumstances. Table 12.8 presents data from one experiment in which Wells (1989) asked participants to indicate which sexual terminology they used with different listeners. References to body parts and sexual acts depend on who is listening. If you consider gender orientation as arising from a CoP, the gender differences make sense. Lesbians use more female-oriented words than male-oriented words for the female genitalia than other subjects do. Gay males use more sexual slang with their partners than other groups do. Heterosexual males show the greatest variety across contexts, indicating that male gender orientation is less rigid than others are. Language use consistent with gender identity is more stable among gay men and lesbians than among heterosexuals. Finally, parents and dissimilar other listeners elicit the most conservative terminology. Speakers shift to clinical terms or none at all with parents.

Some of this sexual terminology may be offensive to readers, but these are the words Americans use to talk about sex. Psychologists know that people talk with their lovers about sexuality with casual terms in intimate situations. Clinical terms are just too formal and unsexy. Most public communication contexts are not intimate and call for some censorship and self-restraint, causing a shift to formal speech styles. Many Americans struggle to talk about sex, and because of this, sexual slang is an important topic for students of psychology. Many psychologists work in mental health settings, where they have to communicate effectively with clients and their families about sexual matters. Mays et al. (1992) made the case for studying sexual slang, proving that many social workers and psychologists are unprepared to work with clients who have nontraditional sexual orientation. Mays et al. noted that many counselors were ignorant of how gay African American men talk about sex. Without knowledge of the gay African American man's lexicon, mental health workers will not fully understand their clients' problems. Even though sexual slang is taboo for

Table 12.8. Preferred Terms by Context, Gender, and Sexual Orientation

Term and Context	Heterosexual Male	Gay Male	Heterosexual Female	Lesbian
Male Genitalia				
Same-sex	dick	cock	penis	penis
Mixed-sex	penis	penis	penis	penis
Parents	penis	penis	penis	penis
Lover	penis	cock	penis	cock
Female Genitalia				
Same-sex	pussy	cunt	vagina	clitoris
Mixed-sex	vagina	vagina	vagina	vagina
Parents	vagina	vagina	vagina	(no resp.)
Lover	vagina	cunt	vagina	clitoris
Coitus				
Same-sex	fuck	fuck	have sex	make love
Mixed-sex	have sex	have sex	have sex	make love
Parents	have sex	have sex	make love	(no resp.)
Lover	make love	fuck	make love	make love
Oral-Genital Contact				
Same-sex	blow job	blow job	blow job	oral sex
Mixed-sex	oral sex	oral sex	oral sex	oral sex
Parents	(no resp.)	(no resp.)	(no resp.)	(no resp.)
Lover	blow job	blow job	oral sex	suck
Hand-Genital Contact				
Same-sex	hand job	jerk off	masturbate	masturbate
Mixed-sex	masturbate	masturbate	masturbate	masturbate
Parents	masturbate	(no resp.)	(no resp.)	(no resp.)
Lover	hand job	jerk off	foreplay	masturbate

Note. From Jay, T. B. (2000). *Why We Curse: The Neuro-Psycho-Social Model of Speech.* Reprinted by permission of John Benjamins N.A. Inc.

many Americans, slang and euphemism are how we talk about sex, and psychologists must be prepared for it.

TABOO, NAME-CALLING, AND INSULTS

Another form of identity comes out of the use of ethnic and racial **insults.** Slang, jargon, and slurs are both personal and social (Jay, 2000). Some forms of name-calling and insulting are derived from gender identity, others are associated with race, religion, and culture. The name-calling rituals are used to mark people on the basis of real or assumed differences.

Leach (1966) used a sociocultural model to explain how animal names are used as insults. The guiding principle is that of **taboo,** forbidden behavior and speech. The speech associated with any taboo behavior is also taboo. Taboos produce social norms of avoidance, and they also become personally relevant. Taboos become embodied through the process of classically conditioned avoidance. The more frequent the pairing of taboo terms and behaviors with negative consequences, the stronger the avoidance of the taboos. The culture's values are represented in taboos on language. Taboos on animal names (e.g., *ass* or *bitch*) are derived in part from rituals regarding killing and eating animals. The animal taboos are not natural; they are constructed categorically. Many animal names are used as insults (e.g., *pig, ass, bitch, cow, horse*). These names refer to animals that are fairly well known. They occupy the intermediate semantic space between pets and wild or exotic animals. The intermediacy or closeness factor (e.g., neither close nor far) produces the taboo. Hence we can insult using *You pig* but not *You kitten* or *You marmot.* Interestingly, Leach's principle of closeness and taboo can be used to predict what animals are edible and those that are not. We do not eat our pets; nor do we eat exotic animals. He also used closeness to predict marriage sanctions; one does not marry members of one's family (too close) or total strangers (too far).

I. L. Allen (1983, 1990) has written extensively on the history of ethnic and racial insults in America. This history shows that ritualized insults are also the result of economic and social problems in culture. The use of ethnic, racial, and religious insults encapsulates both speakers and victims within a social context. The knowledge and use of ethnic and racial terms are the product of one's personal history and identity, as well as the linguistic history of ethnic and racial insults in the culture. For example, when a person utters a racial slur to insult another person, the insult comes from the speaker's bigotry, and at the same time, the slur reproduces the history of the word being used. Calling someone a *chink, greaseball, mick, nigger,* or *spic* reproduces the speaker's racism through the history of the racist use of each term. Learning and then uttering insults reproduces the prejudices in the culture and helps maintain a status quo.

Saying insulting words is not always immediately perceived as an insulting act. Some situations are friendly in-group playing. In word play, insults should not be interpreted as insults on a personal level, even though a particular word has a history of use as an insult. It should be mentioned that minority in-group members use insulting terms between themselves as terms of endearment, which complicates the notion of prejudice and raises questions about the appropriation of meaning. For example, African American high school students in urban schools freely refer to themselves as *niggers* or *niggas.* Some might argue that any use of an ethnic or racial slur marks the speaker as prejudiced to a degree. The perceived meaning of racial or ethnic insults or **derogatory ethnic labels** (DEL) like *nigger, spic, kike,* or *wop* depends heavily on the context in which they are used (Greenberg, Kirkland, & Pyszczynski, 1988). The use of a DEL by a nonmember of that ethnicity in the presence of a targeted minority group member reflects a degree of hostility or prejudice on the part of the speaker. In the absence of the minority, the use of the word may produce solidarity with in-group members.

We cannot assume that knowledge of DELs is the same in all ethnic groups. One common finding is that members of minority groups have a greater awareness of DELs than nonminority speakers do. Meeker and Kleinke (1972) asked African American, white, and Chicano youths to list names for African Americans, whites, and Chicanos. African American and Chicano informants listed significantly more names for themselves and for whites than white subjects did. Whites listed very few names for themselves, but African American and Chicanos listed many names for themselves. Some of these names were used exclusively by group members. The suggestion is that minority group members have a greater knowledge of the names for themselves and whites than whites do.

We have focused on ethnic labels in this section, but discrimination goes beyond race to find reasons to be insulting. Religion, food preferences, body size, social class, gender identity, mental health, education, and income are used to insult people who are viewed as different (Jay, 1992a, 2000). Van Dijk (1987), who has conducted a great deal of research on the subject of linguistic racism and elitism, noted that psycholinguists and cognitive psychologists rarely talk about either elitism or racism and likewise rarely conduct research on the topic that might add insight or help ameliorate these worldwide problems. It is important to address issues of racism and sexism in a course on language because language is so inexorably bound to prejudice and elitism.

The notion of CoPs and accommodating speaking styles provides the basis for a segue into the topic of language registers.

Language Registers and Standards

Speech registers are styles of formality that range from casual slang to the erudite speech of the rhetorician. The TV newscaster's speech lies somewhere in the middle. You might think of registers as markers of linguistic etiquette. Compliant speakers adapt their speech to fit the power and dominance demands in a given setting. Some speakers rebel against norms and choose substandard registers and use slang. As an alternative to the standard, slang affronts dominance. Any register, whether standard or not, includes and excludes speakers at the same time, depending on whether one can speak the register in question.

English has both standard and nonstandard forms. Either form can be adopted regardless of racial or ethnic background. Because registers are correlated with power, standard English is marked with status indicators like wealth or education. Every culture has standard registers and nonstandard (lower-class) registers. Standard registers reinforce a status quo power structure by discriminating against lower-class, minority, and undereducated speakers. English-speaking countries have a long history of discriminatory practices on the basis of speech registers.

Bernstein (1961, 1974) studied middle-class and lower-class **dialect** differences in England and suggested that lower-class speech produces a context-bound **restricted code.** Middle-class speech uses an **elaborate code** in which less is taken for granted and speech is more explicit and specific. Whereas both lower-class and middle-class speakers can use the restricted code from time to time, only the middle-class can switch to the elaborate code. The lower class is stuck with the context-bound dialect. One of the problems with Bernstein's distinction is that dialect differences were confounded with race when it was applied to registers in the United States.

In the early 1970s, some American scholars adopted Bernstein's distinction and applied it to differences in African American and white English even though there was little evidence that supported the distinction (Glucksberg & Danks, 1975). Labov (1970) looked at standard English (SE) and nonstandard English (NE) dialects as equally successful forms of expression. Labov realized that the reason African American children performed less well than white children on standardized tests, in interviews, and when reading out loud was due to the interview situation itself, especially the race of the interviewer. He viewed the social context of the language sample as the most powerful influence on the child's speech. Problems arose for reading teachers who were uncertain what to do when African American children read school texts in African American dialect. Should they be corrected or not? Baratz (1969) showed that both African American and white children make errors when they read and that their errors reflected their underlying dialects rather than deficiencies. One solution to reading differences was to make sure white teachers were familiar with African American dialects so that they would be more aware of reading problems that were not dialect differences.

The work of Baratz (1969) and Labov (1970) showed that dialect use is a function of the situation. In a school setting, there is an inherent power inequity because teachers and other adults dominate minority children. In the end, it is difficult to prove that differences in language reflect deficiencies in intellect. What dialect differences seem to produce is a continuing form of racism or classism on the basis of dialect.

DIALECTS AND DISCRIMINATION: RACE AND POWER

The dialects of English present many similarities but only a few differences compared to SE. Dialects of any main language are by definition *mutually intelligible* to the speakers of that language (Crystal, 1987). But mutual intelligibility is a matter of degree, and some dialects are more easily understood than others. Most speakers of English will understand SE. Americans use dialect differences to make (false) assumptions about language, as if one dialect were superior to another. Then the assumed superiority of a dialect is used to discriminate against speakers who deviate from the standard dialect. It is important to note that all Americans speak a dialect of English, even if it does not sound like we do. We see the nature of discrimination in three separate studies.

Giles and Powesland (1975) reported a study where African American and white speakers read identical answers to two questions. The black speakers used NE and the white speakers used SE. Although exactly the same answers were read, judges consistently evaluated the SE versions as better, indicating that it is not what is said that is so important but *how* it is said. Gaetner and Bickman (1971) had African American and white phone callers make a call for help. Callers pretended to have called the wrong number when they were stranded; they said they did not have any more coins to make another call. The person on the other end of the phone line was asked to call another number (a research assistant) to provide the help. African American subjects helped African American and white callers to the same degree, but white subjects helped African American callers less frequently than white callers. Finally, Giles, Baker, and Fielding (1975) had two groups of British students listen to the same speaker give a speech. One group heard the SE version, and the other heard an NE version. Subjects were asked to evaluate the speaker on rating scales and to write a letter of recommendation stating their opinion of the speaker as a lecturer. In their letters, the students wrote 82 percent more about the SE speaker than the NE speaker. As for the ratings, 72 percent of the SE audience found him "well-spoken," while only 7 percent of the NE audience found him well-spoken. Elitism is clearly at work, especially in academic settings, where proper language use is crucial.

Can you see how the question of linguistic relativity extends to dialect differences? Some people believe that one dialect is intellectually inferior to another. Using NE is assumed to be the basis for thinking and writing unclearly. Teachers are supposed to fix the deficiencies by making students speak and write in SE. In status-marked situations, like the college classroom, an "inferior" dialect becomes a basis for discrimination. Alternatively, Kochman (1981) suggested that dialect and racial differences are only differences of style, not intellect. He noted that some situations provide conflicting discourse goals for nonwhites.

Dialect studies show that all of us carry mental models of vocal stereotypes in our heads, which allow us to discriminate speakers on the basis of age, gender, and dialect. Problems arise when we use these stereotypes to discriminate on the basis of assumed personality or intellectual deficiencies. Mental models are used to distinguish African American from white speech, urban from rural speakers, Canadian French from Parisian French, northern speech from southern speech. Americans have debated the nature of African American and SE differences for some time, which seems to mask an implicit SE elitism.

ELITISM

Speaking "properly" for the middle class is a very important social goal because SE is considered superior to NE. For academics, one of the worst social blunders is to misspeak in public—to use the wrong word or wrong word form is a terrible mistake. People make value judgments about the way we speak, and speaking NE is viewed negatively in middle-class circles. We saw these kinds of prejudice and stereotyping in the studies reported in this chapter.

Academics have the power to change how we analyze discourse and discrimination (Smitherman-Donaldson, 1988). Cognitive psychologists and psycholinguists have all but ignored the influence of group-based ethnic dominance of human communication. Unfortunately, our ignorance promotes a form of linguistic **elitism** and discrimination in psycholinguistic research. Ignoring racial problems perpetuates the problem of prejudice. Prejudice is reproduced through the form and content of discourse (van Dijk, 1987).

Discourse through face-to-face conversation is the central element in communicating prejudice to others. Discourse has been undervalued as a source of prejudice relative to TV, radio, newspapers, and mass communication. Discourse analysis of prejudice talk reveals a speaker's underlying attitudes and beliefs about ethnic differences. The social function of prejudiced talk is to provide evidence, opinions, persuasion, self-presentation, and other-presentation. Through discourse, we share ideas and cognitions (e.g., *we, they*) about others and try to present a positive face to listeners.

What is the discourse of elitism? For van Dijk (1987), the topic of prejudice itself can be realized at micro- and macropropositional levels. The topics associated with prejudice include crime, cruelty, primitivism, poverty, and stupidity. Macropropositions about national policy, work, and education are represented at the micropropositional level with statements like *They should be sent back, They cause unemployment,* or *Education should be in one language only.* Prejudiced discourse produces and reinforces a prejudice schema about differences, deviance, and threats regarding origins, socioeconomic status, cultural differences, and personal characteristics. Prejudice schemas flourished in stories about foreigners analyzed by van Dijk. In conjunction, elitism produces another agenda in prejudiced talk: The cultural elite actively work to interpret, reformulate, and redistribute racist models among the population at large so as to maintain an elitist status quo. Racism and elitism always go hand in hand, and they should not be ignored by students of psycholinguistics.

AFRICAN AMERICAN VERNACULAR ENGLISH

American educators and language scholars in the 1960s debated the history and nature of **African American Vernacular English** (AAVE). Was AAVE a variant of English, or was it a creolized form of English? A **creole** is a mixture of two (or more) languages that takes phonological and grammatical characteristics from both (or all) source languages. Creoles evolve from **pidgins,** which are simplified mixed languages used for communication in a diverse speech community. A pidgin is the accepted language for conducting business and conversation between language groups who do not speak a common language.

During the early stages of contact between two or more groups such as slaves, traders, and landowners, pidgins were used for business transactions. The conversants

retained their native languages, which were used at home. But when the new generation of babies were raised in the pidgin environment, the babies learned the pidgin as
a native language. When a pidgin language is used as a native language, the language
has become creolized. A creolized language like AAVE could become decreolized if
there is enough pressure to shift to a standard language, but this has not happened.
Today, many language scholars believe that AAVE is a creolized form of English. AAVE
presents several grammatical differences relative to English. For example, AAVE has

No final *-s* on third person singular verbs: *She walk to school.*

No copular verb in the present tense: *They real fine.*

A habitual *be: They be walkin* (i.e., *They always walk*).

These kinds of grammatical differences, the deletion or insertion of different
syntactic elements where another dialect or language uses the constituent, are also
present in some form in SE. Remember that these examples represent differences,
not deficiencies. If scholars were to use dialect issues to promote equality and understanding between speakers, we might view these comparisons more favorably.
Instead, differences have been used to reinforce prejudice toward African Americans and the dialects they speak.

How can members of one CoP understand the practices of another group? It
would seem that differences in worldview are bound to produce misunderstandings.
There is evidence that people acculturated in white culture do not fully understand
communication practices in African American communities. What functions in
African American dialect as verbal dueling and playing with language appears to
whites as a form of verbal aggression. SE-speaking whites often misconstrue a form
of verbal play because whites rarely speak African American dialects or play games of
verbal dueling. African Americans appear to white Americans to be more aggressive
and verbally confrontational than whites because African Americans have learned to
converse with higher thresholds for verbal aggression (Kochman, 1981; Smitherman, 1977; Smitherman-Donaldson & van Dijk, 1988). Studies that suggested that
African Americans are more verbally aggressive than whites failed to recognize base
rates of aggressive verbal word play. It is noteworthy that many dialect comparisons
focused exclusively on male speakers and failed to provide a careful analysis of gender, income, education, and status. Several lines of research confound race with register: SE samples are white speakers, and NE samples use African American speakers.
SE and NE forms exist in both groups.

How a child pronounces words and uses the grammar at home makes little
difference as long as the child's language choices conform to the local dialect rules.
However, once the AAVE speaker enters school, things change. Children who
speak, write, or read aloud in NE have to learn to use SE at school. This was never
clearer than during the controversy over AAVE in the late 1960s or more recently
with the Ebonics debate in the 1990s. Suffice it to say that there are no "primitive"
languages or "primitive" dialects; all languages are equally sufficient. The "primitive" label is merely a form of linguistic racism and not a valid distinction of lan-

guage. The dialect that the child acquires depends heavily on the parents' social class, education, and geographic origin. During the school years, children learn to speak the dialect of peers in CoPs. The emerging CoPs have more influence over the child's colloquial speech and slang than the parents do.

During the school years, the AAVE-speaking child will learn when to use AAVE and when it is appropriate to use SE as a second dialect. When children enter school speaking AAVE, they may not be prepared for classmates and teachers who speak SE and do not understand AAVE. De Stefano (1972) found that children who spoke AAVE in the first grade used SE 56 percent of the time, but in the fifth grade, SE was used 70 percent of the time in repetition tasks.

Wyatt and Seymour (1990) found that dialect switching from SE to AAVE also depends on the topic of discussion. In their study, a 5-year-old African American girl with a white teacher used AAVE 25 percent of the time and SE 75 percent of the time at school overall. But she used AAVE 43 percent of the time when talking about feelings and characteristics and 40 percent of the time when talking to African American mates. She never used AAVE when talking to the teacher or to two or more adults at once. AAVE-speaking African American children either knew SE and were reluctant to use it or were learning to use SE over time as the appropriate dialect in the classroom. The ability to speak in both SE or AAVE provides African American children with a useful tool, switching dialects to fit the situation.

EDUCATION, EBONICS, AND CODESWITCHING

The recent debate about dialect differences has centered on **Ebonics,** which is another name for AAVE used to define the speech of urban African Americans (see Rickford & Rickford, 2000). In 1997, school officials in Oakland, California, proposed to allow Ebonics to become the standard for African American children to use in school. Reading and classroom discussions were to be conducted in Ebonics. The policy would have a tremendous effect on how African American children were educated. The use of Ebonics is a complex issue, and the Ebonics movement may perpetuate what it seeks to overcome.

Speakers learn to switch dialects to meet the needs of particular social situations. Generally, African American speakers become bidialectical, but whites do not. There is no pressure on whites to switch dialects in educational settings. Myers-Scotton and Ury (1977) used the idea of **codeswitching** to describe how speakers shift from one dialect to another. Codeswitching is the use of two or more linguistic varieties in the same conversation or interaction (see Myers-Scotton & Lake, 2000). It may involve the insertion of a word or phrase of one dialect (language) other than the one being spoken into a single sentence, or it may involve movement back and forth between languages or dialects. An African American student may use standard dialect in the classroom during a question-and-answer session led by a white teacher but switch to AAVE to talk to friends sitting nearby. Codeswitching occurs because the African American child is cognizant of the social variables at play.

Review Question

As linguistics or psychology students, what is the importance of dealing with sexism, racism, and elitism in personal and professional settings?

There is some implicit elitism at work in this codeswitching research, however. Codeswitching has been defined mainly in terms of switching to a standard dialect but not about switching back to AAVE. Little attention is given to what makes switching to AAVE advantageous. What does AAVE do that the standard dialect cannot do? The pragmatic variables underlying codeswitching to AAVE, with respect to greetings, openings, turn taking, closings, or situational cues, have not been studied (Smitherman-Donaldson, 1988) because language scholars are mainly concerned with structural differences and not the social functions of AAVE. Because codeswitching from English to AAVE is common for African American children and adults (Rickford & Rickford, 2000), the conditions that promote switching should receive more attention. What causes a speaker to switch? What is the consequence of not switching? These questions are important. Consider the social, emotional, and cultural variables involved in codeswitching in the following passage from Adele Givens's "Fake Bitch" comedy routine (Rickford & Rickford, 2000, p. 59), in which Givens recalls how her mother used to switch from vernacular to straight English, depending on who was on the telephone. Givens's mother conducts different social and emotional business with each form; one is informal for family and friends, and the other is more formal for conversations with professionals. What is the consequence of switching? Koch, Gross, and Kolts (2001) examined African American adults' attitudes regarding African Americans who use AAVE or SE exclusively or codeswitch between the two languages. They presented African American college students with an audiotape of a man using AAVE, SE, appropriate codeswitching (SE in a formal setting, AAVE in an informal setting), or inappropriate codeswitching (AAVE in a formal setting, SE in an informal setting). Subjects were asked to rate the speaker on a variety of personality characteristics and indicate if they wanted to know or work with the speaker. The college students rated the SE and appropriate-codeswitching speaker more favorably than either the AAVE speaker or the inappropriate codeswitcher. They indicated that they would like to work with the SE speaker and appropriate codeswitcher more than the AAVE speaker or inappropriate codeswitcher. Codeswitching is not bad per se; it depends on the situation.

Review Question
Exactly what are the changes from the AAVE version to the standard version?

Bilingualism and Second Language Acquisition

Bilingualism is the proficiency or ability to speak two languages. There are different paths to bilingualism. Native bilingualism occurs when children acquire two languages simultaneously. Another path to bilingualism is through immigration, when a family moves from one country to another, and the child has to learn a new language. Several cultures (e.g., India) have one language that is used in school and another that is used in nonschool settings. A different path occurs after a native language has been acquired and a second is attempted; this has been called foreign-language learning or **second language acquisition** (SLA). There are several theories of how bilingualism and SLA unfold (Kilborn, 1994; Snow, 1998). These include points of view centered on the biases of foreign-language educators, child language researchers, linguists, psycholinguists, and sociolinguists. Since this chapter focuses on culture, we concentrate on the sociolinguists' view and contrast it with that of psycholinguistics. I aim to concentrate on the psychological and social consequences of speaking two or more languages rather than give a complete account of bilingualism.

PSYCHOLINGUISTS' APPROACH TO SLA: THE COMPETITION MODEL

Psycholinguists look at language processing as the task of parsing a string of words and connecting them with meaning. Complex sentences or those containing novel lexical items may be difficult to process. Learning a language is a processing skill, and novices are less skilled than experts are. One gets better with practice. Now we bring in the learning of a second language. Some of what we have learned will help us learn that second language, and some will cause interference. The processing model focuses more on performance than on competence. It focuses on the strategies that people use rather than rule learning. One model that has been helpful when applied to SLA is the **competition model** (Bates & MacWhinney, 1981; Kilborn, 1994; MacWhinney, 1987).

The competition model views language learning as knowledge that certain "cues" indicate certain semantic roles. In English, an SVO language, the first noun encountered in a sentence is probably the actor, as in *John whispered to Mary*. This cue can also conflict with other competing cues, for example, when the initial noun is inanimate, as in *The idea whispered to Mary*, or when the noun and verb do not agree, as in *His students laughs at a good joke*. In the SLA situation, some of the cues learned in the first language will be transferred to the new language. English speakers are likely to think of the first noun in the sentence as the actor of the sentence, which may or may not facilitate learning the second language. English, Italian, and Dutch use position, animacy, and agreement as cues to who is the actor; and when these cues are in conflict within a sentence, English speakers will weight noun position more heavily than animacy and agreement in the early phases of SLA. Dutch speakers rely more on agreement and Italians more on animacy (Kilborn & Cooreman, 1987). In other words, SLA will be slowed by established tendencies in the speaker's native language.

When native speakers begin learning a second language, many of them develop systems that rely on native strategies. Others take a compromise position and merge the two systems in social settings that permit codeswitching. The types of mistakes and compromises that are made can be predicted by the relationship between the native and target languages (Kilborn, 1994). Since German speakers do not rely on word order as much as English speakers, it will take some time for them to pay attention to the leading noun to find the actor in English sentences. Because English is an SVO language, English speakers pay attention to word order more than morphology to decide which noun represents the actor. Using English speakers and German-English speakers with different degrees of experience, Kilborn had subjects listen to different types of sentences in English and decide quickly which of two nouns was the actor or grammatical subject in the string. An NVN sentence (e.g., *The waitress pushes the cowboys*) accentuates the SVO cue more than a VNN (e.g., *Kisses the table the apple*) or NNV sentence (e.g., *The baskets the teacher kicks*). It was expected that English speakers would always pick the first noun in NVN sentences but rarely in the NNV and VNN sentences. It was expected that German bilinguals' application of the strategy of using the first-noun cue would depend on their experience with English.

The results are plotted in Figure 12.6. The advanced bilingual group relied more on word order as a cue to meaning than the novices did. The NVN sentences represent the fundamental word order in English, and the advanced group is leaning in this direction toward the English-only speakers. However, for the novices, the effect of word order is very weak. The adoption of word order as a cue to sentence meaning in the advanced group is evidence for the emerging awareness of the importance of this kind of cue in SLA. As fluency increases, so does sensitivity to word order.

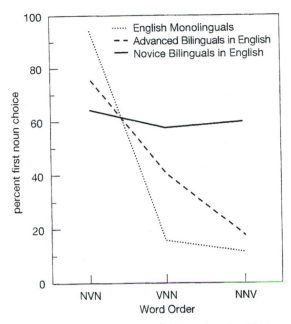

Figure 12.6. Mean Percentage Selecting the First Noun as the Agent *Note.* Figure from "Learning a language late: Second language acquisition in adults" by Kilborn, K., in *Handbook of Psycholinguistics,* edited by Morton A. Gernsbacher, copyright 1994, Elsevier Science (USA), reproduced by permission of the publisher.

A CONTRASTIVE ANALYSIS OF ADULT FOREIGN-LANGUAGE LEARNING

One way to predict where foreign-language learners will have difficulties is through the use of **contrastive analysis,** which uses language differences to predict errors (Snow, 1998). Contrastive analysis compares grammatical rules in one language to those in a second language, looking for similarities and differences.

When foreigners attempt to learn English, certain difficulties are predictable. Because Chinese and Japanese do not contain articles (*a* or *the*), Chinese and Japanese speakers have difficulty learning how articles are used in English (Thomas, 1989). French and German speakers have trouble with adverbials in English, tending to order them as they would in their native languages (e.g., *I go tomorrow to school*). Spanish, German, and Chinese speakers experience difficulties using *do* and ordering auxiliary verbs in questions and negations (Snow, 1998). Finally, speakers of Hebrew have difficulty with perfect and progressive forms in English because Hebrew does not distinguish between ongoing and punctual action or between finished past actions and past actions with relevance in the present. Bilingualism and foreign-language learning continue to be informative about the nature of cross-linguistic differences and similarities.

The psycholinguistic approach suggests that SLA is a matter of experiencing a foreign language and trying to make sense of it. Learning a new lexicon may produce slower reading times in either language or confusion between phonetic systems. Learning a new language may also cause a loss of proficiency, referred to as language attrition, in the native language, or attrition in the second language if it is not practiced regularly. With its focus on cognitive and processing skills, the psycholinguistic approach reveals little about motivational or cultural factors that affect SLA. The sociolinguists' approach is much better at uncovering how personal identity and acculturation affect language learning.

SOCIOCULTURALISTS' APPROACH TO SLA

Sociolinguists, sociologists, and anthropologists focus on the social context of bilingualism. In their view, language performance is closely tied to the speaker's personal identity and identification with the culture of the second language. Social factors such as ethnic pride, racism, communication situations, prejudice, and attitudes are important variables here. Learning a second language has both benefits and costs. A person will not be motivated to learn a second language if it has negative effects or associations for the learner. What is important is the communicative effectiveness and social appropriateness of the new language (Snow, 1998). Becoming bilingual in the sociocultural perspective is a means of being a more effective and competent person in another culture.

A perennial question about bilingualism is whether bilinguals profit or lose because they have to maintain two languages. The advantage of having two languages is referred to as **additive bilingualism; subtractive bilingualism** is the case when one language detracts from the other. Generally, developmental research has shown that bilingualism is not a reason for concern. Little evidence has been found to indicate that bilingual children suffer a disadvantage because of their knowledge of two languages (Crystal, 1987). Wallace Lambert devoted his academic career to demonstrating the social and psychological advantages of bilingualism in Canada. Lambert (1977) found that French Canadian bilinguals were more likely than monolinguals to be advanced academically in French schools and that they develop a more diversified and more flexible intelligence. English Canadian children also do better when their elementary school courses are conducted in French.

The sociocultural perspective helps language professionals understand the cultural and social problems associated with SLA in contexts where the native language and foreign language are associated with conflicting cultural values. This happens when immigrant families move to the United States and the children want to quickly identify with American children by learning to speak English. The motivations here are not about becoming proficient but about avoiding being marked or stigmatized as a speaker of another tongue. When the new language provides cultural, personal, educational, or financial benefits for the learner, motivation and progress in SLA will be greater than when the second language confers no apparent advantage (Schumann, 1997). In two-way Spanish- and English-language learning settings, children learning English progress faster than children learning Spanish because

English has greater positive associations than Spanish does. One of the other consequences of these kinds of programs is that Spanish-speaking children tend to experience attrition in Spanish while learning English, whereas English-speaking children retain English when learning Spanish. This is a clear instance of subtractive and additive bilingualism.

The sociolinguistic perspective also provides answers for why people switch from one language or dialect to another in different social situations.

BILINGUAL CODESWITCHING

Bilingual codeswitching—switching from one language to another, depending on the situation—is a fact of life in bilingual communities and a universal phenomenon wherever languages are in contact. Residents switch between French and English in Quebec, Spanish and English in California, French and German in Switzerland. Codeswitching also occurs in signed language, as when a signer switches from American Sign Language to cued English (a system of hand shapes and mouth shapes). Codeswitching between ASL and cued English follows a similar pattern found in codeswitching in spoken language (Hauser, 2001).

Bilingual communities in North America, South America, and Europe present social and personal reasons for codeswitching strategies. For example, in a bilingual population like Paraguay, where bilinguals use both Spanish and Guaraní, which language is spoken depends on what one is doing and with whom. Spanish is used with strangers and in formal situations where there are differences in power, such as teacher-student interactions or doctor-patient dialogues. In rural Paraguay, Guaraní is used in intimate situations and those that require solidarity, for example, a joke-telling session among workers of equal status. Interestingly, a romantic courtship in rural Paraguay will begin in Spanish, but as the relationship becomes more intimate, Guaraní will be used (Crystal, 1987). In this example, the social or pragmatic functions of bilingualism are important. But like the question of codeswitching, psycholinguists have been more interested in the cognitive cost of using two languages or dialects rather than the social benefits of having two dialects or languages. What is the importance of slower lexical access or slower reading comprehension if the social benefits of switching are advantageous?

According to the sociocultural view, speaking two languages is not much different from what all monolinguals must do from time to time, as when addressing babies in motherese. In both cases, we adjust words, grammar, and morphology in different contexts in order to accommodate the needs of different listeners. Snow (1998, p. 469) put it this way:

> Socially appropriate speakers of English may use an expletive to express anger to a colleague but say, "Darn!" to a child or a minister; similarly, a bilingual says, "chair," to an English listener and "silla," to a Spanish listener. Failure to make these kinds of adjustments might reflect feelings of hostility to the addressee or a need to project a certain kind of personal and social identity for oneself. It need not be seen as a failure of "proficiency."

Snow's comment reveals that codeswitching and bilingual switching are products of the social and emotional environment. To switch codes affords the speaker the flexibility to adapt to shifting contexts and speak a language or register that will serve the speaker's needs the best. For example, Puerto Rican migrants who lived in New York City and later returned to Puerto Rico switch between Spanish and English to invoke an attachment to the American part of their identities (Clachar, 2000). This kind of switching was most common when the returned migrants interacted among themselves, an event not unlike African American children speaking in one dialect to the teacher and a different dialect with classmates. The ability to switch language for personal or social reasons is an advantage that the monolingual lacks in a bilingual setting.

Foreign-language learning success depends on the nature of the two languages in transition and the strategies the language learner transfers from the native language to the second language. Success at SLA is also dependent on emotional and motivational factors that are themselves products of the way our brains function and develop.

BIOLOGICAL AND EMOTIONAL CONSEQUENCES OF BILINGUALISM

Over the course of more than two decades working in the field of SLA, Schumann (1997) developed a theory predicated on the idea that success in SLA is emotionally driven and the product of acculturation. One of the crucial variables in SLA is integration or contact with target language speakers. The desire for contact is a matter of necessity, desire, or both. Acculturation is influenced by two sets of variables, one social and the other psychological-affective. Social forces are factors like dominance (e.g., economic or political superiority) and integration strategies that are at work in the contact situation. These factors will cause one either to seek to preserve one's own culture, to adapt to a new lifestyle while retaining one's own culture, or to assimilate into the new culture, which fosters maximum acculturation.

Schumann (1997) proposed that the cognitive and neurobiological processes that underlie the social and psychological factors of acculturation are rooted in the neural architecture underlying stimulus appraisal that governs approach and avoidance tendencies. He located the mechanisms of motivation in SLA in the amygdala, frontal cortex, and the body proper. We have read elsewhere that the amygdala is critical in emotion perception and production. The frontal cortex is important for decision making and risk assessment; people with damage in this area have difficulty making decisions about their personal lives and social relations (Damasio, 1994). For Schumann, neural architecture for stimulus appraisal (approach and avoidance tendencies) constitutes the affective basis for motivation in SLA. Success in SLA is a product of our innate tendencies to seek out interaction with others. As we develop, we construct **emotional schemas** for emotional experiences that act as filters to focus our attention on and generate expectations about upcoming experiences. Two important issues are the emotional schemas that influence our attention and efforts devoted to learning and the patterns of appraisal that underlie our motivation in SLA. In short, people learn second languages when the experience is pleasant and rewarding; in response, changes occur in the neural architecture and emotional schemas associated with SLA. Emotion, biology, culture, and personal motivation become interdependent in SLA.

A subsequent question about SLA is whether the languages operate with a single neural module or with separate modules and what this difference might mean in terms of emotions. This distinction is important because it speaks to the effect of SLA on socioemotional expression. Ojemann and Whitaker (1978) used a brain stimulation technique with two epileptics that sheds some light on the shared versus separate question. When the brain is stimulated electrically, the affected area becomes inactivated. Ojemann and Whitaker wondered how object naming in two languages would be affected by inactivation. The answer was, "It depends." Some areas of the brain are equally developed with both languages; other areas showed separate language areas. Weaker language representations are diffusely developed in the cortex, while strong representations are more unifocal. Some aspects of bilingual speech use single language areas, while others separate the two languages. The idea of representation strength helps explain why one of the languages suffers attrition without practice. Unless both languages are used equally, the language that is not used will undergo language attrition due to forgetting and lack of practice and maintenance. This holds true for both adults and children.

For adults, there is evidence for the modular view of bilingualism in which two languages operate separately. Recent fMRI research in late bilinguals has shown the activation of two separate, nonoverlapping language areas in Broca's region of the frontal lobe when subjects are engaged in a subvocalization task (Kim, Relkin, Lee, & Hirsch, 1997; see also Chapter 2). Further, psycholinguistic experiments show that a written word presented in one language (e.g., *perro* in Spanish, the word for *dog*) usually does not produce long-term transfer for the word in a second language with the same meaning (Scarborough, Gerard, & Cortese, 1984). Now we can look at the socioemotional effect of bilingualism. Dual representation also explains why emotions are not experienced the same way in both languages, and the native language remains the primary outlet for emotional schemas. Recall Lamendella's (1977) view from the end of Chapter 2: Bilinguals may revert to their mother tongue to express strong emotions because that language has the best tie-in to limbic expression. The mother tongue is embodied more deeply through the limbic system than a second language or a less practiced one. The deep emotional work in communication must be expressed in the primary language. The brain develops in response to both cultural and linguistic input. The emotional work that we do in language is better expressed in one language relative to the other. Those expressions, in turn, are culturally dependent and personally relevant. Here one sees the embodiment of language, culture, and personality all at once.

Despite the neurophysiological evidence for separate loci for two languages, there is recent evidence that behaviorally the two languages of a bilingual do interact and can interfere with each other in real time. Bijeljac-Babic, Bairdeau, and Grainger (1997) reported inhibitory orthographic priming in a lexical decision task with French-English bilinguals. When prime and target were from the same language, orthographically similar primes inhibited target recognition, but dissimilar primes did not. When prime and target words were from different languages, the degree of inhibition increased as a function of the person's level of proficiency in the prime word's language. Proficient bilinguals show almost equivalent degrees of within- and across-language inhibitory priming. Spivey and Marian (1999) also demonstrated language overlap with Russian-English bilinguals. They used eye-tracking methodology to show that when instructed to pick up a stamp in Russian ("*Poloji marku*"), bilinguals looked briefly at a *marker* before fixating the stamp and picking it up. The initial phonemes of *marku* were partially processed in English even though the instruction was in Russian. These studies provide support for parallel interactive representations of two languages.

Another place to look for the effects of SLA, emotion, and embodiment is during sleep. Symbolic and emotional activity fluctuates throughout the night. What happens when a bilingual speaker talks in his or her sleep? Pareja, de Pablos, Caminero, Millan, and Dobato (1999) assessed speech used during sleeptalking episodes in bilingual children in the Basque region of Spain. Sleeptalking occurred in 383 out of a sample of 681 children. The dominant bilinguals, those who spoke one language better than the other, did their sleeptalking in the dominant language. Fewer than 4 percent of the children used the nondominant language persistently during episodes of sleeptalking. Pareja et al. concluded that environmental factors, such as cultural and social setting and immediate past use, may influence a given child on a particular night.

Bilingualism and SLA are complex and multifaceted issues; that is why we have addressed the topic in several places in the text. Bilingualism cannot be dissociated from its personal, political, economic, and social consequences. Native language learning and SLA promote both solidarity and distance between speakers. We look at these products in a monolingual context to end this chapter.

The Social Function of Language: Solidarity and Distance

Every language has a powerful interpersonal function. We speak language because it does things to other people. Language brings us together, and it separates us from others. Language forms an initial bond between parent and child. Language connects a child to the social world in which he or she will find a sense of identity within communities of practice. Language establishes who we are and who we are not. Identity can be seen in part by the way we use pronouns like *you* and *we*. English generally relies on *you* as the preferred form of the second person pronoun. Our earlier use of *thou* is all but obsolete today. However, other European languages retain two second-person pronouns for use in intimate versus nonintimate settings.

Brown and Gilman (1960) and Ervin-Tripp (1972) examined how pronouns and **forms of address** reveal our relationships to others. A good example is the use of pronouns, especially in French, German, and Italian. The French pronoun *tu* is used with close friends, and its counterpart *vous* is used with strangers. But pronoun uses are complex and also take into account conversants' age and status. *Vous* will be used with strangers and minor acquaintances, while *tu* is used in situations that are marked as intimate. *Tu* has the effect of promoting solidarity. In a situation where power is marked, for example, at a restaurant, a waiter will be addressed with *vous* in order to maintain social distance. However, an intimate but asymmetric power situation, like a parent and child conversation, will produce the *tu* form. Brown and Gilman (1960) reported that how often these pronoun forms are used in a culture depends on the level of friendliness or openness in the culture. They found that Italians use *tu* forms more than French, who use it more than German speakers do.

As French has *tu* and *vous*, German uses *du* and *Sie* for solidarity and distance, respectively. At the beer festivals in Munich where beer is consumed in a "people-uniting way," two or more people will pledge eternal friendship and agree to change their formal status forms of address, *Sie*, to the intimate *du*. The change is symbolized by drinking beer together with their arms intertwined as part of the ritual of *Brüderschaft trinken* ("drinking brotherhood") (Hage, 1972). This use of pronouns to create solidarity or distance raises questions about forms of address in general.

English speakers do not make the *tu-vous* distinction with personal pronouns, but we do use forms of address asymmetrically, for example, titles and honorifics (Ervin-Tripp, 1972; see also Chaika, 1994). Forms of address in English depend on the familiarity, age, rank, and status of the person addressed. A child whose name is known is addressed by first name (e.g., *Jimmy, do you need some help?*), otherwise no name is used (e.g., *Do you need some help, little boy?*). Adults in a status-marked situation are addressed with titles such as *Your Honor* or *Madam Chairwoman*. Some adults are properly addressed with their occupational titles, such as *Doctor, Father,* or *Professor.* Other untitled adults are addressed with courtesy titles: *Mr., Mrs., Ms., Sir, Ma'am*. Our adult relatives are addressed with kinship references like *Aunt Millie* or *Uncle Sam*. Kinship is not marked with child relatives; we do not refer to our age-mates as *Cousin Jim* or *Niece Sally*. Familiar adults can be addressed by first names (e.g., *Hello, Dave.*). We can also address others through proclamation, as when the speaker proclaims *You can call me Michael.*

The duty to use a form of address is not equivocal but depends on status. A college campus is a good setting in which to observe forms of address. A higher-status or older person makes the proclamation to a person of lower rank in a conversation. For example, I might tell my seminar students, "I am Professor Jay, but you can call me Tim." In these cases, it is prudent to do as one is told, but granting a lower-status person the right to use a familiar form address does not mean the familiar will be used. Professors give students permission to call them by their first names if they do not want to be referred to as *Professor.* On some campuses, only instructors at the rank of professor are called *Professor* and other instructors are called *Doctor* (Chaika,

1994). Not all students or staff members feel comfortable addressing professors and administrators on a first-name basis. On my campus, some of the nonprofessional staff call me *Doc* without using my professional title or last name in an attempt to be friendly but respectful. Even though English speakers do not use the *vous-tu* distinction, our forms of address reveal the social structures in our culture.

The topic of social structure is a good place to end this discussion on language in social contexts. We continue the discussion in the next chapter with language analyses applied to some very specific settings. Let us conclude this chapter with a comment about the social nature of language (see the accompanying box).

The Social Division of the World

Language is, of course, highly impersonal, yet although its categories are by no means products of our own personal imagination, they are not natural either. Since it is one of the foundations of our social reality, we tend to forget that language itself rests on social convention and to regard the mental divisions it introduces as real. When we label our world, we often commit the fallacy of misplaced concreteness and regard the purely conventional mental gaps separating North America from Central America or business from pleasure as if they were part of nature.

It is important, therefore, to avoid the tendency to reify the conventional islands of meaning in which we organize the world in our minds and to remember that the gaps we envision separating them from one another are purely mental. In the real world, after all, there are no actual divides separating the moral from the immoral or the public from the private. Mental divisions as well as the entities they help delineate have no ontological status whatsoever. It is we ourselves who organize reality into separate mental compartments (Zerubavel, 1997, p. 67).

Review Question
Use the quote from Zerubavel to discuss how concepts like marriage and family are social constructs.

Key Terms

additive bilingualism	appropriate speech	bilingual
African American	basic level	codeswitching
Vernacular English	beer categories	bilingualism

category
codable color
codeswitching
communication goal
competition model
concept
contrastive analysis
community of
  practice
creole
derogatory ethnic label
dialect
disgust
Ebonics
elaborate code
elitism
emotional schemas
focal color

food
forms of address
fuzzy category
gender differences
gender identity
health vegetarian
insults
interruptions
jargon
linguistic determinism
linguistic relativity
model of intimacy
moral vegetarian
multidimensional
  scaling
Netpals
odor names
pidgin

prototype
restricted code
second language
  acquisition
sex differences
sexual talk
slang
speech register
subtractive
  bilingualism
taboo
tag questions
turf
tu-vous
well-defined category
Whorf's hypothesis

What Lies Ahead

Chapter 13 presents applications of psycholinguistic research to everyday situations and problems. We examine how political and social institutions manipulate thought through language policies such as censorship, education, and mass communication. We look at the role of language in the courtroom, police interrogations, and interviews. The conversation between doctors and patients is an important area of psychological research, and so is the role of language in business and industry—for example, the nature of advertisements, product labels or warnings, and speech technology.

Chapter 13
Applied Psycholinguistics

Critical Thinking Questions

1. How do social and political institutions create word meaning?

2. What is the function of question asking in educational settings?

3. How is language use regulated through education?

4. What language issues are central to law and police interrogation?

5. How would you characterize the deceptive use of language in the news media and advertising media?

6. What language issues are important to human factors psychology?

7. Describe the nature of doctor-patient discourse.

Exercise 13.1. **Applied Psycholinguistics**
Before reading this chapter, answer the following questions in your notebook.

1. What is obscene speech?

2. Did President Clinton have sexual relations with Monica Lewinsky?

3. In what ways does television news distort reality?

4. What were the positive and negative aspects of the sex education you received in school?

5. Describe how police interrogate witnesses and crime suspects.

Earlier chapters centered on research suggesting a theory of language. In this chapter, we apply what we know about language to real-world situations where language is critical—for example, police interrogation. One aim is to examine speech in a variety of institutional settings to show how discourse analysis can be used to understand what goes on there. Another purpose is to help psychology students understand social problems. By analyzing speech in institutional settings, we can see how an institution works through the use of language. We see how the institution works by looking at the power of language to guide and manipulate people. We explore only a few settings, these include education (classroom instruction), medicine (doctor-patient dialogue), psychotherapy (client-therapist dialogue), law (courtroom conversations, police interrogation), politics (sociopolitical meaning, media presentations of politics), media (violence against women, advertising), and human factors engineering (speech technology and product warnings). The point is to present a wide variety of language situations, as opposed to providing a detailed analysis of a single institution. The citations can direct the interested reader to in-depth analyses. Let us first focus on how political power is used to define words and manipulate citizens.

The Sociopolitical Construction of Meaning

How do social and political institutions create and change word meanings? This is an especially important process for psychology students to understand in their role as informed citizens. The meanings of words are constructed or determined by the people who have the power to do so, especially governmental institutions (e.g., public schools, graduate schools, professional schools) and influential nongovernmental organizations (e.g., the American Psychological Association, network television, the motion picture industry, advertisers, organized religion). These institutions set standards for human behavior and communication. Why is this important for psychology? Because the culturally accepted definitions of words like *sexual relations, sodomy, educated, parent, marriage, family, sexual abuse, hate crime, obscene, indecent, childhood, insane,* and *incompetent* affect us deeply at personal and professional levels. The definitions of these terms affect our behavior, our legal rights, our perceptions of others, and our manner of communication.

DEFINING "SEXUAL RELATIONS"

Nowhere is the social and political manipulation of words more apparent than in the U.S. Congress, where lawmakers have an enormous influence on citizen behavior. A good example of the construction of meaning was evidenced in the House of Representatives' 1999 hearings on the impeachment of President Bill Clinton. The nature of his relationship with White House intern Monica Lewinsky was debated and dissected on the floor of the House and in the press. The issue raised several questions about sexuality and language. The "truth" or "facts" of a legal hearing depend on the power of the individuals in a position to define what truth or fact is. The "truth" about Clinton's affair is not a stable entity; it is a matter of argument.

Perhaps the most fascinating aspect of the trial was the debate over the meaning of the term *sexual relations*. People who followed the impeachment learned that the concept of "sex" is quite complex. Even though many citizens interviewed by the press expressed outrage at the president's behavior, his favorability ratings remained high. The impeachment proceedings had many Americans debating moral and legal issues regarding sexual infidelity, sexual intercourse, and oral sex. One question was whether oral sex constituted "sexual relations." Another question was whether oral sex between a married man and a woman not his wife constituted adultery. On January 21, 1998, Clinton appeared on PBS's *NewsHour with Jim Lehrer*. Here is how the question about Lewinsky was asked and answered at that time:

LEHRER: The news of this day is that Kenneth Starr, the independent counsel, is investigating allegations that you suborned perjury by encouraging a 24-year-old woman, a former White House intern, to lie under oath in a civil deposition about her having had an affair with you. Mr. President, is that true?

CLINTON: That is not true. That is not true. I did not ask anyone to tell anything other than the truth. There is no improper relationship. And I intend to cooperate with this inquiry. But that is not true.

LEHRER: No improper relationship. Define what you mean by that.

CLINTON: Well, I think you know what that means. It means that there is not a sexual relationship, an improper sexual relationship, or any other kind of improper relationship.

LEHRER: You had no sexual relationship with this young woman?

CLINTON: There is not a sexual relationship. That is accurate.

The Judiciary Committee investigating President Clinton demanded his responses to eighty-one questions about the affair. Question 79 asked:

Do you admit or deny that you made a false or misleading public statement in response to a question asked on or about January 26, 1998, when you stated, "But I want to say one thing to the American people—I want you to listen to me. I am going to say this again. I did not have sexual relations with that woman, Ms. Lewinsky"?

The president's answer was as follows:

I made that statement on January 26, 1998, not in response to any question. I was referring to sexual relations, I was referring to sexual intercourse.

What infuriated many Americans was the president's interpretation of the term *sexual relations*. On close examination, students of legal discourse realize that Clinton was responding, as any good lawyer would, to the working definition that he used in his deposition in the earlier Paula Jones sexual harassment case. That definition is shown in Figure 13.1, which is a reproduction of a page from Clinton's deposition in the Jones case. Read the definition and try to determine whether Clinton thought he was telling the truth when he said he "did not have sexual relations" with Monica Lewinsky according to this definition.

Students of language can appreciate the power of institutions to define terms such as *sex, family,* and *marriage*. These constructed meanings of interpersonal relationships and family law have a direct impact on psychologists and on the attitudes and behaviors of American citizens. Fausto-Sterling (2000) provides a cogent analysis of how gender is constructed in American culture and the difficulty of thinking in terms of only two sexes. Homosexuality was classified as a mental disorder until the 1970s, but the politics of homosexuality have changed since then, and so has the meaning of the word. Not only is homosexuality no longer defined as an illness, but the whole concept of "gender identity" has gained legitimacy. Changing sociopolitical attitudes about gender and sexuality soon become translated into educational policy regarding sex education, as we shall see in the next section.

Paula Jones v. *William Jefferson Clinton and Danny Ferguson*
No. LR-C-94-290 (E.D. Ark.)

DEPOSITION OF WILLIAM JEFFERSON CLINTON

Definition of Sexual Relations

For the purposes of this deposition, a person engages in "sexual relations" when the person knowingly engages in or causes-

(1)   contact with the genitalia, anus, groin, breast, inner thigh, or buttocks of any person with an intent to arouse or gratify the sexual desire of any person;

(2)   contact between any part of the person's body or an object and the genitals or anus of another person; or

(3)   contact between the genitals or anus of the person and any part of another person's body.

"Contact" means intentional touching, either directly or through clothing.

Figure 13.1. A Page from the Deposition of President Bill Clinton in the Paula Jones Case *Note.* From www.cnn.com/ALLPOLITICS/1998/03/13/jonesv.Clinton.docs. Accessed June 8, 2000.

Partial Birth Abortion

In June 2000, the U.S. Supreme Court rejected a Nebraska law that prohibited **partial birth abortion**. The Court ruled that the term had no legal meaning and was so broadly defined that the law would make illegal abortions that were constitutionally protected. The term *partial birth abortion* is an inflammatory name made up by conservative anti-abortion protesters. The Nebraska politicians who wrote the law included the term knowing that it was not a legitimate medical or legal term but merely conservative political rhetoric.

Education and Instruction

One of the obvious applications of psycholinguistic research is to the field of education and instruction. We have addressed language topics that are integral to education: literacy, reading, writing, language development, sign language, semantic memory, Ebonics, bilingualism, and foreign-language learning. Most of the time students spend in educational settings involves thinking about, reasoning with, responding to, or comprehending language. In the limited space available here, we concentrate on the use of questions in instruction, reproduction of knowledge and meaning, and the censorship of discourse in public schools.

Students are forced to prove that they understand what is presented in school through writing assignments and examinations. Teacher-led classroom presentations require the judicious use of appropriate pacing, gestures, enthusiasm, clarity and the avoidance of vagueness, ambiguity, and incompleteness. An information processing analysis of the contemporary classroom (e.g., Good & Brophy, 1995) suggests that students are presented with structured information that must first be comprehended and later be integrated with prior knowledge.

Exercise 13.2. **Questions in Lectures**
In your notebook, keep a verbatim record of some questions asked and answered in one of your classes. After you have completed the material in the next section, compare your verbatim notes with the suggestions from Good and Brophy (1995, pp. 276–281).

QUESTION ANSWERING

If we focus on teacher-led question-and-answer sessions, as opposed to lectures or demonstrations, we see that effective questioning relies on several interdependent processes. A good question-and-answer session promotes active learning. It stimulates students to integrate questions with prior knowledge and to look for implications and consequences. Collins (1977) advocated the use of **Socratic dialogue**, as opposed to the lecture format, as a primary method of achieving inductive knowledge and reasoning. The Socratic method uses questions to lead the student to induce knowledge, as opposed to a lecture or presentation format, which tells students the facts. Here is some question-directed dialogue on the topic of growing grain from Collins (p. 351).

TEACHER: Where in North America do you think rice might be grown? (Rule 1: Ask about a known case.)

STUDENT: Louisiana.

TEACHER: Why there? (Rule 2: Ask for any factors.)

STUDENT: Places where there is a lot of water. I think rice requires the ability to selectively flood fields.

TEACHER: OK, do you think there's a lot of rice in, say, Washington and Oregon? (Rule 6: Pick a counterexample for an insufficient factor.)

STUDENT: Aha, I don't think so.

TEACHER: Why? (Rule 2)

STUDENT: There's a lot of water up there too, but there's two reasons. First, the climate isn't conducive, and second, I don't think the land is flat enough. You've got to have flat land so you can flood a lot of it, unless you terrace it.

You can observe how the Socratic dialogue keeps the student actively thinking and searching for the answers.

This type of dialogue is effective for building inductive reasoning and restructuring information. Instructors who use questioning must do so with a few guidelines. For example, one simple mistake that many teachers make is choosing someone to answer the question too quickly without giving all students enough time to think about the question. When the answer arrives, the other students stop working on it. Instructors solicit better and more complete answers when they wait a few seconds before choosing a candidate. Good and Brophy (1995) have outlined several principles of good questioning:

> Ask questions of the entire class.
> Pick students randomly; call on all students.
> Ask a set of questions that produce 75 percent accuracy.
> Vary the difficulty level of questions from knowledge or fact questions to higher-level questions that require analysis, synthesis, or evaluation.
> Adjust questions to the SES levels of the students in the class.
> Choose a pace that reflects the level of difficulty and the number of questions asked.
> Sequence the questions to achieve the goals of the lesson.
> Vary the style and directness of the questions asked.

Wait for students to think about their answer before choosing a student to supply one.

Give hints if students cannot answer the question in its original form.

Give feedback and indicate if the question was answered completely and correctly or if some information was omitted.

Use silence to provide an opportunity for students to think.

Another aspect of instructional discourse and question answering involves the use of **explanatory questions** for reasoning. Graesser, Baggett, and Williams (1996) suggested that explanatory questions are fundamental cognitive components that facilitate and guide reasoning. Explanatory questions are the type that ask *why, how, what if,* or *what are the consequences?* Each type of question evokes a different style of answering and produces a different level of reasoning. The *why* question, for example, produces two general answer formats, a goal orientation answer and a causal antecedent answer. The goal orientation answer searches for that agent in a causal string that will bring about the appropriate goal. The causal antecedent answer leads to a search for the action or event that led up to a current state. Both Graesser et al. and Collins (1977) suggested that the principles of questioning can be built into instructional software that promotes learning entirely through asking questions (also see Jay, 1986). Graesser et al.'s goal is two-way reasoning, which provides new insights and information to both teacher and students. Unfortunately, most contemporary education is one-way, producing new reasoning only for students.

ELITISM IN EDUCATION

Bourdieu and Passeron (1990), in a frequently cited text, *Reproduction in Education, Society and Culture,* show how public education plays a key role in reproducing an arbitrary cultural scheme based on power. The prevailing ideas in the cultural system are legitimated and perpetuated in the classroom. What does this mean about language? Recall the discussion in Chapter 12 of Bernstein's (1961, 1974) claim that the lower classes were limited by their "restricted" code bound to the here and now, while the upper classes use a more abstract "elaborate" code. The discrepancy is between what the privileged and the lower classes bring to school. The school asks all students to speak the language of the privileged classes.

In public education, the instructor essentially trains students to produce, in reading, writing, and discourse, an arbitrary form of language that reflects the cultural elite. The elite or privileged students have less trouble achieving this elaborate level of discourse than students from poorer areas who come to school speaking nonstandard dialects. Making students use the elite dialect reproduces and so perpetuates the power structures of the dominant culture. Instead of allowing the lower classes to achieve equality through education, the educational system reproduces and legitimates the failure of the lower classes to achieve linguistically.

Why do state governments force students to pass standardized tests, knowing that lower-class students' failure is guaranteed? What do we imagine happens to children of recent immigrants, students who do not speak English as a native language, and students who do not speak standard dialects? The issue of language in the classroom confronts a broad sociopolitical perspective where language problems in reading, writing, and comprehension are viewed as systemic failures rather than personal failures.

Bourdieu and Passeron (1990) argue that the economic and social value of different linguistic codes depends on how closely they match the linguistic norm defined by the school as correct. The academic market value of a student's language depends on the level of mastery demanded by the school and the mastery achieved at home. There is a big difference between the experience of a child who is prepared for school by a family who actively promotes literacy and the experience of a working-class child who is raised to speak the vernacular or common code. The working-class child will experience a forced acculturation when he or she arrives at school and will have to decide whether to participate or be excluded. The control over the grammaticality and meaning of words is the product of social and cultural dominance. People and institutions who have the power to define words and name things do exercise that power. Students in public schools must either conform their own speech to the linguistic standards set by the dominant culture, codeswitch between a nonstandard dialect and the standard, or refuse to speak the language of power and fail the educational system.

SEXUALITY, EDUCATION, AND CENSORSHIP

In several places in the text, we have addressed questions about language concepts used to talk about sexuality, including the sexual lexicon, sexual slang, gender-related insults, euphemism, and sexual harassment. Sexuality is a critical issue for psychologists who deal with sexual development, sexual dysfunction, marital counseling, sexually transmitted diseases, and sex education. Of interest here is the language of sexuality and the dilemma it creates in public schools. How are we to talk about sexuality if sexuality is a taboo subject? How are we to educate children about sexuality, sexual identity, contraception, and sexually transmitted diseases if the language surrounding these issues is taboo?

One informative analysis of the role of sexuality and sexual discourse is Foucault's *History of Sexuality* (1978; also see Fausto-Sterling, 2000). Foucault describes how the concept of sexuality is socially constructed by the institutions in power (e.g., church and state) to coerce the populace into a form of sexual conduct and discourse that best suits the needs of those institutions. For example, the role of sexual intercourse in the culture according to church and state is for the purpose of reproduction within the institution of marriage. Sexuality outside of the church and state definition (e.g., homosexuality) becomes contentious and taboo. By placing taboos on sexual behavior and the language that describes it, the culture produces in adolescents a desire to know about sexuality and frequent discourse surrounding sexual desires.

Teachers and parents have great difficulty talking about sexuality with their children (Berges et al., 1986; Jay, 1998). Teachers cannot openly describe common sexual matters such as masturbation, menstruation, oral sex, sexual intercourse, and orgasm. How can they educate our children if they cannot describe sexuality? The responsibility for educating children of sexually anxious parents becomes a problem for educators. Anxious parents do not want educators to be open with students about sex, assuming that such discussions are catalysts for sexual activity. Actually, the opposite would appear to be true. Plenty of evidence shows that students who are given information about sexual intercourse and contraception do not become more promiscuous as a result of that education (Donovan, 1998).

Without proper **sex education** at school or home, children are left to find out what they want to know about sex from peers. Where does one turn for information? Many adolescents cannot talk about sexuality with counselors and physicians in clinical terms because they are ignorant of the clinical terms. The physician and teenager must resort to the use of sexual slang (Levine, 1970). Attempts to provide better public sex education for children have proved controversial. Magic Johnson, a retired professional basketball player and person with HIV, created a pamphlet using sexual slang terminology intended to educate urban children about AIDS. But the pamphlet did not reach its intended audience. Due to the language in the pamphlet, retailers Kmart and Wal-Mart banned it from their stores. The issue of sex education has moved elsewhere. Parents and educators are currently debating access to sexual materials, both educational and sensational, via the Internet as a solution (Baird & Rosenbaum, 1998).

Review Question
Describe some of the language-related problems in educational settings discussed here.

Language and the Law

Forensic psychology is the application of the science and profession of psychology to issues and questions of law and the legal system. It is a growing field of investigation. The study of language in the courts and law is the province of **forensic linguistics**. This discipline examines how people speak in court, language evidence presented in court, expert testimony by linguists, and the language of the law. Forensics can benefit from the insights of modern psycholinguistics on issues of sexual harassment, discrimination, and verbal abuse. Language and meaning are central to law.

In a classic text, *The Language of the Law*, Melinkoff (1963) makes it clear that the words of the law are the law. Within law, the construction of the meaning of a term depends on how the term has been used and interpreted in court and legal opinions. Previous usage is the meaning of a term, and there can be no other meaning. Shades of meaning are very important in **legalese,** the language of the law and of courtroom conduct. In this sense, legalese operates like a jargon to facilitate communication among legal insiders. Words mean what they are demonstrated to mean in court. When President Clinton was asked if he had had sexual relations with Monica Lewinsky, he answered no, knowing full well that he had engaged in oral sex with her. But because the definition of sexual relations given to him by the court defined such relations in terms of sexual intercourse, he answered the question truthfully based on the Jones's definition. Although his answer seemed to evade the question or to constitute a falsehood to many who debated Clinton's fate, these nuances of the meaning of "sexual relations" are the official legal meanings, even if they elude the person on the street. In reality, much of the language in the courts is difficult to understand in layman's terms.

PLAIN ENGLISH

Many of the terms used in court are not **plain English** but Latin (e.g., *mens rea, nulla bona, res judicata*) or French (e.g., *voir dire, chose in action, fee simple*). Without some education in law, the language of the law makes little sense to many Americans. Legalese in contracts, hearings, and courtrooms also seems wordy, in violation of Grice's maxim of conciseness. The language of the law has the effect of separating the activities of everyday life from the activities of the courtroom. From time to time, efforts are made to convert legalese into common language. This would not be an easy task because the use of layman's terms would alter the legal history of the words. Nonexperts fail to grasp the intricacies of the words of the law.

Legal terms cannot be replaced by words that alter in any way their legal precedents. Even if we did replace legalese with plain English, this does not lead to a better understanding of the law. One study casts doubt on the plain English movement. Masson and Waldron (1994) examined how the simplification of legalese affected comprehension of the law. When archaic and redundant words were replaced or simplified, comprehension was enhanced, as measured by question-and-answer and paraphrasing tasks. Unfortunately, plain language changes did not overcome the problems with understanding complex legal concepts that conflicted with the subjects' prior beliefs and knowledge. Plain language revisions may improve the comprehension of sentences in legal documents, but they do not improve our understanding of the law. And what would be gained by understanding the terms of a legal contract without obtaining an overall understanding of what that contract means in a court of law?

The courts cannot exchange historically significant terms, like *obscenity* or *indecency,* for ones that makes more sense to the person on the street, for example, *pornography.* **Obscenity** and **indecency** mean what the court has ruled they mean in cases involving obscenity and indecency (Jay, 1992a). *Pornography* has no meaning in the court because it is not a legal term; *obscenity* does have legal meaning (Baird & Rosenbaum, 1998).

OBSCENITY AND INDECENCY

Both obscenity and indecency are predicated on the notion that language can corrupt or deprave the people who hear it or read it (Jay, 1992a, 2000). The belief is that obscene and indecent language somehow harms us, although that harm has never been clearly defined or demonstrated in psychological research. Research on obscene speech does not show that it has deleterious effects on normal adults (Commission on Obscenity and Pornography, 1970). There are several sociopolitical arguments for and against obscene speech (Baird & Rosenbaum, 1998). The position that words cause harm serves as the basis for antidiscrimination and hate crime laws (Matsuda, Lawrence, Delgado, & Crenshaw, 1993). The libertarian viewpoint (Wolfson, 1997) uses the First Amendment as a basis for supporting the freedom of expression regardless of how offensive it is.

To understand the legal importance of obscenity and indecency, one must be familiar with obscenity cases. There has been very little activity at the federal level to clarify the definition of obscenity established in the 1970s. The current three-prong definition of *obscenity* was refined in a 1973 Supreme Court case, **Miller v. California.** For a literary work to be considered obscene, the average person, applying contemporary standards, would have to find that, taken as a whole, (1) the work appeals to a prurient interest in sex, (2) depicts or describes sexual conduct in a patently offensive way, and (3) lacks serious literary, artistic, political, or scientific value. That is a very strict definition to meet.

Indecency is broader than obscenity. *Indecency* was defined in *FCC* v. *Pacifica,* a case involving George Carlin's twelve-minute "Filthy Words" routine, which was aired following a clear warning during the afternoon on Pacifica's FM radio station, WBAI in New York. The court ruled that Carlin's language was "patently offensive" but not necessarily obscene, which would have clearly violated the broadcast standards in effect at the time. The concept of indecency is intimately tied to the issue of children's exposure to offensive language. Indecent words are those that describe or refer to sexual or excretory activities and organs. The issue of indecency is far from resolved; in fact, it is not clear what indecency is or how sex education materials can be created that are not in some way indecent. Indecency and obscenity continue to be debated in the context of innovations in communication, especially Internet content and access by children.

COURTROOM DISCOURSE

Another source of confusion with legalese and legal discourse arises in the courtroom. Although many Americans are familiar with the pattern of courtroom discourse from portrayals in the popular media, exposure to these media has not produced a greater understanding of the law.

The structure of conversation in a courtroom setting is conventional. A court case has two simple lines of argument, the prosecution of the case and the defense of the case. The structure of the courtroom argument over guilt begins with opening statements, where the prosecutors present their evidence first and then the defense makes its presentation. The cross-examination of evidence and witnesses is adversarial and hostile (Drew, 1992). At the end of the case, after both sides have rested their case, the prosecution and defense make closing arguments. The jurors participate as passive observers who must decide on the basis of the verbal arguments and documentary evidence which side is more persuasive.

Turn taking, as anyone who has been in court can observe, is highly regulated. In a courtroom setting, the judge monitors and controls what is said (Drew, 1992). Participants cannot say whatever they want, nor can they speak when they want. Witnesses cannot give hearsay evidence and cannot render opinions when asked for facts. They must answer the questions as asked and not give more or less information than what is asked for. Although the overall patterns of presentation and turn taking are controlled, each participant's style of presentation can vary.

Witness Talk

The overall presentation of the witnesses' story may be a familiar *narrative* presentation style, or the testimony may take on a **fragmented style,** which is harder to follow and requires more questioning and filling in of gaps to be understood. The narrative style is more convincing than the fragmented style because the narrative witness seems to be stronger and more confident, not hedging or uncertain. O'Barr (1982) examined the nature of conversation in the courtroom and discovered that two distinctive styles emerged. One important dimension of witnesses' verbal style is based on power, which correlates with gender and class. What is important is how speaking style influences jurors.

Most men and powerful women, according to O'Barr (1982), tend to use **powerful language** (PL), which avoids hesitations, uncertainty, and qualification. **Weak language** (WL) is filled with qualifiers and hedges (e.g., *sort of, quite*), empty adjectives (e.g., *terrifically*), repetitions of qualifiers (e.g., *very, very, very*), and inflated language (e.g., *seventy-two hours, rotated, implosion, not cognizant* instead of *three days, turned, explosion, not aware*). O'Barr found that courtroom speech styles depend on how comfortable speakers feel in the courtroom setting. Educated upper- and middle-class men and women use PL. Well-educated professional women exhibit few features of WL in the courtroom. Many working-class, unemployed, or undereducated men use WL—such things as mannered speech, hypercorrection, verbosity and overprecision—because they feel out of place in court.

O'Barr (1982) tested the effect of style on trial outcomes by creating four versions of the same testimony with PL and WL by a man and a woman. He created juries of undergraduate law and psychology students who evaluated the testimony in a mock trial. Even though these students were practiced at listening to educated women, they still revealed gender biases. Women testifying in PL were believed more than women using WL; the same held for men using PL. Testimony in PL tends to be believed more than testimony in WL. However, overall, males were judged to be more convincing, truthful, and trustworthy than women. In other words, there is a tendency to believe men more than women even if the men use WL. Witnesses using formal style were rated as more convincing, intelligent, competent, and qualified than witnesses who used inflated speech or hypercorrection were. O'Barr suggested that when jurors are from the working class, they are less accepting of working-class witnesses who use expressions like *rotated my head* instead of *turned my head*. The jurors form the impression that the witnesses are phonies because of the way they inflate their speech.

Ideally, courtroom discourse between lawyers, witnesses, and judges should follow a predictable order of presentation, but that is not necessarily what happens. Conflicts often arise between witnesses and lawyers, both of whom try to control their own styles of presenting information. Both lawyers and witnesses can end up speaking simultaneously; they interrupt each other and may refuse to fall silent when asked to do so by the judge. These disordered conversational fluctuations occur because lawyers and witnesses attempt to dominate or control their presentations. It is not necessarily bad, in the eyes of the jurors, when witnesses try to preserve their turn and tell their stories. The jurors feel that the controlling witness is trying to present his or her case. Lawyers are perceived as more intelligent and fair if they let such a witness continue. Overall, jurors prefer a situation where there is little bickering or hostility between lawyers and witnesses.

> **Review Questions**
> How would you characterize courtroom language? Why can't the laws be written in plain English?

POLICE INTERROGATIONS AND INTERVIEWS

Some witnesses and suspects end up in court as a result of police **interrogation**, a process that has been shown to be fraught with problems (Kassin, 1997).

We consider two situations where police investigators question people. In both situations, the nature of the discourse, even the use of a single word, is critical. One situation is where police interview a witness or a victim in order to get information about a recent crime. The other situation involves the interrogation of a suspect in a crime, who is questioned to obtain a confession or to obtain enough information to be charged with the crime.

Confessions: How to Get the Suspect to Talk

The literature on the efficacy of police interrogation of suspects paints a disturbing picture of intimidation, trickery, and manipulation of suspects (see Memon, Vrij, & Bull, 1998; Shuy, 1998b). Many police interrogations are predicated on techniques espoused in a popular and standard interrogation manual by Inbau, Reid, and Buckley (1986). A similar interrogation approach is used in the United Kingdom.

Kassin (1997; see also Kassin & McNall, 1991), in a review of literature on confession evidence, found that police throughout the country use deception, trickery, and psychological coercion to extract confessions. Cases in which innocent people have confessed to crimes they did not commit are plentiful. One of the unfortunate consequences of coerced and false confession is that these coerced confessions can be used as evidence in court. Jury members do not distinguish between coerced evidence and evidence obtained in other ways.

The interrogation procedure is by no means random. Interrogators are trained how to do the job they do. Inbau et al. (1986) presented a nine-step approach to "effective interrogation" of suspects whose guilt seems certain. The steps are as follows:

1. Positive confrontation—a direct presentation of real or fictional evidence regarding the suspect's role in the crime

2. Theme development—building rapport with emotional suspects, offering a moral excuse: using a *minimization* approach (Kassin & McNall, 1991), lulling the suspect into a false sense of security; using a *maximization* approach, scaring and intimidating the suspect into confessing through false claims, rigged lie detector tests, and so on

3. Handling denials—ending the suspect's repetition or elaboration of denial (using step 2) because the more the suspect denies, the harder it is to get to the truth

4. Overcoming objections—showing understanding and returning to the theme (e.g., "That may be true, but . . .") in order to keep the suspect's attention

5. Retaining the suspect's attention—moving closer, leaning in, keeping eye contact, using his or her first name, touching gently

6. Handling the suspect's passive mood—focusing on reasons for committing the crime, exhibiting signs of understanding and sympathy, creating a remorseful mood

7. Creating the opportunity to confess—using an alternative question, giving the suspect an opportunity to give an explanation or reason for the crime

8. Oral confession—expanding an initial admission into a detailed confession replete with details

9. Converting the oral confession into a written one—to prevent suspects from denying that they gave an oral confession

This is a very popular technique among law enforcement practitioners, but it has its problems (Memon et al., 1998). Trickery and deceit may be unethical and are unlawful in several countries. Interrogators argue that deception is justified because they are dealing with criminals. But juries, who do not discount these methods for obtaining confessions, might find individuals who confess on the basis of minimization techniques used in interrogation guilty. Trickery and pressuring suspects might backfire; they might produce false confessions or no confessions at all. Suspects interrogated with these techniques can become suspicious and resentful for years after the interrogation. Finally, encouraging the police to lie in the interrogation context may encourage them to do so in other circumstances.

The foregoing analysis applied to situations where the police thought that the suspect was guilty. In other situations, the guilt and cooperativeness of the suspect are not so clear. Kalbfleisch (1994) undertook an extensive review of the literature on police interrogation techniques and discovered fifteen different techniques that are used to encourage uncooperative suspects to talk:

1. Intimidation—accusing the suspect of being a liar, laughing at the suspect, hammering at the suspect

2. Situational futility—telling the suspect that the truth will come out someday

3. Discomfort and relief—pointing out that denial is uncomfortable and confession cleanses the soul

4. Bluffing—pointing to some fabricated evidence, suggesting that the person is lying

5. Gentle prodding—coaxing and encouraging the suspect to reveal information, offering praise

6. Minimization—providing an excuse or a motivation for the crime

7. Contradiction—pointing out contradictions and inconsistencies

8. Altered information—asking questions that contain incorrect information

9. Chink in the defense—gaining a foothold on deception and accusing the suspect of lying

10. Self-disclosure—revealing personal information, expecting reciprocity from the suspect

11. Deception cues—telling the suspect that he or she is giving off cues of deception

12. Concern—showing concern toward the suspect, mention his or her importance to the interviewer

13. Status quo—emphasizing the costs of hiding the truth (e.g., lower self-esteem)

14. Direct approach—ordering the suspect to tell the truth

15. Silence—maintaining silence to make the suspect uncomfortable and want to talk

It is not clear how often these strategies are used in interrogations. Leo (1996) found an average of five to six tactics per interrogation in his sample of 182 police interrogations. British studies of interrogation found that roughly 62 percent of interrogations result in admissions of guilt or confession (see Memon et al., 1998). In the end, it is difficult to determine how effective pressure tactics are in interrogations because police also use "off the record" interviews and exchanges to manipulate or coerce suspects into confessions or making deals or promises. Some of the reasons for admitting guilt may come from off-the-record tactics.

In *How Emotions Work* (1999), Jack Katz provides a chapter on the emotional language that emerges in a four-hour police interrogation of James Martin, a murderer and career criminal. Martin was an experienced suspect, and the manner in which he spoke under interrogation demonstrated his experience in the interrogation room. His interrogation was filled with tactics that career criminals use in police investigations. Katz also recorded the techniques that police use to uncover weaknesses in suspects' stories in order to coerce a confession. One key moment in Martin's interrogation was reached when the police caught him crying briefly; that was enough to tell them he had done something wrong. The importance of a single word or emotion that may be out of place in the interrogation can literally be a matter of life and death.

Martin's interrogation drama is compelling; so are the manipulative tactics police use when they are contrasted with our constitutionally guaranteed civil rights. Constitutional rights issues make interrogations and courtroom conversations of the utmost importance, especially when a suspect is innocent or is not fully aware of his or her right to remain silent or to obtain the services of an attorney before making any statements to the police. Here is a passage from Katz (1999, p. 301) on Martin's interrogation, indicating the importance of his speech and his nonverbal behavior:

> The suspect, we may say, is faced with an asymmetry in the hermeneutic power of his speech. Denials of culpability may be repeated infinitely without achieving probative effect. Admissions, said once, are instantly and irretrievably effective. Speech much of the time means nothing for the suspect's fate as it emerges from his mouth. His speech often is as free, light, and worthless as air. At other times, it is hugely costly and unbearably heavy. A single word, once it jumps a matter of inches from his mouth to a recording tape, can change his life forever. For much of the interrogation, Martin spins out his story casually, elaborating with colorful details . . . that in style and substance gloss his speech with a veneer of truth. That cavalier practice of speech, itself a sign to police that they are dealing with a professional suspect, is also part of the framework that sets up the suspect's crying.

THE COGNITIVE INTERVIEW

Whereas the interrogation studies focus on people who are suspected of committing crimes, another form of interviewing is needed to obtain information from people who have witnessed criminal behavior. Eyewitness interviews are used in these situations.

A recent development in witness interviewing has been the use of the **cognitive interview** (CI). The technique of the CI was developed in the early 1990s in the United Kingdom to get better witness information than that gleaned from traditional techniques. The traditional interview is highly controlled by the interrogator and unfortunately employs leading questions and closed-ended, yes-or-no questions that provide less information than the CI. The CI assumes that by giving the witness more control and flexibility in the interview situation, better and more elaborate information will be obtained about the nature of the crime (Bekerian & Dennett, 1993). The CI uses the following four basic techniques:

1. Develop a re-creation of the physical and personal context of the crime scene. The interviewer tries to help the eyewitness form an image or impression of the environmental aspects of the original scene. This assumes that the witness has multiple retrieval pathways to information about the incident.

2. Report everything that comes to mind. Sometimes witnesses are not sure what is relevant or salient, and they screen out what they consider unimportant. But that additional information may help fill in gaps from interviews with other witnesses.

3. Report the situation in different orders, sometimes starting with the middle or with the end and working backward. Do not rely on a chronology of events, which may bias the account or cause the omission of details. The idea is that changing the order of recall may help the witness remember information that may not fit the original story schema.

4. Think of the situation from different perspectives or from the points of view of other people at the scene. For example, a child might be asked to recount the event from the point of view of an adult in the setting.

Compared to the standard interview, the CI has led to better recall from adult witnesses (Geiselman, 1999; Geiselman, Fisher, MacKinnon, & Holland, 1985). The CI produced 35 percent more information about persons, events, and objects than a standard control interview did, without increasing errors or confabulations (Geiselman et al., 1985). But the CI does not always work well with children. Recent research has shown that a modified CI produced enhanced accuracy and completeness of recall (Aldridge, 1999), which is good news for social workers interviewing children as witnesses or victims of crimes.

For the purpose of making suspect identifications, as in lineup situations, the CI does not provide better results than standard techniques, which are influenced by demand characteristics. The CI has been found to be most effective when conducted by police trainees because experienced officers tend to revert to standard interview methods. If the CI is to be used in an interview, it might be best to do so using someone trained exclusively in the techniques of the CI.

Review Question
Describe the four features of the cognitive interview.

Doctor-Patient Conversations

For psycholinguists, the importance of studying physician-patient communication or therapist-client communication is twofold: to understand the structure of these therapeutic and diagnostic dialogues by comparing them to "normal" dialogues and to contribute to the improvement of communication between patients and health care providers. We focus on some structural aspects of doctor-patient conversations. These consultations or office visits might be better understood as interviews, since the physician controls most of what happens in the conversation.

SYMPTOMS AND DIAGNOSIS

Nowhere in discourse is the confrontation between the language of science and everyday language more evident than in the conversation between physician and patient. The patient must present evidence or symptoms of illness that are sufficient for the doctor to make a **diagnosis.** The doctor must present the diagnosis to the patient, who tries to understand it. The doctor must deal with unrelated symptoms, as well as the patient's tendency to minimize symptoms or failure to understand what the doctor needs to know. The power or status differential between patient and doctor is enormously asymmetrical, and there is generally little room for the patient to ask questions or deal with misunderstanding. The doctor has to keep the patient on track, answering questions that assist in the diagnosis.

Byrne and Long (1976) found that doctors quickly move through their interview procedures, leaving little time for questions or clarification (also see Drew, 1992; Morris & Chenail, 1995). Here is an example from Byrne and Long's (1976) study. Notice how the doctor moves quickly through the interview to diagnosis in just a few turns.

PATIENT: I'm feeling rundown.

DOCTOR: Mmmmm right, just go into the next room and get undressed. I'll be along in a minute.

PATIENT: I've got a pain in my back and I feel tired all day.

DOCTOR: Tell me, where is this pain? When do you feel tired? In the morning when you get up or in the afternoon?

PATIENT: (silence)

DOCTOR: I think you are depressed. How do you feel about that?

Heath (1979) studied how consistent these one-way conversations were in medical practice. He surveyed journals for information about how physicians communicated with patients, determining several general strategies that doctors use. The results indicated that physicians' interview strategies could be characterized as follows:

- Topics of discussion are restricted to the patient's body and conditions of the disease.
- The doctor talks only to the patient, not family or friends.
- The doctor asks the questions.
- The doctor avoids the entire truth and discourages elaboration.
- Patients are told that they are responsible for getting better and that they have to follow the doctor's advice.

Proper treatment and diagnosis depend on the doctor's ability to understand what the patient is unable to put into clinical terms. These interviewing strategies work for verbally capable patients, but they will not work for all patients. Culture, age, dialect, and education are sources of communication breakdown. For example, in a study of inner-city adolescent patients with medical problems, Levine (1970) found that the use of slang with patients was essential to understanding their problems, since they were not well versed in medical terminology. The interview could not be conducted using clinical terms.

Diagnosis is the pivotal point in the medical interview. Generally, there is no discussion of why the doctor made the diagnosis because the patient feels powerless to ask questions. C. Heath (1992) studied how the doctor communicated the diagnosis and found that responses ranged from a single word (e.g., "bronchitis") to lengthy descriptions. The physician's diagnosis is treated as if it is a fact, which the patient cannot question. However, if a doctor gives a tentative presentation or uses qualifiers, a patient is more likely to ask questions. With the use of computer data banks and computerized patient profiles, analysis of a patient's problems begins when the patient registers for a consultation. Likewise, doctors tailor diagnoses to the menu of diagnoses covered by a patient's health insurance.

THREE PSYCHOTHERAPIES

Psychotherapy generally consists of one or more weekly fifty-minute sessions between a client and a therapist during which the client discusses emotions, problems, and experiences with the nonjudgmental therapist. The therapist listens to the client and attempts to make the client's life more effective by helping with problems or the answers to questions. The nature of therapy is to establish an interpersonal helping relationship between client and therapist based on warmth, understanding, and insight. Exactly how discourse is used in psychotherapy depends on the training of the therapist and nature of the client's problems.

Freud's **psychoanalytic approach** to therapy (1916/1963, 1940) has been stereotyped as the prototypical mode of psychotherapy in popular culture. The stereotypes are not accurate, however, nor do they reflect an understanding of how psychoanalysis works (Gabbard & Gabbard, 1987). One simple way to understand psychotherapy is that it relies on talking about problems. The Freudian model proposes that the patient's current problems are derived from unresolved unconscious conflicts, which can be tapped through several avenues: hypnosis, transference, dream analysis, or free association. The analyst and client repeatedly work through and reevaluate conflicts to make the client more aware of the nature of the problems. One goal is to understand them better as a means of improving quality of life. The alternatives to psychoanalysis are less familiar to the American public.

Cognitive behavior therapy uses direct questioning about the client's present situation by the therapist. The cognitive therapist tries to make the client more aware of currently held irrational beliefs and behaviors. Irrational beliefs may be at the core of problems with depression, eating disorders, anxiety, or sexual dysfunction. The cognitive behavior therapist works to change the irrational behaviors and thoughts and replace them with more effective ones. Notice in the following example from Beck (1976, pp. 280–291) how the therapist makes the client aware of her unrealistic beliefs.

THERAPIST: Why do you want to end your life?

CLIENT: Without Raymond, I am nothing. . . . I can't be happy without Raymond. . . . But I can't save our marriage.

THERAPIST: What has your marriage been like?

CLIENT: It has been miserable from the very beginning. . . . Raymond has always been unfaithful. . . . I have hardly seen him in the past five years.

THERAPIST: You say that you can't be happy without Raymond. . . . Have you found yourself happy when you are with Raymond?

CLIENT: No, we fight all the time and I feel worse.

THERAPIST: You say you are nothing without Raymond. Before you met Raymond, did you feel you were nothing?

CLIENT: No, I felt I was somebody.

THERAPIST: If you were somebody before you knew Raymond, why do you need him to be somebody now?

CLIENT: (*puzzled*) Hmmm . . .

THERAPIST: If you were free of the marriage, do you think that men might be interested in you—knowing that you were available?

CLIENT: I guess that maybe they would be.

THERAPIST: Is it possible that you might find a man who would be more constant than Raymond?

CLIENT: I don't know. . . . I guess it's possible. . . .

THERAPIST: Then what have you actually lost if you break up the marriage?

CLIENT: I don't know.

THERAPIST: Is it possible that you'll get along better if you end the marriage?

CLIENT: There is no guarantee of that. . . .

THERAPIST: Do you have a real marriage?

CLIENT: I guess not.

THERAPIST: If you don't have a real marriage, what do you actually lose if you decide to end the marriage?

CLIENT: Nothing, I guess.

The third discourse-oriented therapy is **client-centered therapy,** which emphasizes the individual's subjective interpretation of events and emotions. In client-centered therapy, the therapist acts as a sounding board or facilitator for the client. The belief is that the client can arrive at his or her own solutions to the problem through the natural tendency for growth and self-actualization, according to Rogers (1951, 1970). Rogers believed that the client held the solution to these problems. It is important for the therapist to understand the client's feelings and to communicate this understanding to the client. One therapeutic goal is to get the client's current self-concept aligned with his or her ideal self-concept.

Through discourse analysis, therapy can be viewed as a conversation between the therapist and client wherein the client makes narrative statements about emotions and experiences (Labov & Fanshel, 1977). These statements can be accepted or challenged by the therapist. The client is the authority on his or her experiences, but the therapist is the authority on the interpretation of the experiences. One goal of therapy is to discuss the client's problems so as to bring about understanding and insight. Sometimes the client and therapist disagree about what is happening in therapy. What should happen when the therapist and client have different versions of the problem at hand? In many cases, this situation requires a *reformulation* of the client's statements (Grossen & Apotheloz, 1996).

Reformulation has three phases: the client makes a statement, the therapist utters a phrase that serves as a reformulation marker, and then the therapist restates the comment in a new way. The reformulation may be preceded by a metadiscursive clause such as *"You mentioned that . . ."* or *"You told me that . . ."* or a marker such as *"How can I put it?"* or *"I mean . . ."* Grossen and Apotheloz (1996, p. 115) documented how reformulation worked with a male client who expressed difficulty about talking with his wife:

CLIENT: When I'm with my wife we talk about problems, which I try to avoid talking about but all the same there are times when we're alone when we don't have anything else to talk about but then the how can I put it the dialogue is almost completely broken off because we are OK together without talking to each other even if sometimes we feel that there is a *dialogue* there is there is we *want* to say something but we don't know, we can't, we don't *dare* there are a lot of things we don't dare that we come up against a brick wall.

THERAPIST: One could say there are some things which are unspoken uh in a way what isn't said.

CLIENT: Yes.

THERAPIST: What isn't said is hence unspoken and it's a burden isn't it?

CLIENT: Yes it's a burden yes yes.

In this passage, the client is having difficulty expressing the exact nature of his communication problems with his wife. The therapist reformulates the first statement using the marker "*one could say*" followed by the reformulation. The client then agrees with and accepts the reformulation by saying "*yes*." Not all reformulations are agreeable; sometimes the client challenges what the therapist reformulates, and a search for an agreeable meaning ensues. Reformulation adds a different dimension to normal turn taking in nontherapeutic discourse. The therapist works to help the client make better sense of what is happening. In everyday conversation, reformulation of what someone says is not essential to the discourse and may come off as condescending.

Therapy can be thought of as an interactive process in which the client and therapist use their roles to construct the meaning of the problems they discuss (Gordon & Efran, 1997). In constructivist theory, a client's problems and the words used to describe them in therapy have no independent, context-free meanings. The problem and word meanings in therapy are all constructed within a particular therapeutic relationship. Therapeutic conversation constantly evolves collaborative meaning between the therapist and client, who pay close attention to the words and **figurative language** used in therapy (Chenail & Fortugno, 1995). Each figure of speech takes on meaning within a larger pattern of figures that emerges in the therapy setting.

Figurative Language in Therapy

We covered the topic of figurative language in conversations in Chapter 9. Here we are interested in figurative language used to describe emotions in a therapeutic setting. For example, it is common in therapy to hear figurative expressions like *I was hot under the collar, I hit the roof, I felt down, I feel blue,* or *I felt empty.* Several studies of discourse in therapy have explored the use and value of figurative language (Angus, 1996; Chaika, 2000; Ferrara, 1994; Karp, 1996; McMullen & Conway, 1996; Pollio & Barlow, 1975). These investigations have shown that figures of speech are common in clients' speech and also to a lesser extent in therapists' comments. From a sample of fifty former and current patients with depression, Karp (1996) found uniformity in how they described the troubling emotional state. Common expressions involved falling down a pit, suffocating, drowning, or being in a dark tunnel. These kinds of expressions apparently capture the downward spiral of depression, where victims become increasingly focused on negative thoughts of sadness and self-hatred.

Figurative statements used over the course of therapy exhibit some consistency. McMullen and Conway (1996) examined twenty-four client-doctor dialogues over a number of sessions and found that many clients presented themselves as fragmented, using phrases like *falling apart* and *at loose ends*. Their degree of fragmentation was related to their therapeutic outcome. The repeated use of figures for sadness and anger fit conceptual metaphors such as ANGER IS HEAT and ANGER IS INSANITY, according to McMullen and Conway.

In the discourse of therapy, clients and therapists construct or collaborate on metaphors that can be repeated and expanded on over sessions (Ferrara, 1994). The meanings of these metaphors have to be understood within the context of the conversational interaction between client and therapist. For example, Ferrara showed that one metaphor, floating down the river, needed to be discussed and clarified to understand what the client was expressing. Here's a sample of that dialogue:

THERAPIST: What's it like to be floating down the river? Tell me more.

CLIENT: It's comfortable. It's safe. Everything keeps on an even keel, you know.

THERAPIST: *Mhm.*

CLIENT: You're kinda floating.

THERAPIST: Kind of in a canoe? . . .

CLIENT: No, more like a great big ole barge. . . . (p. 140)

The therapist needed to clarify how the client felt floating down the river. It wasn't quite clear in the beginning whether this was a pleasant experience or an unpleasant one. Ferrara's research suggests that the meaning of the metaphor must be understood within the context of the session or sessions in which they occur.

Many more techniques and strategies used in therapy are of interest to psycholinguists but cannot be covered in the space available here. Discourse structured around turn taking is more like a question-and-answer format in which the therapist attempts to find out something from the client. The therapist elicits information. Sometimes the client may make straightforward statements that answer the questions that arise; at other times, the therapist must try to find information in the client's statements. A direct question such as *How are you feeling today?* may not elicit a direct response. Clients use indirectness (e.g., *I'm OK*) and negation of the opposite (e.g., *Not bad*). Clients also qualify and mitigate their answers (e.g., *A little bit, Kind of*), which may be interpreted as defensiveness. Therapists also qualify their language and are not always direct, sometimes using euphemisms (e.g., *You have been with us before*) rather than direct speech (e.g., *You have been hospitalized here for depression once before*). In the therapeutic setting, the language that is used and not used between client and therapist is of critical importance.

Review Question

Compare and contrast medical interviews with discourse in psychotherapy. How are they similar, and how are they different?

Mass Communication

How is language in the mass media used by the social and political elite to manipulate us? Why did Noam Chomsky, the father of modern linguistics, focus his attention on how the media shape us through language? There are important issues related to the way the media's use of language influences society at large.

REPORTING THE NEWS

There are many ways of going about analyzing news content and structure, too many to consider here. We focus on cases where language is very manipulative, such as the reporting of political news. Clayman (1992) examined the nature of live news interviews offering an informative approach, which can be used to analyze other forms of discourse. Clayman shows that the interviewer and interviewee collaborate to maintain a level of objectivity and neutrality and what happens when the neutral footing is thrown off course. As in the case of the police interrogation, the interviewer's choice of words is critical to the responses elicited from the interviewee. The wrong word can send the interview in a different direction, put the interviewee on the defensive, or produce opinionated answers. The interviewer has the ability to control much of what happens in the interview.

Prerecorded interviews create problems for viewers who seek the news. Unless interviews are shown in their entirety, which they rarely are, the questions and comments in the interview will be taken out of context, altering their meaning. While the edited news formats give the viewer the appearance of neutrality and objectivity, this is not always the case. News is produced in a corporate framework that interprets the facts. Chomsky was quick to observe that the invisible framework behind the news supported the goals and values of the corporate media elites who manufacture the news.

In *Necessary Illusion* (1989), Chomsky develops the **propaganda model**, showing how the press serves the needs of the elites in power. In the propaganda model, very little in the news can be taken at face value. We must understand the nature of the people who own the media, their advertisers, other corporate elites in America, and what their political motives are. In the propaganda model, the media do not inform us; they manipulate us:

> The major media—particularly, the elite media that set the agenda that others generally follow—are corporations "selling" privileged audiences to other businesses. It would hardly come as a surprise if the picture of the world they present were to reflect the perspectives and interests of the sellers, the buyers, and the product. Concentration of ownership of the media is high and increasing. Furthermore, those who occupy the managerial positions in the media, or gain status within them as commentators, belong to the same privileged elites, and might be expected to share the perceptions, aspirations, and attitudes of their associates, reflecting their own class interests as well. Journalists entering the system are unlikely to make their way unless they conform to

these ideological pressures, generally by internalizing the values; it is not easy to say one thing and believe another, and those who fail to conform will tend to be weeded out by familiar mechanisms.

The influence of the advertisers is sometimes far more direct. "Projects unsuitable for corporate sponsorship tend to die on the vine," the London *Economist* observes, noting that "stations have learned to be sympathetic to the most delicate sympathies of corporations." The journal cites the case of public TV station WNET, which "lost its corporate underwriting from Gulf+Western as a result of a documentary called *Hunger for Profit* about multinationals buying up huge tracts of land in the Third World." (p. 8)

What the media and cultural elites promulgate is a form of thought control through the manipulation of language in the news. According to Chomsky, the media control and advance their agendas in part by controlling how local and world events are interpreted:

> The most effective device is the bounding of the thinkable, achieved by tolerating debate, even encouraging it, though only within proper limits. But democratic systems also resort to cruder means, the method of "interpretation of some phrase" being a notable instrument. Thus aggression and state terror in the Third World become "defense of democracy and human rights"; and "democracy" is successfully achieved when the government is safely in the hands of "the rich men dwelling at peace within their habitations," as in Winston Churchill's prescription for world order. (pp. 105–106)

The point is that the media, in conjunction with the political and corporate elites, control the limits of debate and the definition of the terms used in the debate. Maybe these forms of thought control are clearest in times of war, when a warring government consciously constructs euphemisms to sanitize what is really happening.

Allan and Burridge (1991) provide a number of examples of the use of euphemistic military jargon, cr **militarese**, to hide the workings of the killing machine. During the Nazi *final solution*, the term *look after* was used to mean *commit to a concentration camp*, where identity papers were stamped *"return unwanted,"* meaning that they received the *special treatment*. Euphemistic militarese reached another high point during the Vietnam War under the Nixon administration in the United States. References to killing were replaced with terms that are usually used to refer to living things: a *bombing raid* became a *protective reaction, precision bombing* was called a *surgical strike*, a *concentration camp* was referred to as a *pacification center,* and the *bombing of one's own village* came to be known as *friendly fire*. The manipulative use of euphemism allows the corporate, political, and military elites to justify and conduct their business without arousing the ire of the general public, whose thoughts are manipulated and molded through word meanings.

POLITICAL NEWS

Citizens count on the media, especially the news media, to deliver some objective truth about what is happening in the world around us, but that is a lofty ideal that gets corrupted when filtered through the point of view of the news media, which have corporate interests of their own. Words have the power not only to recast the public impression of events, as when employing palatable euphemisms for ugly realities, but also to make things happen in the news, especially in politics. In political debates, name-calling and labeling are essential ingredients in efforts to sway voters' opinions.

One effective way to label people is by comparison to other groups (e.g., liberal, right-wing conservative) or to other people (e.g., John Kennedy, Richard Nixon), as if making the analogy amounts to making a statement of truth rather than expressing the speaker's opinion. This works through a form of higher-order classical conditioning, where the meaning of a new name is associated with a familiar name. One of the best examples of the use of names comes from the 1988 vice-presidential debate between Lloyd Bentsen and Dan Quayle. Quayle had compared himself to President Kennedy, to which Bentsen replied in the most memorable scene from the debate: "I knew Kennedy. He was a friend of mine; and Senator, you're no Jack Kennedy."

American political discourse is filled with examples like the exchange between Quayle and Bentsen. For example, President Richard Nixon's vice president, Spiro Agnew, was known for his controversial and angry speeches. Agnew referred to Vietnam War protesters as "an effete corps of impudent snobs," "ideological eunuchs," and "vultures who sit in trees." On the other hand, political action groups also criticize the government as in a 1995 fund-raising letter from the National Rifle Association, which warned members against "jack-booted government thugs." Name calling and insulting occurs at all levels of politics, from local to national. President Ronald Reagan is remembered for his "evil empire" speech, wherein he used the word "evil" to describe the former Soviet Union. In a related and more recent speech, President George W. Bush made reference to Iran, Iraq, and North Korea as an "axis of evil."

Have you ever wondered why the media portray psychologists and psychiatrists in such stereotypical ways? Gabbard and Gabbard (1987) in *Psychiatry and the Cinema* reported that Hollywood images of psychologists fall into three simple stereotypical categories: the quack who is funny and silly, the evil psychologist who seduces and exploits patients, and (the least commonly encountered) the realistic psychologist who helps people get healthier. News reports dealing with psychological theory are equally problematic, especially when it comes to complex mental health issues.

VIOLENCE AGAINST WOMEN

A final example of manipulative reporting involves cases of violence against women. These reports are significant in the degree to which they affect our view of the world and how we believe that men and women live in the world. Meyers (1997) reported evidence that news coverage in American cities depicts violence against women differently from violence against men in a way that perpetuates traditional stereotypes of men and women. Consider the following sentences.

1. In the United States, a man rapes a woman every six minutes.

2. In the United States, a woman is raped by a man every six minutes.

3. In the United States, a woman is raped every six minutes.

News media report violence against women in the passive-verb format, as in sentence 2, which removes the agency for the act and can even truncate agency further, as in sentence 3. This puts the focus of the crime on the victim and erases the role of the agents, the men who commit rape and sexual violence. The passive language makes it seem as if rape and violence are something women experience, not something men do to women. It sets up a language of victimization rather than a language of criminalization. Active news language (sentence 1) reports rape and violence as something that men do to women, but such straightforward reporting is rare; the agency is usually removed from reports of violence, especially sexual violence. Passive voice lets the perpetrator off the hook linguistically.

What effect does the language of reporting violence against women have on us? Studies of media reports of violence toward women have found that passive-verb reporting leads readers to be more accepting of the sexual violence than in cases where the active voice is used (Henley, Miller, & Beazley, 1995). The framework of the reporting and the words in the reporting affect how we comprehend acts of violence.

In the Henley et al. study (1995), males but not females attributed less harm to the victim. Males were more accepting of the violence against women when reported in the passive voice. This is but one example of how language in the news affects how we view the world. The unconscious cultural attitudes underlying the construction of news reports on violence against women may perpetuate that violence, treating women as victims and minimizing what happens to them rather than constructing the problem as one of male violence.

ADVERTISING

Complete Exercise 13.3 before you continue.

Exercise 13.3. **Misinformation and Deceptive Advertising**
Read the following statements from a mouthwash label, and answer the questions that follow based on the language on the label.

   KILLS GERMS BY THE MILLIONS ON CONTACT FOR GENERAL ORAL HYGIENE
   FIGHTS BAD BREATH, COLDS, AND RESULTANT SORE THROATS

   1. Do you think the mouthwash stops bad breath?

   2. Do you think the mouthwash cures sore throats?

   3. Do you think the mouthwash cures colds?

Although the manipulation of thought through political and news language is subtle, it is obvious that the language of print and electronic advertising is carefully selected to attract, seduce, and manipulate consumers to spend money. As E. Clark (1985, p. 20) put it:

> Advertising is far from impotent or harmless; it is not a mere mirror image. Its power is real, and on the brink of a great increase. Not the power to brainwash overnight, but the power to create subtle and real change. The power to prevail.

Few scientific articles have shown how language in advertisements affects speakers. I suggest that what is known about how and when advertising works is confidential and proprietary information between the researchers and the corporations.

Advertising emerges as a system of styles to the linguists and psychologists who have studied it (see Crystal, 1987). Advertising style presents us with frequently used words and phrases that emphasize the uniqueness of the product (e.g., *You'll never find an X like this one*), make vague comparisons and claims about the product (e.g., the mouthwash example in Exercise 13.1), use rhythm and rhyme (e.g., *Leggo my Eggo*), create odd grammatical constructions (e.g., *Nobody doesn't like Sara Lee*), and construct unique spellings of words and products names (e.g., *Cheez Whiz*).

Advertisements rely on the illusions they create, but sometimes things go too far. What advertisers do is questionable, especially when they make false claims, urge people to buy unhealthy foods, or convince children to smoke cigarettes. We have all been witnesses to the great efforts that were made by health advocates and politicians to get cigarette advertisements taken off television, as just one example of problematic advertising.

Another linguistic problem arises when advertisers make fraudulent or unsubstantiated claims to sell products. For example, Warner-Lambert, the maker of Listerine, was sanctioned by the Federal Trade Commission for using advertising that made consumers believe that Listerine prevented colds. The advertisement language, similar to that in Exercise 13.3, set up viewers to make an inference that led them to construct a false belief about the product. It was not what the ad said per se that was being challenged but what it led viewers to infer, to make them misbelieve. Consumers linked the *kills germs* in the first statement with the word *colds* in the second. Recall from Chapter 5 the powerful effect that inferences have on sentence comprehension and subsequent recall. Listeners and readers in these studies commonly fill in missing information in sentences that would otherwise leave them with an incomplete picture (Harris & Monaco, 1978).

Braun and Loftus (1998) demonstrated that inferential advertising misinformation effects extend beyond claims about the product itself. The **misinformation effect** extends to viewers' personal memory of experiences with products. Viewers use the advertising misinformation to construct distorted memories of their own experiences with products. For example, after seeing ads in an experimental setting, subjects produced distorted reconstructed memories involving their own use of the products in the ads. This kind of cognitive research can be used to change policies regarding deceptive advertising.

Prozac and "Antidepressant Discontinuation Syndrome"

In a recent book on the dangers of antidepressants, Glenmullen (2000) reports how Eli Lilly, the manufacturer of Prozac, dealt with the problem of weaning patients off antidepressant drugs. A 1996 meeting was sponsored by Eli Lilly to address the problem. One result of the meeting was a change in the language describing Prozac so that no one used the term *withdrawal* to describe its side effects. Glenmullen wrote, "The sanitized term 'antidepressant discontinuation syndrome' is the kind of well-funded obfuscation doctors and patients frequently face when trying to get honest, reliable information on these powerful drugs" (p. 22).

Review Question
What are some of the common features of advertising language?

Human Factors and Ergonomics

One of the most fascinating areas of applied psychology is the field of **human factors,** or ergonomics. Human factors psychologists use their knowledge of human characteristics and behaviors to design environments and objects to fit human needs (see Sanders & McCormick, 1993). The goal of human factors is to enhance human values by making home, leisure, and work environments and the products in them safer, more satisfying, and more effective. The range of applications is vast, from computer screen displays to snow shovels, from office chairs to shopping malls, from space exploration to warning devices, from safety equipment to instructional manuals, from product labeling to military command, from food intake and metabolism to motor skill acquisition. There is a great deal of applied psycholinguistics in human factors. Consider the role of language in problems underlying speech synthesis, auditory warning systems, speech perception, speech intelligibility in noise, speech filtering, product warning labels, instructional warnings, highway signage, and the electronic display of information. With limited space here, we focus on two areas of human factors research, speech technology and warnings on products.

SPEECH TECHNOLOGY

Human factors psychologists have been interested in language processes since the development of the Morse code in the late 1800s. Current concerns involve the computerization of speech comprehension and production processes. Two lines of technology have emerged over the past fifty years in speech technology: speech production, dedicated to producing humanlike speech via computer, and speech recognition technology, which has as its goal the recognition and comprehension of human speech. In Chapter 4, I mentioned George Miller's speech technology work on WordNet, which is an attempt to construct a computer lexicon that captures the characteristics of the human lexicon (Fellbaum, 1998).

There are numerous practical applications of speech technologies. For instance, speech recognition systems can be used to control any number of laborsaving devices, security systems, vending machines, word processors, and data entry systems. A good example of speech recognition technology is Dragon Systems' NaturallySpeaking, a dictation package marketed for basic dictation. To train the dictation system, the user reads excerpts to it from preselected books for thirty minutes. The system keeps 30,000 words in memory and has a backup lexicon of 230,000 words. These systems are not perfect. One problem with dictation systems like NaturallySpeaking is that they do not recognize all of the words the user says. The accuracy rate of this software is about 90 percent, leaving the user to make corrections with the keyboard, mouse, or less easily, voice commands (corrections can be made by saying "scratch that" or "correct that"). You can imagine how important these systems are to people who cannot write using the common keyboard.

Another application of speech technology is to software products that can convert text input into vocal output. Imagine how helpful this software would be to someone who could not speak a foreign language or could not speak at all. Bell Labs' Lucent Technologies offers multilingual text-to-speech systems (TTS) that can read e-mail messages, generate voice prompts in voice response systems, and provide an ordering system for salespeople. The software uses a pronunciation module for ordinary words and derivatives along with default strategies for words not stored in the dictionary. Demonstrations and opportunities to generate samples of TTS are available at the Bell Labs Web site listed at the end of this chapter. Aspects of the speech sample can be adjusted for volume, words per minute, intonation, and breathiness. The visitor can sample TTS technology and create a TTS sample, manipulating some of the speech production variables discussed in Chapter 3 (e.g., intonation, speech rate). Bell Labs maintains a state-of-the-art approach to speech technology and employs many theoretical and applied scholars and engineers.

WARNINGS ON PRODUCTS

Another area of human factors research that affects consumers is product warnings. **Warnings** are verbal messages and **pictographs** attached to products (e.g., on the side of a cigarette package) or embedded in the instructions for proper use of the product (e.g., the instructions for how to set up and use a lawnmower) for the purpose of informing users about the dangers of improper use and giving information about how to avoid those dangers. Warnings on products and in instructions are becoming increasingly prevalent for two reasons: manufacturers are becoming more aware of how dangerous some of their products and contents are, and they also want to reduce the legal liability associated with selling such products. A warning is intended to explain the proper use of a product and to inform the user of the dangers of any conceivable misuse. To be effective, warnings have to capture the owner's attention with effective size, shape, color, placement, and graphic design.

Edworthy (1998) noted four aspects of warnings: iconic, alerting, attention-getting, and informational content. Each has a different function in the process of affecting the users' behavior in light of potential hazards. Of most interest here is the language used in the informational role of the warning. The language of warnings reflects three levels of hazard (Sanders & McCormick, 1993):

> *Danger* is used where there is an immediate hazard.
> *Warning* means that a hazard could occur as the result of unsafe use.
> *Caution* is used when hazards or unsafe use would result in injury or product damage.

Guidelines suggest that a warning should include a signal word (e.g., one of the three italicized in the list) and information describing the hazard, consequences, and necessary behavior (Shuy, 1998a; Wogalter, Desaulniers, & Brelsford, 1987):

1. Signal word conveying seriousness—*danger, warning, caution*

2. Description of the hazard—*contains acid*

3. Consequences associated with the hazard—*severe burns*

4. Behavior needed to avoid the hazard—*shake well before opening*

Whether people read these warnings is another matter. Generally, the more familiar we are with a product or device we are using, the less likely we are to read warnings on it because we are confident about how to use it. Another factor affecting attention to warnings is how dangerous the product appears to be. For example, Otsubo (1988) found that 52 percent of subjects in his study read the warning for a circular saw, but only 25 percent read warnings for a less hazardous-looking jigsaw.

Human factors psychologists usually field-test the efficacy of warnings with a sample of potential users. The design of the warning is of little import if people do not understand what it means or their attention is not drawn to the warning. In product liability cases, courts have ruled for greater specificity in the wording used in warnings. Manufacturers should mention in the warning the important dangers and misuses of the product, but obviously, not all misuses can be mentioned. Increased specificity is not 100 percent successful at reducing risk. Just because the warning is properly worded and placed on the product or instruction does not mean it will be heeded.

When was the last time you read all of the warnings and instructions for a product you purchased? Few of us read all of the warnings on all products we encounter. People read warnings in instructions when they are not confident about how to use the product. When hazardous properties do exist, the warnings about them should be prominently displayed in the instructions, but where to put them in the instructions is another matter. Placing the warnings at the beginning of the instructions is more effective than placing them at the end (Wogalter et al., 1987).

Unfortunately, people do not always read the instructions, thereby nullifying the warnings they contain. One solution to instructional warnings is to place the warning directly on the product, as we find on cigarettes and alcoholic beverages. How effective are on-product warnings? In one study, Strawbridge (1986) had subjects read a warning label on a bottle of liquid adhesive:

DANGER

Contains acid.

To avoid severe burns, shake well before opening.

The label was placed in different locations on the bottle (e.g., top, middle, or bottom of the label) and in different formats (e.g., highlighted with reversed type). Highlighting had little effect on compliance, and embedding the warning in the instructions reduced compliance. The bad news is that some people who saw the warning never bothered to read it. Only 81 percent of the subjects who noticed the warning actually read it, and of them, only 47 percent complied with it. Some subjects claimed that they "forgot" the warning, but this seemed like an illogical excuse, as the time between reading it and opening the bottle was only ten seconds.

Many forms of product warnings display a verbal warning with a pictograph and caution icon (Dingus, Hathaway, & Hunn, 1991). This type of format is illustrated in Figure 13.2. The example has the hazard information spelled out in text. But one of the problems with using pictographs is that their meanings are not always recognized or remembered. Examples of mandatory-action symbols, like the eyewear pictograph in the figure, and their recognition (O) and recall (R) rates are illustrated in Figure 13.3. The bottom of the figure gives examples of exit signs and the percentage of people who made errors in identifying them as exit signs. One would hope that failures in reading a written warning could be offset by pictographs, but these are not entirely unambiguous either; that is why the two forms of information in warnings are better when combined—redundancy helps aids attention, memory, and perceptual processes.

Not all studies of on-product warnings paint this bleak picture of consumer safety. Fortunately, other studies on warnings for different products have produced compliance rates between 67 and 100 percent, indicating that some warnings are quite effective. Of course, compliance depends on alternative uses of the product, the cost of compliance, and the social influence of users who comply with warnings. Wogalter, Young, Brelsford, and Barlow (1999) noted that people base their judgments of product hazards as a function of two perceptions, the severity of potential injury and the likelihood of being injured. Their research suggested that injury severity was the foremost predictor of hazard perception and that higher-severity warnings produced higher hazard perceptions and greater behavioral compliance than low-severity warnings. Manufacturers might communicate

WEAR EYE PROTECTION
SERIOUS EYE INJURY SUCH
AS BLINDNESS, RETINAL
DETACHMENT, SECONDARY
GLAUCOMA, AND EYE GLOBE
RUPTURE MAY OCCUR WHEN
NOT WEARING EYE PROTECTION

Figure 13.2. Warning Label with Pictograph, Caution Icon, and Hazard Information
Note. Reprinted by permission of the Human Factors and Ergonomics Society and the author from Proceedings of the *Human Factors Society 35th Annual Meeting,* 1991. Copyright 1991 by the Human Factors Society. All rights reserved.

hazards better to users if they focus on injury severity rather than likelihood when using a product.

As you can imagine, we have only scratched the surface of product warnings in this overview. There is a whole world of human factors applications that would benefit from the wisdom of an applied human factors psychologist or psycholinguist.

Review Questions
What kinds of warnings appear on consumer products? What effects do these warnings have on consumers?

Key Terms

client-centered
  therapy
cognitive behavior
  therapy
cognitive interview
diagnosis
elitism
explanatory question
figurative language
forensic linguistics

fragmented style
human factors
indecency
interrogation
legalese
militarese
Miller v. *California*
misinformation effect
obscenity
pictograph

plain English
powerful language
propaganda model
psychoanalytic
  approach
sex education
Socratic dialogue
warnings
weak language

1. Must use ear protection	2. Must use eye protection	3. Must use foot protection	4. Must use hand protection	5. Must use head protection	6. Must use breathing protection
O – 10%	20%	30%	50%	37%	13%
R – 73	96	100	97	97	97

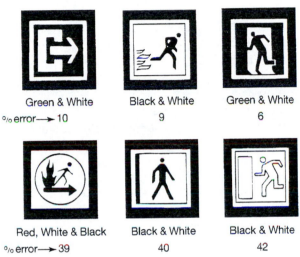

Green & White	Black & White	Green & White
% error ⟶ 10	9	6

Red, White & Black	Black & White	Black & White
% error ⟶ 39	40	42

Figure 13.3. Symbols of Mandatory-Action Messages Used in a Study of Warning Symbol Recognition and Recall

Note. From M. S. Sanders & E. J. McCormick, *Human Factors in Engineering and Design*, 1993, McGraw-Hill. Reprinted with permission of The McGraw-Hill Companies.

Suggested Web Sites

http://www-clg.bham.ac.uk/forensic/index.html
Bell Labs TTS: http://www.bell-labs.com/project/tts/voices.html

Glossary

AAVE African American Vernacular English. Also known as Ebonics.

acoustic Pertaining to the physical aspects of sound.

acoustic cue Any of the physical properties of sound that are used in speech perception.

acquired dyslexia Loss of the ability to read by people who were previously literate.

acquisition The developmental course of language.

ACT model A network model of semantic memory, adaptive control of thought, or adaptive character of thought.

additive bilingualism Case where learning one language helps learning another.

adjacency pair A conversational pattern that unfolds in a stimulus-response format (e.g., speaker complains, and listener apologizes).

affective prosody The emotional quality of an utterance in terms of stress or volume.

African American Vernacular English A variant or dialect of English that incorporates certain African linguistic forms; technically, a creole. Also known as Ebonics.

alexia Inability to read printed words.

allgone Holophrastic utterance used prior to the two-word stage.

allophone A phone recognized as a member of a phoneme category (e.g., [pʰ] and [p] are allophones of /p/).

alphabetic system A writing system that uses symbols (letters) to stand for the sounds in a language.

ambiguity A word, phrase, or sentence with multiple meanings.

American Sign Language (ASL) Sign language used by the deaf community in the United States.

amygdala Almond-shaped structure in the limbic system involved with anger and fear.

anaphor A pronominal or similar expression such as a reflexive pronoun whose reference is determined by an antecedent in the same discourse.

anomia The inability to retrieve the names for objects, common in old age.

anticipation error Producing a sound that will occur later in the utterance (e.g., "leading list" instead of "reading list").

anticipations Speech errors that anticipate what is going to be said (e.g., "see sells" for "she sells").

aphasia   Speech disturbances or loss due to brain damage.

approach or avoidance   The human tendency to approach pleasant things and avoid unpleasant things.

appropriate speech   Acceptable or standard speech, as opposed to substandard or taboo speech.

aprosodia   Loss of the prosodic features of speech.

arbitrary reference   Giving names to objects or events that bear no clear relationship to those objects or events; a property of language.

arguing   A form of child anger expression that appears around age 3 years.

articulation   The physiology of producing speech sounds in the vocal tract.

ASL   American Sign Language.

autism   Disorder that includes such symptoms as failure to establish social contact, failure to maintain eye contact, unresponsiveness, lack of emotional speech, mutism, echolalia, and ritualistic behavior.

automatic speech   Nonpropositional speech produced predominantly by the right cerebral hemisphere that includes clichés, proverbs, taboo words, or jingles.

autonomous search model   A model of word recognition that converts input stimuli to perceptual representations that are submitted to "files" for analysis; the search proceeds until the most likely candidate is found; similar to the ACT model.

babbling   Prelinguistic speech beginning with the production of simple syllables and ending with the production of strings of different syllables.

basal ganglia   Subcortical area of the brain associated with motor movement.

basic level   Concept level that is most informative; for example, "tool" is a basic-level concept; "thing" is more general, and "socket wrench" is more specific.

beat   Hand or arm movements that mark the structure of discourse.

behaviorism   A movement in psychology that opposed structuralism and mentalistic concepts; proposed that psychology should be the study of observable behavior.

behaviorist-learning theory   View that language, like other behaviors, is learned through operant and classical conditioning.

bias effect   In phoneme restoration research, the tendency to be biased to perceiving a particular phoneme due to top-down activation; contrasted with the sensitivity effect.

bilingual codeswitching   Switching from one language to another language in a communication context.

bilingualism   Proficiency in two languages, learned either separately or, in native bilingualism, simultaneously. Compare second language acquisition.

bottom-up processing   Using perceptual information to derive higher-level conceptual information.

bound morpheme   A unit of meaning that is attached to a word but cannot stand alone, such as a prefix or suffix.

bridging inference   An inference made to fill in the missing gaps in discourse to aid comprehension.

Broca's aphasia   Difficulty producing articulate speech as a result of brain damage. Speech is slow, lacking grammatical morphemes, and agrammatical.

Broca's area   Portion of the left cerebral cortex involved with articulation of speech.

case grammar An alternative to transformational grammar that focuses on the relationship between verbs and nouns and their thematic roles or cases in a sentence.

CAT Computerized axial tomography, a brain imaging technique that uses multiple X-rays of the brain.

categorical perception The tendency to perceive similar stimuli (e.g., [p] and [pʰ]) as the same general category of sounds (e.g., /p/) but not similar to those from a different category (e.g., /t/).

categorization The process of assigning objects to concepts.

category A fundamental class to which entities belong (e.g., birds).

causal chain The sequence of events described in a sentence or discourse that relates causes to their effects.

causal inference Bridging an inference framed in terms of the cause of an event.

cerebral cortex The outer layer of the brain, divided into two hemispheres with four lobes.

child-directed speech Communication used by caregivers to infants, accentuating important words, repeating them, and pronouncing them more slowly; also called motherese.

CHILDES Child Language Data Exchange System, a computer-based child language archive.

classical conditioning Learning to associate an originally neutral stimulus (e.g., bell) with a reflexive action (e.g., salivating); also called Pavlovian conditioning.

client-centered therapy Psychotherapy in which the therapist's goal is to help the client clarify feelings and subjective experiences.

closed-class words Words such as articles, prepositions, and conjunctions that are function-oriented and do not change over time; compare open-class words.

coarticulation The influence of adjacent phonemes on each other during continuous speech.

codable color A color that is readily named by consensus; from linguistic relativity research.

codeswitching Switching from one dialect to another or from one language to another in a conversation (as when a bilingual child uses one language with the teacher and another with classmates).

cognitive behavior therapy Psychotherapy in which the therapist's role is to change the patient's irrational thoughts and behaviors.

cognitive interview A method of interviewing eyewitnesses to get better information than traditional techniques by giving the witness more control and flexibility in the situation; uses reinstatement, "report everything," differential ordering, and differential perspective techniques.

cognitive revolution The shift in psychology from behaviorism to cognitive psychology following the Skinner-Chomsky debate.

cognitive science The multidisciplinary study of higher mental processes that includes psychology, computer science, anthropology, linguistics, and philosophy.

coherence Linkages among propositions in one's mental representation of a text.

cohesion Linguistic devices that are used to make text or conversation coherent (e.g., pronouns).

cohesive gesture   A gesture that refers to a previous concept in a conversation, as a pronoun does.

cohort theory   A model of word recognition based on the generation of words (the cohort) that are similar to the target word.

collective monologue   Children's presocial speech, in which they appear to be engaged in dialogue but each child is speaking his or her own mind and not taking into account the needs or thoughts of the other children.

common ground   Mutual shared beliefs, knowledge, and understanding between speakers.

communication   Behavior directed at a recipient that affects the recipient's behavior and the initiator's subsequent behavior.

communication goal   What a speaker is trying to achieve in a communicative exchange.

community of practice   A social group (e.g., rugby players or drug users) whose interactions require the understanding of specific speech practices.

competition model   A model of second language learning that looks at the important features of the native language and compares them to a second language; learners begin learning a second language using the strategies that exist in their native language and eventually shift toward the important features of the foreign language.

complement   A word or phrase that completes the sense of a subject, object, or verb (e.g., the tree *that you trimmed*).

complementary gesture   A gesture that is redundant with what is said, such as pointing to a shoe and saying "shoe."

complex   An underlying or unconscious psychological or emotional problem (e.g., jealousy) that is difficult to deal with consciously but can be tapped through the word association technique.

comprehension   Understanding what is written or said.

concept   A set of properties that are ascribed to a class of constructs; for example, a bird (concept) has wings, feathers, a song, and other features (properties).

conceptual metaphor   Part of the unconscious conceptual system that reflects how people think about an object or situation (e.g., "Time is money").

condition-action rules   Rules that tell what action to take under a given circumstance (e.g., "If the light is red, then I stop my car"); also known as if-then rules.

confusability   The potential for one phoneme to be mistaken for another (e.g., /m/ for /n/).

connectionism   A parallel distributed process or network model.

connectionist model   A theory of learning based on a network configuration of nodes of information acquired through experience and feedback processes.

connotation   The emotional or affective meaning of a word, along with its culturally supported assumptions, that are associated with its denotative or literal meaning.

consonant   Any nonvowel speech sound that employs blocking or partial blocking of the airflow during production.

constituent   A syntactic unit in a phrase structure tree.

constituent structure   Hierarchically arranged syntactic units (e.g., NP, VP) that underlie every sentence.

constraint hierarchy   In optimality theory, the ordering of constraints on language that range from those that are rarely or never violated to those that are frequently violated.

constraint satisfaction   The problem of finding the values for a set of variables (e.g., grammatical rules) that will fit the constraints of the model.

constraints   Grammatical rules in a language (e.g., English sentences must have an explicit subject, but Italian sentences do not have this constraint).

context-bound word   A child's word that is produced only in a particular setting (e.g., saying the word *duck* only while taking a bath).

context dependence   The influence of adjacent phonemes on the acoustic form of speech sounds, especially consonants; similar to the coarticulation phenomenon in speech production.

contextual expression   A figurative expression that can only be understood in the context in which it occurs (e.g., "The ham sandwich is getting antsy").

contrastive analysis   A method of predicting where foreign-language learners will have difficulty by using language differences to predict errors.

conversational layers   Different conversational goals and settings used in conversations (e.g., the literal and nonliteral layers in a sarcastic comment).

conversational maxims   Cooperative principles that guide conversations (e.g., quality, quantity, manner, and relevance).

conversational repair   Action taken to maintain cohesion in a conversation.

corpus callosum   A large band of fibers that connects the cerebral hemispheres.

creole   A mixture of two or more languages learned as a native language.

cross-linguistic study   A study that compares one language structure or performance to that of another spoken or signed language.

cross-sectional study   A research method that examines several age ranges or experimental groups simultaneously.

cuneiform   An early form of writing that used marks pressed into clay with a wedge-shaped stylus.

decomposition view   The idea that root words are stored in memory and affixes are appended to them, rather than all forms of a word having an entry in memory.

deep structure   The meaning underlying the surface structure of a sentence; the basic syntactic structures of grammar.

deferred imitation   Imitation of an event some time after it originally occurred.

deictic gesture   A gesture used to direct attention to an object (e.g., pointing).

DEL   Derogatory ethnic label; ethnic or racial slur.

denotation   The referential meaning of a word.

dependent variable   In experimental situations, the variable that is recorded or measured (e.g., reaction time, percent correct).

derivational morpheme   A morpheme that is added to a root morpheme to produce a new word or stem.

derogatory ethnic label   An ethnic or racial slur.

Descartes' error Trying to separate the mind from the body or brain, referred to as an error because brain and thought are inseparable.

descriptive grammar The rules that are needed to produce sentences and meaningful sequences of sentences in a language.

developmental approach The view of language acquisition that seeks to explain the course of language development; opposed to the learnability approach.

diagnosis The conclusions drawn by a physician following medical examination of a patient and analysis of the patient's symptoms.

dialect A variant of a main language that is intelligible to a speaker of the main language.

differentiation The idea that concepts that are important to speakers of one language show greater discrimination of differences that are minor or ignored in other languages (e.g., beer categories are more differentiated in Germany than in the United States).

discourse A sequence of written statements or spoken utterances that attempts to achieve some communication goal.

disgust Revulsion at the thought of consuming something or placing it in one's mouth.

distinctive features Properties of sound waves or articulations that are used to distinguish one phoneme from another.

dominant meaning The meaning accessed first during the lexical access process; followed by the subordinate meaning.

Ebonics African American Vernacular English.

echoic mention Repeating a word or phrase from an ironic statement to emphasize its incongruity.

editing expression Utterance indicating that repair of a speech error is to follow (e.g., "er," "I mean," "uh").

elaborate code Educated speech, as opposed to the restricted code of the lower classes.

elicitation method A research method that asks the listener to "fill in the blank" in a particular statement or question.

elitism Point of view that one form of a language (and hence the people who speak it) is superior to others.

embedding Including a sentence or clause within another sentence (e.g., "The music *that Orpheus loved* is harp music").

emblematic Representing speech with a socially constructed type of gesture (e.g., forming a circle with the thumb and forefinger to signal "OK" in English).

embodiment The idea that language is represented in memory in reference to events, objects, and situations experienced in the real world; during language comprehension, words are connected to their embodied representations.

emergence The view that language comprehension is a process of perspective taking on what is happening in an utterance, relating words to experiences in the real world to provide deeper meaning.

emotion Basic affect or feeling, such as anger, fear, or joy.

emotional involvement   The degree to which the listener is emotionally involved in a conversation.

emotional schemas   Mental frameworks constructed using our experiences to predict what kinds of emotional experiences are likely to occur in a given social setting.

emotional Stroop task   A color-naming task that uses words that are personally provocative to the reader (e.g., spider-related word such as *web* for a spider phobic).

emotion gap   The failure to account for how emotional phenomena affect speech processing.

ERP   Event-related brain potential.

euphemism   A word or phrase that replaces a taboo word (e.g., *passed away* for *died*).

event-related brain potential   Electrical signals emitted from different areas of the brain in response to different types of stimuli.

exchanges   Speech errors in which one unit of speech is exchanged with another.

exhaustive access   In the ambiguity literature, the theory that all meanings are accessed when an ambiguous word is activated; compare selective access.

expansion   Creating a well-formed expression from a child's primitive utterance (e.g., child says "Throw Daddy," and father expands, "Throw it to Daddy").

explanatory question   Asking why, what if, or what are the consequences to evoke reasoning more thoroughly than a yes-no question might.

expressive learner   A child who uses language to emphasize social interaction.

eye fixation   During reading, the period of time when the eye is focused on text.

eye movements   Motions of the eyes during reading, with eye fixations used to diagnose relationships among words and events in comprehension.

eye-voice span   The time interval between seeing a word and saying that word aloud.

face   One's public presentation of oneself; negative face is the desire to be autonomous, and positive face is the desire to be connected to others.

figurative language   Nonliteral expressions that use imagery to make a comparison between two things or make a situation more concrete (e.g., "My roommate is a pig"); simile and metaphor are common forms.

filled pause   A pause in the flow of speech that is filled with sound or a word (e.g., *er, well*).

first words   A child's first utterances, usually nouns or verbs that are important and frequently heard.

***fis* phenomenon**   The observation that children can hear differences in phonemes before they can produce them, so they say fis instead of fish even though they know the two sounds are different.

fixation   The point during reading where the eye stops moving to focus on a section of text.

fluent aphasia   Decreased ability to understand speech due to brain damage; the patient can hear words but does not know their meanings; also known as Wernicke's aphasia.

fMRI   Functional magnetic resonance imaging, which measures increases in oxygen consumption to construct brain images.

focal color   The best example of a primary color.

food   What a particular culture deems edible.

forensic linguistics   Application of the study of language to questions of law and the legal system.

formalism   The idea that language and language acquisition have nothing to do with communication.

formant   A band of energy on a speech spectrogram.

forms of address   Honorific, professional, or courtesy titles used to refer to another person (e.g., *Your Honor, Doctor, Mrs.*).

foveal region   Central part of the back of the eye on which text is fixated.

fragmented style   Type of witness talk that is not narrative and is difficult to follow because it presents the facts as unconnected fragments.

free association   Method of word association used in psychotherapy in which the client responds to a word with the first word that comes to mind.

free morpheme   A root word, to which bound morphemes and inflectional morphemes may be added to alter meaning.

Freudian slip   A mistake in speaking that purportedly reveals an underlying thought, desire, or motivation.

functionalism   The idea that the mind is defined by the functions it performs and that language and language acquisition are rooted in communication.

fundamental frequency   The rate at which the vocal cords vibrate, perceived as pitch.

fuzzy category   A class in which membership is not entirely clear (e.g., art).

galvanic skin response   Physical test used as a measure of emotional arousal.

garden path sentence   A sentence that leads the reader to parse it incorrectly (go down the wrong linguistic path) and then backtrack and parse it again (e.g., "Fat people eat accumulates").

gaze duration   How long the reader fixates on the text.

gender differences   Differences in language use attributed to gender identity.

gender identity   The degree to which a person regards himself or herself as a male, female, lesbian, gay male, bisexual, or transgender.

Geschwind model   A model of language production and perception based on the symptoms of patients with aphasia.

gestures   Meaningful body movements and facial expressions that complement or supplement speech.

gist effect   The tendency to forget the surface details of a sentence but retain its meaning.

global aphasia   Loss of all speech abilities.

good reader   Readers who have good phonological awareness, take in large amounts of text per eye fixation, and make few regressive eye movements.

good writers   Writers who make certain they comprehend their assignments, use a wide range of ideas, incorporate documentation, spend time revising their texts, are knowledge restructurers, do a lot of reading, use outlines, and reallocate strategies as their writing tasks change.

graded salience   The hierarchy of meanings associated with a word; priority tends to be given to the most salient meaning of a word regardless of the context in which it occurs.

grammatical gender   Gender assigned somewhat arbitrarily to nouns and pronouns in a language, as opposed to natural gender, which reflects the actual sex of the person or thing being referred to.

grammatical rules   Rules for combining words and phrases.

grapheme   Any symbol of an alphabetic writing system; a letter of the alphabet.

grapheme-to-phoneme correspondence (GPC)   How well the symbols of a language correspond to the sounds in the language.

ground   The similarity between the topic and the vehicle in a metaphor.

grounding   In conversation, attending to, identifying, and comprehending each speaker's utterance before moving on to the next statement.

growth point   The beginning of conceptualization in the speech production process.

head-turning procedure   Measure of an infant's preferences for stimuli by monitoring head turning in response to a new stimulus.

health vegetarians   Vegetarians who do not eat meat or other animal products in the belief that these items are not healthy for them personally; compare moral vegetarians.

high-amplitude sucking procedure (HAS)   Measure of an infant's perception by monitoring sucking responses to different stimuli.

High RA   Style of speaking in which the speaker is effective at connecting words to experiences and describing them in detail.

homophones   Words with different spellings that sound the same (e.g., *their* and *there*).

Huey, Edmond Burke   Early psychologist who pioneered the study of reading.

human factors   The study of how human characteristics are applied to the environment and to the objects we use; also called ergonomics.

hyperbole   Deliberate exaggeration (e.g., "The line was a mile long").

iconic gesture   A representational image of an object made with the hands and arms (e.g., cupping the hands together to convey the meaning of the word *ball*).

ideogram   Any abstract or conventional symbol used in a writing system that has no immediate links to the object or sound it represents; compare pictogram.

idiom   A conventionalized figurative expression (e.g., "kick the bucket").

imagery   Discourse that evokes the concrete image of an object or a scene.

indecency   Legal standard that focuses on body parts, products, and processes deemed to be "patently offensive."

independent variable   In experimental design, the variable of interest, which is manipulated or controlled by the experimenter; compare dependent variable.

indirect access   Reading by decoding words into sounds on the path to meaning.

indirect request   Requesting something obliquely, assuming that the recipient will infer what is being asked for (e.g., asking, "Are you wearing a watch?" instead of "What time is it?").

inference   An attempt to fill in what is missing in a text; information that is activated but not explicit during reading or listening.

inflectional morpheme   A grammatical morpheme or word ending that changes the meaning of a word in some way (e.g., *-ed, 's*).

innateness   Hypothesis that humans are genetically equipped to acquire universal grammar, which is the basis for all languages.

inner speech   Verbalized thought or silent self-talk that accompanies thinking.

insisting   A child's persistence at asking for something.

instrumental conditioning   Conditioning in which the consequence of a behavior (punishment or reward) determines whether the behavior is repeated or not; also known as Skinnerian conditioning.

insults   Offensive language used to denigrate another person.

integrated model   A model of speech production that incorporates gestures into the production stream.

interactive model   A model of reading that views the process as an interaction between top-down and bottom-up processes.

interrogation   The verbal interview of a suspect by the police.

interruptions   Disruptions of the speech production process.

intonation   Changes in pitch (frequency) over time.

invariance   The acoustic or articulatory property of speech that does not change from context to context.

irony   Making a statement that is intended to be understood as the opposite of its literal meaning (e.g., "I love to pay taxes").

irregular verb   A verb that does not follow the usual morphosyntactic rules.

IRT   Interference reaction time, the time to respond to a stimulus in the context of a secondary task that interferes with it.

jargon   Idiomatic speech used by a social group to facilitate communication within the group.

joint attention   Focusing on an object or event unrelated to the speaker or listener to shift attention to that object or event.

joint pretense   Awareness on the part of both speaker and listener that their conversation takes place on two layers simultaneously, the figurative and the literal.

joint project   Discourse regarded as a collaborative effort between the speaker and listener who are trying to attain a particular goal by talking.

joking narrative   Form of humor achieved by telling the joke in the form of a story.

knowledge restructurer   Writer who reformulates the facts to create a more cohesive essay.

knowledge teller   Writer who merely restates the facts.

LAD   Linguistic acquisition device, Chomsky's mechanism to explain how language is acquired, assuming that the capacity or propensity for language is inborn.

language   A structured system for combining words that makes it possible to communicate with others and that has notable properties (e.g., communicativity, arbitrariness, multiple structures, productivity, and evolutionary).

language acquisition   The process or developmental course of language learning.

language lateralization   The notion that certain language functions are carried out by either the left or the right cerebral hemisphere.

language production   Speaking or signing a language, as opposed to comprehension.

late closure   Parsing strategy that attaches incoming words to the phrase under construction.

learnability approach   The view that children acquire language by imputing linguistic rules.

Leborgne   Broca's patient who had difficulty speaking but retained his ability to curse.

left-hemisphere damage   Damage that usually results in a form of aphasia.

legalese   Legal language used in legal documents and courtroom proceedings.

lemma   The word as a grammatical entity, such as a noun or a verb.

lexeme   The word as a morphological and phonological entity.

lexical ambiguity   A word's having more than one meaning.

lexical bias effect   In speech error research, the phenomenon that the tendency to make an error that produces a word outweighs the tendency to produce a nonword.

lexical frame analysis   Grammatical analysis that looks at a sentence as a framework into which certain word slots must be filled, depending on the particular verbs and nouns involved, similar to case grammar or thematic analysis.

lexical semantics   The meanings of words and meaning relationships among words.

lexicon   Each person's mental dictionary of words.

limbic system   Subcortical area of the brain associated with instinctive behaviors (e.g., the fight-or-flight response).

linguistic determinism   Stronger version of linguistic relativity where thoughts are governed by the words that are available to express them.

linguistic relativity   The idea that thought depends on or is relative to the language used for thinking.

literacy   The ability to read and write functionally.

localization   The notion that brain functions are restricted to specific areas of the brain.

logogen model   A model for retrieving words from memory through activation rather than searching.

logogram   A word-sized grapheme, such as Japanese *kanji*.

longitudinal study   Research method that studies individuals over a long period of time; compare cross-sectional study.

Low RA   Style of speaking in which the speaker describes experience in vague, nonemotional terms.

macrostructure   Overall structure or theme of a text.

malapropism   Replacing an intended word or phrase with one that is similar but different in meaning (e.g., using *minor brain headache* instead of *migraine headache*).

manner   The action in a motion event, conveyed by the verb in some languages and outside the verb in others.

mapping problem   A child's problem of associating a new word with its proper meaning.

meiosis   Deliberate underemphasis; understatement (e.g., "Mozart wrote some decent music").

memory span   Number of items that can be recalled in exact serial order—a capacity of working memory.

mental model   A reader's mental representation of a text.

mentalese   Language used in thinking.

merge model   A model of speech perception that is predicated on the idea that feedback is not an essential part of the process, operating instead on bottom-up information flow.

mesh   The notion that language (e.g., a word) interacts with properties of an object that is stored in memory; for example, *twisting* has to interact with properties in memory that represent what the word means in the real world.

metalinguistic awareness   Awareness of the components and structures of language.

metaphor   The implicit comparison of two things by saying that one thing is the other (e.g., "My roommate is a pig").

metonymy   Reference to an object or situation through one aspect of it (e.g., "Wall Street reacted favorably").

microstructure   Individual sentences or propositions in a text supporting the macrostructure.

militarese   Euphemistic jargon used to hide the true workings of the war machine (e.g., calling a concentration camp a "pacification center").

Miller **v.** *California*   Supreme Court case that refined the three-pronged test for determining obscenity.

minimal attachment   A parsing strategy that attaches incoming words to the existing tree structure, adding the fewest possible branches (nodes).

minimal pair   Words or syllables that differ in only one sound that makes a difference in meaning (e.g., *tap* and *pap*).

misinformation effect   In advertising, the use of language that leads the consumer to make inferences that are incorrect.

MLU   Mean length of utterance, a measure of grammatical development.

model of intimacy   A culture's model of how people should behave in intimate situations.

modularity   Organization of the brain and mind into distinct, independent, and autonomous parts.

moral vegetarians   People who do not eat meat because they believe doing so is immoral.

morpheme   A unit of meaning—a word, prefix, or suffix.

morphological rules   Rules for combining morphemes in a language.

morphology   The study of the structure of words.

motion event   The movement, duration, and direction of objects as described by verbs, prepositions, adjectives, and adverbs in an utterance.

Motor theory   A speech perception theory predicated on the idea that listeners simulate what the speaker is saying in order to perceive what was said.

multidimensional scaling   A data analysis technique that displays n-dimensional structure (e.g., size and ferocity, or any number of dimensions) of a category of objects on the basis of similarity ratings of pairs of examples (e.g., lion and mouse).

multiple code theory   An attempt to integrate language, memory, and emotional phenomena in one network-type representation.

muting function   The effect of figurative language to attenuate the emotional aspects of what is being said; for example, sarcasm mutes anger with humor.

N400   An aspect of an evoked potential that is sensitive to semantic anomalies in sentences.

name-calling   A form of emotional speech in which the speaker calls the listener an insulting name (e.g., "pig").

narrative   Real or constructed memory of an event from the past.

nativist-linguist theory   The view that language is innate, not learned.

natural language processor   A computer program designed to parse everyday speech.

nature versus nurture   In the language literature, the question of whether language is learned or inborn.

negation   The use of negative sentences, which in children takes a predictable developmental course.

negative evidence   Feedback on ungrammatical utterances.

negative face   Aspect of politeness in which the speaker attempts to be autonomous.

neighborhood   The semantic or orthographic associates of a target word.

Netpals   The Internet or e-mail equivalent of penpals, people who communicate with each other over the Internet.

nonfluent aphasia   Speech produced in a halting, partial manner; also known as Broca's aphasia.

nonpropositional speech   Automatic, noncreative speech (e.g., clichés, expletives, idioms).

nonsense word   A permissible phonological form that has no meaning (e.g., *shime*).

nonstandard English   Substandard or lower-class speech registers; similar to a restricted code.

object permanence   The notion that during the sensorimotor stage of development, children develop the ability to think about objects that are not present.

obscenity   A legal concept refined in *Miller* v. *California* that compares speech to a three-pronged test.

odor names   Example of a category in which it is difficult to label the individual entities.

open-class words   Nouns, adjectives, verbs, and adverbs, which evolve over time; compare closed-class words.

operant conditioning   An organism's learning to behave on the basis of the consequences of its behavior (e.g., in response to punishment or reward).

operating principles   The limited number of strategies children use to figure out what is important in their native language (e.g., pay attention to word endings).

optimality theory   A connectionist-inspired perspective on the nature of linguistic knowledge and linguistic constraints on sentence production.

orthography   Method of mapping the sounds in a language onto written symbols; the written form of a language; spelling.

overextension   A child's tendency to use a word overbroadly (e.g., calling all four-legged animals "cows").

overregularization   A child's tendency to regularize irregular verbs (e.g., *goed*).

P600   A positive deflection of an event-related potential that occurs 600 ms after a syntactic anomaly in a stimulus sentence.

parafoveal region   The area of about 5 degrees of visual angle on each side of the fixation point during eye fixation on text.

parallel model   A model of language processing that integrates ongoing lower-level and higher-level processes, as opposed to a linear model that progresses through a series of stages from bottom to top.

parallel processing   The ability to carry out several tasks simultaneously.

parallel transmission Simultaneous transmission of information about adjacent phonemes in the speech flow, as opposed to serial transmission.

parameters Regular features of language, such as word order or the requirement for an explicit subject in an English sentence but not in an Italian sentence.

parental feedback Parents' responses to children's verbal expressions.

parsing Assigning words in a sentence to linguistic categories; determining the relationships of sequences of words according to the rules of grammar.

partial processing Failure to fully comprehend an utterance or a bit of text, indicating that speech is not always fully processed.

path In a motion event, the trajectory or direction of motion conveyed by the verb or its appurtenances.

Pattern-Playback A speech synthesizer that converts hand-painted images of speech (spectrograms) into speech.

pause A point in the speech production process where the speaker stops speaking, usually at a phrase boundary or the end of a sentence.

peek-a-boo A social interaction game that helps a child learn to use language.

peripheral region During eye fixation, the area beyond the parafoveal region.

perseveration Speech error that repeats a previously spoken constituent (e.g., "she shells" for "she sells").

perspective taking The listener's attempt to understand by taking a perspective on the scene described by the speaker.

PET Positron emission tomography, a brain-imaging technique that monitors cerebral blood flow.

phone A phonetic segment that is a member of a category of sounds that are contrastive (e.g., [p] versus [pʰ]).

phoneme A contrastive phonological segment of speech (e.g., /t/ versus /d/).

phoneme monitoring Listening carefully to speech for the presence of a target phoneme, as in an experimental task.

phonemic confusions Sets of phonemes that sound similar and are mistaken for each other (e.g., *mice* and *nice*).

phonemic restoration Notion that when a speech sound is omitted from a speech segment, the listener fills in or restores the missing sound.

phonetic alphabet Alphabetic symbols used to represent phonetic segments of speech so that there is a one-to-one correspondence between a sound and its symbol.

phonological awareness Awareness of the phonological properties of language, such as the ability to count the syllables in a word or identify words that rhyme with it.

phonological dyslexia Selective problems reading nonwords compared to words but without related semantic errors; patients can read words both regular and irregular but are much better with nonwords; closely related to deep dyslexia.

phonological memory Retention of speech sounds, words, or sentences in short-term memory.

phonological rules The rules speakers instinctively follow regarding the phonological regularities or predictable aspects of speech sounds in their native language.

phonotactic rules Rules dictating which combinations of phonemes are permissible in a language.

phrase structure The structure of noun phrases and verb phrases in sentences.

pictograms Primitive writing symbols that look like their referents.

pictograph Any nonverbal symbol used to represent an object or condition (e.g., skull and crossed bones to indicate poison).

picture naming An experimental task that measures how long it takes for a subject to name a picture.

pidgin A language that borrows from the various native languages spoken in a region to facilitate communication between speakers of the different languages; a pidgin learned as a native language is a creole.

pitch Fundamental frequency as perceived by a listener.

pitch contour Intonation of a sentence.

plain English Straightforward language intended to replace legalese in legal documents.

poor readers Readers who lack alphabetic principal or phonological awareness, have poor phonological memory and word recognition skills, and have difficulty with analogies, pronunciation, morphemic strategies, and inferencing.

poor writers Writers who do not make an effort to comprehend their assignments, use a wide range of ideas, incorporate documentation, revise their texts, restructure, do outside reading, use outlines, or adapt their writing strategies as their writing tasks change.

positive face A form of politeness in which the speaker desires to be connected to others.

poverty of stimulus Nativists' argument that there is insufficient information in the environment for children to acquire language only by hearing people speaking.

powerful language Courtroom discourse that avoids hesitations, uncertainty, and qualification.

pragmatics A focus on how social situations constrain language usage.

pragmatic strategies Production or comprehension strategies that focus on social variables in a speech situation (e.g., age, gender, politeness).

preclosing statement Comments made prior to ending a conversation (e.g., "Look at the time").

preferential looking A method used to determine visual preferences by measuring the amount of time spent looking at one stimulus relative to another.

prelinguistic gestures The communicative hand movements and pointing that a child uses before learning to speak.

prescriptive grammar Attempts to legislate what grammatical rules should be followed rather than to determine what rules actually are followed in speech.

preservation error Speech error in which a speaker continues to use a previous sound in an utterance (e.g., saying, "phonological fool" instead of "phonological rule").

prestige dialect Dialect spoken by individuals in positions of power, deemed to be correct by prescriptive grammarians.

pretend play A child's symbolic use of toys and other objects.

primate communication Laboratory or field studies of how nonhuman primates can communicate under artificial conditions or natural conditions, respectively.

priming The effect on response time of words previously heard or read on lexical access to subsequent words.

processing impairment Language difficulties resulting from the failure of a language process (e.g., lexical access) to be completed successfully.

productivity Quality of language that allows a large number of utterances to be generated from a small number of components.

pronoun reversal Using the wrong pronoun to apply to oneself (e.g., a child's referring to himself as "him" instead of "me"); common in autism.

propaganda model The theory that the news is biased to fit the needs of major corporations who wield the power to control it.

proposition A statement that expresses a factual claim.

propositional speech Novel and articulate speech; impaired by left-brain damage.

prosody Duration (length), pitch, or loudness of speech sounds.

prototype The average or standard example of a category.

psychoanalytic approach Freud's technique for conducting therapy.

put-on A teasing form of figurative language.

question asking One of several pedagogical techniques that builds intuition by asking for answers rather than giving answers (as in a lecture).

reading span Processing and storage capacity during a reading task; highly correlated with listening span.

reference Aspect of meaning that relates words to objects in the environment.

referent Entity designated by a noun phrase.

referential activity A speaker's attempt to connect experiences and emotions to language; may be high or low.

referential learners Children who focus on references to their immediate environment, as opposed to social interactions.

regularization error An error that regularizes an irregular word (e.g., *goed* for *went*).

Remote Associates Test (RAT) Word association test that asks the subject to supply a word that is related to three other words.

representational gesture A symbolic gesture that has semantic content (e.g., waving bye-bye or opening and closing mouth to mean "fish").

restricted code The notion that the lower classes speak a nonstandard form of English.

retold story A narrative that repeats a previously told tale.

reversible sentence A sentence in which nouns can be exchanged (e.g., "The mouse bit the cat"), as opposed to a nonreversible sentence, in which they cannot be exchanged (e.g., "The girl ate the cookie").

revision A stage of writing that improves overall quality.

rewrite rule A syntactic rule that converts one form of a sentence into another form (e.g., from active to passive).

rhetorical question An assertion framed as a question to which no answer is expected (e.g., "How many times have I told you to wash your hands before dinner?").

right-hemisphere damage   Brain damage that usually results in the disruption of emotional qualities of speech perception and production as well as spatial and imagery aspects of speech.

r_m The behaviorist's notion of meaning as an internal response to a stimulus.

RRWUs   Recurrent real-word utterances, commonly as a result of brain damage.

rule learning   The notion that children acquire language by learning rules (e.g., past tense).

saccade   Rapid eye movement that does not extract information from text.

sarcasm   The use of satirical or ironic language to convey a negative attitude.

schema   A mental framework used to organize meaningful material on the basis of prior experience.

script   A short and detailed description of a sequence of events that unfold chronologically.

second language acquisition   Learning a second language after a native language has been acquired; also known as foreign-language learning.

segmentation problem   A listener's difficulty deciding where one word ends and another begins in the continuous flow of speech.

selective access   In the ambiguity literature, the theory that a particular meaning is accessed when an ambiguous word is activated; compare exhaustive access.

selective adaptation   Decreased sensitivity to a phoneme due to repeated exposure to it; used in phonemic restoration research.

self-repair   In the speech production process, an interruption of speech to correct a phonological, morphological, syntactic, or lexical error.

semantic differential   Evaluation using a series of bipolar rating scales (e.g., *good–bad*) to measure the emotional or connotative meaning of words.

semantic features   A bundle of features or aspects of meaning, such as (for the concept "bird") "is alive" or "has feathers."

semantic inhibition   Suppression of one aspect of a word's meaning in favor of another interpretation.

semantic memory   The part of memory that contains words, concepts, and facts about the world.

semantic network   A network of links and nodes used to represent semantic information about sentences.

semantic priming   The phenomenon of one word's activating others that are related (e.g., *doctor* eliciting *nurse*).

semantic verification   In an experimental setting, judging as quickly as possible whether a sentence is true or false.

sense   The part of the meaning of an expression that along with the context determines its referent.

sensitivity effect   A proposal to account for the phonemic restoration effect that occurs because the listener shifts the level of sensitivity to incoming signals.

sensorimotor thinking   In Piaget's theory, the first mode of thought, in which thinking is connected to objects in the environment and the actions they perform.

serial model   A model of language processing that unfolds one stage at a time rather than in parallel.

sex differences Differences in language usage attributed to biological sex.

sex education Topic that illustrates the problem with speaking about sexuality in public schools.

sexual talk References to sex acts or sexual body parts.

simile An explicit comparison using *like* or *as* (e.g., "Marriage is like a trap").

situational model A framework created during discourse comprehension whereby the listener or reader constructs a model of what is being described, for example, the relationship between objects and people in a setting.

Skinner-Chomsky debate Argument about whether language is inborn or learned; gave birth to the cognitive revolution in cognitive psychology.

slang Informal, nonstandard lexicon used between members of a social group that marks membership in that group, affronts authority, and promotes secrecy.

slip of the tongue Involuntary deviation from an intended utterance.

slip of the hand Speech error in sign language similar to a slip of the tongue.

social interaction theory The view that language structure is acquired through social interaction with adults and older children.

sociolinguistics The branch of linguistics that focuses on the social forces that affect language use (e.g., gender, politeness).

Socratic dialogue A method of building intuition through asking questions.

span of perception The amount of information that can be apprehended simultaneously. In reading, it is two to three words per fixation (known as the perceptual window).

spatial model A mental representation of objects in relation to other objects or people.

speaking rate The pace of verbal output in words per minute or syllables per minute.

spectrogram The image of speech sounds produced by spectrograph.

spectrograph Device that analyzes speech sounds and converts acoustical energy to a spectrogram.

speech Spoken language (not "ideal" language).

speech act The speaker's intention to do things with words (e.g., a commisive commits the speaker to do something, as in "I promise to . . .").

speech register Style of formality in speech, ranging from formal to casual slang.

spider phobic A person who fears spiders.

split-brain patient Individual in whom the corpus callosum has been severed (usually to eliminate seizures in epilepsy) and the two hemispheres do not communicate with each other.

spreading activation model A network model that posits the migrating activation of adjacent nodes that are related in meaning.

standard English The accepted norm or speech register for conducting business, education, or other formal social affairs; similar to the elaborate code.

standard pragmatic view A model of figurative language comprehension that proposes that a literal interpretation of a figure of speech is obligatory, contradicted by several lines of research.

statistical learning Learning language not by rules but by how frequently words and word endings are used.

story grammar   The structure of a story in terms of its setting, episodes, characters, and goals.

storytelling   Narrative form of discourse that uses conventional tales and stories or novel stories that follow the conventional format.

stress   The length, loudness, or pitch of a syllable; also called accent.

stress-timed   Of a language, having interstress intervals of equal duration regardless of how many syllables fall in the intervals.

Stroop task   Experimental exercise in which the subject is presented with stimuli (the names of colors) and required to respond with the color of the stimulus rather than that of the writing; the semantic meaning of the stimulus interferes with the perceptual judgment (e.g., RED written in black ink).

style   A situational dialect or register.

subordinate meaning   In the lexical access process, the meaning understood after the dominant meaning has been accessed.

subtractive bilingualism   The case where learning one language detracts from fluency in another language.

sucking rate   An indication of how much attention a nursing newborn is paying to a stimulus; as interest goes up, so does the sucking rate.

supplementary gesture   A gesture that accompanies speech that contains different but related information (e.g., pointing to a cup while saying "mommy").

surface dyslexia   Reading limited almost entirely to phonological recoding; the reader can decode pseudowords but has trouble with irregular words; errors will be ones like reading "decease" instead of "disease"; compare with deep dyslexia.

surface memory   Memory for the microstructure of discourse (e.g., structure of a particular sentence).

surface structure   The linear constituent ordering of a written or spoken sentence; the end result of applying transformational rules to a deep structure.

SVO (subject-verb-object) order   The conventional order of primary constituents in simple sentences in English.

syllabary   The symbols of a syllabic writing system, each representing a syllable rather than a letter or sound.

synonyms   Different words with roughly the same meaning (e.g., *pants* and *trousers*).

syntactic bootstrapping   A child's strategy to find the meaning of a novel word through syntactic structure.

syntax   The grammatical rules of a language.

taboo   Social prohibition dictated by cultural practices.

taboo words   Words that are not supposed to be used in public.

tag question   An interrogative tacked on the end of a statement (e.g., "It's getting late, *don't you think?*").

task environment   The writer's understanding of the writing assignment and the physical context of producing the subsequent text.

teasing   Figurative use of speech, similar to a put-on or insult.

telegraphic speech   A child's tendency to omit prepositions and articles in early multiword utterances (e.g., "Mommy sock").

text base   The macrostructure of discourse, or an understanding of it (e.g., the overall structure of a text).

text-to-speech system   Software that generates a voiced response to typed input.

thematic structure analysis   A type of grammatical analysis that looks for thematic roles in a sentence (e.g., patient, agent, and goal); similar to lexical frame analysis or case grammar.

threatening   A form of anger expression that appears between 2 and 3 years of age.

time course   The unfolding of psycholinguistic or cognitive processes over time.

tip-of-the-tongue state (TOT)   A failure at lexical access that produces guesses that are phonologically or semantically similar to the target word.

tongue twister   An utterance that is difficult to produce because the words use similar sounds (e.g., "She sells seashells by the seashore").

top-down processing   Using higher-level conceptual information to process perceptual information.

topic   The main point or subject matter of a discourse or narrative; in metaphor, the subject of the sentence (e.g., *love* in "Love is a growing plant").

topic-centered story   A form of narrative that focuses on a central theme and unfolds around that theme.

total communication   A form of deaf education that uses speech and sign language.

TRACE   A parallel distributed process type of model of language processing developed by McClelland and Rumelhart.

transformational rules   Rules that describe the relationship between sentences (e.g., how to transform an active sentence into a passive one).

transition   The upward or downward movement in pitch as viewed on a spectrogram.

tree diagram   A layout of the constituent structure of a phrase or sentence.

turf   The speaker's ownership or jurisdiction over the physical location of a conversation.

turn taking   The shifting pattern of speakers in a conversation as each takes and relinquishes the opportunity to speak.

tu-vous   The French pronouns for *you*, the familiar one (*tu*) used with listeners who are close to the speaker and the formal one (*vous*) used with other people.

two-word stage   The period of language acquisition that follows the one-word stage.

typicality   A measure of how closely an exemplar matches the prototype of a category; for example, a robin is a typical bird, but an ostrich is not typical.

underextension   A child's tendency to use a word too narrowly (e.g., using *Daddy* to refer only to her father).

ungrammatical   Violating the grammatical rules of the language.

universal grammar   The inborn set of grammatical parameters, to be set by hearing the local language; the principles or properties that pertain to the grammars of all human languages.

vehicle   The part of a metaphor that is simple and concrete or mutually known (e.g., *plant* in "Love is a growing plant").

verbal protocol   A form of thinking aloud that provides a window into what the speaker is thinking or planning.

verbal refusal   A form of anger expression that occurs with 2-year-olds.

verbatim memory   The ability to recall exactly what happened or was said.

visual window   The amount of information that can be processed during the fixation period in reading.

VO strategy   A comprehension strategy used by children that provides the correct parsing for an active sentence but not for passive or interrogative sentences.

vocal expression of emotion   Quality of speaker's voice that indicates emotion, such as high pitch or wavering voice.

voice onset time   The lag after the onset of a voiced phoneme before the voicing begins.

voicing   Speech sounds that are produced using the vocal cords.

vowel   A sound produced without significant restrictions of the airflow through the mouth.

Wada test   A test used to assess language lateralization by deactivating one hemisphere with sodium amytal.

warnings   Verbal and pictographic information attached to products or embedded in the instructions that specify the proper uses of the product.

Washoe   A chimpanzee that was taught American Sign Language.

weak language   Courtroom language that is filled with qualifiers, hedges, and empty adjectives.

well-defined category   A category in which members are easily identified (e.g., the category "odd numbers").

Wernicke's aphasia   Fluent aphasia.

Wernicke's area   A portion of the left cerebral cortex involved with language understanding.

Whorf's hypothesis   The theory that the words and grammar of the native language influence the way we view the world; also known as linguistic relativity.

word association   Saying the first word that comes to mind when a target word is given, used as a measure of semantic meaning.

word fluency   The ability to produce a number of verbal responses to a question or prompt.

word magic   The notion that uttering a word or hearing a word produces a physical effect (e.g., cursing someone, "I hope you die," causes the person to die).

word mapping   Establishing a relationship between words and the objects to which they refer.

word processor   Device used in writing documents to prepare and correct text.

word spurt   Rapid growth in word production starting at around age 16 to 22 months.

WordNet   A self-contained electronic lexical database.

working memory   Short-term memory; a pool of resources that perform mental operations.

writer's block   An inability to write text, usually due to emotional or motivational problems.

Wundt, Wilhelm   The father of experimental psychology in Germany; a proponent of structuralism.

Zipf's law   The theory that the probability of hearing or reading a word depends on its statistical frequency.

Bibliography

Acredolo, L., & Goodwyn, S. (1985). Symbolic gesturing in language development: A case study. *Human Development, 28,* 40–49.

Acredolo, L., & Goodwyn, S. (1988). Symbolic gesturing in normal infants. *Child Development, 59,* 450–466.

Adachi, T. (1996). Sarcasm in Japanese. *Studies in Language, 19,* 1–36.

Adolphs, R., Russell, J. A., & Tranel, D. (1999). A role for the human amygdala in recognizing emotional arousal from unpleasant stimuli. *Psychological Science, 10,* 167–171.

Aitchison, J. (1987). *Words in the mind: An introduction to the mental lexicon.* Oxford: Blackwell.

Aksu-Koc, A., & Slobin, D. I. (1985). The acquisition of Turkish. In D. I. Slobin (Ed.), *The crosslinguistic study of language acquisition: Vol. 1. The data.* Hillsdale, NJ: Erlbaum.

Albert, S., & Kessler, S. (1978). Ending social encounters. *Journal of Experimental Social Psychology, 14,* 541–553.

Alberts, J., Kellar-Guenther, Y., & Corman, S. (1996). That's not funny: Understanding recipients' responses to teasing. *Western Journal of Communication, 60,* 337–357.

Aldridge, N. C. (1999). Enhancing children's memory through cognitive interviewing: An assessment technique for social work practice. *Child and Adolescent Social Work Journal, 16,* 101–126.

Allan, K., & Burridge, K. (1991). *Euphemism and dysphemism.* New York: Oxford University Press.

Allen, I. L. (1983). *The language of ethnic conflict.* New York: Columbia University Press.

Allen, I. L. (1990). *Unkind words: Ethnic labeling from Redskin to WASP.* New York: Bergin & Garvey.

Allen, J., & Seidenberg, M. (1999). The emergence of grammaticality in connectionist networks. In B. MacWhinney (Ed.), *The emergence of language* (pp. 115–151). Mahwah, NJ: Erlbaum.

Allen, L. S., Richey, M. F., Chai, Y. M., & Gorski, R. A. (1991). Sex differences in the corpus callosum of the living human brain. *Journal of Neuroscience, 11,* 933–942.

Altmann, G. T. M., Garnham, A., & Dennis, Y. (1992). Avoiding the garden path: Eye movements in context. *Journal of Memory and Language, 31,* 685–712.

Altmann, G. T. M., & Steedman, M. (1988). Interaction with context during human sentence processing. *Cognition, 30,* 191–238.

Anderson, J. R. (1983). *The architecture of cognition.* Cambridge, MA: Harvard University Press.

Anderson, J. R. (1993). *Rules of the mind.* Hillsdale, NJ: Erlbaum.

Anderson, J. R. (1996). ACT: A simple theory of complex cognition. *American Psychologist, 51,* 355–365.

Andrews, S. (1982). Phonological recoding: Is the regularity effect consistent? *Memory and Cognition, 10,* 565–575.

Angus, L. (1996). An intensive analysis of metaphor themes in psychotherapy. In S. Mio & N. Katz (Eds.), *Metaphor: Implications and applications* (pp. 73–84). Mahwah, NJ: Erlbaum.

Ardila, A. (in press). Spanish-English bilingualism in the United States. In F. Babbro (Ed.), *Brain and mind in bilinguals.*

Athey, I. (1970). Affective factors in reading. In H. Singer & R. B. Ruddell (Eds.), *Theoretical models and processes of reading* (pp. 98–123). Newark, DE: International Reading Association.

Atkinson, R. C., & Shiffrin, R. (1968). Human memory: A proposed system and its control processes. In K. Spence & J. Spence (Eds.), *The psychology of learning and motivation* (Vol. 2, pp. 89–195). New York: Academic Press.

Austin, J. L. (1962). *How to do things with words.* New York: Oxford University Press.

Ayers, T. J. (1984). Silent reading time for tongue-twister paragraphs. *American Journal of Psychology, 97,* 607–609.

Baars, B. J., Motley, M. T., & MacKay, D. G. (1975). Output editing for lexical status in artificially elicited slips of the tongue. *Journal of Verbal Learning and Verbal Behavior, 14,* 382–391.

Babcock, R. L., & Salthouse, T. A. (1990). Effects of increased processing demands on age differences in working memory. *Psychology and Aging, 5,* 421–428.

Bachorowski, J. (1999). Vocal expression and perception of emotion. *Current Directions in Psychological Science, 8,* 53–56.

Bachorowski, J., & Owren, M. J. (1995). Vocal expression of emotion: Acoustic properties of speech are associated with emotional intensity and context. *Psychological Science, 6,* 219–224.

Baddeley, A. D. (1976). *The psychology of memory.* New York: Basic Books.

Baddeley, A. D. (1986). *Working memory.* New York: Oxford University Press.

Baddeley, A. D., & Hitch, G. (1974). Working memory. In G. Bower (Ed.), *The psychology of learning and motivation* (Vol. 8, pp. 47–89). New York: Academic Press.

Baddeley, A. D., & Lewis, V. (1981). Inner active processes in reading: The inner voice, the inner ear, and the inner eye. In A. M. Lesgold & C. A. Perfetti (Eds.), *Interactive processes in reading* (pp. 107–129). Hillsdale, NJ: Erlbaum.

Baillargeon, R., Spelke, E., & Wasserman, S. (1985). Object permanence in five-month-old infants. *Cognition, 20,* 191–208.

Baird, R. M., & Rosenbaum, S. E. (1998). *Pornography: Private right or public menace?* Amherst, NY: Prometheus.

Baker, N., & Nelson, K. (1984). Recasting and related conversational techniques for triggering syntactic advances by young children. *First Language, 5,* 3–22.

Ball, E. W., & Blachman, B. A. (1991). Does phoneme awareness training in kindergarten make a difference in early word recognition and developmental spelling? *Reading Research Quarterly, 25,* 49–66.

Balota, D. A. (1994). Visual word recognition: The journey from features to meaning. In M. A. Gernsbacher (Ed.), *Handbook of psycholinguistics* (pp. 303–358). New York: Academic Press.

Balota, D. A., & Chumbley, J. I. (1984). Are lexical decisions a good measure of lexical access? The role of word frequency in the neglected decision stage. *Journal of Experimental Psychology: Human Perception and Performance, 10,* 340–357.

Balota, D. A., & Spieler, D. H. (1999). Word frequency, repetition, and lexicality effects in word recognition tasks: Beyond measures of central tendency. *Journal of Experimental Psychology: General, 128,* 32–55.

Baratz, J. C. (1969). Teaching reading in an urban Negro school system. In J. C. Baratz & R. Shuy (Eds.), *Teaching black children to read* (pp. 92–116). Washington, DC: Center for Applied Linguistics.

Baron, J. (1973). Phonemic stage not necessary for reading. *Quarterly Journal of Experimental Psychology, 25,* 241–246.

Baron, J., & Strawson, C. (1976). Use of orthographic and word-specific knowledge in reading words aloud. *Journal of Experimental Psychology: Human Perception and Performance, 4,* 207–214.

Barrett, M. (1986). Early semantic representations and early word usage. In S. Kuczaj & M. Barrett (Eds.), *The development of word meaning* (pp. 39–67). New York: Springer-Verlag.

Barron, R. W. (1992). Proto-literacy, literacy, and the acquisition of phonological awareness. *Learning and Individual Differences, 3,* 243–255.

Barsalou, L. (1983). Ad hoc categories. *Memory and Cognition, 11,* 211–217.

Bartlett, F. C. (1932). *Remembering.* Cambridge: Cambridge University Press.

Bates, E. (1976). *Language and context: The acquisition of pragmatics.* New York: Academic Press.

Bates, E. (1979). *The emergence of symbols: Cognition and communication in infancy.* New York: Academic Press.

Bates, E., Benigni, L., Bretherton, I., Camaioni, L., & Volterra, V. (1979). *The emergence of symbols: Cognition and communication in infancy.* New York: Academic Press.

Bates, E., Camaioni, L., & Volterra, V. (1975). The acquisition of performatives prior to speech. *Merrill-Palmer Quarterly, 21,* 205–226.

Bates, E., & Elman, J. (1996). Learning rediscovered. *Science, 247,* 1849–1850.

Bates, E., & Goodman, J. (1999). On the emergence of grammar from the lexicon. In B. MacWhinney (Ed.), *The emergence of language* (pp. 29–80). Mahwah, NJ: Erlbaum.

Bates, E., & MacWhinney, B. (1981). Second language acquisition from a functionalist perspective: Pragmatic, semantic, and perceptual strategies. In H. Winitz (Ed.), *Annals of the New York Academy of Sciences Conference on Native and Foreign Language Acquisition.* New York: New York Academy of Sciences.

Bates, E., & MacWhinney, B. (1982). Functionalist approaches to grammar. In E. Wanner & L. R. Gleitman (Eds.), *Language acquisition: The state of the art* (pp. 173–218). Cambridge: Cambridge University Press.

Bates, E., Marchman, V., Thal, D., Fenson, L., Dale, P., Reznick, J. S., Reilly, J., & Hartung, J. (1994). Developmental and stylistic variation in the composition of early vocabulary. *Journal of Child Language, 21,* 85–123.

Bates, E., O'Connell, B., & Shore, C. (1987). Language and communication in infancy. In J. Osofsky (Ed.), *Handbook of infant development* (pp. 149–203). New York: Wiley.

Bates, E., & Snyder, L. (1987). The cognitive hypothesis in language development. In I. Uzgiris & J. Hunt (Eds.), *Research with scales of psychological development in infancy* (pp. 168–206). Champaign-Urbana: University of Illinois Press.

Bates, E., Wulfeck, B., & MacWhinney, B. (1991). Cross-linguistic research in aphasia: An overview. *Brain and Language, 41,* 123–148.

Batic, N., & Gabassi, P. G. (1987). Visual dominance in olfactory memory. *Perceptual and Motor Skills, 65,* 88–90.

Bavelier, D., Corina, D., Jezzard, P., Clark, V., Karni, A., & Lalwani, A. (1998). Hemispheric specialization for English and ASL: Left invariance, right variability. *Neuroreport, 9,* 1537–1542.

Beach, C. M. (1991). The interpretation of prosodic patterns at joints of syntactic structural ambiguity: Evidence for cue trading relations. *Journal of Memory and Language, 30,* 644–663.

Beattie, G., & Coughlan, J. (1999). An experimental investigation of the role of iconic gestures in lexical access using the tip-of-the-tongue phenomenon. *British Journal of Psychology, 90*(1), 35–56.

Beck, A. T. (1976). *Cognitive therapy and the emotional disorder.* New York: International Universities Press.

Beck, I. L., Perfetti, C. A., & McKeown, M. G. (1982). Effects of long-term vocabulary instruction on lexical access and reading comprehension. *Journal of Educational Psychology, 74,* 506–521.

Becker, C. A. (1979). Semantic context and word frequency effects in visual word recognition. *Journal of Experimental Psychology: Human Perception and Performance, 5,* 252–259.

Beeman, M., & Chiarello, C. (Eds.). (1998). *Right hemisphere language comprehension: Perspectives from cognitive neuroscience.* Mahwah, NJ: Erlbaum.

Beeman, M., & Gernsbacher, M. A. (1992). *Structure building and coherence inferencing during comprehension.* Unpublished manuscript, University of Oregon, Eugene.

Bekerian, D. A., & Dennett, J. L. (1993). The cognitive interview: Reviewing the issues. *Applied Cognitive Psychology, 7,* 275–297.

Bellugi, U. (1967). *The acquisition of negation.* Unpublished doctoral dissertation, Harvard University, Cambridge, MA.

Benedict, H. (1979). Early lexical development: Comprehension and production. *Journal of Child Language, 6,* 183–200.

Benjamin, L. T., Jr. (1997). *A history of psychology: Original sources and contemporary research.* New York: McGraw-Hill.

Benton, S. L., Kraft, R. G., Glover, J. A., & Plake, B. S. (1984). Cognitive capacity differences among writers. *Journal of Educational Psychology, 76,* 820–834.

Bereiter, C., & Scardamalia, M. (1987). *The psychology of written composition.* Hillsdale, NJ: Erlbaum.

Berges, E. T., Neiderbach, S., Rubin, B., Sharpe, E. F., & Tesler, R. W. (1983). *Children and sex: The parents speak.* New York: Facts on File.

Berko, J. (1958). The child's learning of English morphology. *Word, 14,* 47–56.

Berko, J., & Brown, R. (1960). Psycholinguistics research methods. In P. H. Mussen (Ed.), *Handbook of research methods in child development* (pp. 517–557). New York: Wiley.

Berko-Gleason, J. (1977). Talking to children: Some notes on feedback. In C. E. Snow & C. Ferguson (Eds.), *Talking to children: Language input and acquisition.* Cambridge: Cambridge University Press.

Berko-Gleason, J. (1997). *The development of language.* Needham Heights, MA: Allyn & Bacon.

Berko-Gleason, J., Hay, D., & Cain, L. (1989). The social and affective determinants of language development. In M. Rice & R. Schiefelbusch (Eds.), *The teachability of language* (pp. 171–186). Baltimore: Brookes.

Berko-Gleason, J., & Melzi, G. (1997). The mutual construction of narrative by mothers and children: Cross-cultural observations. *Journal of Narrative and Life History, 7,* 217–222.

Berlin, B. & Kay, P. (1969). *Basic color terms: Their universality and evaluation.* Los Angeles: University of California Press.

Berman, R., & Slobin, D. I. (1994). *Relating events in narrative: A crosslinguistic developmental study.* Hillsdale, NJ: Erlbaum.

Bernstein, B. (1961). Social class and linguistic development: A theory of social learning. In A. Halsey, J. Floud, & C. D. Anderson (Eds.), *Education, economy, and society* (p. 228). New York: Free Press.

Bernstein, B. (1974). *Class, codes, and control: Theoretical studies towards a sociology of language.* London: Routledge & Kegan Paul.

Best, C. (1994). The emergence of native-language phonological influences in infants: A perceptual assimilation model. In J. Goodman & H. Nusbaum (Eds.), *The development of speech perception: The transition from speech sounds to spoken words* (pp. 167–224). Cambridge, MA: MIT Press.

Bhatia, R., & Ritchie, W. (1999). The bilingual child: Some issues and perspectives. In W. Ritchie & T. Bhatia (Eds.), *Handbook of child language acquisition* (pp. 569–646). San Diego, CA: Academic Press.

Bialystok, E., & Hakuta, K. (1994). *In other words: The science and psychology of second-language acquisition.* New York: Basic Books.

Bijeljac-Babic, R., Bertoncini, J., & Mehler, J. (1993). How do 4-day-old infants categorize multisyllabic utterances? *Developmental Psychology, 29,* 711–721.

Bijeljac-Babic, R., Biardeau, A., & Grainger, J. (1997). Masked orthographic priming in bilingual word recognition. *Memory and Cognition, 25,* 447–457.

Black, M. (1962). *Models and metaphors: Studies in language and philosophy.* Ithaca, NY: Cornell University Press.

Black, M. (1979). More about metaphors. In A. Ortony (Ed.), *Metaphor and thought* (pp. 19–43). New York: Cambridge University Press.

Blasko, D. (1999). Only the tip of the iceberg: Who understands what about metaphor? *Journal of Pragmatics, 31,* 1675–1683.

Bleasdale, F. A. (1987). Concreteness-dependent associative priming: Separate lexical organization for concrete and abstract words. *Journal of Experimental Psychology: Learning, Memory, and Cognition, 13,* 582–594.

Bloom, L. (1991). *Language development from two to three.* Cambridge: Cambridge University Press.

Bloom, L., Lifter, K., & Hafitz, J. (1980). Semantics and verbs and the development of verb inflections in child language. *Language, 56,* 386–412.

Bloom, P. (Ed.). (1993). *Language acquisition: Core readings.* Cambridge, MA: MIT Press.

Bloom, P. (1994). Recent controversies in the study of language acquisition. In M. A. Gernsbacher (Ed.), *Handbook of psycholinguistics* (pp. 741–779). New York: Academic Press.

Blumenthal, A. L. (1970). *Language and psychology: Historical aspects of psycholinguistics.* New York: Wiley.

Bock, K., & Levelt, W. J. M. (1994). Language production: Grammatical encoding. In M. A. Gernsbacher (Ed.), *Handbook of psycholinguistics* (pp. 945–984). New York: Academic Press.

Bohannon, J. N., MacWhinney, B., & Snow, C. E. (1990). Negative evidence revisited: Beyond learnability, or who has to prove what to whom? *Developmental Psychology, 26,* 221–226.

Bohannon, J. N., & Stanowicz, L. (1988). Adult responses to children's language errors: The issue of negative evidence. *Developmental Psychology, 24,* 684–689.

Bohannon, J. N., & Warren-Leubecker, A. (1988). Recent developments in child-directed speech: You've come a long way, baby-talk. *Language Science, 10,* 89–110.

Bonvillian, J. D., Orlansky, M. D., & Novack, L. L. (1983). Developmental milestones: Sign language acquisition and motor development. *Child Development, 54,* 1435–1445.

Bourdieu, P., & Passeron, J. C. (1990). *Reproduction in education, society and culture* (2nd ed.). Thousand Oaks, CA: Sage.

Bowerman, M. (1976). Semantic factors in the acquisition of rules for word use and sentence conduction. In D. Morehead & A. Morehead (Eds.), *Normal and deficient child language* (pp. 99–180). Baltimore: University Park Press.

Bowerman, M. (1979). The acquisition of complex sentences. In P. Fletcher & B. MacWhinney (Eds.), *Language acquisition* (pp. 285–306). Cambridge: Cambridge University Press.

Bowerman, M. (1982). Reorganizational processes in lexical and syntactic development. In E. Wanner & L. R. Gleitman (Eds.), *Language acquisition: The state of the art* (pp. 319–346). Cambridge: Cambridge University Press.

Bowers, J. S., Vigliocco, G., Stadthagen-Gonzalez, H., & Vinson, D. (1999). Distinguishing language from thought: Experimental evidence that syntax is lexically rather than conceptually represented. *Psychological Science, 10,* 310–315.

Bradley, D. C. (1983). *Computational distinctions of vocabulary type.* Bloomington: Indiana University Linguistics Club.

Bradley, D. C., Garrett, M. F., & Zurif, E. B. (1980). Syntactic deficits in Broca's aphasia. In D. Caplan (Ed.), *Biological studies of mental processes* (pp. 269–286). Cambridge, MA: MIT Press.

Bradley, L., & Bryant, P. E. (1983). Categorizing sounds and learning to read: A causal connection. *Nature (London), 301,* 419–421.

Braine, M. (1994). Is nativism sufficient? *Journal of Child Language, 21,* 9–32.

Brakke, K. E., & Savage-Rumbaugh, E. S. (1996). The development of language skills in pan: II. Production. *Language and Communication, 16,* 361–380.

Brand, A. (1991). Social cognition, emotions, and the psychology of writing. *Journal of Advanced Composition, 11,* 395–407.

Brandt, A. M., & Rozin, P. (1997). *Morality and health.* New York: Routledge.

Bransford, J. D., Barclay, J. R., & Franks, J. J. (1972). Sentence memory: A constructive versus interpretive approach. *Cognitive Psychology, 3,* 193–209.

Braun, K. A., & Loftus, E. F. (1998). Advertising's misinformation effect. *Applied Cognitive Psychology, 12,* 569–591.

Breetvelt, I., van den Bergh, H., & Rijlaarsdam, G. (1994). Relations between writing processes and text quality: When and how? *Cognition and Instruction, 12,* 103–123.

Brodmann, K. (1909). *Vergleichende Lokalisationlehre der Großhirnrinde in ihren Prinzipien dergestallt auf des zallenbaves* [Comparative localization theory of the cerebral cortex]. Leipzig, Germany: Barth.

Brody, L., Zelazo, P., & Chaika, H. (1984). Habituation-dishabituation to speech in the neonate. *Developmental Psychology, 20,* 114–119.

Brown, A. S. (1991). A review of the tip-of-the-tongue experience. *Psychological Bulletin, 109,* 204–223.

Brown, R. (1965). *Social psychology.* New York: Free Press.

Brown, R. (1968). The development of *Wh*-questions in child speech. *Journal of Verbal Learning and Verbal Behavior, 7,* 279–290.

Brown. R. (1973). *A first language: The early stages.* Cambridge, MA: Harvard University Press.

Brown, R., Cazden, C., & Bellugi, U. (1967). *The child's grammar from 1 to 3.* Paper presented at the Minnesota Symposium on Child Psychology, Minneapolis.

Brown, R., & Fraser, C. (1963). The acquisition of syntax. In C. Cofer & B. Musgrave (Eds.), *Verbal behavior and learning: Problems and processes* (pp. 158–201). New York: McGraw-Hill.

Brown, R., & Gilman, A. (1960). The pronouns of power and solidarity. In T. A. Sebeok (Ed.), *Style in language* (pp. 253–276). Cambridge, MA: MIT Press.

Brown, R., & Gilman, A. (1989). Politeness theory and Shakespeare's four major tragedies. *Language in Society, 18,* 159–212.

Brown, R., & Hanlon, C. (1970). Derivational complexity and order of acquisition in child speech. In J. Hayes (Ed.), *Cognition and the development of language* (pp. 11–54). New York: Wiley.

Brown, R., & Lenneberg, E. (1954). A study in language and cognition. *Journal of Abnormal and Social Psychology, 49,* 454–462.

Brown, R., & Levinson, S. (1987). *Politeness: Some universals in language usage.* Cambridge: Cambridge University Press.

Brown, R., & McNeill, D. (1966). The "tip of the tongue" phenomenon. *Journal of Verbal Learning and Verbal Behavior, 5,* 325–337.

Brownell, H. H., Potter, H. H., Michelow, D., & Gardner, H. (1984). Sensitivity to lexical denotation and connotation in brain-damaged patients: A double dissociation? *Brain and Language, 22,* 253–264.

Bruner, J. S. (1975). The ontogenesis of speech acts. *Journal of Child Language, 2,* 1–19.

Bruner, J. S. (1983). *Child's talk: Learning to use language.* New York: Norton.

Bruner, J. S. (1990). *Acts of meaning.* Cambridge, MA: Harvard University Press.

Bruner, J. S. (1995). From joint attention to the meeting of minds: An introduction. In C. Moore & P. J. Dunham (Eds.), *Joint attention: Its origins and role in development* (pp. 1–14). Hillsdale, NJ: Erlbaum.

Bruning, R. H., Schraw, G. J., & Ronning, R. R. (1995). *Cognitive psychology and instruction* (3rd ed.). Upper Saddle River, NJ: Prentice Hall.

Bryant, P. E., & Bradley, L. (1985). *Children's reading problems.* Oxford: Blackwell.

Bucci, W. (1984). Linking words and things: Basic processes and individual variation. *Cognition, 17,* 137–153.

Bucci, W. (1993). The development of emotional meaning in free association. In J. Gedo & S. Wilson (Eds.), *Hierarchical conceptions in psychoanalysis* (pp. 3–47). New York: Guilford Press.

Bucci, W. (1995). The power of the narrative: A multiple code account. In J. Pennebaker (Ed.), *Emotion, disclosure, and health* (pp. 93–122). Washington, DC: American Psychological Association.

Bucci, W. (1997). Symptoms and symbols: A multiple code theory of somatization. *Psychoanalytic Inquiry, 17,* 151–172.

Bucci, W. (2000). The need for a "psychoanalytic psychology" in cognitive psychology. *Psychoanalytic Psychology, 17,* 203–224.

Bucci, W., & Freedman, N. (1978). Language and hand: The dimension of referential competence. *Journal of Personality, 46,* 594–622.

Buckner, J., & Fivush, R. (1998). Gender and self in children's autobiographical narratives. *Applied Cognitive Psychology, 12*, 407–429.

Burke, D., MacKay, D., Worthley, J., & Wade, E. (1991). On the tip of the tongue: What causes word finding failures in young and older adults? *Journal of Memory and Language, 30*, 542–579.

Butterfield, J. (Ed.). (1986). *Language, mind, and logic.* New York: Cambridge University Press.

Byrne, P. S., & Long, B. (1976). *Doctors talking to patients: A study of the verbal behavior of general practitioners consulting in their surgeries.* London: Her Majesty's Stationery Office.

Cabeza, R., & Nyberg, L. (2000). Imaging cognition II: An empirical review of 275 PET and fMRI studies. *Journal of Cognitive Neuroscience, 12*, 1–47.

Caccaiari, C., & Glucksberg, S. (1994). Understanding figurative language. In M. A. Gernsbacher (Ed.), *Handbook of psycholinguistics* (pp. 447–477). New York: Academic Press.

Cain, W. (1979). To know the nose: Keys to odor identification. *Science, 203*, 467–470.

Canary, D. J., & Dindia, K. (Eds.). (1998). *Sex differences and similarities in communication: Critical essays and empirical investigations of sex and gender in interaction.* Mahwah, NJ: Erlbaum.

Capirci, O., Iverson, J., Pizuto, E., & Volterra, V. (1996). Communicative gestures and the transition to two-word speech. *Journal of Child Language, 23*, 645–673.

Caplan, D. (1994). Language and the brain. In M. A. Gernsbacher (Ed.), *Handbook of psycholinguistics* (pp. 1023–1053). New York: Academic Press.

Caplan, D., & Waters, G. (1990). Short-term memory and language comprehension: A critical review of the neuropsychological literature. In G. Vallar & T. Shallace (Eds.), *Neuropsychological impairments of short-term memory* (pp. 337–389). New York: Cambridge University Press.

Caramazza, A., & Zurif, E. B. (1976). Dissociation of algorithmic and heuristic processes in language comprehension: Evidence from aphasia. *Brain and Language, 3*, 572–582.

Carey, L. J., Flower, L., Hayes, J. R., Schriver, K. A., & Haas, C. (1989). *Differences in writers' initial task representatives.* Berkeley, CA: Center for the Study of Writing. (ERIC Document Reproduction Service No. ED 310 403)

Carey, S. (1978). The child as word learner. In M. Halle, J. Bresnan, & G. A. Miller (Eds.), *Linguistic theory and psychological reality* (pp. 264–293). Cambridge, MA: MIT Press.

Carmichael, L., Hogan, H., & Walter, A. (1932). An experimental study of the effect of language on representation of visually perceived form. *Journal of Experimental Psychology, 15*, 73–86.

Carpenter, M., Nagell, K., & Tomasello, M. (1998). Social cognition, joint attention, and communicative competence from 9 to 15 months of age. *Monographs of the Society for Research in Child Development, 63*(4, Serial No. 255).

Carpenter, P. A., & Just, M. A. (1989). The role of working memory in language comprehension. In D. Klahr & K. Kotovsky (Eds.), *Complex information processing: The impact of Herbert A. Simon* (pp. 31–68). Hillsdale, NJ: Erlbaum.

Carpenter, P. A., Miyake, A., & Just, M. A. (1994). Working memory constraints in comprehension: Evidence from individual differences, aphasia, and aging. In M. A. Gernsbacher (Ed.), *Handbook of psycholinguistics* (pp. 1075–1122). New York: Academic Press.

Carpenter, P. A., Miyake, A., & Just, M. A. (1995). Language comprehension: Sentence and discourse processing. *Annual Review of Psychology, 46*, 91–120.

Carr, A. G. (1991). *Theoretical considerations of the Daneman and Carpenter paradigm for the study of working memory span.* Unpublished doctoral dissertation, New School for Social Research, New York.

Carroll, D. (1999). *Psychology of language.* Pacific Grove, CA: Brooks/Cole.

Caselli, M., Bates, E., Casadio, P., Fenson, J., Fenson, L., Sanders, L., & Weir, J. (1995). A cross–linguistic study of early lexical development. *Cognitive Development, 10*, 159–199.

Cassady, M. (1990). *Storytelling, step by step.* San Jose, CA: Resource Publications.

Cattell, J. M. (1885). The time to recognize and name letters, pictures, and colors. *Philosophische Studien, 2*, 635–650.

Chafe, W. (1992, August). *Intonation units and prominences in English natural discourse.* Paper submitted at the University of Pennsylvania Prosodic Workshop, Philadelphia.

Chafe, W. (1998). Things we can learn from repeated tellings of the same experience. *Narrative Inquiry, 8,* 269–285.

Chaika, E. (1994). *Language: The social mirror.* Boston: Newbury House.

Chaika, E. (2000). *Linguistics pragmatics and psychotherapy: A guide for therapists.* London: Whurr.

Chall, J. (1983). *Stages of reading development.* New York: McGraw-Hill.

Chenail, R. J., & Fortugno, L. (1995). Resourceful figures in therapeutic conversations. In G. H. Morris & R. J. Chenail (Eds.), *Talk of the clinic: Explorations in the analysis of medical and therapeutic discourse* (pp. 71–88). Hillsdale, NJ: Erlbaum.

Cheney, D. L., & Seyfarth, R. M. (1990). *How monkeys see the world: Inside the mind of another species.* Chicago: University of Chicago Press.

Cheney, D. L., & Seyfarth, R. M. (1999). Recognition of other individual's social relationships by female baboons. *Animal Behaviour, 58,* 67–75.

Chiappe, D., & Kennedy, J. (2000). Are metaphors elliptical similes? *Journal of Psycholinguistic Research, 29,* 371–398.

Chomsky, N. (1957). *Syntactic structures.* The Hague, Netherlands: Mouton.

Chomsky, N. (1959). A review of Skinner's *Verbal Behavior. Language, 35,* 26–58.

Chomsky, N. (1965). *Aspects of the theory of syntax.* Cambridge, MA: MIT Press.

Chomsky, N. (1981). *Lectures on government and binding.* Dordrecht, Netherlands: Foris.

Chomsky, N. (1982). Discussion of Putnam's comments. In M. Piatelli-Palamarini (Ed.), *Language and learning: The debate between Jean Piaget and Noam Chomsky* (pp. 310–324). Cambridge, MA: Harvard University Press.

Chomsky, N. (1988). *Language and problems of knowledge.* Cambridge, MA: MIT Press.

Chomsky, N. (1989). *Necessary illusions: Thought control in democratic societies.* Boston: South End Press.

Chomsky, N. (1991). Linguistics and cognitive science: Problems and mysteries. In A. Kasher (Ed.), *The Chomskian turn* (pp. 26–53). Cambridge, MA: Blackwell.

Chomsky, N., & Halle, M. (1968). *The sound pattern of English.* New York: Harper & Row.

Clachar, A. (2000). Redressing ethnic conflict through morphosyntactic "creativity" in code mixing. *Language and Communication, 20,* 311–327.

Clancy, P. (1985). The acquisition of Japanese. In D. I. Slobin (Ed.), *The crosslinguistic study of language acquisition: Vol. 1. The data.* Hillsdale, NJ: Erlbaum.

Clark, E. (1978). From gesture to word: On the natural history of deixis in language acquisition. In J. S. Bruner & A. Garton (Eds.), *Human growth and development* (pp. 85–120). Oxford: Oxford University Press.

Clark, E. (1982). The young word maker: A case study of innovations in the child's lexicon. In E. Wanner & L. R. Gleitman (Eds.), *Language acquisition: The state of the art* (pp. 390–425). Cambridge: Cambridge University Press.

Clark, E. (1993). *The lexicon of acquisition.* Cambridge: Cambridge University Press.

Clark, E. (1995). Later lexical development and word formation. In P. Fletcher & B. MacWhinney (Eds.), *The handbook of child language* (pp. 393–412). Oxford: Blackwell.

Clark, H. H. (1977). Inferences in comprehension. In D. La Berge & S. J. Samuels (Eds.), *Perception and comprehension* (pp. 243–263). Hillsdale, NJ: Erlbaum.

Clark, H. H. (1983). Making sense of nonce sense. In G. Flores d'Arcais & R. Jarvella (Eds.), *The process of language understanding* (pp. 297–331). Chichester: Wiley.

Clark, H. H. (1994). Discourse in production. In M. A. Gernsbacher (Ed.), *Handbook of psycholinguistics* (pp. 985–1021). New York: Academic Press.

Clark, H. H. (1996). *Using language.* Cambridge: Cambridge University Press.

Clark, H. H., & Clark, E. (1977). *Psychology and language: An introduction to psycholinguistics.* New York: Harcourt Brace Jovanovich.

Clark, H. H., & Gerrig, R. J. (1983). Understanding old words with new meanings. *Journal of Verbal Learning and Verbal Behavior, 22,* 591–608.

Clark, H. H., & Gerrig, R. J. (1984). On the pretense theory of irony. *Journal of Experimental Psychology: General, 113,* 121–126.

Clark, H. H., & Haviland, S. E. (1977). Comprehension and the given-new contract. In R. O. Freedle (Ed.), *Discourse production and comprehension* (pp. 1–40). Norwood, NJ: Ablex.

Clark, H. H., & Lucy, P. (1975). Understanding what is meant from what is said: A study in conversationally conveyed requests. *Journal of Verbal Learning and Verbal Behavior, 14,* 56–72.

Clark, H. H., & Schaefer, E. F. (1989). Contributing to discourse. *Cognitive Science, 13,* 259–294.

Clark, H. H., & Schunk, D. (1980). Polite responses to polite requests. *Cognition, 8,* 111–143.

Clark, H. H., & Schunk, D. (1981). Politeness in requests: A rejoinder to Kemper and Thissen. *Cognition, 9,* 311–315.

Clayman, S. E. (1992). Footing in the achievement of neutrality: The case of news-interview discourse. In P. Drew & J. Heritage (Eds.), *Talk at work: Interaction in institutional settings* (pp. 163–198). Cambridge: Cambridge University Press.

Clifton, C. (1992). Tracing the course of sentence comprehension: How lexical information is used. In K. Rayner (Ed.), *Eye movements and visual cognition: Scene perception and reading* (pp. 397–414). New York: Springer-Verlag.

Clifton, C., & Ferreira, F. (1987). Discourse structure and anaphora: Some experimental results. In M. Coltheart (Ed.), *Attention and performance: Vol. 12. The psychology of reading* (pp. 635–654). London: Erlbaum.

Code, C. (1987). *Language, aphasia, and the right hemisphere.* New York: Wiley.

Code, C. (1989). Speech automatisms and recurrent utterances. In C. Code (Ed.), *The characteristics of aphasia* (pp. 155–177). London: Taylor & Francis.

Collins, A. M. (1977). Processes in acquiring knowledge. In R. C. Anderson, R. J. Spiro, & W. E. Montague (Eds.), *Schooling and the acquisition of knowledge* (pp. 339–363). Hillsdale, NJ: Erlbaum.

Collins, A. M., & Loftus, E. F. (1975). A spreading activation theory of semantic processing. *Psychological Review, 82,* 240–248.

Collins, A. M., & Quillian, M. R. (1969). Retrieval time from semantic memory. *Journal of Verbal Learning and Verbal Behavior, 8,* 240–247.

Collins, A. M., & Quillian, M. R. (1972). How to make a language user. In E. Tulving & W. Donaldson (Eds.), *Organization of memory* (pp. 309–351). New York: Academic Press.

Colston, H., & Keller, S. (1998). You'll never believe this: Irony and hyperbole in expressing surprise. *Journal of Psycholinguistic Research, 27,* 499–513.

Colston, H., & O'Brien, J. (2000). Contrast and pragmatics in figurative language: Anything understatement can do, irony can do better. *Journal of Pragmatics, 32,* 1557–1583.

Coltheart, M. (1978). Lexical access in simple reading tasks. In G. Underwood (Ed.), *Strategies of information processing* (pp. 151–216). New York: Academic Press.

Coltheart, M., Curtis, B., Atkins, P., & Haller, M. (1993). Models of reading aloud: Dual-route and parallel distributed-processing approaches. *Psychological Review, 100,* 589–608.

Coltheart, M., Davelaar, E., Jonasson, J. T., & Besner, D. (1977). Access to the internal lexicon. In S. Dornic (Ed.), *Attention and performance* (Vol. 6, pp. 535–555). Hillsdale, NJ: Erlbaum.

Coltheart, M., Rastle, K., Perry, C., Langdon, R., & Ziegler, J. (2001). DRC: A dual route cascaded model of visual word recognition and reading aloud. *Psychological Review, 108,* 204–256.

Commission on Obscenity and Pornography. (1970). *The report of the Commission on Obscenity and Pornography.* New York: Bantam.

Conrad, C. (1972). Cognitive economy in semantic memory. *Journal of Experimental Psychology, 92,* 149–154.

Conrad, R. (1972). Speech and reading. In J. Kavanagh & I. Mattingly (Eds.), *Language by ear and by eye* (pp. 205–240). Cambridge, MA: MIT Press.

Conrad, R. (1977). The reading ability of deaf school-leavers. *British Journal of Educational Psychology, 47,* 138–148.

Cooper, R., & Aslin, R. (1990). Preference for infant-directed speech in the first month after birth. *Child Development, 61,* 1584–1595.

Corteen, R., & Woods, B. (1972). Autonomic response to shock-associated words in an unattended channel. *Journal of Experimental Psychology, 94,* 308–313.

Corts, D., & Pollio, H. R. (1999). Spontaneous production of figurative language and gesture in college lectures. *Metaphor and Symbol, 14,* 81–100.

Cowan, N. (1988). Evolving conceptions of memory storage, selective attention, and their mutual constraints within the human information-processing system. *Psychological Bulletin, 104,* 163–191.

Cuetos, F., & Mitchell, D. C. (1988). Cross-linguistic differences in parsing: Restrictions on the use of the late closure strategy in Spanish. *Cognition, 30,* 73–105.

Curtiss, S. (1981). Dissociations between language and cognition: Cases and implications. *Journal of Autism and Developmental Disorders, 11,* 15–30.

Cutler, A. (1982). Idioms: The colder the older. *Linguistic Inquiry, 13,* 317–320.

Cutler, A. (1994). Segmentation problems, rhythmic solutions. In L. R. Gleitman & B. Landau (Eds.), *The acquisition of the lexicon* (pp. 81–104). Cambridge, MA: Elsevier/MIT Press.

Damasio, A. R. (1994). *Descartes' error.* New York: Putnam.

Daneman, M., & Carpenter, P. A. (1980). Individual differences in working memory and reading. *Journal of Verbal Learning and Verbal Behavior, 19,* 450–466.

Danks, J. H. (1977). Producing ideas and sentences. In S. Rosenberg (Ed.), *Sentence production: Developments in research and theory* (pp. 229–258). Hillsdale, NJ: Erlbaum.

Daugherty, K., & Seidenberg, M. (1994). Beyond rules and exceptions: A connectionist approach to inflectional morphology. In S. D. Lima, R. L. Corrigan, & G. K. Iverson (Eds.), *The reality of linguistic rules* (pp. 353–388). Philadelphia: Benjamins.

Davies, I., & Corbett, G. (1997). A cross-cultural study of colour grouping: Evidence for weak linguistic relativity. *British Journal of Psychology, 88,* 493–517.

Davies, I., Sowden, P., Jerrett, D., Jerrett, T., & Corbett, G. (1998). A cross-cultural study of English and Setswana speakers on a colour triads task: A test of the Sapir-Whorf hypothesis. *British Journal of Psychology, 89,* 1–15.

de Boysson-Bardies, B., Halle, P., Sagart, L., & Durand, C. (1989). A cross-linguistic investigation of vowel formants in babbling. *Journal of Child Language, 16,* 1–17.

de Boysson-Bardies, B., Sagart, L., & Durand, C. (1984). Discernable differences in babbling of infants according to target language. *Journal of Child Language, 8,* 511–524.

de Boysson-Bardies, B., Vihman, M., Roug-Hellichius, L., Durand, C., Landberg, I., & Arao, F. (1992). Material evidence of infant selection from target language: A cross-linguistic study. In C. Ferguson, L. Menn, & C. Stoel-Gammon (Eds.), *Phonological development* (pp. 369–391). Timonium, MD: York Press.

De Casper, A., & Fifer, W. (1980). Of human bonding: Newborns prefer their mothers' voices. *Science, 208,* 1174–1176.

De Casper, A., & Spence, M. (1986). Prenatal maternal speech influences newborns' perception of speech sounds. *Infant Behavior and Development, 9,* 133–150.

Deese, J. (1970). *Psycholinguistics.* Baltimore: Johns Hopkins University Press.

de Groot, A. M. B. (1989). Representational aspects of word imageability and word frequency as assessed through word associations. *Journal of Experimental Psychology: Learning, Memory, and Cognition, 15,* 824–845.

de Houwer, A. (1995). Bilingual language acquisition. In P. Fletcher & B. MacWhinney (Eds.), *The handbook of child language* (pp. 219–250). Oxford: Blackwell.

de Klerk, V. (1990). Slang: A male domain? *Sex Roles, 22,* 589–606.

de Klerk, V. (1991). Expletives: Men only? *Communication Monographs, 58,* 156–169.

de Klerk, V. (1992). How taboo are taboo words for girls? *Language in Society, 21,* 277–289.

Delattre, P., Liberman, A. M., Cooper, F. S., & Gerstman, L. J. (1952). An experimental study of the acoustic determinants of vowel color: Observations on one- and two-formant vowels synthesized from spectrographic patterns. *Word, 8,* 195–210.

Dell, G. S. (1985). Positive feedback in hierarchical connectionist models: Applications to language production. *Cognitive Science, 9,* 3–23.

Dell, G. S. (1986). A spreading activation theory of retrieval in sentence production. *Psychological Review, 93,* 283–321.

Dell, G. S. (1995). Speaking and misspeaking. In L. R. Gleitman & M. Liberman (Eds.), *An invitation to cognitive science: Vol. 1. Language* (pp. 183–208). Cambridge, MA: MIT Press.

Dell, G. S., Burger L. K., & Svec, W. R. (1997). Language production in serial order: A functional analysis and a model. *Psychological Review, 104,* 123–147.

Dell, G. S., Chang, F., & Griffin, Z. M. (1999). Connectionist models of language production: Lexical access and grammatical encoding. *Cognitive Science, 23,* 517–542.

Dell, G. S., Reed, K. D., Adams, D. R., & Meyer, A. (2000). Speech errors, phonotactic constraints, and implicit learning: A study of the role of experience in language production. *Journal of Experimental Psychology: Learning, Memory, and Cognition, 26,* 1355–1367.

Della Corte, M., Benedict, H., & Klein, D. (1983). The relationship of pragmatic dimensions of mother's speech to the referential-expressive distinction. *Journal of Child Language, 10,* 35–43.

Demetras, M., Post, K., & Snow, C. E. (1986). Feedback to first language learners: The role of repetitions and clarification questions. *Journal of Child Language, 13,* 275–292.

Demuth, K. (1994). On the underspecification of functional categories in early grammars. In B. Lust, M. Suner, & J. Whitman (Eds.), *Syntactic theory and first language acquisition: Cross-linguistic perspectives* (pp. 119–134). Oxford: Blackwell.

Denes, P. B., & Pinson, E. N. (1993). *The speech chain: The physics and biology of spoken language* (2nd ed.). New York: Freeman.

de Ruiter, J. P. (2000). The production of gesture and speech. In D. McNeill (Ed.), *Language and gesture* (pp. 284–311). New York: Cambridge University Press.

Desor, J. A., & Beauchamp, G. K. (1974). The human capacity to transmit olfactory information. *Perception and Psychophysics, 16,* 551–556.

De Stefano, J. (1972). Social variation in language: Implications for teaching reading to black ghetto children. In J. A. Figurel (Ed.), *Better reading in urban schools* (pp. 18–24). Newark, DE: International Reading Association.

de Villiers, J. G., & de Villiers, P. A. (1973). A cross-sectional study of the acquisition of grammatical morphemes in child speech. *Journal of Psycholinguistic Research, 2,* 267–278.

de Villiers, J. G., & de Villiers, P. A. (1985). The acquisition of English. In D. I. Slobin (Ed.), *The crosslinguistic study of language acquisition: Vol. 1. The data.* Hillsdale, NJ: Erlbaum.

de Villiers, J. G., & Roeper, T. (1995). Relative clauses are barriers to wh- development for young children. *Journal of Child Language, 22,* 389–405.

de Villiers, J. G., Roeper, T., & Vainikka, A. (1990). The acquisition of long-distance rules. In L. Frazier & J. G. de Villiers (Eds.), *Language processing and acquisition.* Dordrecht, Netherlands: Kluwer.

de Vries, B., Blando, J. A., & Walker, L. J. (1995). An exploratory analysis of the content and structure of the life review. In B. Haight & J. Webster (Eds.), *The art and science of reminiscing. Theory, research, methods, and applications* (pp. 123–137). Washington, DC: Taylor & Francis.

Dews, S., & Winner, E. (1997). Attributing meaning to deliberate false utterances: The case of irony. In C. Mandell & A. McCabe (Eds.), *The problem of meaning: Behavioral and cognitive perspectives* (pp. 377–414). Amsterdam: North Holland/Elsevier.

Dews, S., & Winner, E. (1999). Obligatory processing of literal and nonliteral meanings in verbal irony. *Journal of Pragmatics, 31,* 1579–1599.

Dews, S., Winner, E., Kaplan, J., Rosenblatt, E., Hunt, M., Lim, K., McGovern, A., Qualter, A., & Smarsh, B. (1996). Children's understanding of the meaning and functions of verbal irony. *Child Development, 67,* 3071–3085.

Dingus, T. A., Hathaway, J. A., & Hunn, B. P. (1991). A most critical warning variable: Two demonstrations of the powerful effects of cost on warning compliance. *Proceedings of the*

Human Factors Society 35th Annual Meaning (pp. 1034–1038). Santa Monica, CA: Human Factors Society.

Donovan, P. (1998). School-based sexuality education: The issues and challenges. *Family Planning Perspectives, 30,* 188.

Dooling, D. J., & Lachman, R. (1971). Effects of comprehension on retention of prose. *Journal of Experimental Psychology, 88,* 216–222.

Drew, P. (1992). Contested evidence in a courtroom cross-examination: The case of a trial for rape. In P. Drew & J. Heritage (Eds.), *Talk at work: Interaction in institutional settings* (pp. 470–520). Cambridge: Cambridge University Press.

Dromi, E. (1987). *Early lexical development.* Cambridge: Cambridge University Press.

Du Bois, J. W. (1974). Syntax in mid-sentence. In *Berkeley studies in syntax and semantics* (Vol. 1, pp. III-1–III-25). Berkeley: University of California, Institute of Human Learning and Department of Linguistics.

Duffy, S. A., Morris, R. K., & Rayner, K. (1988). Lexical ambiguity and fixation times in reading. *Journal of Memory and Language, 27,* 429–446.

Duncan, S., & Fiske, D. W. (1985). *Interaction structure and strategy.* Cambridge: Cambridge University Press.

Durgunoglu, A. Y., & Oeney, B. (1999). A cross-linguistic comparison of phonological awareness and word recognition. *Reading and Writing, 11,* 281–299.

Eble, C. (1996). *College slang: In-group language among college students.* Chapel Hill: University of North Carolina Press.

Eckert, P. (1989). *Jocks and burnouts: Social categories and identity in the high school.* New York: Teachers College Press.

Eckert, P., & McConnell-Ginet, S. (1999). New generalizations and explanations in language and gender research. *Language in Society, 28,* 185–201.

Edworthy, J. (1998). Warnings and hazards: An integrative approach to warning research. *International Journal of Cognitive Ergonomics, 2*(1–2), 3–18.

Ehri, L. C. (1985). Effects of printed language acquisition on speech. In D. Olson, N. Torrance & A. Hildyard (Eds.), *Literacy, language and learning: The nature and consequences of reading and writing* (pp. 333–367). New York: Cambridge University Press.

Ellis, A. W. (1980). On the Freudian theory of speech errors. In V. A. Fromkin (Ed.), *Errors in linguistic performance: Slips of the tongue, ear, pen, and hand* (pp. 123–131). New York: Academic Press.

Elman, J. L., Bates, E., Johnson, M., Karmiloff-Smith, A., Parisi, D, & Plunkett, K. (1996). *Rethinking innateness: A connectionist perspective on development.* Cambridge, MA: Bradford Books.

Elman, J. L., & McClelland, J. L. (1986). Exploiting lawful variability in the speech waveform. In J. S. Perkell & D. H. Klatt (Eds.), *Invariance and variability in speech processes* (pp. 360–385). Hillsdale, NJ: Erlbaum.

Engen, T. (1991). *Odor sensation and memory.* New York: Praeger.

Engen, T., & Engen, E. (1997). Relationship between development of odor perception and language, *Enfance, 1,* 125–140.

Erickson, T. A., & Mattson, M. E. (1981). From words to meaning: A semantic illusion. *Journal of Verbal Learning and Verbal Behavior, 20,* 540–552.

Ervin, S. M. (1957, September). *Grammar and classification.* Paper presented at the annual meeting of the American Psychological Association, New York.

Ervin-Tripp, S. (1972). On sociolinguistic rules: Alternation and co-occurrence. In J. J. Gumperz & D. Hymes (Eds.), *Directions in sociolinguistics* (pp. 213–250). New York: Holt, Rinehart and Winston.

Esposito, A. (1979). Sex differences in children's conversations. *Language and Speech, 22,* 213–220.

Falk, J. (1980). The conversational duet. *Berkeley Linguistics Society: Proceedings of the 6th Annual Meeting,* 507–514.

Fausto-Sterling, A. (2000). *Sexing the body: Gender politics and the construction of sexuality.* New York: Basic Books.

Fellbaum, C. (Ed.) (1998). *WordNet: An electronic lexical database.* Cambridge, MA: MIT Press.

Fernald, A. (1989). Intonation and communicative intent in mothers' speech to infants: Is the melody the message? *Child Development, 60,* 1497–1510.

Fernald, A. (1992). Human maternal vocalizations to infants as biologically relevant signals: An evolutionary perspective. In J. Barkow, L. Cosmides, & J. Tooby (Eds.), *The adapted mind: Evolutionary psychology and the generation of culture* (pp. 391–428). New York: Oxford University Press.

Fernald, A., & Kuhl, P. K. (1987). Acoustic determinants of infant preference for motherese speech. *Infant Behavior and Development, 10,* 279–293.

Fernald, A., & Morikawa, H. (1993). Common themes and cultural variations in Japanese and American mothers' speech to infants. *Child Development, 64,* 637–656.

Fernald, A., Taeschner, T., Dun, J., Papousek, M. de Boysson-Bardies, B., & Fukui, I. (1989). A cross-language study of prosodic modifications in mothers' and fathers' speech to preverbal infants. *Journal of Child Language, 16,* 477–501.

Ferrara, K. (1994). *Therapeutic ways with words.* New York: Oxford University Press.

Ferreira, F. (1993). Creation of prosody during sentence production. *Psychological Review, 100,* 233–253.

Ferreira, F., & Clifton, C. (1986). The independence of syntactic processing. *Journal of Memory and Language, 25,* 348–368.

Ferreira, F., Henderson, J. M., Anes, M. D., Weeks, P. A., & McFarlane, D. K. (1996). Effects of lexical frequency and syntactic complexity in spoken-language comprehension: Evidence from the auditory moving-window technique. *Journal of Experimental Psychology: Learning, Memory, and Cognition, 22,* 324–335.

Fillenbaum, S., & Rapoport, A. (1971). *Structure in the subjective lexicon.* New York: Academic Press.

Fillmore, C. (1968). The case for case. In E. Bach & R. T. Harms (Eds.), *Universals in linguistic theory* (pp. 1–90). New York: Holt, Rinehart and Winston.

Firth, U. (1985). Beneath the surface of dyslexia. In K. Patterson, J. Marshall, & M. Coltheart (Eds.), *Surface dyslexia* (pp. 301–330). London: Erlbaum.

Fisher, D. F., & Shebilske, W. E. (1984). There is more that meets the eye than the eyemind assumption. In R. Groner, G. McConkie, & C. Menz (Eds.), *Eye movements and human information processing.* Amsterdam: North Holland.

Fishman, P. (1978). Interaction: The work women do. *Social Problems, 25,* 397–406.

Fitzpatrick, M., Mulac, A., & Dindia, K. (1995). Gender-preferential language use in spouse and stranger interaction. *Journal of Language and Social Psychology, 14,* 18–39.

Flege, J. (1995). Second language speech learning: Theory, findings, and problems. In W. Strange (Ed.), *Speech perception and linguistic experience: Issues in cross-language research* (pp. 233–277). Baltimore: York Press.

Fletcher, C. R. (1994). Levels of representation in memory for discourse. In M. A. Gernsbacher (Ed.), *Handbook of psycholinguistics* (pp. 589–607). New York: Academic Press.

Fletcher, C. R., & Bloom, C. P. (1988). Causal reasoning in the comprehension of simple narrative texts. *Journal of Memory and Language, 27,* 235–244.

Fletcher, C. R., & Chrysler, S. T. (1990). Surface forms, textbases, and situation models: Recognition memory for three types of textual information. *Discourse Processes, 13,* 175–190.

Flexner, S. (1976). *I hear America talking.* New York: Van Nostrand Reinhold.

Flower, L., & Hayes, J. R. (1980). The cognition of discovery: Defining a rhetorical problem. *College Composition and Communication, 31,* 21–32.

Flower, L., & Hayes, J. R. (1983). *A cognitive model of writing processes in adults (final report).* Pittsburgh: Carnegie-Mellon University. (ERIC Document Reproduction Service No. ED 240 608)

Flower, L., & Hayes, J. R. (1984). The representation of meaning in writing. *Written Communication, 1,* 120–160.

Flower, L., Hayes, J., Carey, L., Schriver, K., & Stratman, J. (1986). Detection, diagnosis, and the strategies of revision. *College Composition and Communication, 37,* 16–55.

Fodor, J. A. (1983). *The modularity of mind.* Cambridge, MA: MIT Press.

Folven, R. J., & Bonvillian, J. D. (1991). The transition from nonreferential to referential language in children acquiring American Sign Language. *Developmental Psychology, 27,* 806–816.

Ford, M., Bresnan, J. W., & Kaplan, R. M. (1982). A competence based theory of syntactic closure. In J. W. Bresnan (Ed.), *The mental representation of grammatical relations* (pp. 727–796). Cambridge, MA: MIT Press.

Forster, K. I. (1976). Accessing the mental lexicon. In F. Wales & E. Walker (Eds.), *New approaches to language mechanisms* (pp. 257–287). Amsterdam: North-Holland.

Forster, K. I. (1979). Levels of processing and the structure of the language processor. In W. Cooper & C. Walker (Eds.), *Sentence processing* (pp. 27–85). Hillsdale, NJ: Erlbaum.

Forster, K. I. (1987). Form-priming and masked primes: The best match hypothesis. In M. Coltheart (Ed.), *Attention and performance: Vol. 12. The psychology of reading* (pp. 127–146). Hillsdale, NJ: Erlbaum.

Forster, K. I. (1989). Basic issues in lexical processing. In W. Marslen-Wilson (Ed.), *Lexical representation and processes* (pp. 75–107). Cambridge, MA: MIT Press.

Forster, K. I., & Chambers, S. M. (1973). Lexical access and naming time. *Journal of Verbal Learning and Verbal Behavior, 12,* 627–635.

Foss, D. (1969). Decision processes during sentence comprehension: Effects of lexical item difficulty and position upon decision times. *Journal of Verbal Learning and Verbal Behavior, 8,* 457–462.

Foss, D. (1970). Some aspects of ambiguity on sentence comprehension. *Journal of Verbal Learning and Verbal Behavior, 9,* 699–706.

Foucault, M. (1977). *The history of sexuality: Vol. 1. An introduction.* New York: Pantheon.

Fowler, C. A. (1984). Segmentation of coarticulated speech in perception. *Perception and Psychophysics, 36,* 359–368.

Fowler, C. A. (1986). An event approach to the study of speech perception from a direct-realist perspective. *Journal of Phonetics, 14,* 3–28.

Fowler, C. A., & Rosenblum, L. D. (1991). The perception of phonetic gestures. In I. G. Mattingly & M. Studdert-Kennedy (Eds.), *Modularity and the motor theory in speech perception: Proceedings of a conference to honor Alvin M. Liberman* (pp. 33–59). Hillsdale, NJ: Erlbaum.

Frazier, L. (1979). *On comprehending sentences: Syntactic parsing strategies.* Bloomington: Indiana University Linguistics Club.

Frazier, L. (1987). Sentence processing: A tutorial review. In M. Coltheart (Ed.), *Attention and performance: Vol. 12. The psychology of reading* (pp. 559–586). Hillsdale, NJ: Erlbaum.

Frazier, L., & Clifton, C. (1996). *Construal.* Cambridge, MA: MIT Press.

Frazier L., & Rayner, K. (1982). Selection mechanisms in reading lexically ambiguous words. *Journal of Experimental Psychology: Learning, Memory, and Cognition, 15,* 779–790.

Frazier, L., & Rayner, K. (1987). Resolution of syntactic category ambiguities: Eye movements in parsing lexically ambiguous sentences. *Journal of Memory and Language, 26,* 505–526.

French, L., Lucariello, J., Seidman, S., & Nelson, K. (1985). The influence of discourse content and context on preschoolers' use of language. In L. Galda & A. Pellegrini (Eds.), *Play, language, and stories* (pp. 1–27). Norwood, NJ: Ablex.

Freud, S. (1940). *An outline of psycho-analysis.* New York: Norton.

Freud, S. (1963). *Introductory lectures on psychoanalysis.* New York: Norton. (Originally published 1916)

Frisson, S., & Pickering, M. (1999). The processing of metonymy: Evidence from eye movements. *Journal of Experimental Psychology: Learning, Memory, and Cognition, 25,* 1366–1383.

Fromkin, V. A. (1971). The nonanomalous nature of anomalous utterances. *Journal of Linguistics, 4,* 47–68.

Fromkin, V. A. (1973). *Speech errors as linguistic evidence.* The Hague, Netherlands: Mouton.

Fromkin, V. A., & Bernstein Ratner, N. (1998). Speech production. In J. Berko-Gleason & N. Bernstein Ratner (Eds.), *Psycholinguistics* (pp. 309–346). Orlando, FL: Harcourt Brace.

Fromkin, V. A., & Rodman, R. (1998). *An introduction to language.* Orlando, FL: Harcourt Brace.

Frost, R., Katz, L., & Bentin, S. (1987). Strategies for visual word recognition and orthographical depth: A multilingual comparison. *Journal of Experimental Psychology: Human Perception and Performance, 13,* 104–115.

Fussell, S. R. (1992). *The role of metaphor in written descriptions of emotional states.* Unpublished manuscript, Carnegie Mellon University.

Fussell, S. R., & Moss, M. (1998). Figurative language in emotional communication. In S. R. Fussell & R. J. Kreuz (Eds.), *Social and cognitive approaches to interpersonal communication* (pp. 113–141). Mahwah, NJ: Erlbaum.

Gabbard, K., & Gabbard, G. O. (1987). *Psychiatry and the cinema.* Chicago: University of Chicago Press.

Gaetner, S., & Bickman, L. (1971). Effects of race on the elicitation of helping behaviour: The wrong number technique. *Journal of Personality and Social Psychology, 20,* 218–222.

Gardner, B. T., & Gardner, R. A. (1969). *Teaching sign language to a chimpanzee.* Albany: State University of New York Press.

Gardner, H. (1975). *The shattered mind.* New York: Knopf.

Gardner, H. (1985). *The mind's new science: A history of the cognitive revolution.* New York: Basic Books.

Gardner, R. A., Gardner, B. T., & Van Cantfort, T. E. (Eds). (1989). *Teaching sign language to chimpanzees.* Albany: State University of New York Press.

Garrett, M. F. (1975). The analysis of sentence production. In G. Bower (Ed.), *Psychology of learning and motivation: Advances in research and theory.* (Vol. 9, pp. 133–177). New York: Academic Press.

Garrett, M. F. (1976). Syntactic processes in sentence production. In R. Wales & E. Walker (Eds.), *New approaches to language mechanisms* (pp. 231–256). Amsterdam: North Holland.

Garrett, M. F. (1980). The limits of accommodation. In V. Fromkin (Ed.), *Errors in linguistic performance* (pp. 263–271). New York: Academic.

Garrett, M. F. (1984). Disorders of lexical selection. *Cognition, 42,* 143–180.

Garrett, M. F. (1988). Processes in language production. In F. J. Newmeyer (Ed.), *Linguistics: The Cambridge survey: Vol. 3. Language: Psychological and biological aspects* (pp. 69–96). Cambridge: Cambridge University Press.

Garrod, S., & Sanford, A. (1990). Referential processing in reading: Focusing on roles and individuals. In D. A. Balota, G. B. Flores d'Arcais, & K. Rayner (Eds.), *Comprehension processes in reading* (pp. 465–484). Hillsdale, NJ: Erlbaum.

Gathercole, V. (1989). Contrast: A semantic constraint. *Journal of Child Language, 16,* 685–702.

Gathercole, V. (2002). Monolingual and bilingual acquisition: Learning different treatments of *that*-trace phenomena in English and Spanish. In D. K. Oller & R. E. Eilers (Ed.), *Language and literacy in bilingual children.* Clevedon, England: Multilingual Matters.

Gazzaniga, M. S., & Hillyard, S. A. (1971). Language and speech capacity of the right hemisphere. *Neuropsychologia, 9,* 273–280.

Gazzaniga, M. S., Ivry, R. B., & Mangun, G. R. (1998). *Cognitive neuroscience: The biology of the mind.* New York: Norton.

Geiselman, R. E. (1999). Commentary on recent research with cognitive interview. *Psychology, Crime, and Law, 5,* 197–202.

Geiselman, R. E., Fisher, R., MacKinnon, D., & Holland, H. (1985). Eyewitness memory enhancement in the police interview: Cognitive retrieval mnemonics versus hypnosis. *Journal of Applied Psychology, 70,* 401–412.

Gernsbacher, M. A. (1989). Mechanisms that improve referential access. *Cognition, 32,* 99–156.

Gernsbacher, M. A. (1990). *Language comprehension as structure building.* Hillsdale, NJ: Erlbaum.

Gernsbacher, M. A. (1991b). Comprehending conceptual anaphors. *Language and Cognitive Processes, 6,* 81–105.

Gernsbacher, M. A. (Ed.). (1994). *Handbook of psycholinguistics*. New York: Academic Press.

Gernsbacher, M. A., & Robertson, R. R. W. (1995). Reading skill and suppression revisited. *Psychological Science, 6*, 165–169.

Gernsbacher, M. A., Varner, K., Faust, M. (1990). Investigating differences in general composition skill. *Journal of Experimental Psychology: Learning, Memory, and Cognition, 16*, 430–445.

Gerrig, R. (1986). Process models and pragmatics. In N. Sharkey (Ed.), *Advances in cognitive science* (pp. 23–39). Chichester, England: Horwood.

Gerrig, R. (1989). The time course of sense creation. *Memory and Cognition, 17*, 194–207.

Gerrig, R., & Goldvarg, Y. (2000). Additive effects in the perception of sarcasm: Situational disparity and echoic mention. *Metaphor and Symbol, 15*, 197–208.

Gerrig, R., & Murphy, G. (1992). Contextual influences on the comprehension of complex concepts. *Language and Cognitive Processes, 7*, 205–230.

Geschwind, N. (1970). The organization of language and the brain. *Science, 170*, 940–944.

Gibbs, R. W. (1979). Contextual effects in understanding indirect requests. *Discourse Processes, 2*, 1–10.

Gibbs, R. W. (1980). Spilling the beans on understanding and memory for idioms. *Memory and Cognition, 8*, 449–456.

Gibbs, R. W. (1984). Literal meaning and psychological theory. *Cognitive Science, 8*, 431–444.

Gibbs, R. W. (1985). On the process of understanding idioms. *Journal of Psycholinguistic Research, 14*, 465–472.

Gibbs, R. W. (1986a). Comprehension and memory for nonliteral utterances: The problem of sarcastic indirect requests. *Acta Psychologica, 62*, 41–57.

Gibbs, R. W. (1986b). On the psycholinguistics of sarcasm. *Journal of Experimental Psychology: General, 115*, 1–13.

Gibbs, R. W. (1986c). What makes some indirect speech acts conventional. *Journal of Memory and Language, 25*, 181–196.

Gibbs, R. W. (1989). Understanding and literal meaning. *Cognitive Science, 13*, 243–251.

Gibbs, R. W. (1990a). Comprehending figurative referential descriptions. *Journal of Experimental Psychology: Learning, Memory, and Cognition, 16*, 56–66.

Gibbs, R. W. (1990b). Psycholinguistic studies on the conceptual basis of idiomaticity. *Cognitive Linguistics, 1*, 417–451.

Gibbs, R. W. (1994). Figurative thought and figurative language. In M. A. Gernsbacher (Ed.), *Handbook of psycholinguistics* (pp. 411–446). New York: Academic Press.

Gibbs, R. W., Bogdanovich, J., Sykes, J., & Barr, D. (1997). Metaphor in idiom comprehension. *Journal of Memory and Language, 37*, 141–154.

Gibbs, R. W., & Nayak, N. (1989). Psycholinguistic studies on the syntactic behavior of idioms. *Cognitive Psychology, 21*, 100–138.

Gibbs, R. W., Nayak, N., Bolton, J., & Keppel, M. (1989). Speakers' assumptions about the lexical flexibility of idioms. *Memory and Cognition, 17*, 58–68.

Gibbs, R. W., Nayak, N., & Cutting, C. (1989). How to kick the bucket and not decompose: Analyzability and idiom processing. *Journal of Memory and Language, 28*, 576–593.

Gibbs, R. W., & O'Brien, J. (1990). Idioms and mental imagery: The metaphorical motivation for idiomatic meaning. *Cognition, 36*, 35–68.

Gibson, E. J., & Levin, H. (1975). *The psychology of reading*. Cambridge, MA: MIT Press.

Gibson, J. J. (1966). *The senses considered as perceptual systems*. Boston: Houghton Mifflin.

Gildea, P., & Glucksberg, S. (1983). On understanding metaphor: The role of context. *Journal of Verbal Learning and Verbal Behavior, 22*, 577–590.

Giles, H., Baker, S., & Fielding, G. (1975). Communication length as a behavioral index of accent prejudice. *International Journal of the Sociology of Language, 6*, 73–81.

Giles, H., & Powesland, P. (1975). *Speech style and social evaluation*. New York: Academic Press.

Gilligan, C. (1982). *In a different voice*. Cambridge, MA: Harvard University Press.

Giora, R. (1999). On the priority of salient meanings: Studies of literal and figurative language. *Journal of Pragmatics, 31*, 919–929.

Giora, R., & Fein, O. (1999a). Irony: Context and salience. *Metaphor and Symbol, 14*, 241–257.

Giora, R., & Fein, O. (1999b). On understanding familiar and less-familiar figurative language. *Journal of Pragmatics, 31,* 1601–1618.

Giora, R., Fein, O., & Schwartz, T. (1998). Irony: Graded salience and indirect negation. *Metaphor and Symbol, 13,* 83–101.

Glanzer, M., & Erhenreich, S. (1979). Structure and search of the internal lexicon. *Journal of Verbal Learning and Verbal Behavior, 18,* 381–398.

Glaser, W. R. (1992). Picture naming. *Cognition, 42,* 61–105.

Glaser, W. R., & Dungelhoff, F.-J. (1984). The time course of picture-word interference. *Journal of Experimental Psychology: Human Perception and Performance, 10,* 640–654.

Glick, J. (1987). Bilingualism: Cognitive and social aspects. In P. Homel, M. Palij, & D. Aaronson (Eds.), *Childhood bilingualism: Aspects of linguistic, cognitive, and social development* (pp. 171–180). Hillsdale, NJ: Erlbaum.

Glucksberg, S., & Danks, J. H. (1968). Effects of discriminative labels and of nonsense labels upon availability of novel function. *Journal of Verbal Learning and Verbal Behavior, 7,* 72–76.

Glucksberg, S., Gildea, P., & Bookin, H. B. (1982). On understanding nonliteral speech: Can people ignore metaphors? *Journal of Verbal Learning and Verbal Behavior, 21,* 85–98.

Glucksberg, S., & Keysar, B. (1990). Understanding metaphorical comparisons: Beyond similarity. *Psychological Review, 97,* 3–18.

Glucksberg, S., Keysar, B., & McGlone, M. (1992). Metaphor understanding and accessing conceptual schema: A reply to Gibbs (1992). *Psychological Review, 99,* 578–581.

Glucksberg, S., Krauss, R., & Weisberg, R. (1966). Referential communication in nursery school children: Method and some preliminary findings. *Journal of Experimental Child Psychology, 3,* 333–342.

Glucksberg, S, Kreuz, R. J., & Rho, S. H. (1986). Context can constrain lexical access: Implications for models of language comprehension. *Journal of Experimental Psychology: Learning, Memory, and Cognition, 12,* 323–335.

Glushko, R. J. (1979). The organization and activation of orthographic knowledge in reading aloud. *Journal of Experimental Psychology: Human Perception and Performance, 5,* 674–691.

Goffman, E. (1967). *Interaction ritual: Essays on face-to-face behavior.* Garden City, NY: Anchor Books.

Goffman, E. (1971). *Relations in public.* New York: Basic Books.

Goffman, E. (1976). Replies and responses. *Language in Society, 5,* 257–313.

Goldfield, B. A., & Reznick, J. S. (1990). Early lexical acquisition: Rate, content, and the vocabulary spurt. *Journal of Child Language, 17,* 171–184.

Goldinger, S. D., Pisoni, D. B., & Logan, J. S. (1991). On the locus of talker variability effects in recall of spoken word lists. *Journal of Experimental Psychology: Learning, Memory, and Cognition, 17,* 152–162.

Goldin-Meadow, S. (1999). The development of gesture with and without speech in hearing and deaf children. In L. S. Messing & R. Campbell (Eds.), *Gesture, speech, and sign* (pp. 117–132). Oxford: Oxford University Press.

Goldman-Eisler, F. (1968). *Psycholinguistics: Experiments in spontaneous speech.* New York: Academic Press.

Goldshmidt, O., & Weller, L. (2000). "Talking emotions": Gender differences in a variety of conversational contexts. *Symbolic Interaction, 23,* 117–134.

Golinkoff, R. M. (1983). The preverbal negotiation of failed messages: Insights into the transition period. In R. M. Golinkoff (Ed.), *The transition from preverbal to verbal communication* (pp. 57–78). Hillsdale, NJ: Erlbaum.

Golinkoff, R. M., Hirsh-Pasek, K., Cauley, K. M., & Gordon, L. (1987). The eyes have it: Lexical and syntactic comprehension in a new paradigm. *Journal of Child Language, 14,* 23–45.

Good, T. L., & Brophy, J. (1995). *Contemporary educational psychology.* White Plains, NY: Longman.

Goodenough, F. L. (1931). *Anger in young children.* Westport, CT: Greenwood.

Goodenough, W. (1956). Componential analysis and the study of meaning. *Language, 32,* 195–216.

Goodman, K. S. (1970). Reading: A psycholinguistic guessing game. In H. Singer & R. B. Ruddell (Eds.), *Theoretical models and processes of reading* (pp. 259–272). Newark, DE: International Reading Association.

Goodman, J., & Nusbaum, H. (1994). *The development of speech perception: The transition from speech sounds to spoken words.* Cambridge, MA: MIT Press.

Gopnik, A., & Choi, S. (1995). Names, relational words, and cognitive development in English and Korean speakers: Nouns are not always learned before verbs. In M. Tomasello & W. Merriman (Eds.), *Beyond names for things: Young children's acquisition of verbs* (pp. 83–90). Hillsdale, NJ: Erlbaum.

Gopnik, A., & Meltzoff, A. (1986). Relations between semantic and cognitive development in the one-word stage: The specificity hypothesis. *Child Development, 57,* 1040–1053.

Gordon, D. E., & Efran, J. S. (1997). Therapy and the dance of language. In T. L. Sexton (Ed.), *Constructivist thinking in counseling practice* (pp. 101–110). New York: Teachers College Press.

Gorrell, P. G. (1987). *Studies of human sentence processing: Ranked parallel versus serial models.* Unpublished doctoral dissertation, University of Connecticut, Storrs.

Gough, P. B. (1972). One second of reading. In J. F. Kavanagh & I. G. Mattingly (Eds.), *Language by ear and by eye* (pp. 331–358). Cambridge, MA: MIT Press.

Graesser, A. C., Baggett, W., & Williams, K. (1996). Question-driven explanatory reasoning. *Applied Cognitive Psychology, 10,* S17–S31.

Graesser, A. C., & Clark, L. F. (1985). *The structures and procedures of implicit knowledge.* Norwood, NJ: Ablex.

Graham, K. S., Hodges, J. R., & Patterson, K. (1994). The relationship between comprehension and oral reading in progressive fluent aphasia. *Neuropsychologia, 32,* 299–316.

Green, D. M., & Swets, J. A. (1966). *Signal detection theory and psychophysics.* New York: Wiley.

Greenberg, J., Kirkland, S. L., & Pyszczynski, T. (1988). Some theoretical notions and preliminary research concerning derogatory ethnic labels. In G. Smitherman & T. van Dijk (Eds.), *Discourse and discrimination* (pp. 74–92). Detroit: Wayne State University Press.

Greene, J. (1972). *Psycholinguistics: Chomsky and psychology.* Baltimore: Penguin.

Greene, J. O., & Cappella, J. N. (1986). Cognition and talk: The relationship of semantic units to temporal patterns of fluency in spontaneous speech. *Language and Speech, 29,* 141–157.

Grice, H. P. (1975). Logic and conversation. In P. Cole & J. L. Morgan (Eds.), *Syntax and semantics* (Vol. 3, pp. 41–58). New York: Seminar Press.

Grice, H. P. (1978). Some further notes on logic and conversation. In P. Cole (Ed.), *Syntax and semantics* (Vol. 9, pp. 113–128). New York: Academic Press.

Griffin, Z., & Bock, K. (2000). What the eyes say about speaking. *Psychological Science, 11,* 274–279.

Gropen, J., Pinker, S., Hollander, M., & Goldberg, R. (1991). Affectedness and direct objects: The role of lexical semantics in the acquisition of verb argument structure. In B. Levin & S. Pinker (Eds.), *Lexical and conceptual semantics* (pp. 153–195). Cambridge, MA: Blackwell.

Grosjean, F., Grosjean, L., & Lane, H. (1979). The pattern of silence: Performance structure in sentence production. *Cognitive Psychology, 11,* 58–81.

Grossen, M., & Apotheloz, D. (1996). Communicating about communication in a therapeutic interview. *Journal of Language and Social Psychology, 15,* 101–132.

Haber, R. N., & Haber, L. R. (1982). Does silent reading involve articulation? Evidence from tongue-twisters. *American Journal of Psychology, 95,* 409–419.

Hage, P. (1972). Münchner beer categories. In J. Spradley (Ed.), *Culture and cognition: Rules, maps, and plans* (263–278). Prospect Heights, IL: Waveland Press.

Haiman, J. (1998). *Talk is cheap: Sarcasm, alienation, and the evolution of language.* Oxford: Oxford University Press.

Halliday, M. A. K., & Hasan, R. (1976). *Cohesion in English.* London: Longman.

Hamblin, J., & Gibbs, R. W. (1999). Why you can't kick the bucket as you slowly die: Verbs idiom comprehension. *Journal of Psycholinguistic Research, 28,* 25–39.

Hanson, V., & Bellugi, U. (1982). On the role of sign order and morphological structure in memory for American Sign Language sentences. *Journal of Verbal Learning and Verbal Behavior, 21,* 621–633.

Harris, M., Barrett, M., Jones, D., & Brookes, S. (1988). Linguistic input and early word meaning. *Journal of Child Language, 15,* 77–94.

Harris, R. (1986). *The origin of writing.* La Salle, IL: Open Court.

Harris, R. J., & Monaco, G. E. (1978). Psychology of pragmatic implication: Information processing between the lines. *Journal of Experimental Psychology: General, 107,* 1–22.

Hauser, P. (2001). An analysis of codeswitching: American sign language and cued English. In M. Metzger (Ed.), *Bilingualism and identity in deaf communities* (pp. 43–78). Washington, DC: Gallaudet University Press.

Havelock, E. A. (1982). *The literate revolution in Greece and its cultural consequences.* Princeton, NJ: Princeton University Press.

Havelock, E. A. (1986). *The muse learns to write: Reflections on orality and literacy from antiquity to the present.* New Haven, CT: Yale University Press.

Haviland, S. E., & Clark, E. (1974). "This man's father is my father's son": A study of the acquisition of English kin terms. *Journal of Child Language, 1,* 23–47.

Hayes, J. R., & Flower, L. (1986). Writing research and the writer. *American Psychologist, 41,* 1106–1113.

Hayes, K. J., & Hayes, C. (1952). Imitation in a home-raised chimpanzee. *Journal of Comparative and Physiological Psychology, 45,* 450–459.

Heath, C. (1992). The delivery and reception of diagnosis in the general-practice consultation. In P. Drew & J. Heritage (Eds.), *Talk at work: Interaction in institutional settings* (pp. 235–267). Cambridge: Cambridge University Press.

Heath, S. B. (1979). The context of professional languages: An historical overview. In J. E. Alatis & G. R. Tucker (Eds.), *Language in public life* (pp. 102–118). Washington, DC: Georgetown University Press.

Heath, S. B. (1983). *Ways with words.* Cambridge: Cambridge University Press.

Heider, E. (1972). Universals in color naming and memory. *Journal of Experimental Psychology, 93,* 10–20.

Heider, E., & Oliver, D. (1972). The structure of the color space in naming and memory for two languages. *Cognitive Psychology, 3,* 337–354.

Henley, N. (1995a). Body politics revisited: What do we know today? In P. J. Kalbfleisch & M. J. Cody (Eds.), *Gender, power, and communication in human relationships* (pp. 27–61). Hillsdale, NJ: Erlbaum.

Henley, N. (1995b). Ethnicity and gender issues in language. In H. Landrine (Ed.), *Bringing cultural diversity to feminist psychology: Theory, research, and practice* (pp. 361–395). Washington, DC: American Psychological Association.

Henley, N., Miller, M., & Beazley, J. (1995). Syntax, semantics, and sexual violence: Agency and the passive voice. *Journal of Language and Social Psychology, 14,* 60–84.

Herrnstein, R. J., & Boring, E. G. (1965). *A sourcebook in the history of psychology.* Cambridge, MA: Harvard University Press.

Hickok, G., Say, K., Bellugi, U., & Klima, E. S. (1996). The basis of hemispheric asymmetries for language and spatial cognition: Clues from focal brain damage in two deaf native signers. *Aphasiology, 10,* 577–591.

Hickok, G., Wilson, M., Clark, K., Klima, E. S., Kritchevsky, M., & Bellugi, U. (1999). Discourse deficits following right hemisphere damage in deaf signers. *Brain and Language, 66,* 233–248.

Hilgard, E. R. (1987). *Psychology in America: A historical perspective.* Orlando, FL: Harcourt Brace.

Hinton, G. E., & Shallice, T. (1991). Lesioning an attractor network: Investigations of acquired dyslexia. *Psychological Review, 98,* 74–95.

Hirsh-Pasek, K., & Golinkoff, R. M. (1991). Language comprehension: A new look at some old themes. In N. A. Krasnegor, D. M. Rumbaugh, R. L. Schiefelbusch, & M. Studdert-Kennedy

(Eds.), *Biological and behavioral determinants of language development* (pp. 301–320). Hillsdale, NJ: Erlbaum.

Hirsh-Pasek, K., Kemler-Nelson, D.G., Jusczyk, P. W., Cassidy, K. W., Druss, B., & Kennedy, L. (1987). Clauses are perceptual units for young infants. *Cognition, 26*, 269–286.

Hockett, C. F. (1960). The origin of speech. *Scientific American, 203*, 88–96.

Hockett, C. F. (1977). Jokes. In C. Hockett (Ed.), *The view from language* (pp. 257–289). Athens: University of Georgia Press.

Hoff, E. (2001). *Language development*. Belmont, CA: Wadsworth.

Hoff, E., & Naigles, L. (1999, July). *Fast mapping is only the beginning: Complete word learning requires multiple exposures.* Paper presented at the 8th International Conference for the Study of Child Language, San Sebastian, Spain.

Hoffman, C. (1991). *An introduction to bilingualism.* White Plains, NY: Longman.

Holland, D., & Quinn, N. (Eds.). (1987). *Cultural models in language and thought.* New York: Cambridge University Press.

Holland, D., & Skinner, D. (1987). Prestige and intimacy: The cultural models behind Americans' talk about gender types. In D. Holland & N. Quinn (Eds.), *Cultural models in language and thought* (pp. 78–111). New York: Cambridge University Press.

Holmes, J. (1984). "Women's language": A functional approach. *General Linguistics, 24*, 149–178.

Holtgraves, T. (1998). Interpersonal foundations of conversational indirectness. In S. R. Fussell & R. J. Kreuz (Eds.), *Social and cognitive approaches to interpersonal communication* (pp. 71–89). Mahwah, NJ: Erlbaum.

Holtgraves, T., & Yang, J. (1990). Politeness as universal: Cross-cultural perceptions of request strategies and inferences based on their use. *Journal of Personality and Social Psychology, 59*, 719–729.

Holtgraves, T., & Yang, J. (1992). The interpersonal underpinnings of request strategies: General principals and differences due to culture and gender. *Journal of Personality and Social Psychology, 62*, 246–256.

Howard, D. (1997). Language in the human brain. In M. D. Rugg (Ed.), *Cognitive neuroscience* (pp. 277–304). Cambridge, MA: MIT Press.

Howes, D. H. (1957). On the relation between intelligibility and frequency of occurrence of English words. *Journal of the Acoustical Society of America, 29*, 296–305.

Huey, E. B. (1968). *The psychology and pedagogy of reading.* Cambridge, MA: MIT Press. (Originally published 1908)

Hugdahl, K. (1995). *Psychophysiology: The mind-body problem.* Cambridge, MA: Harvard University Press.

Hughes, S. E. (1992). Expletives of the lower working-class women. *Language in Society, 21*, 291–303.

Ikeda, M., & Saida, S. (1978). Span of recognition in reading. *Vision Research, 18*, 83–88.

Inbau, F. E., Reid, J. E., & Buckley, J. P (1986). *Criminal interrogation and confessions.* Baltimore: Williams & Wilkins.

Irigaray, L. (1967). Approche psycholinguistique du langage des déments [Psycholinguistic approach to language in the demented.] *Neuropsychologia, 5*, 25–52.

Iverson, J., Capirci, O., & Caselli, M. (1994). From communication to language in two modalities. *Cognitive Development, 9*, 23–43.

Iverson, J., & Thal, D. J. (1998). Communicative transitions: There's more to the hand than meets the eye. In A. Wetherby, S. Warren, & J. Reichle (Eds.), *Transitions in prelinguistic communication* (pp. 59–86). Baltimore: Brookes.

Jackson, H. (1958). *Selected writings of John Hughlings Jackson: Vol. 2. Evolution and dissolution of the nervous system speech. Various papers, addresses and lectures.* New York: Basic Books. (Originally published 1874)

Jaeger, J. J., Lockwood, A. H., van Valin, R. D., Kemmerer, D. L., Murphy, B. W., & Wack, D. S. (1998). Sex differences in brain regions activated by grammatical and reading tasks. *Neuroreport, 9*, 2803–2807.

James, W. (1890). *Principles of psychology* (Vol. 1). New York: Holt.

Jared, D., McRae, K., & Seidenberg, M. S. (1990). The basis of consistency effects in word naming. *Journal of Memory and Language, 29,* 687–715.

Jay, T. B. (1980). Sex roles and dirty word usage: A review of the literature and a reply to Haas. *Psychological Bulletin, 88,* 614–621.

Jay, T. B. (1981). Comprehending dirty word descriptions. *Language and Speech, 24,* 29–38.

Jay, T. B. (1986). Computers and psychology. In V. P. Makosky (Ed.), *The G. Stanley Hall lecture series* (Vol. 7, pp. 84–120). Washington, DC. American Psychological Association.

Jay, T. B. (1991, March). *Metaphors of lust and love.* Paper presented at the annual meeting of the Popular Culture Association, San Antonio, TX.

Jay, T. B. (1992a). *Cursing in America.* Philadelphia: Benjamins.

Jay, T. B. (1992b, April). *Women cursing women.* Paper presented at the annual meeting of the Eastern Psychological Association, Boston.

Jay, T. B. (1996). Cursing: A damned persistent lexicon. In D. J. Herrmann, C. McEvoy, & C. Hertzog (Eds.), *Basic and applied memory research: Theory in context* (Vol. 2, pp. 301–313). Mahwah, NJ: Erlbaum.

Jay, T. B. (1998). *What to do when your kids talk dirty.* San Jose, CA: Resource Publications.

Jay, T. B. (2000). *Why we curse: The neuro-psycho-social model of speech.* Philadelphia: Benjamins.

Jay, T. B., & Danks, J. H. (1977). Ordering of taboo adjectives. *Bulletin of the Psychonomic Society, 9,* 405–408.

Jay, T. B., King, K., & Dunan, T. (2002, March). *Soap in my mouth: College students' narratives of being punished for cursing.* Paper presented at Eastern Psychological Association Meeting, Boston, MA.

Jay, T. B., & Richard, D. (1995, April). *Verbal sexual harassment, figurative language, and gender.* Paper presented at the annual meeting of the Eastern Psychological Association, Boston.

Jenkins, J. J. (1970). The 1952 Minnesota word association norms. In L. Postman & G. Keppel (Eds.), *Norms of word association* (pp. 1–38). New York: Academic Press.

Johnson, A. (1996). Comprehension of metaphors and similes: A reaction time study. *Metaphor and Symbolic Activity, 11,* 145–159.

Johnson-Laird, P. N. (1981). Mental models of meaning. In A. Joshi, I. Sag, & B. Nash (Eds.), *Linguistic structure and discourse setting* (pp. 106–126). Cambridge: Cambridge University Press.

Johnson-Laird, P. N. (1983). *Mental models.* Cambridge, MA: Harvard University Press.

Johnston, J. R., & Slobin, D. I. (1979). The development of locative expressions in English, Italian, Serbo-Croatian, and Turkish. *Journal of Child Language, 6,* 529–545.

Johnstone, B. (1993). Community and context: Midwestern men and women creating their worlds in conversational storytelling. In D. Tannen (Ed.), *Gender and conversational interaction* (pp. 62–80). New York: Oxford University Press.

Jonsson, L. (1995). *Sarcasm in German.* Unpublished dissertation, Macalester College, St. Paul, MN.

Jorgensen, J., Miller, G., & Sperber, D. (1984). Test of the mention theory of irony. *Journal of Experimental Psychology: General, 113,* 112–120.

Jung, C. G. (1910). The association method. *American Journal of Psychology, 31,* 219–269.

Jung, C. G., & Ricklin, F. (1904). Experimentelle Untersuchungen über Assoziationen Gesunder: 1. Beitrag diagnostische Assoziations-studien [Experimental studies of associations in healthy subjects: 1. Contribution of diagnostic association studies]. *Journal für Psychologie und Neurologie, 3,* 55–308.

Jusczyk, P. W. (1999). Word segmentation abilities and their contribution to language acquisition. In A. Greenhill, H. Littlefield, & C. Tano (Eds.), *Proceedings of the 23rd Annual Boston University Conference on Language Development* (pp. 1–19). Somerville, MA: Cascadilla Press.

Jusczyk, P. W., & Derrah, C. (1987). Representation of speech sounds by young infants. *Developmental Psychology, 23,* 648–654.

Jusczyk, P. W., Friederici, A., Wessels, J., & Svenkerud, V. (1993). Infants' sensitivity to the sound patterns of native language words. *Journal of Memory and Language, 32,* 402–420.

Just, M. A., & Carpenter, P. A. (1980). A theory of reading from eye fixations to comprehension. *Psychological Review, 87,* 329–354.

Just, M. A., & Carpenter, P. A. (1987). *The psychology of reading and language comprehension.* Needham Heights, MA: Allyn & Bacon.

Just, M. A., & Carpenter, P. A. (1992). A capacity theory of comprehension: Individual differences in working memory. *Psychological Review, 99,* 122–149.

Just, M. A., Carpenter, P. A., & Woolley, J. D. (1982). Paradigms and processes in reading comprehension. *Journal of Experimental Psychology: General, 111,* 228–238.

Kalbfleisch, P. (1994). The language of detecting deceit. *Journal of Language and Social Psychology, 13,* 469–496.

Karp, D. (1996). *Speaking of sadness: Depression, disconnection, and the meanings of illness.* New York: Oxford University Press.

Kassin, S. M. (1997). The psychology of confession evidence. *American Psychologist, 52,* 221–233.

Kassin, S. M., & McNall, K. (1991). Police interrogations and confessions: Communicating promises and threats by pragmatic implication. *Law and Human Behavior, 15,* 233–251.

Katz, J. (1999). *How emotions work.* Chicago: University of Chicago Press.

Kellas, G., Ferraro, F. R., & Simpson, G. B. (1988). Lexical ambiguity and time course of attentional allocation in word recognition. *Journal of Experimental Psychology: Human Perception and Performance, 14,* 601–609.

Kellogg, R. T. (1987). Writing performance: Effects of cognitive strategies. *Written Communication, 4,* 269–298.

Kellogg, R. T. (1994). *The psychology of writing.* New York: Oxford University Press.

Kellogg, W. N., & Kellogg, L. A. (1933). *The ape and the child: A study of environmental influence upon early behavior.* New York: Whittlesey House.

Kelly, S., Barr, D., Church, R., & Lynch, K. (1999). Offering a hand to pragmatic understanding: The role of speech and gesture in comprehension and memory. *Journal of Memory and Language, 40,* 577–592.

Keltner, D., Capps, L., Kring, A., Young, R., & Heerey, E. (2001). Just teasing: A conceptual analysis and empirical review. *Psychological Bulletin, 127,* 229–248.

Kemler Nelson, D., Hirsh-Pasek, K., Jusczyk, P. W., & Wright Cassidy, K. (1989). How the prosodic cues in motherese might assist language learning. *Journal of Child Language, 16,* 55–68.

Kennedy, M. L. (1985). The composing process of college students writing from sources. *Written Communication, 2,* 434–456.

Kent, G. H., & Rossanoff, A. J. (1910). A study of association in insanity. *American Journal of Insanity, 67,* 37–96, 317–390.

Kess, J. F. (1992). *Psycholinguistics: Psychology, linguistics, and the study of natural language.* Philadelphia: John Benjamins.

Keysar, B., Barr, D., & Horton, W. (1998). The egocentric basis of language use: Insights from a processing approach. *Current Directions in Psychological Science, 7,* 46–50.

Keysar, B., & Bly, B. (1999). Swimmers against the current: Do idioms reflect conceptual structure? *Journal of Pragmatics, 31,* 1559–1578.

Kilborn, K. (1994). Learning a language late: Second language acquisition in adults. In M. A. Gernsbacher (Ed.), *Handbook of psycholinguistics* (pp. 917–944). New York: Academic Press.

Kilborn, K., & Cooreman, A. (1987). Sentence interpretation strategies in adult Dutch-English bilinguals. *Applied Psycholinguistics, 8,* 415–431.

Killen, M., & Naigles, L. R. (1995). Preschool children pay attention to their addressees: Effects of gender composition on peer disputes. *Discourse Processes, 19,* 329–346.

Kim, K., Relkin, N., Lee, K., & Hirsch, J. (1997). Distinct cortical areas associated with native and second languages. *Nature, 388,* 171–174.

Kimball, J. P. (1973). Seven principles of surface structure parsing in natural language. *Cognition, 2,* 15–47.

King, J., & Just, M. A. (1991). Individual differences in syntactic processing: The role of working memory. *Journal of Memory and Language, 30,* 580–602.

Kintsch, W. (1974). *The representation of meaning in memory.* Hillsdale, NJ: Erlbaum.

Kintsch, W. (1994). The psychology of discourse processing. In M. A. Gernsbacher (Ed.), *Handbook of psycholinguistics* (pp. 721–739). New York: Academic Press.

Kintsch, W., & Bates, E. (1977). Recognition memory for statements from a classroom lecture. *Journal of Experimental Psychology: Human Learning and Memory, 3,* 150–159.

Kintsch, W., & van Dijk, T. A. (1978). Toward a model of text comprehension and production. *Psychological Review, 85,* 363–394.

Kintsch, W., Welsch, D., Schmalhofer, F., & Zinny, S. (1990). Sentence recognition: A theoretical analysis. *Journal of Memory and Language, 29,* 133–159.

Kita, S. (2000). How representational gestures help speaking. In D. McNeill (Ed.), *Language and gesture* (pp. 162–185). New York: Cambridge University Press.

Klatt, D. H. (1989). Review of selected models of speech perception. In W. Marslen-Wilson (Ed.), *Lexical representations and processes* (pp. 169–226). Cambridge, MA: MIT Press.

Klima, E. S., & Bellugi, U. (1966). Syntactic regularities in the speech of children. In J. Lyons & R. Wales (Eds.), *Psycholinguistic papers* (pp. 183–208). Edinburgh: Edinburgh University Press.

Kluender, K., Diehl, R. L., & Killeen, P. R. (1987). Japanese quail can learn phonetic categories. *Science, 237,* 1195–1197.

Kluender, K., Diehl, R. L., & Wright, B. A. (1988). Vowel-length difference before voiced and voiceless consonants: An auditory explanation. *Journal of Phonetics, 2,* 153–169.

Koch, L., Gross, A., & Kolts, R. (2001). Attitudes toward Black English and code switching. *Journal of Black Psychology, 27*(1), 29–42.

Kochman, T. (1981). *Black and white styles in conflict.* Chicago: University of Chicago Press.

Kollock, P., Blumstein, P., & Schwartz, P. (1985). Sex and power in interaction: Conversational privileges and duties. *American Sociological Review, 50,* 34–46.

Kosslyn, S. (1987). Seeing and imagining in the cerebral hemispheres: A computational approach. *Psychological Review, 101,* 211–221.

Kövecses, Z. (1988). *The language of love.* London: Associated University Presses.

Kowalski, R. (2000). "I was only kidding!" Victims' and perpetrators' perceptions of teasing. *Personality and Social Psychology Bulletin, 26,* 231–241.

Krauss, R. M. (1998). Why do we gesture when we speak? *Current Directions in Psychological Science, 7,* 54–60.

Krauss, R. M., Chen, Y., & Gottesman, R. F. (2000). Lexical gestures and lexical access: A process model. In D. McNeill (Ed.), *Language and gesture* (pp. 261–283). New York: Cambridge University Press.

Krauss, R. M., & Hadar, U. (1999). The role of speech-related arm/hand gestures in word retrieval. In L. S. Messing & R. Campbell (Eds.), *Gesture, speech, and sign* (pp. 93–116). Oxford: Oxford University Press.

Kreuz, R. J., & Glucksberg, S. (1989). How to be sarcastic: The echoic reminder theory of verbal irony. *Journal of Experimental Psychology: General, 118,* 374–386.

Kreuz, R. J., Kassler, M., & Coppenrath, L. (1998). The use of exaggeration in discourse: Cognitive and social facets. In S. R. Fussell & R. J. Kreuz (Eds.), *Social and cognitive approaches to interpersonal communication* (pp. 91–111). Mahwah, NJ: Erlbaum.

Kreuz, R. J., Kassler, M., Coppenrath, L., & Allen, B. (1999). Tag questions and common ground effects in the perception of verbal irony. *Journal of Pragmatics, 31,* 1685–1700.

Kreuz, R. J., Roberts, R. M., Johnson, B., & Bertus, E. (1996). Figurative language occurrence and co-occurrence in contemporary literature. In R. J. Kreuz & M. S. MacNealy (Eds.), *Empirical approaches to literature and aesthetics: Vol. 52. Advances in discourse processes* (pp. 83–97). Norwood, NJ: Ablex.

Kroll, J. F., & Merves, J. S. (1986). Lexical access for concrete and abstract words. *Journal of Experimental Psychology: Learning, Memory, and Cognition, 12,* 92–107.

Kuhl, P. K. (1987). Perception of speech and sound in early infancy. In P. Salapatek & L. Cohen (Eds.), *Handbook of infant perception* (pp. 275–382). New York: Academic Press.

Kuhl, P. K. (1991). Human adults and human infants show a "perceptual magnet effect" for the prototypes of speech categories, monkeys do not. *Perception and Psychophysics, 50,* 93–107.

Kuhl, P. K. (1993). Innate predispositions and the effects of experience in speech perception: The native language magnet theory. In B. de Boysson-Bardies, S. de Schonen, P. W. Jusczyk, P. MacNeilage, & J. Morton (Eds.), *Developmental neurocognition: Speech and face processing in the first year of life* (pp. 259–274). Dordrecht, Netherlands: Kluwer.

Kuhl, P. K., & Meltzoff, A. (1997). Evolution, nativism and learning in the development of language and speech. In M. Gopnik (Ed.), *The inheritance and innateness of grammars* (pp. 7–44). New York: Oxford University Press.

Kuhl, P. K., & Miller, J. (1975). Speech perception by the chinchilla: Voiced-voiceless distinction in alveolar plosive consonants. *Science, 190,* 69–72.

Kuhn, T. (1962). *The structure of scientific revolutions.* Chicago: University of Chicago Press.

Kutas, M., & Hillyard, S. A. (1980). Reading senseless sentences: Brain potentials reflect semantic incongruity. *Science, 207,* 203–205.

Kutas, M., & Hillyard, S. A. (1983). Event-related brain potentials to grammatical errors and semantic anomalies. *Memory and Cognition, 11,* 539–550.

Kutas, M., Hillyard, S. A., & Gazzaniga, M. (1988). Processing of semantic anomaly by right and left hemispheres of commissurotomy patients. *Brain, 111,* 553–576.

Kutas, M., & Van Petten, C. K. (1994). Psycholinguistics electrified: Event-related brain potential investigations. In M. A. Gernsbacher (Ed.), *Handbook of psycholinguistics* (pp. 83–143). New York: Academic Press.

La Berge, D, & Samuels, S. J. (1974). Toward a theory of automatic information processing in reading. *Cognitive Psychology, 6,* 293–323.

Labov, W. (1970). The logic of nonstandard English. In F. Williams (Ed.), *Language and poverty* (pp. 153–189). Chicago: Markham.

Labov, W. (1972c). The transformation of experience in narrative syntax. In. W. Labov (Ed.), *Language in the inner city.* Philadelphia: University of Philadelphia Press.

Labov, W. (1973) The boundaries of words and their meanings. In C. Bailey & R. Shaw (Eds.), *New ways of analyzing variations in English.* Washington, DC: Georgetown University Press.

Labov, W., & Fanshel, D. (1977). *Therapeutic discourse: Psychotherapy as conversation.* New York: Academic Press.

Labov, W., & Waletzky, J. (1967). Narrative analysis: Oral versions of personal experience. In J. Helm (Ed.), *Essays on the verbal and visual arts* (pp. 12–44). Seattle: University of Washington Press.

Lakoff, G., & Johnson, M. (1980). *Metaphors we live by.* Chicago: University of Chicago Press.

Lakoff, R. (1975). *Language and a woman's place.* New York: Harper & Row.

Lambert, W. (1977). The effects of bilingualism on the individual: Cognitive and sociocultural consequences. In P. Hornby (Ed.), *Bilingualism: Psychological, social, and educational implications* (pp. 15–27). New York: Academic Press.

Lamendella, J. T. (1977). The limbic system in human communication. In H. Whitaker & H. A. Whitaker (Eds.), *Studies in neurolinguistics* (Vol. 3, pp. 157–222). New York: Academic Press.

Lashley, K. S. (1950). In search of the engram. *Symposia of the Society for Experimental Biology, 4,* 454–482.

Lashley, K. S. (1951). The problem of serial order in behavior. In L. A. Jeffress (Ed.), *Cerebral mechanisms in behavior* (pp. 112–136). New York: Wiley.

Lave, J., & Wenger, E. (1991). *Situated learning: Legitimate peripheral participation.* New York: Cambridge University Press.

Leach, E. (1966). Anthropological aspects of language: Animal categories and verbal abuse. In E. H. Lenneberg (Ed.), *New directions in the study of language* (pp. 23–63). Cambridge, MA: MIT Press.

Lee, C., & Katz, A. (1997). The differential role of ridicule in sarcasm and irony. *Metaphor and Symbol, 13,* 1–15.

Lenneberg, E. H. (1967). *Biological foundations of language.* New York: Wiley.

Leo, R. (1996). Inside the interrogation room. *Journal of Criminal Law and Criminology, 86,* 266–303.

Levelt, W. J. M. (1983). Monitoring and self-repair in speech. *Cognition, 14,* 41–104.

Levelt, W. J. M. (1989). *Speaking: From intention to articulation.* Cambridge, MA: MIT Press.

Levelt, W. J. M., Roelofs, A., & Meyer, A. S. (2000). A theory of lexical access in speech production. *Behavioral and Brain Sciences, 22,* 1–75.

Levine, C. C. (1970). Doctor-patient communication with the inner-city adolescent. *New England Medical Journal, 282,* 494–495.

Levinson, S. (1983). *Pragmatics.* Cambridge: Cambridge University Press.

Levy, C. M., & Ransdell, S. (1995). Is writing as difficult as it seems? *Memory and Cognition, 23,* 767–779.

Levy, J. (1972). Lateral specialization of the human brain: Behavioral manifestations and possible evolutionary basis. In J. A. Kiger (Ed.), *The biology of behavior* (pp. 159–180). Corvallis: Oregon State University Press.

Li, P., Bates, E., & MacWhinney, B. (1993). Processing a language without inflections: A reaction time study of sentence interpretation in Chinese. *Journal of Memory and Language, 32,* 169–192.

Liberman, A. M., Cooper, F. S., Shankweiler, D. P., & Studdert-Kennedy, M. (1967). Perception of the speech code. *Psychological Review, 74,* 431–461.

Liberman, A. M., Harris, K. S., Hoffman, H. S., & Griffith, B. C. (1957). The discrimination of speech sounds within and across phoneme boundaries. *Journal of Experimental Psychology, 54,* 358–368.

Liberman, A. M., & Mattingly, I. G. (1985). The motor theory of speech perception revised. *Cognition, 21,* 1–36.

Liberman, A. M., & Mattingly, I. G. (1989). A specialization for speech perception. *Science, 243,* 489–494.

Liberman, I. Y., Shankweiler, D. P., Fischer, F. W., & Carter, B. (1974). Explicit syllable and phoneme segmentation in the young child. *Journal of Experimental Child Psychology, 18,* 201–212.

Lieberman, P. (1991). *Uniquely human.* Cambridge, MA: Harvard University Press.

Lima, S. D. (1987). Morphological analysis in sentence reading. *Journal of Memory and Language, 26,* 84–99.

Limber, J. (1973). The genesis of complex sentences. In T. Moore (Ed.), *Cognitive development and the acquisition of language* (pp. 169–186). New York: Academic Press.

Lindholm, K. (1980). Bilingual children: Some interpretations of cognitive and linguistic development. In K. Nelson (Ed.), *Children's language* (Vol. 2, pp. 215–266). New York: Gardner Press.

Linebarger, M., Schwartz, M., & Saffran, E. (1983). Sensitivity to grammatical structure in so-called agrammatic aphasics. *Cognition, 13,* 361–393.

Lively, S. E., Pisoni, D. B., & Goldinger, S. D. (1994). Spoken word recognition. In M. A. Gernsbacher (Ed.), *Handbook of psycholinguistics* (pp. 265–301). New York: Academic.

Loftus, E. F., & Palmer, J. C. (1974). Reconstruction of automobile destruction: An example of the interaction between language and memory. *Journal of Verbal Learning and Verbal Behavior, 13,* 585–589.

Loftus, E. F., Schooler, J. W., & Wagenaar, W. A. (1985). The fate of memory: Comment on McCloskey and Zaragosa. *Journal of Experimental Psychology: General, 114,* 375–380.

Long, D., & Graesser, A. C. (1988). Wit and humor in discourse processing. *Discourse Processes, 11,* 35–60.

Lowe, R. C., Kegl, J. A., & Poizner, H. (1997). Fractionation of the components of role play in a right-hemispheric-lesioned signer. *Aphasiology, 11,* 263–281.

Lucariello, J. (1987). Concept formation and its relation to word learning and use in the second year. *Journal of Child Language, 14,* 309–332.

Luce, P. A., Pisoni, D. B., & Goldinger, S. D. (1990). Similarity neighborhoods of spoken words. In G. Altman (Ed.), *Cognitive models of speech processing: Psycholinguistic and computational perspectives* (pp. 122–147). Cambridge, MA: MIT Press.

Lundberg, I., Frost, J., & Petersen, O. (1988). Effects of an extensive program for stimulating phonological awareness in preschool children. *Reading Research Quarterly, 23,* 263–284.

Lupker, S. J. (1984). Semantic priming without association: A second look. *Journal of Verbal Learning and Verbal Behavior, 23,* 709–733.

Luria, A. R. (1964). The development of the regulatory role of speech. In R. Harper, C. Anderson, C. Christensen, & S. Hunka (Eds.), *The cognitive processes* (pp. 601–621). Englewood Cliffs, NJ: Prentice Hall.

Lyons, J. (1970). *Noam Chomsky.* New York: Viking.

MacDonald, M. C., Just, M. A., & Carpenter, P. A. (1992). Working memory constraints on the processing of syntactic ambiguity. *Cognitive Psychology, 24,* 56–98.

MacDonald, M. C., Pearlmutter, N. J., & Seidenberg, M. S. (1994). The lexical nature of syntactic ambiguity resolution. *Psychological Review, 101,* 676–703.

MacKay, D. G. (1969). Effects of ambiguity on stuttering: Toward a model of speech production at the semantic level. *Kybernetik, 5,* 195–208.

MacKay, D. G. (1972). Lexical insertion, inflection, and derivation: Creative processes in word production. *Journal of Psycholinguistic Research, 8,* 477–498.

MacKay, D. G. (1978). Derivational rules and the internal lexicon. *Journal of Verbal Learning and Verbal Behavior, 17,* 61–71.

Macnamara, J. (1972). Cognitive basis of language learning in infants. *Psychological Review, 79,* 1–13.

MacNeilage, P. (1972). Speech physiology. In J. H. Gilbert (Ed.), *Speech and cortical functioning* (pp. 1–72). New York: Academic Press.

MacWhinney, B. (1987). Applying the competition model to bilingualism. *Applied Psycholinguistics, 8,* 315–328.

MacWhinney, B. (1999a). *The emergence of language.* Mahwah, NJ: Erlbaum.

MacWhinney, B. (1999b). The emergence of language from embodiment. In B. MacWhinney (Ed.), *The emergence of language* (pp. 213–256). Mahwah, NJ: Erlbaum.

MacWhinney, B., & Bates, E. (1989). *The cross-linguistic study of sentence processing.* New York: Cambridge University Press.

MacWhinney, B., Bates, E., & Kliegl, R. (1984). Cue validity and sentence interpretation in English, German, and Italian. *Journal of Verbal Learning and Verbal Behavior, 23,* 127–150.

MacWhinney, B., Keenan J. M., & Reinke, P. (1982). The role of arousal in memory for conversations. *Memory and Cognition, 10,* 308–317.

MacWhinney, B., & Snow, C. E. (1985). The child language data exchange system. *Journal of Child Language, 12,* 271–296.

Maddieson, I. (1984). *Patterns of sound.* Cambridge: Cambridge University Press.

Maltz, D., & Borker, R. (1982). A cultural approach to male-female miscommunication. In J. J. Gumperz (Ed.), *Language and social identity* (pp. 196–216). Cambridge: Cambridge University Press.

Mamet, D. (1992). *Oleanna.* New York: Pantheon.

Mandler, J. M. (1984). *Stories, scripts, and scenes: Aspects of schema theory.* Hillsdale, NJ: Erlbaum.

Mandler, J. M., & Johnson, N. S. (1977). Remembrance of things past: Story structure and recall. *Cognitive Psychology, 9,* 111–151.

Mani, K., & Johnson-Laird, P. (1982). The mental representation of spatial descriptions. *Memory and Cognition, 10,* 181–187.

Mann, V. A., Madden, J., Russell, J. M., & Liberman, A. M. (1981). Further investigation into the influence of preceding liquids on stop consonant perception [Abstract]. *Journal of the Acoustical Society of America, 69*(Suppl. 1), S91.

Marcus, G. F., Vijayan, S., Bandi, S., Rao, S., & Vistron, P. (1999). Rule learning by seven-month-old infants. *Science, 283,* 77–80.

Markman, E. (1991). The whole-object, taxonomic, and mutual exclusivity assumptions as initial constraints on word meanings. In S. A. Gelman & J. Byrnes (Eds.), *Perspectives on language and thought: Interrelations in development* (pp. 72–106). Cambridge: Cambridge University Press.

Markman, E. (1994). Constraints on word meaning in early language acquisition. In L. R. Gleitman & B. Landau (Eds.), *The acquisition of the lexicon* (pp. 199–229). Cambridge, MA: Elsevier/MIT Press.

Marsh, G., & Desberg, P. (1983). The development of strategies in the acquisition of symbolic skills. In D. Rogers & J. Slaboda (Eds.), *The acquisition of symbolic skills* (pp. 149–154). New York: Plenum Press.

Marshall, J. C., & Newcombe, F. (1973). Patterns of paralexia: A psycholinguistic approach. *Journal of Psycholinguistic Research, 2,* 175–200.

Marslen-Wilson, W. D. (1985). Speed shadowing and speech comprehension. *Speech Communication, 4,* 55–73.

Marslen-Wilson, W. D. (1987). Functional parallelism in spoken word recognition. *Cognition, 25,* 71–102.

Marslen-Wilson, W. D. (1990). Activation, competition, and frequency in lexical access. In G. T. M. Altmann (Ed.), *Cognitive models of speech processing: Psycholinguistic and computational perspectives* (pp. 148–172). Cambridge, MA: MIT Press.

Marslen-Wilson, W. D., & Tyler, L. K. (1980). The temporal structure of spoken language understanding. *Cognition, 8,* 1–71.

Marslen-Wilson, W. D., & Welsh, A. (1978). Processing interactions during word recognition in continuous speech. *Cognitive Psychology, 10,* 29–63.

Martin, J. G. (1972). Rhythmic (hierarchical) versus serial structure in speech and other behavior. *Psychological Review, 79,* 487–509.

Martin, L. (1986). Eskimo words for snow: A case study in the genesis and decay of an anthropological example. *American Anthropologist, 88,* 418–423.

Massaro, D. W. (1975). *Understanding language: An information-processing analysis of speech perception, reading, and psycholinguistics.* New York: Academic Press.

Massaro, D. W. (1994). Psychological aspects of speech perception. In M. A. Gernsbacher (Ed.), *Handbook of psycholinguistics* (pp. 219–263). New York: Academic Press.

Masson, M., & Miller, J. A. (1983). Working memory and individual differences in comprehension and memory of text. *Journal of Educational Psychology, 75,* 314–318.

Masson, M., & Waldron, M. A. (1994). Comprehension of legal contracts by non-experts: Effectiveness of plain language redrafting. *Applied Cognitive Psychology, 8,* 67–85.

Matlin, M., & Foley, H. (1997). *Sensation and perception.* Needham Heights, MA: Allyn & Bacon.

Matsuda, M. J., Lawrence, C. R., III, Delgado, R., & Crenshaw, K. W. (1993). Words that wound: Critical race theory, assaultive speech, and the First Amendment. Boulder, CO: Westview.

Mattingly, I. G., & Liberman, A. M. (1988). Specialized processing system for speech and other biologically significant sounds. In G. M. Edelman, W. E. Gall, & W. M. Cowan (Eds.), *Functions of the auditory system* (pp. 775–793). New York: Wiley.

Mayberry, R. I., & Eichen, E. (1991). The long-lasting advantage of learning sign language in childhood: Another look at the critical period for language acquisition. *Journal of Memory and Language, 30,* 486–512.

Mayberry, R. I., & Jaques, J. (2000). Gesture production during stuttered speech: Insights into the nature of gesture-speech integration. In D. McNeill (Ed.), *Language and gesture* (pp. 199–214). New York: Cambridge University Press.

Mayberry, R. I., & Nicoladis, E. (2000). Gesture reflects language development: Evidence from bilingual children. *Current Directions in Psychological Science, 9,* 192–199.

Mays, V. M., Cochran, S. D., Ballinger, G., Smith, R. G., Henley, N., Daniels, M., Tibbits, T., Victorianne, G. D., Osei, O. K., and Birt, D. K. (1992). The language of black gay men's sexual behavior: Implications for AIDS risk reduction. *Journal of Sex Research, 29,* 425–434.

McCabe, A. (1996). *Chameleon readers: Teaching children to appreciate all kinds of good stories.* New York: McGraw-Hill.

McCabe, A. (1998). Sentences combined: Text and discourse. In J. Berko-Gleason & N. Bernstein Ratner (Eds.), *Psycholinguistics* (pp. 275–308). Orlando, FL: Harcourt Brace.

McClelland, J. L. (1991). Stochastic interactive processes and the effect of context on perception. *Cognitive Psychology, 23,* 1–44.

McClelland, J. L., & Elman, J. L. (1986). The TRACE model of speech perception. *Cognitive Psychology, 18,* 1–86.

McClelland, J. L., & Rumelhart, D. (1981). An interactive-activation model of context effects in letter perception: Part 1. An account of the basic findings. *Psychological Review, 88,* 375–407.

McClelland, J. L., Rumelhart, D., & the PDP Research Group. (1986). *Parallel distributed processing: Vol. 2. Explorations in the microstructure of cognition.* Cambridge, MA: Bradford.

McCutchen, D., & Perfetti, C. A. (1982). The visual tongue-twister effect: Phonological activation in silent reading. *Journal of Verbal Learning and Verbal Behavior, 21,* 672–687.

McElree, B., & Nordlie, J. (1999). Literal and figurative interpretations are computed in equal time. *Psychonomic Bulletin and Review, 6,* 486–494.

McGhee, P. E. (1979). *Humor: Its origin and development.* San Francisco: Freeman.

McKoon, G., & Ratcliff, R. (1980). Priming in item recognition: The organization of prepositions in memory of text. *Journal of Verbal Learning and Verbal Behavior, 19,* 369–386.

McKoon, G., & Ratcliff, R. (1988). Contextually relevant aspect of meaning. *Journal of Experimental Psychology: Learning, Memory, and Cognition, 14,* 331–343.

McKoon, G., & Ratcliff, R. (1989). Semantic associations and elaborative inference. *Journal of Experimental Psychology: Learning, Memory, and Cognition, 15,* 326–338.

McMullen, L. & Conway, J. (1994). Dominance and nurturance in the figurative expression of psychotherapy clients. *Psychotherapy Research, 4,* 43–57.

McMullen, L., Vernon, A., & Murton, T. (1995). Division of labor in conversations: Are Fishman's results replicable and generalizable? *Journal of Psycholinguistic Research, 24,* 255–268.

McNeill, D. (1966). Developmental psycholinguistics. In F. Smith & G. Miller (Eds.), *The genesis of language* (pp. 15–84). Cambridge, MA: MIT Press.

McNeill, D. (1987). *Psycholinguistics: A new approach.* New York: Harper & Row.

McNeill, D. (1992). *Hand and mind: What gestures reveal about thought.* Chicago: University of Chicago Press.

McNeill, D. (1999). Triangulating the growth point: Arriving at consciousness. In L. S. Messing & R. Campbell (Eds.), *Gesture, speech and sign* (pp. 77–92). Oxford: Oxford University Press.

McNeill, D. (Ed.). (2000). *Language and gesture.* New York: Cambridge University Press.

McNeill, D., & Duncan, S. (2000). Growth points in thinking-for-speaking. In D. McNeill (Ed.), *Language and gesture* (pp. 141–161). New York: Cambridge University Press.

McQueen, J. M., Norris, D., & Cutler, A. (1999). Lexical influence in phonetic decision making: Evidence from subcategorical mismatches. *Journal of Experimental Psychology: Human Perception and Performance, 25,* 1363–1389.

Mednick, S. A., & Mednick, M. T. (1967). *The remote associates test.* Boston: Houghton Mifflin.

Meeker, F. B., & Kleinke, C. L. (1972). Knowledge of names for in- and outgroup members of different sex and ethnic groups. *Psychological Reports, 31,* 832–834.

Mehler, J., Jusczyk, P. W., Lambertz, G., Halsted, N., Bertoncini, J., & Amiel-Tison, C. (1988). A precursor of language acquisition in young infants. *Cognition, 29,* 143–178.

Melinkoff, D. (1963). *The language of the law.* Boston: Little, Brown.

Memon, A., Vrij, A., & Bull, R. (1998). *Psychology and law: Truthfulness, accuracy, and credibility.* New York: McGraw-Hill.

Mental lexicon [Special issue]. (1999). *Brain and Language, 68*(1–2).

Meringer, R., & Mayer, K. (1895). *Versprechen und verlesen: Ein psychologisch-linguistiche studie* [Misspeaking and misreading: A psycholinguistic study]. Stuttgart, Germany: Göschense Verlagsbuchhandlung.

Mervis, C. B., & Bertrand, J. (1994). Acquisition of the novel name-nameless category (N3C) principle. *Child Development, 65,* 1646–1662.

Mervis, C. B., & Bertrand, J. (1995). Early lexical acquisition and the vocabulary spurt: A response to Goldfield & Reznick. *Journal of Child Language, 22,* 461–468.

Mervis, C. B., & Rosch, E. (1981). Categorization of natural objects. In M. R. Rosenz & L. W. Porter (Eds.), *Annual review of psychology* (Vol. 21). Palo Alto, CA: Annual Reviews.

Metcalfe, J., Funnell, M., & Gazzaniga, M. (1995). Right hemisphere memory superiority: Studies of a split-brain patient. *Psychological Science, 6,* 157–164.

Meyer, D. E., & Schvaneveldt, R. W. (1971). Facilitation in recognizing pairs of words: Evidence of a dependence between retrieval operations. *Journal of Experimental Psychology, 90,* 227–234.

Michaels, S. (1983). The role of adult assistance in children's acquisition of literate discourse strategies. *Volta Review, 85,* 72–85.

Miller, G. A. (1967). *The psychology of communication.* New York: Basic Books.

Miller, G. A. (1995). *The science of words.* New York: Scientific American Library.

Miller, J. F., & Chapman, R. S. (1981). The relation between age and mean length of utterance. *Journal of Speech and Hearing Research, 24,* 154–161.

Miller, J. F., Wier, C., Pastore, R., Kelley, W., & Dooling, R. (1976). Discrimination and labeling of noise-buzz sequences with varying noise lead times: An example of categorical perception. *Journal of the Acoustical Society of America, 60,* 410–417.

Miller, P., Wiley, A., Fung, H., & Liang, C. (1997). Personal storytelling as a medium of socialization in Chinese and American families. *Child Development, 68,* 557–568.

Minami, M., & McCabe, A. (1995). Rice balls and bear hunts: Japanese and North American family narrative patterns. *Journal of Child Language, 22,* 423–446.

Mitchell, D. C. (1987). Lexical guidance in human parsing: Locus and processing characteristics. In M. Coltheart (Ed.), *Attention and performance XII: The psychology of reading* (pp. 601–618). Hillsdale, NJ: Erlbaum.

Mitchell, D. C. (1994). Sentence parsing. In M. A. Gernsbacher (Ed.), *Handbook of psycholinguistics* (pp. 375–409). New York: Academic Press.

Mitchell, D. C., Corley, M. B., & Garnham, A. (1992). Effects of context in human sentence parsing: Evidence against a discourse-based proposal mechanism. *Journal of Experimental Psychology: Language, Memory, and Cognition, 18,* 69–88.

Mitchell, D. C., & Holmes, V. M. (1985). The role of specific information about the verb in parsing sentences with local structural ambiguity. *Journal of Memory and Language, 24,* 542–559.

Miyake, A., Just, M. A., & Carpenter, P. A. (1994). Working memory constraints on the resolution of lexical ambiguity: Maintaining multiple interpretations in neutral contexts. *Journal of Memory and Language, 33,* 175–202.

Moerk, E. L. (1989). The LAD was a lady, and the tasks were ill-defined. *Developmental Review, 9,* 21–57.

Moerk, E. L. (1990). Three-term contingency patterns in mother-child verbal interactions during first-language acquisition. *Journal of the Experimental Analysis of Behavior, 54,* 293–305.

Moerk, E. L. (1991). *Language training and learning: Processes and products.* Baltimore: Brookes.

Monsell, S., Patterson, K., Graham, A., Hughes, C. H., & Milroy, R. (1992). Lexical and sublexical translations of spelling to sound: Strategic anticipation of lexical status. *Journal of Experimental Psychology: Learning, Memory, and Cognition, 18,* 452–467.

Morais, J., Bertelson, P., Cary, L., & Alegria, J. (1986). Literacy training and speech segmentation. *Cognition, 24,* 45–64.

Morgan, J., & Demuth, K. (1996). *Signal to syntax: Bootstrapping from speech to grammar in early acquisition.* Mahwah, NJ: Erlbaum.

Morgan, J., Bonamo, K. M., & Travis, L. (1995). Negative evidence on negative evidence. *Developmental Psychology, 31,* 180–197.

Morris, G. H., & Chenail, R. J. (1995). *Talk of the clinic: Explorations in the analysis of medical and therapeutic discourse.* Hillsdale, NJ: Erlbaum.

Morrison, R. E., & Imhoff, A. W. (1981). Visual factors and eye movements in reading. *Visual Language, 15,* 129–146.

Morton, J. (1969). Interaction of information in word recognition. *Psychological Review, 76,* 165–178.

Morton, J. (1970). Word recognition. In J. Morton & J. Marshall (Eds.), *Psycholinguistics 2: Structure and processes* (pp. 107–156). Cambridge, MA: MIT Press.

Morton, J. (1979). Facilitation in word recognition: Experiments causing change in the logogen model. In P. Kolers, M. Wrolstad, & H. Bouma (Eds.), *Processing of visual language* (pp. 259–268). New York: Plenum.

Morton, J. (1982). Disintegrating the lexicon: An information processing approach. In J. Mehler, E. Walker, & M. F. Garrett (Eds.), *On mental representation* (pp. 89–109). Hillsdale, NJ: Erlbaum.

Morton, J., & Patterson, K. (1980). A new attempt at an interpretation, or an attempt at new interpretation. In M. Coltheart, K. Patterson, & J. Marshall (Eds.), *Deep dyslexia* (pp. 91–118). London: Routledge.

Motley, M. T. (1980). Verification of "Freudian slips" and semantic prearticulatory editing via laboratory-induced spoonerisms. In V. A. Fromkin (Ed.), *Errors in linguistic performance* (pp. 133–147). New York: Academic Press.

Motley, M. T., & Baars, B. J. (1976). Semantic bias effects on the outcomes of verbal slips. *Cognition, 4,* 177–187.

Motley, M. T., Camden, C. T., & Baars, B. J. (1981). Toward verifying the assumption of laboratory-induced slips of the tongue: The output-error and editing issues. *Human Communication Research, 8,* 3–15.

Motley, M. T., Camden, C. T., & Baars, B. J. (1982). Covert formulation and editing anomalies in speech production: Evidence from experimentally induced slips of the tongue. *Journal of Verbal Learning and Verbal Behavior, 21,* 578–594.

Mowrer, O. H. (1960). *Learning theory and the symbolic process.* New York: Wiley.

Mullennix, J. W., & Pisoni, D. B. (1990). Stimulus variability and processing dependencies in speech perception. *Perception and Psychophysics, 47,* 379–390.

Murphy, G. L., & Shapiro, A. M. (1994). Forgetting of verbatim information in discourse. *Memory and Cognition, 22,* 85–94.

Myers, J. L., Shinjo, M., & Duffy, S. A. (1987). Degree of causal relatedness and memory. *Journal of Memory and Language, 26,* 453–465.

Myers-Scotton, C., & Lake, J. (2000). Explaining aspects of codeswitching and their implications. In J. Nichol (Ed.), *One mind, two languages: Bilingual language processing* (pp. 91–125). Oxford, UK: Blackwell.

Myers-Scotton, C., & Ury, W. (1977, June 2). Bilingual strategies: The social functions of codeswitching. *International Journal of Sociology of Language, 13,* 193.

Naigles, L. (1990). Children use syntax to learn verb meanings. *Journal of Child Language, 17,* 357–374.

Naigles, L. (1995). The use of multiple frames in verb learning via syntactic bootstrapping. *Cognition, 58,* 221–251.

Naigles, L., & Hoff-Ginsberg, E. (1998). Why are some verbs learned before other verbs? Effects of input frequency and structure on children's early verb use. *Journal of Child Language, 25,* 95–120.

Navarro, A. M. (1998). *Phonetic effects of the ambient language in early speech: Comparisons of monolingual- and bilingual-learning children.* Unpublished dissertation, University of Miami, Coral Gables, FL.

Neely, J. H. (1991). Semantic priming effects in visual word recognition: A selective review of current findings and theories. In D. Besner & G. Humphreys (Eds.), *Basic processes in reading: Visual word recognition* (pp. 236–264). Hillsdale, NJ: Erlbaum.

Nelson, K. (1973). Structure and strategy in learning to talk. *Monographs of the Society for Research in Child Development, 38*(1–2, Serial No. 149).

Nelson, K. (1981). Individual differences in language development: Implications for development and language. *Developmental Psychology, 17,* 170–187.

Neville, H. J., Coffey, S. A., Lawson, D. S., Fischer, A., Emmorey, K., & Bellugi, U. (1997). Neural systems mediating American Sign Language: Effects of sensory experience and age of acquisition. *Brain and Language, 57,* 285–308.

Newkirk, D., Klima, E. S., Pedersen, C. C., & Bellugi, U. (1980). Linguistic evidence from slips of the hand. In V. A. Fromkin (Ed.), *Errors in linguistic performance* (pp. 165–197). New York: Academic Press.

Newport, E. L. (1990). Maturational constraints on language learning. *Cognitive Science, 14,* 11–28.

Newport, E. L., & Ashbrook, E. F. (1977). The emergence of semantic relations in ASL. *Papers and Reports on Child Language Development, 13,* 16–21.

Newport, E. L., Gleitman, L. R., & Gleitman, H. (1977). Mother, I'd rather do it myself: Some effects and non-effects of motherese. In C. E. Snow & C. Ferguson (Eds.), *Talking to children: Language input and acquisition* (pp. 109–150). Cambridge: Cambridge University Press.

Nicoladis, E., & Genesee, F. (1997). Language development in preschool bilingual children. *Journal of Speech-Language Pathology and Audiology, 21,* 258–270.

Nieh, J. (1999). Stingless-bee communication. *American Scientist, 87,* 428–435.

Ninio, A., & Bruner, J. S. (1978). The achievement and antecedents of labeling. *Journal of Child Language, 5,* 1–15.

Ninio, A., & Snow, C. E. (1996). *Pragmatic development.* Boulder, CO: Westview.

Nissen, H. J. (1986). The archaic texts from Uruk. *World Archeology, 17,* 318–334.

Nooteboom, S. (1980). Speaking and unspeaking: Detection and correction of phonological and lexical errors in spontaneous speech. In V. A. Fromkin (Ed.), *Errors in linguistic performance* (pp. 87–95). New York: Academic Press.

Norman, D. (1989). Cognitive artifacts. In J. M. Carroll (Ed.), *Designing interaction: Psychology at the human-computer interface* (pp. 17–38). New York: Cambridge University Press.

Norrick, N. R. (1987). Functions of repetition in conversation. *Text, 7,* 245–264.

Norrick, N. R. (1993a). *Conversational joking: Humor in everyday talk.* Bloomington: Indiana University Press.

Norrick, N. R. (1993b). Repetition in canned jokes and spontaneous conversational joking. *Humor, 6,* 385–402.

Norrick, N. R. (2000). *Conversational narrative: Storytelling in everyday talk.* Philadelphia: John Benjamins.

Norris, D., McQueen, J. M., & Cutler, A. (2000). Merging information in speech recognition: Feedback is never necessary. *Behavior and Brain Sciences, 23,* 299–325.

O'Barr, W. (1982). *Linguistic evidence: Language, power, and strategy in the courtroom.* New York: Academic Press.

O'Brien, E. J. (1987). Antecedent search processes and the structure of text. *Journal of Experimental Psychology: Learning, Memory, and Cognition, 13,* 278–290.

O'Brien, E. J., & Albrecht, J. E. (1991). The role of context in accessing antecedents in text. *Journal of Experimental Psychology: Learning, Memory, and Cognition, 17,* 94–102.

O'Brien, E. J., & Myers, J. L. (1987). The role of causal connections in the retrieval of text. *Memory and Cognition, 15,* 419–427.

O'Brien, E. J., Plewes, P. S., & Albrecht, J. E. (1990). Antecedent retrieval processes. *Journal of Experimental Psychology: Learning, Memory, and Cognition, 16,* 241–249.

O'Brien, E. J., Shank, D., Myers, J. L., & Rayner, K. (1988). Elaborative inferences during reading: Do they occur on-line? *Journal of Experimental Psychology: Learning, Memory, and Cognition, 14,* 410–420.

Ochs, E. (1982). Talking to children in Western Samoa. *Language in Society, 11,* 77–104.

Ohala, J. J. (1986). Against a direct realist view of speech perception. *Journal of Phonetics, 14,* 75–82.

Ojemann, G. A., & Whitaker, H. A. (1978). The bilingual brain. *Archives of Neurology, 35,* 409–412.

Oller, D. K. (1980). The emergence of sounds of speech in infancy. In G. H. Yeni-Komshian, J. F. Kavanaugh, & C. A. Ferguson (Eds.), *Child phonology: Vol. 1. Production* (pp. 93–112). New York: Academic Press.

Oller, D. K., & Eilers, R. E. (1988). The role of audition in babbling. *Child Development, 59,* 441–449.

Oller, D. K., & Eilers, R. E. (1998). Interpretive and methodological difficulties in evaluating babbling drift. *Parole, 7–8,* 147–164.

Oller, D. K., & Eilers, R. E. (Eds.). (2002). *Language and literacy in bilingual children.* Clevedon, England: Multilingual Matters.

Oller, D. K., Eilers, R. E., Urbano, R., & Cobo-Lewis, A. (1997). Development of precursors to speech in infants exposed to two languages. *Journal of Child Language, 24,* 407–425.

Olson, D. (1996). Toward a psychology of literacy: On the relations between speech and writing. *Cognition, 60,* 83–104.

Onifer, W., & Swinney, D. (1981). Accessing lexical ambiguities during sentence comprehension: Effects of frequency of meaning and contextual bias. *Memory and Cognition, 9,* 225–236.

Ortony, A. (1975). Why metaphors are necessary and not just nice. *Educational Theory, 25,* 45–53.

Ortony, A. (1979). Beyond literal similarity. *Psychological Review, 86,* 161–180.

Ortony, A. (1980). Some psycholinguistic aspects of metaphor. In R. Honeck & R. Hoffman (Eds.), *Cognition and figurative language* (pp. 69–83). Hillsdale, NJ: Erlbaum.

Ortony, A., & Fainsilber, L. (1987). The role of metaphor in descriptions of emotions. In Y. Wilks (Ed.), *TINLAP 3: Theoretical issues in natural language processing: Position papers* (pp. 181–184). Las Cruces: New Mexico State University, Computing Research Lab.

Ortony, A., Schallert, D. L., Reynolds, R. E., & Antos, S. J. (1978). Interpreting metaphors and idioms: Some effects of context on comprehension. *Journal of Verbal Learning and Verbal Behavior, 17,* 465–477.

Osaka, N. (1987). Effect of peripheral visual field size on eye movements during Japanese text processing. In J. O'Regan & A. Levy-Schoen (Eds.), *Eye movements: From physiology to cognition* (pp. 421–429). Amsterdam: Elsevier.

Osgood, C. E. (1953). *Method and theory in experimental psychology.* New York: Oxford University Press.

Osgood, C. E., Suci, G. J., & Tannenbaum, P. H. (1957). *The measurement of meaning.* Urbana: University of Illinois Press.

Osterhout, L. (1990). *Event-related brain potentials elicited during sentence comprehension.* Unpublished doctoral dissertation, Tufts University, Medford, MA.

Osterhout, L., & Holcomb, P. J. (1992). Event-related brain potentials elicited by syntactic anomaly. *Journal of Memory and Language, 31,* 785–806.

O'Sullivan, C., & Yeager, C. P. (1989). Communicative context and linguistic competence: The effects of social setting on a chimpanzee's conversational skill. In R. A. Gardner, B. T. Gardner, & T. E. Van Cantfort (Eds.), *Teaching sign language to chimpanzees* (pp. 269–279). Albany: State University of New York Press.

Otsubo, S. (1988). A behavioral study of warning labels for consumer products: Perceived danger and the use of pictographs. In *Proceedings of the Human Factors Society 32nd Annual Meeting* (pp. 536–540). Santa Monica, CA: Human Factors Society.

Paap, K. R., & Noel, R. W. (1991). Dual-route models of print to sound: Still a good horse race. *Psychological Research, 53,* 13–24.

Paivio, A. (1969). Mental imagery in associative learning and memory. *Psychological Review, 76,* 241–263.

Paivio, A. (1986). *Mental representations: A dual coding approach.* New York: Oxford University Press.

Palmeri, T. J., Goldinger, S. D., & Pisoni, D. B. (1993). Episodic encoding of voice attributes and recognition memory for spoken words. *Journal of Experimental Psychology: Learning, Memory, and Cognition, 19,* 309–328.

Palermo, D. S. (1963). Word associations and children's verbal behavior. In L. Lipsitt & C. Spiker (Eds.), *Advances in child development and behavior* (Vol. 1). New York: Academic Press.

Pareja, J., de Pablos, E., Caminero, A., Millan, I., & Dobato, J. (1999). Native language shifts across sleep-wake states in bilingual speakers. *Sleep, 22,* 243–247.

Partridge, E. (1984). *Dictionary of slang and unconventional English.* New York: Macmillan.

Patterson, K., Graham, N., & Hodges, J. R. (1994). Reading in Alzheimer's-type dementia: A preserved ability? *Neuropsychology, 8,* 395–412.

Paul, S. T., Kellas, G., Martin, M., & Clark, M. B. (1992). The influence of contextual features on the activation of ambiguous words meanings. *Journal of Experimental Psychology: Learning, Memory, and Cognition, 18,* 703–717.

Pearson, B., Fernandez, S., & Oller, D. K. (1993). Lexical development in bilingual infants and toddlers: Comparisons to monolingual norms. *Language Learning, 43,* 93–120.

Pearson, B., Fernandez, S., & Oller, D. K. (1995). Cross-language synonyms in the lexicons of bilingual infants: One language or two? *Journal of Child Language, 22,* 345–368.

Penfield, W., & Roberts, L. (1959). *Speech and brain mechanisms.* Princeton, NJ: Princeton University Press.

Pennebaker, J. W. (1990). *Opening up: The healing power of confiding in others.* New York: Morrow.

Pennebaker, J. W., Kiecolt-Glaser, J. K., & Glaser, R. (1988). Disclosure of traumas and immune function: Health implications for psychotherapy. *Journal of Consulting and Clinical Psychology, 56,* 239–245.

Perani, D., Dehaene, S., Grassi, F., Cohen, L., Cappa, S. F., Dupoux, E., Fazio, F., & Mehler, J. (1996). Brain processing of native and foreign language. *Neuroreport, 7,* 2439–2444.

Perfetti, C. A. (1985). *Reading ability.* New York: Oxford University Press.

Perfetti, C. A., & Goldman, S. R. (1976). Discourse memory and reading comprehension skill. *Journal of Verbal Learning and Verbal Behavior, 14,* 33–42.

Perfetti, C. A., Zhang, S., & Berent, I. (1992). Reading in English and Chinese: Evidence for a "universal" phonological principle. In R. Frost & L. Katz (Eds.), *Orthography, phonology, morphology, and meaning* (pp. 227–248). Amsterdam: North-Holland.

Perrig, W., & Kintsch, W. (1985). Propositional and situational representations of text. *Journal of Memory and Language, 24,* 503–518.

Peters, A. (1995). Strategies in the acquisition of syntax. In P. Fletcher & B. MacWhinney (Eds.), *The handbook of child language* (pp. 462–483). Oxford: Blackwell.

Petitto, L. A., & Marentette, P. F. (1991). Babbling in manual mode: Evidence for the ontogeny of language. *Science, 251,* 1493–1496.

Pezdek, K., & Prull, M. (1993). Fallacies in memory for conversations: Reflections on Clarence Thomas, Anita Hill, and the like. *Applied Cognitive Psychology, 7,* 299–310.

Piaget, J. (1926). *The language and thought of the child.* New York: Harcourt Brace.

Piaget, J. (1954). *The origins of intelligence.* New York: Basic Books.

Piaget, J. (1962). *Play, dreams, and imitation in childhood* (C. Gattegno & F. M. Hodgson, Trans.). New York: Norton.

Pine, J. (1994). Environmental correlates of variation in lexical style: Interactional style and the structure of the input. *Applied Psycholinguistics, 15,* 355–370.

Pinker, S. (1994). *The language instinct: How the mind creates language.* New York: Morrow.

Pinker, S. (1997). *How the mind works.* New York: Norton.

Pinker, S. (1999). *Words and rules: The ingredients of language.* New York: Basic Books.

Pinker, S., Lebeaux, D., & Frost, L. (1987). Productivity and constraints in the acquisition of the passive. *Cognition, 26,* 195–197.

Pinker, S., & Prince, A. (1988). On language and connectionism: An analysis of a parallel distributed processing model of language acquisition. *Cognition, 28,* 73–193.

Pinker, S., & Prince, A. (1994). Regular and irregular morphology and the psychological rules of grammar. In S. Lima, R. Corrigan, & G. Iverson (Eds.), *The reality of linguistic rules* (pp. 321–352). Philadelphia: John Benjamins.

Pisoni, D. B., Nusbaum, H., Luce, P., & Slowiaczek, L. (1985). Speech perception, word recognition, and the structure of the lexicon. *Speech Communication, 4,* 75-95.

Plaut, D. C. (1999). A connectionist approach to word reading and acquired dyslexia: Extension to sequential processing. *Cognitive Science, 23,* 543–568.

Plaut, D. C., McClelland, J. L., Seidenberg, M., & Patterson, K. (1996). Understanding normal and impaired word reading: Computational principles in quasi-regular domains. *Psychological Review, 103,* 56–115.

Plunkett, K., & Schafer, G. (1999). Early speech perception and word learning. In M. Barrett (Ed.), *The development of language* (pp. 51–72). East Sussex, England: Psychology Press.

Plutchik, R. (2001). The nature of emotions. *American Scientist, 89,* 344–350.

Poizner, H., Klima, E. S., & Bellugi, U. (1987). *What the hands reveal about the brain.* Cambridge, MA: MIT Press.

Polanyi, L. (1979). So what's the point? *Semiotica, 25,* 207–241.

Polanyi, L. (1981). Telling the same story twice. *Text, 1,* 315–336.

Polanyi, L. (1989). *Telling the American story.* Cambridge, MA: MIT Press.

Pollatsek, A., Bolozky, S., Well, A. D., & Rayner, K. (1981). Asymmetries in the perceptual span for Israeli readers. *Brain and Language, 14,* 174–180.

Pollio, H. R. (1974). *The psychology of symbolic activity.* Reading, MA: Addison-Wesley.

Pollio, H. R., & Gerow, J. R. (1968). The role of rules in recall. *American Journal of Psychology, 81,* 303–313.

Pollio, H. R., Smith, M., & Pollio, M. (1990). Figurative language and cognitive psychology. *Language and Cognitive Processes, 5,* 141–167.

Posner, M. I., & Raichle, M. E. (1994). *Images of mind.* New York: Freeman.

Prather, P., Zurif, E. B., Stern, C., & Rosen, T. J. (1992). Slowed lexical access in nonfluent aphasia: A case study. *Brain and Language, 43,* 336–348.

Premack, D. (1971). Language in chimpanzees? *Science, 172,* 808–822.

Premack, D. (1986). *Gavagai! or the future history of the animal language controversy.* Cambridge, MA: Bradford.

Prince, A., & Smolensky, P. (1991). *Notes on connectionism and harmony theory in linguistics.* Boulder, CO: University of Colorado, Department of Computer Sciences.

Prince, A., & Smolensky, P. (1997). Optimality: From neural networks to universal grammar. *Science, 275,* 1604–1610.

Prinz, P. M., & Prinz, E. A. (1979). Simultaneous acquisition of ASL and spoken English (in a hearing child of a deaf mother and hearing father): Phase I. Early lexical development. *Sign Language Studies, 25,* 283–296.

Pritchett, B. L. (1988). Garden path phenomena and the grammatical basis of language processing. *Language, 64,* 539–576.

Pullum, G. K. (1991). *The great Eskimo vocabulary hoax, and other irreverent essays on the study of language.* Chicago: University of Chicago Press.

Rabin, M. D., & Cain, W. S. (1986). Determinants of measured olfactory sensitivity. *Perception and Psychophysics, 39,* 281–286.

Rasmussen, T., & Milner, B. (1977). The role of early left-brain injury in determining lateralization of cerebral speech functions. *Annals of the New York Academy of Sciences, 299,* 355–369.

Rauscher, F. B., Krauss, R. M., & Chen, Y. (1996). Gesture, speech, and lexical access: The role of lexical movements in speech production. *Psychological Science, 7,* 226–231.

Rayner, K., Carlson, M., & Frazier, L. (1983). The interaction of syntax and semantics during sentence processing: Eye movements in the analysis of semantically biased sentences. *Journal of Verbal Learning and Verbal Behavior, 22,* 358–374.

Rayner, K., & Duffy, S. A. (1986). Lexical complexity and fixation times in reading: Effects of word frequency, verb complexity, and lexical ambiguity. *Memory and Cognition, 14,* 191–201.

Rayner, K., & Frazier, L. (1989). Selection mechanisms in reading lexically ambiguous words. *Journal of Experimental Psychology: Learning, Memory, and Cognition, 15,* 779–790.

Rayner, K., & McConkie, G. W. (1976). Asymmetry of the perceptual span in reading. *Bulletin of the Psychonomic Society, 8,* 365–368.

Rayner, K., & Morris, R. K. (1991). Comprehension processes in reading ambiguous sentences: Reflections from eye movements. In G. Simpson (Ed.), *Understanding word and sentence* (pp. 175–198). Amsterdam: North-Holland.

Rayner, K., & Morris, R. K. (1992). Eye movement control in reading: Evidence against semantic preprocessing. *Journal of Experimental Psychology: Human Perception and Performance, 18,* 163–172.

Rayner, K., & Pollatsek, A. (1989). *The psychology of reading.* Englewood Cliffs, NJ: Prentice Hall.

Rayner, K., & Sereno, S. C. (1994). Eye movements in reading: Psycholinguistic studies. In. M. A. Gernsbacher (Ed.), *Handbook of psycholinguistics* (pp. 57–81). New York: Academic Press.

Razran, G. A. (1939). A quantitative study of meaning by a conditioned salivary technique (semantic conditioning). *Science, 90,* 89–90.

Razran, G. A. (1961). The observable unconscious and the inferable conscious in current Soviet psychophysiology. *Psychological Review, 68,* 81–147.

Read, C. (1981). Writing is not the inverse of reading for young children. In C. Frederiksen & J. Dominic (Eds.), *Writing: The nature, development, and teaching of written communication* (pp. 105–115). Hillsdale, NJ: Erlbaum.

Read, C., Zhang, Y., Nie, H., & Ding, B. (1986). The ability to manipulate speech sounds depends on knowing alphabetic reading. *Cognition, 24,* 31–44.

Reder, L. M., & Kusbit, G. W. (1991). Locus of the Moses illusion: Imperfect encoding, retrieval, or match? *Journal of Memory and Language, 30,* 385–406.

Reese, E. (1995). Predicting children's literacy from mother-child conversations. *Cognitive Development, 10,* 381–406.

Reich, P. A. (1986). *Language development.* Englewood Cliffs, NJ: Prentice Hall

Reilly, J., Klima, E. S., & Bellugi, U. (1990). Once more with feeling: Affect and language in atypical populations. *Development and Psychopathology, 2,* 369–391.

Remez, R. (1994). On the perception of speech. In M. A. Gernsbacher (Ed.), *Handbook of psycholinguistics* (pp. 145–172). New York: Academic Press.

Remez, R., Rubin, P. E., Pisoni, D. B., & Carrell, T. D. (1981). Speech perception without traditional speech cues. *Science, 212,* 947–950.

Repp, B. (1992). Perceptual restoration of a "missing" speech sound: Auditory induction or illusion? *Perception and Psychophysics, 51,* 14–32.

Reynolds, A. G. (1990). The cognitive consequences of bilingualism. In A. G. Reynolds (Ed.), *Bilingualism, multiculturalism, and second language learning: The McGill Conference in honor of Wallace E. Lambert* (pp. 145–182). Hillsdale, NJ: Erlbaum.

Rickford, J. R., & Rickford, R. J. (2000). *Spoken soul: The story of Black English.* New York: Wiley.

Rieben, L., & Perfetti, C. A. (Eds.). (1991). *Learning to read: Basic research and its implications.* Hillsdale, NJ: Erlbaum.

Rips, L. J., Shoben, E. J., & Smith, E. E. (1973). Semantic distance and the verification of semantic relations. *Journal of Verbal Learning and Verbal Behavior, 12,* 1–20.

Roberts, R. M., & Kreuz, R. J. (1994). Why do people use figurative language? *Psychological Science, 5,* 159–163.

Rogers, C. R. (1951). *Client-centered therapy.* Boston: Houghton Mifflin.

Rogers, C. R. (1970). *On becoming a person: A therapist's view of psychotherapy.* Boston: Houghton Mifflin.

Root, R. L. (1985). *Assiduous string-savers: The idea-generating strategies of professional expository writers.* Paper presented at the annual meeting of the Conference of College Composition and Communication. (ERIC Document Reproduction Service No. ED 258 205)

Rosch, E. H. (1973). On the internal structure of perceptual and semantic categories. In T. E. Moore (Ed.), *Cognitive development and the acquisition of language* (pp. 111–144). New York: Academic Press.

Rosch, E. H. (1974). Linguistic relativity. In A. Silverstein (Ed.), *Human communication: Theoretical perspectives*. New York: Halsted Press.

Rosenberg, S. (1987). *Advances in applied psycholinguistics*. Cambridge: Cambridge University Press.

Ross, E. D., Homan, R. W., & Buck, R. (1994). Differential hemispheric lateralization of primary and social emotions: Implications for developing a comprehensive theory of emotions, repression, and the subconscious. *Neuropsychiatry, Neuropsychology, and Behavioral Neurology, 7*, 1–19.

Ross, E. D., Thompson, R. D., & Yenkosky, J. (1997). Lateralization of affective prosody in brain and the callosal integration of hemispheric language functions. *Brain and Language, 56*, 27–54.

Rosten, L. (1968). *The joys of Yiddish*. New York: McGraw-Hill.

Rozin, P., Bressman, B., & Taft, M. (1974). Do children understand the basic relationship between speech and writing? The mow-motorcycle test. *Journal of Reading Behavior, 6*, 327–334.

Rozin, P., & Fallon, A. (1987). A perspective on disgust. *Psychological Review, 94*, 23–41.

Rubenstein, H., Garfield, L., & Millikan, J. A. (1970). Homographic entries in the internal lexicon. *Journal of Verbal Learning and Verbal Behavior, 9*, 487–494.

Rubin, G. S., Becker, C. A., & Freeman, R. H. (1979). Morphological structure and its effect on visual word recognition. *Journal of Verbal Learning and Verbal Behavior, 18*, 757–767.

Rumbaugh, D. (1977). *Language learning by a chimpanzee: The Lana project*. New York: Academic Press.

Rumelhart, D. E. (1975). Notes on a schema for stories. In D. Bobrow & A. Collins (Eds.), *Representation and understanding: Studies in cognitive science* (pp. 211–236). New York: Academic Press.

Rumelhart, D. E., McClelland, J. L., & the PDP Research Group. (1986). *Parallel distributed processing: Vol. 1. Explorations in the microstructure of cognition*. Cambridge, MA: MIT Press.

Sachs, J. (1987). Preschool boys' and girls' language use in pretend play. In S. Phillips, S. Steele, & C. Tanz (Eds.), *Language, gender and sex in comparative perspective* (pp. 178–188). Cambridge: Cambridge University Press.

Sachs, J. S. (1967). Recognition memory for syntactic and semantic aspects of connected discourse. *Perception and Psychophysics, 2*, 437–442.

Sacks, H. (1972). On the analyzability of stories by children. In J. J. Gumperz & D. Hymes (Eds.), *Directions in sociolinguistics* (pp. 325–345). New York: Holt, Rinehart and Winston.

Sacks, H. (1974). An analysis of the course of a joke's telling. In R. Bauman & J. Sherzer (Eds.), *Explorations in the ethnography of speaking* (pp. 337–353). Cambridge: Cambridge University Press.

Sacks, H. (1992). *Lectures on conversation* (Vols. 1–2). (Ed. G. Jefferson). Oxford: Blackwell.

Sacks, H., Schegloff, E. A., & Jefferson, G. (1974). A simplest systematics for the organization of turn-taking for conversation. *Language, 50*, 696–735.

Saffran, J., Aslin, R., & Newport, E. (1996). Statistical learning by 8-month-old infants. *Science, 274*, 1926–1928.

St. George, M., Mannes, S., & Hoffman, J. (1997). Individual differences in inference generation: An ERP analysis. *Journal of Cognitive Neuroscience, 9*, 776–787.

Samuel, A. G. (1981). Phonemic restoration: Insights from a new methodology. *Journal of Experimental Psychology: General, 110*, 474–494.

Samuel, A. G. (1986). The role of the lexicon in speech perception. In H. Nusbaum & E. Schwab (Eds.), *Pattern recognition by humans and machines: Speech perception* (Vol. 1, pp. 89–111). Orlando, FL: Academic Press.

Samuel, A. G. (1996). Does lexical information influence the perceptual restoration of phonemes? *Journal of Experimental Psychology: General, 125*, 28–51.

Samuel, A. G. (1997). Lexical activation produces potent phonemic percepts. *Cognitive Psychology, 32*, 97–127.

Samuelsson, I., Mauritzson, U., Carlsson, M., & Ueda, M. (1998). A mother and friend: Differences in Japanese and Swedish mothers' understanding of a tale. *Childhood, 5,* 493–506.

Sanders, M. S., & McCormick, E. J. (1993). *Human factors in engineering and design.* New York: McGraw-Hill.

Sandra, D. (1990). On the representation and processing of compound words: Automatic access to constituent morphemes does not occur. *Quarterly Journal of Experimental Psychology, 42A,* 529–567.

Sanford, A. J., & Garrod, S. C. (1994). Selective processing in text understanding. In M. A. Gernsbacher (Ed.), *Handbook of psycholinguistics* (pp. 699–719). New York: Academic Press.

Saussure, F. de. (1966). *Course in general linguistics.* New York: McGraw-Hill. (Originally published 1916)

Savage-Rumbaugh, E. S., & Lewin, R. (1994). *Kanzi: The ape at the brink of the human mind.* New York: Wiley.

Savage-Rumbaugh, E. S., McDonald, K., Sevik, R. A., Hopkins, W. D., & Rubert, E. (1986). Spontaneous symbol acquisition and communicative use by pygmy chimpanzees (*Pan paniscus*). *Journal of Experimental Psychology: General, 115,* 211–235.

Savage-Rumbaugh, E. S., Shanker, S. G., & Taylor, T. J. (1998). *Apes, language, and the human mind.* New York: Oxford University Press.

Savin, H. B. (1963). Word-frequency effect and errors in the perception of speech. *Journal of the Acoustical Society of America, 35,* 200–206.

Scarborough, D., Gerard, L., & Cortese, C. (1984). Independence of lexical access in bilingual word recognition. *Journal of Verbal Learning and Verbal Behavior, 23,* 84–99.

Scarborough, H., & Dobrich, W. (1990). Development of children with early language delay. *Journal of Speech and Hearing Research, 33,* 70–83.

Schachter, S., Christenfeld, N., Ravina, B., & Bilous, F. (1991). Speech disfluency and the structure of knowledge. *Journal of Personality and Social Psychology, 60,* 362–367.

Schachter, S., Rauscher, F., Christenfeld, N., & Crone, K. T. (1994). The vocabularies of academia. *Psychological Science, 5,* 37–41.

Schank, R. C. (1977). Rules and topics in conversations. *Cognitive Science, 1,* 421–441.

Schank, R. C., & Abelson, R. P. (1977). *Scripts, plans, goals, and understanding.* Hillsdale, NJ: Erlbaum.

Schegloff, E. A., & Sacks, H. (1973). Opening up closings. *Semiotica, 8,* 289–327.

Scherer, K. R., Banse, R., & Wallbott, H. G. (2001). Emotion inferences from vocal expressions correlate across language and cultures. *Journal of Cross-Cultural Psychology, 32,* 76–92.

Scherer, K. R., Banse, R., Wallbott, H. G., & Goldbeck, T. (1991). Vocal cues in emotion encoding and decoding. *Motivation and Emotion, 15,* 123–148.

Schieffelin, B., & Ochs, E. (1986). Language socialization. *Annual Review of Anthropology, 15,* 163–191.

Schmandt-Bessarat, D. (1986). Tokens: Facts and interpretations. *Visible Language, 20,* 250–272.

Schmandt-Bessarat, D. (1987). *Oneness, twoness, threeness: How ancient accountants invented numbers.* New York: New York Academy of Sciences.

Schmandt-Bessarat, D. (1992). *Before writing.* Austin: University of Texas Press.

Schooler, J. (1993). *Memory and the statistical structure of the environment.* Unpublished doctoral dissertation, Carnegie Mellon University, Pittsburgh.

Schreuder, R., Flores d'Arcais, G. B., & Glazenborg, G. (1984). Effects of perceptual and conceptual similarity in semantic priming. *Psychological Research, 45,* 339–354.

Schriefers, H., Meyer, A. S., & Levelt, W. (1990). Exploring the time course of lexical access in language production: Picture-word interference studies. *Journal of Memory and Language, 29,* 86–102.

Schumann, J. (1997). *The neurobiology of affect in language.* Malden, MA: Blackwell.

Schvaneveldt, R. W., Meyer, D. E., & Becker, C. A. (1976). Lexical ambiguity, semantic context, and visual word recognition, *Journal of Experimental Psychology: Human Perception and Performance, 2,* 243–256.

Schwanenflugel, P. J., Harnishfeger, K. K., & Stowe, R. W. (1988). Context availability and lexical decisions for abstract and concrete words. *Journal of Memory and Language, 27,* 499–520.

Schwartz, A. E. (1984). Earliest memories: Sex differences and the meaning of experience. *Imagination, Cognition, and Personality, 4,* 43–52.

Schwartz, B. L., Benjamin, A. S., & Bjork, R. A. (1997). The inferential and experiential bases of metamemory. *Psychological Science, 6,* 132–137.

Schwartz, B. L., & Smith, S. M. (1997). The retrieval of related information influences tip-of-the tongue states. *Journal of Memory and Language, 36,* 68–86.

Schwartz, B. L., Travis, D. M., Castro, A. M., & Smith, S. M. (2000). The phenomenology of real and illusory tip-of-the-tongue states. *Memory and Cognition, 28,* 18–27.

Schwoebel, J., Dews, S., Winner, E., & Srinivas, K. (2000). Obligatory processing of the literal meaning of ironic utterances: Further evidence. *Metaphor and Symbol, 15(1–2),* 47–61.

Scribner, S., & Cole, M. (1981). *The psychology of literacy.* Cambridge, MA: Harvard University Press.

Searle, J. R. (1969). *Speech acts: An essay in the philosophy of language.* New York: Cambridge University Press.

Searle, J. R. (1975a). Indirect speech acts. In P. Cole & J. L. Morgan (Eds.), *Syntax and semantics* (pp. 59–82). New York: Seminar Press.

Searle, J. R. (1975b). A taxonomy of illocutionary acts. In K. Gunderson (Ed.), *Minnesota studies in the philosophy of language* (pp. 344–369). Minneapolis: University of Minnesota Press.

Segalowitz, N. (1997). Individual differences in second language acquisition. In A. M. B. de Groot & J. F. Kroll (Eds.), *Tutorials in bilingualism: Psycholinguistic perspectives* (pp. 85–112). Mahwah, NJ: Erlbaum.

Segui, J., Frauenfelder, U., & Mehler, J. (1981). Phoneme monitoring, syllable monitoring, and lexical access. *British Journal of Psychology, 72,* 471–477.

Seidenberg, M. S., & McClelland, J. L. (1989). A distributed, developmental model of word recognition and naming. *Psychological Review, 96,* 523–568.

Seidenberg, M. S., Tanenhaus, M. K., Leiman, J. M., & Bienkowski, M. (1982). Automatic access of the meanings of ambiguous words in context: Some limitations of knowledge-based processing. *Cognitive Psychology, 14,* 489–537.

Seidenberg, M. S., Waters, G. S., Barnes, M. A., & Tanenhaus, M. K. (1984). When does irregular spelling or pronunciation influence word recognition? *Journal of Verbal Learning and Verbal Behavior, 23,* 383–404.

Sell, M., Kreuz, R. J., & Coppenrath, L. (1997). Parents' use of nonliteral language with preschool children. *Discourse Processes, 23,* 99–118.

Service, E. (1992). Phonology, working memory, and foreign-language learning. *Quarterly Journal of Experimental Psychology, 45,* 21–50.

Service, E., & Kohonen, V. (1995). Is the relation between phonological memory and foreign language learning accounted for by vocabulary acquisition? *Applied Psycholinguistics, 16,* 155–172.

Shafto, M., & MacKay, D. (2000). The Moses, Mega-Moses, and Armstrong illusions: Integrating language comprehension and semantic memory. *Psychological Science, 11,* 372–378.

Shankweiler, D. P., Cain, S., Katz, S., Fowler, A. E., Liberman, A. M., Brady, S. A., Thornton, R., Lundquist, E., Dreyer, L., Fletcher, J. M., Stuebing, K. K., Shaywitz, S. E., & Shaywitz, B. A. (1995). Cognitive profiles of reading-disabled children: Comparison of language skills in phonology, morphology, and syntax. *Psychological Science, 6,* 149–156.

Shannon, C. E. (1948). A mathematical theory of communication. *Bell System Technical Journal, 27,* 379–423, 623–656.

Shatz, M. (1978). On the development of communicative understandings: An early strategy for interpreting and responding to messages. *Cognitive Psychology, 10,* 271–301.

Shatz, M., Hoff-Ginsberg, E., & MacIver, D. (1989). Induction and the acquisition of English auxiliaries: The effects of differentially enriched input. *Journal of Child Language, 16,* 121–140.

Shaywitz, B. A., Shaywitz, S. E., Pugh, K. R., Constable, R. T., Skudlarski, P., Fulbright, R. K., Bronen, R. A., Fletcher, J. M., Shankweiler, D. P., Katz, L., et al. (1995). Sex differences in functional organization of the brain for language. *Nature, 373,* 607–609.

Shell, D. F., Colvin, C., & Bruning, R. H. (1995). Self-efficacy, attribution, and outcome expectancy mechanisms in reading and writing achievement: Grade-level and achievement-level differences. *Journal of Educational Psychology, 8,* 386–398.

Shiffrin, D. (1981). Tense variation in narrative. *Language, 57,* 45–62.

Shinjo, M., & Myers, J. (1987). The role of context in metaphor comprehension. *Journal of Memory and Language, 26,* 226–241.

Shuy, R. (1998a). *Bureaucratic language in government and business.* Washington, DC: Georgetown University Press.

Shuy, R. (1998b). *The language of confessions, interrogation, and deception.* Thousand Oaks, CA: Sage.

Silva, M. J., & McCabe, A. (1996). Vignettes of the continuous and family ties: Some Latin American traditions. In A. McCabe (Ed.), *Chameleon readers: Teaching children to appreciate all kinds of good stories* (pp. 116–136). New York: McGraw-Hill.

Simpson, G. B. (1981). Meaning dominance and semantic context in the processing of lexical ambiguity. *Journal of Verbal Learning and Verbal Behavior, 20,* 120–136.

Simpson, G. B. (1994). Context and the processing of ambiguous words. In M. A. Gernsbacher (Ed.), *Handbook of psycholinguistics* (pp. 359–374). New York: Academic Press.

Simpson, G. B., & Burgess, C. (1985). Activation and selection processes in the recognition of ambiguous words. *Journal of Experimental Psychology: Human Perception and Performance, 11,* 28–39.

Simpson, G. B., & Burgess, C. (1988). Implications of lexical ambiguity resolution for word recognition and comprehension. In S. I. Small, G. W. Cottrell, & M. K. Tanenhaus (Eds.), *Lexical ambiguity resolution* (pp. 271–288). San Mateo, CA: Morgan Kaufman.

Singer, M. (1980). The role of case-filling inferences in the coherence of brief passages. *Discourse Processes, 3,* 185–201.

Singer, M. (1994). Discourse inference processes. In M. A. Gernsbacher (Ed.), *Handbook of psycholinguistics* (pp. 479–515). New York: Academic Press.

Singer, M., Andrusiak, P., Reisdorf, P., & Black, N. (1992). Individual differences in bridging inference processes. *Memory and Cognition, 30,* 539–548.

Singer, M., & Ferreira, F. (1983). Inferring consequences in story comprehension. *Journal of Verbal Learning and Verbal Behavior, 22,* 437–448.

Skinner, B. F. (1957). *Verbal behavior.* Englewood Cliffs, NJ: Prentice Hall.

Slobin, D. I. (1973). Cognitive prerequisites for the development of grammar. In C. Ferguson & D. I. Slobin (Eds.), *Studies of child language development* (pp. 175–208). New York: Holt, Rinehart and Winston.

Slobin, D. I. (1982). Universal and particular in the acquisition of language. In E. Wanner & L. R. Gleitman (Eds.), *Language acquisition: The state of the art* (pp. 128–170). Cambridge: Cambridge University Press.

Slobin, D. I. (1985). Crosslinguistic evidence for the language-making capacity. In D. I. Slobin (Ed.), *The crosslinguistic study of language acquisition: Vol. 2. Theoretical issues* (pp. 1157–1256). Hillsdale, NJ: Erlbaum.

Slowiaczek, M. L. (1983). What does the mind do while the eyes are gazing? In K. Rayner (Ed.), *Eye movements in reading: Perceptual and language processes.* New York: Academic Press.

Slugoski, B., & Turnbull, W. (1988). Cruel to be kind and kind to be cruel: Sarcasm, banter, and social relations. *Journal of Language and Social Psychology, 7,* 101–121.

Smith, E. E., Shoben, E. J., & Rips, L. J. (1974). Structure and process in semantic memory: A featural model for semantic decisions. *Psychological Review, 81,* 214–241.

Smith, F. (1971). *Understanding reading: A psycholinguistic analysis of reading and learning to read.* New York: Holt, Rinehart and Winston.

Smith, L. (1995). Self-organizing processes in learning to learn words: Development is not induction. In C. Nelson (Ed.), *Basic and applied perspectives on learning, cognition, and development* (Vol. 28, pp. 1–32). Mahwah, NJ: Erlbaum.

Smitherman, G. (1977). *Talkin and testifyin: The language of Black America.* Boston: Houghton Mifflin.

Smitherman-Donaldson, G. (1988). Discriminatory discourse on Afro-American speech. In G. Smitherman-Donaldson & T. van Dijk (Eds.), *Discourse and discrimination* (pp. 144–175). Detroit: Wayne State University Press.

Smitherman-Donaldson, G., & van Dijk, T. (Eds.). (1988). *Discourse and discrimination.* Detroit: Wayne State University Press.

Smoczynska, M. (1985). The acquisition of Polish. In D. I. Slobin (Ed.), *The crosslinguistic study of language acquisition: Vol. 1: The data.* Hillsdale, NJ: Erlbaum.

Smolensky, P. (1988). On the proper treatment of connectionism. *Behavior and Brain Sciences, 11,* 1–22, 59–74.

Snow, C. E. (1977). The development of conversation between mothers and babies. *Journal of Child Language, 4,* 1–22.

Snow, C. E. (1981). Social interaction and language acquisition. In P. Dale & D. Ingram (Eds.), *Child language: An international perspective* (pp. 195–213). Baltimore: University Park Press.

Snow, C. E. (1998). Bilingualism and second language learning. In J. Berko-Gleason & N. Bernstein Ratner (Eds.), *Psycholinguistics* (pp. 453–481). Orlando, FL: Harcourt Brace.

Snow, C. E. (1999). Social perspectives on the emergence of language. In B. MacWhinney (Ed.), *The emergence of language* (pp. 257–276). Mahwah, NJ: Erlbaum.

Snow, C. E., & Ferguson, C. A. (1977). *Talking to children: Language input and acquisition.* Cambridge: Cambridge University Press.

Snow, C. E., & Hoefnagel-Hohle, M. (1978). The critical period for language acquisition: Evidence from second language learning. *Child Development, 49,* 1114–1128.

Soderfeldt, B., Ingvar, M., Ronnberg, J., Eriksson, L., Serrander, M., & Stone-Elander, S. (1997). Signed and spoken language perception studied by positron emission topography. *Neurology, 49,* 82–87.

Sommers, M. S., Nygaard, L. C., & Pisoni, D. B. (1992). The effects of speaking rate and amplitude variability on perceptual identification. *Journal of the Acoustical Society of America, 91,* 23–40.

Sperber, D., & Wilson, D. (1981). Irony and the use-mention distinction. In P. Cole (Ed.), *Radical pragmatics* (pp. 295–318). New York: Academic Press.

Sperry, R. W. (1968). Hemisphere disconnection and unity in conscious awareness. *American Psychologist, 23,* 723–733.

Sperry, R. W., Gazzaniga, M. S., & Bogen, J. F. (1969). Interhemispheric relationships: The neocortical commissures: syndromes of hemispheric disconnection. In P. J. Vinken & G. W. Bruyn (Eds.), *Handbook of clinical neurology* (Vol. 4, pp. 273–290). New York: Wiley.

Spivey, M., & Marian, V. (1999). Cross talk between native and second languages: Partial activation of an irrelevant lexicon. *Psychological Science, 10,* 281–284.

Staats, A. W. (1964). *Human learning: Studies extending conditioning principles to complex behavior.* New York: Holt, Rinehart and Winston.

Staats, A. W. (1968). *Learning, language, and cognition.* New York: Holt, Rinehart and Winston.

Staats, A. W. (1971). Linguistic-mentalistic theory versus an explanatory S-R learning theory of language development. In D. I. Slobin (Ed.), *The ontogenesis of grammar* (pp. 103–150). New York: Academic Press.

Staats, A. W., & Staats, C. K. (1958). Attitudes established by classical conditioning. *Journal of Abnormal Social Psychology, 57,* 37–40.

Staats, A. W., & Staats, C. K. (1959). Effect of number of trials on the language conditioning of meaning. *Journal of General Psychology, 61,* 211–223.

Staats, A. W., & Staats, C. K. (1963). *Complex human behavior.* New York: Holt, Rinehart and Winston.

Staats, A. W., Staats, C. K., & Crawford, H. L. (1962). First-order conditioning of meaning and the paralleled conditioning of GSR. *Journal of General Psychology, 67,* 159–167.

Staats, C. K., & Staats, A. W. (1957). Meaning established by classical conditioning. *Journal of Experimental Psychology, 54,* 74–80.

Stanners, R. F., Neiser, J. J., Hernon, W. P., & Hall, R. (1979). Memory representation for morphologically related words. *Journal of Verbal Learning and Verbal Behavior, 18,* 399–412.

Stanners, R. F., Neiser, J. J., & Painton, S. (1979). Memory representation for prefixed words. *Journal of Verbal Learning and Verbal Behavior, 18,* 733–743.

Stanovich, K. E., Cunningham, A. E., & Cramer, B. (1984). Assessing phonological awareness in kindergarten children: Issues of task comparability. *Journal of Experimental Child Psychology, 38,* 175–190.

Stapley, J. C., & Haviland, J. M. (1989). Beyond depression: Gender differences in normal adolescents' emotional experiences. *Sex Roles, 20,* 295–308.

Stein, N. L., & Glenn, C. G. (1979). An analysis of story comprehension in elementary school children. In R. Freedle (Ed.), *New directions in discourse processing* (Vol. 2, pp. 53–120). Hillsdale, NJ: Erlbaum.

Stein, R. (1991). *Psychoanalytic theories of affect.* New York: Praeger.

Stemberger, J. P. (1985). An interactive activation model of language production. In A. W. Ellis (Ed.), *Progress in the psychology of language* (Vol. 1, pp. 143–186). Hillsdale, NJ: Erlbaum.

Stoel-Gammon, C., & Otomo, K. (1986). Babbling development in hearing-impaired and normally hearing subjects. *Journal of Speech and Hearing Disorders, 51,* 33–41.

Strawbridge, J. (1986). The influence of position, highlighting, and imbedding on warning effectiveness. *Proceedings of the Human Factors Society 30th Annual Meeting* (pp. 716–720). Santa Monica, CA: Human Factors Society.

Stroop, J. R. (1935). Studies of interference in serial verbal reactions. *Journal of Experimental Psychology, 18,* 624–643.

Studdert-Kennedy, M. (1976). Speech perception. In J. J. Lass (Ed.), *Contemporary issues in experimental phonetics* (pp. 243–293). New York: Academic Press.

Swaab, T. Y., Brown, C. M., & Hagoort, P. (1997). Spoken sentence comprehension in aphasia: Event-related potential evidence for a lexical integration deficit. *Journal of Cognitive Neuroscience, 9,* 39–66

Swinney, D. (1979). Lexical access during sentence comprehension: (Re)consideration of context effects. *Journal of Verbal Learning and Verbal Behavior, 18,* 645–659.

Swinney, D., & Cutler, A. (1979). The access and processing of idiomatic expressions. *Journal of Verbal Learning and Verbal Behavior, 18,* 523–534.

Tabossi, P. (1988). Accessing lexical ambiguity in different types of sentential context. *Journal of Memory and Language, 27,* 324–340.

Tabossi, P., Columbo, L., & Job, R. (1987). Accessing lexical ambiguity: Effects of context and dominance. *Psychological Research, 49,* 161–167.

Taft, M. (1981). Prefix stripping revisited. *Journal of Verbal Learning and Verbal Behavior, 20,* 289–297.

Taft, M., & Forster, K. I. (1975). Lexical storage and retrieval of prefixed words. *Journal of Verbal Learning and Verbal Behavior, 14,* 638–647.

Taft, M., & Forster, K. I. (1976). Lexical storage and retrieval of polymorphemic and polysyllabic words. *Journal of Verbal Learning and Verbal Behavior, 15,* 607–620.

Tanenhaus, M. K., Carlson, G., & Trueswell, J. C. (1989). The role of thematic structures in interpretations and parsing. *Language and Cognitive Processes, 4,* 211–234.

Tanenhaus, M. K., Leiman, J. M., & Seidenberg, M. S. (1979). Evidence for multiple stages in the processing of ambiguous words in syntactic contexts. *Journal of Verbal Learning and Verbal Behavior, 18,* 427–440.

Tannen, D. (1984). *Conversational style: Analyzing talk among friends.* Norwood, NJ: Ablex.

Tannen, D. (1987). Repetition in conversation as spontaneous formulaicity. *Text, 7,* 215–244.

Tannen, D. (1989). *Talking voices: Repetition, dialogue, and imagery in conversational discourse.* New York: Cambridge University Press.

Tannen, D. (1994). *Gender and discourse.* New York: Oxford University Press.

Taraban, R., & McClelland, J. L. (1988). Constituent attachment and thematic role assignment in sentence processing: Influences of content-based expectations. *Journal of Memory and Language, 27,* 597–632.

Tardif, T. (1996). Nouns are not always learned before verbs: Evidence from Mandarin speakers' early vocabularies. *Developmental Psychology, 70,* 620–635.

Terrace, H. S., Petitto, L. A., Sanders, R. J., & Bever, T. G. (1979). Can an ape create a sentence? *Science, 206,* 891–902.

Terwilliger, R. F. (1968). *Meaning and mind: A study in the psychology of language.* New York: Oxford University Press.

Thomas, M. (1989). The acquisition of English articles by first- and second-language learners. *Applied Psycholinguistics, 10,* 335–357.

Thompson, R. B. (1999). Gender differences in preschoolers' help-eliciting communication. *Journal of Genetic Psychology, 160,* 357–368.

Thomson, R. B., Murachver, T., & Green, J. (2001). Where is the gender in gendered language? *Psychological Science, 12,* 171–175.

Thorndyke, P. (1977). Cognitive structures in comprehension and memory of narrative discourse. *Cognitive Psychology, 9,* 77–110.

Thorne, A. (1995). Developmental truths in memories of children and adolescence. *Journal of Personality, 63,* 139–163.

Thorne, B., & Henley, N. (1975). *Language and sex: Difference and dominance.* Rowley, MA: Newbury House.

Till, R. E., Mross, E. F., & Kintsch, W. (1988). Time course of priming for associate and inference words in a discourse context. *Memory and Cognition, 16,* 283–298.

Titon, J. T. (1994). *Early downhome blues: A musical and cultural analysis.* Chapel Hill: University of North Carolina Press.

Titone, D., & Connine, C. (1999). On the compositional and noncompositional nature of idiomatic expressions. *Journal of Pragmatics, 31,* 1655–1674.

Tomasello, M. (1992). Author's response: On defining language: Replies to Shatz and Ninio. *Social Development, 1,* 159–162.

Tomasello, M. (1995). Joint attention as social cognition. In C. Moore & P. J. Dunham (Eds.), *Joint attention: Its origins and role in development* (pp. 103–130). Hillsdale, NJ: Erlbaum.

Tomasello, M., & Farrar, J. (1986). Joint attention and early language. *Child Development, 57,* 1454–1463.

Tomasello, M., Kruger, A., & Ratner, H. (1993). Cultural learning. *Behavioral and Brain Sciences, 16,* 495–552.

Tomasello, M., & Todd, J. (1983). Joint attention and lexical acquisition style. *First Language, 4,* 197–212.

Tourangeau, R., & Sternberg, R. (1982). Understanding and appreciating metaphors. *Cognition, 11,* 203–244.

Trabasso, T., Secco, T., & van den Broek, P. (1984). Causal cohesion and story coherence. In H. Mandl, N. L. Stein, & T. Trabasso (Eds.), *Learning and comprehension of text* (pp. 83–111). Hillsdale, NJ: Erlbaum.

Trabasso, T., & Sperry, L. (1985). Causal relatedness and importance of story events. *Journal of Memory and Language, 24,* 595–611.

Trabasso, T., & van den Broek, P. (1985). Causal thinking and the representation of narrative events. *Journal of Memory and Language, 24,* 612–630.

Trabasso, T., van den Broek, P., & Suh, S. Y. (1989). Logical necessity and transitivity of causal relations in stories. *Discourse Processes, 12,* 1–25.

Trehub, S. (1976). The discrimination of foreign speech contrasts by infants and adults. *Child Development, 47,* 466–472.

Treiman, R. (1993). *Beginning to spell: A study of first-grade children.* New York: Oxford University Press.

Treiman, R. A., & Baron, J., & Luk, K. (1981). Speech recoding in silent reading: A comparison of Chinese and English. *Journal of Chinese Linguistics, 9,* 116–124.

Treiman, R. A., & Hirsh-Pasek, K. (1983). Silent reading: Insights from second-generation deaf readers. *Cognitive Psychology, 15,* 39–65.

Trueswell, J. C., & Tanenhaus, M. K. (1994). Toward a lexicalist framework of constraint-based syntactic ambiguity resolution. In C. Clifton, K. Rayner, & L. Frazier (Eds.), *Perspectives on sentence processing* (pp. 155–180). Hillsdale, NJ: Erlbaum.

Trueswell, J. C., Tanenhaus, M. K., & Garnsey, S. M. (1994). Semantic influences on parsing: Use of thematic role information in syntactic disambiguation. *Journal of Memory and Language, 33,* 285–318.

Tunmer, W. E., Herriman, M. L., & Neesdale, A. R. (1988). Metalinguistic abilities and beginning reading. *Reading Research Quarterly, 23,* 134–158.

Tzeng, O. J. L., & Hung, D. L. (1980). Reading in a nonalphabetic writing system. In J. Kavanagh & R. Venezky (Eds.), *Orthography, reading, and dyslexia* (pp. 211–226). Baltimore: University Park Press.

Tzeng, O. J. L., Hung, D. L., & Wang, W. (1977). Speech recoding in reading Chinese characters. *Journal of Experimental Psychology: Human Learning and Memory, 3,* 621–630.

Umbel, V., Pearson, B., Fernandez, S., & Oller, D. (1992). Measuring bilingual children's receptive vocabularies. *Child Development, 63,* 1012–1020.

Vakoch, D. A., & Wurm, L. H. (1997). Emotional connotation in speech perception: Semantic associations in the general lexicon. *Cognition and Emotion, 11,* 337–349.

van den Broek, P. (1990). The causal inference maker: Toward a process model of inference generation in text comprehension. In D. A. Balota, G. B. Flores d'Arcais, & K. Rayner (Eds.), *Comprehension processes in reading* (pp. 423–445). Hillsdale, NJ: Erlbaum.

van den Broek, P. (1994). Comprehension and memory of narrative texts: Inferences and coherence. In M. A. Gernsbacher (Ed.), *Handbook of psycholinguistics* (pp. 539–588). New York: Academic Press.

van den Broek, P., Rohleder, L., & Narvaez, D. (1996). Causal inferences in the comprehension of literary texts. In R. J. Kreuz & M. S. MacNealy (Eds.), *Empirical approaches to literature and aesthetics. Advances in discourse processes* (Vol. 52, pp. 179–200). Stamford, CT: Ablex.

van den Broek, P., & Trabasso, T. (1986). Causal networks versus goal hierarchies in summarizing text. *Discourse Processes, 9,* 1–15.

van Dijk. T. (1972). *Some aspects of text grammars.* The Hague, Netherlands: Mouton.

van Dijk, T. (1987). *Communicating racism: Ethnic prejudice in thought and talk.* Newbury Park, CA: Sage.

van Dijk, T., & Kintsch, W. (1983). *Strategies of discourse comprehension.* New York: Academic Press.

Van Lancker, D. (1972). *Heterogeneity in language and speech: Neurolinguistic studies* (Working Paper in Phonetics No. 29). Los Angeles: University of California Press.

Van Lancker, D. (1987). Nonpropositional speech: Neurolinguistic studies. In A. W. Ellis (Ed.), *Progress in the psychology of language* (Vol. 3, pp. 49–118). Hillsdale, NJ: Erlbaum.

Van Lancker, D. (1991). The neurology of proverbs. *Behavioral Neurology, 3,* 169–187.

Van Lancker, D., & Cummings, J. L. (1999). Expletives: Neurolinguistic and neurobehavioral perspectives on swearing. *Brain Research Reviews, 31,* 83–104.

Van Larwick-Goodall, J. (1971). *In the shadow of man.* Boston: Houghton Mifflin.

Van Petten, C., & Kutas, M. (1987). Ambiguous words in context: An event-related potential analysis of the time course of meaning activation. *Journal of Memory and Language, 26,* 188–208.

Varga, D. (2000). Hyperbole and humor in children's language play. *Journal of Research in Childhood Education, 14,* 142–151.

Vellutino, F. R., & Scanlon, D. (1987). Phonological coding, phonological awareness, and reading ability: Evidence from a longitudinal and experimental study. *Merrill-Palmer Quarterly, 33,* 321–363.

Vellutino, F. R., Scanlon, D., & Spearing, D. (1995). Semantic and phonological coding in poor and normal readers. *Journal of Experimental Child Psychology, 59,* 76–123.

Venesky, R. L. (1970). *The structure of English orthography*. The Hague, Netherlands: Mouton.

Verbugge, R. R., & McCarrell, N. S. (1977). Metaphoric comprehension: Studies in reminding and resembling. *Cognitive Psychology, 9*, 494–533.

Vigliocco, G., Antonini, T., & Garrett, M. F. (1997). Grammatical gender is on the tip of Italian tongues. *Psychological Science, 8*, 314–317.

Vihman, M. (1996). *Phonological development: The origins of language in the child*. Cambridge, MA: Blackwell.

Von Frisch, K. (1962). Dialects in the language of the bees. *Scientific American, 207*, 79–87.

Vucinich, S. (1977). Elements of cohesion between turns in ordinary conversation. *Semiotica, 20*, 229–257.

Vygotsky, L. S. (1962). *Thought and language*. Cambridge, MA: MIT Press.

Wada, J. (1949). A new method for the determination of the side of cerebral speech dominance. *Igaka to Seibutsugaku, 24*, 221–222.

Wagner, R. K., & Stanovich, K. E. (1996). Expertise in reading. In K. A. Ericsson (Ed.), *The road to excellence* (pp. 159–227). Mahwah, NJ: Erlbaum.

Wallace, A. (1962). Culture and cognition. *Science, 135*, 351–357.

Warren, R. M. (1970). Perceptual restoration of missing speech sounds. *Science, 167*, 392–393.

Warren, R. M., & Warren, R. P. (1970, December). Auditory illusions and confusions. *Scientific American*, pp. 30–36.

Wells, J. W. (1989). Sexual language use in different interpersonal contexts: A comparison of gender and sexual orientation. *Archives of Sexual Behavior, 18*, 127–143.

Wells, J. W. (1990). The sexual vocabularies of heterosexual and homosexual males and females for communicating erotically with a sexual partner. *Archives of Sexual Behavior, 19*, 139–147.

Wenger, E. (1998). *Communities of practice: Learning, meaning, and identity*. New York: Cambridge University Press.

Werker, J., Gilbert, J., Humphrey, K., & Tees, R. (1981). Developmental aspects of cross-language speech perception. *Child Development, 52*, 349–355.

Werker, J., & Polka, L. (1993). Developmental changes in speech perception: New challenges and new directions. *Journal of Phonetics, 21*, 83–101.

Werker, J., & Tees, R. C. (1984). Cross-language speech perception: Evidence for perceptual reorganization during the first year of life. *Infant Behavior and Development, 7*, 49–64.

Werner, H., & Kaplan, B. (1963). *Symbol formation*. New York: Wiley.

Wexler, K. (1996). The development of inflection in a biologically based theory of language acquisition. In M. Rice (Ed.), *Toward a genetics of language* (pp. 113–144). Mahwah, NJ: Erlbaum.

Wexler, K., & Culicover, P. (1980). *Formal principles of language acquisition*. Cambridge, MA: MIT Press.

Whorf, B. L. (1956). Science and linguistics. In J. B. Carroll (Ed.), *Language, thought, and reality: Selected writings of Benjamin Lee Whorf* (pp. 207–219). Cambridge, MA: MIT Press.

Wiener, N. (1948). *Cybernetics: Or control and communication in animal and the machine*. Cambridge, MA: MIT Press.

Williams, J. M. G., Mathews, A., & MacLeod, C. (1996). The emotional Stroop task and psychopathology. *Psychological Bulletin, 120*, 2–24.

Willingham, D. B. (2001). *Cognition: The thinking animal*. Upper Saddle River, NJ: Prentice Hall.

Wingfield, A., & Klein, J. F. (1971). Syntactic structure and acoustic pattern in speech perception. *Perception and Psychophysics, 9*, 23–25.

Winner, E., & Gardner, H. (1977). The comprehension of metaphor in brain-damaged patients. *Brain, 100*, 717–729.

Winner, E., Windmueller, G., Rosenblatt, E., Bosco, L., Best, E., & Gardner, H. (1987). Making sense of literal and nonliteral falsehood. *Metaphor and Symbolic Activity, 2*, 13–32.

Winslow, D. J. (1969). Children's derogatory epithets. *Journal of American Folklore, 82*, 255–263.

Wogalter, M. S., Desaulniers, D., & Brelsford, J. Jr. (1987). Consumer products: How are hazards perceived? *Proceedings of the Human Factors Society 31st Annual Meeting* (pp. 615–619). Santa Monica, CA: Human Factors Society.

Wogalter, M. S., Young, S. L., Brelsford, J. W., & Barlow, T. (1999). The relative contributions of injury severity and likelihood information on hazard-risk judgments and warning compliance. *Journal of Safety Research, 30,* 151–162.

Wolf, M. (1991). Naming speed and reading: The contribution of the neurosciences. *Reading Research Quarterly, 26,* 123–141.

Wolfe, G. I., & Ross, E. D. (1987). Sensory aprosodia with left hemiparesis from subcortical infarction. *Archives of Neurology, 44,* 668–671.

Wolfson, N. (1997). *Hate speech, sex speech, free speech.* Westport, CT: Praeger.

Wong-Filmore, L. (1991). Second-language learning in childhood: A model of language learning in social context. In E. Bialystok (Ed.), *Language processing in bilingual children* (pp. 49–69). Cambridge: Cambridge University Press.

Wootten, J., Merkin, S., Hood, L., & Bloom, L. (1979, March). Wh- questions: Linguistic evidence to explain the sequence of acquisition. Paper presented at the biennial meeting of the Society for Research in Child Development, San Francisco.

Wundt, W. (1970). The psychology of the sentence. In A. Blumenthal (Ed. & Trans.), *Language and psychology: Historical aspects of psycholinguistics* (pp. 20–31). New York: Wiley. (Original work published 1900)

Wurm, L. H., & Vakoch, D. A. (1996). Dimensions of speech perception: Semantic associations in the affective lexicon. *Cognition and Emotion, 10,* 409–423.

Wyatt, T., & Seymour, H. (1990). The implications of code-switching in Black English speakers. *Equity and Excellence, 24*(4), 17–18.

Yeni-Komshian, G. H. (1998). Speech perception. In J. Berko-Gleason & N. Bernstein Ratner (Eds.), *Psycholinguistics* (pp. 107–156). Orlando, FL: Harcourt Brace.

Yeni-Komshian, G. H., & Lafontaine, L. (1983). Discrimination and identification of voicing and place contrasts in aphasic patients. *Canadian Journal of Psychology, 37,* 107–131.

Zanarini, M., & Frankenburg, F. (1994). Emotional hypochondriasis, hyperbole, and the borderline patient. *Journal of Psychotherapy Practice and Research, 3,* 25–36.

Zerubavel, E. (1997). *Social mindscapes: An invitation to cognitive psychology.* Cambridge, MA: Harvard University Press.

Ziegler, J. C., Tan, L. H., Perry, C., & Montant, M. (2000). Phonology matters: The phonological frequency effect in written Chinese. *Psychological Science, 11,* 234–238.

Zimmerman, D. H., & West, C. (1975). Sex roles, interruptions, and silences in conversation. In B. Thorne & N. Henley (Eds.), *Language and sex: Differences and dominance* (pp. 105–129). Rowley, MA: Newbury House.

Zipf, G. K. (1949). *Human behavior and the principle of least effort.* Reading, MA: Addison-Wesley.

Zurif, E. B. (1995). Brain regions of relevance to syntactic processing. In L. R. Gleitman & M. Liberman (Eds.), *An invitation to cognitive science: Vol. 2. Language* (pp. 381–397). Cambridge, MA: MIT Press.

Zurif, E. B., & Swinney, D. (1994). The neuropsychology of language. In M. A. Gernsbacher (Ed.), *Handbook of psycholinguistics* (pp. 1055–1074). New York: Academic Press.

Zurif, E. B., Swinney, D., Prather, P., Solomon, J., & Bushell, C. (1993). An on-line analysis of syntactic processing in Broca's and Wernicke's aphasia. *Brain and Language, 45,* 448–464.

Zwann, R. A., & van Oostendorp, U. (1993). Do readers construct spatial representations in naturalistic story comprehension? *Discourse Processes, 16,* 125–143.

Index

Page numbers followed by italicized *f* and *t* refer to figures and tables, respectively.